THE OTHER SIDE OF THE WIRE
VOLUME 1

With the German XIV Reserve Corps
on the Somme,
September 1914 – June 1916

Ralph J. Whitehead

**Hardback edition produced
in a strictly limited printing
of 750 individually numbered
and signed copies**

This is copy number 600 of 750

THE OTHER SIDE OF THE WIRE VOLUME 1

With the German XIV Reserve Corps on the Somme, September 1914 – June 1916

Ralph J. Whitehead

Helion & Company Ltd

For *Landwehrmann* Jakob Hönes, 7th Company, Reserve Infantry Regiment 121 (fallen on the Somme 13 June 1915) and *Vizefeldwebel* Albert Thielecke, 7th Company, Reserve Infantry Regiment 121 (fallen on the Somme 11 June 1915) whose remains were discovered 88 years after their deaths, and for the thousands of men from both sides of the wire that still lie undiscovered under the soil of the Somme. They are not forgotten

Helion & Company Limited
26 Willow Road
Solihull
West Midlands
B91 1UE
England
Tel. 0121 705 3393
Fax 0121 711 4075
Email: info@helion.co.uk
Website: www.helion.co.uk

Published by Helion & Company 2010

Designed and typeset by Farr out Publications, Wokingham, Berkshire
Cover designed by Bookcraft Ltd, Stroud, and Farr out Publications, Wokingham, Berkshire
Printed by The Cromwell Press Group, Trowbridge, Wiltshire

© Ralph J. Whitehead 2009

ISBN 978 1 906033 29 3

British Library Cataloguing-in-Publication Data.
A catalogue record for this book is available from the British Library.

For details of other military history titles published by Helion & Company Limited contact the above address, or visit our website: http://www.helion.co.uk.

We always welcome receiving book proposals from prospective authors.

Contents

Preface

E ver since I was a small boy I was fascinated by family history. I would often sift
through albums and boxes of photographs in the attic. I occasionally came across
a few of men wearing uniforms. When I asked my parents about them I began to
find out the history of my family and the Great War.

The two closest relatives on my father's side, my grandfather 2nd Lieutenant Frank J.
Whitehead, Liaison Officer, Camp Mills, Long Island and my Great-Uncle Private Charles
Mutter, Company B, 306th Machine Gun Battalion had died before I was born. When
I discovered that my maternal grandfather had brothers who served in the war I found I
was too late, they had all passed away. All I could rely upon were a few old photographs
and the stories passed down from my parents. I eventually learned that I had relatives
who had served in Württemberg regiments during the war and had apparently survived
but there were no other details beyond this basic information. For all I know they could
have served in one of the regiments attached to the XIV Reserve Corps. I suspect that
I had relatives who served in the British army from Rugby, England but at this time I
cannot verify this information.

I did learn that the war apparently spilled over to the backyard of a house in Queens
County, New York. The Haufler family was divided when it came to the war. My great-
grandfather who was born in Marbach am Neckar and who emigrated to the United
States in the late 1880's was pro-American when the U.S. entered the war in April 1917.
However, his sons were pro-German and when my maternal grandfather, Arthur Lynch,
came over for a visit or Sunday dinner the discussion often turned to the war. The Haufler
boys voiced their opinions that the U-boats should sink the American troop ships as they
crossed the Atlantic while my grandfather, who had brothers onboard these troop ships
obviously felt differently. These arguments generally led to a violent fistfight behind the
house and afterward everyone would go their separate ways without ever coming to a
consensus on the issue.

As I grew older my interest in the war increased and I looked for any reading material
I could find. I started reading the classic books on the war such as *The Guns of August* by
Barbara Tuchman, *Goodbye to all that* by Robert Graves and *Old Soldiers never Die* by
Frank Richards. One item I found interesting was the almost complete lack of information
on the German side of the war, they were always the 'enemy' and not given much more
substance than this simple word.

I had always found books written at the personal level more interesting than general
histories and began my search for German accounts of the war. I was only able to find a
few books on the market including *All Quiet on the Western Front* and *The Advance from
Mons*. Then there were two events in the early 1970's that became the catalyst for what
would eventually become this book. The first dealt with Martin Middlebrook's book *First
Day on the Somme*. It was one of the only books I had read that used first hand accounts
from soldiers who had fought in the war.

The second event occurred shortly after reading Middlebrook's book. My wife and
I were dating at that time and we would often attend antique shows. One in particular

always had a good selection of items that fit our collecting habits and it was held at a local racetrack.

I was going through a box of postcards when I came across the lone card dealing with the Great War. It was a photograph of British prisoners being interrogated by a group of German officers. I recognized the postmark for Reserve Infantry Regiment 99 as being a regiment that had been featured in Middlebrook's book.

After spending a ridiculously small sum to purchase the card I took it home and always wondered what events led to the photograph being taken and who the men were. This started a long process of obtaining any references to RIR 99 that I could find and then learning to read and translate German. Once I discovered how the men in the photograph were captured I was hooked. I needed to know more about the Somme and the German army. I expanded my search into the regiments that made up the 26th Reserve Division and once finished with this group I went further to research the 28th Reserve Division completing the units within the XIV Reserve Corps that existed in 1914.

Now came the hard part, translating the materials needed to complete my project. At first I concentrated on the period at the start of the battle of the Somme but then realized that the period from 1914 through June 1916 had been ignored in most histories and apparently never covered from the German perspective.

After translating hundreds of pages and documents from numerous sources I had a collection of information that needed some form. I eventually came to the idea of compiling all of the information by time periods and formed a narrative of events from the initial invasion in September 1914 to the point just before the British attack on 1 July 1916 as the first part of a larger project. It is my intention to continue the history of these divisions through the end of the war including the momentous battle of the Somme.

I feel that as most books only deal with the British, French or American point of view the reader is missing half of the story, the events and experiences of the 'enemy', the men in Field Grey who fought on the other side of the wire. Hopefully this book will help fill this void and provide the reader with a new perspective on the war.

Acknowledgements

This book has taken many years to complete and I am the first to admit that I was not the best person at keeping legible records of my sources. As such I want to state that if I have left anyone out of the acknowledgements that played a role in compiling the materials used in this book I offer my apologies. Your efforts were of great value and most appreciated by the author.

For help in locating many of the German sources used in preparation of this book: Jack Sheldon and Frank Grosse. Frank in particular has been involved in the preparation of this book almost since the beginning and has acted in the capacity of a lending library by providing books from his vast collection for use in the manuscript. His advice and encouragement has been gratefully welcomed during the times when I had almost given up finishing this book, thank you Frank.

For advice and encouragement and the source of unique material: Graham Stewart, Desmond Blackadder, Alastair Fraser, Paul Reed, Terry Reeves, Egbert Sandrock, Paul Hederer, Ian Forsdike, Andrew Hesketh, David Neale, Sebastian Laudan and Brian Ludwig, among others I have been fortunate to meet through Chris Baker's Great War forum from The Long, Long Trail website (http://www.1914-1918.net/). I would like to add a special thank Felix Fregin from Simpelveld, Netherlands for his assistance in translating hundreds of *Feldpost* letters by Karl Losch and allowing me to use portions in this book.

For proofreading and advice on publishing: Bill MacCormick, author of *Pro Patria Mori: The 56th (1st London) Division at Gommecourt, 1st July 1916* and Jack Alexander, author of *McCrae's Battalion: The Story of the 16th Royal Scots*. Both Bill and Jack demonstrated a great deal of patience with a novice writer who found their advice invaluable. I would highly recommend both books to anyone with an interest in the Great War.

I am especially indebted to the Hönes and Rapp families from Württemberg, Germany for allowing me to use family photographs of *Landwehrmann* Jakob Hönes, 7th Coy, RIR 121. I would like to thank the following authors for allowing me to use excerpts from their books; Jimmy Taylor - *The 1st Royal Irish Rifles in the Great War*; Martin Middlebrook - *The First Day on the Somme*; Michael Stedman – *Salford Pals*; Michael Rossor, H Bruce Rossor and Ron Shephard who have allowed me to use quotes from the *A Sergeant-Major's War* as well as providing access to the unpublished portions of the diary of Ernest Shephard. I would like to thank Lee Samson of the Naval & Military Press for allowing me to use quotations from *A War Weary Road* by Charles Douie. I would like to thank Emma Golding, Trainee Archivist at the Imperial War Museum for her assistance in attempting to obtain permission to use first hand accounts from the museum's vast collection. I am particularly grateful to Brian Ludwig and his family for allowing me to read his great uncle's story of the Great War with Reserve Infantry Regiment Nr. 120 and allowing me to use parts of this story in my book. I want to extend my gratitude to David Rametta of the Medici Society for allowing me to quote portions of *The History of the South Wales Borderers 1914-1918*. I would like to thank Richard Baumgartner of Huntington, West Virginia for allowing me to use quotes from his publication *Der Angriff*. I would like to thank Michelle Griffin for allowing me to use several quotes from Philip Orr, *The Road to the Somme* (Blackstaff Press) reproduced by permission of Blackstaff Press on behalf of the author.

Where possible I have attempted to gain permission for the use of quotations and photographs used in the book, however, if I have unknowingly infringed copyright in the writing of this book I would hope that my apologies are accepted.

Lastly, I want to thank my family, my son Andrew and his wife Nole and my daughter Julia and her husband Todd for patiently listening to my stories of the Great War all of these years. I would like to thank my granddaughter Clara and grandson Owen in advance for all of the time they will spend in the future listening to my stories of the war. Above all else I would like to express my deepest gratitude and love to my wife Elizabeth who has put up with my interest, or as she would say my obsession with the Great War for almost 40 years. Her support and encouragement has made this book possible. While looking at the German soldier on the right of the photograph found on page 527 she noticed an extremely strong resemblance to my face, stance, and size and commented that she now understood my obsession. I was not just interested in the Germans on the Somme I had apparently been there.

Ralph J. Whitehead
June 2007

German Army Organization and Rank Comparison

I n order for the reader to better understand the military terms and ranks mentioned in this book I have prepared a basic breakdown of the formation of the German army and the comparison of ranks between the German Army and the British Army.

The German Army consisted of several parts including Active regiments, Reserve regiments, *Landwehr* regiments and *Landsturm* units. All qualified German males would be required to serve 2 years in the Active Army starting at age 20. 4-5 years in the Reserve, 11 years in the Landwehr and 7 years in the Landsturm 2nd Ban followed this.

The basic infantry regiment consisted of three battalions of infantry, designated I, II and III. Each battalion consisted of four companies (1-4, 5-8 and 9-12 respectively) that were further broken down into three platoons (*Zug*) and then into sections or *Gruppe* that consisted of 1 Non-Commissioned Officer and 8 men. Each soldier in a reserve regiment would have been armed with the M98 Mauser rifle or the M88 rifle. Each regiment would normally contain one Machine Gun Company armed with six MG08 heavy machine guns and one spare gun. The average strength of the regiment would have been 83 officers and 3,204 men.

The XIV Reserve Corps consisted of two reserve divisions, the 26th and 28th. A complete breakdown of the two divisions can be found in Appendix I. The 26th Reserve Division was formed from reserve units and one active infantry regiment from Württemberg. The men for the most part had already served their two-year tour of active duty and were now listed as Reserve or *Landwehr* men. This division was formed from men who lived in the towns and villages surrounding Stuttgart, Tübingen, Gmünd, Ludwigsburg, Heilbronn, Hall, Calw, Ulm, Rottweil, Reutlingen, Leonberg and Esslingen among others. Reserve Infantry Regiment 99, added to the division on 19 August 1914, came from the areas around Zabern and from Pfalzburg and was considered a Prussian regiment. The men came from a wide variety of backgrounds, from farm workers to office and factory workers and many other professions, including a large number of miners in the ranks of RIR 99.

The breakdown of professions in one sample regiment, Reserve Infantry Regiment Nr. 121, provides the reader with some idea of the variety of backgrounds the men brought to the war.

This regiment included men who were employed in the agricultural and horticultural fields including many who were farmers and farm workers as well as vine growers, tradesmen, factory workers, Government officials, students, domestic employees, active officers and Non Commissioned officers, judges, teachers, merchants, railway and postal officials, bankers, financiers, builders and shop keepers to office managers. The different regiments represented a cross-section of German society at the outbreak of the war.

The 28th Reserve Division was formed from men in the Duchy of Baden. The men in both divisions came from a similar variety of backgrounds from farmers in rural towns and villages to factory workers and professional men from the larger cities. This division was formed from men who lived in and around Mannheim, Karlsruhe, Neubreisach, Konstanz, Reuchen, Bruchsal, Emmendingen and Rastatt and others.

The two *Jäger* Battalions assigned to the 28th Reserve Division each consisted of 4 companies of *Jägers*. They did not have a machine gun company at the outbreak of the war. These battalions were formed from men in the vicinity of Schlettstadt (Strassburg i.E.) and Ratzeburg (Schleswig-Holstein and Mecklenburg) respectively.

The field artillery was normally established into three sections or *Abteilung*. The I and II *Abteilung* consisted of 3 batteries each of M96 7.7cm field guns while the III *Abteilung* consisted of 3 batteries of M98.09 10.5cm light field howitzers.

As in most cases there were always exceptions to the rules. RIR 99 was one of the regiments in the army that had 4 battalions (I, II, III, IV) instead of the normal 3 and therefore had 16 companies of infantry at the start of the war.

The 27th RFAR assigned to the 28th Reserve Division consisted of two *Abteilung* (I and II) and was not equipped with the light field howitzers, something not uncommon in reserve units.

Abbreviations used to designate the different military units found in this book.

RIR 99	Reserve Infantry Regiment Nr. 99
IR 180	Infantry Regiment Nr. 180
II/RFAR 26	II *Abteilung* Reserve Field Artillery Regiment Nr. 26
4/R109	4th Company Reserve Infantry Regiment Nr. 109
III/R111	III Battalion Reserve Infantry Regiment Nr. 111
9/180	9th Company Infantry Regiment Nr. 180

Reservists from RIR 109 at the start of the war. (Author's collection)

III(F)/FAR 12   III *Abteilung*, (howitzers), Field Artillery Regiment Nr. 12
1R/Pioneer Bn 13   1st Reserve Company 13th Pioneer Battalion

Rank Comparison
Grenadier }
Musketier }   Ranks equivalent to a Private Soldier. The different terms were
Füsilier }   due to the type of unit the soldier belonged to, the military
Jäger }   class of the soldier or from tradition.
Wehrmann }
Landsturmmann }
Landsturmpflichtiger }
Reservist}
Infanterist }
Soldat }
Ersatz-Reservist}
Schütze} (Normally associated with Machine Gun troops)
Einjährig Freiwilliger   One Year Volunteer
Kriegsfreiwilliger   War Volunteer
Kanonier   Gunner
Radfahrer   Cyclist
Pionier   Sapper
Fahrer   Driver
Hornist   Trumpeter
Tambour   Drummer
Krankenträger   Stretcher bearer
Gefreiter   Lance Corporal
Oberjäger   Corporal (*Jäger* units)
Unteroffizier   Corporal
Sergeant   Sergeant
Vizefeldwebel   Staff Sergeant
Vizewachtmeister   Staff Sergeant (Cavalry, artillery, train)
Feldwebel   Sergeant Major
Wachtmeister   Sergeant Major (Cavalry, artillery)
Fähnrich   Officer Cadet
Offizier Stellvertreter Acting officer
Feldwebelleutnant   Sergeant Major Lieutenant
Leutnant   Second Lieutenant
Oberleutnant   Lieutenant
Rittmeister   Captain (Mounted unit, Transport)
Hauptmann   Captain
Major   Major
Oberstleutnant   Lieutenant Colonel
Oberst   Colonel
Generalmajor   Major General
Generalleutnant   Lieutenant General
General der Artillerie   General of Artillery

| *General der Infanterie* | General of Infantry |
| *General der Kavallerie* | General of Cavalry |

Medical Staff

Sanitäter	Medical Assistant
Assistentzarzt	Second Lieutenant
Oberarzt	Lieutenant
Stabsarzt	Captain
Oberstabsarzt	Major or higher

Chaplains

| *Pfarrer* | Padre |

One final note regarding terminology used in the Great War. The reader will note the use of terms such as shrapnel and shellfire. These represent two different types of ammunition used during the war. High explosive shells formed fragments or splinters when exploding and were set off by impact fuzes.

Shrapnel shells were basically large shotgun shells. Each shrapnel shell was filled with numerous lead balls that were expelled by an explosive charge inside the shell casing. This was accomplished with the use of a time fuze so that the shell would burst at an appropriate height above enemy troops scattering the lead balls over a wide area.

The term shrapnel only applies to the latter type of shell and should not be confused with the modern version of this term.

Introduction

In the decades following the end of the Great War many families made pilgrimages to visit the graves of fallen fathers, sons and brothers. It is a practice that has continued to the present day.

One such visitor to Northern France in the summer of 1926 was Waldemar Stöckle from Mannheim, Germany. Waldemar was a former *Unteroffizier* in Reserve Infantry Regiment Nr. 111. He was returning to the Somme to visit the village of Le Sars where he had lived and fought for nearly two years during the war.

Waldemar had first gazed upon the rolling hills of the Somme twelve years earlier in the autumn of 1914 as part of an invading army with the XIV Reserve Corps. As his goal grew closer the familiar terrain brought back many forgotten memories.

Much had changed since then. The green fields were no longer crisscrossed with ribbons of white trenches. White clouds filled the deep blue sky instead of the yellowish bursts of exploding shrapnel shells. He could only hear the sound of birds and the wind as he drove instead of the crack of the rifle or staccato burst of machine gun fire.

The route traveled by Waldemar took him past numerous well-kept British cemeteries that stood as mute reminders of the death and destruction that had once held sway over the bucolic countryside. Waldemar was also visiting a cemetery, the final resting place of so many friends and comrades from his regiment that had been buried under the French soil.

The men of RIR 111 had created a fitting resting place for the regimental fallen just outside of Le Sars. A large stone pedestal had been erected at the entrance with the inscription 'RIR 111 Einen Toten' on one side and the regimental battle honors on the reverse: 'Fricourt, Mametz, Montauban, la Boisselle'. An artist in the regiment, carving it from a single block of white sandstone, had created a griffin. It was placed atop the stone pedestal. A gravestone marked each burial and their regimental comrades maintained the cemetery as an act of love and friendship.

When Waldemar arrived at the cemetery he could barely believe what he found. The pedestal was covered in a dense growth of nettles while the once beautiful stone griffin lay shattered in pieces at the base. Search as he might he could not find a single gravestone from the many men who had been laid to rest. It was as if the memory of his friends had been erased from existence much as the old trenches had been filled in and leveled.

What of the men from RIR 111 who had fought and died on the Somme? What of the men from the XIV Reserve Corps that had come to the Somme in September 1914 and fought both the French and British for nearly two years? It was as if they had all been simply forgotten. Once all of the veterans from the war had passed away who would be left to remember the men who had sacrificed everything for their country?

The story of the men of the XIV Reserve Corps who came to the Somme in the autumn of 1914 filled with expectations of victory, the story of the men who transformed the rolling farmland and small villages into one of the strongest defensive positions constructed during the war needs to be told. Without it the full story of the Somme will never be fully understood.

This, at long last, is their story.

1

Prelude to the Battle of the Somme: On the Offensive in Northern France, September 1914

Until September 1914 the area by the rivers Somme and Ancre had not seen any fighting since the Franco-Prussian War. By late September it had suddenly become the focus of the fighting at the beginning of what became known by the opposing armies as the Race to the Sea.

The initial German offensive into Belgium and Northern France was over; the German army had been forced to retreat at the Battle of the Marne. The German plans of a swift and decisive victory had not been fulfilled and the Western front was in a state of confusion. The trench lines had not come into existence and many areas of the front were open and undefended by either side.

When General Erich von Falkenhayn, Prussian War Minister, took over the position as Chief of General Staff from General Helmuth von Moltke in mid-September he found the situation in northern France of great concern. The German right wing on the Oise was hanging in the air. The British and French forces had numerical superiority after three German army corps had been transferred to the Eastern Front. The French railway network allowed the Allies to move troops around the front faster than the Germans. In fact the western units of the German army were operating from a single supply line running from Belgium to St. Quentin and Falkenhayn realized that enemy cavalry could easily cut this line.

In addition the German forces in the west faced a shortage of ammunition; the pre-war estimates had proven to be inadequate. As a result the army received orders to conserve their ammunition, from artillery shells to rifle cartridges. In view of the overall situation some commanders argued that the wisest course would be to withdraw on the right flank to prevent the Allies from enveloping it.

Falkenhayn would not tolerate the idea of a withdrawal and wanted the offensive to continue. He felt that if the front further south could be maintained it should still be possible 'to bring the northern coast of France, and therefore the control of the English Channel, into German hands.'[1] Arrangements were made for reinforcements to be sent to the northern flank as rapidly as possible. If this could be accomplished then victory was still possible. Everything depended upon speed and the use of all available forces in order to achieve this goal.

Meanwhile the expected Allied left hook did not take long to materialize. On 17 September the French Sixth Army under General Michel-Joseph Maunoury struck north on both sides of the Oise and threatened the German right flank. However the threat was short lived. The Germans brought down the IX Reserve Corps from Antwerp, supported by four cavalry divisions. The French Sixth Army was brought to a halt after advancing some four miles on the line Carlepont-Noyon. The first attempt to outflank the Germans had failed and the only result was that the line of battle had now been extended a short distance to the sea. The gap between Noyon and the coastal ports was still 160 kilometers wide.

The Germans established their plan of action at a conference called by Falkenhayn on 21 September. The Sixth Army under Crown Prince Ruprecht of Bavaria would concentrate west of Cambrai with the task of advancing towards the coast, then curving south toward the Somme thereby enveloping the French left wing. Meanwhile XXI Corps and I Bavarian Corps would come up on the left and threaten Péronne.

Before this plan could get under way General Joseph Joffre made his next move. General Edouard de Castelnau's Second Army advanced across the River Avre and headed west for Lassigny, Roye and Chaulnes. By 23 September the French Second Army was threatening German communications near Ham and St. Quentin and a breakthrough did not seem impossible. At this critical moment the German XVIII Corps arrived from Rheims, supported by II Corps and drove back de Castelnau's right wing but not before de Castelnau's left wing had reached Péronne and formed a bridgehead on the eastern bank of the Somme, but even this limited success could not be maintained. On 26 September

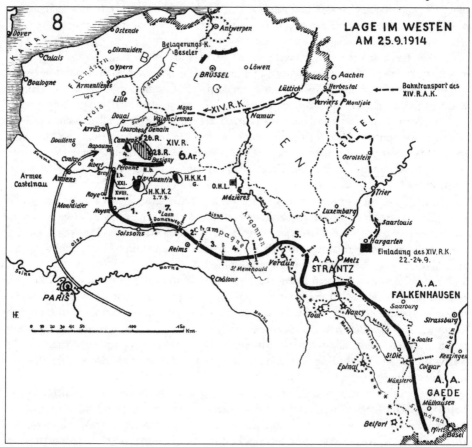

Transport of the XIV Reserve Corps from the Vosges to the Somme, September 1914.

General der Infanterie Frhr. von Soden, Commander 26th Reserve Division. (*Das Württembergisches Reserve-Feldartillerie Regiment Nr. 26 im Weltkrieg 1914-1918*)

the German XXI Corps arrived and drove the French out of Péronne with the help of I Bavarian Corps and pushed them back over the river. This sector became stabilized and the fighting moved further north.

By the latter half of September 1914 the German right flank ended near the river Somme. The terrain further north was open and only guarded by elements from German cavalry divisions. The opposing French army also had an open flank beyond where their troops were actively engaged in fighting the I and II Bavarian Corps.[2] Both sides desperately combed their existing forces for additional units they could send to the northern flank.

New formations were quickly coming to the front: the II Cavalry Corps under *Generalleutnant* Georg von der Marwitz advanced to the north by 27 September and pushed back French Territorial troops under General Henri Brugère. The task of the cavalry was to clear the way for the XIV Reserve Corps that was coming up on the right of the II Bavarian Corps that would then advance toward Albert. One of the formations destined to be sent to assist in the north was the XIV Reserve Corps.

The XIV Reserve Corps had already seen extensive fighting in the Vosges in August and early September as part of the opening German offensives. It consisted of two divisions, the 26th (Württemberg) Reserve Division and the 28th (Baden) Reserve Division. The Corps had been involved in heavy fighting against active French divisions specially trained in mountain warfare. The Germans were generally older *Reservists* and *Landwehr* men with a mix of young *Kriegsfreiwilliger*.[3] Most had already served in the German army before the war and in August 1914 were assigned to reserve units. The strain on the soldiers in the XIV Reserve Corps who were unaccustomed to fighting at high altitudes under arduous conditions had been considerable.

The Corps had received a new commander in early September, *Generalleutnant* Hermann von Stein, former Quartermaster General of the German Army on the staff of von Moltke. Toward the end of September these divisions were ordered north in order to participate in the siege of Antwerp. In order for the XIV Reserve Corps to move to Antwerp it was necessary to arrange its relief by several *Landwehr* Divisions. Once this was accomplished it could move to a location where it could be loaded aboard troop trains and transported north.

Rows of transport trains arrived to carry the XIV Reserve Corps north. There was no commotion; no concerns among the men and everyone knew their orders. On the evening of 21 September the first train was loaded for the journey to Belgium. Over the next few days the remainder of the Corps would follow.

The men did not know where they were headed and there were many rumors and wagers as to their destination. Some thought the Corps was headed to the Eastern front, others to the Western front. A few felt that the Corps was being assigned to the siege of Antwerp.

In the early stages of the trip, the trains passed through an area unfamiliar to most on board. The scenery in Germany was beautiful and the patriotic inhabitants of the countryside greeted the men enthusiastically as the trains rolled past. It was a stark contrast to the scenes of destruction they had witnessed a short time earlier in France. The trains moved slowly due to the congestion on the rail system and the accommodations were cramped and uncomfortable but food was plentiful. At each stop the men were issued rations as well as food from the German Red Cross and civilian volunteers. The men in Field Grey were lavished with gifts of coffee, bread and cakes of all kinds at every station they passed. The soldiers appreciated the kindness and generosity of their fellow countrymen. In the words of the men of Reserve *Jäger* Bn 8, they were beautiful days on the train.

The question concerning their destination was answered quickly as the trains moved north via Saar-Louis-Trier and through the Eifel; the trains were headed west. During the

XIV Reserve Corps medical column preparing to move
north, September 1914. (Author's collection)

Train journey through Belgium, RIR 99. (Author's collection)

journey toward Antwerp the Corps received orders to proceed to Cambrai where it was needed to extend the existing front to the north. The change in orders caused some delay in the movement of the Corps as new routes were required and the carefully planned movement of the trains was thrown into confusion.

Upon crossing the Belgian frontier the situation changed drastically. The supply of food was not as efficient as it had been at home and both quantity and regularity of rations decreased as the trains moved further into Belgium. The German Army had worked wonders with the rail system of Belgium but was not prepared to feed such large numbers of men. The damage caused by the invaders and more so by Belgian authorities was soon repaired so that the trains could move along the railway lines. Still, delays were common and trains were often forced to stop for long periods of time. The trains traveled over bridges and through tunnels that had been damaged or destroyed by the Belgians and many admired the replacement structures that allowed them to continue their journey in relative safety.

The troops tried to pass the time as pleasantly as possible. Each car had its political discussion group, *Skat* club[4] or men who simply sat at the doors, enjoying the weather dangling their legs in the breeze as they rolled along. However the vast majority of men simply slept on the long journey. *Telephonist* Krehl, 9/R40, assigned to the regimental staff wrote in his diary:

We have passed Verviers. Now we travel upon Belgian soil. The traces of war are essentially less here. In general everything gave a peaceful impression. What attracted my attention the most were the clean little houses and well-groomed gardens. Young and old looked between or over the slat fences. Many waved to us, but many men stood there like a real Belgian country type, mutely watching us, drawing powerfully on a clay pipe. The picture quickly changed. Magnificent deep-green meadows, on which four-footed herds with spotted hides grazed, stretching their breadth. Working windmills animated the countryside. Trains rolled past us to the east, alternating

Infantryman – RIR 119. (Author's collection)

with wounded, prisoners and other booty. You almost forgot that the war had left this countryside and moved further via Liège only a short time before. The train went day and night. Now however we were on French soil. We appeared to be approaching the enemy.[5]

Fewer people were seen along the route than in Germany. The mood of the civilians had changed dramatically since entering Belgium. The railway stations were filled with curious onlookers and many had dark, hate-filled faces as they watched the trains roll by. A few however realized that they could make a profit out of the situation and sold wine, cigarettes, cigars and chocolate at profiteering prices to the eager soldiers.

The trains passed Liège, Namur and Charleroi, the rich industrial areas of Belgium where steelworks, coal production and factories were prevalent. Once the trains crossed the French frontier rumors of *Franktireurs* spread among the troops. Everyone had heard stories of these civilians ambushing the lines of supply and communications. Additional security was ordered and each locomotive had an officer and a detachment of armed soldiers aboard whose job was to protect the train crew. At last the trains approached their destination, officers and non-commissioned officers shouted orders as the men disembarked and assembled into their units.

Among the first to be unloaded was Reserve *Jäger* Bn 8. The men were quickly formed and began to march through the streets of Cambrai singing *Die Wacht am Rhein* at the top of their lungs. Their singing attracted the attention of a General Staff officer who inquired if they were fresh troops from Germany. When the *Jägers* heard the question they redoubled their efforts and sang even louder while the local inhabitants watched their antics and shook their heads in disbelief.

The battalion received orders to proceed to Masnières and billet there for the night. When the *Jägers* reached the village it appeared to be uninhabited and the men began to knock on the doors of the houses and cottages; no one answered. Finally the men began forcing in doors as they were tired and did not want to wait any longer.

One group was billeted in the home of a local factory owner. When the building was searched they discovered a solidly built wine cellar, a large stone vault structure. The greatest discovery was a large cache of 1875 Burgundy buried under a thin layer of sand. They quickly relieved the owner of the contents of his wine collection allegedly to increase their headroom. When they left the following morning a number of angry villagers complained loudly about the destruction of their homes and theft of property to no avail.

25 September 1914

Units from the 26th Reserve Division disembarked in the early morning at Denain and Lourches north of Cambrai. The men were very happy to finally be free of their cramped quarters and able to stretch their limbs. The Corps staff remained in Cambrai while the division staff moved into quarters in Villers-Plouich and the vanguard of the Corps advanced towards Fins-Gouzeaucourt. Units from the 28th Reserve Division arrived at 4 a.m. and disembarked near Busigny, southwest of Le Cateau and at Cambrai. During the unloading the II/R109 was ordered to march to Gonnelieu, south of Cambrai, because French infantry and cavalry had been reported to be in Le Pave.

Each regiment had a different impression of the city as they arrived in Cambrai. The first noticed an absence of civilians while units arriving later were confronted with a city filled with people apparently untouched by the destruction of war. Large numbers of women moved about the streets in pretty dresses while there was a noticeable absence of men. Some people fled at the report of the advancing Germans but many had stayed to take their chances. Several hotels were giving out free champagne. It took great effort to keep the men from imbibing too much alcohol especially since they had not received regular supplies of food on the last stages of their journey and were quite tired and famished. The lead units were assigned billets in the vicinity of Cambrai. RIR 119 reported many of the inhabitants they passed on the march route offered water and refreshments, in some

Cambrai, September 1914. (*Die 26. Reserve Division 1914-1918*)

Infantryman – RIR 109. (Author's collection)

cases wine. When marching through Cambrai the regiment passed the magnificent town hall that shone in the glowing sunshine.

The gunners in the 4/RFAR 26 were relieved to be free from the confinement of the railway cars where they shared accommodations with the battery horses. The guns were unloaded at Lourches. The members of the battery heard wild rumors of *Franktireurs* and more realistic predictions of hard fighting ahead, but they were confident of their fighting ability and the German army as a whole.

The weather was hot and humid and the men were not accustomed to marching in such heat and many became fatigued. However they were much happier to march on the rolling terrain of the Somme instead of the high passes of the Vosges. They were quite pleased to sleep in real beds at night or locate comfortable quarters supplied with ample amounts of straw.

The Corps was attached to the Sixth Army under Crown Prince Ruprecht von Bayern, which constituted the extreme right wing of the German Army. Two Bavarian Corps had previously arrived in the vicinity and had been fighting against the French. With the arrival of the XIV Reserve Corps the front could be extended north and the French Army could hopefully be encircled.

The main drawback to this plan was that the French had also been shifting troops and were extending their lines north as fast as the Germans were. The French forces facing the XIV Reserve Corps were a mix of regular infantry regiments, territorial troops and cavalry from the French Second Army under General Castelnau that had been formed at Amiens.

The French XI Corps was forming opposite the XIV Reserve Corps. The XI Corps, under General Eydoux consisted of the 21st and 22nd Divisions. This Corps had arrived at Amiens on the 25th; it had previously been attached to the French Ninth Army east of Rheims. Reports were received that four French territorial divisions were entrenched between Doullens and Amiens in the line Doullens – Contay. One advanced French

Gunner – RFAR 26. (Author's collection)

detachment was reported to be between Arras and Bapaume and there was active aerial reconnaissance above Cambrai.

While the newly formed Sixth Army was to envelop the French left flank it would take time to place the XIV Reserve Corps in motion. Thousands of men, horses and guns had to be unloaded and assembled into their units. II Bavarian Corps fought on the left of the Corps, south and west of Le Transloy. The plans called for the 28th Reserve Division to advance on the right flank of II Bavarian Corps while the 26th Reserve Division would advance along the National road from Cambrai to Albert and turn the French flank.

The two greatest obstacles facing the XIV Reserve Corps were a lack of information on the location and strength of the French forces in their vicinity, and, insufficient information of when and where their own forces were being unloaded and where they were located at any given point in time.

The 26th Reserve Division ordered the Württemberg Reserve Dragoon Regiment to reconnoiter the area around Cambrai and report their findings as soon as possible. Reports soon arrived that Arras, Bapaume and Douai were occupied by the French, apparently Territorial troops. Intelligence gathered by the patrols revealed that German Cavalry units were fighting in a westerly direction at Sailly-Saillisel.

Reserve *Jäger* Bn 8 advanced on the morning of the 25th. Shortly after leaving Masnieres they came upon the wreckage of 19 German supply wagons in a long line upon the highway. The wagons had probably belonged to a cavalry division located nearby. They were able to determine that French cavalry, supposedly North African *Spahis*, had attacked the supply column from which only one wagon had been able to escape capture or destruction. When the *Jägers* arrived they discovered the drivers had been killed and their eyes had been gouged out. This enraged the men and they were eager to take revenge against the French.

Cavalry patrols advised the *Jägers* that they were unsupported and that a French Cavalry division operating nearby could attack them at any time. The main body of German cavalry was some 20 kilometers distant and was unable to assist them. The *Jägers* took additional security measures during the march and they began to burn everything in sight in revenge for the massacred supply column.

The *Jägers* arrived in the village of Gouzeaucourt in the evening where the inhabitants were quite friendly towards their new guests, providing comfortable billets and anything the men asked for. They only asked in return that the *Jägers* would not take anything with them. Individual doors were already marked in chalk 'Good people live here,'[6] left behind by the Württemberg Dragoons that had passed through the village earlier. The *Jägers* followed their example.

26 September 1914

It was a hot day and considerable demands were placed upon the men whose legs were still stiff from the long journey. There were still conflicting accounts of French forces and their locations. The Reserve Dragoon Regiment received orders to send out five long-range patrols. The 1st Squadron went toward Queant-Croisilles-Boisleux-Avesnes-Rebreuviette. The 2nd Squadron sent two patrols; the first toward Vaulx-Courcelle-Doullens and the second in the direction of Bapaume-Sailly-Marieux. The 3rd Squadron also sent two patrols; the first in the direction of Douai-Lille-Dunkirk and the second to Arras-St. Pol then toward the sea.

In the morning Reserve *Jäger* Bn 8 was ordered to protect the right wing of II Bavarian Corps that was marching from Manancourt to Bray. The *Jägers* were accompanied by the I/R109, the Machine Gun Coy/R109 and 1/Reserve Dragoon Regiment 8 designated as Detachment Kachel.

Detachment Kachel advanced through Fins toward Recquigny, which was occupied by French Territorial troops. The French moved to the vicinity of Barastre when the vanguard of the Guard Cavalry accompanied by one battery from FAR 15 galloped past Detachment Kachel. The artillery quickly took the French under fire while the cavalry advanced to the north in order to block off any French advance from this direction. When the German attacked Barastre and Recquigny the French Territorials quickly withdrew from the field in every direction.

The *Jägers* noted the Reserve Dragoons were unable to maintain the speed and maneuverability demonstrated by the Guard Cavalry as they sat on their 'field nags and let their heads hang down'. *Oberleutnant* von Löbenitz noted that 'Dragoons ride like the wind if they first sat up.'[7] Unfortunately the observations were true in many cases. The Dragoon Regiment had received their mounts from horses brought in under the requirements of mobilization. Most of the horses had been used to pull delivery carts, milk and farm wagons. They were not in the best condition and unused to rigorous conditions in the field. Many broke down under the strain of the long-range patrols that could be 40 kilometers or more.

The 1/Reserve *Jäger* Bn 8 was on outpost duty during the night when the company commander, *Hauptmann* Siewert, reported hearing a French baggage column marching in the twilight. The rattle of wagons could be heard clearly in the direction of Villers au Flos. When dawn broke on the 27th Siewert discovered that the enemy baggage column was in reality a creaking windmill, much to his chagrin.

Infantryman – RIR 120. (Author's collection)

Leutnant Karl Egelhaaf, RFAR 26. (Sebastian Laudan)

The 26th Reserve Division sent out a detachment to protect the disembarkation of the remainder of the division. Detachment von Ziegesar consisted of RIR 119, the Reserve Dragoon Regiment, 4/RFAR 26 and the 4/Pioneer Bn 13. Detachment von Ziegesar advanced towards Bapaume, traveling through Havrincourt, Hermies and reached the Cambrai-Bapaume road at Beugny. They had the honor of forming the extreme right wing of the German Army.

News about the French was scarce during the advance; however sounds of artillery fire could be heard indicating heavy fighting was going on nearby. German cavalry rode through the terrain individually as well as in close formations. French cavalry could be seen at the edge of the forest of Havrincourt on the left flank. Additional reports arrived of French forces north of the Cambrai-Bapaume road, from Vaulx-Vraucourt, Bullecourt, up to Cambrai.

When the detachment advanced toward Vélu it came under machine gun fire from the village. White shrapnel clouds suddenly burst over the men but French gunnery was poor and their shots much too high to cause any damage. The 4/RFAR 26 went into position east of the village and provided support for the infantry. The advance continued and in the afternoon made contact with the 4th Cavalry Division Garnier near the small village of Beugny. The 4th Cavalry Division had been ordered to push forward to Albert but had not been able to reach the city due to the increasing number of French forces in their path.

Generalleutnant von Auwärter, commanding Reserve Infantry Brigade 52, ordered Detachment von Ziegesar to hold the line Morchies-Lebucquiere along with *Jäger* Bn 7 and one battery from FAR 3 from the 4th Cavalry Division. Two battalions from RIR 120 advanced towards Bapaume and were ordered to cover the right flank.

Jäger Bn 7 had occupied Beugny with cyclist troops. They were expected to check any French attack from Frémicourt with their machine guns. The battery from FAR 3 was positioned at the crossroads northeast of the village with cavalry in the rear in support. The 5/R119 relieved the cyclist troops in Beugny while the 6/R119 was positioned on the road to Morchies. The rest of the men were in reserve nearby.

Cavalry scouts advised von Ziegesar that strong French forces were reported to be advancing from Bapaume as well as via Beugnatre and Vaulx-Vraucourt on their right flank. French reconnaissance units of cyclists and *Chasseurs d'Afrique* had been observed everywhere, encompassing the right flank at Inchy, Pronville and Lagnicourt.

Towards evening waves of French infantry suddenly poured out of Beugnatre and Vaulx-Vraucourt. FAR 3 and the 4/RFAR 26 opened fire upon the advancing infantry. Shell after shell fell in the middle of the French lines and the attack began to falter. However French forces continued their advance and now shrapnel screamed from the north and burst in the tops of the trees lining the National road. Everything was thrown into confusion and soon men were running in every direction. Additional French batteries joined the fighting from the vicinity of Haplincourt. The arrival of the 5th and 6/RFAR 26 and light ammunition column from the II *Abteilung* provided much needed support and ammunition.

The 5/R119 was forced to withdraw from Beugny in the face of superior French forces that continued to advance beyond the village. The 5th Coy withdrew and the III/R119 was ordered to occupy the Bois des Chaufours while the 12/R119 occupied Morchies to protect the right flank.

Reports were coming in from all directions that the French stood on the flank at Bullecourt, Riencourt, Lagnicourt and Noreuil. At least two French infantry regiments and three field gun batteries opposed RIR 119 and the situation was critical. Then just before the onset of dusk the most unexpected thing happened, the French retreated.

Von Ziegesar was ordered to recapture Beugny in the night. Provisions were made for an advance by two battalions from RIR 119, the third was ordered to occupy Delsaux Farm south of Beugny.

At 9.30 p.m. two machine-guns swept the main street of Beugny and the battalions advanced with fixed bayonets. The French waited until the bulk of both battalions were inside the village and then opened fire from the houses and walls while machine-guns fired from the church. Flames rose up at the village edge and the 'defenders jumped out of the burning barns like frogs.'[8] The dark night was illuminated with the burning buildings and flashes from rifles and machine guns from both sides. RIR 119 was able to take Beugny from the French and in the process captured 130 prisoners from the *84e Régiment Territoriale*. It was reported that some of the prisoners were nabbed as they hid under the benches inside the school.

During the fighting the companies became hopelessly mixed together. Suddenly a message arrived that the enemy was attacking the village from the rear. The men in RIR 119 began to retreat toward Cambrai. They could see a burning village off to their left and many wondered what was happening.

The burning village was Morchies occupied by the 12/R119. The company had entered the village in the afternoon and occupied the northern edge without opposition. The company was positioned to block the French coming from the direction of Lagnicourt. While two platoons prepared trenches in the hedges and gardens in the village a Hussar patrol pushed on to Lagnicourt and found it to be free of French forces.

Pioneer – 4/Pionier Battalion 13. (Author's collection)

At dusk the village of Lagnicourt came alive and troops could be heard marching on the hill to the north at the Bois de Maricourt. Orders could be heard and there was a distinct sound of clinking spades. The 12/R119 sent a patrol to determine what was happening and they sneaked up on a French outpost approximately 600 meters away. Behind the outpost they could make out a French camp being set up. As darkness fell the patrol returned to Morchies and reported their findings.

The field kitchens arrived in the darkness and stopped alongside a small group of cyclists that accompanied the 12/R119. *Feldwebel* Gräter was distributing food when he heard the sound of marching on the road to Beugny and saw a column approaching. He called out, 'Halt, who goes there?' receiving infantry fire in response. The cooks banged the lids down on their kettles, the drivers jumped into their seats and whipped the horses while the cyclists jumped on their bicycles and rode off.

The men lined up to receive their rations ran back to the defenses and in a few moments the village was empty. Since the 12/R119 faced an enemy force assumed to be larger the men moved around the village dodging French troops and were able to exit the village without suffering many losses. They withdrew until they were approximately 500 meters away from Morchies on the road to Lebucquiere where the company halted; the 4/Pioneer Bn 13 joined them.

When the report of the fighting in Morchies reached RIR 119 it was realized they had not been attacked from the rear. Beugny was reoccupied and entrenchments were constructed at the village edge and patrols were sent to Fremicourt to clarify the situation. After questioning the prisoners and village inhabitants they learned that the *84e Régiment Territoriale* and one battery of artillery had occupied Beugny. The night passed quietly with the exception of one incident. A French sergeant came up in the darkness and encountered a German sentry. The sentry was wounded in the leg by a bayonet thrust but he was able to strike down the sergeant using his rifle butt.

Regiments were still arriving by train near Cambrai and it would take time to assemble all of the men. IR 180 and RIR 121 were being unloaded at Denain and Cambrai. The 28th Reserve Division was awaiting reports from Detachment Kachel that was to have joined the Guard Cavalry Division fighting against the French at Le Transloy.

The advance units of XIV Reserve Corps in conjunction with the cavalry had upset French plans against Cambrai. Based upon reports after the fighting the Corps had come into contact with portions of at least two Territorial divisions (Cure and Brugere), which were withdrawn behind the Ancre where they joined the French XI Corps.

The main forces of the XIV Reserve Corps were finally unloaded and assembled on 27 September. The senior command placed high hopes on an advance against Albert and the Corps received orders to relieve the pressure on the right wing of the II Bavarian Corps that was suspected to be at Combles. The 26th Reserve Division would advance on the National road via Boursies to Bapaume while the 28th Reserve Division would advance from Bertincourt via Haplincourt to Ligny-Thilloy.

The AOK Sixth Army[9] Liaison Officer, Major von Xylander, depended on the rapid advance of XIV Reserve Corps to bring assistance to the Bavarians who would overwhelm the allegedly inferior French forces facing the II Bavarian Corps. The Cavalry Corps HKK 1[10] would protect and clear the right flank of XIV Reserve Corps up to Arras. However this was not to prove as easy as they had hoped. Considerable French forces were being assembled in Bapaume and to the north, apparently protecting the left wing of the French army and to disrupt the disembarkation of German troops. The new French forces consisted of four Territorial divisions under Brugere, the 81st, 82nd, 84th and 88th Infantry Divisions and the Provisional Cavalry Division Beaudemoulin. They would have to be dealt with before any advance could be made.

Infantrymen and musicians – IR 180. (Author's collection)

27 September 1914

In the early morning hours the 28th Reserve Division advanced toward Ligny-Thilloy. RIR 109 protected the main body of the division with the I *Abteilung* RFAR 29 and 1R/ Pioneer Bn 13 in support. The rest of the division followed at large intervals, some having just been unloaded earlier that morning.

The division marched toward Bapaume until the lead units were in position south of Ligny-Thilloy and Warlencourt where the 1st and 2/R109 deployed in a sunken road south of le Barque and opened fire upon the edge of a nearby forest. At 1 p.m. heavy artillery and machine gun fire suddenly struck these companies and the 3rd and 4/R109 positioned further in the rear. This short fight resulted in 2 men killed and 16 men wounded in the 1st and 2/R109; the dead were buried on the road to Flers.

During this action the III/R109 was forced to dig-in due to infantry fire coming from the direction of Bapaume. The 9th and 11/R109 entered the city and expelled French cavalry and cyclist patrols and then rejoined the battalion. The III Battalion moved to Ligny-Thilloy and occupied the village edge. All the while the regiment received strong shell and shrapnel fire, which was responded to by guns from RFAR 29.

French cavalry units then advanced against the companies in the sunken road, which were repelled by infantry fire. Once the 26th Reserve Division continued to advance on the road to Albert the French opposition in front of RIR 109 disappeared. The regiment continued toward Flers where the men received billets. The regiment lost a total of 2 men killed and 32 wounded.

While in Flers the men discovered large egg warehouses in the form of concrete basins. They devoured the eggs throughout the night using every available piece of cookware. Every container of the field kitchens, cookware and pockets of the men were then filled with eggs for use in the coming days.

RIR 111 had deployed for an attack upon Ligny-Thilloy when the regiment reached Haplincourt, following behind RIR 110. The regiments advanced until they reached the Bapaume-Le Transloy road where they heard sounds of skirmishing coming from Ligny-Thilloy. RIR 110 came up against light resistance, reportedly French Colonial troops who were quickly driven back. The regiment stopped when they reached Le Transloy because the Bavarians were reported to be fighting in Les Boeufs to the south and might require support. Later the 110th occupied a support line south of Bancourt because of reports received of a French advance from the direction of Arras in the north.

RIR 111 received orders to send one battalion to protect the right flank and occupy Bapaume in connection with the 26th Reserve Division. During the advance the 10/R111 found the contents of the municipal savings bank hidden in a cellar and confiscated it.

RIR 40 was one of the last regiments to reach the front at Flers in the evening, in part due to taking the wrong road on the march and in part due to enemy aerial activity. French planes frequently flew overhead forcing the men to constantly lie down. This seriously disrupted the mobility of the regiment.

The 4th Bavarian Division had been brought to a stop in the area of Bazentin le Petit - Longueval in the afternoon by French forces advancing from Albert. The Bavarians sent a request for support to the 28th Reserve Division and the II/R111 was sent to Flers in response. However when the battalion arrived their help was no longer required.

The 26th Reserve Division made substantial advances on the 27th. There was a skirmish in the morning as the 12/R119 recaptured Morchies. Afterward the 12th Coy could see marching columns behind Vaulx-Vraucourt to the northwest in the early morning fog. However they were unable to determine if they were friend or foe. The division assembled on the National road leading from Cambrai to Albert. The vanguard was located in Beugny while the main body was located in Boursies. IR 180 and RIR 121 had still not finished unloading and assembling and because of neglect the division orders had not reached RIR 120, which delayed the advance until 9 a.m. During the march toward Bapaume the II/RFAR 26 moved through Beugny that still bore the gruesome signs of the nighttime attack made upon the French Territorials by RIR 119.

Reserve Infantry Brigade 52 led the vanguard to Bapaume. Reserve Infantry Brigade 51 formed the main body of the division. The column was fired upon at intervals during the advance but the French afforded only weak opposition, especially at Sapignies, and withdrew behind the Bapaume-Arras road. While the men marched they observed *Chasseurs à Cheval* ride out from nearby copses and then race northward. The village of Favreuil was supposed to be occupied by the enemy but when the 11/R119 reached the Château Park they found that the village was empty of any French troops.

Bapaume was reached about midday, the French yielded in the face of the advance and offered little opposition. The city was peacefully occupied and the men were allowed a short rest. Meanwhile the batteries of RFAR 26 took position at the northern and southern exits of the city and fired into the ranks of the withdrawing French infantry. The II/R119 observed a large force of French cavalry by Avesnes and the battalion quickly deployed to meet the threat. The battery assigned to the regiment took the new target under fire and the cavalry withdrew out of range. The terrain between Behucourt and the National road north of Ligny-Thilloy was also cleared of any French troops.

According to Corps headquarters the vanguard of the 26th Reserve Division was supposed to reach Ovillers-La Boisselle by night with the rest of the regiments receiving

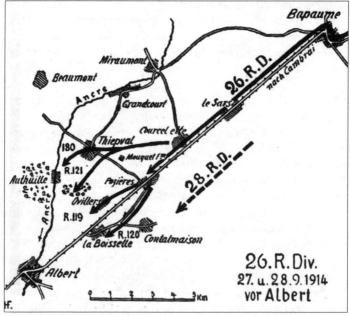

Advance by the 26th Reserve Division from Bapaume.

billets to the rear. During the day the last regiments of the 26th Reserve Division were unloaded and by 4 p.m. the division continued to advance towards Albert. Suddenly a French aircraft flew over the division at a low altitude. A frenzied fire was directed at the plane but without any visible success as it flew off into the distance. The last regiment in the division, RIR 99 finally reached Cambrai by late afternoon where it advanced as far as Fontaine Notre-Dame by late evening.

There was a short pause before the final descent towards Le Sars, during which sounds of fighting could be heard coming from Grevillers where Brigade Wundt was fighting with the French rearguard. The advance continued in the dark, lights flashed on here and there, however no sound, no people, no French troops could be seen. The village of Courcelette lay far away hidden in a dark group of trees.

Just as the lead units of RIR 119 reached the sugar factory by Le Sars a shot rang out in the darkness, like the sound of a whip through the night. The men listened to see if anyone was hit but no one called out, and the advance continued towards Pozières. Hans Ludwig, 6/R120, recalled the night the regiment reached the village:

> September 27, 1914 found our regiment advancing down the road from Cambrai to Amiens and we reached the small hamlet Le Sars about ten miles west of Bapaume. That day we found very little resistance on the part of the retreating French infantry. Night was rapidly approaching and we were told we would spend the night in the village of Pozières about 4 miles distant. At the rate we were going this meant about an hour's march before we had a chance to rest our tired limbs. A bone-dry brook

Baggage train RIR 110 entering a village on the Somme, September 1914.
(*Reserve-Infanterie Regiment Nr. 110 im Weltkrieg 1914-1918*)

cut through the middle of the village and my company had been assigned quarters on the other side. By the time we reached Pozières, however, it was pitch dark and when the first patrols tried to enter a house they were driven off by rifle and machine gun fire. We could not see how in the world we should be able to occupy our quarters when every house of Pozières was a miniature fort.[11]

As RIR 120 and the 2/R119 moved towards Pozières infantry fire suddenly twinkled at them from the village, trees and hedges, striking into the marching column. There was an indescribable turmoil in the ranks for a few moments. The officers quickly brought the men back into order and the companies were placed into position along the main road, awaiting orders to attack.

Von Auwärter ordered RIR 119 and RIR 120 to capture Pozières. The village was attacked in a pincer movement using fixed bayonets. The regiments penetrated into the burning village and in a short time it was taken.

It was so dark that we could see nothing but the flashes from the rifles and machine-guns, so, we set fire to some of the houses on the main road, Frenchmen in them or not. Soon we had all the light we wanted. My company was not in the first line but after a while there were no lines at all. There just was a grand mix up in the streets, hallways, barns, in fact all over the place. Until midnight, one of the fiercest hand-to-hand fights of the war was staged in Pozières. Hans Ludwig, 6/R120 [12]

Infantry column RIR 110 entering a village on the Somme, September 1914. (*Reserve-Infanterie Regiment Nr. 110 im Weltkrieg 1914-1918*)

Hans Ludwig, 6/R120. (Brian Ludwig)

The defenders consisted of two companies from the *22e Régiment Territoriale* that had been sent from Albert to occupy Pozières a few hours earlier. Since the XIV Reserve Corps did not know the strength or location of French forces on their front and because of the late hour no further advance was considered possible.

The XIV Reserve Corps would have to encompass the French flank and bring about a decision on another day. Besides, it was felt that Pozières must be held at all cost and prepared for defense and RIR 119 and RIR 120 occupied the village. The French defenders had prepared comfortable positions in the hedges at the village edge and had cushioned them with straw. The troops of RIR 119 found a warm camp while the opposing sentries kept up a sporadic fire during the night. The flash of guns on the left flank illuminated the black night where the Bavarians were still heavily engaged with the French while the men took up their quarters.

28 September 1914

On 28 September AOK Sixth Army ordered the XIV Reserve Corps to advance against Albert. As soon as sufficient ground had been gained the II Bavarian Corps (Line Montauban-Maricourt) would accompany it in the crucial advance towards the south over the Somme. I Cavalry Corps von Richthofen would support the operation by advancing on the right bank of the Ancre against the line Hedauville-Bouzincourt. However the attack did not come off as planned because French forces fighting in front of Albert as well as against the right flank of the 26th Reserve Division had increased in strength almost hourly until even the rear of the division was threatened.

The morning started off misty and rainy with many areas covered in dense fog as the regiments were formed. It was the first day that the entire 28th Reserve Division was assembled since arriving in northern France. The men of RIR 111 were awakened by the sounds of a large number of horses as a German cavalry division rode through their quarters

Pozières before the attack. (*Das Reserve-Infanterie-Regiment Nr. 111 im Weltkrieg 1914 bis 1918*)

in the early morning hours. The bulk of the division was then assembled at crossroad 110 about one kilometer west of Gueudecourt where the regiments received their orders.

RIR 40 and RIR 109 proceeded in the direction of Contalmaison. When the regiments reached Bazentin le Petit wood RIR 109 was ordered to attack Contalmaison while RIR 40 was positioned in Bazentin le Petit wood and the Bois de Mametz. RIR 40 determined that RIR 120 was on their right while Bavarian IR 5 (4th Bavarian Division) was in front of them. While the regiments were taking up their positions both woods and the surrounding terrain came under French shell and shrapnel fire.

French infantry had prepared positions in Contalmaison and at Contalmaison farm. It was the task of RIR 109 to drive the French out. The regiment was supported by RIR 120 and the 1st and 2R/Pioneer Bn 13.

RIR 109 advanced towards Contalmaison, the left wing taking direction on the village church steeple. The first detachments reached Contalmaison shortly after 11 a.m. The hill north of the village was captured despite heavy losses where approximately 20 prisoners were taken.

Other battalions advanced and skirmish line after skirmish line could be observed moving to the south and southwest as far as the men could see. The French continued to scatter shrapnel over the countryside. The II/R109 reached the northern edge of Contalmaison at 11.45 a.m. and by noon they had taken the southern exit of the village. The battalion lost only 3 men killed and 21 wounded in the attack. During the fighting at Contalmaison the men of RIR 109 had a very unpleasant surprise. They discovered that the heat of the action had caused the eggs stuffed into nearly every soldier's pocket to liquefy and had an unpleasant glue-like aftereffect. There was a lot of quiet cursing among the ranks of the regiment.

When the I/R109 attacked strong flanking fire caused the men to move too far to the right and the battalion ended up advancing towards La Boisselle with RIR 120. RIR 120 proceeded against La Boisselle via Hill 129 north of Contalmaison.

> Later that night the French evacuated Pozières and retreated to La Boisselle which is more or less a suburb of the large town of Albert. In the morning we had to advance to La Boisselle over an absolutely flat stretch and found bodies of dead French soldiers who had been hit by our shrapnells [sic]. The French put these bodies off of the road but did not take the time to bury them. In fact the corpses were never to be buried

as this part of France was to become one of the most dangerous, if not *the* most dangerous place on the whole Western front. Hans Ludwig, 6/R120 [13]

The advance continued as Ludwig recalled:

Shortly before entering La Boisselle, which stretches from a valley up to the hilltop, we were received by steady rifle fire. Again the village had to be cleaned out in hand-to-hand fighting, only this time it was daylight; the losses were heavier and the French appeared determined to hold on to this place. During this mess a goat with a rooster sitting on its back was running aimlessly and bewildered up and down the main street. Both animals were scared to death and therefore ran up and down the street between the French and German lines, finally deciding to stay with us. Both the rooster and the goat were sent back to our replacement battalion and after the rooster died, it was stuffed and mounted in a conspicuous place in the barracks to remind the old-timers of the rooster of La Boisselle. We were outnumbered by fresh troops but managed to throw them out of the village, experience being the better of quantity. But we again found stiff resistance on top of the hill where a lonely farm was situated, long remembered as the Grenate Farm. Hans Ludwig, 6/R120 [14]

Karl Metzger, 8/R120 was also involved in the heavy fighting in the village:

With this fighting the war becomes quite real before our eyes. For example my comrade Jakob Schlecht … had gotten a severe stomach shot next to me so that his intestines fell out, and after a few hours he died from this wound. Another comrade had his head formally separated from his body by a shell splinter and that head lay before our feet. Enemy shells struck the church of Pozières and wounded and killed many German soldiers. My own brother Albert, 7/R120, was shot through the arm

Pozières after the attack. (*Das Württembergische Reserve-Infanterie-Regiment Nr. 119 im Weltkrieg 1914-1918*)

The Last Cock of La Boisselle (*Der letzte Hahn von 'La Boisselle'*). (Author's collection)

on the La Boisselle road.… The entire village of La Boisselle was immediately taken under heavy enemy shellfire; it burned in every corner and death held a rich harvest.[15]

The village was captured at 5 p.m. and the men from RIR 120 were reformed and continued to advance. When La Boisselle fell the 1/R109 was sent to the right to counter strong French flanking forces and eventually ended up being involved in the attack against Ovillers with RIR 119. They stayed in this village for the next fourteen days along with one platoon of the 9/R109, as their presence was urgently needed.

During the attack the 3/R109 had worked forward to within 200 meters of the French line when the company was suddenly struck by severe flanking fire. Two of the three platoons were withdrawn behind a nearby hillside. This left the 3rd Platoon in a serious predicament. The men increased their fire in order to hold off any potential French counterattack. However this rate of fire would soon consume their small supply of cartridges and subsequently the men began to run out of ammunition one by one.

Gefreiter Erne acted decisively in the situation and crawled through the heavy French fire. He took the cartridge belts off of the dead and wounded men lying around the position. Laden with as much ammunition as he could carry he crawled back to his comrades where his haul was distributed. His actions enabled the 30 or so remaining men to hold out until assistance arrived. The French were soon outflanked from the right by the remainder of the I/R109 and the survivors were able to rejoin their company.

During the attack RIR 40 remained in the Bois de Mametz and Bazentin le Petit wood. The commander, *Oberstleutnant* John von Freynd and three officers went forward to find Bavarian IR 5 in Bazentin le Petit wood in order to determine what was happening. On their way to the Bavarian lines the patrol met a *Vizefeldwebel* from the Bavarian regiment who had been sent to establish a connection with them.

Oberstleutnant John Von Freynd. (*Das Reserve-Infanterie-Regiment Nr. 40 im Weltkrieg*)

The officers were led to a hillside southeast of Bazentin le Grand covered in dense undergrowth where they met with the staff of Bavarian IR 5. Von Freynd was unable to learn anything new from his visit and decided to return to his command. On the return journey the four officers met the commander of the II/R40 where the dense undergrowth and tree line met.

French artillery was scattering the area with shrapnel fire and several officers urged the group to enter the relative safety of the forest but Freynd ignored their suggestions. The group was standing and sitting along an elevated portion of the roadway surveying the situation along their front and giving orders when there was a sudden deafening explosion over their heads. A shrapnel shell had exploded just above the group of officers.

Von Freynd sank to the ground without a sound; he had been struck in the right temple by a shrapnel ball and killed instantly. The remaining officers were wounded, some severely. The body of von Freynd was carried to the rear and buried near the front line transport. RIR 40 was even more in the dark than before because the commander had taken most of the orders and instructions he had received from brigade headquarters to the grave.

At 5.35 p.m. the I/R109 in La Boisselle was replaced by RIR 120 and the battalion rejoined the regiment in order to take part in an attack against Fricourt. Units from RIR 40, Reserve *Jäger* Bn 8 and Bavarian IR 5 joined the battalion for the attack. The rolling hills provided some protection from French fire but once the men moved closer to Fricourt the terrain flattened out and the artillery and infantry fire increased. They were forced to halt due to the heavy fire.

During the advance from the Bois de Mametz RIR 40 had to cross a hollow and then ascend the last hill before the village. The new regimental commander, Major Käther, and his adjutant had joined the main line. They looked to the rear and saw a battalion commander and his adjutant running down the hill when a French shell exploded directly in front of them. Both men were enveloped in a black cloud of smoke and dirt and it was believed they had been killed. Amazingly, both men emerged from the cloud unscathed and joined the line. RIR 40 took position along the crest of a hill just outside of Fricourt and the men lay prone.

They could see Fricourt if they raised their heads up slightly. Even this position was dangerous however as the French continued to cover the terrain with shell and shrapnel fire. One man close to the regimental adjutant was killed instantly when he was struck in the head by a dud shell.

RIR 111 now joined in the attack against Fricourt. Two battalions formed up in the hollow running along the eastern side of the Bois de Mametz and advanced. The sun was already sinking and the sky was red and overcast as the regiment attacked. In the darkness the units became badly mixed together and RIR 111 ended up in the rear of RIR 40. The officers made an attempt to reform the regiment for the attack but their orientation in the unfamiliar terrain without proper reconnaissance was greatly impeded and they could not establish the direction towards Fricourt.

Stacks of grain in nearby fields caught fire and spread an eerie glow of light through the area. The men were in position a few hundred meters in front of a forest but could not see Fricourt in the darkness. The order to capture Fricourt was given again but where was the village? The commander of the *Jägers* decided the attack could not take place under the circumstances and the battalion bivouacked in the hollow.

The 4/Reserve *Jäger* Bn accompanying RIR 40 did not hear the orders and joined the attack of the I/R40. The men had become too eager and had taken the wrong direction along with parts of RIR 111. The battalions assumed a burning village was Fricourt and veered too far to the left and ran straight towards Mametz that was already in possession of Bavarian *Jäger* Bn 2. The attackers reached the burning village amidst a frenzied fire coming from other German troops.

The 4th *Jäger* Coy that followed the main body of infantry described the night attack. When the infantry were within 100 to 200 meters of the village they were struck by a hail of rapid machine gun and light infantry fire. The effect was startling. The infantry immediately turned around and ran back in the direction they had come only a few minutes before.

Oberleutnant Richard Müller, commander of the 4th Coy immediately had his men lay down as they had drilled in the past and the infantry ran through their ranks. The *Jägers* were in a bad spot, they were facing an enemy of unknown strength and their rifles were unloaded in order to prevent any casualties from occurring if they fired into their own men in the darkness. Now they lay under fire without having the opportunity of replying in kind.

Müller used his Alpine *Jäger* horn to assemble his men behind a straw rent. All of the men answered the call and had apparently not suffered a single casualty. They assumed that the 'enemy' had set their sights too high to be much of a danger; it was just a lot of noise. The battalion diary had a dry and factual account of the nighttime disaster:

> Nighttime attacks on villages promise little success if the roads, foreground and the exact position of the neighboring troops were not duly explored and connections on all sides had been established.[16]

Fricourt farm. (Author's collection)

In the background, towards the west, one burning village could be seen next to another. The remainder of RIR 111 decided that the attack was no longer feasible and the men took advantage of the hollows to avoid artillery fire and bursts of fire from French infantry. They withdrew to the Contalmaison-Fricourt road north of the Fricourt Farm and spent the night protected in a sunken road.

At the same time the III/R111 had reached the heights north of Mametz and formed for an attack upon Fricourt. Officer patrols had been sent forward on reconnaissance of the French position but none had returned before darkness had fallen. Time was running out if Fricourt was to be captured this day.

RIR 109 sent out patrols to establish the French positions and strength. Twelve volunteers from the 6/R109 proceeded towards Fricourt. They made their way up to the village and determined there were French pickets at the northern exit and that strong forces occupied the village. Based upon the findings of this patrol the capture of Fricourt was postponed until the following morning.

However the brigade commander wanted to capture Fricourt before the end of the day. At 11p.m. orders were issued for the village to be taken by bayonet attack. The only units available for the attack were the III/R111, parts of RIR 40 and Reserve *Jäger* Bn 8.

The men were positioned in three columns in a hollow northwest of Mametz and advanced with fixed bayonets. They had gotten to within 300 meters of the edge of the village without any opposition when they encountered wire entanglements. Just as the men attempted to cut through the entanglements heavy fire struck into their ranks coming from the village and nearby hills. The men began to take losses in the fire and the attack was smashed.

The III/R111 remained in the position where it had stopped. The 9/R111 managed to advance to the southern edge of Fricourt and penetrated into the flank of Hill 110. The battalion could no longer hold its exposed position and was withdrawn behind a hill north of Mametz. The regimental aid post east of Mametz was kept busy through the night where the medical officers and one nurse did their best with the large number of wounded.

The two regiments made another attempt to capture the terrain toward the east in the valley between Mametz and Fricourt and to occupy the village. The assault failed again as a result of darkness and lack of maps as the battalions could not maintain their lines or direction. One battalion of RIR 111 strayed so far from the others that it ended up being collected by RIR 109. The mood of the III/R111 was somber as the battalion had taken heavy losses and had nothing to show for it.

The early casualties: Reservist Karl Fuchs, Reservist Gottlob Lauer, Reservist Jakob
Wörner RIR 119. Killed on 28 September 1914 at Pozières. (Author's collection)

Overall the mood of the men was poor. Troops swarmed everywhere around the
terrain. Everywhere one could hear shouting 'Don't shoot', followed by short commands,
all of which indicated great chaos.

The regiments of the 26th Reserve Division were assembled early in the morning to
continue the advance upon Albert. The two brigades received their orders for the day.
Reserve Infantry Brigade 51 would protect the right flank of the division. Reserve Infantry
Brigade 52 would attack on the line Ovillers-La Boisselle.

The dense early morning fog made it difficult to see anything and in some cases it was
hard to see the outline of the ground. By 6 a.m. RFAR 26 was formed in columns on the
National road by the entrance of Le Sars as if on maneuvers. The thick fog had slowed the
column down considerably. Fortunately the regimental commander had ridden ahead on
a reconnaissance and was able to rapidly lead the batteries into position. The I *Abteilung*
was placed in position 2 kilometers east of Pozières while the II and III *Abteilung* were
positioned west of Courcelette.

While the dense early morning fog made the deployment of the troops difficult it
had the added benefit of concealing the Germans from French observation. RIR 119
attacked in the direction of Contalmaison, the right wing passing by Ovillers and the
left wing passing by Pozières where units from RIR 120 joined in the attack. During the
initial advance the troops received only scattered fire from the direction of Contalmaison.

When the fog began to lift French troops could clearly be seen digging trenches.
Machine gun fire quickly forced them to abandon their work and withdraw. At 9.30 a.m.

two French batteries were observed driving up along the road from Albert. They were quickly taken under fire from the guns of RFAR 26 positioned nearby. Within a few minutes a hurricane of fire broke over the village of Pozières and according to a company lying in a garden it felt like a stay in hell.

While Contalmaison was being attacked RIR 119 was suddenly ordered to attack Ovillers. This change of plans required the regiment to alter direction from the south toward the west. The regiment was realigned and attacked with the two battalions. The companies worked forward slowly in face of the heavy French fire. The 4th and 5/RFAR 26 provided support and opened fire upon the village and surrounding terrain.

Rows of French dead in their blue uniform jackets and bright red trousers lay in the fields between Ovillers and La Boisselle, the majority coming from the *64e Régiment d'Infanterie* who had offered stubborn resistance against the German assault.

At 1 p.m. the attack faltered when *Oberstleutnant* von Ziegesar was wounded and the II Battalion ran out of ammunition. With fresh supplies of ammunition and close artillery support provided by RFAR 26 the infantry attack continued against Ovillers. Faced with this threat the French garrison occupying Ovillers withdrew to the hills in front of Albert. However French batteries showered the village with fire so that the II/R119, which had suffered the most from this shelling, was forced to take cover in the sunken road leading towards Authuille.

The III/R119 that had been in reserve was ordered forward and advanced behind a thin veil of skirmishers until they had reached the edge of the Forest of Authuille. Later the battalion was moved closer towards Ovillers where the men began to dig trenches along the road leading towards Authuille. During the night the men could hear trains rumbling through Albert bringing fresh troops and batteries that were being positioned in the hills surrounding the city and north of the Ancre.

In the early morning hours of 28 September RIR 99 assembled in Fontaine Notre Dame and was on the road by 6 a.m. The regiment marched more than 30 kilometers on the National road towards Bapaume. Along the march route the regiment began to pick up stray children from the surrounding areas. The regimental commander, *Oberst* Grall, was concerned that due to the uncertain conditions the children might not have sufficient food.

As they approached Bapaume the regimental mess officer was sent ahead in an automobile in order to arrange for supplies, particularly bread, fodder for the horses and wine. During the long march the regiment passed a number of burning farmsteads and wounded French soldiers alongside the road, testimonials to the fighting that had gone on ahead of them.

The regiment reached Bapaume at midday and entered an empty city. They confiscated the weapons of a few lightly wounded French soldiers they encountered and found a large number of French General staff maps of the area that were most welcome. After a short rest the march was resumed.

RIR 121 also assembled in the morning except for the 4th Coy. The 4/R121 was sent to occupy the village of Thiepval to the west of Courcelette. As the company approached the village the men came under infantry fire from several gardens and nearby streets. The village was apparently occupied by a French cyclist patrol. The 4/R121 rushed the village and quickly overcame the weak resistance. One *Feldwebel* who came across two French soldiers with their hands raised high still holding their rifles was almost killed when he

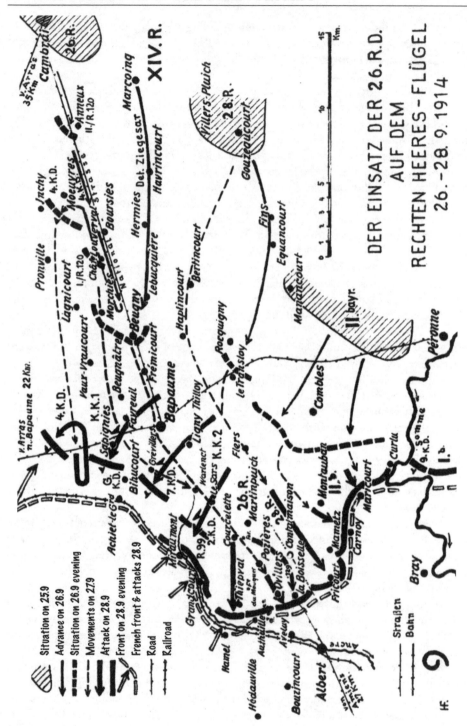

Somme Front: 26-28 September 1914.

Pre-war souvenir postcard of Thiepval Church. (Author's collection)

approached them. As the *Feldwebel* came closer one man suddenly lowered his rifle and shot the *Feldwebel* through the mouth.

Several prisoners were taken in the short fight with most of the Frenchmen fleeing leaving their bicycles behind. The prisoners claimed that the XIV Reserve Corps was facing no less than 40,000 Territorial troops on their front.

While the regiment assembled several cavalry divisions were nearby. For many of the men it was the first and last time they had seen such a huge mass of cavalry in one place. Later in the morning the II/R121 was sent to Thiepval to relieve the 4th Coy. The battalion sent out patrols that reported French troops at Mesnil-Hamel that had also sent patrols across the Ancre. The French were found south of Thiepval in the forest of Aveluy and west of Ovillers. The regiment was ordered to prepare to attack.

At 11 a.m. the II/180 replaced the II/R121 in Thiepval to allow this battalion to participate in an attack against the heights northwest of Ovillers. The II/180 and one platoon from the Machine Gun Company reached Thiepval at noon and immediately sent out patrols to the Ancre valley.

The 2nd Cavalry Division under General *Freiherr* George von Thumb from the II Cavalry Corps was assigned to provide support on the right flank of the 26th Reserve

Mouquet Farm. (*Das Württembergische Reserve-Infanterie-Regiment Nr. 121 im Weltkrieg 1914-1918*)

Division. The cavalry moved into position north of Courcelette to protect the Ancre crossings at Grandcourt and Miraumont. The III/180 (less the 9th and 11/180) was detached from the regiment and placed under the orders of Cavalry Division von Thumb. The 10th and 12/180 occupied the Ancre crossing at Grandcourt and later helped drive French troops out of the village of Beaucourt on the northern bank of the river. When this was completed the companies were placed at the disposal of General von Wundt. He ordered the companies to capture a mill located 500 meters east of the village of Hamel after receiving reports that French infantry occupied it. The companies rejoined the regiment the following day after suffering minor losses.

At 5.30 p.m. the I/180, 9th and 11/180 and two-thirds of the Machine Gun Coy took possession of Authuille Wood, occupying the northwestern edge of the forest. They were supported by the 6/RFAR 26 located near Mouquet Farm.

The II and III/R121 attacked the forest and hills west of Ovillers at 4 p.m. The skirmish line received only weak fire from French troops positioned on the hills and forest. The regiment then received artillery fire, which caused a number of casualties. During the bombardment French artillery observers mistakenly targeted four cows that were evenly spaced in the same manner as a German battery in firing position. Unfortunately the cows and the men of the III/R121 nearby paid for this error with their lives. By the time darkness had fallen, the II and III/R121 had taken up positions upon the hill facing south while the I/R121 with the Machine Gun Company were positioned behind the right wing inside Aveluy Wood.

Orders to capture the villages of Authuille and Aveluy and encircle Albert from the right bank of the Ancre could not be executed because of the increasing French threat to the right flank. The railway-line in the Ancre valley from Albert to Achiet le Grand and Arras was still occupied by the French.

Numerous French batteries located north of the Ancre caused considerable losses to the men in Reserve Infantry Brigade 51. The number and caliber of the French guns also demonstrated the inferiority of the artillery attached to XIV Reserve Corps that was having difficulty countering French artillery fire.

Beauregard Farm. (Sebastian Laudan)

The last regiment from Reserve Infantry Brigade 51 to arrive on the field was RIR 99. During the day two companies were assigned to assist the cavalry on the right flank and provide support in any fighting in the direction of Puisieux on the hills dominating the Ancre valley. At 8 p.m. the II/R99 occupied the crossings over the Ancre at Miraumont and Grandcourt on the right flank. The battalion quickly established a connection with IR 180 on the left in Thiepval and with the III/R99 on the right in the village of Miraumont. Every attempt by the French to cross the Ancre at Hamel, Grandcourt and Miraumont was repelled.

The II/R99 was ordered to proceed to Beauregard farm across the Ancre located at the northern exit of Miraumont. The farm was surrounded by a high wall and was currently occupied by a *Jäger* cyclist company. The battalion advanced through Irles and reached Miraumont receiving shrapnel fire during most of its journey but was able to reach the farm without suffering any casualties.

After the *Jäger* Coy returned to the rear the II/R99 came under fire from French artillery using high explosive shells. The commanding officer realized his battalion would not be able to hold the farm under the current conditions and ordered the men to withdraw and seek cover in a nearby sunken road. When darkness fell the battalion was ordered to withdraw to Miraumont where the men entrenched at the edge of the village.

When the battalion reached Miraumont the village was searched for any French soldiers. All they found were two dead infantrymen. One was a sergeant who was carrying a company payroll. His comrades were probably cursing the unfortunate NCO for failing to deliver their money. The field kitchens came up at night and provided the men with a hot meal.

The XIV Reserve Corps had made headway against the French forces opposing it but the main goal, the capture of Albert had not been realized. Many of the officers and men later wondered what might have been if the journey from the Vosges had not taken as long as it had. Their goal was so close the men of RFAR 26 reported being able to see the cathedral with the golden Virgin and child gleaming in the afternoon sunshine. Despite the possibility that the cathedral was being used as an observation post the artillery was prohibited from shelling it by direct orders of the Corps commander.

One of the most important positions captured on 28 September was the village of Thiepval. Located some 60 meters above the Ancre valley it dominated the terrain to the south and east. It was a small village of some 200 inhabitants and a spacious Château, which had been abandoned in some haste. The Château was occupied in the evening by the staff of several units. The officers held a comfortable meeting at a large dining room table drinking wine that had been found in the cellar. They all admired the fine furnishings and accessories throughout the splendid home.

Many of the difficulties experienced by the XIV Reserve Corps on 28 September were the result of poor intelligence concerning the French forces opposing it. General Castelnau had moved fresh forces around Albert including throwing the lead elements of the French XI Corps against the Germans. At the same time Territorial Divisions had been sent north of the Ancre to encompass the XIV Reserve Corps. Without knowing this information the main German thrust was directed to the south and was not prepared to change direction to the west in sufficient numbers to counter the new French threat.

Another problem experienced by the XIV Reserve Corps was the failure of the cavalry to protect the right flank while forcing the French back at the same time. The I Cavalry Corps von Richthofen did not advance across the railway line Achiet le Grand-Arras, similarly the 7th Cavalry Division had very little success advancing on the west bank of the Ancre.

29 September 1914

The advance towards Albert was resumed. The 28th Reserve Division would attack to the south while the 26th Reserve Division would attack in the direction of Albert and provide protection against the growing French threat to the right flank.

THIEPVAL (Somme) — Le Château

Pre-war souvenir postcard of Thiepval Château. (Author's collection)

German wounded, French prisoners. (*Die 26. Reserve Division 1914-1918*)

The main thrust by the 28th Reserve Division would be against Fricourt and the heights on both sides of the village. The 4th Bavarian Division had already occupied Mametz and protected the left flank of the division. Parts of four regiments would attack Fricourt while RIR 111 and Reserve *Jäger* Bn 8 would attack Hill 110, one kilometer south of the village.

At 5.30 a.m. the Machine Gun Coy/R109 deployed south of a small copse to support the attack upon Fricourt. The regiments prepared for the attack, as described by *Oberleutnant* Guksch, RIR 40:

> We moved sideways a considerable distance, sheltered in the hollow and deployed behind the wood in order to break forth in the direction of Fricourt from here. When the regimental staff was in the valley behind the hollow fierce enemy artillery fire was placed on the edge of the wood above and the hollow. The shrapnel hailed into the wood.[17]

The I and II/R40 and Reserve *Jäger* Bn 8 formed the main line along with RIR 109 while the III/R40 remained in reserve. The attack began at 5.45 a.m. in semi-darkness as the men quickly rushed towards the village. The French covered the advancing German lines with shell, shrapnel, rifle and machine gun fire. The first houses at the northern edge of the village were stormed at 6 a.m.; there was no opposition inside the village.

What the attackers did not know was that the night before the French decided they could not hold Fricourt and had evacuated the village under cover of darkness. The French had taken up new positions on the heights south and west of the village. The village had already been entered by several detachments from Reserve *Jäger* Bn 8 before dawn.

The *Jägers* had pressed forward past the Château and into the village. The artillery fire was quite strong and many of the men sought cover in the houses and shops. These proved to be inadequate protection against the shellfire as one house after the other was destroyed.

Oskar Lipp
Oberleutn. u. Kompagnieführer im
Ref.-Inf.-Regt. 121, gest. 30. Sept.
an den bei Thiepval erlitt. Wunden

Fischer
Leutnant d.R. i. Ref.-Inf.-Regt. 119
(Justiz-Ref.), gest. 30. Sept. an einer
in Ovillers erlittenen Verwundung

Oberleutnant Oskar Lipp (Ulm), Supply
Officer II/R121. Wounded 29 September
1914 at Authuille, died 2 October 1914
Reserve Field Hospital 1, Bapaume.
(*Kriegstagbuch aus Schwaben*)

Leutnant der Reserve Walter Fischer
(Heidenheim) 1/R119. Wounded 29
September 1914, died 30 September
1914 Reserve Field Hospital 1, Bapaume.
(*Kriegstagbuch aus Schwaben*)

Many *Jägers* were wounded or killed in the heavy fire. The wounded suffered a particularly horrible fate. They had been collected and taken into a large barn in the village. The barn was later hit by shells and set on fire, killing all of the men trapped inside.

Just as RIR 111 reached the Fricourt Château French infantry fire suddenly struck the right flank. The advance continued and when the regiment entered the village the companies quickly became mixed together in the maze of houses. The 1st and 4/R111 advanced past the church to the southern edge of the village. Parts of these companies attempted to capture the Fricourt Railway station located just outside of the village but heavy French resistance drove them back. *Jäger* companies also attempted to capture the railway station without success. The survivors occupied the houses and gardens located at the southern edge of the village.

At 7.30 a.m. a French counterattack approaching Fricourt from the southwest was repelled. The machine guns from RIR 109 caused particularly heavy losses to the French troops. Everything had gone surprisingly quickly. Fricourt had been occupied and prepared for defense when the first orders arrived at 8 a.m. to capture the village.

Fricourt formed a narrow projection from the German lines because troops on the left at Mametz and on the right at La Boisselle were not able to advance from their positions. This meant that key positions at the Forest of Bécourt and the Bécourt Château remained in French hands. The Germans wanted to expand their gains by attacking the French lines to the west of the village in order to straighten their line and relieve the pressure. *Oberstleutnant* von Baumbach, commander of RIR 109, advanced three separate times but in each case the attacks were forced back by French fire.

The final attempt could not take place as ordered. The heavy bombardment greatly impeded the transmission of orders and made the assembly of the forces required impossible. Afterward the men were put to work strengthening the positions and preparing the buildings for defense by creating loopholes in the walls and roofs and setting up barricades in the streets leading out of the village. The situation became critical when French artillery opened a particularly heavy fire upon the village at 10 a.m. that continued for the rest of the day.

Further French attacks against Fricourt occurred during the afternoon, all of which were repelled. The fighting did not die down until darkness had fallen and even at that point the French made at least one further attempt to recapture the village. Machine-gun fire and spotlights supported the attacking French troops, but these attempts also failed. While the men began to dig trenches and improve their positions burning houses scattered throughout the village and French spotlights lit up the night. The stony, hard ground made digging almost impossible. The men used their small entrenching tools as best they could but the results were far from adequate. The first foot of ground was easy to dig through, after that however it became difficult to make any progress in the hard ground. These shallow positions were fully exposed to French fire.

In order to prevent a French surprise night attack two *Jägers* volunteered to set fire to several large piles of straw. *Jägers* Baldus and Jansen crawled out into the open field some 200 meters in front of the village and set both piles alight. They made it safely back to Fricourt amid a hail of French bullets. The light given off by the straw effectively prevented any attack approaching from this direction unseen.

The village was exposed to hellish fire from three sides. When darkness fell the regiments attempted to bring some order to the confused situation while the wounded were carried to the rear for treatment. *Oberleutnant* Guksch:

> Strong enemy fire was placed on Fricourt. Many homes rose up in flames and illuminated the surrounding area during the night. As soon as it had become dark the regimental staff also went forward toward Fricourt in order to be able to assess the situation better. We arrived at the Château together with the brigade staff. Burning Fricourt was a scary and beautiful sight as we walked through it, and as so many bullets flew around, whilsth our soldiers on the hillside or the supports in the village

Fricourt Château before the war. (*Reserve-Infanterie Regiment Nr. 110 im Weltkrieg 1914-1918*)

further prepared for the night defense, and spent their night's rest there. We felt like victors and despite the fiercest enemy resistance we had advanced several kilometers further forward again. The hope that a further advance to victory on the next day filled us all, however, things turned out differently.[18]

The French employed larger caliber guns against Fricourt during the evening and some thought they might include naval guns. *Leutnant* Kehr, 3/Reserve *Jäger* Bn 8, described the effect of these larger guns on the defenders of Fricourt:

Suddenly we hear a sinister roaring in the air, like the close proximity of a severe thunderstorm. Then a crazy noise, everything was shrouded in a sulfur yellow vapor and dust. Bits of clay, hard pieces of stone came rushing down. Since then we have often had this pleasure however the very first impression was terrible. One feels his own impotence very much in such a moment and if one is not cowardly it results in a quiet communion with God. This bombardment is nerve rending as soon as you allow yourself to lose composure for only a moment. It has a completely different effect on each individual. The moral effect however is the most malign because the 3rd Company did not lose a single man in the approximately one half hour continuous bombardment of this evening.[19]

The last French counterattack against Fricourt took place at midnight; it broke down completely in the fire of the III/R40.

The German attack against Hill 110 south of Fricourt had also taken place this day. The hill was heavily defended because the French knew how important this position was in dominating the surrounding countryside.

Fricourt Château after the bombardment. (*Reserve-Infanterie Regiment Nr. 110 im Weltkrieg 1914-1918*)

Officers indicating where RIR 111 attacked on Hill 110. (Author's collection)

The III/R111 waited until word arrived that Fricourt had been taken before attacking Hill 110. Once this had been confirmed RIR 111 and RIR 40 gradually ascended the side of the hill in the face of heavy French fire. Casualties increased quickly and before too long a large number of killed and wounded were lying on the grass. The French concentrated their fire upon the 1/R40 on the right wing and tore it apart. The men were pinned down and the slightest movement resulted in heavy fire. Many men were recently arrived replacement troops and quickly became casualties because they had not learned to protect themselves against this kind of fire. The survivors waited hungry and exhausted as they had not eaten in the last 36 hours and were at the end of their strength.

The center and right had better results. The attackers slowly worked forward to the summit aided by machine-gun fire from the rear. The hill was taken at noon and the defenders slowly withdrew over the crest, the 9th and 10/R111 following closely on their heels. They were forced to halt their pursuit when their advance was blocked by German shellfire.

French batteries covered Hill 110 and the surrounding terrain with shrapnel and shellfire preventing any further advance by the III/R111 or Bavarian troops on the left by Mametz. Their first task was to prepare the ground they had captured for defense against French counterattacks. The men on Hill 110 could not count on support by fresh troops because all available reserves had already been committed elsewhere.

Wecker

Oberleutnant d. R. im Ref.-Inf.-
Regt. 121, gefallen bei Thiepval
am 29. September 1914

Schmid (Lothar)

Leutnant d. R. im Reserve-Inf.-
Regt. 120 (Kaufmann), gestorben
am 30. September 1914 an den bei
La Boisselle erhaltenen Wunden

Oberleutnant der Reserve Friedrich
Wecker (Heilbronn) 8/R121. Killed
in action 29 September 1914.
(*Kriegstagbuch aus Schwaben*)

Leutnant der Reserve Lothar Schmid
(Horb) RIR 120. Died from wounds
received at La Boisselle 30 September
1914. (*Kriegstagbuch aus Schwaben*)

Throughout the night the French made numerous attempts to recapture Hill 110 and penetrate into the village, all were repelled. Again and again all available troops were called to the front to beat back the attacks. No one got any rest this night.

The exhausted men dug-in during the night and were in the process of creating a crude trench line when the French attacked at 11.30 p.m. The French lost heavily in this attack, especially from the fire from a machine gun brought up from the rear. Afterward the men rested in their shallow trenches with their rifles cradled in their arms.

The 26th Reserve Division planned to continue the attack against Albert. The division staff arrived at the battle headquarters located in the *Café Nationale*, a small tollhouse where the National road and the Martinpuich-Courcelette road intersected. The situation facing the division had worsened in the course of the last 24 hours because the French continued to reinforce their front and left flank.

HKK 1 (Guard and 4th Cavalry Divisions) protected the right flank and rear of the division north of the Ancre. HKKII (7th and 9th Cavalry Divisions) was under the unified command of General von Richthofen. The 2nd Cavalry Division von Thumb was south of the Ancre under the orders of the XIV Reserve Corps. However the cavalry force, five full divisions, failed to advance across the Arras-Miraumont railway line and did not fulfill their task to protect the right flank of the division. This failure proved to be incomprehensible to many in the 26th Reserve Division.

In order to reinforce the right wing of the German army and outflank the French additional forces were extracted from other parts of the front. The Guard Corps, IV Corps and I Bavarian Reserve Corps were being assembled to form an army group that would advance against Arras in the north while the 4th Cavalry Division von Hollen located

French prisoners captured 29 September 1914. (*Die 26. Reserve Division 1914-1918*)

above Lille would clarify the situation further north. Unfortunately these events would not occur before the beginning of October.

Considering all factors the offensive by the XIV Reserve Corps had to be temporarily postponed. It grew increasingly obvious that it was imperative to hold the ground already captured by the Corps and wait for the arrival of IV Corps and protect the right flank of the Sixth Army.

The situation faced by Reserve Infantry Brigade 51 in the Forest of Authuille was especially difficult. RIR 121 and IR 180 suffered losses from the concentrated fire of numerous French batteries located on the northern bank of the Ancre and by Mesnil. As a result the brigade commander decided to withdraw them to a position further in the rear.

The position of the I and II/R121 was untenable because it ran at right angles to the main German line, which allowed the French artillery to fire into their flank and rear. The main body withdrew to the hills southeast of Thiepval at 10 a.m. It was accomplished as if it had been on the parade ground in peacetime.

Hauptmann von Raben and approximately 35 men from the 5th and 7/R121 were ordered to hold their position under all circumstances and act as rearguard for the withdrawal. They remained in their exposed position until nightfall when they made their way back to the German lines. Their action allowed the stretcher-bearers to remove most of the wounded men from the forest and carry them back to the dressing station for medical care.

IR 180 had also suffered in the French fire, part of which consisted of flanking fire. When RIR 121 withdrew IR 180 had to follow and took up positions around Thiepval as well as Hill 150 north of the village.[20] Hill 141 south of Thiepval had to be temporarily abandoned.[21]

Thiepval Château was being used as the Battle Headquarters by Reserve Infantry Brigade 51 but the close proximity to the front line made it an obvious target for French guns. The Château was shelled heavily and caught fire causing the brigade to transfer headquarters to Mouquet Farm while the Château and all of its contents were destroyed.

Infantryman – RIR 40. (Author's collection)

RIR 119 in Ovillers had been subjected to heavy artillery fire starting at 1 a.m. The shells fell into the densely occupied village, shattered walls and buildings, setting houses on fire and forcing the field kitchens to withdraw to the rear. Later in the morning the French transferred the heaviest fire onto the village edge and trenches of the regiment. The feared *Rimailho* howitzers joined the fire from the French field guns.[22]

Losses quickly mounted and soon surpassed those of the previous days. When Brigade Wundt withdrew from the Forest of Authuille the situation became even worse as the right flank of RIR 119 hung in the air. When Reserve Infantry Brigade 51 withdrew it also placed RIR 120 in a precarious position. RIR 120 held the line Ovillers-La Boisselle on the left of RIR 119 and the withdrawal also exposed its right flank. One officer in RIR 120, *Leutnant* Julius Marx, proceeded to Pozières in order to see the situation facing the regiment first hand. From his vantage point he could see the panorama of the fighting along the entire front of the division. He was joined by the brigade commander, who sat in a folding chair because of a sore leg. The brigade commander noticed French troops to the north of La Boisselle and had *Leutnant* Marx contact the artillery to target them. Within a short time German shells fell among the French lines causing the infantry to withdraw behind the heights in their rear.

Marx and the brigade commander watched the heavy fire falling upon Ovillers and La Boisselle, and saw them covered in smoke and dust while fires broke out among the buildings. They knew the terrible conditions must have also been bringing heavy losses to the men fighting in these villages.

The previous mornings had started with a dense fog. RIR 120 had expected this to happen on the 29th and made plans to utilize the fog to capture the heights in front of Albert by surprise, without artillery preparation. The next day the morning sun climbed high into the sky and there was no sign of fog. The division staff quickly prohibited the

Infantryman – RIR 110. (Author's collection)

undertaking as being too risky. The regiment was disappointed and waited for the German artillery to prepare the heights for an attack.

The guns opened fire at 7.30 a.m. but by 9 a.m. division orders arrived that the regiment should remain on the defensive for the next few days. Later, additional orders arrived to prepare trenches, the first sign they were there to stay.

After the close fighting in the village we were again grouped into fighting units, which brought my company into the first line. Under heavy losses we cleaned out 'Granate farm' and the following lines of trenches and took prisoners. We were about to enter Albert when we received orders to retreat and hold La Boisselle until the divisions on our right and left had moved up into line with us. We expected to stay a few hours, a day at most, but we never left La Boisselle until March 1915 when we were relieved by another unit.

We occupied the buildings of La Boisselle, which were built of brick with strong cellars and offered fair protection. La Boisselle was a typical French village, built along one main street, barns facing the road to escape the window tax and living houses in the rear. In these living houses we made ourselves comfortable. Approximately half of the village was situated on the hill and from there we could look into Albert and also over the plateau to our right and left, which was occupied by the French. Our neighboring regiments were in the valley with no field of vision whatsoever. A French attack could be built up safely right in front of their noses without them seeing it. From La Boisselle however, we could overlook the hill and send an alarm to our comrades even if we were unable to help otherwise.

Not figuring on a long stay, we did not bother digging holes or trenches and were instead posted in a room with windows. During the night French patrols advanced, feeling out our position, but they were sent home with a bloody nose without finding out anything. In the morning we saw trenches dug out by the French one to one and a half miles from La Boiselle. They must have worked all night while we were loafing, taking it easy.

During the day we were very careless and moved unconcernedly about the village, expecting an order to advance any minute. But no such orders came. In the afternoon shells from French 75s fell into the village. We looked around for shelter and found cellars big enough to hold us all and also strong enough to protect us, especially well-built brick buildings were still standing.

That night, in order to protect our sentries and also to cover our movements during the day, we started to build a trench around the village but we did not get very far with our portable trench equipment as it was too light and weak.

The first foot down was easy but then we struck a mixture of rock and steel-hard flint stone which soon ruined our tools. At least we had some protection from bullets and splinters. Hans Ludwig, 6/R120 [23]

The positions along the Ancre became increasingly threatened during the day. All river crossings up to Miraumont were protected by French artillery and occupied by French infantry. The French made numerous attempts to cross the river and roll up the position of the division from the exposed right flank, all had failed.

The protection of the flank between Thiepval and Miraumont was assigned to RIR 99. The area south of Grandcourt was assigned to the Württemberg Reserve Dragoon Regiment while the crossings at Thiepval and St. Pierre-Divion were assigned to IR 180. The Dragoons only numbered 155 men in three squadrons but they did provide long-range fire against advancing French troops and reserves, their sights set between 1,000 and 1,800 meters.

The increased threat to the right flank required new artillery placement. The 6th and 7/RFAR 26 moved to the hollow east of Thiepval while the 9th Battery was positioned to cover the forest of Authuille. The I *Abteilung* was ordered to proceed with RIR 99 to Grandcourt where its guns would cover the extreme right flank. The batteries of the I *Abteilung* were positioned on Hill 131 south of Miraumont where they had a wide field of fire on the opposite bank of the Ancre.

RIR 99 received orders from the division to capture the hills north of the Ancre at Grandcourt and Miraumont; however it was impossible due to heavy French pressure. The French made three attempts to cross the Ancre in force on the right wing of the division against RIR 99. All three attacks were repelled with the help of artillery support.

RFAR 26 received support from the Mounted *Abteilung* of FAR 35 (2nd Cavalry Division). These guns were very helpful stopping a French attack against Miraumont from the direction of Serre-Puisieux.

The additional support was appreciated as the French continued to probe the right flank of the division. At 2 p.m. dense lines of French infantry advanced against the 12/R99 in the Ancre valley. The attack was quickly shattered in the fire of the 12th and 5/R99 along the Ancre and from the rapid fire provided by RFAR 26 from Hill 131.

The constant French attacks along the Ancre resulted in a shifting of all available forces needed to hold the line. This caused a gap to arise between the Württemberg Reserve Dragoon Regiment and IR 180 at Thiepval. The II/R110 was transferred from the 28th

Grandcourt Church after being struck by French shells. (Author's collection)

Reserve Division for this purpose. The 6th and 7/R110 filled the gap along the Ancre while the remaining two companies were assigned to positions at Courcelette and Le Sars.

The constant fighting along the line made any movement in or around the positions very dangerous. French shrapnel fire burst along the front throughout the day and infantry fire was continuous. The men had not yet learned how to take cover and protect themselves from this type of fire. In the late afternoon the regimental commander of IR 180, *Oberst* von Haldenwang, was proceeding to Thiepval when he was struck by a rifle bullet and severely wounded. As he was being carried past the division headquarters the division commander awarded him with the Iron Cross II Class. Von Haldenwang died a short time afterward.

French artillery fire was becoming particularly annoying. The guns assigned to the XIV Reserve Corps consisted of modern field guns and light field howitzers in two field artillery regiments, RFAR 26 and 29. The only other guns available to the Corps were two older model heavy field howitzer batteries (6th and 8/Reserve Foot Artillery Regiment 10) and one 10cm battery. These guns were not equipped with recoil systems and modern sights. They were also spread across the Corps front so that their overall effect on any given point was diminished.

Officer in RIR 111 standing in front of Thiepval Château. (Author's collection)

In the early evening a car approached Pozières from the rear. It contained the Sixth Army Commander, Crown Prince Ruprecht von Bayern. He had come to the front in order to find out about the situation directly from General von Auwärter. When Ruprecht was about to leave he told the assembled officers:

> You must still endure for a few days, then however reinforcements will arrive, and then we can advance again.[24]

The fighting was nearly over for the day. The 7/R99 sent a reconnaissance patrol toward Beauregard farm. They discovered a French battalion and staff had occupied the farm. When theirs report reached the I *Abteilung* RFAR 26 it immediately opened fire and drove the French out. Prisoners taken on the following day gave French losses at approximately 100 dead and 200 wounded.

The front at the end of the day had not changed much from the previous day. When the fighting died down at night the lines were reformed and the troops were rearranged according to the situation. A new problem faced the XIV Reserve Corps involving the preparation and distribution of rations. Until now the field kitchens had followed the regiments and distributed rations when needed. Now the regiments were stationary and occupying rudimentary field works. The positions offered little protection against enemy fire as well as against the wind and weather.

The last food ration had been issued to the troops on the previous day. It was impossible for the field kitchens to approach the forward line due to heavy fire and as a result remained in the rear on the 29th. When darkness fell the field kitchens advanced as far as possible. The rations were distributed to food carriers who had the difficult task of locating their units in the dark. The bearers also had to carry cumbersome food containers with both hands across shell holes and other obstacles while carrying rifles slung over their backs while French shells and infantry fire caused casualties among the men. If the troops in the front line received any warm food they could consider themselves lucky.

Most felt the offensive would begin again once fresh troops arrived on their right flank. The new type of warfare they faced, trench warfare, was not yet a fact of life. The next few days would prove whether they were right or wrong.

30 September 1914

There was little change in the line held by the troops of the XIV Reserve Corps. Units were reorganized and the defensive positions were improved as much as possible. Artillery fire continued to cause losses among the men in their exposed positions.

In the pre-dawn darkness the French attacked RIR 40. The French used spotlights to illuminate the German lines and blind the defenders. However the spotlights had illuminated their own troops and they suffered considerable losses, approximately 100 killed and wounded and 60 men taken prisoner. Spotlights were also used along the front of RIR 111 until dawn when their effect was diminished and the men in the regiment were able to move about once more.

The situation on Hill 110 was very tense and the men rested on their arms awaiting the inevitable French attack. Towards dawn the *Jägers* were surprised to see a large French force in a turnip field just in front of their position. They quickly opened fire, joined by two machine-guns from Bavarian IR 5 that were positioned with the *Jägers*. The French soldiers were surprised by the volume of fire and tried to flee but the rifles and machine-guns reaped a grisly harvest. A small group of 40 Frenchmen who were protected by a small embankment were all that were left of the attacking force. They were soon taken prisoner.

It was soon apparent that they would not be advancing any further for the time being. *Oberjäger* Balfranz, 1/Reserve *Jäger* Bn 8, recalled that:

> On September 30th the commander gave the order that the position had to be held to the last man and that we should take provisions out of the packs of the wounded and dead if we were in need of food.[25]

While large-scale infantry attacks had ceased for the time being there was still the danger of local attacks and from marksmen on both sides of the front. The men quickly learned that individual French soldiers were crack shots and if they exposed any part of their person it drew fire. A number of men were hit while observing the enemy positions including one company officer who was severely wounded while scanning the French lines through his binoculars. A marksman fired a bullet that went through the binoculars and struck the officer in the head.

The *Jägers* made every attempt to improve their positions but all that most could accomplish during the night was to dig out a small hole barely large enough for one man. Still they continued their attempts to enlarge the small holes in the hard chalk ground. *Oberjäger* Balfranz recalled:

> About 9 o'clock in the morning *Oberjäger* Probst suddenly came running until he was in front of my cover, both hands pressed to his left side. At this point he stopped and sank to his knees. I called to him as I remained stationary under cover that he should jump into one of our holes as quickly as possible because bullets continuously smashed into the position, 'In a minute!' he replied, then, 'I can no longer!' He had barely allowed himself to lie down when an enemy bullet shattered both of his knees. In spite of the fire I jumped over to him in order to pull him into my hole. He resisted it with his last strength and said 'let me lie here'. Nevertheless I had reached him. 'Save yourself and go back!' A bullet went past me through my tunic and cartridge box and I jumped back into my hole.

After a short time I heard him weakly call my name. I tied my handkerchief onto my bayonet and jumped up again going towards him, waving it in the air towards the enemy. Oddly I was not fired at now. He said to me 'give my regards to my father in Brodenbach on the Moselle, *Leutnant* Müller and the company!' and stretched out his hand towards me with the paleness of a corpse already cast on his face. A few bullets struck near us again and I jumped back into my hole.

I later heard that *Leutnant* Müller had already been killed an hour earlier. A few times I heard *Oberjäger* Probst groan out again seemingly caused by being hit again. A strong firefight now cut off any contact with him. I could not see to him again until the onset of darkness. He was dead. He had pulled down the chinstrap and his *Tschako* softened the dreadful picture.[26]

However the danger of being exposing was not restricted to the German side as Balfranz recalled:

About 3 o'clock I noticed an enemy infantryman climbing out of a trench in full height at 900 meters distance through my binoculars. He might assume that we could not reach him there. I gave the binoculars to the next man for observation, got into position, fired and immediately my comrade notified me of a hit. I assumed that he was severely wounded and asked my platoon leader to prohibit any firing on the wounded man. My wish was fulfilled. After approximately two minutes the wounded Frenchman was on the pile of the spoil thrown out of the trench from where he was drawn into the trench.[27]

The French troops located at the Fricourt railway station were particularly annoying during the day. They made repeated attacks against the southeast corner of the village from their location, all of which were preceded by a strong artillery bombardment but every attack was repelled. There were also small French attacks against Hill 110 and the nearby quarry, all of which were also repelled.

The artillery fire was perhaps the most annoying to the men in their crude trenches. Casualties began to mount and the Fricourt was reduced to ruins by the hour. The men took whatever cover they could inside the village, usually the undamaged stone cellars of the buildings. Despite the gradual destruction of the village many of the inhabitants had remained behind and were sharing the cellars with the German troops including the owner of the Château. His splendid home was heavily shelled in the early morning and it was soon set on fire and destroyed.

With the destruction of the Château RIR 109 was forced to relocate regimental headquarters into nearby cellars. The new location was described as having a tottering stairway leading into the depths where an enormous vaulted ceiling spanned the room. The regimental office was located in one corner with a typewriter and a constantly ringing telephone. Next to it were makeshift night beds used by the staff, functional but not very comfortable. There was a desk in the center that was always strewn with cards and where daily meals were taken. Throughout the cellar was the dull glimmer of smoking oil lamps that threw giant shadows on the walls as people came and went.

Several heavy shells struck the dressing station of RIR 109 located in Fricourt. The attending physician, *Oberarzt* Dr Gumprich, was so severely wounded he had to have his

Field Kitchen – IR 180. (Author's collection)

leg amputated. *Stabsarzt* Dr Meyerhoff was also wounded but he was able to remain at his post and care for the ever-increasing number of wounded coming in. He later received the Iron Cross II Class for his devotion to duty.

The II and III/R109 suffered the most from the fire. The I Battalion suffered the least, possibly as a result of its close proximity to the French lines. The French gunners appeared to be afraid of hitting their own men if they fired upon this battalion.

The German response to the enemy artillery fire was inadequate. The guns were suffering from a shortage of shells and only French attacks and other worthwhile targets could be taken under fire. The German infantry restricted their actions to defensive firing and strengthening their positions. *Unteroffizier* Breinlinger, 10/R111, observed three French trenches and reported their location to the artillery, and they were identified as a worthwhile target. The resulting bombardment caused the French garrison to abandon their trenches and once in the open they became easy targets for the combined rifle and machine-gun fire from the regiment.

There were still many gaps in the front and every attempt was being made to connect the individual trenches. However many areas that the men needed to cross were under French observation and this generally meant that they were subject to artillery fire. At one point *Radfahrer* Strübel, 4/R109 was bringing important orders to the regimental staff in the cellar of the badly damaged Château grounds. In order to get there he needed to cross a portion of the road that was clearly visible to the French.

As Strübel made a dash across the exposed portion the French immediately opened fire with shrapnel, followed shortly afterward with high explosive shells. He took cover behind a straw pile when a shell came down and exploded in the middle of a team of horses and wagon.

The shell tore the legs off of the lead horse and killed the driver. Strübel rushed over to the wagon and found it contained a badly wounded officer and a doctor. A *Jäger* taking cover nearby gave the wounded horse a mercy shot and then helped Strübel and the

Comfortable quarters, the cellar vaults of Fricourt Château. (*Reserve-Infanterie Regiment Nr. 110 im Weltkrieg 1914-1918*)

doctor's orderly, *Reservist* Stumpf, 3/R109, move the wagon off of the exposed roadway while shells burst around them. The men received the Iron Cross II Class for their bravery.

RIR 109 received orders to hold their position at all cost and up to the last man. The regiment expected the French to target Fricourt as the main focus of any counterattack and the men made use of their time to make the village as defensible as possible. All day the observers could see continuous movement of infantry columns behind the French lines however no attack occurred.

The French artillery had been noticeably strengthened during the day. The German guns did their best to counter the French artillery presence but could not match their caliber or range. The few German heavy guns available did play an important part in protecting the German line by directing their fire to the areas where it was needed most. They were able to shell the city of Albert and fires could be seen breaking out in several areas. The cathedral with its Golden Virgin and child however were still off limits to the German gunners. Requests for increased artillery support had to go unfulfilled due to the critical shortage of ammunition.

Gradually the villages of Thiepval, Ovillers, Pozières and La Boisselle became badly damaged under the constant French fire. Mouquet Farm, the headquarters of IR 180, was set on fire. French aircraft flew low over the German positions and in some cases dropped bombs or steel darts. French aviators had one small success for the day when one of their bombs destroyed the bedroom of General von Soden in Martinpuich.

Pozières suddenly became the target of numerous French guns. Confusion reigned as baggage wagons, artillery limbers being pulled by frenzied horses rushed out of danger amidst the shouts of the drivers and the men running alongside them. In some situations it was not possible to take cover. Men like *Leutnant* Marx, RIR 120, remained with their horses while the shells fell all about them.

After 30 minutes of fire it became quiet once more. Miraculously Marx and the horses came through unscathed though the horses were still terrified from the noise and smoke. Afterward Marx was able to see how close they had come to being killed or wounded when he discovered a dud French shell in one stall while another had apparently exploded at the entrance to the barn. In an understatement of the events Marx felt that being exposed under such fire was really not that much fun.

The two regiments along the right flank of the division, IR 180 and RIR 99 were subjected to a series of French attacks and strong reconnaissance probes. Another gap formed between the regiments between Thiepval and Grandcourt and reinforcements were urgently needed. Two companies from RIR 110 were brought up once again to the threatened area and remained for the rest of the day.

RFAR 26 continued to provide much needed support against the frequent French attacks. The artillery received some additional relief when an *Abteilung* of howitzers from a Bavarian Artillery regiment from the IV Corps arrived in the afternoon.

The cavalry were to make one further attempt to relieve pressure on the flank. The 2nd Cavalry Division assembled and prepared for action at Irles and Pys. Observers in RFAR 26 had a clear view of the front to the north toward Arras. Shrapnel clouds were hanging in the sky everywhere they could see in the north and northeast, from Serre to Puisieux, Achiet-Bihucourt. They whistled and hissed into the positions from the flank and rear.

Rumors began to circulate that local civilians had been in contact with the French Army by means of light signals. However the civilians that had been caught up in the fighting had no opportunity to send any type of signal whatsoever. The occupants of the villages would be found hiding in the cellars of their homes along with the German troops.

Grandcourt church after further shelling. (Author's collection)

It was clear that they were more concerned with their personal safety than in acting as espionage agents. They were as vulnerable to French fire as the troops and during the day French shells killed 5 inhabitants of Grandcourt and the village church was heavily damaged.

The 26th Reserve Division anxiously awaited the arrival of the IV Corps (General Sixt von Armin), the lead elements of which had reached Péronne. It would allow the 26th Reserve Division to resume the offensive and relieve the pressure on the right flank of the Corps. The division was highly disappointed when it learned that the IV Corps was ordered to continue to march north toward Arras.

The division did obtain some relief on its right flank with the arrival of the 7th Division (IV Corps) in the evening at Bapaume. The division sent a detachment to Grevillers as protection for the right flank of the XIV Reserve Corps in response to the French occupation of the line Achiet le Petit-Gomiecourt. Later reports indicated that the 1st Guard Division was disembarking in St. Quentin. Their quick arrival on the scene was even more eagerly awaited. Then the right wing of the 26th Reserve Division would no longer hang in the air. The first week of fighting in northern France for the XIV Reserve Corps was over.

Chapter notes

1. A. Swanson, 'Race to the Sea'. *History of the First World War,* p. 298.
2. I Bavarian Army Corps fought in the area near Péronne, south of the river Somme. II Bavarian Army Corps was positioned on the right of the I Bavarian Army Corps and fought near Maricourt and Montauban just north of the river Somme. A large concentration of German cavalry divisions were in the area, the Guard and 4th Cavalry Divisions in the Independent Cavalry Command 1, the 2nd, 7th and 9th Cavalry Divisions in the Independent Cavalry Command 2 were positioned to protect the right flank of the Sixth Army.
3. 'War Volunteer'. A certain number of young men between the ages of 17 and 20 were allowed to volunteer for active service before their Class was called up.
4. Skat is a popular German card game generally played with a dealer and from 3 to 4 players
5. W. Gallion, *Das Reserve-Infanterie-Regiment Nr. 40 im Weltkrieg,* p. 35.
6. W. Jecklin, *Das Reserve-Jäger-Bataillon Nr. 8 im Weltkrieg 1914-1918,* p. 43.
7. Ibid.
8. M. Gerster, *Das Württembergische Reserve-Infanterie-Regiment Nr. 119 im Weltkrieg 1914-1918,* p. 24.
9. AOK 6 = Sixth Army Headquarters (Staff).
10. HKK1 was the abbreviation for 'Independent Cavalry Corps 1'.
11. H. Ludwig, Manuscript, 6th Company RIR 120, p.4.
12. Ibid.
13. Ibid.
14. Ludwig, op. cit. pp. 4-5. Also K. Metzger, *Vom Weltkrieg 1914/18. Selbsterlebnisse eines Frontsoldaten,* p. 9. The rooster was first kept in a cage, after its death it was sent to Germany by *Hauptmann* Dorn where it was stuffed and kept as a souvenir of the war. The stuffed rooster eventually came into the possession of Cornille Zach-Dorn, wife of *Hauptmann* Dorn.

15. Metzger, op. cit., pp. 7-8.
16. Jecklin, op. cit., p. 45.
17. Gallion, op. cit., p. 40.
18. Jecklin, op. cit., pp. 46-47
19. Jecklin, op. cit. p. 48.
20. Later the site of the Schwaben Redoubt.
21. Called the 'Granatloch' by the Germans and the 'Leipzig Redoubt' by the British.
22. The Model 1904 Rimailho howitzer was first adopted by the French Army in 1906. The caliber was 155mm. It had a maximum range of 6,285 meters and fired a shell weighing 95 pounds.
23. Ludwig, op. cit., pp. 5-6.
24. Soden, Die 26. (Württembergische) Reserve-Division im Weltkrieg 1914-1918, p. 55.
25. Jecklin, op. cit., p. 48.
26. Ibid
27. Ibid

2

October 1914 – Period of Transition

On 1 October the IV Corps reached the area southeast of Arras. The I Bavarian Reserve Corps occupied a large part of the Scarpe and advanced from the direction of Douai. The 1st Guard Division reached Bapaume and the area north of Péronne. The Achiet le Grand-Arras railway was still in French hands and aerial reconnaissance reported French troops advancing upon Arras from the west and south. Reinforcements had not arrived as quickly as expected but were at last approaching the front. The Army High Command was counting on the quick capture of Arras, which could then be used as a strategic base to outflank the French. In accordance with the grand plan the Sixth Army issued the following notice:

> Soldiers of the Sixth Army! The moment has arrived in which the Sixth Army should bring about the decision from the weeks of continuous hard fighting at the right wing of the army. I am confident that everyone in his position will prove worthy of the meaning of our task for the salvation of our Fatherland. Therefore onward without stopping until the enemy has been entirely thrown down.
>
> Ruprecht Crown Prince of Bavaria[1]

The XIV Reserve Corps was in transition. The momentum of the first week of fighting on the Somme had been lost. The front facing the 28th Reserve Division had become stagnant while the 26th Reserve Division faced the unenviable position of being the right wing of the German army with an exposed right flank. The French continued to extend the front northward and at the same time maintained a steady pressure against the XIV Reserve Corps. Artillery fire continued to pour onto the positions held by the men with no sign of letting up.

All along the front the French were reported to be digging into the earth like moles, in particular at Hill 141 south of Thiepval and the Grove of Bécourt where the positions were being transformed into fortresses. However there was hope that the offensive could be resumed once reinforcements arrived and the exposed right flank could be protected. Many considered the current situation as a slight interruption in the overall offensive plan. In response to increasing French resistance the regiments of the 28th Reserve Division were deployed along the front and ordered to dig in where the men stood.

The morning of 1 October was marked with a heavy fog that made it difficult to see anything. Between 5 and 6 o'clock *Oberjäger* Balfranz noticed a shape in the fog about 50 meters away. It turned out to be a French officer crouching low to the ground; he was followed by more figures. Balfranz quickly realized it was a skirmish line moving parallel to the German position.

He quickly alerted the men around him and when the signal was given the *Jägers* opened a devastating fire. The French responded and for a few moments there was a terrifying firefight going on with each side hidden by the smoke and fog. Once the firing

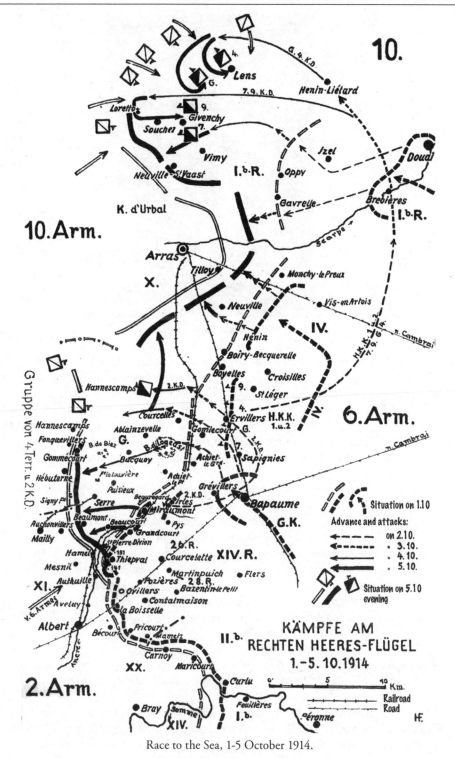

Race to the Sea, 1-5 October 1914.

Infantryman – RIR 111. (Author's collection)

stopped and the fog lifted at about 7 a.m. the *Jägers* could see about 20 'Red Trousers' lying in front of their position. Afterward the *Jägers* continued to improve their crude defensive holes after receiving reinforcements from the RIR 111. In the first two days of October RIR 111 reported seven attacks on their front causing numerous casualties on both sides.

Once the fog lifted both sides turned to sniping at any movement observed in the opposing line. This sporadic fire continued for the remainder of the day and many men were killed and wounded by head and upper body shots. *Oberjäger* Balfranz:

> Shortly after we received reinforcements from [Reserve] Infantry Regiment 111. I received two infantrymen into my group and placed them into the holes of two of the casualties. One, a small man with a goatee, fell a short time after with a headshot and was killed instantly. We have not seen any warm food for three days now. In quieter moments I jumped out of my hole and got the knapsacks and rifles lying around nearby and stacked everything beside my hole as flanking cover.[2]

Besides providing additional protection the knapsacks yielded much needed food. In one Balfranz discovered a letter from the wife of a *Jäger* who had been killed a short time before:

> She wrote that he should not let his courage sink as she went to church every morning with their children and prayed for him so that he would surely come home again.[3]

The main problem with the position occupied by the *Jägers* was that the French flanked them from both sides. The French had occupied the Fricourt railway station and adjacent buildings and could see straight into the position of the 3rd Coy where they could observe every movement. The position of the 1st Coy was so exposed the men were unable to move at all during daylight.

In order to relieve the pressure *Hauptmann* Kachel procured a field gun and placed it close to the 1st Coy under cover of the early morning fog. Once in position the gun opened fire into the railway station at point blank range and quickly silenced the French infantry. Later the gun was moved to the 4th Coy where it drove the French out of the railway station. Unfortunately the French reoccupied the position by late afternoon. Several small French attacks were repelled throughout the next few days. Everything possible was being done to prevent the French from taking the village. The *Jägers* had already received word that Fricourt was to be held to the last man.

The 6th and 7/R110 attempted to push their lines forward but were forced to stop after receiving heavy artillery fire that resulted in 7 men killed and 14 wounded. The two companies maintained their position with the help of one company from RIR 119 from Pozières. Fricourt and Hill 110 were held under continuous shellfire and French snipers fired on anyone foolish enough to expose themselves.

The French developed new tactics in an attempt to entice the Germans to leave their holes. It was called 'Attaque sans quitter les tranchees'. The French pretended to attack by prominently displaying fixed bayonets above their trenches, shouting 'en avant!', blowing calls on bugles and wild firing. These crude attempts to deceive the Germans were not very successful.

French artillery fire continued to plague the men. However on one occasion the 28th Reserve Division was able to strike back. On 3 October 30 marksmen from the I/R109 fired at a French artillery battery at a distance of 1,200 meters with good results. The enemy response came at noon when the battalion came under heavy artillery fire that continued until every house in Fricourt had been set on fire.

RIR 119 occupied Ovillers and was ordered to dig in as deep as possible and to use the stone cellars in the village for cover. They shared these shelters with civilians who were trapped by the fighting while the French slowly pounded the village into ruins. Once it was quiet the civilians were assembled and deported to rear areas to safety.

The soldiers had constructed shallow holes where they received some protection from French fire. However the line was far from solid. Large gaps existed between many of the regiments as well as smaller gaps between units within the regiments.

The right wing of the 26th Reserve Division was of great concern to General von Soden. One location in particular was the French occupation of Hill 141 south of Thiepval. This spot threatened the German lines to the north and south. Fortunately the only French activity along the front of the division was an attempt to occupy a new trench at Beauregard farm. The French were taken under fire by the I *Abteilung* RFAR 26 and 7/R99 and forced to withdraw. During the mopping up operation the 7th Coy captured 120 men from the *18e Régiment Territoriale*.

Subsequent to the notice issued by Crown Prince Ruprecht the XIV Reserve Corps received the outline of an ambitious attack plan scheduled to take place the following day:

> On the 2nd of October the Sixth Army will attack with both wings. The Army cavalry, I Bavarian Reserve Corps and IV Army Corps would go to Mailly via Arras, the left wing of the 1st Guard Division would advance and attack alongside the Achiet le Petit-Puisieux-Mailly road against the left flank and left wing of the

enemy – approximately against the line Doullens-Albert. The I Bavarian Corps and the XXI Army Corps would attack the enemy before their front at daybreak south of the Somme and the XIV Reserve Corps and II Bavarian Corps would initially hold their positions.

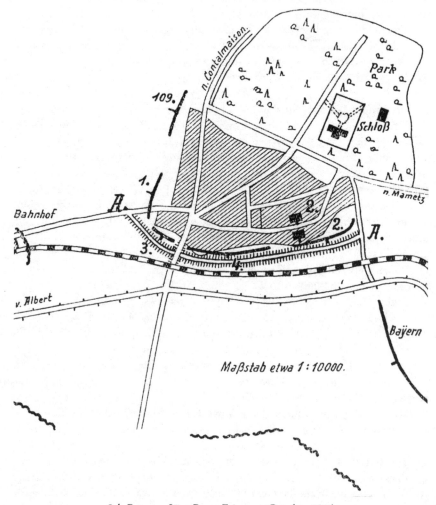

8th Reserve *Jäger* Bn at Fricourt, October 1914

General Major von Fölkersamb, commander of Reserve Infantry
Brigade 56, and staff. (Author's collection)

The XIV Reserve Corps would then thrust forward from its right wing just in time to correspond with the advance of the 1st Guard Division. The 2nd Cavalry Division would protect the right flank of the XIV Reserve Corps.[4]

The XIV Reserve Corps ordered RFAR 26 to support the Guard Corps from the southern bank of the Ancre and have RIR 99 join in the attack upon Beaucourt. There was a great deal of preparation to be made if this plan had any chance of success.

In the end nothing came from this elaborate plan. The cavalry remained too close to the infantry and did not perform the larger task of reconnaissance and outflanking the French. The Guard Corps did not arrive on the field until the middle of the afternoon when it was reported advancing from Sapignies toward the line Achiet-Puisieux. RIR 99 reported hearing artillery fire to the north at 4 p.m. that continued until the early morning hours of 3 October. RIR 99 waited the moment when they could join the attack but the order never came.

Everyone eagerly awaited reports of the fresh attacks and the relief they would bring. However French resistance increased in front of the IV and Guard Corps, especially at Arras and very little progress could be made. The Guard Corps had deployed between Ervillers and Sapignies but was still fighting around Achiet le Grand on the evening of 2 October. French artillery fire against the XIV Reserve Corps lessened noticeably on 2 October and appeared to have shifted further north to face the new German threat.

The situation did not improve on 3 October. The 1st Guard Division was to advance via Bucquoy to Hebuterne while the 2nd Guard Division advanced via Achiet le Petit to Puisieux-Serre. The 4th Guard Infantry Brigade and artillery were missing from the latter division and would not join it until 4 October at the earliest.

The Guard Corps attacked in the afternoon and by evening it had reached the line Courcelles-Bois de Logeast-Achiet le Petit after heavy fighting. The IV Corps failed to advance via the line Henin-Neuville while Arras remained in French hands. Under these circumstances RIR 99 could not advance from the Ancre and used all available forces just to hold its current position.

The artillery however was able to provide support for the Guard Corps. The I *Abteilung* RFAR 26, four field gun batteries and one howitzer battery from Bavarian FAR 5 and two 10cm batteries poured fire into the French flank. Two heavy field howitzer batteries from the 1st Bavarian Foot Artillery Regiment also joined in. RFAR 26 observed:

> The 'red trousers' of the Territorials dropped in rows upon the tawny clay of the autumn fields northwest of Miraumont under this devastating fire.[5]

Finally, on 4 October the Guard Corps made some progress against the French. The 1st Guard Division advanced via Ablainzeville-Bucquoy while the 2nd Guard Division advanced via Puisieux-Serre. The 3rd Guard Infantry Brigade attacked Puisieux and Serre in the afternoon with support from RFAR 26. By evening the Guard Corps reached the line Bois du Biez-La Louviere Farm-Serre while the IV Corps advanced to the Bapaume-Arras road north of Boiry Becquerelle-Boyelles.

The recent successes could be shared with the Kaiser who arrived at the Guard Corps Headquarters on 4 October where he optimistically said: 'Well children, once the leaves fall we will be in Berlin again.'[6] The Kaiser sent his greetings to the XIV Reserve Corps saying that he was counting on it and the IV Corps to deliver the attack along with the Guard Corps.

French prisoners captured on 4 October 1914 by the 10/R99. (Author's collection)

On 4 October von Soden met with the commander of the 2nd Guard Division, *Generalleutnant* von Winckler, in Achiet le Grand where they discussed the situation. They decided the right wing of the 26th Reserve Division would advance to the southwest. IR 180 and RIR 121 would attack on the southern bank of the Ancre near Thiepval while RIR 99 would attack north of the Ancre supported by other regiments. Patrols from the I/R110 on 3 October reported the heights south of Beaucourt on the left bank of the Ancre were unoccupied. However they were in error as on 4 October the 5th and 8/R110 located in Courcelette came under heavy French fire from these heights.

RIR 99 advanced in the morning and occupied Beauregard farm and the nearby ruined mill capturing numerous prisoners. The regiment then reformed for an advance against Beaucourt and Beaumont. That afternoon RIR 99 came under heavy French artillery fire, however losses were light as the men were widely scattered and under cover. The battalion commander was among the wounded, being hit by a shrapnel ball; he remained with his men even after relinquishing command. The regiment entrenched west of the ruined mill-Puisieux road with their right flank resting against the Guard Corps. During the night the regiment lost contact with the Guard units.

On 4 October RIR 40 reported strong artillery fire on their position at Fricourt followed by an attack later in the afternoon from the direction of Bray. The group from RIR 109 positioned between the 3rd and 4/R40 was overrun and approximately 30 to 40 Frenchmen penetrated into the village near the *Café du Commerce*.

Oberleutnant Richard Müller, 4/Reserve *Jäger* Bn 8, ran to the position in heavy fire to determine what had happened. When he returned he collected the reserve platoons and proceeded to the threatened area along with part of the 2/R109. Müller sent one group after the other against the French in order to close the gap in the line. They gained the western edge of the road leading to Bray and opened fire into the French flank approximately 100 meters distant. Their fire was too great and the French were forced to retreat, and the ground was soon seeded with corpses according to the *Jägers*.

The fighting ended with darkness. The French artillery fired throughout the fighting and the last shots destroyed several houses at the edge of Fricourt. The position was mopped up afterward by the *Jägers* and to their surprise a number of prisoners were found taking cover inside the village. The men came from the *156e* and *160e Régiments d'Infanterie*. According to statements by the prisoners their own artillery fire had caused them considerable casualties.

Beaumont

At 7 p.m. on 4 October RIR 99 was ordered to capture the heights east of Beaumont and Beaucourt along with the Ancre bridges southwest of Beaucourt. According to the orders the French were in full retreat in front of the Guard Corps. The attack would include units from RIR 99, RIR 110 and 4/Pioneer Bn 13 designated as Detachment Grall supported by RFAR 26. Reserve Infantry Brigade 51 received additional orders to throw the French holding the ground east of the St. Pierre-Divion – Thiepval road back across the Ancre.

Detachment Grall formed for the attack at 10 p.m. on the 4th between the railway embankment at Grandcourt to a point 100 meters north of the ruined mill. While a heavy battery bombarded the French position an officer's patrol was sent forward on reconnaissance. When the patrol did not return as scheduled the attack was postponed from 2 a.m. to 3 a.m. on 5 October.

Pietzcker
Leutnant b. R. und Komp.-Führer
im Inf.-Regt. 180 (K. Geologe Dr.),
gefallen am 1. Oktober bei Thiepval

Leutnant der Reserve Franz Pietzcker (Tübingen) 8/180. Killed in
action 1 October 1914. (*Kriegstagbuch aus Schwaben*)

Sauter
Leutnant im Inf.-Regt. 180, gest.
am 2. Oktober 1914 an den bei
Thiepval erhaltenen Wunden

Körbling
Leutnant in der 2. Res.-Pionier-
Komp. XIII. A.-K., gefallen am
3. Oktober 1914 bei Fricourt

Leutnant Klaus Sauter (Augsburg)
2/180. Severely wounded in the stomach
at Thiepval 29 September 1914, died
2 October 1914 at Field Hospital 1,
Bapaume. (*Kriegstagbuch aus Schwaben*)

Leutnant Körbling 2/Pioneer Bn 13.
Killed in action 3 October 1914 at
Fricourt. (*Kriegstagbuch aus Schwaben*)

The attack began promptly at 3 a.m. The men had to cross the hollow that ran from
Beaucourt to the west of Serre in order to attack the French trenches on Beaumont heights;
the main body was protected by a line of skirmishers. Due to the nature of the ground
the village of Beaumont was lost to sight for most of the time.

The ranks needed to be reformed when they reached the crest of the heights and they found they were still quite a distance from the village. Because of the delay in starting the attack and an inaccurate estimate of the distance needed to travel the advance had taken far too long. An especially bright moon appeared between the clouds gave away their position. The French opened fire into the German ranks and forced them to look for cover before the final attack could begin.

The skirmish line was reinforced and attempted to advance but heavy fire prevented it. The men began to dig in with their shovels while under fire from the front as well as the right flank. The 9th and 12/R99 used the protection offered by a hollow east of Hill 143 and proceeded toward the village. When they reached their assigned positions the men were ordered to take cover. They received light infantry fire from Beaumont while they were digging but did not suffer many casualties.

When the signal was given both companies assaulted the village. *Leutnant der Reserve* Müller and 25 men entered Beaumont from the northeast, the remainder soon followed. They discovered most of the French garrison had already fled toward Auchonvillers. The

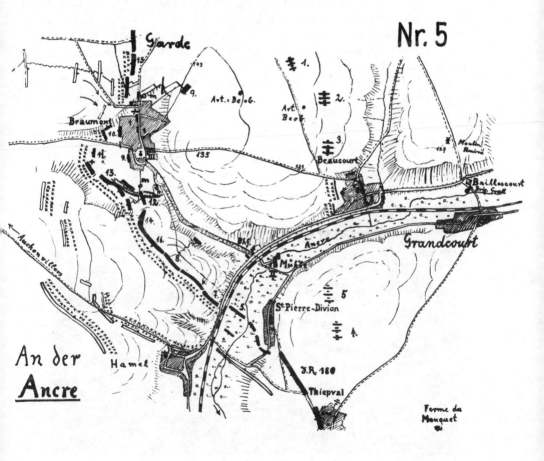

Fighting north of the Ancre.

houses were thoroughly searched and turned up 50 prisoners, an ammunition wagon and a military hospital with an additional 50 wounded soldiers and medical staff. While the exits of the village were occupied and prepared for defense *Vizefeldwebel* Schleicher, 9/R99, with three groups forced the last French troops from their trenches at the southern edge of the village. Afterward one platoon advanced almost to the village of Auchonvillers before returning.

Schleicher observed approximately three French companies advancing from Auchonvillers towards Beaumont. He gave the order for volley fire on the lead company. This company hesitated before the unexpected fire and then turned back toward Auchonvillers while the remaining companies continued to advance. The French were eventually stopped northwest of Beaumont by the heavy fire. Two French field gun batteries joined in the fighting making further advances toward Auchonvillers impossible. During the fighting the II/R110 occupied positions east of the village and dug in.

Units from the IV/R99 had started their attack at 2 a.m. The companies reached the Beaucourt-Serre road at 4 a.m. and were prepared to attack when the French suddenly evacuated their positions. Apparently pressure from the right by the rest of RIR 99 and RIR 110 had forced them to abandon their position. The battalion entrenched on both sides of the road, facing west losing only a few men from artillery fire.

The connection between RIR 110 and RIR 99 had been broken during the attack. French batteries effectively held both forces in their newly won positions and made it impossible for RIR 99 to report the capture of Beaumont to the rear or to RIR 110 on their right. RIR 110 was also prevented from sending reports to the rear or determining the fate of RIR 99.

Non-commissioned officer and enlisted man RIR 119 in
the ruins of Beaumont. (Author's collection)

Memorial card: 30 year old Johann Breunig, 9/R110. Killed in
action 5 October 1914 at Beaumont. (Author's collection)

At daybreak artillery fire fell on the German positions. The guns could easily be
seen on the heights beyond Beaumont and they fired throughout the day. The German
commanders in the rear were unaware of the progress made in the attack and thought
that the road east of Beaumont had not been reached by friendly forces. Therefore they
ordered the heavy artillery to bombard the reverse slope east of the Beaumont heights
as well as the village.

The fire from both French and German guns had become too much for some of the
men of RIR 110 in their exposed positions and several groups were forced to withdraw
to the nearby hollow. These men were collected, reformed and placed in position in the
rear as support. The troops in Beaumont took cover when the friendly fire began and at
first suffered no casualties. Once they began to lose men one platoon shifted into nearby
farm buildings while the remainder stayed behind to hold the village. RIR 110 suffered
the most in the concentrated artillery fire. Adjutant *Leutnant* Huber and 48 men had
been killed, 5 officers and 166 men were wounded, mostly by shrapnel fire.

During this time the French evacuated most of their positions on the heights east of
Beaumont and only left behind small patrols. The German guns continued to shell the
empty positions all morning and finally stopped at midday.

Reinforcements arrived on 5 October from II Bavarian Corps consisting of four
battalions from the Bavarian IR 17 and one battalion from Bavarian IR 5 commanded

by *Oberst* Meyer. They were ordered to advance against Beaumont. The battalions formed near Beauregard and were set to attack through the artillery hollow at 2 p.m.

RIR 110 also decided to attempt to reach Beaumont. At 4 p.m. *Oberst* von Vietinghoff successfully reached the village with 70 men. He was surprised to find RIR 99 already occupying it. Later in the evening Bavarian IR 17 and IR 5 also reached the village. Von Vietinghoff considered any further advance against Auchonvillers impossible considering the concentrated French artillery fire. Instead he prepared the village and surrounding vicinity for defense. Communications to division headquarters were still unavailable.

Many problems encountered at Beaumont were the result of poor communications with headquarters. Division headquarters had changed its location to Beauregard Farm on 5 October while RFAR 26 moved into the home of Notary Turlot in the village of Miraumont. The regiments in the field had no knowledge about these moves and due to the heavy fighting there had been no opportunity to advise the different commands of the changes.

Beaucourt

Beaucourt formed the key to the French position north of the Ancre. The village was positioned on a hillside overlooking the river where the prominently situated château offered the French machine guns a wide field of fire. The attack against Beaucourt was to take place in conjunction with the advance against Beaumont.

The task of taking the village fell to units from RIR 99 and Pioneer Bn 13 who would act as bombers. The advance reached a point about 300 meters from the village without a shot being fired. Then the French suddenly opened fire and the attack was pressed with all possible speed.

The village of Beaumont. (Author's collection)

The French fired from behind barricades and nearby houses. The flashes from the weapons gave away their positions to the men of RIR 99. The Pioneers threw hand grenades at the makeshift barricades opening a way to the interior of the village. The 8/R99 thrust into the village and captured the western edge. Strong fire forced them to stop and fighting broke out against the machine guns located in the château.

The barricades at the southern edge of the village had still not been taken. The 5/R99 advanced into the village and quickly became embroiled in a firefight at the railway embankment. The company forced its way deeper into the village until it was almost in the rear of these barricades. Then the 8/R99 and part of the 14/R99 attacked the barricade from the front.

At 6.30 p.m. French resistance was finally broken and the last Frenchmen were chased out of the château yard. Later the 6th and 10/R99 advanced toward a railway station southwest of the village and a mill in the Ancre valley to create advance posts to protect the main line.

They could not pursue the French retreating from Beaumont because of the gap between the 26th Reserve Division and Guard Corps on the right. An officer from the Guard arrived a short time later and reported the gap was approximately 800 meters wide. As a result the heights to the north and south were prepared for defense.

In the evening the field kitchens arrived and distributed hot meals as well as packages and the first letters from home the men had had received in some time. The artillery finally grew silent and all that could be heard was the clinking of spades in the rocky soil.

At 8 a.m. on 5 October the French advanced toward Beaumont and halted at a trench approximately 800 meters west of the village. It was suspected they were providing protection for their artillery positioned by Auchonvillers. The French had not discovered the gap between the divisions and made no effort to exploit the weakness in the German lines or attempt to recapture Beaumont. They were content with intensive shelling of the village throughout the day.

The home of Notary Turlot (*Das Württembergisches Reserve-Feldartillerie Regiment Nr. 26 im Weltkrieg 1914-1918*)

The men in the village took advantage of every piece of cover. They occupied the cellars of the houses and successfully limited their losses to 10 killed and 16 wounded. The French sent out strong patrols during the day and intense infantry and artillery fire gave the impression that an attack was imminent, however none occurred.

German patrols in the night of 5 October from RIR 110 were sent out without caps or coats. Reports were received that French patrols were wearing captured German helmets and coats as a deception. No chance was being taken of firing on friendly troops or the possibility of being deceived by the enemy.

St. Pierre-Divion

The third part of the plan called for the capture of the village of St. Pierre-Divion. Units from RIR 110, RIR 119 and IR 180 would attack the village. The advance took place early in the morning of 5 October. RIR 110 quickly cleared a small copse in front of the village then continued to advance using the light from burning stacks of straw.

The attack drove the French out of St. Pierre-Divion at bayonet point and continued toward the village mill in the face of rifle fire coming from a nearby forest. At 1 a.m. French fire also came from the mill that was soon set on fire by the attackers. The light from the fire illuminated the French infantry who were in full retreat towards Mesnil. The advance continued to the village of Hamel but stopped when the men realized they could become cut off. The final act was to prepare the heights east of the village for defense.

On 5 October the 1st Guard Infantry Division (Group Hutier – 2nd and 3rd Guard Infantry Brigades) attempted to reach the line Gommecourt-Hebuterne-La Signy Farm but due to strong French opposition only captured a small amount of terrain. The 2nd Guard Infantry Division (Group von Winckler – 1st and 4th Guard Infantry Brigades) had been diverted to support the IV Corps at Arras.

German trenches at the edge of Beaumont-Hamel, 7/R99. (Author's collection)

Zur frommen Erinnerung im Gebete an

O
Herr
gib ihm
die
ewige
Ruhe!

Und
das
ewige
Licht
leuchte
ihm!

Anton Saile, Zimmermann
Landwehrmann im Pion.-Bat. Nr. 13, 4. Komp.
geboren den 10. Juni 1884 in Hirrlingen
geft. den Heldentod am 5. Oktbr. 1914
in Nordfrankreich.

Memorial Card: 30 year-old *Landwehrmann* Anton Saile 4/Pioneer
Bn 13. Killed in action 5 October 1914. (Author's collection)

The 26th Reserve Division moved headquarters one further time to the village of Miraumont where it remained until the end of 1915. The division staff occupied the Château of Miraumont, the summer home of a wealthy Parisian *Monsieur* Mercier.

Thiepval

In conjunction with the fighting north of the Ancre the 26th Reserve Division advanced south of the river. The plan called for the I and III/180 to attack the French inside Thiepval Wood while the 11/180 was given the separate assignment to attack the mill by Hamel. The intent was to throw the French back into the Ancre valley.

The attacks were a success and the French in Thiepval Wood were temporarily thrown back. Several prisoners were captured along with numerous rifles, ammunition and sandbags while the 11/180 captured the mill and set it on fire. However it had been realized before the attack that it would be impossible to hold these positions so the men were ordered back to the original German line of St. Pierre-Divion – Thiepval.

The one place the Germans wanted to capture and hold was Hill 141 located at the tip of the ridge south of the village of Thiepval. It was assumed the French had constructed a strong position, as soldiers were observed coming up the hill and disappearing into a trench inside a small group of trees. RIR 121 was ordered to capture the hill on the evening of the 5th.

The II and III/R121 were assigned to capture the position. The battalions formed at 9 p.m. with the II Battalion in the main line while the III/R121 formed the second line. The attack started at 9.15 p.m. from the vicinity of Ovillers-La Boisselle. The battalions first had to cross the hollow between Ovillers and the opposite ridge near Thiepval.

The bulk of the men advanced in impeccable order and as they began their ascent not a shot had been fired. Once the line almost reached the crest of the slope the French opened a murderous fire. Both battalions dropped to the ground immediately and the fire went safely over their heads and into the ranks of a few stragglers who had lagged behind. The stragglers quickly ran back and reported that everyone in both battalions had been killed. However this was not the case.

The French continued to fire over the heads of the men lying down. After a short pause the battalion commanders ordered everyone to shout and cheer. The sudden commotion caused the garrison to stop firing while they tried to determine where the noise was coming from. The commanders now ordered their men to attack and both battalions surged forward with fixed bayonets and drove the French garrison out of their trenches. Many in RIR 121 eagerly pursued the French, following them down the opposite slope before the officers could stop them. The men were eventually called back and reformed on Hill 141.

The attack resulted in few casualties for RIR 121 but approximately 100 enemy dead were counted around the hill. The position was quickly reinforced and the existing French trenches were expanded and improved. The main feature of the hill was the clay mine approximately 60 meters long by 40 meters wide bordered by high poplar trees. This spot was given the designation '*Granatloch*' by the regiment.

The men continued to work on the trenches in the expectation of a counterattack. One gun from the regimental Machine Gun Coy was brought up and placed into position. The French made numerous small attacks at night in an attempt to recapture the position but were repelled each time with help from the machine gun that afforded excellent service.

One drawback of the new position was the lack of safe access to Thiepval and the main German line. The French made several attempts to recapture the hill in the following night as well but failed each time. In the morning the defenders fell into a deep sleep after being awake since the previous day. They could sleep undisturbed, as French artillery fire normally did not begin until after midday.

The men could only leave the trenches at night when they could stretch their limbs in relative safety. Rations had to be brought up by food carriers who walked to Thiepval in the open where they met the field kitchens. When they carried their heavy loads back to the hill many became casualties from random French fire. Labor parties were formed immediately after the capture of the hill to expand the position as well as prepare secure communication trenches to the main German line.

On 9 October the Priest from Thiepval came out to the *Granatloch* with several local farmers carrying white flags. They wanted permission to bury the numerous French dead lying around the position. *Leutnant* Lichtenfels and the priest went across to the French

16th Company RIR 99. (Author's collection)

lines under the flag of truce. A French officer agreed to an armistice lasting 45 minutes which both sides used to bury the fallen men.

A few days previously, on 6 October, the 26th Reserve Division ordered Brigade Meyer (Bavarian IR 5 and 17) to attack Auchonvillers. RIR 99 was ordered to attack the village of Hamel while Reserve Infantry Brigade 51 would attack Authuille. It was an ambitious plan that did not take place for several reasons. The battalions had insufficient strength to participate in any attack and would not be able to make any headway against the strong position created by the French along the line Auchonvillers – La Signy Farm – Hebuterne. The regiments remained in their current positions and made improvements in the defenses.

The II/R99 did attempt to enlarge the gains made in the previous days with a reconnaissance in force against the village of Hamel. Major Laue and a group of cyclist troops approached Hamel in the early morning. The detachment came under fire from a house located just outside the village and came to a halt. The 6th Coy quickly captured the French position and continued the advance.

A group of children was suddenly spotted between the Germans and withdrawing French troops. *Oberleutnant der Landwehr* Vonnegut, 6/R99, realized the danger and ordered his men to cease fire and only allowed his men to continue to fire after the children were safely out of harm's way. The 6th Coy then advanced and occupied the southern edge of the village, reinforced later in the day by one platoon from the 10th Coy. Additional companies attempted to follow but were stopped by French artillery fire. It was then decided the regiment did not have sufficient strength to maintain a hold on the village.

Hamel was evacuated and the men were withdrawn east of the railway embankment. The brief occupation of Hamel resulted in moderate losses for the 6/R99 and the resulting field position occupied by the regiment ran from Auchonvillers to the Mesnil Grove southeast of Authuille. Hamel lay between 200 and 400 meters in front of the new line. The regiment was deployed to cover the new line and Bavarian artillery units were moved to Beaucourt to provide support.

Infantrymen – RIR 111. (Author's collection)

The men were immediately put to work preparing the villages of Beaucourt and Beaumont for defense. Embrasures were created in the walls of the houses; the window openings were filled with earth and clay behind wooden panels. Small openings were left for the rifle barrels. The men dug crude trenches between the buildings and tree barriers and 'wolf pits'[7] were created to make the line as secure as possible.

Fighting continued to rage north of the 26th Reserve Division but little headway was made. The 1st Guard Division Group Hutier captured Gommecourt with Guard IR 4. However several determined attacks by 2nd Guard Regiment *zu Fuss* against Hebuterne had failed. The attack by the 3rd Guard Infantry Brigade against Mailly was unsuccessful in part due to the strong French position located at La Signy Farm. Further north the reinforced IV Corps had still not captured Arras after repeated attempts.

The race to the sea continued to move north and new units were being brought up for the task. The VII Army Corps was being assembled at Cambrai while six new army Corps, XXII through XXVII were being formed and were scheduled to march by 10 October. The continuation of the offensive by the XIV Reserve Corps would prove to be even more elusive in the following days. Because of the difficulties encountered by Arras the Guard Corps shifted forces from the left wing by Serre and transferred them to the right wing near Arras. With the reduction of strength the attack against Hebuterne had to be cancelled. The Guard Corps did manage to maintain control of Gommecourt despite heavy pressure by French troops.

On 7 October Brigade Meyer was transferred from the 26th Reserve Division and sent to assist the 1st Guard Division. This meant that the 26th Reserve Division needed to find additional troops to hold the line and the division was temporarily given RIR 110. Even with the addition of Brigade Meyer the 1st Guard Division was not able to capture Fonquevillers and Hannescamp on 8 October while the 2nd Guard Division Group Winckler with the 2nd Cavalry Division made only modest gains against the French.

The 26th Reserve Division now occupied a line almost 15 kilometers long and according to the division commander did not have sufficient strength to continue the offensive. It was time to change to a defensive posture.

The artillery fire from both sides continued without abatement with the advantage lying with the French and a seemingly plentiful supply of ammunition. The German guns replied when necessary but every attempt was being made to conserve ammunition.

Disaster at Bécourt

On the evening of 7 October General von Stein issued orders to the 28th Reserve Division to attempt an undertaking against the French positions in the village of Bécourt and neighboring Hill 106. There were several reasons given for this hastily planned attack. Earlier in the same morning a patrol from the 6/R111 reported that a French battery was in position along the La Boiselle-Bécourt road. In addition to destroying or incapacitating this annoying battery the attack would capture Hill 106 thereby preventing the French from using it as an observation post. The capture of Bécourt would straighten the line between La Boiselle and Fricourt and by doing so would relieve the pressure on Fricourt.

The 28th Reserve Division assigned the task of leading the attack to *Oberstleutnant* Weiss, commander of the III/R111. Weiss would have his battalion (minus the 7th Coy) and two companies from RIR 40 (4th Coy and 2 platoons from the 1st and 3rd Companies) in the attack. Two companies from RIR 109 would provide support while the III/R120

Eigene Aufnahme f. d. Kriegstagbuch   Hofphot. A. Hirrlinger

Die vom König verliehene neue Fahne des Ref.-Jnf.-Regts. 120

Regimental colors - RIR 120. (*Kriegstagbuch aus Schwaben*)

under Major von Zeppelin would attack on the right wing. The orders for the attack did not reach Weiss until 8 o'clock in the evening; it was set for 11.30 p.m.

Due to the limited amount of time before the attack was to start and darkness *Oberstleutnant* Weiss was unable to make any type of reconnaissance of the French position. When it was decided that the attacking force was insufficient Reserve *Jäger* Bn 14 was ordered to send two companies to join them.

The units needed to be contacted, informed of their part in the attack and assembled with all of the equipment and supplies needed in order to proceed at the scheduled time. The troops were assembled in a hollow north of Fricourt with Reserve *Jäger* Bn 14 and RIR 40 forming the skirmish line, RIR 111 following as the main body. Both the III/R111 and I/R40 brought their battalion flags with them for the attack. The lack of reconnaissance and hasty planning in implementing the attack would have serious consequences in the next 24 hours.

The units proceeded with the attack as scheduled. They advanced across the stubble fields towards the copse that surrounded Bécourt. The night was pitch black and the men relied upon the dim moonlight to guide them to their destination. They were awaiting the first enemy response and nerves were tense when a German voice suddenly called out to the advancing column from the darkness. It turned out to be a patrol from RIR 120. The column had apparently gone astray in the darkness and was in front of La Boisselle instead of approaching Bécourt. The patrol also advised Detachment Weiss that RIR 120 was not scheduled to attack until the following day. Weiss decided to continue the attack regardless of the lack of support on the right wing. The column was realigned to face Bécourt and advanced.

When the column came to within 400-500 meters from the edge of the dark wood the French opened fire from the left flank. The 1/R40 was ordered to deal with it. Part of the 1st Coy changed direction and engaged the French in a trench located on a nearby hillside. The remainder of the company lost contact with their comrades during the change of direction and proceeded against Bécourt Wood with the main body.

The fight on the flank grew in intensity until the Germans were forced to take cover on a small rise of ground. They 1st Coy began to take heavy casualties and realized that their right flank was exposed and had lost contact with the main body. *Leutnant* Vohl was ordered to take a small group of men from the line and extend the front toward the wood and find out what was happening. Vohl went down the line and grabbed the legs of eight men, two of them slid down the slope lifeless shot through the head.

Detachment Weiss approached the wood and were within 200 meters when the French opened fire. The men surged forward and quickly overcame the light resistance; actually they had more trouble with the wire fences and dense hedges than with French fire while entering the wood. The detachment met with sporadic resistance advancing through the dense undergrowth until an open area was reached near Bécourt Château.

The companies were in a state of confusion from moving through the trees and the next few minutes were taken up organizing the men back into their units. While this was happening Weiss and two orderlies continued toward Hill 106. They were followed a short time later by the main body and the attack continued in the pale moonlight. When the line got to within 200 meters of the hill they were struck by heavy fire coming from a myriad of communication trenches in their front as well as from both flanks from French reinforcements who had seemingly appeared as if by magic.

The Germans attempted to storm Hill 106 but the fire was too severe and the attack failed. Now the men were faced with a dilemma, they could not remain in such an open position under the heavy fire as their casualties were growing by the minute. Weiss was among the first to be wounded when a rifle bullet shattered his left hand. The order was finally given to withdraw into the wood. The western edge of the wood was occupied and prepared for defense before the French fire grew too intense.

Weiss had expected to receive support from Fricourt or from La Boisselle but there was no sign that it was coming. He sent messages to the rear asking for support but the runners could not get through the heavy volume of fire. The French had recovered from the shock of the initial attack and had reoccupied the trenches at the eastern edge of the wood; Detachment Weiss was cut off and surrounded.

Wolde

Hauptmann und Kompagnieführer
im Res.-Inf.-Regt. 120, gefallen am
8. Oktober bei La Boiselle

Hauptmann Richard Wolde (Hamburg)
12/R120. Killed in action 8 October at La
Boisselle. (*Kriegstagbuch aus Schwaben*)

Derksen

Leutnant d. R. im Inf.-Regt. 120,
gest. am 8. Okt. 1914 an den bei
La Boiselle erhaltenen Wunden.

Leutnant der Reserve Heinrich Derksen
(Wesel, Düsseldorf) 9/R120. Reported
wounded and missing in action at
La Boisselle. Died 8 October 1914.
(*Kriegstagbuch aus Schwaben*)

There were attempts to relieve the trapped detachment by a reinforced battalion from RIR 120 under Major von Zeppelin. However they ran into heavy French resistance and were unable to make any headway toward Bécourt Wood. After suffering casualties the battalion returned to La Boisselle.

Weiss decided they needed to force their way through to the German lines. Five separate attempts were made in the direction of Fricourt and La Boisselle but each time heavy French fire from trenches and behind felled trees forced them back into the wood.

As if to make matters worse the German artillery opened fire upon the wood in a misguided attempt to assist the trapped men. By now most of the officers had either been killed or wounded and casualties among the men continued to increase by the hour. By 8 a.m. it was over, the bulk of Detachment Weiss that still remained was forced to surrender to the French and the men were led away into captivity.

Scattered groups of men still had hopes of breaking through to their own lines under cover of darkness. One included the commander of Reserve *Jäger* Bn 14. He crawled through the wood with several officers and men in order to locate a suitable spot where they could make their way back to Fricourt. As they approached the tree line they noticed a French infantry company marching alongside the edge of the wood, fortunately the *Jägers* were not discovered. However their luck ran out when two of the *Poilus* left the column in order to relieve themselves in the wood and stumbled into the hidden *Jägers*. Any opposition was useless. Within a few seconds the French company had surrounded the small group and the French captain said, '*La Guerre est finie pour vous*'.

Not all of the scattered remnants of Detachment Weiss were as unlucky as the *Jägers*. The 1/R40 that had been sent to the left flank to engage the French at the beginning of the attack found that they were in danger of being overwhelmed by the increasing number of enemy troops. The survivors were ordered to disengage as best they could and make their way back to their battalion position. The men worked their way back individually and in groups and many successfully made their way back to Fricourt.

Meanwhile Vohl and his men had reached the edge of Bécourt Wood in the morning and found it was strangely silent. They found the wood edge was unoccupied and almost impossible to enter due to a thick hedge. When they located a gap they discovered a French position that had obviously been strongly occupied. Vohl found a spot where he could observe the edge of the wood and waited to see what was happening. In a few moments he spotted three French officers on the other side of the hedge. They discussed the situation in the wood and then departed in three different directions. Vohl also observed French infantry crawling towards the wood from the direction of the hillside where the 1/R40 was still engaged.

He rejoined his group and decided to make their way out of the wood towards a railway embankment and then back to the German lines. As they left the wood they were spotted by French infantry and fired upon. The seven men spread out in an arc as they worked their way towards the nearest cover and all of them made it without any losses. When they reached safety they discovered other men had made their way there before them. These men were from different companies that had become separated from their units in the fighting in the dense wood. Many had lost their bearings and crawled around the wood in circles until they had no idea which side had been shooting at them. Other members of the 1/R40 that had been able to elude the French eventually made their way towards the German lines when they were fired upon by friendly troops. *Unteroffizier* Wilhelm, 1/R40, who successfully made his way through several French trenches without suffering losses shouted out: 'Comrades, don't shoot' and to his great joy the firing stopped and they were able to cross the last 100 meters to the German lines at the run and safety.

Patrols from Fricourt and La Boisselle tried to determine fate of the rest. They were able to report Bécourt was strongly occupied by the French and there was no expectation any more men would return.

However more men did make their way through to the German lines. The largest group belonged to Reserve *Jäger* Bn 14. *Leutnant* von Pentz, the last remaining officer, successfully led 95 men back to the German lines during the night. What had happened to the others was not known for some time. The fate of *Oberstleutnant* Weiss and the others was eventually determined when a French soldier was taken prisoner who carried a postcard depicting the public entry of German prisoners on the boulevards of Paris; it was a picture of the missing men. The French lists of prisoners eventually made its way through channels to the German authorities that published the names of the missing men in the *Verlustlisten*.

The remnants of Detachment Weiss were assembled in Bazentin le Petit where the true cost of the disaster could be determined. The II/R111 had suffered the most; the battalion could only muster approximately 150 men. Combined with the losses from the other units it meant an entire battalion had been lost in the undertaking.

What of the fate of the two flags? The flag of RIR 40 was brought back intact while the flag of RIR 111 was missing. When the flag bearer, *Vizefeldwebel* Stöckmann, realized he would not be able to escape he buried the flag at the base of an oak tree. Once inside a Prisoner of War camp Stöckmann was able to send a message to the adjutant of his battalion and relay the story about the flag.[8] The XIV Reserve Corps issued orders that from this time forward regimental flags would not be taken into action again. The remaining flags were cased and returned to Germany and placed in storage.

Soon after the failed attack the German line was subjected to heavy French artillery fire. The I/R40 near the copse on the left of the Contalmaison-Fricourt road became a devilish place from the roar of exploding French shells that reportedly made the lives of the defenders as hot as hell.

The bombardment fell upon the house where the battalion ambulance stood. *Stabsarzt* Dr. Wossidlo was working on repacking the medicine box that had become disorganized over the last few days:

> We have a splendid Medical Captain. He is always in front in the fighting and retains a classic calmness in the heaviest shellfire. On 8 October when he was in Fricourt in the heaviest bombardment we had experienced he did not leave his ambulance until he had carefully wrapped up all of the medicine inside it. A *Gefreiter* next to him had his head torn off. He did not let this interrupt him. Everything around him was burning, the heavy shells exploded in close proximity. He remained until everything had been brought to safety. The man accordingly enjoys the greatest trust and became greatly admired by all.[9]

The fighting to the north of the XIV Reserve Corps continued. The 1st Guard Division failed to take Fonquevillers and Hannescamp on the 8th even with the support of Brigade Meyer. The 2nd Guard Division Group Winckler and the 2nd Cavalry Division only made slight headway against the French on their front. The 3rd Guard Infantry Brigade von Petersdorff with two battalions from the Kaiser Alexander Guard Grenadier Regiment Nr. 1 and one battalion from the 4th Guard Regiment *zu Fuss* occupied the Serre Sector.

The artillery batteries reinforcing the 26th Reserve Division were withdrawn on 7 October. The division now relied solely upon RFAR 26 for artillery support and the batteries were stretched to their limit.

Horse-drawn field ambulance, XIV Reserve Corps. (Author's collection)

The 'Race to the Sea' continued in the manner of a chess game. Each side maneuvered their units in order to counter the opposing side. The Guard and IV Corps were fighting south of Arras then the I Bavarian Reserve Corps came into line followed by the VII and XIV Corps north of Arras. The XIX Corps followed by the XIII Corps occupied the heights by Lille. HKK 1, 2 and 4 attempted to protect the right flank of the army and veiled the advance of the newly formed Fourth Army commanded by Duke Albrecht von Württemberg. The Fourth Army consisted of the III and XXVII Reserve Corps, the XXII, XXIII, XXVI and XXVII Corps that closed the gap between Lille and the sea. Finally Group Fabeck consisting of the XV and II Bavarian Corps was pushed into the gap between the Fourth and Sixth Armies. The opposing lines now ran from the sea to the Alps.

On 10 October General Karl von Bülow issued the following order:

I have taken over the supreme command over the newly-formed Second Army. Our supreme war leader has entrusted five battle-proven Corps to my leadership. With the help of God I will lead them to victory. Von Bülow, *General-Oberst*, Army Headquarters St. Quentin.[10]

The XIV Reserve Corps along with the XVIII, XXI, I and II Bavarian Corps formed the new army; the official date of transfer was 11 October. The Sixth Army as well as the Second Army issued the following instructions on 13 October:

The general situation requires temporarily giving up the attack. Therefore the army corps will immediately limit themselves to the ground they have captured and will immediately develop their positions. Only attack activity with limited goals will be allowed.[11]

It was the start of almost two years of trench warfare on the Somme for the men of the XIV Reserve Corps. Events in the second half of October required that all reinforcements attached to the Corps become immediately withdrawn. Corps and army reserves were to be eliminated. This required the divisions of the XIV Reserve Corps to make some changes in the units holding the line. The front of the 26th Reserve Division was approximately 12 kilometers in length. When RIR 110 was withdrawn from Beaumont and returned to the 28th Reserve Division the remaining troops in the division had to fill the gap and were being stretched very thin. The situation was made even worse on 23 October when one battalion from RIR 119 was sent to the 28th Reserve Division and occupied Fricourt.

The Reserve Dragoon Regiment was moved to Flers to act as a temporary army reserve while the 26th Reserve Division was fortunate in obtaining one battalion from the 1st Guard Division that was quartered in Miraumont.

8 October would prove to be the last strategic offensive movement attempted by the XIV Reserve Corps for some time to come. The period of mobile warfare was finished and was being replaced by spade warfare. The weather was still moderate at the beginning of the month but as time passed nights grew colder and early morning fog usually lasted until midday. The second half of the month was marked with a sharp increase in cold weather; it was the start of winter. Harsh autumn winds swept over the flattened fields of wheat and rotting turnips, rain soon followed. Idle limbs became sensitive against the

dampness and the only cure was to work on the position. Still morale among the troops was good and the men joked and had hopes for a better future.

The XIV Reserve Corps was now concerned with trench construction, distribution of troops within assigned sectors, housing of reserves and the seemingly endless details required by position warfare.

The men fully expected to continue their advance against the French once the current situation had improved and new forces became available. As a result the idea of constructing a permanent trench system or shelters was unthinkable. Everything had changed after 8 October when the regiments were ordered to dig-in. Very little pre-war training had prepared the men for this type of fighting. The spade had been universally despised by most of the men who now suddenly found it to be their best friend and the savior of the Field Grey.

The first orders directed the men to create trenches between 1.2 and 1.5 meters deep with a parapet and firing steps. The early trenches were shallow and in many instances traverses were lacking allowing the French to fire down the length of the trench. The shallow trenches did provide some degree of protection against French field guns but as artillery grew in quantity and size of caliber these trenches proved to be inadequate. Trenches needed to be deepened; where traverses did exist they needed to be widened and strengthened. The work was difficult and at first many of the men did not want to take on the gigantic task of improving the defenses until they realized that there was a correlation between the depth of the trench and the reduction in their losses.

At first many of the trenches were not connected to one another and gaps were present all along the line. The individual holes used by the men were gradually connected into small trenches. The individual trenches were then quickly joined to one another but despite the attempts by both divisions to create a unified trench system there were several areas

Aerial photograph of the Beaumont Sector. (*Das Württembergische Reserve-Infanterie-Regiment Nr. 119 im Weltkrieg 1914-1918*)

where large gaps still existed. One existed between the 26th Reserve Division and the Guard Corps in the valley between the Serre-Mailly road and Beaumont. Another between Reserve Infantry Brigades 52 and 51 in the hollow between Thiepval and Ovillers and one between La Boisselle and Contalmaison where the 26th and 28th Reserve Divisions joined. The XIV Reserve Corps attempted to close these gaps by the use of wire obstacles and patrols. Still the danger existed that French troops could force a breakthrough at these points.

The need for secure communication trenches leading toward the rear became evident from the start. All movement to and from the trenches had to take place at night as men traveled along the surface of the ground and were exposed to French fire during daylight.

Supplying adequate food to the front line was a problem from the start of position warfare. Most of the food was brought up from the rear and the men had to walk 3 to 4 kilometers a night in each direction.

> All this time our food had to be carried on a post between two men from Contalmaison, about 3 miles away. We never got any warm food unless we had a chance to warm it over in a cellar. The food consisted of coffee and bread in the morning and rice soup and boiled beef at night. On Sundays we had pork, sauerkraut and hot wine and this crazy combination of a meal was the only thing that reminded us that another week had gone by.
>
> The food expeditions to Contalmaison were no joke. First we carried about 15 small aluminum mess kits on our posts. As these pots were very much battered, the covers did not hold and sometimes when we had to speed up a little, we spilled more than half of the contents. Then there was the trouble of picking up one of the darned covers when it came off, with a cartridge belt around our bellies and rifles slung over our shoulders, without spilling the whole thing.
>
> Once when I was on food duty the two of us were knocked down by the air pressure from an exploding shell and both of us were half dizzy. When we finally arrived at the trench in La Boisselle, our mess kits were mostly minus their covers and half empty. We acted like drunken sailors and by the time we reached our hole we had a mixture of half soup and half mud. As the others saw that we were in no condition to be argued with, they got some bread down from the shelf and whatever their own folks at home had sent them in small packages through the mail and made their own supper. The two of us had lost our appetite and were glad to be alive after being so close to croaking for no good reason at all. Hans Ludwig, 6/R120 [12]

After a while the aluminum mess kits were replaced with 10-gallon jugs in baskets that did not make as much noise as the mess kits and aluminum pots clinking together. But more often than not the glass jugs were shattered by random rifle fire or by being dropped and the men had to go back for a replacement.

Almost all work had to be done at night under the cover of darkness. Even companies that were relieved from front line duty were often recalled each evening to the front to dig. The first wire obstacles were erected in front of the trenches wherever possible. The sound of the mallets being used to drive in the wire stakes often brought down French fire that resulted in casualties and a great deal of damage to the trenches and wire obstacles that had to be repaired night after night.

The men in the rear were not immune from hard work and danger. Other Ranks from the First Line Transport and Baggage Section of the Train had little time to rest. They spent their time during the daylight hours receiving the materials needed in the trenches and loading the wagons for transport and caring for the horses. During the night the same men would travel to and from the front line with loads of supplies. Losses were inevitable from the constant shellfire directed against the suspected supply routes. Regardless of the French fire or weather the transport wagons continued their nightly journey to and from the front. Each day passed in the same manner.

The construction of the trenches proved to be quite difficult. The ground consisted of a thin layer of humus that covered a dense layer of chalk and flint. Many men were not accustomed to heavy work and the short handled infantry tools were not adequate for the task at hand. Pickaxes and long-handled shovels were desperately needed.

The XIV Reserve Corps had three pioneer companies assigned to the two divisions. The pioneers were in great demand for their expertise in all forms of trench construction and related defensive works ranging from building bridges across the Ancre to creating strong points out of existing houses or tunneling under the railway line near Fricourt. The pioneers were distributed throughout the front and would act as supervisors and instructors while the infantry performed most of the labor.

The pioneers began the process of accumulating the massive amounts of material needed for trench construction in Pioneer parks located behind the lines. Iron rails were collected from far and wide. Trees were felled and cut up; barbed wire was removed from pasture fences and sent to the front.

In addition to creating new defensive position the pioneers provided assistance in actually defending the trenches. At this point in the war pioneers were the only men trained in the use of hand grenades and other explosives used by the army. The pioneers began the process of teaching the infantry how to use the early hand grenades and introduced the first flare pistols for use in lighting up the dark nights. Steel shields were placed along the parapet and mirrors were positioned in order to allow observation of the French lines without exposing the sentries to enemy fire. Screens were set up along roads and villages that would prevent any observation of German traffic.

In some instances the infantry were able to provide valuable assistance to the pioneers by utilizing their pre-war skills. RIR 99 had more than its share in this aspect. Many of the Other Ranks in the regiment had been miners in Westphalia.

The regiment was assigned to the Beaumont – Beaucourt sector. The regimental miners used their talents to drive tunnels into the clay and chalk hillsides along the Ancre, constructed bombproof dug-outs, created deep trenches with breastworks and traverses on each flank. Numerous latrines were created and made accessible through safe communication trenches. Tunnels were created to connect different trench sections.

The large ravine located near Beaumont was a natural choice for creating large tunnels. *Hauptmann* Leiling, 16/R99, was placed in charge of the fortification work in the ravine that received the designation the *Leiling Schlucht*.[13]

Several modifications needed to be made as trenches were improved and expanded. As they went deeper into the ground the trench walls became steeper and had a tendency to collapse. It became standard practice to line trench walls with boards, rolls of wire or woven mats constructed of reeds and thin branches taken from nearby sources.

Hauptmann Leiling (sitting below dog on the left) 16/R99 in the
Leilingschlucht. (*Geschichte des Reserve-Infanterie-Regiment Nr. 99*)

RIR 99 set up alarm bells in every trench through the hard work of *Gefreiter* Fischer, a telegraph wire inspector in civilian life. The bells could be used to alert the different companies whenever needed. Fischer used French civilian telephone lines that he integrated into the army lines. Now each company was connected by telephone with regimental headquarters and the artillery headquarters.

The XIV Reserve Corps was concerned with providing shelter for the men while at the front. Instructions were issued to create shelters with a minimum of 30 inches of earth on top. The earliest shelters were generally no more than shallow depressions or holes scooped out of the side of the trench. The temporary shelters appeared to be more than adequate protection for the moment when the men did not expect to stay long and the advance would continue.

Despite orders to construct shelters some men still held to the belief they were unnecessary and therefore ignored them. This was particularly true of units that were stationed inside several of the villages that dotted the German front line. The men of RIR 99 had resisted making shelters underground at first and utilized the existing buildings in the villages of Beaumont and Beaucourt for living quarters, medical dug-outs and battalion headquarters.

The 10/R99 was quartered with 7 cows inside of a 2-cow barn in Beaumont. The 10th Coy regarded their quarters as being invulnerable because when the French shelled Beaumont on two days not a single shell struck the barn despite at least 98 shells per minute striking the village as crater after crater appeared around the structure. The barn remained untouched in subsequent bombardments and was always considered to be a lucky spot.

Two residential homes were turned into a battalion headquarters. In order to protect the occupants from French fire a massive wall several meters thick was constructed out of poplars taken from the Ancre valley on the side facing the enemy. The protective wall became so enormous that even the men constructing it felt the logs might completely collapse the lightly constructed homes.

The regiment constructed a medical dug-out for Dr Amels, the regimental surgeon. His structure was popularly called the 'Stable Bethlehem' and was located in Beaucourt. It was constructed out of large poplar trees that had once lined the streets of Irles that were covered in layers of manure. The interior of the dug-out was covered with wallpaper obtained from Cambrai.

RIR 120 was holding the village of La Boisselle. They had decided to take advantage of the brick buildings that made up the majority of the village structures. At the beginning of October the men were posted in rooms that had windows facing the opposing lines and whenever the French came too close to the village they were driven off by rifle and machine gun fire.

During one day the men carelessly moved about the village while still hoping to advance once more. By the afternoon no such orders had arrived, instead French 75's fired into the village forcing the men to seek shelter inside large stone cellars. The men continued to occupy the village buildings despite increasing French activity.

All night while we were working, French bullets crashed against the brick walls of the houses. This at first made us uneasy, but later on we could not have slept any more without hearing the then familiar noise of a bullet crashing against a brick, making a noise like a whip.

One day we were amusing ourselves by playing one of those penny-in-the-slot music machines, which could be found in every French restaurant, one of which served as our quarters. Suddenly some 75's came tearing past the cellar. While the music box was still playing the *Marseillaise*, a direct hit went into it and stopped the music. The shooting was over after a while and we went upstairs to inspect the damage. We had lost one wall and instead of a music box we had a heap of rubbish. A gear of this machine cut the throat of a picture of Napoleon I on one wall, which was still standing. The other two were tottering and the fourth was gone altogether. After this, we moved such of our belongings as we could still locate and identify into the cellar and made our quarters down there. A few fresh air fiends continued to sleep upstairs, claiming that they still had a roof even if one wall was missing, which could happen in any war. The buildings of La Boisselle were systematically

Reinforcing walls - the village of Beaucourt – RIR 119. (Author's collection)

Friends, RIR 120 (L), IR 180 (R). (Author's collection)

destroyed one by one and everybody was in a cellar before long, joining the other cave dwellers. Hans Ludwig, 6/R120 [14]

The crude shelters were eventually expanded and covered with tree branches, wooden planks, old doors, and corrugated iron, anything the men could find. Then they would be covered with straw, earth or manure in order to provide some camouflage against enemy observation and protection against shrapnel balls or shell splinters. The men who were fortunate enough to be positioned in a village also utilized the stone cellars of the village buildings as pre-made dug-outs. The cellars were covered with a makeshift roof made from any form of debris and rubbish at hand, then covered with bricks, straw, earth or manure.

There was a shortage of materials needed to provide a roof for the shelters for RIR 121 on Hill 141. The nearest source of supplies was the village of Thiepval that was occupied by IR 180. Nevertheless many roof rafters ended up in dug-outs on Hill 141. Even the street door of the village commander's residence went missing one night. It was later seen in a dug-out at the *Granatloch*. The men of IR 180 called the action 'theft', while the men of RIR 121 considered it a 'stratagem'.

While the early shelters offered some protection against French shrapnel balls and rifle bullets they were completely ineffective against shells. Many early shelters were destroyed by shellfire. On 5 October the French shelled the 6/R109 at the western edge of Fricourt.

One shell struck a shelter causing it to collapse upon the sole occupant, *Reservist* Oswald Troetschler and he became crushed under the tangle of smashed planks. Several men spent 20 minutes under heavy French fire trying to rescue Troetschler from the collapsed dug-out. They finally succeeded and carried the injured man to a neighboring shelter where his wounds were bandaged. Troetschler was then carried to the medical facility in the rear after darkness had fallen.

The need to provide prompt medical care was critical, as it would provide the injured man the greatest chance of surviving his injuries. A series of medical dug-outs were created along the front in order to treat the sick and wounded, usually in stone cellars. Temporary cases would still be taken care of in regimental patient rooms while additional facilities were set up to treat serious cases.

The artillerymen had also prepared crude shelters near their guns. What started as simple holes dug alongside the guns grew in size over time. Boards and planks were used to support the walls and act as a roof. The men felt they were as safe as if they were in Abraham's lap. French shells soon demonstrated how the feeling of safety was only an illusion. On 19 October a heavy French shell struck the 2nd Battery. The shell not only destroyed gun No. 5, it also killed 3 men in the adjoining dug-out and wounded 2 others.

The shallow shelters proved to be ineffective against French shells and something needed to be done. Different types of dug-outs were constructed in both divisions but nothing seemed to be adequate in protecting the men. The men in RIR 120 tried something new.

> Though our losses were small at first, they were consistent and we realized that we needed better protection if we did not want every man in the regiment to bite the dust. First we heaped all rubbish on top of the cellars, then bricks, straw, and earth dug from the trenches and whatever else we could find. Then the French started to train heavier guns on our position, and while we still stuck to the cellars as the best we had, we began to dig holes about ten yards square and covered them with four layers of raw logs and about two feet of dirt and bricks and finished them off with more dirt, planting beets to camouflage them. One bright soul built a dug-out all for himself consisting of a box spring he had salvaged from some bed which he used to cover his hole. He considered this ample protection until one day he nearly choked to death when his piece of art collapsed while he was asleep in it. We pulled him out by his hind legs and he was glad to come out with us, giving up the idea of individual dug-outs as unhealthy.
>
> One platoon in another company had used the immensely big doors of a barn to cover their hole with some few feet of dirt on top of it which weakened the whole thing. A direct hit wiped them out and the loss was 16 men. They were buried in one grave which later played an important part in the life of my group. Hans Ludwig, 6/R120 [15]

In one part of the front the men were faced with an unusual dilemma. The ground along the Ancre was unsuited for digging shelters of any kind due to the high water table. Building above ground solved the problem. The position held by the 5/R99 in front of the mill in the swampy Ancre valley was soon known as the *'Biber Kolonie'* from the strong

Crude trench shelter in the copse near Mouquet farm. (*Das Württembergische Reserve-Infanterie-Regiment Nr. 121 im Weltkrieg 1914-1918*)

resemblance the structures had to beaver lodges. A long raised barricade also gave the impression of a beaver dam adding to the appropriateness of the name.

Trees and pastures concealed the position from French observers and the ground provided one more beneficial service. Many shells that impacted in the soft ground failed to explode. However the men reported that when a shell exploded in a tree it made an eerie sound and scattered shell splinters far and wide. With the large number of unexploded shells at hand the men from the 5/R99 decided to play a trick upon the French.

The dud French shells were fitted with explosive charges supplied by the pioneers. Then they were placed inside a small barrel and floated down river toward the French lines. All of the bombs were successfully grounded before they could do any harm but their actions did make it into the French army reports when it was announced that the Germans had unleashed fire ships on the Ancre. Paris radio announced the new German 'barbarism' to the rest of the world from the transmitter atop the Eiffel Tower.[16]

Shortly after the episode involving the fire ships an impromptu information exchange started between the sentries from RIR 99 and their French counterparts. One sentry in RIR 99 tied a newspaper to a tree between the opposing lines with a message asking the French about any victory news.

The following day the sentries found a response in the same manner touting supposed Allied successes including the Russian advance into Germany, the breakdown of the Austrian army and the inevitable withdrawal of the German army from France. On the reverse side the French had sent another message, one aimed at enticing the German soldiers to desert. The French claimed that the only way the Germans would see Paris would be if they joined their comrades who had already been captured. The French promised a good life, plenty of wine and very beautiful women if the Germans would simply come over and give up. If they did it would not be long before they were reunited with their families. The final message in the package was a copy of a sumptuous menu from the officer's mess.

The men from RIR 99 responded that it was unworthy for a cultured people to try to induce their comrades in the opposing army to desert. They also explained that the German officer shared the meals given to the men. When this form of communication reached the attention of the senior commanders it quickly came to an end.

Early reinforced trench dug-out – XIV Reserve Corps. (*Die 26. Reserve Division 1914-1918*)

At the end of October the 7/R99 made a fantastic discovery in Beaumont. A sentry discovered a concealed corridor in a cellar while taking shelter from a bombardment. Pioneers opened it up and discovered a stairway leading down 6-8 meters ending at a long corridor from which other tunnels branched off. The entrance was widened and the tunnels were cleaned up. A second exit was constructed leading to the nearby road. On 25 October the 10/R99 was assigned to occupy the new tunnel complex.

Experienced miners from the regiment widened the tunnels and provided additional support for the roof. Fabrics taken from the surrounding villages were used to cover the bare chalk walls and a third emergency exit was constructed. The first tunnel became utilized as a courtroom, the Justice Palace. A sleeping area was located behind it while another tunnel became used as a writing room. The middle of the corridor widened into a circular room large enough for the company to assemble for roll call. Rifle racks and storage areas for hand grenades and other supplies were installed.

Religious services were often held inside the center tunnel and the sound of singing was accompanied by the distant sound of exploding shells on the surface far above. Candles were placed at regular intervals to provide sufficient illumination.

The men attempted to make their crude homes as comfortable as possible. Frames were carved from the chalk that held photographs of loved ones at home. Tables and benches were taken from local houses and brought into the dug-outs. Large quantities of wheat, hay and straw were gathered up and used to manufacture makeshift beds. Some men went as far as to make chairs from chalk and bricks.

No improvement or comfort could take away the knowledge that the men were faced with living underground. Water dripped into the underground shelters constantly after the weather turned to rain and fog. With the onset of cold weather the men needed some method to keep warm. Small iron stoves were obtained from the local communities and supplemented by a supply taken from St. Quentin and installed inside the dug-outs.

Stoves were also made using local chalk and bricks. These also allowed the men to prepare hot tea and coffee in the front line. At first wood was used to heat the small stoves, later Thuringian charcoal burners began to produce charcoal to be used as fuel. Afghans confiscated from the population of Antwerp arrived and were distributed among the men for additional warmth.

Lighting the numerous dug-outs started to become an issue when the supply of candles began to run out. Candles and paraffin were taken from the local population as well as being manufactured in the rear but it was still not enough to fill the need. Hundreds of empty preserve bottles were accumulated and sent to the front. A soap boiler in RIR 99 showed his comrades how to make lights using cans or jars, filled on the bottom with clay and with chalk on top to hold the fuel. A piece of straw and tow obtained from the armourer would be used as a wick. Other methods of producing lamps included using empty bottles with the neck broken off. The men of RIR 99 were more fortunate than most. A generator placed in a mill in the Ancre valley supplied electric power for lighting many of the dug-outs.

Still, despite all efforts the shelters and dug-outs were gloomy and damp. A typical scene inside a shelter could include men smoking pipes or cigars and playing *Skat*, or shrouded by heavy coats lying on straw beds while writing a letter to their family or trying to sleep. Folk songs and the sound of harmonicas could be heard coming from many of the dug-outs.

The numerous dug-outs soon became infested with rats and many items needed to be kept out of reach.

> Our cellars looked funny enough with all kinds of boxes, tins, etc. hanging on wires or strings. Once in the dug-out of the colonel somebody was cursing very loud and very well. It was the adjutant of the colonel, who at home was a minister in the church. The other officer asked him what was wrong and he got the very short answer 'rats in the bed'. 'Oh', said the other one, 'that's Ok, I can pat mine on the back already, they're tame.' Hans Ludwig, 6/R120 [17]

Charcoal burners, RIR 110. (*Reserve-Infanterie Regiment Nr. 110 im Weltkrieg 1914-1918*)

One man in RIR 109 apparently had similar ideas concerning rats.

We hung our bread from the ceiling on strings because of the many rats. One man had a trained rat that had a string around its neck and he walked it just like a dog. Emil Goebelbecker, 9/R109 [18]

Supplying food to the front lines was more difficult than expected. Everything had to be done under the cover of darkness until adequate communication trenches were in place. During October the food service slowly improved and better organized. Army provisions were supplemented with food taken from the land; meat, vegetables and wine. Potatoes and turnips were often dug up at night by the men and eaten.

The range of food provided to the men consisted of coffee in the morning followed by warm food that included turnips, rice, potatoes, Swiss cheese, coffee, tea, wine or mulled wine and plentiful amounts of army bread and white bread supplied by the battalion bakers, tobacco, newspapers and as often as possible, fresh straw. Fruit was a luxury that was supplied far less frequently than desired by the men. The idea of using sugar beets that were plentiful to feed the men was quickly abandoned. One item that was lavishly distributed was sugar that was taken from the numerous factories that dotted the terrain in the rear areas.

Two wine cellars were discovered in Miraumont containing 10,000 liters of wine that was distributed to the men in the trenches and was considered a Godsend during the cold and rainy nights. In Le Transloy a warehouse was discovered in a remote cellar containing 900,000 eggs that were stored in glass jars. This find allowed the regular distribution of eggs to everyone in the XIV Reserve Corps, so much that each battalion could be allotted over 20,000 eggs apiece.

One source of food came from the numerous livestock wandering around the countryside that had been rounded up and were looked after by men, many of who were farmers in civilian life. The II/R99 alone managed to gather a herd of several hundred sheep. Small amounts of wine were discovered from time to time hidden in the deep cellars and not infrequently inside the large piles of manure found at almost every household and farm. The men from RFAR 26 became adept at locating the hidden bottles using a variety of tools including hoes and pitchforks used as divining rods as every hiding place was thoroughly searched.

When in rest quarters many men had taken to hunting rabbits and searching for stray chickens in order to increase the food supply. A badly damaged mill on the Ancre was found to be quite useful. A large supply of wheat was found there and was ground into flour. RIR 99 brought up French railway coaches and filled them with the flour and delivered it to the field bakery. The mill was later turned into a bathhouse and a canteen until it was eventually destroyed.

The men had taken to keeping chickens, piglets and rabbits in small pens inside the trenches. This was soon stopped as it became difficult to maintain the sanitary conditions of the trenches.

Supply wagons brought construction materials for the trenches and dug-outs as well as mail and newspapers. The French could easily identify the routes the wagons used to approach the front during daylight hours by the tracks left behind. This allowed their

Vizewachtmeister der Reserve/Offizier Stellvertreter Hans Weerth (Stuttgart-Cannstatt) 1/RFAR 26, killed near Beaumont. (*Kriegstagbuch aus Schwaben*)

Leutnant der Landwehr (*Vizefeldwebel/Offizier Stellvertreter*) Eugen Heinrich (Stuttgart-Cannstatt), 1R/Pioneer Bn 13, died 14 October 1914 from wounds received at Fricourt. (*Kriegstagbuch aus Schwaben*)

Oberleutnant der Reserve Christian Flogaus (Rosswälden) 4/180. Killed in action 28 October 1914 near Mouquet farm.(*Kriegstagbuch aus Schwaben*)

artillery to fire randomly along the route at night in an attempt to disrupt the delivery of the supplies and to cause casualties.

At the end of September *Hauptmann* Kachel, commander of Reserve *Jäger* Bn 8 brought up four field kitchens to the southeastern part of the village of Fricourt:

> Only our battalion had dared this. However we have our commander to thank for it because now good food was guaranteed in this difficult situation.[19]

However the field kitchens were forced to withdraw to Bazentin le Petit as a result of heavy French fire, a distance of about 10 kilometers. This meant that the luxury of hot food during daylight hours had to be abandoned and all food was brought up during the night as with the other units in the Corps.

The field mail started regular delivery of packages from home. They included many items needed by the men such as underwear, stockings, handkerchiefs, suspenders, cigarettes, tobacco, pipes, cookies, cheese and chocolate.

One problem facing the men was a lack of water for drinking and bathing. Many units had access to local facilities and wells that allowed a regular supply of water. However there were some that did not have access to water at all. RIR 121 located at the *Granatloch* was still an isolated position. The regiment still did not have any safe access to Thiepval. Food and water were carried up each night over open ground. Only a limited supply could be carried on each trip. This meant the men were forbidden to use water for any purpose other than drinking or cooking. All bathing was prohibited and it would be weeks or months in most cases before they were able to have a proper bath or clean their clothing.

RIR 120 was in such an exposed position that the men were forbidden to take off their uniforms or equipment or even put on a change of underwear. Cartridge boxes and boots remained on at all times and the men slept with their rifles close at hand, 1 cartridge in the chamber, 5 cartridges in the magazine. The normal routine for October was 2 hours on guard, 2 hours digging and 2 hours of rest. This routine lasted 24 hours a day for over 3 weeks, all in the event of a French attack. Washing was considered a crime and all water was to be strictly used for coffee and drinking.

The Corps artillery fell into a daily routine during the month. The Light Ammunition Columns were positioned where they could reach the batteries quickly. The battery horses were kept in the rear and provided with comfortable stables. The problem of supplying sufficient hay and straw for the horses and men was solved when threshers arrived and began to harvest the fields behind the lines. As the weather grew colder the horse's hair grew longer and many of the gunners remarked that they appeared to look like orangutans. The regimental commander of RFAR 26 remarked that 'one could stuff mattresses with their hair.'[20]

Artillery fire was severely restricted due to the ongoing ammunition shortage. The guns were only authorized to fire against French attacks and particularly worthwhile targets. The French apparently did not have the same restrictions and fired at the German lines on a daily basis causing extensive damage.

The village of Fricourt and the ruins of Fricourt Château were favorite targets of French gunners in October. On 12 October heavy French fire fell on the village and the few remaining houses were turned into rubble and ash. Two ammunition wagons and teams were lost; fortunately the men were able to escape injury.

The troops were suffering losses every day in their poorly developed positions from the constant shellfire. RIR 109 reported losses of 1 officer, 34 Other Ranks killed; 157 Other Ranks wounded in the first six days of October. Reserve *Jäger* Bn 8 reported losses of 3 officers, 1 *Unterarzt*, 87 *Oberjäger* and *Jäger* killed; 1 officer, 156 *Oberjäger* and *Jäger* wounded and 8 *Oberjäger* and *Jäger* missing between 28 September and 31 October, mainly from artillery fire. Other regiments reported similar losses. A member of the *Jägers* described the artillery fire:

In general the French daily menu for us…was approximately the following: Early at 12 o'clock some infantry fire soup with shrapnel inserted. A long pause for digestion. 2-3 o'clock in the afternoon shrapnel with shell broth. On many days instead of that it was heavy digestible scrap that however was served one or more hours later. From 5 to 7 o'clock light artillery dinner. Shortly after the onset of darkness and toward 11 o'clock at night watery infantry soup with meager shell crumbs. Therefore there was not much to worry about fluctuation but however we gradually became tired of the rich food.[21]

One complaint voiced by many men in the Corps was the lack of artillery support. The close cooperation between the infantry and artillery found later in the war had not been established. The shortage of shells was becoming critical. The number of rounds fired since the beginning of the war had far exceeded all pre-war estimates. It would be some time before sufficient replacements could be obtained. Until that happened the artillery would make do as best it could.[22]

Positioning artillery observers with the infantry slowly became an accepted practice. Over time observers established close working relations with the infantry units and both sides became familiar with the needs of the other. The observers would go out each morning before dawn to the observation post where they had the best view of the French lines. They remained in their holes until after darkness had fallen before they could return to the rear. No light was allowed, no fire could be lit that would betray their position. They sat in their cramped holes in the wet and cold without the chance of any relief. Nothing should betray their location to the French, especially any identifiable path leading to their post.

The benefits of having observers connected to the artillery batteries were evident from the start. Telephone lines gradually connected every part of the line with headquarters and the batteries. It was time consuming and difficult work and no one was eager to do

The church bell from Ovillers in the garden at the Miraumont Château.
(*Die 26. Reserve Division 1914-1918*)

The Leaning Virgin, Albert Cathedral. Postcard sent by a Machine
Gun *Schützen*, RIR 119. (Author's collection)

it. However, now the French could be taken under accurate fire almost immediately after
the observer made the decision that the target was worthwhile.

A French attack on 25 October against RIR 109 was successfully repelled with
the assistance of a field gun from RFAR 29 positioned nearby under the command of
Vizewachtmeister Maurer. On the evening of the same day a French attack against the
III/R110 was repelled by fire called in by the local artillery observer. On 29 October the
1st and 7/RFAR 26 located in the copse of Serre successfully stopped a French attack
north of Beaumont.

Each side tried to locate the artillery observers and eliminate them whenever possible.
The obvious locations that might be used by observers were the numerous church steeples
located along the front. On 26 October the French shelled the church tower of Ovillers
that was suspected of concealing an observation post. The tower was destroyed and
afterward the church bell was brought to Miraumont where it was placed in the park of
the 26th Reserve Division headquarters.

The XIV Reserve Corps also looked to destroy possible French observation posts
and fired at the high chimney at La Signy Farm as well as the steeple of the cathedral of
Albert using the 8/Reserve Foot Artillery Regiment 10 and one 21cm mortar battery. The
previous restrictions placed on firing at the cathedral were lifted in order to eliminate
the suspected observation post. The 8th Battery succeeded in part and nearly caused

the statue of the Madonna and Child to lean forward, suspended over the edge of the cathedral where it remained for almost 4 years.

Chapter Notes

1. Soden, *Die 26. (Württembergische) Reserve-Division im Weltkrieg 1914-1918,* p. 55.
2. W. Jecklin, *Das Reserve-Jäger-Bataillon Nr. 8 im Weltkrieg 1914-1918,* p. 49.
3. Jecklin, op. cit., p. 50.
4. Soden, op. cit., p. 61.
5. M. Klaus, *Das Württembergisches Reserve-Feldartillerie-Regiment Nr. 26 im Weltkrieg 1914-1918,* p. 21.
6. Soden, op. cit., p. 59.
7. 'Wolf Pits' were small holes with a sharp stake located in the center placed inside wire entanglements.
8. During the post-war cleanup of Northern France a detachment of German prisoners were assigned to Bécourt Wood and came across the buried flag. They burned the flagpole and a man named Weber took the flag and wrapped it around his body under his uniform. In August 1920 Weber returned to Germany and turned the flag over to the former War Ministry in Berlin where it was transferred to the Army Museum in Baden.
9. Jecklin, op. cit. p. 52.
10. Soden, op. cit., p.
11. Ibid.
12. H. Ludwig, Manuscript, 6th Company RIR 120, p. 7.
13. The *'Leiling Schlucht'* was known to the British troops as the 'Y' ravine after its unique shape.
14. Ludwig: op. cit. p. 6.
15. Ludwig, op. cit. pp. 6-7.
16. P. Müller, *Geschichte des Reserve-Infanterie-Regiment Nr. 99,* pp. 38-39.
17. Ludwig, op. cit, p. 8.
18. R. Baumgartner (Ed.), 'An der Somme, An interview with Soldat Emil Goebelbecker', *Der Angriff, A Journal of World War 1 History,* No. 3, p. 5.
19. W. Jecklin, *Das Reserve-Jäger-Bataillon Nr. 8 im Weltkrieg 1914-1918,* p. 51.
20. M. Klaus, *Das Württembergisches Reserve-Feldartillerie-Regiment Nr. 26 im Weltkrieg 1914-1918,* p. 23.
21. Jecklin, op. cit., p. 50.
22. At the outbreak of war each field gun was supplied with 987 rounds. Each Light Field Howitzer was supplied with 973 rounds of ammunition.

3

November 1914

At the start of November the heaviest fighting on the Western Front was taking place north of the Somme by the River Yser and near Ypres in Belgium. By the middle of the month the worst of the fighting was over and the Western Front began to solidify.

Further south the men of the XIV Reserve Corps had been directed to create an impregnable position; the Corps was determined not to lose a single foot of ground that it had captured. To accomplish this gigantic task every available man would be needed to work on the defenses.

The biggest problem to overcome was the lack of troops. One manpower issue was directly related to the defensive works already occupied by the regiments. The current trench system was very rudimentary. It lacked sufficient communication trenches leading to the rear. It consisted of only one defensive line in many areas and did not have any supporting trenches nearby and wire entanglements were inadequate for the task of protecting the trenches. The present setup required nearly every available soldier in the Corps to man the defensive works in case of an attack.

The lack of replacements for men lost in the previous three months was compounding the problem. While some replacements had arrived in October the majority of the regiments were still well below normal strength. The mechanism that ensured a steady

Sigel

Leutnant d. R. im Inf.-Regt. 180, gefallen bei Thiepval am 6. November 1914

Keiper

Leutnant im Res.-Inf.-Regt. 119, gest. am 26. Nov. 1914 an den bei Ovillers la Boisselle erh. Wunden

Leutnant der Reserve or *Vizefeldwebel/ Offizier Stellvertreter* Karl Sigel (Oppelsbohn) 1 MG Coy/180. Died from illness 10 November 1914, Thiepval. (*Kriegstagbuch aus Schwaben*)

Leutnant Gustav Keiper (Landau i.d. Pfalz) 8/R119. Wounded in action 24 November 1914 at Ovillers-La Boisselle, died 26 November 1914 at Reserve Field Hospital 1, Bapaume. (*Kriegstagbuch aus Schwaben*)

flow of replacements was not yet in place. The speed of the early fighting and the heavy losses suffered both in the West and in the East had strained the German supply system to the limit.

In October several regiments had received an influx of men that helped to maintain the regiments close to full strength. RIR 99 received the largest number, 1,800 men. When additional replacements arrived in November RIR 99 was able to fully reform all four battalions once more.[1] RIR 99 was also one of the first regiments in the corps to establish a second machine gun company. On 21 October Fortress Machine Gun Detachment 8 from Mainz joined the regiment and was assigned to the II Battalion. This increase in firepower was a welcome addition.

RIR 110 received 250 replacements that allowed the regiment to maintain company strength at approximately 200 men each. The regiment now consisted of 19 Officers, 22 officer replacements and 2,135 men. RIR 109 received replacements in late October when Battalion Karlsruhe arrived with 5 officers, 4 *Offizier Stellvertreter* and 122 men; more were to arrive on 1 November. Most of the men in Battalion Karlsruhe were familiar faces as the men were returning to the regiment after convalescing from illnesses and wounds. Reserve *Jäger* Bn 8 received much needed support when a machine gun company of four guns was assigned to the battalion.

Any benefit from the increase of troops in the Corps was almost immediately lost when RIR 109 was sent south on 6 November to act as the reserve for the VIII Corps that was involved in heavy fighting near Gruny. The regiment was used to dig trenches as well as hopefully deceiving the enemy about the number of reserves present in the Corps area. The regiment was broken up into separate battalions and each would march in the rear accompanied by squadrons of *Ulans*. At times they would march to a railway station

Replacements – RIR 120. (Author's collection)

Replacements – Infantryman, *Ersatz* Battalion RIR 119. (Author's collection)

where they would board trains and become shifted around the front. The regiment finally returned to the XIV Reserve Corps at the end of the month.

Despite these problems the front of the XIV Reserve Corps was worked on feverishly day and night in order to have the position ready for the coming winter. As the trenches were extended and improved it was discovered that fewer troops were needed to man them on a daily basis. This freed up more men for work on the defenses and allowed some regiments to start a regular schedule of relief. Some men were now kept in the front line for four weeks, followed by two weeks at rest in the rear.

Building supplies, tools and shovels collected from the Line of Communication troops as well as from Germany began to arrive that allowed faster work on improving the trenches. The first crude trenches were now being transformed into a well-developed trench system. An oven in Miraumont made floor tiles that were produced from the abundant supply of chalk. Traverses were constructed, new communication trenches were established and improvements were made in the housing found within the trenches.

Among the biggest complaints made by the men in the trenches were the lack of wood for trench construction and cooking fires and the lack of drinking water. Once a new sawmill located in Bapaume was operating at full capacity the supply of wood improved. The water problem would take longer to resolve.

New weapons began to make an appearance in the trenches and many required the construction of special facilities. Frames were constructed to fire rifle grenades; *minenwerfer* positions were excavated and concealed as well as positions for oxyacetylene searchlights. Armored loopholes and telescopic sights were provided for snipers. Tests were held on new methods of producing smoke used for cover and concealment. During one test on 18 November a sack of powder ignited and flared up burning several pioneers on their faces, some severely. Other tests were performed on the use of contact mines and flame-throwers.

The improvement and expansion of the trenches went beyond the first line. Preparations for a second and third line were started. Strongpoints were created in the rear, Hill 143

Pioneer depot 200 yards from the front line, La Boisselle. (Author's collection)

north of Beaumont, Beaucourt Manor, Hill 151 north of Thiepval, the *Wundtwerk* south of Thiepval[2], and Mouquet Farm. Many of the front line villages were prepared for defense. An alarm service was created in case of emergencies. Rear area billets were inspected and improvements were made wherever possible.

There was a concern that the spirit of the offensive would be lost with all of the entrenching and construction. It was determined that in order to maintain the spirit of the offensive among the men regular patrols had to be sent out each night all along the front.

Patrols would provide valuable intelligence regarding French positions and helped to determine the identity of the opposing French units through prisoners and identification marks and documents found on dead enemy soldiers. One patrol discovered the location of a French battery behind the copse near Bécourt-Becordel. Another patrol from RIR 110 crawled to within 20 meters of the French trenches on the night of 1 November. They located two dead French soldiers and cut off their regimental markings. Before they left the area the members of the patrol threw several hand-grenades into the enemy trench. The same men went out in the night of 2 November and discovered another body about 80 meters in front of the French trench. The regimental markings were also taken from this body and as a result of these patrols the presence of the *26e, 81e* and *160e Régiments d'Infanterie* was established.

The patrols went out into no-man's-land as quietly as possible, usually at the onset of darkness. At times the French sentries either heard a noise or suspected German patrols were out and opened fire blindly into the foreground. This un-aimed fire caused few losses and eventually died down. While the men at the front grew accustomed to this it still startled the staff located in the rear into thinking that the French were attacking. Over time they also grew accustomed to the sound of firing and took little notice of it. Few French patrols were encountered and it was generally felt that they were not as aggressive as the German patrols. Many nights the French apparently did not send any out at all.

Patrol Schiedel, 3/R119. (*Die 26. Reserve Division 1914-1918*)

However on at least one occasion it was an alert sentry who may have prevented a large French patrol from entering the German lines.

Once I was on duty in a wet hole directly in front of the ruins of a lonely house between the lines, known as the blacksmith's shop. A strong French patrol was feeling around in the outfield in front of me. I warned the regiment with a few shots which were not aimed at the moon either. The whole crowd behind me was out in a jiffy and started shooting with everything they had. This was not very much but it was too much for me, as most of the bullets came traveling a hand's breadth from the ground in my direction. I wished that I had not been too lazy to make a hole a few inches deeper while I had the time to do it. The only thing I could do was to get down as low as I could and it was certainly a form-fitting affair. Nothing could be seen of the Frenchmen, and when I heard footsteps behind me I was out of the hole quicker than I got into it, with my hand on the trigger. But they were some men from my company with a corporal to find out why I had interrupted their slumber. I told them, and they said I was crazy and had seen fairies floating in the moonlight. But they proceeded anyhow to search the outfield, very carefully hugging the ground in spite of their belief that no one had been there. We found two dead Frenchmen only 200 feet from my hole and took the bodies back. I again occupied my hole but after this I was no longer sleepy. I expected the French to come back any minute to look for their dead. After a while I was satisfied they would not come, and then began to deepen and widen the hole. The next man continued the work and after this we had a nice comfortable hole in the mud with an old horse blanket at the bottom of it. Hans Ludwig, 6/R120 [3]

A larger French patrol attempted to attack the German lines near Beaumont on a foggy morning where RIR 99 was positioned. An alert sentry spotted the French troops and notified his company commander. The 10/R99 moved out of the trenches along the enemy flank and waited for the French to get within 30 meters of the German trench at the edge of the wire entanglements. They opened a devastating fire into the flank of the unsuspecting French. The survivors quickly withdrew to the French lines.

Not long afterward the French made a second attempt to attack the German lines at Beaumont. A sentry spotted this attack as well and alerted the garrison. The attack was stopped cold in the heavy defensive fire and as the French survivors withdrew the 10/R99 followed them approximately 500 meters until they ran into the German artillery fire. The 10/R99 lost 3 men killed, 11 wounded, while the French losses were more substantial, approximately 50-60 dead and 21 prisoners who belonged to the 2nd Coy, *65e Régiment*

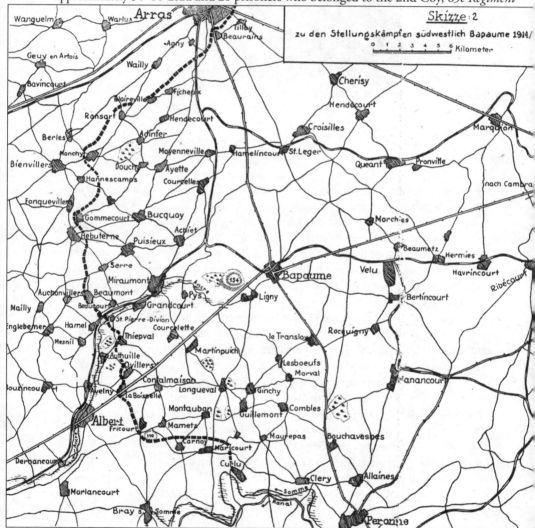

General map of the Somme front.

d'Infanterie. Documents found on the body of a captain indicated that the French had planned on capturing Beaumont with a total of 330 men. The first man to step foot in the village would receive the *Légion d'honneur*. When the French dead were brought in it was dicovered that they were wearing steel body protection and breast armour while every second man carried a steel shield that was supposed to protect them while they dug entrenchments.

One of the first German raids on the Somme took place in the afternoon of 7 November when groups from the 1st and 15/R99 accompanied by pioneers attacked a French trench sap. The attackers managed to reach the French line but could not advance any further due to flanking fire. The raiders had to withdraw before they were able to place contact mines inside the sap, however they claimed to have caused heavy enemy losses and they returned with approximately 20 armored shields. The patrol lost 2 men killed.

During the latter half of November heavy fighting was taking place on the Eastern Front at Łódź. In order to prevent the Germans from shifting any troops to the east the Allies attempted to hold the German forces in the West with small undertakings and attacks.

On 11 November a French officer attempted to cut through the wire entanglements in front of RIR 111. A sentry spotted him and alerted the garrison and the crew of a nearby machine gun post. The machine gun opened fire and the officer was killed. His body was recovered and based on the uniform markings it was established that he belonged to the *236e Régiment d'Infanterie*. Another German patrol on Hill 110 near Fricourt also found a tin of explosives near the wire, which indicated that the French were trying new methods to get through the German wire.

The French became especially active in front of the II/180, in particular in front of the 6th Coy. A French infantry company approached the German lines under cover of

Machine Gun section RIR 119. (Author's collection)

Infantryman – IR 180. (Author's collection)

darkness with support from heavy artillery fire. The attack was repelled with well-aimed rifle fire and the support of machine gun No. 4. On the following morning the French could still be seen in a position 50 meters in front of the German line, inside of a small copse. A patrol was sent out from the 6th Coy under *Unteroffizier* Lorch. Patrol Lorch approached the French position and using newly-issued hand grenades was able to capture 22 prisoners consisting of 1 sergeant major, 2 sergeants, 3 corporals and 14 men from the *337e Régiment d'Infanterie* and 2 men from the *19e Régiment d'Infanterie.* In addition the patrol brought back rifles, ammunition, numerous entrenching tools and wire cutters.

Because so many dead Frenchmen lay in front of the 6th Coy *Leutnant* Fussbahn went over to the enemy lines under a flag of truce at 3 p.m. on 14 November and asked the French to bury their dead, his request was refused.

The men of the XIV Reserve Corps also faced another enemy in November, the weather. The rainy weather started at the beginning of November and the clay ground grew thicker and heavier each day. Any movement became extremely difficult in the mud, where each step threatened to pull off the men's boots and sometimes did. Everything became covered in a brownish yellow crust of mud; faces, hands, uniforms, rifles and food. So many of the rifles had become dirty and clogged with mud that the men found that they could no longer be loaded. It became so bad at times that new construction had to be postponed and all efforts were directed in draining the position so it would not turn into a bog. Fortunately the men's humor was not completely gone. One chalkboard in the front line of RIR 111 was inscribed with 'Only for good swimmers'.[4]

When the weather allowed work to continue on the position it proved almost more than the men could bear. When one trench section was finally completed it was followed by the collapse of another trench wall or dug-out time after time. The problems associated with weather continued throughout the month and did not improve until the first frost occurred and the ground began to solidify. This was short-lived however and when the ground thawed trench walls and dug-outs collapsed all across the front of the Corps. There could be fatal consequences to the bad weather as well. In the sector of the III/R111 a trench collapse cost the lives of 1 *Unteroffizier* and 3 men.

Many men wore long faces because of the horrible conditions they had to endure. There was some improvement in their mood when the prospect of relief approached or when they received a warm cup of tea or occasionally Schnapps.

The wet weather also brought about an increase in illnesses among the troops including the threat of typhoid. Fortunately an effective vaccine was available and the first inoculations had been planned to begin on 30 October. Because of the infectious nature of this disease the relief so many expected had to be postponed until all of the men received their vaccinations. The medication resulted in swelling of the chest where the vaccine was applied as well as a slight fever and general feeling of discomfort. Considering the desire for relief from the trenches it was a small price to pay to be under a warm roof, being able to wash for the first time in weeks and receive good, hot food.

Medical inspection rooms for mild cases of illness were established behind each regiment. RIR 109 set up its medical inspection room in the Lamarck house, the home of the 18th Century French naturalist located in Bazentin-le-Petit.[5] Directions were also issued that provided for greater maintenance and care of the latrines that would decrease the possibility of typhoid in the future. The vaccinations continued until all of the men had received their shots.

Some of the health issues involved the local civilian population. Every attempt was made to enlist the aid of the populace to maintain the cleanliness of the lavatories in the villages, which many claimed ridiculed any description. Many of the Germans considered

RIR 121 in the trenches. (Author's collection)

Field Church service - XIV Reserve Corps. (*Die 26. Reserve Division 1914-1918*)

the local people to be good natured but extraordinarily unclean and the local men were given the job of cleaning and sanitizing all facilities under the watchful eyes of regimental adjutants and supply officers.

The regimental physicians held regular office hours in each command and set aside time to treat local civilians including providing obstetric services as if they were back

The Lamarck House, Bazentin-le-Petit. (*Der Schützengraben*)

Uniform and equipment repairs - RIR 119. (Author's collection)

in Germany. The ability to provide medical services expanded when a second medical column arrived in Miraumont from Württemberg. The men in this column had been led to believe that they were intended for the 'Line of Communications,' safely in the rear and not close to the actual front. It only took them a short time to get accustomed to French fire.

Once the men were relieved they moved into quarters in the rear areas where they found life was taking on more of a normal routine. The first field religious services were started inside the village churches throughout the sector held by the Corps. Minister Lempp and Father Wahr acted as clergy for the 26th Reserve Division.

The well at Villers aux Flos was equipped with an electric pump as an aid to the military hospital established there. A cyclist company delousing station was established. A bathhouse was placed in the sugar factory at Longueval where the large tanks and heating equipment could be put to use for the benefit of the men. Regular hot meals from the field kitchens and warm, dry quarters made life quite comfortable. The ability to keep dry was well received by the men. The wet weather had played havoc with the men's uniforms, especially their boots and shoes. The company shoemakers and tailors were kept quite busy during this period.

By far the most desired item was mail from home and as each week passed more and more flowed to the front. Large numbers of gifts also began to arrive in the Corps. The biggest demand was for woolen items and smoking materials.

Some attempts were made to salvage and protect civilian property whenever possible but for the most part the local population was required to give up any item considered a necessity by the XIV Reserve Corps. One valuable collection of historic importance was saved. It consisted of a large collection of primitive flint tools together with the research notes of a local teacher in Beaucourt. The items were packed and sent to the rear for safe storage as was the family photographs and souvenirs from the mill owner in Hamel.

The division commanders and other high-ranking officers were regular visitors to the front lines where they gave encouragement to the men and offered advice on improvements

Oberst Friedrich Grall RIR 99. (*Geschichte des Reserve-Infanterie-Regiment Nr. 99*)

to the trenches and dug-outs. *Freiherr* von Soden was often seen accompanying *Oberst* Grall, RIR 99, on tours along the front. *Oberst* Grall was easy to identify with his grey white beard wearing a white winter fur coat, Alpine *Jäger* stick and his pockets filled with gifts for the men.[6]

One visit to the front was made by a member of the staff of the 28th Reserve Division. He toured the front line occupied by RIR 40 at Montauban, the left wing regiment of the Corps. After his visit he was encouraged by what he saw but he also felt that a number of improvements were needed and that his recommendations should be acted upon with some haste. However, the meticulous staff officer also noted in his report that the left wing Company, the 9/R40, had barely 80 men fit for duty.

Despite this last observation he continued to stress the need for improved wire entanglements as in some areas it consisted of a single trip wire. The trenches still had to be deepened and he suggested that the earth removed by deepening the trenches could be used to fill sandbags and then used to construct loopholes in the parapets. Many old earthen holes in the sides of the trench were left over from the prior occupants, Bavarian troops, and were still in use while many of the entrances to dug-outs had their opening facing the enemy. The company leaders and their men were not in a position to correct many of these deficiencies due to more pressing concerns defending large sections of trenches with the overall shortage of men.

A number of high-ranking visitors also arrived in the Corps sector including military representatives from various neutral countries. *General der Pioneer* Fremel visited the XIV Reserve Corps following a request from Army Headquarters. After touring the positions he recommended a number of improvements in the construction of the second line and dug-outs.

On 3 November a *Hubertus Schnitzeljagd*[7] took place under the leadership of the commander of the Reserve Dragoon Regiment between Le Sars and Pys. The riders assembled at a farm 300 meters southwest of Le Sars, the finish was located at the churchyard of Pys, a distance of 3,200 meters. Duke Adolf Friedrich von Mecklenburg was present as well as the noted Swedish explorer and scholar Sven Hedin who rode in the car of the commanding general of the Guard Corps along with *Hauptmann* Schlüter as spectators. A total of 55 mounted officers had gathered at Le Sars for the 3 p.m. start of the hunt including General von Soden and *Generalleutnant* von Pavel. The horsemen rode the course through fields and obstacles and over hills. Most of the horses were not used to this type of activity as they were recently requisitioned from farms in France and Germany.

When the *Schnitzeljagd* ended the participants and their guests assembled for a cold collation including sandwiches and hot punch. The festivities were briefly disrupted when a French airplane flew overhead and forced the party to take cover under nearby trees until it flew off.

The local French population was still living within many of the villages along the front in November. Many of them would not be separated from their homes or possessions, in spite of the ever-increasing danger. Their presence became an issue of personal safety as well as the possibility of espionage.

There had been several incidents in Pozières in October where suspected spies were found. The first man turned out to be a German agent who was eventually released to go about his duty of collecting intelligence information. The second came close to being shot.

Leutnant Julius Marx, RIR 120, was billeted in a house on the outskirts of Pozières. One day a small Frenchman came down from the hayloft in the adjoining barn. He was wearing tattered clothing and was so gaunt he looked like a ghost according to Marx. The man was frightened at being caught and when questioned denied that he was a soldier. After a quick search Marx discovered his military identity disc and the poor man confessed that he was indeed a French soldier. He had apparently been hiding in the hayloft since the French had been driven out of the village. He had put on civilian clothing and remained in hiding when the Germans took over the area. He claimed to be 38 years old, married with 5 children.

Marx watched as another officer in the regiment told the man in barely comprehensible French that he was to be shot immediately. The reaction was inevitable. The poor man broke down and fell to his knees while crying about his poor wife and children and desperately pleading with *Leutnant* Marx to save him.

When Marx tried to reassure the man that he would do what he could the other members of the regiment standing nearby began to berate Marx and laugh at his attempts at sympathy. Marx was not going to take this lying down and he ran through the heavy fire coming down on the village at the time and provided a full account of the situation to the Town Major.

The Town Major interviewed the prisoner who could barely walk as a result of fear and physical weakness. He was soon also convinced that the man was harmless and ordered him to be placed under guard where he would receive food before being taken to the rear. The Frenchman was overjoyed at his good fortune as he was led away.

Infantry group, RIR 120. (Author's collection)

Everything appeared to be in order and Marx went back to his duties. However an hour later he received a call from a *Hauptmann* on brigade staff who had heard of the matter and who proposed that the man be court-martialed and shot immediately. It seems that a dead pigeon had been found in the hayloft and it was assumed that the prisoner had been sending messages to the enemy by carrier pigeon.

Marx searched the loft for any evidence of espionage or proof that the man was innocent as he proclaimed. He found nothing more than a torn letter, leftover pieces of fruit and the bones of an uncooked pigeon. Marx turned over his findings to the *Hauptmann* who confronted the prisoner. The poor Frenchman claimed he had stayed alive by eating the fruit he stole from the nearby garden at night as well as the pigeon he caught.

He apparently became separated from his regiment during the fighting in Pozières and hid himself in order to stay alive for his 5 children. He was afraid to turn himself in to the Germans out of fear.

Marx was able to convince the officer in charge of the case that the man deserved a full hearing at a court-martial and he was taken away once more. Marx felt that he would rather die than allow a man whose innocence he was convinced of to be shot out of hand.

Krämer
Leutn. d. R. im Feldminenwerferzug
XIV. Reservekorps (cand. arch.), gef.
am 11. Dezember 1914 bei Thiepval

Zeller
Leutnant d. R. im Pionier-Bat. 13
(stud. electr.), gefallen am 17. November 1914 bei Beaumont

Leutnant der Reserve Albert Krämer (Hoheneck, Ludwigsburg), Field *Minenwerfer* Platoon XIV Reserve Corps. Killed in action 11 December 1914 near Thiepval. (*Kriegstagbuch aus Schwaben*)

Leutnant der Reserve Eugen Zeller (Backnang) Pioneer Bn 13, Attached to XIV Reserve Corps Field *Minenwerfer* Platoon. Died from severe wounds or killed in action 17 November 1914 near Beaumont. (*Kriegstagbuch aus Schwaben*)

In another instance the men of RIR 40 had been reminded to maintain the strictest discipline and to treat the occupants of Montauban with consideration. This was because the allegedly innocent owner of a small house had been shot by the Germans shortly before.[8]

The 1/R40 was scheduled to go into the trenches on the evening of 4 November. While the men were waiting they noticed unusually heavy civilian traffic to one particular home. The people appeared to be furtive and were often seen carrying small bundles or baskets. The soldiers felt that the home might conceal a secret shop of some sort.

One and a half hours before leaving for the trenches a man from the listening post with glowing red cheeks approached a company officer and whispered into his ear in slurred speech, 'we have discovered a good cellar, your water bottle will soon be filled with champagne'. The officer found out that his men had discovered a hidden wine cellar in the suspicious home. The entire 1st Platoon was stretched out from the cellar up to the straw beds, along the stairway and floors in a queue. Full bottles of wine and liquor were being passed from hand to hand silently through an opening in a wall and being placed into knapsacks or being poured into water bottles or thirsty throats.

While the wine, champagne and cognac bottles were being handed up a uniform suddenly came to light from the cellar. The officer immediately recognized it as French Fire Brigade uniform.

The occupants of the house were not sitting idly by while their property was being pilfered. They ran around the house cursing and swearing at first and finally brought the Mayor of Montauban to confront the thieves. The Mayor threatened to hold the officer responsible for the theft of the wine using all of the authority of his dignified office. The officer would have nothing to do with the threats made by the Mayor. Speaking in crude

RIR 40 in the trenches near Mametz. (Author's collection)

French the officer showed the Mayor the uniform stating they had discovered a French military uniform and pieces of equipment concealed in the cellar and if the entire matter was not immediately cleared up the Mayor and the owner of the house would be placed under arrest. The bluff worked and the civilians dropped their protests concerning the theft.

Now it was time for the relief and the men gathered their equipment and assembled on the road. Apparently the news concerning the wine cellar had spread quickly through the ranks of the 1st Coy. The line was very crooked and wavy; helmets were slanted and even backward on some men. Their equipment was unbuckled and often just hanging. Water bottles were uncorked and cognac, wine and champagne seemed to flow from them. Everyone appeared to have a huge grin on his face.

Once some semblance of order had been restored the company moved off to the front. The march to the front was described as being more like a walk home after midnight from a party rather than anything remotely military. Once in the trenches the effect of the alcohol began to be felt even more. The men fought to stay awake and alert while on guard duty. Many of the sentries had heavy eyelids and the officers were constantly running back and forth in their sectors acting as a second set of eyes and arousing sleeping sentries from their stupor. The sentries that were able to stay awake were constantly seeing 'ghosts' in front of the unfamiliar trenches.

However the night passed without incident and some men began to recover from their indulgences of the previous evening. Others were still celebrating and while the French bombarded the line with artillery fire the sound of the exploding shells was intermingled with the sound of corks being pulled from fresh bottles.

Some welcome relief for the Corps artillery arrived in November in the form of antiquated artillery pieces. The 26th and 28th Reserve Divisions each received four Model 73 9cm. (88mm) field guns that had been taken from storage. The guns had no shields, no recoil system that resulted in the guns jumping like Billy goats when fired, and medieval

Model 73 9cm (88mm) field gun – RFAR 26. (*Das Württembergisches Reserve-Feldartillerie Regiment Nr. 26 im Weltkrieg 1914-1918*)

sights. However the tubes were extremely accurate and the most important point was they had an ample supply of ammunition. Once the guns were in position they formed the bulk of routine German artillery fire for some months to come.

The obsolete guns were also used for anti-aircraft purposes. *Hauptmann* Frohlich, RFAR 29, would use his M73 guns to fire at French aircraft, without much success. In revenge the French artillery would sporadically cover the suspected German gun positions with heavy fire so that sport shooting against aircraft soon died down.

The French still did not seem to be affected by any shortage of artillery ammunition. The German lines were bombarded on a daily basis and at the end of each day the enemy fired the 'evening benediction' from railway guns. These guns generally fired at the division headquarters located in Miraumont. The XIV Reserve Corps responded to this fire whenever possible by using the heavy guns from the 8/Reserve Foot Artillery Regiment 10, which were located in the churchyard hollow south of Grandcourt. The guns would shell various French villages as well as any other worthwhile target such as the tall chimney of the sugar factory south of Colincamps. The mortars brought it down as it was suspected of being used as an observation post.

Even with a shortage of ammunition the critical issue was still the need to provide close support for the infantry. The answer came in the form of mine throwers, more commonly known as *minenwerfer*. There were a number of existing models of *minenwerfer* available at the outbreak of the war. These were quickly supplemented by a number of new models of various caliber and construction, many of which were still very primitive. Training locations were set up behind the front where the men could be introduced to the new weapons and learn to operate them.

The first use of the heavy *minenwerfer*, (25cm), took place with RIR 110 in early November. A heavy *minenwerfer* was installed into a position in the regiment in the evening of 2/3 November under the guidance of *Pionier Hauptmann* Rettig. It was to be used to destroy a group of houses located at the southern exit of Fricourt.

Light *Minenwerfer* emplacement, *Minenwerfer* Coy 226.
(Author's collection)

The bombardment began at 7.30 a.m. on 4 November. The guns of RFAR 29 supported the *minenwerfer* by firing on the French artillery positions. After the seventh shot the buildings were on fire and almost completely destroyed. A loophole was discovered in the wall of one barn from the light of the fire behind it. The *minenwerfer* was then turned against the Fricourt railway station, a source of annoying French fire and patrols. The station was destroyed after the eleventh shot.

At first the French were silent, then, after the houses were destroyed the French opened fire on Fricourt and the surrounding trenches. The bombardment lasted the rest of the day and night.

On 5 November a reconnaissance patrol was sent out from RIR 110 to explore the ruined houses. They were able to confirm that the ruins were free from the enemy but they were unable to actually enter them due to heavy fire coming from the French

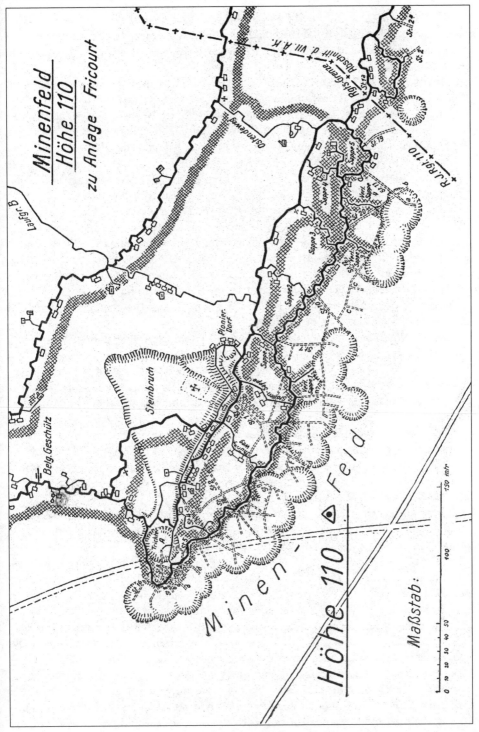

Start of mining – Hill 110.

trenches. On the same afternoon 3 more shots were fired from the heavy *minenwerfer* to completely destroy a portion of the houses that were still intact. Afterward the gun was withdrawn to Courcelette. The French response was haphazard with wild fire from the infantry and artillery.

The men of RIR 110 noted that the moral effect of the 200-pound *minenwerfer* shell was not insignificant. The effect against living targets as opposed to inanimate targets was not as great because the shell could be seen in flight and the impact area could be guessed and avoided at times. However the effect against inanimate targets was devastating. Anything within 10 meters from the point of impact was considered a direct hit. One major drawback in using the *minenwerfer* was that the French could usually determine the gun location quickly and it needed to be moved after it was finished firing. In addition the infantry did not appreciate the vengeance fire that usually followed.

Something new occurred at the end of November. It was to have a major impact upon the lives of the men in the XIV Reserve Corps; mine warfare. The start of mine warfare on the Somme took place near Beaumont and La Boisselle. RIR 99 along with the 4/Pioneer Bn 13 began to drive several mines towards the French lines in an area that would become known as the 'Mine Field'. It was an area deemed suitable for this type of warfare, something the French would also not ignore. Other mines were started near La Boisselle also with the assistance of Pioneer Bn 13. Neither of these undertakings would be completed at any time before December.

In late November the men positioned on Hill 110 heard strange noises coming from the earth. The pioneers were brought up and they determined it was the sound of the French mining under the German lines. In response the XIV Reserve Corps also began to send mines out from Hill 110. A new nerve-wracking time was starting for the men in the affected areas. They would never be sure when a mine might suddenly go off below their feet.

The need to manage the food supply for the divisions took on even greater importance in November. With the prospect of long-term occupation of the region a better method was needed to supply sufficient quantities of food and find the best method of distribution to the men. By the middle of the month the order had been issued that the troops had to nourish themselves from the resources of the land.

Detachments from the different regiments were established whose sole purpose was to scour the surrounding countryside and requisition the supplies needed for the thousands of men and horses in the Corps. Officers that spoke French were assigned to this duty whenever possible.

The 2nd Squadron of the Württemberg Reserve Dragoon Regiment was assigned to proceed to Gouzeaucourt, Honnecourt, Gonnelieu, Banteux and other nearby villages in the rear and pick up all available food stocks including livestock, grain, cabbage and wine.

The infantry regiments also sent out detachments to search the areas to the rear of their sector. *Leutnant* Marx, RIR 120, was one of the officers assigned to this duty as he spoke French fluently. In most cases the detachments were successful in obtaining the supplies they requested. From time to time however the local farmer offered some resistance.

When Marx and his men came to a farm in Lagnicourt and began to requisition cattle the farmer objected and suddenly reached for a hatchet in his anger. Marx considered having the man shot but then thought that by doing so it would not have been good for their reputation and would add very little to their prestige. Marx solved the problem

Schweikle

Leutn. d. L. i. Res.-Jnf.-Regt. 121,
gefallen bei Thiepval
am 5. Dezember 1914

Leutnant der Reserve Eugen Schweikle
(Sulz am Neckar) 6/R121. Killed in
action 5 December 1914 near Thiepval.
(*Kriegstagbuch aus Schwaben*)

Mayer (Hermann)

Leutn. d. R. i. Res.-Jnf.-Regt. 121,
gefallen bei Thiepval
am 5. Dezember 1914

Leutnant der Reserve Hermann Meyer
(Stuttgart) 6/R121. Killed in action
5 December 1914 near Thiepval.
(*Kriegstagbuch aus Schwaben*)

by clearly explaining the mechanism of his revolver to the man and promising him he would come back again quite soon.[9] Once again Marx had been able to resolve a problem without spilling any blood.

The occupying forces tried to maintain the best possible relationship with the civilian populace. It was normal practice to issue slips or certificates to civilians in the event an item was confiscated for use by the German army. At times soldiers played jokes on the local people by giving them certificates containing crude jokes. When these infractions were reported to the authorities the local Town Major did everything in his power to correct the abuse but in most cases it was impossible to track down the guilty parties.

The first half of December was relatively quiet for the men stationed on the Somme. They continued the hard work maintaining the trenches, a task made more difficult in the heavy rain and thick mud. The troops had little time to rest whether in the front trenches or in the rear. Most spent their time engaged in the war of attrition against mud and water, digging new entrenchments and preparing the villages in the rear for defense. The heavy rain continued to cause trench walls and dug-outs to collapse and in some areas the men took bricks from ruined villages to pave the trench floor, which helped to keep their feet dry. One account of the conditions and activities of the troops in early December came from the diary of *Offizier Stellvertreter* Gerstner, 10/R110:

> On December 7th our company was withdrawn to Bazentin as the support company where we could recover somewhat again from the fatigue of our 14 days of 'position time' and also bring the outer person who had been quite neglected into order again. Although the housing was an overcrowded nest of staffs and wagon lines, all others were pleased however at being in a human dwelling once again, in which one was far away from the shells and could spend their time in regular activities. So the

Men of the 3/R119 in the trenches, note herringbone
brickwork on the fire step. (Author's collection)

days passed good and bad and apart from the nightly entrenching work that we
performed near the Château Park of Fricourt, nothing disagreeable disturbed our
preparation time. At about 11 o'clock we received the completely unexpected order
that we were to replace the 11th Company in the Château garden of Fricourt. We
began the advance at the onset of darkness during the pouring rain and reached the
park about midnight where we received our support line behind the foremost park
wall, therefore at the eastern edge of Fricourt. Good dug-outs were not available to
us. The few holes were poorly covered with bed slats and doors and offered no sort
of protection against the already day long prevailing rain and from the disgusting
weather. The rain came in everywhere and no one could even think of resting in
this cold and dampness. We were always reasonably happy if the morning dawned
and we could make frozen limbs warm and nimble again through entrenching.
Fortunately the rain lessened in the next days so that we were able to provide our
Other Ranks with a slightly more advantageous constitution and the construction
of the position also came along beautifully.[10]

RIR 109 set up a construction material detachment in a large sheet metal shed in Bazentin le Petit under the command of *Leutnant der Reserve* Ganter. The *'Ganterwerk'*, as it became known, manufactured and distributed trench construction materials for the regiment.

The construction detachment consisted of three to four groups from each of the two reserve companies, the regimental Armourer and the regimental entrenching tool wagon. When more wood was required a tree felling detachment was formed and sent to Foureaux Wood[11] where the trees were cut and split into planks. The fresh lumber was then distributed to the various Pioneer parks and the *Ganterwerk* where it was transformed into materials destined for the front such as knife rests[12], wooden loopholes, boards and slats for dug-outs and trench floors.

Railroad rails, armor plate, wood and iron beams were brought to the front and used to reinforce the crude dug-outs and trenches. Many dug-outs were expanded when possible and decorated to make them more like home.

Pioneer troops were also kept very busy giving instruction to the troops on the handling and use of hand grenades, light pistols and installing heavy belts of wire entanglements at weak points along the front. The pioneers worked on the new mine tunnels under the French lines as well as manning various listening posts set up in galleries driven deep out into No Man's Land in order to counteract enemy mining attempts. The steeples of the churches of Courcelette and Beaumont were brought down because they had served as aiming points for French artillery. Armor piercing K-Ammunition[13] began to arrive in quantities and was distributed to the regiments for use against enemy armored loopholes.

There were unforeseen dangers associated with bringing up trench stores to the front.

Once I was carrying a 50 lb. bundle of barbed wire when a major coming from a side trench stopped me and ordered me to button up my coat, informing me that a soldier should never walk around half-naked. He should have been in the cemetery with us. Then he would have taken his trousers off to keep them clean, not just unbutton his coat. He was killed a few days later by a direct hit into his cellar. In the meantime I was so mad that when coming down with the next bundle of wire and my coat still open, I walked down the main street of La Boisselle rather than chancing another meeting with this officer. Bullets whistled past me and I didn't feel so smart after all, but was too thickheaded to go over to the trench.

In the center of the village was a big heap of rocks, once the church of La Boisselle. I left the road in front of the church and cut over to the right where several things began to happen which made my hair stand up. The first thing was that my bundle of wire went flying through the air and landed about 5 feet from the place where I came down myself. I didn't have my senses back yet when a flame shot out from the pile of rocks and a loud crash followed immediately. The smoke drifting by could not be mistaken for anything else but gunpowder. I was too stunned to get away when another crash knocked me down again, but this time I started to crawl in the direction of the trench as this mystery was too deep and the explosions a bit too close. When I reached the trench I didn't know if I was drunk, dead or alive. Those explosions were very close, not more than 2 feet away and yet all I got were the free air rides and scratches from hitting the ground too hard. I looked over toward the church and there was another crash again. I ducked down and waited for the

The destruction of the church steeple at Guillemont at the moment of the explosion
to prevent the French from using it as an aiming point. (Author's collection)

splinters to pass but none came. The next time I saw more and finally decided to ask
the men in a nearby dug-out what all this monkey business was about. I was told
that a new type of field gun had been placed into the cellar of the church and that
it was firing through a cellar window. Like a damn fool, I had been right next to
this window, not knowing I was due for a haircut and shave if I waited long enough
and moved just a little to the left. I had gone to the right, why, I don't know myself,
but still had I gone to the right. Remember it was dark and the men in the cellar
could not see me as they were firing at a fixed target and the muzzle of the gun was
in the only window they could have used for looking for fools like me. This was the
end of my carrier duty for that night and when I told the story to my friends they
had a good laugh and asked me how it felt to go flying without an aircraft. Hans
Ludwig, 6/R120 [14]

Infantrymen – RIR 120. (Author's collection)

Pioneer duties could be quite dangerous and there were inevitable accidents. Hans Ludwig recalled a close call in early December near La Boisselle while part of the regiment was digging a new trench:

At about 5.30 excited whispering went along the line and everybody went down into the unfinished trench, getting our rifles into position as a line of men were advancing toward us clad in overcoats with rifles in their hands. Since we never took our belts off, we wore our overcoats over our cartridge belts but these men out there had no belts at all as far as we could see in the dim light. They must be Frenchmen trying to cut through this hitherto unoccupied part to cut off La Boisselle from the rear, but we were there waiting for them. My rifle had been alongside of me by force of habit and it did not take long to get ready. After a while the line came closer and we could see a little more but not enough. Waiting for a signal to let go with our rifles we heard one of them say 'where in hell is that damn infantry, they have gone home without waiting for us.' We then found out that the line coming toward us consisted of pioneers returning after putting up a barbed wire defense for the new trench. Their officer did not feel so good after we told them what nearly happened to them and he promised to keep the infantry posted about his movements the next time he was out.[15]

Another wiring party was not as fortunate when *Pionier* Gairing was killed by friendly fire while out repairing the wire obstacles. Apparently a trench sentry mistook him for a member of an enemy patrol. On the same day *Pionier* Werner Dubs was accidentally killed by his own hand grenade.

Wiring parties also had to contend with the French searchlights that were positioned at intervals along the front line. The powerful lights swept along the German trenches and could be quite dangerous if a man was caught in the open. The lights did not follow a set pattern and would appear suddenly at one location only to be switched off and appear at another spot in the line.

We had to be very careful when we left our trenches. Formerly we had walked upright and not too fast but now we had to move cautiously. During the nights and also during a few foggy mornings we laid a barbed wire defense in front of our trenches, and through it zig-zagged a small path, wide enough only to let one man pass without tearing his uniform on the shoulders. Our 'private parts' were always in danger of being damaged by barbs on the wire. Several times when returning from duty in the lookout holes, we were caught by this searchlight just when we were wiggling our way though the barbed wire boulevard. The only thing that was safe in such a case was to stand perfectly still, taking a chance that the French might mistake us for posts holding the barbed wire, until the light had passed on. Detection was then nearly impossible. One night with two other men, I was detailed to show some engineer officers around the outfield. On our return to the barbed wire, the beam of light suddenly sprung out of the night and changed the scene from dark to bright light. The three of us froze stiff wherever we were at the moment but the officers, not used to this special and added feature of ours, picked up their hind legs and disappeared with incredible speed into the trenches. They left behind some cloth, some skin, some blood and three privates with as many curses as these three privates could think of in that second......We knew that standing still now would be suicide in the first degree and we hopped to. The zig-zag path might have been there, but for all we cared it could have been in China. We crossed from where we were standing, accompanied by the now familiar sound of bullets hissing past us. I am sure a slow motion picture camera would have shown three black lines shooting past and we dived into the trench head first, just in time to hear the first shrapnels [sic] and high explosives howl over and burst. They were short with the first delivery and when the second one came we were in a cellar trying to catch our breath, not from running but from cursing while running. None of us had stopped a bullet, but I had a long slit on my shoulder. As the barbed wire was not high, it must have been a bullet going through there, but I did not feel or hear it. One of the other two had a similar slit in the side of his coat and the third one had the seat of his trousers torn off but he was quite sure this was done by barbed wire, which he proved with plenty of scratches on the extension of his spine. Hans Ludwig, 6/R120 [16]

The ruins of La Boisselle. (Author's collection)

Something needed to be done about the French searchlights.

This experience was too much for us and we requested our officers to get some help from our artillery to blow that candle out or to pieces. But they had no ammunition and so we made arrangements with the company next to ours. Whenever the searchlight was on us their sentries would try to blow it out and vice versa. For more than ten nights we drilled holes into the atmosphere. One night when we were being looked over by the light a lucky shot from the next company hit the troublesome apparatus. A greenish-blue flame shot out and the light went out, never to come back anymore. Hans Ludwig 6/R120 [17]

Events in the next few weeks would clearly indicate that the war would last far longer than most had anticipated and that the men would not be going home by Christmas as many had hoped.

Chapter Notes

1. RIR 99 was one of the regiments in the German army that consisted of four battalions as opposed to the normal complement of three.
2. Called 'Wonderwork' by the French.
3. H. Ludwig, Manuscript, 6th Company RIR 120, p. 8.
4. E. Bachelin, *Das Reserve Infanterie Regiment Nr. 111 im Weltkrieg 1914 bis 1918*, p. 47.
5. Jean-Baptiste Antoine de Monet, Chevalier de Lamarck (August 1, 1744 – December 28, 1829). Recognized as a great Zoologist and as a forerunner of the theory of evolution. Lamarck's works were never popular during his lifetime. He died in poverty and obscurity and was buried in a rented grave. Five years later his remains were moved to an unknown location.
6. *Oberst* Friedrich Grall was born on 1 March 1859 and joined the army in 1879 with IR 57. He was promoted to *Leutnant* in 1880, *Hauptmann* in 1894 and in 1899 he joined the newly formed IR 159. In 1913 he reached the rank of *Oberstleutnant* in IR 136 in

Strasburg and at the outbreak of the war he commanded Landwehr Infantry Regiment 99 until being assigned to RIR 99. *Oberst* Grall was 55 years old at the start of the war.

7. Hubertus is the Patron Saint of all huntsmen. A *Schnitzeljagd* can be described as a paper chase. Horsemen would ride a course following a paper trail or in some cases a scented trail or rider wearing a foxtail. It is celebrated on 3 November each year.

8. W. Gallion, *Das Reserve-Infanterie-Regiment Nr. 40 im Weltkrieg*, p. 46.

9. J. Marx, *Kriegs Tagebuch eines Juden*, pp. 38-39.

10. Greiner, *Reserve-Infanterie-Regiment Nr. 110 im Weltkrieg 1914-1918*, p. 62.

11. Foureaux Wood was also known as High Wood.

12. Knife-rest: Portable barbed wire entanglement; stretched on an X-shaped frame and used for stopping gaps in no-man's land and trenches.

13. K Ammunition = Armor piercing ammunition for rifles and machine guns.

14. Ludwig, op. cit., p pp. 13-14.

15. Ludwig, op. cit. p. 11.

16. Ludwig, op. cit. pp. 8-9.

17. Ludwig, op. cit., p. 9.

4

December 1914

Continued heavy fighting in Russia at the end of 1914 required the use of all available
German reserves. As a result several army Corps were transferred to the Eastern
Front and thus seriously reduced German forces in the West. This reduction
provided an opportunity for the Entente to take advantage of the weaker German front
in order to prevent any further transfer of German troops to the East and if possible force
a breakthrough in the West at the same time.

General Joffre planned a series of attacks along the entire front, from Flanders to the
Vosges. French and British units not involved in the main attacks would provide support
with diversionary attacks. However these smaller attacks should also be ready to exploit
any successes. Since the beginning of December preparations for French attacks against
the XIV Reserve Corps were clearly noticeable, especially on the left bank of the Ancre
opposite the 26th Reserve Division.

Trench periscope. L –R: *Lt.* Weynert, *Lt.* Kaüffmann, *Oblt.*
Haug, *Lt.* Düsbeck, RIR 111. (Author's collection)

Klemm

Leutnant b. Res. im Reserve-Inf.-
Regt 119 (wissenschaftl. Hilfslehrer),
gefallen am 17. Dez. bei Ovillers

Örtle

Leutnant b. R. im R.-Inf.-Regt. 120
(Geometer), gefallen am 19. Dez.
bei La Boiselle

Leutnant der Reserve or *Vizefeldwebel/Offizier Stellvertreter* Adolf Klemm (Lossburg) 2/ R119. Killed in action 17 December 1914 at Ovillers. (*Kriegstagbuch aus Schwaben*)

Leutnant der Reserve Richard Örtle (Stuttgart) RIR 120. Killed in action 19 December 1914 at La Boiselle. (*Kriegstagbuch aus Schwaben*)

Observers reported movement and troop accumulations behind Albert. Captured French newspapers openly discussed stories of the expected breakthrough of the German lines and there were always persistent rumors of a French offensive. Warnings were issued to all commands to remain vigilant.

In an attempt to obtain information regarding French activities RIR 121 planned a raid against the opposing trenches. The undertaking was set for the night of 10/11 December and the target was the French line in the forest of Authuille. The attack would be supported by heavy *minenwerfers*. However the attempt failed. In part this was because the French were well entrenched and partly because cooperation between the infantry and the *minenwerfers* was not coordinated properly and the trench mortar fire was directed at the wrong location.

French artillery grew increasingly active against the position of RIR 119 at Ovillers and the 6/R119 suffered particularly heavy losses at the western edge of the village. When darkness fell on the 16th a patrol was sent out under *Unteroffizier* Böcker. 30 to 40 French soldiers were discovered advancing between the lines with parcels in their hands. Several rounds from the artillery drove the French back but Böcker had become curious about their activities and stayed out in No Man's Land. He found the French were conspicuously restless; there was a lot of talk as they entrenched. Böcker had the impression that they were preparing for something unusual.

He reported to his superiors and was ordered to prepare a position 150 meters from an outpost occupied by 8–10 Frenchmen and then open fire on them. When Böcker's men tried to dig out their position the shovels made too much noise and it was decided to sneak up on the French outpost instead. They managed to get on the flank of the French and shouted as they opened fire. The occupants quickly withdrew to the main French line. Patrol Böcker explored the abandoned outpost and found steel protective shields

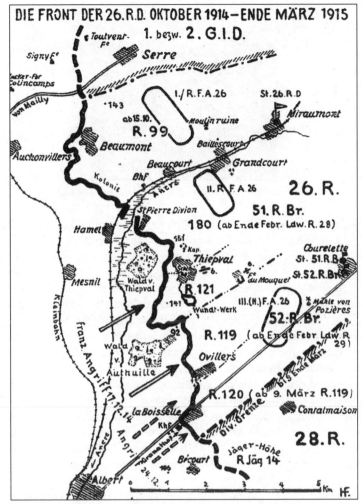

17 December attacks against the 26th Reserve Division.

and strange wooden racks that were up to 4 meters long and placed on wheels. The racks had been hollowed out and filled with explosives.

The pioneers examined the devices and concluded they were torpedoes designed to blow up wire obstacles. Corps headquarters was convinced an attack was imminent and ordered all regiments to be on alert. By the morning of 17 December the XIV Reserve Corps was ready for action.

French attacks did take place at several locations on the morning of 17 December. On the far right of the Corps, near Beaumont, an attack struck the 1/R99 where the opposing lines were less than 80 meters apart and where *Pionier Hauptmann* Neininger had constructed several tunnels under the French lines. On 14 December *Pionier Unteroffizier* Klopfgeräusche reported one tunnel was complete and loaded with explosives in preparation for detonation.

French prisoners – RIR 99. (*Geschichte des Reserve-Infanterie-Regiment Nr. 99*)

The French set off a mine at the start of their attack. The mine fell short of the German lines by 30 meters and the detonation was badly timed. It took place directly under the advancing waves of French infantry and many were thrown into the air by the explosion. Others caught in front of it surrendered to the 1/R99 while those on the sides and rear sought cover behind the lip of earth spoil thrown up after the explosion had settled.

This mine also set off the German mine and a secondary explosion tore through No Man's Land near the French trench. An examination afterward revealed one crater to be 6 meters deep and 16 meters across while the other was 25 meters in diameter. The explosions resulted in the collapse of a German listening gallery and listening post in which several pioneers from the 4/Pioneer Bn 13 were killed.

RIR 99 directed rifle and machine gun fire against the attackers. A homemade trench mortar dropped shells among the French lines with devastating effect until the barrel burst while being fired. The crew then joined *Unteroffizier* Hasselmann, 10/R99, and began to throw the trench mortar bombs toward the French while the RFAR 26 opened fire and brought heavy losses to the enemy. The 15/R99 and 11/R119 counterattacked and were able to penetrate the French trenches. Heavy flanking fire caused them to withdraw but not before they captured 35 prisoners from the *137e Régiment d'Infanterie*.

The main French thrust against the 26th Reserve Division occurred between Thiepval and Ovillers where RIR 121 and IR 180 were positioned. The French had assembled five regiments of infantry to participate in the attack; the *19e, 116e, 118e, 215e Régiment d'Infanterie* and the *41e Régiment Coloniale*. RIR 121 on Hill 141 was subjected to strong artillery fire at 6 a.m. followed by infantry and machine gun fire. The men were on alert and waited calmly at their firing positions for the attack to begin.

The French attacked only at the left wing of the regiment, in the hollow between Ovillers and La Boisselle. This part of the line was not occupied by any troops as most of the position was under water due to weather conditions. RIR 121 did however have two companies flanking the gap, the 5th and 11/R121. The French came up to the trench in the dark and as it grew lighter they realized they were in a trap. There was a short exchange of fire but in the end the French were forced to surrender. RIR 121 captured two officers and 149 men while another 25 dead were left in front of the wire entanglements.

At the same time *Leutnant* Härter, 2/180 at the left wing of IR 180 observed another strong French infantry force advancing through the hollow between Hill 141 and Ovillers. The French troops were heading for a communication trench that connected RIR 121

French prisoners captured by RIR 119 near Ovillers, 17 December 1914.
(*Die 26. Reserve Division 1914-1918*)

with RIR 119. Härter quickly decided to attack the French and sent two detachments under *Leutnant der Reserve* Maier and *Leutnant* Blank.

The detachments drove the French towards the trenches held by RIR 121 and after a short fight captured 91 prisoners. The remainder of the French force had been killed or captured by RIR 121. The 2/180 suffered minor losses in their counterattack, 3 men killed and 3 men wounded.

When the blood red sun finally appeared and lit up the battlefield the men on Hill 141 could see a company of French infantry lying in front of the German wire by Ovillers. They could neither go forward nor retreat. Suddenly, as if ordered, the French jumped up as a group and tried to run to the rear. A machine gun from RIR 119 fired into the mass at point blank range. Some of the men fell while the others turned around and threw their rifles away, running toward the German lines with their hands raised.

Shortly after this attack new waves of infantry appeared in front of the 8/R119 by Ovillers in close columns. The infantry and machine guns immediately opened fire, supported on their right flank by the 5/R119. Rows of attacking French infantry were cut down in the defensive fire, however new masses of infantry seemed to appear out of the ground from the forest of Authuille.

The French attack had been directed against the II/R119. An advanced outpost occupied by the 7/R119 was in danger of being cut off and captured so the men were withdrawn to the main German line. The French immediately occupied the outpost and prepared it for defense. The attack spread to the portion of the line being held by the 6th and 7/R119 and before the French could clear the top of the small hill in front of Ovillers the defenders in both companies were pouring fire into the French ranks.

The 4/R119 and parts of RIR 120 at the quarry position near La Boisselle joined in the fighting on the left flank.

On 17 December just before sunrise, all of our outposts came back reporting that large groups of French infantry were building up for an attack on the regiment to our right. I was asleep when these men came in and when I reached my assigned post I was still asleep. I pushed my rifle out through the steel shield and rubbed some dirt from my hands into my eyes. In an instant I was as wide awake as anybody can be. There, right in front of us but facing the next regiment were three lines of French infantry, officers on horseback and flags lazily floating in the light breeze, apparently waiting for an order to go ahead….a frantic call went our for machine guns and as we only had six in the whole regiment, just two were down near the *Granathof* where we were. The others came shortly and were thrown on top of the trenches without any protection.

The French were still in formation, officers going up and down the line, which showed signs of unrest. An officer raised his hand and they fixed bayonets. Our orders were to not start shooting until we were told. We were getting restless as it must have taken the French about 15 minutes to get ready. They paid no attention whatsoever to us and concentrated only on the unsuspecting Regiment 119 to our right, who, on account of being down in the valley could not see what was happening on the plateau in front of us.

Finally a red flare went up just as the French lines started to move. I never saw any attack that was as thoroughly killed before it got under way as this one. Two machine guns on the tip of La Boisselle covered the territory behind the French third line, cutting them off from any chance of getting back into their trenches. The other four, together with the infantry, fired right into the thick masses. The steel shield was hindering us and soon all of us were on top of the trench together with

10.5cm Light Field Howitzer in firing position, RFAR 26. (Author's collection)

the machine guns, firing lying flat on our stomachs. An officer on horseback tried to reorganize the French lines but they drifted aimlessly back and forth. Then this officer pitched down from his horse, the animal racing madly towards the German lines where Regiment 119 had been warned by us to be on the lookout. They knew by this time what was going on and our men were in telephone contact with them all the time. The French force of about 3,000 had dwindled to not more than 500 and they raised their hands over their heads, the signal for us to stop firing with the exception of those covering the lines of retreat….The French losses during the brief space of about 20 minutes were over 2,500 dead and wounded. The dead were still on the plateau when we left La Boisselle later in March 1915. Hans Ludwig, 6/R120 [1]

Guns from the III *Abteilung* RFAR 26[2] joined the fighting. Batteries Burk, Fuchs and Reinmöller were prepared to open fire as soon as the command was given. When French artillery fire was directed against the southwestern edge of Pozières the howitzers opened fire in a single salvo and then proceeded to fire at will.

Shrapnel shells burst in yellowish-white clouds above the French lines and cut down dozens of the attackers. The howitzers continued to fire at the enemy infantry using their best shells, the grey peacetime ammunition, not the new red, Az-projectiles[3] that were considered to be almost ineffective by the gunners and the attack faltered in the face of this destructive barrage. A short time afterward barn doors swung open in Thiepval. The building had concealed two field guns and they opened fire upon the French lines. Additional field guns joined in from Battery Preysing, 6/RFAR 26 near Mouquet Farm and the Thiepval Château Park. They poured a devastating fire into the left flank of the attackers.

When the field guns joined in the howitzers lengthened their range in order to place a wall of fire between the attacking infantry and their trenches. French reserves did not dare to leave their trenches despite the officers clearly heard giving the order *'en avant!'* The field was soon covered with dead and wounded. Those who had been able had already retreated to the safety of their trenches while others could neither retreat through the wall of shellfire or advance into the rifle and machine gun fire of the defenders. Finally the survivors threw away their weapons and raised their arms in surrender, 465 men were led away as prisoners. The French *19e Régiment d'Infanterie* had virtually ceased to exist.

One of the few gains made by the French in their early morning attack was the capture of the outpost of RIR 119. The outpost was connected to the main German line by a long communication trench and was now filled with French infantry. RIR 119 was determined to recapture the position. Machine guns were brought forward and positioned at elevated locations where they could fire into the post. The light field howitzers were brought to bear on this target and after a few well-placed shots into the dense ranks of the French troops the garrison surrendered. 293 unwounded and 56 wounded prisoners were brought in along with their weapons and equipment.

New French attacks against the post at midnight failed in heavy defensive fire. It was a ghastly picture in front of the regiment. The dead lay in piles and rows just as they had dropped during the attack. The wounded attempted to crawl to the rear but could go no further and cried for help. Compassionate *Swabians* attempted to help the wounded but rifle fire from the French trenches drove them back. The whimpering of the wounded and

7.7cm Field guns inside a barn near Thiepval, RFAR 26. (Lawrence Brown)

dying men could be heard throughout the day. At nightfall most of the wounded could be brought into the German lines where they were sent to the rear for medical treatment.

> It was a very disagreeable duty left to us to go out during the following nights to bring in the wounded. The French made no effort to do this and many a life could have been saved if they had taken their wounded in. During the first night our men refrained from shooting towards the direction from whence the moaning and wailing of the wounded came, but the French did not move and made no effort to come out. So it was left to our men to recover as many as we could bring in, at the same time all of the equipment of the dead and wounded, but progress was slow and we were hindered by the French sentries who realized what was going on and tried to keep us off. Later, when decay set in, parties had to go out and cover the bodies with lime and other chemicals as the odor was getting unbearable. Hans Ludwig, 6/R120 [4]

French attacks against the 28th Reserve Division were concentrated near the village of Mametz that was held by RIR 111 and Reserve *Jäger* Bn 14. The attack took place at 5 a.m. in the morning in darkness where the opposing trenches were very close together.

The *Jägers* reported hearing unfamiliar bugle calls in the distance and then close by. French infantry suddenly appeared in front of their trench shouting '*Urra*! *Urra*!' The *Jägers* opened fire into the dense waves of attackers and killed or wounded numerous French soldiers in front of the wire obstacles. Some had managed to penetrate the German lines and entered the main trench and a communication trench about 100 meters away and a force the size of a company was seen advancing towards Mametz.

A weak spot had been discovered in the German lines at the right wing of RIR 111 by the Mametz-Carnoy road. There was a gap approximately 200 meters wide between the left wing of the 6/R111 and the *Jägers*. The gap had been closed using patrols, sentries and an old trench lying a short distance in front of the main German line.

Krais
Leutnant d. L. im R.-Inf.-Regt. 119
(Kaufmann), gefallen am 20. Dez.
bei Braumont

Leutnant der Reserve Hermann Krais
(Reutlingen) 11/R119. Killed in action
20 December 1914 near Beaumont.
(*Kriegstagbuch aus Schwaben*)

Bezel
Leutn. d. R. im Ref.-Inf.-Regt. 119
(Hotelier), gest. am 27. Dez. 1914 a.
d. b. Ovillers l. Boiffelle erh. Wunden

Leutnant der Reserve Karl Bezel
(Friedrichshafen) 5/R119. Wounded in
action 25 November 1914, died 17 December
1914, Reserve Field Hospital 1, Bapaume.
(*Kriegstagbuch aus Schwaben*)

The attack had overwhelmed the sentries and the French advanced up to a hedge. From this position some of the French soldiers continued toward Mametz and the rear of the *Jägers*. Joseph Amann, 6/R111 tells of the fighting at the gap:

> In the night from the 16th to the 17th of December I was at a listening post several times. Our position was at a right angle and pointed out a gap that it flanked and in which the connection was maintained at night only by patrols. At dawn we heard the shouts from the corner sentry: 'The French have broken through and stand behind us!' then there was a runner, 'the company leader needs everyone at the right wing'.
>
> 'No', I said, 'then we would just be a large target'…we are 60 brave soldiers, 'out to the rear!' I called and they moved. Already during our initial fire the Frenchmen became unsteady and tried to save themselves in our unoccupied trench. We followed after them as fast as possible on their heels. The command 'lay down!' was given when they disappeared into the trench.
>
> Now the most interesting part comes – how those in the trench were lost – because when shooting their torsos had disappeared as targets; naturally only their heads showed. However that resulted in shooting too high and my command 'shoot at the edge of the trench!' allowed us to take the trench in a half-hour with the approach of our reinforcements. 60 prisoners were taken, the remaining were dead, shot in the head. We had 4 dead to mourn…[5]

The *Jägers* attacked the French troops remaining in the trench at dawn aided by men of the 1R/Pioneer Bn 13. The French put up a stubborn resistance as the *Jägers* forced them from traverse to traverse with the help of *Pionier Leutnant der Reserve* Gobrecht,

Communication trench in La Boisselle, 16 December 1914. (Author's collection)

Unteroffizier Meyer and *Gefreiter* Geyer. The French did not surrender until the Germans used hand grenades. 1 officer and 79 men were captured in the counterattack.

The captured officer obtained permission to go into No Man's Land in order to bring in four of his men who were trapped. After 30 minutes the officer returned with his men and they joined the considerable number of prisoners assembled at the foot of *Bayern Höhe* awaiting transport to the rear. The officer was wounded during his rescue attempt when he was shot through both cheeks by French rifle fire.

The extreme left wing of the XIV Reserve Corps near Montauban was attacked where RIR 40 was holding the line. The regiment had been under heavy fire, especially the village of Montauban. Telephone *Unteroffizier* Esperstedt provided this description from his observation post:

> The heavy shells crashed and smashed, covering Montauban with smoke, the town hall of the mayor blew up with a lot of noise, leaving windows and doorframes hanging on the tops of poplar trees. A few shells hissed and exploded. Mud, stones

and dust pattered down taking your breath away. The whirl of the heavy artillery fire made the connection with the battle line almost impossible; the cables had already been broken long before.[6]

The men had already been alerted by the sound of rifle fire coming from Mametz and Hill 110 and were ready. In the early morning darkness a listening post of the 6/R40 observed the approach of a thin skirmish line.

The French were allowed to come up to the wire entanglements before the defenders opened fire. Almost at the same time a second wave of French troops was observed. The heavy fire forced the attackers to withdraw behind a small hill 300 meters in front of the 6/R40 where they were hidden from view, carrying their wounded with them.

At 7.45 a.m. a smaller French detachment approached the trench held by the 9/R40. However they were also forced to withdraw due to fire from a listening post and from the machine guns of Bavarian *Leib* Regiment on the left flank. Many dead were counted in the foreground on the following day.

It appeared the French planned on overrunning the German sentries with hand grenades and makeshift trench mortar bombs. Two trench mortar bombs were discovered and detonated with rifle fire from a safe distance. A similar advance from the railway hollow east of the Montauban-Carnoy road against the 8/R40 at 10.30 a.m. met with the same fate.

After the initial reports of the breakthrough by Mametz were received RIR 111 ordered an immediate counterattack. All available men were assembled from the battalion staff and one group from the reserve company. *Leutnant* Sigel assembled all of the men he could find in Longueval for the attack, Other Ranks from the first line transport, from the construction materials yard, guards, orderlies, clerks and officer's servants. This makeshift unit proceeded against the village. *Radfahrer* Wilhelm Klein, 5/R111, who was with the staff of the II Battalion, described the counterattack:

Active firing suddenly began at 5 o'clock in the morning at the front; about 5.30 *Landwehrmann* Sinnwell, 6th Company telephoned that the French had occupied the trenches that had been dug out over the last few nights. Sinnwell was going through the new trench to get coffee and at this time he was struck in the ear with a bayonet by a Frenchman. Approximately two French companies had come up to Mametz where they fixed themselves in the houses. *Oberstleutnant* von Schweinichen immediately ordered the battalion staff to assemble for a counterattack. *Leutnant* Munding, leader of the 8th Company, came toward us accompanied by *Offizier Stellvertreter* Wöhrle and a few men from the 8th Company. With the three officers we were altogether 24 men. We quickly filled our tunic pockets with ammunition and then followed at a run through the communication trench to the front. *Oberstleutnant* von Schweinichen went outside along the trench and stopped to assess the enemy. When we were past the position of the 5th Company we could also see the enemy.

We left the trench in the direction of the Mametz-Carnoy road, formed a skirmish line and advanced in the direction of Carnoy. We immediately received infantry fire from the front and machine gun fire from Hill 110. After a short firefight we stormed the trench. We took 36 or more unwounded French prisoners, amongst them a second lieutenant and a sergeant major. The French had lost approximately 70 men killed,

Infantryman – RIR 109. (Author's collection)

amongst them 2 officers; furthermore many more wounded lay in the trenches and in the terrain between the lines. 538 unwounded prisoners were taken in the entire battle sector. One of the fallen officers had over 2,000 Francs on his person that was turned over to the regiment. Our losses amounted to 8 killed, amongst them *Offizier Stellvertreter* Wöhrle from the 8th Company and a few wounded, amongst them *Leutnant* Mathy, our adjutant. He received a gunshot in the thigh and lay in a shell hole with Cyclist Mück until the onset of darkness where he was wounded twice by shell splinters.[7]

RIR 109 had just relieved RIR 110 at Fricourt and the men had barely become familiar with the trenches when a telephone message arrived that the French had penetrated the line and that strong French forces occupied Mametz. They could hear the sound of fighting nearby but could not see any part of the attack from their position.

The men of RIR 110 also heard the sounds of heavy fighting as they marched toward the long-awaited rest quarters. The III/R110 had just left the line at 4 a.m. on the 17th and was marching toward Le Transloy when the sounds of the attack were heard. They were simply turned around and headed back to the front, tired, wet and hungry. The other parts of the regiment that had arrived in their billets had started to wash their underclothes when the regiment was ordered back into the line. The men did not have any spare underwear and were forced to put on the freezing wet clothing as they marched off into the cold December day.

The counterattacks against Mametz were not well coordinated. Whenever the different composite units arrived they were quickly thrown into action. One group managed to enter the village and make their way up to the church. However they were forced to withdraw before superior French fire.

Another group of 35 men from RIR 109 succeeded in getting into the *Trockengraben* where they joined a detachment from RIR 40. The combined unit crawled to within 50 meters of the village edge then rushed the village. The French quickly withdrew from the walls and hedges and retreated deeper in to the village. The attackers followed and took their first prisoner. The mixed detachment headed toward the village pond but heavy fire from the houses along the street forced them to stop. They tried to advance up the Contalmaison-Mametz road however it was also held under strong fire.

When the third company arrived from RIR 109 there were finally enough men to penetrate the village. The company reached the northern edge of the village without suffering any losses. The 1st Platoon was sent to the right to encompass the village. The 2nd and part of the 3rd Platoon advanced on the left. The remainder of the 3rd Platoon guarded the southern exit of the village in order to cut off the French retreat.

When the signal was given the company attacked with fixed bayonets. They climbed over walls, hedges and fences and jumped over trenches during the advance. The first houses were reached and quickly cleared. The groups penetrated into the center of the village where bitter fighting arose; the French were fighting back desperately.

The fighting moved from house to house, pressing the French back into the middle of the village until they were completely surrounded and forced to surrender. 98 unwounded men were captured; many more dead and wounded lay in the village including a captain.

An der Somme durch deutsche M.G. gefallene Franz. Jnf.

French infantry killed by German machine gun fire on the Somme. (Author's collection)

They belonged to a company from the *236e Régiment d'Infanterie*. The German losses in this last attack were reported as 7 men killed, 17 men wounded.

The French were not finished for the day and additional attempts were made along the front of the 28th Reserve Division. The *Jägers* repelled several smaller attacks throughout the afternoon with the help of flanking machine gun fire and the use of the new auxiliary trench weapons that were found to be very useful in their baptism of fire.[8]

At 3 p.m. the French made use of the natural terrain and nearby structures as they worked closer to the German lines. However, flanking machine gun fire from the neighboring Bavarian regiment quickly forced them to withdraw. At 4 p.m. similar attempts was made against the 9/R40. French troops attacked the mangled wire entanglements with an '*Urra!*' A whistle blown in the German trenches signaled the men to open fire. The heavy fire struck into the attacker's ranks like a blow and the French faltered, hesitated and then stopped. A few groups managed to advance into the withering fire and made their way up to a German trench. However there was no escape for them as it was filled with deep mud. Whoever did not surrender was killed.

At 6 p.m. the *Jägers* observed a French column approaching its position. They were allowed to come within 30 meters of the German lines when they were swept away in a murderous fire from rifles and machine guns. Approximately 150 men were taken prisoner from this last attack. The *Jägers* had taken almost 400 prisoners and approximately 500 dead lay in front of their position. French dash and bayonet attacks with unloaded rifles made little headway against the German lines. The brief French success at Mametz could not be maintained without further support from the rear.

The XIV Reserve Corps reported approximately 1,000 prisoners had been captured. The enemy dead and wounded could only be estimated and was placed at 2,000. The defenders were cold, wet and exhausted after fighting all day. Rations had not been able to be brought up into the trenches because ammunition, reinforcements and the artillery were given priority.

In the evening of the 17th German reserves were distributed, especially in areas that appeared to be the most threatened. They found movement in the trenches in the thick mud and dark night very difficult but most eventually reached their destination. They were put to work repairing the trenches and shoveling mud in order to stay warm.

The numerous prisoners taken during the fighting on the 17th had to be transported to the rear. For many of the men assigned as escorts it was the first time they had been out of the front line for two months or more. Hans Ludwig was assigned to escort a large group of French prisoners to the rear:

> With a few other men, I was detailed to take the prisoners back to Courcelette where they were questioned at division headquarters. It was indeed a surprise to see houses again with walls and windows after having spent two months in the ruins of La Boisselle. After a short stay we were ordered to take the prisoners to Bapaume. The French had been issued blue overalls of thin cloth to cover their red trousers but on the way to Bapaume they all discarded these over-trousers, proudly displaying the red trousers, the pride of any Frenchman. We passed through several villages and the French women came running out of their houses, crying and bringing their fellow countrymen wine and food. I distinctly remember one old woman sitting on the doorstep of her home in Le Sars with tears running down her cheeks always

repeating 'and they are so young.' The difference was only that we were old soldiers, whereas the French had come directly from Paris and represented the cream of the French capital's young men, drafted for service after the beginning of the war. They never before had been in the trenches and considered the time they spent there too long. They certainly got a dirty deal and somebody must have been court-martialed [sic] for the way they were led to slaughter. We asked them why they had not tried to take La Boisselle, but they knew of the *Granate* farm and the men holding La Boisselle. We were known to them as the devils of La Boisselle. They were surprised to learn that it was these devils who had stopped them ... .

In Bapaume we were put on a train, one of us with about 50 'red trousers' in a cattle wagon. I got tired of holding my rifle and stuck the bayonet of it into the wooden roof of the car, leaving the rifle dangling in the air, opening one can of sardines after the other for the Frenchies from whom all knives had been taken. One fellow made more noise than the others when the train stopped in an open stretch. He came forward and asked to be allowed to leave the train for a minute. I declined to do so as I could not very well leave the rest of them alone and did not also feel like shooting him if he should desire to run away. He was very nice about it and said quietly that it had to go into those nice red trousers then. This remark made a hit with his friends, who laughed and roared for a long time. He also made a hit with me, and I let him go and did not even watch him, not because I did trust him but because I did not want to turn my back on the other 49 in the car who might get fooled by my rifle swinging from the roof. Long before I could have gotten that bayonet out of the roof, I would have been pushed out of commission, at least as far as they could see it. I did not tell them that I had a miniature Mauser pistol with ten bullets ready in my pocket and any attempt of mutiny would have been costly for them.

The man who was in such a hurry to go for a walk came back and everything was fine until we reached Cambrai. We expected to turn our prisoners over to somebody else here but were told that we might have to take them to Germany. The 15 of us were already figuring on a trip home when some convalescent men from hospitals in Cambrai showed up and took over the transport. We enjoyed ourselves for a few hours and got drunk. When the time came to assemble at the railway station we were all more or less stewed to the ears. Even the comm. officer in charge of the party forgot what he was doing and made us present arms, on which occasion five rifles of the 15 fell on the floor and one of them went off. After that we stopped drilling and got into the train as well as we could.[9]

The Corps expected the attacks to continue the following day, probably before dawn as it had on the 17th. This was confirmed by constant artillery fire, aerial observation and from captured French orders. One set of orders indicated the French had planned a larger attack in the night of 17 December but it did not occur. The Corps artillery was ordered to fire into the French trenches in order to disrupt troop concentrations and prevent any further attacks. *Offizier Stellvertreter* Gerstner:

The fire that did not quiet down the entire night also increased to the greatest intensity towards morning. A stronger bellow of the guns always mingled in the crash of the infantry fire. The ground shook under their projectiles.[10]

French attacks did continue before dawn on the 18th. Several attempts were made against RIR 111 and the *Jägers* near Mametz. Each was repelled leaving behind a large number of French dead lying in No Man's Land. Of the approximately 60 men in one attack RIR 40 shot down almost 50 of them, the remainder turned and fled towards the French lines. One company leader of RIR 40 sent in his after action report with a short sentence: 'I believe the 11/R40 had done their bit very well.'[11]

German artillery was still very active in trying to disrupt any new French attacks. Observers noted a large accumulation of troops nearby and called in their artillery. Telephone *Unteroffizier* Esperstedt in the headquarters of the III/R40 wrote:

I called the artillery with the receiver in my hand.

'*Hauptmann* Leinekugel here' came the reply.

'Telephone Operator III/R40 here. *Herr Hauptmann*, substantial accumulation of the enemy in the Carnoy Copse, attack expected, please fire'.

'We must save ammunition; I will fire if it is urgently necessary'.

'It is worth the trouble'.

'Good, you also agree',

'Yes indeed'. I then heard: 'First gun – fire!'

I replied: 'Fifty too short'.

'Second gun – fire!' 'Well placed'.

'Battery – salvo fire!' Several salvoes moved over our heads that smoked out the copse. The *Poilus* scattered like wasps and offered a good target for our machine guns and rifles.[12]

The French were particularly active in front of the 6/R40. They had worked closer to the German lines during the night. Heavy artillery fire fell on the position in the early morning causing damage to the trenches. When the French attacked they were taken in the flank by the 6/R40 firing from a tunnel driven out from the right flank of the company and the French retreated behind a small hill. The 6/R40 contacted the artillery and directed fire upon the hidden troops.

Repeated attacks against the company were all repelled. *Leutnant* Westermann, 6/R40, reported: 'The French were hopping around like scared chickens in their helplessness.'[13] The defenders suffered far fewer losses than the French. The trenches, even in their poor condition, provided good protection. The French artillery concentrated its fire upon recently-constructed dug-outs and destroyed nearly every one of them, fortunately they were not occupied. It was thought that the French considered the fresh earth works as being special defensive positions.

When the attacks ended the men had been standing at their posts for several days during prolonged rain without sleep or food. The trenches were in a terrible condition between the heavy rain and constant artillery fire. Trench walls had collapsed and required urgent repairs. The construction supply yards brought up wood for dug-outs and trench walls; slats for duckboards, fascines and new wire for obstacles. Pumps were brought up to clear out the extra water. As much work was completed as possible in the lull of the fighting. Rations were brought up in the evening and distributed to the men. Spare cooking kettles were installed in many places so that they could at least make coffee in the trenches. The wounded were transported to the rear to the field hospitals.

RIR 111 suffered a particularly heavy blow in the afternoon of the 18th. *Hauptmann* von Zingler, III/R111, assembled the company officers for a meeting about the situation. While they were in a shallow shelter a French shell struck it and Zingler and six other officers, including several company commanders, were killed instantly and a number of other officers and men were wounded. *Offizier Stellvertreter* Gerstner, RIR 110 provided an account of the situation on this day:

Towards midday we received marching orders. First we were to proceed without food via Bazentin then towards Mametz where we would be in a hollow immediately behind the position of the 4th Battery Res. F.A. 29 and expected further orders. On the way we had already found out that the battalion would not be used intact but with two companies each being made available to the 111th Reserve and 40th Reserve. The 9th and 10th Companies became subordinate to the II/R111 (position west of Mametz); the 11th and 12th Companies became subordinate to R.I.R. 40 (positioned at Montauban).

The 9th and 10th Companies remained in the hollow for the time being. The stay was quite disagreeable since in the meantime rain had set in again. Camping on the dank ground was impossible. So everyone stood around in groups and tried to protect themselves as well as possible against the rain and cold with tent squares and blankets.

Since no orders had arrived because of a lack of any connection with our battalion our battalion commander, *Major* von Szczepanski, decided to establish a connection through an officer's patrol and towards evening I received the task to report about our prepared position to the commander of the II/R111 (*Oberstleutnant* von Schweinichen) and to accept further orders from him…I picked out two reliable men, amongst them *Wehrmann* Helmstädter. When darkness fell we went forth over the terrain that was unfamiliar to us and after a long march we came to a poorly-covered dug-out that was being used as a depot and simultaneously also as a wounded collecting point.

There we bumped into some returning food carriers who gave us further directions and showed us a communication trench that represented the only connection to the front and that had to be used to go any further. At first I followed these instructions, however I had already determined after a short time that any swift advance in this trench was as good as being ruled out. It was partially filled with meter deep mud and water into which one sank up to the hips so that we had to work ourselves out again and again with help from our rifles.

In addition you stepped upon corpses every few feet, mainly French who had fallen here or as severely wounded and had been ground down into the mud before anyone could have brought them help. Under these circumstances I decided to proceed across the open field and only if one of the many flares came down nearby and brightly illuminated the terrain would we quickly take cover again because we immediately received heavy fire.

After marching approximately ¾ of an hour we finally reached the foremost trench and after a short search I also found the battalion commander, *Oberstleutnant* von Schweinichen there, an older gentleman with a white beard. He had assembled a few officers of his battalion for a discussion in his dug-out as I reported to him and I still have the picture in my memory how this old gentleman quietly and matter-of-factly explained the situation and clearly and definitely gave his orders in the poorly covered dug-out and by the sparse glimmer of a flickering candle.

The mood was confident however there was a deep solemnity on their faces. It appeared to me as if everyone was still under the effect of a painful incident and I also learned of the cause a little later. A direct hit had smashed into a dug-out situated nearby a few hours earlier and killed or severely wounded several company leaders assembled there for a discussion…

We began the return march again when I had received my orders from the sector commander. We repeatedly came through strong enemy fire, nevertheless we reached our troops safely again after midnight who were still camped in the hollow

Construction of the 26th Reserve Division cemetery monument, Miraumont. The monument was officially dedicated in December 1914. (Author's collection)

during the pouring rain…the previous orders calling for the participation of both companies in the front line could be disregarded because it would only result in wasteful victims in the already strongly occupied fire trench.[14]

Over the following days the French were quiet however their artillery remained active through this period, as did aerial observation from numerous aircraft. During the night of 20/21 December the French artillery fire increased in strength and became very heavy by 3 a.m. on the villages of Mametz and Montauban. Listening posts reported much activity in the French lines.

At 7.30 a.m. strong skirmish lines suddenly appeared 200 meters away from the 6th and 7/R40. The attackers advanced in waves shouting 'en avant!' Well-aimed infantry fire mowed down the French in rows. Defensive artillery fired in the rear of the attackers blocked any reserves. The survivors flooded to the rear in a short time and the attack was over. The men of RIR 40 observed that some of the French troops were equipped with incendiary flares that caught fire as soon as any projectile struck them.

400-500 French dead lay in a very narrow area in front of the companies. They were later interred by a French detachment that approached under the protection of a Red Cross flag. All activity ceased on both sides of the line during the burial.

It would seem humanity was not lost even during the heavy and brutal fighting. Just a short time before these men had been trying to kill one another by any means possible, from rifle and bayonet to sharpened spades and trench knives. *Leutnant* Westermann, 6/R40, provided an account of such an incident a day after the heavy fighting:

Suddenly I saw a Red Cross flag far behind the hillock. I immediately hurried to my company, placed everyone in position and strongly prohibited anyone from looking out above the fire trench because I was very careful. The French would gladly act deviously and were unscrupulous in the choice of their methods. I accepted that perhaps a surprise was planned by which they expected the 'Barbarians' to respect the Red Cross flag as an international contrivance or that they would be curious and would try to determine the identity of our regiment and the strength of our trench garrison.

Therefore my strict order was to also remain under cover in all circumstances and to wait for my further instructions. Meanwhile the Red Cross flag moved slowly towards us and was always clearly visible behind the hillock. I now told my platoon leaders that I would go over and gave them instructions that if there were any hostile actions against me they were to open fire without regard to me because being overrun must be avoided under all circumstances.

The men should also open fire if I gave the signal for it from over there. Meanwhile it was a peaceful intention by the enemy so I did not want to neglect the opportunity of studying the enemy position and especially the earthworks also for once during the day and to study it exactly.

As I swung over the parapet and followed a laborious crossing through the wire entanglements – the same had been thoroughly shot up for a long time, but I did not allow the enemy to notice anything of it – I also saw two men from the left wing of the company approach the Red Cross flag. It was *Unteroffiziers* Riesner and Stotz. We arrived together approximately 100 meters in front of our position and stopped as one French medical soldier gave a sign with his hand. I also waved to him that he should approach. Hereupon he gave a signal to the rear and now 4 men with 2 stretchers appeared. They now came toward us more and I asked them in French for the purpose of their advance.

The medical soldier replied that they wanted to fetch some badly wounded men in the foreground that were helpless since yesterday morning and were groaning loudly. I gave my consent to this and granted a short ceasefire, whereupon we shook hands at which opportunity I expressed my respect to the enemy medical soldier about his way of acting and said to him that he could have already done this yesterday where we would also not have treated him differently despite the day long fighting. He might now tell his comrades that the *Boches* are completely different than Barbarians. While the French rescued 5 badly wounded men I looked about in detail and made useful observations. Of course I was especially interested in the earthworks in front of our nose. After the French went back into their positions again we also went back into our trench, enriched with extremely valuable observations. The fighting gradually picked up again.[15]

Another attack took place against Mametz and once again the French were able to break through the line. At 7 a.m. several enemy waves attacked RIR 111 and Reserve *Jäger* Bn 14. The assault was broken by rifle and machine gun fire but the French did have some momentary success. A machine gun positioned by the 6/R111 jammed at the outset of the attack. This allowed the French to penetrate into a communication trench that led toward Mametz.

When the attackers entered the German line they threatened the rear of the *Jägers*. Two flanking companies changed front to face the new threat and opened fire, trapping the French between them.

The French were pressed back traverse by traverse with hand grenades. During the fighting the 6/R111 reported the French artillery was shelling their own men causing even more losses. Finally, when the French had been pushed back as far as possible a *Fähnrich* shouted '*a bas les armes*' and as a result 2 officers and 160 men surrendered.

The French finally realized that their attempts had failed. There were no further attacks but their artillery continued to shell the German lines. During a search of the trenches RIR 111 discovered 60 French soldiers taking refuge in the trenches of the I Battalion; they were quickly rounded up and taken to the rear.

What of the position? What the artillery had not destroyed the weather had. The trenches were in terrible condition, in some cases completely leveled. The defenders had no protection from the dampness coming up from below or snow and rain penetrating from above. The men were exhausted from the fighting in the last four days. Many were buried in the shallow dug-outs as they collapsed from the shelling and poor weather. Men were being dug out of the mud everywhere.

While repairs were started on the trenches and wire entanglements and fresh reserves were brought forward the senior commanders realized that the French attacks demonstrated a critical weakness of the German line. The front line had to be held at all costs as there were no other defensive lines further to the rear. The plans to create a second and third line had to be implemented with all possible haste in order to prevent a future disaster from occurring.

Christmas inside a dug-out, RIR 109. (*Das Reserve-Infanterie-Regiment Nr. 109 im Weltkrieg 1914 bis 1918*)

The first Christmas in the field

Christmas was quickly approaching but just how would the French behave on this Holy day? Considering the recent fighting was there the possibility of an attack? In the words of one man, 'would the Frog disturb the holiday?'[16] These were some of the questions on the minds of the men in the XIV Reserve Corps. Another less worrisome problem facing the Corps was the massive amount of mail, gifts and packages that were causing great strain on the field post office. It could barely keep up with the huge volume.

The issue of how Christmas would be observed was left up to the individual regimental commanders. Many things were taken into account, in particular the activities of the enemy at the different parts of the front. It was a somber holiday for the parts of RIR 111 in the front line. When the men placed Christmas lights along the parapet of the trenches the French fired off Very pistols. The glow from the burning flares illuminated the gruesome battlefield in front of the regiment with the distorted bodies of French soldiers killed only a short time before. Only the parts of the regiment occupying warm billets in Longueval were able to celebrate the holiday. They enjoyed a religious service, good food and decorated Christmas trees while the regimental band played holiday music. The men had time to look back at the last four months of the war and took note of the many friends who were not present to celebrate the holidays with them. RIR 111 had lost 24 Officers, 390 Other Ranks killed; 43 Officers, 1,377 Other Ranks wounded for a total of 1,834 officers and men lost since the start of the war.

In RIR 109 only the 2/R109 celebrated the holiday as this company was in the rear in rest billets. The rest of the regiment would not hold any celebrations according to orders issued on 24 December:

> The actions of the enemy allow us to recognize his intentions as to also attempt an attack upon Fricourt. Therefore no Christmas celebrations can take place; rather the further extension of the position is to be worked on nonstop. Hopefully we will be able to celebrate our beautiful festival next time.[17]

Friends and family from home had sent thousands of packages and letters to men in the regiments. Each day wagons arrived piled to overflowing. It was probably the hardest Christmas of the war for the men in the Corps. The men's hearts were not yet dulled from the fighting and many had the hope that they would be home by next Christmas sitting around with their family and telling stories of the war to their children. Many thoughts wandered to home and family and the men temporarily forgot that they were standing in water up to their ankles.

For the men standing in the trenches the weather had improved dramatically and the skies turned clear and the rain stopped. Men in RIR 109 heard singing coming from the French trenches, otherwise there was silence everywhere. On Christmas day sentries noticed several French soldiers waving white cloths on rifles in front of the regiment. It appeared the French were trying to achieve a Christmas truce.

Several men from RIR 109 accompanied by *Jägers* went up to the French line under a flag of truce in order to trade cigars and Christmas pastries. When the senior commands learned of the unofficial truce they were apparently not upset about the fraternization.

Afterward monotonous rifle fire started along the entire line and by evening the French started a lively artillery bombardment. Three men were killed and one man was wounded on this first Christmas of the war. The wounded man died several days later.

The men in RIR 40 anxiously anticipated the approaching holiday, wondering how the French would react. On the morning of 24 December a heavy bombardment began on the sector of the 26th Reserve Division north of the regiment. By the afternoon the firing diminished and then ceased all together. This had prevented the 40th Reserve from celebrating the holiday but the men were still in a contented mood with thoughts of home and missing comrades.

However they were very disappointed that most of the gifts, Christmas delicacies and mail that had been sent from home had not been distributed due to the recent fighting. Despite this the night was quiet and the weather turned cold and dry. They lit candles on small evergreens and along the parapet. However when flares illuminated No Man's Land it proved to be a grisly sight, with sickly white bodies of fallen Frenchmen lying in heaps in grotesque positions with contorted and twisted limbs.

On Christmas day frost glittered upon the trees in Bazentin le Petit Wood in the morning light. The men celebrated the holiday quietly in their dug-outs while sentries manned the line. There was sporadic French machine gun fire and two French artillery rounds were fired into Mametz from the direction of Bouillon Wood, otherwise it was a quiet day. The silence was described as being almost unbearable. Once each company was relieved the men celebrated Christmas in the rear.

Reserve *Jäger* Bn 14 found that recent events had left little time to prepare for Christmas celebrations. When the battalion was relieved the men rushed to spruce up their quarters. Uniforms and equipment were placed in good order and makeshift decorations were set up.

The battalion received a large amount of gifts and packages from home that helped to add some joy to the celebration. They covered small Christmas trees with candles and decorations and many thoughts turned to home and family. The Christmas mood was shaken when news arrived that the active unit, *Jäger* Bn 14, had suffered huge losses in heavy fighting at the *Buckenkopf* in the Vosges.

'Attack' on a Bundt cake, NCOs, RIR 110. (Author's collection)

In the weeks before Christmas hundreds of packages, gifts and letters arrived daily at the 26th Reserve Division. They came from friends and family and from anonymous civilians, the Red Cross and officers' wives. The division provided Christmas trees, larger ones for the rest quarters, smaller ones for the dug-outs.

> I can really use the sausage and cheese in the trench, but it must not always be Camembert, Swiss or any other Allgauer cheese would also suffice. I have not yet received the cognac. When I have the opportunity I will send you the metal flask I received from H. Backer. *Kriegsfreiwilliger* Karl Losch, 3/R119 [18]

Despite the appearance of Christmas in the trenches many men were simply not in the mood to celebrate. They were worried about their families at home having enough to eat, worrying about the prospect of death at the front. However wine and Christmas folk songs from the trenches and dug-outs soon lifted their spirits. While they had been told to expect a French attack, for most of the regiments it was a relatively quiet time.

The number and size of the letters from home for RIR 99 had increased daily in the weeks before Christmas. In addition each battalion was given 800 Marks to use to buy supplies for their celebration. Huge amounts of gifts and packages arrived including a large crate of presents sent from the Strasbourg streetcar conductors that was divided evenly among the men.

Warm cardigans were sent from Westphalia, as well as wool, chocolate, cakes, smoking items from the officers' wives and from anonymous friends. The men who received gifts and letters shared with those who did not. One group of men who held their officer in such high esteem ordered a large pie from Cambrai with his name on it.

The rear areas were covered with small firs. Most were cut down and distributed among the men and candle decorations were purchased from the small shops in the villages. When darkness fell gifts were exchanged and Christmas songs sounded everywhere. One man rode to battalion headquarters where he came through the doorway wearing a white sheepskin coat carrying a barn lantern, sack and fir in his arms. His field grey cap and pistol on his belt testified to his true profession. His long beard reminded everyone of Armourer Weg. He distributed presents, provided cheerful verses and spoke seriously about distant loved ones, of German festivities and many of the rough looking men around him had tears in their eyes.

The sentries in the sapheads had been instructed to maintain a watchful eye for the French because it was expected that they would make Christmas as disagreeable as possible. No attack occurred but as Silent Night was being sung in the church in Beaumont it was accompanied by the crash of 'rum jars' when the enemy artillery joined in. The church fell apart under the shellfire and ambulances carried the casualties of the first war Christmas to Bapaume. Many were wounded and a few killed.

The men of one battalion of RIR 99 had sent some Christmas cheer home of their own. In October 1914 a fund had been set up that taxed cigars and smoking items. The money was used to provide assistance to the families of men who needed it most. By Christmas the battalion was able to send 1,300 Marks to Germany where it was distributed. This brightened the lives of many families according to the letters the men later received.

The highlights of trench life in the holiday season for the men of IR 180 were the presents from home sent by family and friends and the Red Cross. On Christmas Eve

The *Granathof* near La Boisselle. (Author's collection)

each battalion held a banquet that included sauerkraut, smoked meats, cheese, potato salad, pastries and mulled wine.

The French apparently believed that the Germans held drinking parties at this time of year and that everyone would be inebriated. On the evening of 25 December the 12/180 fired at a French patrol and a severely wounded prisoner was brought in. Before he died he told his captors that his mission was to determine if the Germans were celebrating and were drunk.

> At Christmas time we let the French rest a little; I still have not come under rifle fire (it seems they also shoot so many bullets around the head) however under shell fire, against that one is completely powerless. Now it is getting better again, however the entrenching and guard duty with frost and night.... [are] our permanent tasks.
> Karl Losch, 3/R119 [19]

The regiment that had the worst Christmas in the Corps was RIR 120. The men had been anticipating the festive holiday as best they could under the trying circumstances at La Boisselle. Letters and packages from home were piling up. Plans for small celebrations were under way when everything was thrown into turmoil.

The 'Granathof'

The only permanent success made by the French on 17 December was the occupation of the cemetery of La Boisselle. The village of La Boisselle jutted out of the line and was overlooked by the French on three sides. There were two smaller positions that extended even further towards the enemy; the La Boisselle cemetery and the adjoining farmstead known as the *Granathof* by the German defenders. The *Granathof* was a small French farm with several outbuildings surrounded by a wall that stood on a hill just outside of the village limits. The position had little strategic value to either side but over time it had turned into a point of honor that must be held at all cost.

In the weeks prior to the December attacks the French had been sapping closer toward the cemetery and the *Granathof*. The German artillery did not have sufficient ammunition to stop the work and by early December the enemy was within 15 meters of the German trenches. Two companies from RIR 120 held the cemetery and the *Granathof*. These companies were in a precarious position. German marksmen occasionally hit one of the French soldiers while they were digging but still could not prevent them from sapping closer and closer.

The defenders used the strong cellars of the *Granathof* as their headquarters and occupied a semi-circular trench that surrounded the cemetery. The trenches in the cemetery sometimes ran over the boards of coffins. The men had to be very careful not to make any noise with the French so close by as any disturbance usually resulted in shellfire.

When stationed in the cemetery they utilized the civilian monuments to the dead. Many were in the shape of small houses with a door over every grave. The men called these impromptu shelters doghouses. Generally two men would rest inside of the doghouse with their knees pulled up to their chins due to a lack of space. The third member of the group would be outside on guard duty. After a period of two hours the man on guard would pull a string attached to the finger of the next man scheduled for guard duty and they would silently exchange places.

The defenders of the cemetery and the *Granathof* were under constant fire and several improvised weapons were developed to assist in the defense of the position. One invention consisted of a catapult using a flexible plank of wood. A box was filled with broken bottles, nails, splinters and an explosive charge. When the catapult was fired the box would both sail across and explode inside the French trenches or as in many cases fall off of the plank and explode inside the German trench. In either instance the explosion threw the debris at friend and foe alike.

Probably the most effective weapon was a makeshift trench mortar. An empty shrapnel shell was mounted on a base and used as a mortar to fire beer bottles filled with glass, nails, metal splinters and an explosive charge. The French response when these bottle mortars were fired indicated that they were effective.

The French finally pushed their advance post to within 3 meters of the German line. One night they attempted to capture the cemetery position. The defenders were on alert and stopped the attack before the French soldiers could completely leave their trench.

> The French pushed their advanced post up to 10 feet from ours and one night they went over the top with the intention of taking the cemetery away from us. We were prepared, however and they were surprised to find the place alive with our men. We sent them back without much trouble, but they had heavy losses as they had been careless and thought that only a few men were in the cemetery whereas a whole company was stationed there. One of their officers clad in the new light blue uniform dropped halfway between us and the French outpost and we decided to get him in as we had never seen that uniform before and wanted to know what it was all about. The

Granathof trenches, 6/R120. (Brian Ludwig)

next night was dark and stormy when one man went out and fastened a rope under the dead man's arms. As they tried to pull him over, a hand-grenade sailed into the trench. This was repeated every time the rope was pulled tight, then the other end of the rope started to disappear over the edge of the trench. One man hung on to it and another threw a hand-grenade, whereupon the pulling stopped. The French had been just as wise as we and had tied the officer on his legs. There followed the most dangerous tug of war I had ever heard of, with hand-grenades as the means of stopping the pulling for a short while. This thing only came to an end much later when the Frenchman's leg was actually pulled out and the rest of the body pulled into our trench. It was an awful mess. Hans Ludwig, 6/R120 [20]

The cemetery position became too difficult to hold and RIR 120 was ordered to abandon the trench and use the windows in the cellars of the *Granathof* as sentry posts. French troops quickly took over the abandoned German position during the attacks made on 17 December.

At noon on 24 December the headquarters of the 26th Reserve Division received a report that the enemy had attacked the projecting point at La Boisselle. Parts of the *118e, 62e* and *64e Régiment d'Infanterie* had attacked the *Granathof* from the cemetery of La Boisselle. Thousands of shells were fired at the village and the *Granathof* prior to the attack.

Forty thousand shells fell on our regiment, more than two-thirds of which came down on the three companies holding the forward positions near the *Granathof.* I slept during the morning as I had been on guard all night and was too tired to wake

Granathof trenches, 6/R120. (Brian Ludwig)

up even if all hell was breaking loose. About half our dug-out collapsed around noon and this woke me up. The first thing I thought was that I was on a boat on the ocean. I crawled out and saw nothing but dust and smoke. Shells were exploding all around and when I asked someone what was going on I couldn't hear myself talk. But he knew what I meant and he pointed towards the machine gun, which was firing steadily. I stuck my rifle through the slit of a shield and immediately received an awful wallop on the cheek with the butt of my rifle. I tried to pull it back out but it would not go and after I pulled down the shield and everything else I saw that the front part of my nice rifle was all bent up like a pretzel. Either something had hit it or I had stuck it in the mud without knowing it, which could have also caused it to split open.

I looked for a new rifle but was stopped on the left by shells dropping regularly as if controlled by a clock. It would have been suicide to pass through that barrage twice. I then remembered an old communication trench which we had barricaded and which once connected the cemetery with the trenches we were now holding. I jumped over the sandbag barricade and proceeded on my stomach. About 20 yards out and coming around a corner, I spied a Frenchmen kneeling down with his rifle all set ready to shoot. I knew I was cooked unless I could get him first. He must have seen me. In order to get back I had to climb over the sandbags, offering a fine target, but I knew this and had my little Mauser ready. As quickly as I could I faced him and let go with three shots. He was still sitting there motionless like a statue, so I must have killed him. But when I reached the spot I realized that he must have been dead at least a full day. He was cold and his hands gripped the rifle. My object was that rifle but he held on so tightly that I could not move it. My position was none too rosy but I had to have a rifle before the real fun started. I took the dagger which we all carried in our boots and cut the muscles controlling the fingers. Then I had a rifle and plenty of bullets. I stuffed my pockets with them. Hans Ludwig, 6/R120 [21]

Ludwig was able to make sure the rifle was accurate by firing several bullets at a sign on the road to Albert. The men of RIR 120 fired at any Frenchman who dared to show his head while the regimental machine guns emitted a steady stream of fire in order to prevent the French from advancing.

At 4 o'clock in the afternoon the machine gun stationed near us had to cease firing; all reserve barrels had been used up from the steady firing and nothing could be gotten through the still increasing barrage. The crew took to their rifles and came with us. At 5 o'clock the barrage moved towards the center of the village where the church used to be, and the critical hour had come. 2,000 Frenchmen advanced towards the *Granathof*, meeting no resistance at all. The men of our company had left the cellars and had been out in the open and now they were either wounded or dead. The French took 10 prisoners, a fact for us to be proud of but not for them as they outnumbered us 50 to 1. They took possession of the *Granathof* and then proceeded to widen their lines to the right and left. But on the left they had to face the remainder of Companies No. 4 and 5 and on the left they advanced against my group, all that was left of Company No. 6 with a few men of No. 7. Last but not least they faced the crew of the disabled machine-gun. About 300 Frenchmen went

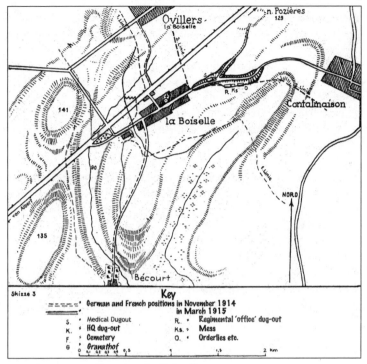

La Boisselle.

up the main street. Then the gun in the cellar of the church, which at one time scared the life out of me, started to bark in quick succession. The shells it fired had a special mixture in them and exploded not more than 200 yards after leaving the gun. Whatever of the French company did not go down or apart tried to escape to the right where they had to face our 9th Company, who turned around and pulled them in. This done, the gun started to get warmed up and spat steel and lead against the strong walls of the *Granathof*. This held the French there in check and they did not try any more to move up into the village. Hans Ludwig, 6/R120 [22]

An additional account of the fighting was made part of the citation for bravery of Karl Metzger, 8/R120:

On 24 December 1914 the French attacked the position of Reserve Infantry Regiment 120 at La Boisselle with strong forces – French divisions against weak Swabian battalions, but their attack was shattered by Swabian bravery. A small detachment at the left wing of the 8th Company was under the leadership of *Unteroffizier* Walker; amongst them was also *Wehrmann* Karl Metzger.

Although the considerable superiority of the enemy that was advancing against the left wing was recognized, the stout little flock made a heroic stand. Metzger especially provided his comrades a good example through his intrepidness and coolness. The well-aimed fire of this small group brought the French onrush to a halt and forced them to go back again to their old position after heavy losses. *Wehrmann* Metzger received the Württemberg Gold Military Merit Medal for this action.[23]

The French advance was brought to a halt in the combined fire from rifles, machine guns and from the artillery piece that had been positioned inside the ruins of the church. The French kept up a steady pressure despite the heavy fire and continued to send small groups against different parts of the German lines trying to locate any weak points. During the fighting the remnants of the 6/R120 were forced to withdraw after having been outflanked.

> Once we got into a jam. We were outflanked and had to retreat about 20 yards and leave the useless machine gun behind. But when a few Frenchmen began to pull on the gun one of our machine gunners went wild, jumped over towards his gun and slammed his rifle down on the fellow nearest him who folded up like a pocket knife. We could not very well leave that one man do all of the work alone and followed him, all with bayonets fixed with the exception of myself. I used my little Mauser, which was excellent in hand-to-hand fighting. The French, never very fond of the German bayonets, retreated in haste and the day was saved. They tried it once more but most of them went down and the rest retreated into the cellars of the *Granathof*. Hans Ludwig, 6/R120 [24]

The French had successfully taken the *Granathof* and 43 prisoners fell into their hands. The 5th and 8/R120 in the trench at the tip of La Boisselle successfully held their line with help from the 4th, 6th, 7th and 9/R120.

Regimental Armourers and damaged weapons – RIR 120. (Author's collection)

Later in the evening the French attacks ceased and the men of RIR 120 set about to prepare new trenches to defend La Boisselle.

We were dead tired and our eyes were inflamed from the gases of the shells and cartridges we had fired all day long. French shells falling into the *Granathof* before

21cm heavy howitzer, Kirchhofmulde, Grandcourt. (*Die 26. Reserve Division 1914-1918*)

Granathof cellars, 6/R120. (Brian Ludwig)

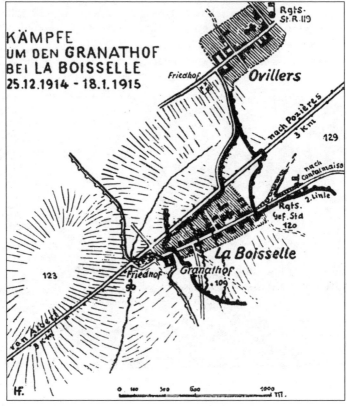

La Boisselle – *Granathof.*

they advanced had set the buildings on fire, and we could overlook very plainly the field in front of us. Half of us were digging and the other half were still sniping at every Frenchman who dared show himself. The French had no connection between the cemetery and the *Granathof* and had put out a line of workers to dig a trench. But here came new barrels for the machine guns and death again reaped a rich harvest. I do not think even one of them escaped. Just then I was on sniping duty and could see by the light of the burning *Granathof.* The French artillery left us alone as we were too close to their own line.

Around midnight I went down to dig in the new trench and must have swung my pick for about 15 minutes when suddenly something swished past us followed by a terrific explosion. All of the snipers were down in the trench, draped all over the place like rag dolls. They did not know whether they had jumped or been kicked. All they saw was a big red flame shooting out from the ground. While we were conversing about what this new thing could be, another swish and another explosion came together, this time closer. We thought that this was the end of it all, but here was another one covering us with dirt. The smoke drifting over the trench was black. We grinned at each other because these were some of the jealously preserved shells from our 21cm howitzers and these were brutes, in my estimation the worst things ever used in trench warfare. One came darn close and up went a green flare to tell

Infantry company – RIR 120. (Author's collection)

them so. The next one nearly took my breath away when it sailed past as we were standing up. Then we got enough courage together to peek out and look when they landed. Unconsciously we pulled our heads in when the next one came but we were up again with the explosion and a cruel spectacle revealed itself to our eyes. There in the cemetery, illuminated by the flickering light of the *Granathof*, a sheet of flame shot up, throwing monuments, crosses and also powerless French infantrymen into the air, rotating their bodies like the wings of a windmill. We turned away and did not want to see any more. One man reminded us it was Christmas Eve or already Christmas Day. It was the first time that we celebrated this holiday in the trenches and what a celebration it was.

Not more than 10 shots were fired by our artillery and then everything was quiet. We stopped digging and with the exception of two men sat down in the dark trench, the fire in the *Granathof* sometimes painting grotesque figures on the opposite wall. Not a word was spoken and the quietness reminded us of the few hours of this Christmas Eve which had brought so much misery for so many here in La Boisselle, more back home and also over in the French lines and in their homes. Hans Ludwig, 6/R120 [24]

The French made further attempts to expand their gains on 25 and 26 December but without success. The loss of this small and unimportant part of the line was considered a court-martial offense and had to be re-captured at all costs.

For men such as Hans Ludwig and his comrades the fighting appeared to be over for the time being. They were among the fortunate ones who were being sent to the rear for some rest, and given their mental and physical state is was long overdue.

We were fagged out and did not know we were sitting in the icy water accumulating on the bottom of the trench. Around 3 o'clock in the morning an officer came, and the first thing he asked was for us to remain seated which was unnecessary as we could not have gotten up for anybody. He asked several questions but we had nothing to say. We did not yet realize the importance of our work. He turned to one man who

Zur frommen Erinnerung
im Gebete an
Anton Elsäßer
geboren am 13. Juni 1887,
gefallen am 24. Dezember 1914 auf
dem Felde der Ehre bei La Boiselle.

Unteroffizier Anton Elsässer, 5/R120 listed as MIA on 24 December 1914 at
La Boisselle. His status was later listed as KIA. (Author's collection)

was sitting in an awkward position and asked him if he was wounded but received
no answer and when he looked closer he found this man was fast asleep. He then
whispered with the corporal who told us then that we were to get a great surprise.
Before daylight we were to be relieved by a company from [Reserve] Regiment 119
who were coming over from Ovillers. Two of our men went back with the officer to
bring that company up to us.

They found the company already waiting in the dug-outs near the entrance into
La Boisselle and shortly afterwards we explained as much as there was to explain.
Their faces showed uneasiness when we told them that they had Frenchmen right in
front of them, on the right and also on the left but when I told one corporal that he
also had Frenchmen in the rear I had to have this confirmed by my corporal as this
man would not believe it and thought I was crazy. They had been in a quiet position
since September 1914 and their losses were one slightly wounded man and a few sick.
The sudden change to the hell of the *Granathof* was too much for them. They had
heard and seen the Frenchmen trying to smoke us out. They had witnessed from a
safe distance the fury of the French artillery hammering away at our trenches and
did not expect anybody to live through this.[25]

The men made their way back to Pozières where they could finally rest after their
long ordeal.

Our progress was very slow, and only after about an hour did we reach Regimental
Headquarters. The night was passing and it was nearly daylight, so instead of being
questioned we were not delayed and ordered to return to Pozières for a good rest.
A trench had been built by the other division leading along the road back into
Contalmaison but we were in too great a hurry to get back before daylight and
climbed out. The bullets whistling around us failed to make an impression. We
reached Pozières at 8 o'clock and went to sleep immediately on a bed of straw on
the floor of a half-wrecked house. We didn't even unhook our belts we were so used

Communication trench to the 4/R120. (Author's collection)

to being dressed up. We had not slept very long when we were roused by one man hollering murder. He had fallen asleep smoking a cigar which dropped out of his hand and now the straw underneath him and the seat of his trousers were on fire. We put it out by dumping a barrel of water on it and then went to sleep again.

Some society back home had sent a barrel of wine for the Christmas celebration and in the afternoon the 17 of us went down the road to drink our share of it. Needless to say we were soon cooked and happy. Without food for a whole day and with our nerves gone, a few glasses made us dizzy and again I slept all through the night. In the morning a shell cracked down on the road in front of the house, another on went into a pile of manure in the backyard. A third one committed suicide in a barrel of rainwater in the same place, splashing the water all over creation. In about 3/5 of a second we were all assembled in the cellar just as a shrapnel [sic] came in through one wall of our one-room apartment and departed through the other one, leaving a perfect air circulation system with room for improvements. Other shells fell into Pozières and we came up again, leaving the badly frightened clerks in the cellar.

After our time in La Boisselle, our appearance had changed so much that the day before when we first entered this holy of holies, a clerk, who never was in a more dangerous place than his office, asked if one of the volunteers had survived. He was looking straight at a man who had been in the same class at school with him for two years. A fine looking bunch of soldiers we must have been, but at least we did not need a shave because we were all too young to be bothered with facial hair.[27]

XIV Reserve Corps headquarters issued orders that the *Granathof* be retaken at once and these orders ruined any possibility of a Christmas celebration in RIR 120. On 26 December, just before the first counter-attack, *Oberstleutnant* Fromm, II/180, replaced *Oberstleutnant* Neumann, the commander of RIR 120. Neumann had reportedly been replaced due to illness but the actual reasons need to be reviewed.

Before all of the events that occurred at La Boisselle in December 1914 Neumann felt that the village of La Boisselle was not defensible. The village thrust out into the enemy lines that surrounded it on three sides from ground that also dominated it. Neumann felt that in position warfare the village of La Boisselle was not worth the effort in holding it.

He sent his superiors a written proposal that La Boisselle should be evacuated and the line should be moved to a new position southwest of Pozières. The new line would have a better field of fire over a foreground area that was similar to a glacis of a fort.

However this idea had some serious problems. No position had been prepared beforehand. It only existed as a sketch on a map. No troops were available to construct it due to the large movement of men to the East. Neumann was also ignoring the price to be paid for the moral effect of abandoning La Boisselle after the army reports had made special mention of the attention directed to the village by friend and foe.

Another crucial issue was the tactical consideration that the advantage the German army expected to gain from the new position would be very little considering that the village with all of its trenches, dug-outs and other facilities would be very close to the new German front. This would offer many advantages to the French when they took over the position.

The hills of Albert would still dominate the new position by Pozières as they had before at La Boisselle. If the lines were withdrawn then the flank by Ovillers would become as untenable as La Boisselle had become. If Ovillers fell or was abandoned then the village of Thiepval would be threatened as well. Thiepval was the key to the position that the

6/R120 after the fighting on 24 December 1914. (Brian Ludwig)

French intended to capture since September. If Thiepval was taken the French artillery could dominate the terrain for a considerable distance to the southeast, east and northeast.

The memorandum sent by Neumann strained the relationship he had with his superiors because they had felt that any implied weakness, any withdrawal, must be avenged aggressively. This seemed to demand the impossible of RIR 120. However Neumann considered all of the casualties caused in its defense as futile and pointless and his ideas slowly gained ground among the officers and men in the regiment.

When Fromm took command on 26 December he too wanted to abandon La Boisselle but instead of withdrawing toward Pozières he felt that the Regiment should go forward and take the heights in front of the village. The high command recognized the pluck and dash of his idea but lacked the manpower to attempt it. His idea would only remain a dream.

The first attempt to recapture the *Granathof* was planned to take place the very night Fromm assumed command. The attack would take place in the early morning hours of 27 December with elements from RIR 120 and the 2nd Reserve and 4/Pioneer Bn 13. *Pionier* Friedrich Frey, 2R/Pioneer Bn 13, provided an account of the attack:

> At 11.30 at night on December 26th we were advised by *Leutnant* Eberhard that we should make ourselves ready for the attack upon the *Granathof* at 6 o'clock the next morning, and that the French had occupied it on December 24th. We therefore brought our affairs in order and saw to our hand grenades, each man was supplied with two apiece. On the next morning we were awakened at 6 o'clock and moved off into our position opposite the *Granathof*. It was a dark but starry night. Our group consisted of eight men and one *Gefreiter* as the group leader. Furthermore *Leutnant* Eberhard was with us.
>
> When we had all taken our positions and we had fixed bayonets the artillery led the storm with heavy mortar fire at 7.30 in the morning. Afterward the heavy *minenwerfer* fired and it was eerie watching this heavy colossus climbing into the air and seeing it fall down again over there. One could follow their trajectory exactly since you could see the glowing fuze. The trench mortar bombs exploded with a terrible crash and generated such an atmospheric pressure that they numbed our heads on this side, approximately 60 meters distant. This entire prelude lasted for only 10 minutes. Then finally the order came: 'Pioneers advance to the storm!' I had already built sortie steps out of sandbags beforehand and had already helped *Leutnant* Eberhard first when he shouted. Then Bühler, Geiwitz, Schauffler and a few volunteer infantrymen and I followed. It had begun with two companies of infantry in the attack.
>
> We immediately rushed off, *Leutnant* Eberhard first; I was on the left of him, Bühler on the right. After approximately 20 steps *Leutnant* Eberhard shouted: 'Oh, I'm hit!' and sank down in front. He still urged us forward: 'further comrades, on them, on them!' then I heard nothing more from him. Bühler jumped along toward him and brought him back and afterward came back to us again and shouted that the *Leutnant* was only slightly wounded, which unfortunately was not true. In the meantime I stormed further with my comrades and luckily we arrived over there in front of the enemy position.
>
> Fortunately there were not any obstacles because neither the French nor we could put such up because of the close distance (60 meters). I knelt down in front

of a low wall between two loopholes and threw my hand grenades. I had, beside the two that belonged to me, still carried forward 2 auxiliary hand grenades into the position, which I attempted to ignite with the matches. This did not happen because the fuze was wet. I tried using my gas lighter and succeeded in lighting the fuze. I had thrown all four away over the wall into the French trench and heard them explode with a loud noise. There was a breach in the wall on the right of me and we five (3 pioneers, 2 infantrymen) took cover there in front of the French trench and fired. We had to wait for reinforcements because we were too few. Suddenly Bühler, who was already by the wall, screamed: 'I have been hit!' I crawled towards him, and he had a gunshot wound in the upper arm. I wanted to take him back but he said he could crawl back. Now there was a heap of straw on the right of the breach directly in front of the wall and the thought went through me like lightning that I could smoke out the Frogs. I had to leave my cover with a spring and luckily made it.

The gas lighter was out and igniting it was the work of an instant. With it the enemy bullets whistled around my head like mad and the terrible rattling dazed me. However marvelously I remained spared. I only got off with a light grazing shot on the left upper arm. Unfortunately the straw pile would not burn because it was very wet yet I attempted to light it twice. Anyhow the French had doused it with water. I now had to go back into the gap – I suddenly received fire from above. When I looked up I saw a Frog standing above me with a cloud of smoke from his rifle. I aimed at him and suddenly there was a blow and something clinked past by my head. As I saw afterward a Frenchman had fired and hit the middle of my fixed bayonet; this bullet was meant for my head and I thanked God that he guarded me so wonderfully. Now I crawled over to Bühler again to see him. However he was no longer there.

Eberhard
Leutn. in der 2. Ref.-Pionier-Komp.
XIII. A.-K. gef. am 27. Dez. 1914
bei la Boisselle

Leutnant Konstantin Eberhard
(Dollenhof) 2R/Pioneer Bn 13. Killed
in action 27 December 1914 at La
Boisselle. (*Kriegstagbuch aus Schwaben*)

Neininger
Hauptmann im Pionierbataillon 13,
gefallen am 27. Dezember 1914
bei La Boisselle

Hauptmann Julius Neininger (Stuttgart)
Pioneer Bn 13. Killed in action
27 December 1914 at La Boisselle.
(*Kriegstagbuch aus Schwaben*)

I imagine that he either crept back or the Frenchmen moved over there during the mad firing at me. I now received six spherical hand grenades from the rear from *Hauptmann* Neininger that I naturally immediately conveyed further, the first thrown at the Frog in his trench. He was not very pleased by it because his fire lessened somewhat. Unfortunately I was only alone with Geiwitz at the gap because Bühler and Schauffler were either wounded or dead and we had received no reinforcements from the rear. A few volunteer infantrymen stoutly held out with us. All at once orders came through from the right: 'Stop, everyone slowly withdraw' and so we jumped back from shell hole to shell hole. The Frenchmen were firing at us but nevertheless did not dare to follow. When we were in our position again we found that *Leutnant* Eberhard would probably die. And indeed, after one hour he was dead. Honor his memory.

Thank God I was unwounded except for a slight grazing shot on the left upper arm that I only noticed afterward. I received the Iron Cross II Class for my participation in this assault along with several more comrades and wear this award in the proud awareness that I had placed my life above all else for my much-loved Fatherland.

From my companion Frey I found out that Pionier Bühler was missing, *Pionier* (*Fahnenjunker*) Schauffler was severely wounded and died. *Leutnant der Reserve* Tochtermann, who had penetrated into the *Granathof* with two groups from the company, was severely wounded along with two *Unteroffizier* and two pioneers. The attack had failed, probably because the infantry was not promptly put in.[28]

RIR 120 now made a request for additional pioneer troops and on 29 December two companies of Bavarian pioneers arrived. The pioneer officers arrived on 28 December and explored the position in order to determine what they could suggest in order to improve the defenses. They decided to develop the existing line into a virtual fortress. Nothing was to interfere with making La Boisselle as secure as possible. Transport horses now traveled to La Boisselle carrying entrenching tools, wood, wire, sandbags, everything possible needed to improve the lines. Supplies and food could only be brought up at night because the Pozières-La Boisselle road was under French observation.

While in the cemetery and *Granathof*, we were excused from any kind of work. After returning to our own trenches we again carried bundles of barbed wire, trench tools and steel posts twisted like cork screws for a new and better barbed wire defense. All this material was dumped during the nights at the entrance into the village, where the wagons bringing it by way of Contalmaison were protected by the barricades during unloading. If possible, the drivers turned their carts over and left as fast as the horses could go.

The successful unloading of these wagons gave our officers the idea that our field kitchens could come up to La Boisselle and keep the men from going to Contalmaison for their food. This would save considerable time and everybody would be ready if an emergency should arise. The first night they tried it was a mess. Supply wagons and field kitchens of twelve companies crammed in a narrow space, and in between were about 200 men trying to get food. In spite of the efforts of the officers, the

Ruins of La Boisselle. (Author's collection)

noise must have reached the ears of the French and a few direct hits caused heavy losses. That was the end of the La Boisselle food deliveries.[29]

The pioneers and infantry worked day and night to create a fortified La Boisselle despite strong French artillery fire. During all of this work the men of RIR 120 could clearly hear the French mining under the ground in La Boisselle.

Karl Metzger sent a letter home to his friends describing the recent events at La Boisselle:

La Boisselle (Northern France) 30 December 1914
I start this time with the words that if our needs are very great next time then God help us. You have received the last two letters I sent and in the meantime Christmas has come. Unfortunately we were not able to enjoy it and my prediction was not fulfilled when I parted on 4 August and said 'until Christmas when we will be home again'. The words 'Peace on Earth' are still far in the future. I will only share with you that we received unceasingly heavy, dreadful shell fire from heavy and light guns on 24 December (Christmas Eve) from 8 o'clock in the morning until 11 o'clock at night on our position in La Boisselle and we actually did not know when the meager cover over our heads would be destroyed. At exactly 11 o'clock the enemy fire was placed further to the rear and the enemy attacked with greatly superior strength. However they found us prepared. We stood in the enemy fire four long hours and my comrades on the right and left fell and the snow was stained red with the blood of faithful German soldiers. The French were everywhere. However after a long and stubborn fight we knocked them back again to their old positions despite their tenfold superiority in strength. Only the victory was very costly for us. 24 December 1914 was very difficult and bloody for us and none of us believed that we would still be alive by the evening. You would not believe at all how depressed I and the other

survivors are. We have become very nervous because we have taken part in so much in the last days; in eight days we have not had more than 15 hours of sleep and then at night at the listening posts with the cold, many of the positions not more than 80 meters from the enemy line. However we do not let our courage sink because we trust in God and we have still come away with our lives. Unfortunately the position of the 5th Company was partly lost to the French, we stood in the enemy fire until evening and many asked what the night would bring because our ranks had been so severely thinned and if the Frenchmen had known how few of us there still were I believe it would have gone badly for us. The night proceeded generally quiet but Christmas morning broke with heavy enemy shellfire again but there was no attack. On the other hand orders came from the division commander General von Soden at 10 a.m. that the 8th and the remnants of the 5th Companies RIR 120 were to be replaced for a few days because of their brave stand in the position at La Boisselle and because of the number of losses. What a shout when this became known by the Company. So we were relieved at 7 o'clock in the evening on Christmas Day by the 9th and 10th Companies RIR 119 and we went back to Pozières. However our rest did not last long. When we arrived at that place we received our Christmas packages towards evening and wanted to unwrap them, then came the terrible order: 'The company will immediately make ready', a French attack was expected at the front in La Boisselle. And so we went forth immediately at the quick march, through a communication trench that was filled with water and snow and half-destroyed and that had been buried. The water was up past our knees but it did not matter at all, we went forward into the position and stood sentry with wet clothes so that our coats froze on us like a stiff boot. We stood guard like this until the morning and

Scene of La Boisselle. The city of Albert (marked by + +) can be seen
to the left of the ruined building. (Author's collection)

then went back to Pozières again. God was thanked and praised; now we could have a good sleep again and wash, because we looked like savages and the horrors of the last terrible days were on every face. Unfortunately I must report to you that Heinrich Siber from Grosssachsenheim has probably been taken prisoner, hopefully he was not killed during the assault on the *Granathof. Pionier* Karl Haug, a carpenter from Kleinsachsenheim was killed; also *Hauptmann* Neininger of the pioneers has fallen at the *Granathof.* I will close now in the hope of a quick peace and that this bloodshed ends quickly. I will remember this Christmas as Long as I live. Goodbye and Heartfelt greetings, Karl.[30]

Elsewhere on the front there was a general silence during the last week of the year. The only activity on New Year's Eve occurred when the French artillery fired a single salvo upon Hill 110. Otherwise the day was marked with songs and humorous shouts all along the line. The first year of the war had come to an end.

Chapter Notes
1. H. Ludwig, Manuscript, 6th Company RIR 120, p. 14.
2. III *Abteilung* RFAR 26 consisted of 3 batteries of 10.5 cm. light field howitzers, each battery contained 4 guns.
3. 'AZ' = *Aufschlag Zünder* (Percussion Fuze).
4. Ludwig, op. cit., pp. 14-15.
5. E. Bachelin, *Das Reserve Infanterie Regiment Nr. 111 im Weltkrieg 1914 bis 1918*, p. 52.
6. W. Gallion, *Das Reserve-Infanterie-Regiment Nr. 40 im Weltkrieg,* p. 52.
7. Bachelin, op. cit., pp. 48-49.
8. Auxiliary trench weapons included *Minenwerfers*, rifle grenades, *Erdmörsers*, etc.
9. Ludwig, op. cit., pp. 15-16.
10. Greiner, *Reserve-Infanterie-Regiment Nr. 110 im Weltkrieg 1914-1918,* p. 62.
11. Gallion, op. cit., p. 53.
12. Ibid.
13. Ibid.
14. Greiner, op. cit., pp. 63-64.
15. Gallion, op. cit., p. 55.
16. Gallion, op. cit., p. 56.
17. G. Frisch, *Das Reserve-Infanterie-Regiment Nr. 109 im Weltkrieg 1914 bis 1918*, p. 41.
18. Losch, Karl, *Kriegsfreiwilliger* 3/R119. *Feldpost* letters 1915-1916, letter dated 11 January 1915.
19. Losch, op cit, *Feldpost* letter dated 5 January 1915.
20. Ludwig, op. cit., pp. 12-13.
21. Ludwig, op. cit., pp. 16-17.
22. Ludwig, op. cit., p. 17.
23. K. Metzger, *Vom Weltkrieg 1914/18. Selbsterlebnisse eines Frontsoldaten,* pp. 8-9.
24. Ludwig, op. cit., pp. 18-19.
25. Ibid.
26. Ludwig, op. cit., p. 19.
27. Ludwig, op. cit., pp. 19-20.
28. L. Knies, *Das Württembergische Pionier Bataillon Nr. 13 im Weltkrieg 1914-1918*, pp. 72-73.

29. Ludwig, op. cit., p. 13.
30. Metzger, op. cit., pp. 35-36. *Gefreiter* Heinrich Siber was later reported as being taken prisoner. Württemberg *Verlustlisten* No. 314, 4 December 1915.

5

January – March 1915

It was the start of a new year, the war had already lasted far longer than many had expected and there was no sign of it ending soon. 1914 had ended in rain and storms, 1915 began with rain and storms. January proved to be a very wet month that caused the trenches and roads to require a great deal of restoration work. The men complained that the sun set too quickly and that the wet fog bothered their throats. Slimy mud still gurgled under their boots and there was a terrible humidity in many of the dug-outs. The Somme was generally an unpleasant place to be.

The prolonged rainy weather had made much of the work done on the position worthless as trench walls collapsed and trenches filled with mud. The men would often wade in water knee deep and had a difficult time getting dry afterward. The mud became so bad by the second week of January that many parts of the trenches were virtually impassable. On 8 January the artillery observation officer in the sector of the III/180 was trying to get to his post. He ended up becoming stuck in the mud and clay up to his stomach and several men had to dig him out when he was unable to free himself.

The position by Montauban held by RIR 40 almost became untenable due to the bad weather as it was constantly under water. A new line was started that was 150 meters closer to the French but until it was finished the old water-filled trench still had to be occupied. Communications and traffic between the different groups holding the waterlogged trench could only be maintained by the use of floating boards.

The common enemy – mud! IR 180. (Author's collection)

Playing *Skat* in the trenches, RIR 121. (Author's collection)

The shallow dug-outs did not offer much help during the first winter of the war. Water dripped constantly from the ceilings while cold air penetrated every corner from poorly connected joints. They were dark, dank holes in the earth for the most part.

> I really could use the candles, because I don't know what to do without light in the cellar or in our dug-outs, it's not too bright even on days when it is clear as a bell. It is not any less pleasant in the trenches with the winter countryside, white fields everywhere, but they normally do not last very long. Karl Losch, 3/R119 [1]

Trench stoves did provide some comfort however and the health of the men was good thanks in part to the distribution of woolen underclothes, deliveries of tea and occasionally mulled wine as well as plentiful food. Some regiments were fortunate to receive special treats. In the case of the men of RIR 120 they received a *Laugenbretzel* each Sunday in addition to their normal rations.

> We have gotten an Afghan from the company in December. I have warm under-clothing, head protection and mittens I have still not used… So far I have remained quite spared from head colds and coughs until now; it is easy to come down with diarrhea from the preserved food and the damp straw ground. Chocolate helps splendidly to prevent it. I received cigars, some pastries, old rum, balaclava (I have never had it on), braces and this stationery from the Red Cross. Karl Losch, 3/R119 [2]

Sketch of entrance to La Boisselle with village well, RIR 120. (Author's collection)

The weather began to improve by 10 January and by February nature had already made a reappearance when snowdrops and daisies bloomed on the slopes of the hills. When spring finally arrived, life in the trenches became more bearable and the position acquired a more pleasing look.

> Presently we have very dry cold (however not too cold) weather. In part we have also installed stoves in our shelters; however they are not necessary now because it is not so cold, and we keep each other warm, in that we (mostly 3 together in a hole) lie quite closely together if we do not stand guard. Tonight I have also gone out on a patrol against the enemy, three of us, out about 300m in front of our position, but saw nothing of the French. On 27th January we picked up a volunteer, who had been sent a small camera. However the pictures are very small and they are developed in Stuttgart so therefore it will still be some time until I could send you a photograph … The day before yesterday we had the most beautiful spring weather, yesterday sunshine and today thawing. On the other hand there is standing guard and observing in the moonlit nights. Karl Losch, 3/R119 [3]

Drinking and washing water was still very scarce on the Somme front. The wells in many of the villages had been rendered useless by French fire. However there was always plenty of rainwater mixed in with the mud. It came flowing into the village in streams into the trenches and low lying places and stood knee deep in many areas but it was useless for drinking.

One group of men in the 4th Battery II/RFAR 29 had acquired a bathtub and carried it to their quarters where the men were able to take a hot bath. The tub was placed in a room that had three walls; a French shell had removed the fourth wall so there was no problem with ventilation according to *Gefreiter* Siegele. Siegele had written home to

Barm-
herziger
Jesus
gib

seiner
Seele die
ewige
Ruhe !

Zur frommen Erinnerung
im hl. Gebet an
an unsern lb. unverg. Sohn und Bruder
Mathias Epp,
Moosbeuren,
geb. den 28. Dezember 1888,
gefallen den 16. Februar 1915
in Thiepval.

Matthias Epp 6/RFAR 26. Killed in action 16 February 1915 at Thiepval. (Author's collection)

explain to his family just how dirty he was after spending 8 days without changing his uniform or being able to wash. They had the appearance of being pulled out of a mud hole so the idea of a warm bath and fresh clothing was a welcome relief.

The early trenches were a dangerous place to be. There were daily losses caused from random fire due to the poorly constructed trenches and on most occasions it was simply a matter of luck whether a soldier became a casualty on any given day. The fighting in 1914 had shown that many times the casualties could be traced back to the leadership. The trenches were not deep enough; traverses not wide enough and the older dug-outs that existed provided virtually no protection against French fire. Karl Losch described what it was like under French fire in Ovillers:

Yesterday was a Sunday again. Our bells tolling at 10 o'clock were cannon thunder and bursting shells. It was a beautiful bright day. Naturally the French made use of it as their pilots circled over our position and transmitted targets through signals to their artillery - our trenches including the dug-outs. So it went the throughout the day until 6 p.m. From 10-11 a.m. it was very severe; then a shell came every 5-10 minutes that almost always smashed into the same hole not far away from us. The French acted similarly at other positions. We sat or lay all day in our dug-out on a piece of ground, often not talking to each other, then tried to sleep or listen to the roaring and whistling of the shells. Sometimes we discussed where that shell had burst or that dud had driven in. The tut rrr-schtschschsch-klatsch (shell exploding with a great crash) or rrrtschschsch-bum (the shell has not burst, it has driven into soft ground, they are called duds). Then there is still the blow out that is when the explosives were driven out without splitting the casing of the shell. The duds are not dangerous in general but later with unskilled handling, as for example when a farmer later plows the field and jostles one it can still explode. There are 2 or 3 that have driven into the ground on the left of our cover and have thrown earth into the trench. We remained preserved from other losses. Further up on the right of us, a shell burst near a dug-out but not through the ceiling, however it buried the entrance. Fortunately nobody was in there. The dug-outs are covered with wood to make them

The result of a French shell – 1 cubic meter of earth, stone and a tree blown into the trench – and the men who had to remove it - RIR 121. (Author's collection)

more resistant; if by chance a shell burst just about the middle of the dug-out or penetrated through the ceiling then everyone was finished. God save us from this.[4]

New orders were issued in January that attempted to address these issues. All dug-outs would be at least 2.5 meters under ground; all parados were to be given a width of 5 meters.[5] Trench walls were to be covered with wickerwork and fascines and duckboards were to be put into place on the trench floor.

Still, even with many of these improvements the trenches could prove to be quite dangerous.

In the morning, one day, I was standing [watch] on the step next to the company commander's dug-out. My rifle had a scope on the top. They only handed them out to about 8 people in the company. *Scharfschütze*, they called that – snipers. They had put some steel plates with an opening there and you could only get the barrel of the rifle through.

The *Leutnant* had a cook – Keller was his name, a real tall guy. He was a Reservist. Well, he came out (of the dug-out) and said, 'Emil, can I look out?' I said, 'Sure, why not.' He went there to look and got shot in the throat. It could have been me. I have always thought that. Emil Goebelbecker, 9/R109 [6]

The gunners in RFAR 29 had already begun to create dug-outs by each battery that exceeded the minimum requirements issued by the XIV Reserve Corps.

Yesterday evening the French fired into our position so that one could believe that no one could have walked away. However we fortunately have very big dug-outs, where altogether no projectile could penetrate. 4-5 meters of earth were placed over these dug-outs. Our position could no longer be seen because of all the smoke. During the day it is generally quiet because aircraft fly around them. If one would fire then our position would be betrayed immediately. A pilot dropped 6 bombs at us a half hour ago. However this was without success because they all landed in a garden. Rudolf Siegele, 4/RFAR 29 [7]

The men quickly became aware of the need for deeper, well-constructed dug-outs when the French began using large caliber guns to bombard the German lines.

One day when we were sitting in our cellar, a big shell coming from a naval gun on rails selected our front yard as its final resting place, giving up the ghost with an explosion which threw us together like pins in a bowling alley. Others followed at short intervals. This was getting serious and for the first time in that war we scratched our heads, knowing very well that one hit was enough to relieve us from our earthly miseries. It would take us months to complete adequate protection against this new weapon if it could be done at all.

The first explosion had torn down the canvas which served as a door and we could see the half round impression of the shell in the mud for a distance of about ten feet ending in a huge crater. It must have slid along the ground before it exploded. We were now huddled together on each side of the entrance to escape the splinters which could come in through the open door. The dizzy druggist sat with his back against the brick wall facing the *Granathof*, from which direction the shells were coming. Then he came hurdling through the cellar to our side for no good reason at all, as far as we could see. He insisted that somebody or something had pushed him. An examination of the place where he had been sitting proved that one of the big ones had dug down into the ground outside the cellar, pushing out a section of the brick wall about 3 inches. If that baby had gone off we all would have been hash.

Another one smashed in the entrance and still another threw a whole mass into the entrance closing it permanently. All our efforts to clear this entrance were in vain and we stopped when we saw a dud among the bricks which could go off when touched.

The bombardment went on. Once in a while, when the air pressure from a close one would make our ears hurt, we would suspiciously eye the dud in our former entrance. All the shells seemed to fall within a short area around or on one side of our cellar between the house and the main road. We could not hear many explosions on the other side of the cellar which faced the trench.

Another one slammed a ton of junk on our entrance and we were faced with the alternative of either suffocating or getting cut up into chopped beef while trying to clear the entrance. Even if we succeeded in doing this without mishap, the first step out would have been sure death. We got worried then and after much talking started to tunnel out of the cellar through the wall opposite the entrance, where the trench was 20 feet away and only a few scattered shells were falling. We worked like wild men and after about ten feet had cut into the corner of the grave of the 16 men we had buried there a month earlier. The odor was terrible and the moral effect was not so good either for our badly shaken nerves. In view of the fact that we had to get out and every minute counted we agreed to keep on working. One man worked with the shovel, frequently relieved, and the other cleared the dirt away, storing it in the corners of the cellar.

After three hours work we hit the trench and daylight and also air and in this trench we saw a fragment of one of the heavy ones. These were about 3 feet long and 9 inches in diameter, with a 3-inch wall on each side and only 3 inches of room for the TNT. This kind of shell is designed to wreck fortifications. What chance would we have had if one of these had landed on our cellar? Hans Ludwig, 6/R120 [8]

Some areas of the front were simply more dangerous than others and only if the sentries and the trench garrison were constantly alert could the men prevent unnecessary losses:

One of our double sentries was posted in a hole about ten feet square alongside the ruins of a house. This corner was one of the favorite targets of a battery of French 75's. They would send over four shells, wait an hour or two and then another quartet would come over. We had lost a dozen men by the time we got to know the direction from whence the shells came. One of the two men on guard always watched in that direction, and as soon as he saw four flashes in rapid succession, the two on guard would go down into the hole as fast as humanly possible. You could not believe how fast this folding up can be done unless you actually saw or had to do it yourself. The shells or shrapnels [sic], whatever they fancied to send over, would be on top of us a fraction of a second after the flashes were seen. After these shrapnels [sic] had spat out their load of lead marbles, we were up again and watching. Once when I was on duty on that spot my friend pulled me down, as he was so excited he could not call me. When we were down on our stomachs, four shells exploded in the house, sending bricks flying in all directions. Glad this was over, we got up again but had a surprise waiting for us. They sent over a double portion and just when we were again upright the second load was on top of us. They were shrapnel [sic] this time, and were clattering all around us. The ruins of the house again received the bulk of the missiles, and this time we took our time getting up. It felt like about five minutes but I am sure we were not down more than 20 seconds. The rest of the watch passed quietly, though my friend nearly had a fit when I went down to light a match to see what time it was as he thought that another present was on the way over. Hans Ludwig, 6/R120 [9]

Sometimes a man was just lucky he did not end up on a *Verlustlisten*:

The French have not forgotten us; they fire daily on our position. However our dug-outs are built solidly against shells so that no ball can penetrate them. Today a shell landed directly at my feet. Fortunately it did not explode otherwise it would have struck me. Rudolf Siegele, 4/RFAR 29 [10]

Ersatz Reservist Thomas Simmendinger 6/R111. KIA 18
February 1915 near Fricourt. (Author's collection)

The trenches had not changed very much since October 1914. The line was still not complete and the ultimate goal was a united front, Badener and Württemberger together, with an effective field of fire towards the French with wire obstacles in place that were 20 meters wide or more.

More work was needed all along the front in order to make it as secure as possible. However not every regiment completed all of the work required on the trenches they occupied. These shortcomings were brought to light when the regiments began to be transferred to different sectors of the front.

When RIR 111 took over the front between La Boisselle and Fricourt the men discovered that the trenches were lacking enough dug-outs to house two full companies. These men were required to stay in billets in the rear during the day and come up each night to construct them.

When RIR 109 occupied the Mametz sector formerly held by RIR 40 and RIR 110 the men complained that almost nothing was found in its proper place. The positions were poorly developed; wire obstacles were weak and missing completely in many places. The dug-outs did not correspond to safety requirements so much so that during repeated bombardments several dug-outs and observation posts collapsed. The access trench was not protected against French observation or fire.

The work needed by RIR 109 to remedy these defects went slowly because all available manpower was being used to sap towards Hill 94. Due to the proximity of the French a network of saps were being driven toward the opposing line. Once completed the head of each was connected, thereby forming a new trench. A great deal of labor was needed to improve the position and it also required a similar amount of supplies to be brought up each day.

Many of the old front line trenches that were now located in the second line showed considerable effects from fighting and poor weather. They were restored to a defensible position and occupied by the reserve platoons.

The rainy weather in February and March made the ground on Hill 110 almost impassable as communication trenches filled with mud. The bearer troops carrying heavy loads of supplies were forced to move outside the trenches and across open ground resulting in unnecessary losses. A new position was created in a sunken road on Hill 110

Horse stalls near Pozières – III/RFAR 26. (Author's collection)

using the sapping method and was later named the *Pionier Graben* after its completion. Travel outside of the communication trenches was officially forbidden. Duckboards were manufactured in quantity and eventually introduced to all of the trenches. While this measure helped the situation it was not a perfect answer. Individual soldiers provided what help they could. *Pionier* Glaser, 4/Pioneer Bn 13 constructed a transfer pump that was used to remove excess water from the trenches and send it in the direction of the French lines.

The trenches on the eastern slope of the high ridge north of Fricourt were too far from the French, there was almost 1 kilometer between opposing lines. The heights were reached by sapping toward the French trenches. The Germans were then able to provide greater fire effect against the French trenches and any activity in the hollow east of Bécourt could be taken under fire.

The right flank of the 28th Reserve Division was still separated from the left flank of the 26th Reserve Division near La Boisselle by a gap that was only protected by wire obstacles and sentries. The French were constantly working closer toward La Boisselle and this represented a danger to the right wing of the 28th Reserve Division. If Bécourt could be taken it would have provided an ideal solution to the problem as well as reducing the length of the front line. However the memory of the disastrous events in October 1914 and lack of sufficient reserves prevented any action from being taken. Work was started to finally connect the two divisions once and for all.

The left wing of the 28th Reserve Division was exposed as well where a gap from 300-400 meters opened up to the *Lehmgrubenhöhe* and the neighboring division. Sentries and wire entanglements provided some protection for this gap. The *Lehmgrubenhöhe* was one of the most unpleasant spots in the line. The position was very exposed to the effects of bad weather and was subject to numerous artillery fire raids.

Construction in the *Lehmgruben* was completely pointless in the wet winter weather. A special trench had to be constructed around the position. Saps 100 meters in length were driven forward; the heads of each were connected forming a new trench. The process was then repeated from the new line until the desired position had been reached. By the beginning of March *Lehmgrubenhöhe* was in the uncontested possession of RIR 111.

The new lines that had been constructed had to be carefully planned beforehand in order to prevent them from coming under enemy fire from Hill 110. The trenches were first drawn on maps; then the parados and trench line was outlined with white tape laid down at night. Patrols were sent out into No Man's Land as protection for the fatigue parties digging out the new line. New communication trenches continued to be constructed to reduce casualties among the men carrying supplies from the rear on a journey that might be 8 kilometers or more each night. They would also allow reserves to come up safely during times of need or being able to exit from a battle if the situation required it

Many of the new communication trenches were being equipped with fire steps and sortie steps in order that they could be easily defended or exited if required. New trenches were constructed in a zigzag method that helped to reduce the effect of French artillery fire. An officer was assigned to each sector as the Communication Trench officer. His sole responsibility was to oversee the construction and maintenance of the communication trenches in his area. All of the trenches were eventually given names so that the men would be less confused when using them. It was common to leave the Communication Trench Officer behind during a relief in order to maintain the continuity of trench construction and maintenance with each new unit.

One particularly important route to the front ran along the Fricourt-Contalmaison road to Foureaux Wood and needed to be free from French observation. New communication trenches were constructed along this route that satisfied this need. Dug-outs were installed for the communication trench sentries and runners and the trench was covered with a belt of wire entanglements and fitted with fire steps and loopholes for defense. It became used as a switch trench and could be used to hold the enemy in check in the event of a breakthrough through as well as a staging area for flanking counterattacks. The most important of the switch trenches was called the *Sigelgraben* that led toward Foureaux Wood; it was named after the former leader of the 5/R111.

The French were able to observe the work on the new trenches and they attempted to disrupt the work with rifle, machine gun and artillery fire. Light rockets and spotlights from the vicinity of Albert would light up the night in order to illuminate any movement and RIR 111 suffered many casualties before the work was completed.

French artillery fire caused losses along the entire front as well as damage to the newly-created positions. It was quickly found that using wicker, fascines and wood to cover the trench walls was not as useful as had been expected. When the trenches became damaged by artillery fire these materials became obstacles in their own right more often than not. Orders were issued to leave the trench walls uncovered whenever possible.

The number of protected sentry posts increased along the front. These positions were often covered with railway rails and provided good locations for observing the French. The relatively few machine guns allocated to each regiment needed to be situated as favorably as possible in order to take advantage of their firepower. The ideal location would allow the guns to bring effective flanking fire against any enemy attack.

Real benefits came with each improvement in the line. The frequent French artillery fire raids caused less damage to the deep, well-constructed trenches than on the less developed approach routes leading from the rear. The more the lines were developed the fewer troops were needed to man them. Every regiment could now institute a regular

German trench near Ovillers – IR 180. (Author's collection)

system of battalion relief. This normally meant that one battalion would hold the front while the second battalion would be positioned nearby in reserve while the third battalion was quartered further to the rear at rest. The time spent in the front line was substantially reduced with these changes.

Despite the improvements made along the front there was still a difficulty in supplying the front with all necessary requirements while under fire. In order to correct these problems small ammunition depots, hand grenade warehouses and stocks of iron rations were positioned in the dug-outs along the front so there would be no shortages of critical items in a crucial moment.

Additional dressing stations were placed at key locations in each regimental sector. Dug-outs were placed in each company sector so that a medical officer and stretcher-bearers could be accommodated. Each medical dug-out or dressing station was equipped with all of the necessary materials, medicine, beds and bandages and could provide help for the wounded in the fastest possible time. It was no longer necessary to wait until darkness had fallen in order to carry the wounded over the open ground and through obstacles.

Many men felt unusually safe while they were in a trench as generally no shells fell near them. This was especially true in instances of foggy mornings. Both the French and Germans used the cover of fog to work outside the trenches during daylight hours that normally could only be done at night. The infantry did not fire in order not to provoke the opposing side. The artillery did not fire because of lack of observation.

Trench with mined dug-out entrance – RIR 110. (*Reserve-Infanterie Regiment Nr. 110 im Weltkrieg 1914-1918*)

However the fog could be treacherous if a gust of wind suddenly blew it away unexpectedly. Woe to those who did not get into the trench quickly enough, many paid dearly with their lives for their slow reaction.

Marksmen were feared on both sides of the wire. The French were very alert and always caused losses whenever possible. One of the most dangerous areas of the front was on the left of the *Granatloch* near Thiepval where enemy marksmen killed several soldiers. It was not until a man coming from rear saw that if you stood outside the trench on a comparatively dark night or in the fog a man could be seen by the French silhouetted against the sky. At another point in the *Granatloch* a steel shield placed upon the parapet was still not enough protection against French fire. After two men had been killed it was discovered that if the sun shone through the observation opening and then went dark it meant that someone was standing behind the shield.

Additional rifles with telescopic sights started to be issued by mid-March to the regiments in the XIV Reserve Corps. In addition to marksmen fixed rifles were fired at regular intervals in order to disrupt any enemy movement and were placed to cover known traffic routes.

Herring cans, wooden hammers and other items were often held high over the trench edges to serve as makeshift targets for the marksmen. Successful hits were applauded and misses were signaled as if in peacetime. This ended when enemy marksmen killed one Group leader and another man from the 2/R40 that were engaged in this activity.

Bringing food and other supplies to the front line held more dangers than just enemy fire. *Unteroffizier* Schultz, 2/R40:

A special detachment was getting the food and materials. No access trench existed there and they had to go over open fields. In order to orient the food carriers on their return from the field kitchens the water carrier fastened a small lantern at the place to slide down over the edge of the trench. On one unkind evening War Volunteer 'B' was also assigned as a food carrier. The small lantern could not be affixed. During the return Comrade 'B' went with the others along the trench edge and called out 'can one enter here?', one of the trench sentries answered 'it is only just a drain'. Upon that 'B' let himself slide down into the trench; however oh woe, instead of sliding into the trench our comrade slid into the latrine that had been thrown up in the course of the evening by the pioneers until he was underneath it up to his arms. Under general grinning the pitiful man had to be extricated out of his helpless situation. Because of his fair smell he got his own 'dug-out' in order to take off his clothes that were skillfully taken back to Flers to be boiled but hopefully not in the field kitchen. 'B' remained like a hermit in underpants and slippers in his earthen hole up to the time of the relief that followed after a few days.[11]

There were also times when danger was more imaginary than real. Hans Ludwig related the following about guiding a replacement company into the trenches at La Boisselle at 2 o'clock in the afternoon in early 1915:

One man standing at the entrance of a dug-out handed cigars to every one of us. I did not smoke but stuck one between my lips anyhow to be sociable. We were forced to use the trench going to La Boisselle as it was not yet night and we had to be careful with the men entrusted into our care. They trusted us and knew that we would take no unnecessary chances.

This darn trench was so narrow at the top that we had to pull like truck horses to get our packs through and the ground was wet and muddy. In several places a shell had filled up the trench and there we had to caution the men to be careful and bend down low as we were moving parallel with the French trenches and they could see every careless move we made. Once they spotted a troop movement we would have been in hot water.

About halfway out, the man ahead of me let out a yell, turned around and tried to push me back which could not be done as two more old-timers were following me. Before we jumped out of the trench we wanted to know what it was all about. The man was all out of breath and stuttered 'hand grenade'. We knew that no hand grenade could be thrown here and besides this, if one had been thrown it would have exploded long ago. So we looked at the thing and found reposing in the muck the tobacco bag of our corporal. He had climbed out of our trench and moved up from the rear to the front of the company and while walking overhead had lost his tobacco pouch, which looked more like an anarchist bomb than a hand grenade. We had a good laugh and went on to the dug-outs near Headquarters in La Boisselle without heavy losses.

Well-constructed trench near Thiepval. (Lawrence Brown)

Once inside the dug-out I wanted to take a drink from my canteen and only then realized that on my way through the trench I had chewed up that cigar and swallowed it hook, line and sinker. Seasickness must be a pleasure compared with the way I then felt. I stuck my finger down my throat and recovered the biggest part of the cigar but still felt like a house on fire. I drained the contents of my canteen which contained wine and not water as it should have. Besides being sick I now also was drunk, but luckily the wine would not stay down and it again came up with the rest of the cigar.[12]

However the ever-present dangers still existed. Later the same day Ludwig was ordered to take 20 men into the trenches:

It was then just twilight as far as I could see from the dug-out but once outside I saw right away that it was still too light. I turned around to see if all my men were following me and then faced the *Granathof*. That same minute, the air pressure from an exploding shell knocked me down face first. My helmet protected my head but the heavy pack was slammed against the back of my neck and for a short time I was knocked stiff. Two of the 20 men had been killed and three wounded. The fallen men were quickly gathered in by doctors and orderlies from headquarters. The neighborhood still looked foggy to me but I was revived quickly and after inspecting myself found that outside of a small piece of steel in my finger I only had a large

Food carriers – RIR 121. (*Das Württembergische Reserve-Infanterie-Regiment Nr. 121 im Weltkrieg 1914-1918*)

lump rising where my pack had struck its knockout blow. This pack had saved my life as it was full of splinters.[13]

Artillery fire was also very dangerous if the food carriers left too early in the evening and despite orders to the contrary left the safety of the communication trenches to travel overland. The French often fired at the men assigned to assist the field kitchens and wagons in the evening. Many fixed positions were taken under artillery fire in the hope of catching large groups of food carriers, wagons or other carrying parties. One favorite target of the French artillery was the eastern edge of Pozières. Supply wagons waited for the shell impacts and then raced past the danger area before the next salvo could arrive.

Drivers were very agile in traveling badly damaged and rough routes at night. Rushing through shell holes occasionally caused some of the cargo to be lost. Sacks of mail, gifts or bread from wagons often fell on to the muddy ground. Many of the items were found on the following days but were rarely returned to the rightful owners as the finders viewed it as their property. The aggrieved men often complained to their officers but little could be done to alleviate the problem.

Cyclists came into the trenches each day and in the evening brought the orders of the day, mail and small purchases for the men from canteens and shops in the rear. Their arrival in trenches was expected with longing. It was a bright spot in the day for many men because even if they were not bringing something for everyone they nevertheless knew the latest piece of news or gossip. Much of their information was only rumor, greatly garbled from being passed from one mouth to another. However most had a core of truth.

If the aides of two staffs discussed something about a relief and were overheard by the cyclists it was a good bet that by evening a rumor of pending relief had spread throughout the entire regiment. Everyone was uplifted by the rumor even though they knew it might not be true. By the time the men realized they had become a victim of a rumor the cyclists or kitchen staff had already brought a new one that would make them happy once again.

The men at the front often envied the cyclists. It was accepted that they had it easy coming into the lines on dry, quiet nights, however if they carried a heavy load in a dark night, waded through mud up to their knees or laboriously working through the lines in artillery fire while bounding from cover to cover they amply atoned for the good times.

Mining began to take on a greater role on the Somme in early 1915. The two most active locations were near Beaumont north of the Ancre and at La Boisselle where the matter concerning the *Granathof* was to be decided once and for all.

The first German mine set off on the Somme north of the Ancre took place on 3 January in the minefield by Beaumont. It was a small mine by later standards, 110 kilograms of *Donarit*[14] and the resulting crater was quite small. On 17 January French artillery heavily shelled a mine tunnel entrance located by the 1/R99. At first it was thought that a traitor had given away the location of the mine entrance. Then it was realized that it was more likely that the mine spoil was being improperly disposed of. The heavy fire caused a great deal of damage to the trenches.

On 1 March observations made by the 2/R110 indicated that the French were mining opposite their position near Fricourt. The men were ordered to cease all noises so that the pioneers could listen for underground activity. Large mounds of earth being thrown up in the French lines also provided confirmation of mining activity. On 19 March the French exploded their first mine under the *Jägerstellung* providing the ultimate verification that the French were starting to mine in the area of Fricourt.

Listening galleries were driven forward toward the French positions near Fricourt while three mine tunnels were started on Hill 110, numbered from right to left I, II and III. The 2R/Pioneer Bn 13 supervised the mining while the infantry performed the work.

Württemberg *Radfahr Kompagnie* 2, XIV Reserve Corps. (Author's collection)

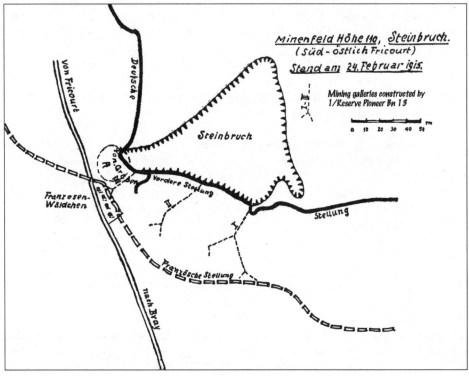

Mining on Hill 110.

The three tunnels were used as attack dug-outs until they had reached French lines and were prepared for detonation.

In an attempt to disrupt French mining activity Mortar Battery Ewers was ordered to fire 60 rounds against the suspected mine position and nearby trenches. The bombardment was successful in damaging the lines but later observations indicated that the mining continued.

The sound of underground activity could be clearly heard In La Boisselle by the Bavarian Pioneer listening posts in late December 1914. It was believed that the French were digging a mine tunnel from under the ruins of the *Granathof* toward the German trenches and something needed to be done about it. At the same time RIR 120 and the pioneers from Pioneer Bn 13 and the Bavarian Pioneer Regiment were also mining under the French trenches at the *Granathof*. It was only a matter of which side would finish first.

> I was to go on duty at midnight together with a non-com and had time to look around. Near the left wing of our company I discovered a hole from which pioneers brought one bag of dirt after the other, carefully distributing the contents all along the line in shell holes if possible. I finally learned that they were digging a tunnel with the intention of mining underneath the cellars of the *Granathof*, blowing that place up as soon as possible. Hans Ludwig, 6/R120 [15]

Miners near Beaumont – RIR 121. (*Das Württembergische Reserve-Infanterie-Regiment Nr. 121 im Weltkrieg 1914-1918*)

The men were kept to their usual routine until 2 January, the date the mine was set to go off. The companies positioned close to the *Granathof* were ordered to withdraw into the trenches of neighboring companies in order to prevent unnecessary casualties from the blast. The mine was detonated at the scheduled time but there was little commotion. They expected a reprisal from the French artillery but it did not take place. It was not until the men returned to their trenches that they discovered the reason for the lack of any French response.

The bird who laid the direction of the tunnel must have been drunk; instead of blowing up the cellars of the *Granathof*, these darned fools had blown up the left wing trenches of our company and the French lines were not damaged at all. But one result became known very quickly. The French smelled trouble and started mining too, but they were amateurs like we were and made a worse job of it than we had done.

One nice afternoon we heard a lot of noise over in the French trenches and then the ground was shaking and out of the French trench came flying dirt, smoke and French soldiers. Their explosives had not been set right and the whole thing had blown backwards instead of upward. In the meantime one of our own mines was ready again and we expected to go to hell this time as long as our pioneers had missed us the first time. The shaking and rocking of the ground was stronger this time and all of the damage done was a big hole between the two lines. Again they missed the cellars.

During the following night the French decided to occupy the hole left by the explosion, as they had also dug emergency dug-outs into the walls of the crater, hand grenades were useless. So we had to try our mine thrower which by that time had been improved and was throwing captured Belgian shells. A few of them went off; most of them did not. The few that did explode were too much for the fellows sitting in the hole. They tried to climb out but were held in check by rifle fire. They had to give up and come over as prisoners. The next night some of our men volunteered to stay in the hole during the following day but when French 75's dropped into the hole they dropped out and the following night we filled the bottom of the hole with barbed wire and this place of dispute remained unoccupied by either side after this. Hans Ludwig, 6/R120 [16]

The 'Granathof'

The *Granathof* had become the main focus of concern for Reserve Infantry Brigade 52 and RIR 120 that occupied La Boisselle. The *Granathof* buildings no longer had any roofs; perforated walls and a few rafters were all that remained of the once prosperous farm. However the *Granathof* still had large shellproof cellars and it was believed picked French marksmen, *Chasseur Alpins*, were occupying these cellars.

The French marksmen were a constant source of aggravation to the men of RIR 120 holding the line near La Boisselle and made the trenches a dangerous place to be. Karl Metzger, 8/R120:

> On 26 January 1915 I stood on sentry in the position of La Boisselle, in the vicinity of the cemetery. The day was bright and clear and light snow lay upon the fields. The French position lay only 100-150 meters distant from us. At 4 o'clock in the afternoon my comrade Gustav relieved me. During the relief I said to him: 'Gustav, it went well for me today, the cursed Frenchman, the shooter behind there shot damned accurately today.' That chap already fired shots a few times that passed by my head by a hair's breadth, likewise he had hit the protective shield so that sparks flew from it. 'Therefore Gustav, pass it with care and especially do not smoke on guard today so you do not give away your sentry position by your rising smoke!'
>
> However my friend Gustav just laughed and said: 'Ah, Karl, you worry too much because of such nonsense, I will smoke my cheap tobacco (Hochwald brand) to my heart's content without any further concern.'
>
> Now I disappeared into the dug-out and joined my other comrades.... Our dug-outs in January 1915 were still inadequate because there were still no shell-proof mined dug-outs of 20 to 30 steps under the chalk. However we had barely become comfortable, when, all at once there was a shot and immediately following a terrible scream. We jumped out of the shelter as fast as lightning in order to see what had happened. O woe, O sorrow, our Gustav had received a terrible head shot, directly over the bridge of the nose and one eye hung from his face; a terrible sight! The Frenchman had aimed only too precisely today and had made a good shot, straight through the loophole opening in the protective shield. We brought Gustav into the sergeant's dug-out where he received first aid. We grudgingly lost him because he was a good and faithful comrade, especially when it was announced that the canteen wagon was in the sunken road. He would start off with his sack and even if there was nothing more to buy our Gustav still succeeded because he knew how to help himself. When he returned fully laden and with a halloo everyone received their share.
>
> After some time we received a message from him, he was in a military hospital in Germany and he is generally feeling well, only naturally his eye is gone forever.[17]

Monument to Woodrow Wilson, the neutral Christian, supplier
of French artillery shells. (*Der Schützengraben*)

The artillery batteries supporting RIR 120 were provided with a small daily allotment
of shells in response to the serious situation existing at La Boisselle. While the regiment
welcomed this support it was insignificant in comparison to the number of shells available
to the French. It was believed at the time that the French were able to obtain unlimited
numbers of shells from suppliers in neutral countries.

> Today at 4 o'clock in the afternoon shells crashed about the different batteries but
> did not do anything to our battery, but at the 5th Battery an *Unteroffizier* and a
> *Kriegsfreiwilliger* were severely wounded (head). The *Unteroffizier* has probably already
> died, and so on it bangs every day. We have noticed quite often that the French have
> a lot of ammunition from America.[18]

The French guns firing upon La Boisselle normally concentrated two-thirds of their
daily fire upon the trenches and the remainder in the vicinity of the regimental battle
headquarters making it possibly the most dangerous place in the village. The regimental
staff of RIR 120 did have the highest percentage of casualties from French fire than any
other part of the regiment.

The German artillery could only bombard the *Granathof* a few minutes each day
even with the increased allotment of shells. During these periods the marksmen would
hide inside the cellars and when the fire stopped re-emerge. An attempt was made in

early January to bombard the *Granathof* using heavy *minenwerfers* but with little effect. Attempts to fire upon the *Granathof* were hampered by the proximity of the opposing lines. Any error in firing could result in German troops being killed or wounded.

The telephone system in early 1915 in La Boisselle was insufficient for the task of providing close artillery support. The artillery observers did not have a direct line to the guns in the rear and could not make adjustments to the fire as needed. All communications between the observers and the gun crews had to be accomplished using runners. As a result of this several guns were moved up into the village at point blank range but were in exposed positions and vulnerable to French fire.

Brigade Headquarters had been pressing Fromm to attack the *Granathof* since he assumed command of RIR 120. However, Fromm felt that he did not dominate his new regiment with his will and vision and as such could not guarantee the success of an attack. He was also worried that in the event of an unsuccessful attack he would not have sufficient reserves at hand to defend the village of La Boisselle against a French counterattack.

Despite the apparent misgivings of Fromm, General von Auwärter continued to urge him to attack. There was a valid reason to attack the *Granathof* other than to satisfy a 'point of honor': to stop French mining. The situation at La Boisselle had become so serious that RIR 120 had been assigned one battalion from RIR 119 for support.

There were a number of small attacks made by RIR 120 over the next two weeks. A mine was set off on 6 January under a portion of the French line but did little damage. This was followed by a brief bombardment of the *Granathof* on 8 January followed by an infantry attack. The attack failed from the outset when French machine guns stopped the men when they had barely left the trench. A similar attack on 10 January ended with the same results.

On 10 January the French also attacked La Boisselle. At 2.50 p.m. the French set off a mine; three companies attempted to attack following the explosion but were cut down

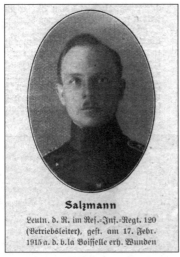

Leutnant der Reserve Walter Salzmann 6/R120. Died 17 February 1915 from wounds received at La Boisselle. (*Kriegstagbuch aus Schwaben*)

Leutnant der Landwehr Schnizer RIR 120. Died 4 June 1916 from wounds received at La Boisselle. (*Kriegstagbuch aus Schwaben*)

by the fire from the 10/R119 and 8/R120 supported by an artillery battery that flanked the French lines.

During the same day pioneer listening posts could hear sounds of French mining activity nearby. The pioneers decided to detonate their mine first. There was a flurry of activity as they made the final preparations for setting off the mine. The explosives were put into place, the electrical leads were set and the tunnel was blocked off with sandbags, timbers and earth. The work was completed and on 11 January the mine was detonated. The explosion was much larger than the pioneers had expected and their conclusion was that their mine had set off the French explosive charge as well. The French mine had been positioned some distance from the German trenches so the pioneers came to the conclusion that the French mine was intended to be used as a countermine and not against their trenches.

When the mine detonated many French soldiers were seen flying through the air from their trench and nearby shell holes. The French were apparently preparing for an attack and the explosion caught them unaware. Some of the survivors fled across open fields and were cut down in the German fire. A number of prisoners were taken including two officers. The prisoners gave their overall losses at approximately 100 men.

Karl Metzger was standing sentry when the explosion occurred:

I want to describe the following brave action that occurred in La Boisselle and that was worth placing under the nose of every Frenchman and their lies and fraud calling us barbarians will collapse miserably. It was on 11 January 1915 as we, RIR 120, 8th Company, blew up a French dug-out immediately in front of our position in La Boisselle. The mine explosion was horrible as masses of earth flew high into the air with Frenchmen in full equipment. Several different severely wounded and half-buried helpless Frenchmen lay directly in front of our sentry post after the mine explosion where my comrade Ernst Faigle from Horrheim and I stood at double sentry post. They screamed pitifully for help and indeed it would have been easy for us to deal with them once and for all.

However we said to ourselves, something happened here and we must allow our humane feelings to prevail because we only conducted war with armed might. I got our platoon leader Leutnant Winter; because I knew he could speak French.....

We wanted him to attempt to shout across to our enemies in French, because we were only 80-100 meters from each other that they should cease fire, we wanted help their severely wounded comrades who lay in front of us and rescue them. He did not think long; then he climbed onto the edge of the trench, waved his white handkerchief and called across in French about the foregoing. There, after 3-5 minutes no more shots fell on our position, it became dead silent and all at once we saw how 8-10 Frenchmen left their trench provided with picks, spades and tent-cloths and approached our position.

Now we also went out of our trenches and greeted the French soldiers in the middle of the heaviest fighting with 'Bonjour, good comrade!' How we reacted to this moment, as we, friend and foe, hand in hand looked each other in the eye. All of us had tears in our eyes and never, never in our lives have we forgotten this moment no matter if you were German or French. Now united we immediately went to the rescue of the severely wounded French, put them on tent-cloths and carried them

8/RIR 120. Man sitting second from left is Karl Metzger. The man sitting far left was his brother. Every man marked with a '+' was killed during the war. (*Vom Weltkrieg 1914/18. Selbsterlebnisse eines Frontsoldaten*)

into the closest of our medical dug-outs where they in part received their first help. They were very grateful to us as they saw they were safe. Now we could not let the Frenchmen who helped carry their comrades across from over there leave because they had entered our position and in consequence a French officer came across toward evening in order to obtain his comrades release; however we also had to take him prisoner because according to the laws of war no enemy is allowed in the position of the other with open eyes. He could only have conferred with us under a flag of truce with his eyes blindfolded. Naturally on the next day the old shooting went on again.[19]

Karl Losch and his companions had a clear view of La Boisselle from their positions in Ovillers.

And now to the 120th. That was a very windy point as a position. In the front is the *Granathof*, it is so-called because the farmyard became buried over and over with shells about Christmas time, so that the 120th could no longer hold it. It was the same with the cemetery. During the shellfire the French advanced into both positions which naturally resulted in costly fighting and from the 5th Company 50 men were captured in a communication trench that had been cut off by the French. Now our pioneers undermined the *Granathof*, in order to blow it into the air. In the cemetery mine after mine was driven in, so that the ground flew into the air under colossal coils of smoke. Simultaneously shrapnel was fired so that the French would be hit by the shrapnel balls if they crawled out of their holes still alive. I do not know if the cemetery is still occupied now. Yesterday the French tried to occupy an empty trench near the 120th; however they were thrown out by the 120th. On the left of La Boisselle the French made an attack yesterday; however it was thrown back by our

Leutnant Winter 8/R120. (*Vom Weltkrieg 1914/18. Selbsterlebnisse eines Frontsoldaten*)

artillery. You can see from the sketch how we are the furthest distance away from the French. The terrain between us and them is not suitable for an attack, however the hollow or the cemetery of Ovillers and on the right of it is good. They had already made an attack on 17 December, but were thrown back. Then Sigle became injured when he jumped inside our trench onto a bayonet. [20]

The French attempted several small attacks in the following days and each one was easily repelled. Another German mine was detonated but without any real success. The Germans tried to retake the *Granathof* on January 14th and 15th but each time the French were alerted by the preparation fire and ready for the attack. Every German attack up to this point had overestimated by far the effect of the artillery and trench mortar preparation fire. It seemed that neither side was able to gain the upper hand at La Boisselle.

At this time each company had at most one platoon in the front line while the rest of the company was in nearby cellars and in the village in reserve. This was satisfactory while the French were still hundreds if not more than a thousand meters away but not when they were barely 40 meters distant. With the French being so close the inability of bringing up reserves in a timely manner in order to meet an attack would be disastrous. The problem was how to protect the reserves and position them at the front at the same time.

This problem was solved by the use of a new concept, mined dug-outs. Two officers in RIR 120; *Hauptmann* Wider and *Oberleutnant* Doll (the latter had been an engineer

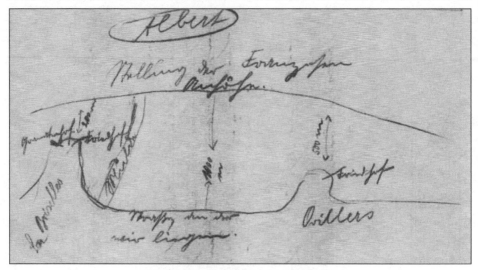

Karl Losch sketch map of La Boisselle

in the Berlin underground in civilian life) came upon the idea that instead of the light shelters cut into the trench walls they should be positioned deep under the floor of the trench, constructed in the manner of a mine. Their idea received approval and work was begun immediately.

The mined dug-outs required an immense amount of wood in their construction. Supply wagons arrived each night by the regimental headquarters dug-out and unloaded the materials needed by the men. The French artillery that normally covered this location in heavy fire each day for some reason failed to shell it at night. Therefore the supply wagons were not disturbed in their nightly work.

At first some officers and men were reluctant to undertake the amount of work required to complete the new dug-outs. But as the work continued and the losses and danger from French fire became less even the most vocal critics became enthusiastic about the task ahead. The losses to the regiment had noticeably reduced from just a few weeks earlier. The work was tedious but once finished the men could be safely quartered in the front line and available at a moment's notice. The new mined dug-outs were between 5 and 7 meters under the ground and safe from most French shells being used at the time.

The construction process included first digging a vertical tunnel deep into the ground and then enlarging the base. The wooden support structure was installed and the excavation was backfilled with earth as needed. The greatest disadvantage for this type of mined dug-out was the need for a ladder to exit or enter the dug-out. Also the dug-out could possibly become a mantrap if the French broke into the trenches.

The solution to this problem came rather quickly with the idea of building a stairway tunnel with wooden frames and steps into the ground. Each dug-out was to have two such exits. They were supplied with plank beds and mattresses, tables and chairs.

Large quantities of earth needed to be removed for each mined dug-out. The spoil needed to be carefully disposed of in order to prevent French observers from spotting the work and targeting the location with artillery fire.

Not everyone held the new mined dug-outs in high esteem. An Examining Commission visited the front in February 1915 and inspected the new dug-outs for the first time.

The structures afforded quite good protection against enemy fire however the amount of work needed in their manufacture bore no relationship to the gain that they promised.[21]

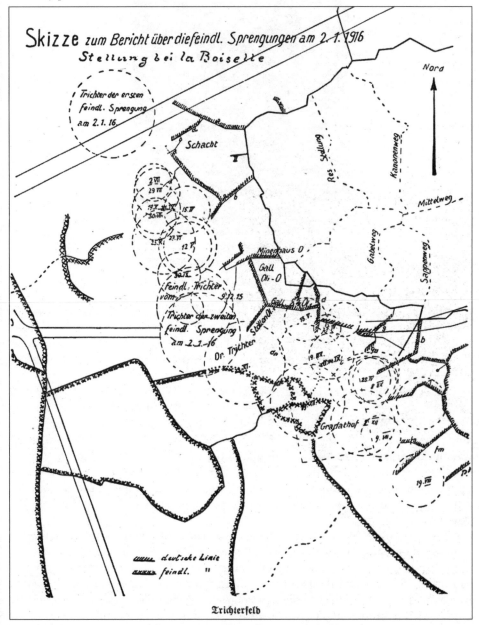

Mines near La Boisselle – *Granathof*

Infantryman – RIR 120. (Author's collection)

The findings of the commission did little to dissuade the XIV Reserve Corps from installing the new dug-outs. Special detachments were formed in each regiment and at the Pioneer depots in order to meet the growing demand for wooden frames used to create the dug-outs. Each regiment could produce approximately 40 frames per day while the Pioneer parks could deliver a further 40 to 60 frames.

In the meantime both sides undertook almost daily attacks at the *Granathof*; the only result was an increase in their casualty lists. Neither side could gain any real advantage over the other. The lines were so close together that setting up wire entanglements was almost impossible due to the diligence of the opposing sentries. Each attempt to attack was quickly discovered by alert sentries and stopped in heavy defensive fire.

Once Fromm had sufficient mined dug-outs to shelter his reserves a plan was drawn up for the final attack upon the *Granathof*. Unlike earlier attempts the attack was not designed to capture the position, instead the senior command had decided to destroy the position once and for all.

The plan called for surprise; no artillery preparation fire would be used, as the men would need to approach the French lines undetected. The attack was to take place shortly after midnight on 18 January. Four companies from RIR 120 would make the assault while the 10/R119 provided support and flanking protection. Pioneer groups that would handle the destruction of the *Granathof* position accompanied the attackers. The composite unit was designated Battalion Todtenberg after the officer in command.

The night of 17/18 January was very dark and still. The assault companies had all taken up their positions beforehand, step ladders and wooden frames were set up to allow a quick exit from the trenches. At 12.10 a.m. a flare was fired off, this was the signal for the attack to begin. The two leading companies quickly crossed the short distance separating the two lines and had gotten to within a few meters of the French trench without a shot being fired. The men quickly began to cut through the few wire obstacles or climbed over them before the first French response.

About 10 o'clock on the night of January 17th, detachments from the different companies came drifting in and half an hour later everybody was ready. The hour was set for five minutes after midnight. This gave the officers a chance to compare their watches at midnight and get back to their places in time. The signal was to be a low blast from the whistle of every officer. We could not afford to make too much noise, as our only chance of success was to surprise the enemy.

The half hour we had to wait seemed like hours to us and we were getting more nervous every minute. When the whistles were blown I was standing in the trench looking at my watch, which was as far out of the way as it could have been. In the scramble to get up the ladders, this timepiece was torn off and lost forever. On account of this I was the last one to leave the trench. When I had finally struggled clear, the first men were already entering the French trenches, only 50 yards away. I started running, when suddenly the ground gave way underneath my feet and I went down and landed on top of a corporal who had fallen into this abandoned trench ahead of me. He acted as a shock absorber for me and I had to absorb the curses from him. We got straightened out but could not get out of the trench, which was deep and narrow. I threw my rifle across the top of the trench and like a monkey started to swing my body gripping my rifle with my hands, very ably assisted by the corporal who pushed me. But a rifle is not built for performances of this kind and the two of us were again in a heap on the bottom of the trench. There was more cursing and the suggestion that he push me out and I try to pull him out afterwards. I got out, dirty beyond belief, and did my best to pull him out, but the closest we got was when he nearly pulled me back again. That guy must have weighed a ton. Along came a fellow who at the start had been hit in the cartridge belt by a bullet, which was followed by miniature explosions around his stomach. After convincing himself that he was not damaged he moved up and helped me pull the third one out of the hole. Hans Ludwig, 6/R120 [22]

The *Granathof* and adjacent cemetery position was occupied by two companies, the 7th and 8/65e *Régiment d'Infanterie*. The French sentries were quickly overpowered or killed and the attackers poured into the trenches. Most of the garrison had either been killed or taken prisoner before the defenders had time to become fully alert. Only a few men were able to escape from the *Granathof* and over 100 men and two officers were taken prisoner in the attack; a third officer was captured the following day from a nearby shell hole.

By this time most of the men had advanced towards the *Granathof* but very few had entered the cemetery. From there came a lot of noise, mixed in with some requests for some of us to come over in a hurry. We sprinted over, looking out for hidden trenches, and soon were hopelessly tangled up in all kinds of barbed wire. While busy getting the wire out of my trousers, a bullet took the tip off my helmet, but that thing was no good anyhow so I let it go.

I held on to the front half of my rifle with the bayonet on top, the other part, the butt, I had left in the trench. The next thing was a Frenchman who left a trench right in front of us and started running. As I could not shoot, I thought to hell with the trousers and started running after the guy, thereby preventing my two companions from taking a crack at him. I invited him to stop but all he did was run. Then he put his rifle underneath his armpit and started firing backwards while running. That was too funny for me and got me mad. I threw the remains of my rifle after him, taking a chance to hit him and I did hit, or better the bayonet did hit. It went into his thigh and he was out. I caught up to him and took his rifle away. For the second time in La Boisselle I had a French rifle and all this time I had my little Mauser in my pocket, like a darned fool forgetting all about it. The other two men came up and we found that the flying Frenchman was not damaged very badly. We bandaged him up in a hurry and told him to stay put until we came back for him.

The request for help from the cemetery came over very clearly and very loud. Then for the first time I noticed that our artillery was laying down a barrage in a half circle around the *Granathof* and the cemetery, thereby cutting off the French reserves. It was not later than 12:15 when the three of us entered the cemetery. There we found about five of our men trying to knock 20 Frenchmen cold. We arrived at the right moment, and, as they did not see us took the French from the rear. A few shots from us and their hands went up. One man took them back with instructions to pick up the wounded one on the way back. Hans Ludwig, 6/R120 [23]

Once in the maze of trenches another light signal was fired into the air, the request for artillery support from the field guns and light field howitzer batteries of RFAR 26. The batteries opened fire and blocked off the *Granathof* and cemetery with a wall of fire. This was a recent innovation and successfully prevented any French reinforcements from coming through the fire barrier. The French artillery remained silent during the attack, not knowing where the opposing lines were located.

We were now seven of us and went deeper into the cemetery, where hand-to-hand fighting was going on. We cleaned up quickly but could not get them out of one corner, which was strongly fortified.

About ten of us went back and went around the cemetery, jumping over the remains of the wall. The fellow with the cartridges blown off saw something in an undamaged doghouse, pulled out a hand grenade, lit the fuze, opened the door, threw the hand grenade in calmly saying 'here, divide this amongst yourselves.' He then put his foot against the weak wooden door and a moment later he went flying through the air together with the door. He was badly scratched and needed a lot of iodine and bandages but was not hurt badly. In the doghouse were three French officers who weren't in too nice a condition but we could do nothing with them until later. Once in the rear of the remaining Frenchmen, we jumped at them from both sides and took 19 more prisoners. One of them was so drunk he had to be dragged along by two other Frenchmen. Hans Ludwig, 6/R120 [24]

Some men were fortunate enough to receive a marked burial, *Feldwebel* August Maus, MG Coy/R119, killed in action 14 January 1915. (Author's collection)

Once the trench garrison had been overwhelmed the defenders taking refuge in the cellars had to be dealt with before the pioneers could begin their work. Platoon Löckle, 10/R119, attacked the French marksmen inside two undamaged cellars.

Our orders were to hold our positions until the engineers were ready with their TNT to blow up the cellar of the *Granathof*. It was not easy to enter these cellars as they were occupied by picked French snipers who were exempt from any kind of work. These brave men would not surrender. They shot through the cellar windows and cellar doors. Only after one window had been cleared and a machine gun nozzle shoved into it, it got more quiet, but these Frenchmen had to be finished with hand grenades, although we had wanted to spare them if possible. Time was limited and the engineers entered the cellars to adjust the explosives while the wounded and dead were carried out. In the meantime a small crowd of us gathered on one side of the cemetery. We continued firing at the French reserve lines through the artillery barrage making them believe we still had not reached our goal. The French reserves could not see what had happened and did not know who was in possession of the cemetery. We were not troubled by their artillery. Hans Ludwig, 6/R120 [25]

Not all of the occupants of the cellars had been killed. Platoon Löckle managed to take 21 prisoners after using hand grenades. It took time for the pioneers to place their explosive charges in the confines of the cellars and pack them with sandbags. The charges were planted so that the cellars and any mine tunnels found would be destroyed. After two hours the pioneers reported 'explosives ready'. It was time to give the signal for everyone to return to the German lines. One long blow on a whistle signaled the men to return to the German lines and in 5 minutes the *Granathof* was empty. A plunger was depressed and the cellar vaults flew into the air with a noise like thunder.

> We waited two hours – to us it looked like two weeks and then a siren howled, the signal for us to return to our trenches. We did not run, we walked back, and were still about ten yards from our trench when the TNT went off. Once more the *Granathof* was burning. The cellars were destroyed and we did not walk any more. We jumped quickly and followed the rest of the crowd into our dug-out after a good night's work. I had to stand a lot of kidding from my old friends on account of the French rifle and the missing tip of my helmet.
>
> Another company relieved us shortly afterwards and we took over their trenches in a much less dangerous position near Ovillers. Later on French prisoners told us that at the time of our attack they had considered the garrison of La Boisselle finished; the village ready to be taken away from us. Our offensive move took all the pep away from them.
>
> Our engineers had destroyed the French mine tunnels while we were waiting and we therefore had a distinct advantage. Hans Ludwig, 6/R120[26]

Afterward it was discovered that several of the charges had failed to go off and that a portion of the cellars still offered protection to small groups of soldiers. However this did not concern the men of RIR 120. The French tunnel system in the cellars had been destroyed and the danger from French mines was over for the time being. If the French wanted to mine under La Boisselle they would have to start from much further back and this would require a great deal of time and effort.

The Germans losses in the attack were 3 officers, 31 Other Ranks killed, wounded or missing. The total French losses are not known but they were estimated to be considerably higher. The attack did result in the capture of 3 officers, 104 unwounded enlisted men as well as the capture of 1 mine thrower, 1 spotlight and 2 machine guns.

The French artillery covered La Boisselle in heavy fire for eight hours after the attack was over. German losses from this fire were low, primarily due to the effectiveness of the deep dug-outs that had just been constructed. Only one dug-out had been damaged, the orderly room dug-out of the regimental headquarters. A shell penetrated into the room and exploded. The only occupant, *Leutnant der Reserve der Feld Artillerie* Hausser had both of his legs blown off and he died a few hours later. Enemy activity died down considerably afterward.

While the fighting at La Boisselle died down it was never completely over. Artillery fire on the village was a daily event but thanks to the newly-created mined dug-outs losses were quite small and life became tolerable once again.

General von Stein wrote a brief article regarding the fighting at the *Granathof*. It was picked up in a number of German newspapers and reprinted. Eventually everyone in the regiment received a copy as a souvenir. RIR 120 received the nickname 'The *Granathof* Regiment' when the fighting was over.

French prisoners captured 18 January 1915 at the *Granathof*. (*Das Württembergische Reserve-Infanterie-Regiment Nr. 120 im Weltkrieg 1914-1918*)

The French prisoners were interrogated afterward and one officer was reported to have said:

> The French II/65 had occupied the position at La Boisselle on 16 January and replaced a battalion of the 118th Regiment that needed recuperation. We already knew the position from an earlier stay in the sector. The bombardment of the *Granathof* by the German artillery had been ineffective; no heavy shells could have hit the buildings. Anyway, early on 16 January we found the cellars still undamaged, the telephones still operating. According to our beliefs the situation was so dangerous that neither side could hold it. The German attack conducted on 18 January that led to our capture demonstrated this.
>
> The churchyard and the *Granathof* were occupied by the 7th and 8/65. When the attack took place out of the German position only 40 meters distant timely support for the two companies was not possible, although the attentiveness of the sentries was not lacking. The French infantry were not very capable in bayonet fighting. The consciousness that we were physically less powerful when the Germans were so strong caused only a few of our men to have the courage to accept the bayonet attack. When they were not able to go back they therefore surrendered.[27]

The French army report on the fighting on 18 January caused everyone in RIR 120 to have a laugh:

> The enemy made a useless attempt to place itself in possession of the blockhouse of La Boisselle. We threw them back and they left 200 dead on the field of battle.[28]

Apparently the French also tried to explain the destruction of the *Granathof* as the result of the explosion of an ammunition dump from artillery fire.

Most men were buried close to where they fell. La Boisselle mass grave:
French and German dead buried together. (Author's collection)

Of La Boisselle the French tell the biggest pile of dung in their report of 19th January
(or 18th January). That was no shell but German mines, there is also no ammunition
depot existing in the hill. Karl Losch, 3/R119 [29]

The French behaved rather calmly after the attack with the exception of continued
mining activity at La Boisselle and Beaumont. The men's nerves continued to be strained
even further due to the constant fear of mine explosions. The 1/R120 attempted to end
the danger once and for all on 7 February when the company set off another mine under
the *Granathof*. It too failed to completely destroy the *Granathof* cellars or the French
mine system.

Some time after the fighting was over the regimental commander came across an
English magazine with an article on the 'Hell of La Boisselle'.

The sketch came from the French officers who conducted me through the position,
christened the Hell of La Boisselle.

The French and Germans share in the possession of the village (the French only
have possession of the forward lying *Granathof*) and the trenches are so close together
that the French in the foremost position were forced to disappear in their dug-outs
in order to escape the splinter effect of their own projectiles, as soon as the fire on
the German trenches became reported by telephone.

The village looks like a mixture of volcanic craters, the ground has become so sowed over by projectiles, and the grey-black smoke of the explosions of the superb French shells that ceaselessly smashed into the German positions make the scene look like a painting of Dante's *Inferno*.

The strategic value of the village made it an important battle objective for many months. The French have sacrificed over 2,000 men among others in the last weeks working forward to their present position.[30]

Now RIR 120 was determined more than ever to transform the village of La Boisselle into an impregnable position. In the period from late December 1914 through March 1915 more than 5,000 cartloads of pioneer materials were brought into the village and used to prepare an elaborate defensive position. After the action of the 18th RIR 120 set about constructing a new trench running north to south from the southwestern tip of the village. The work was being done so close to the new French lines that it could only be done with great caution. Most of the new trench had to be sapped.

At first the amount of supplies required to make this transformation was not clearly understood by the Pioneer parks in the rear. When RIR 120 placed an order for sandbags the regiment received an answer that 500 would be delivered. Fromm replied that they needed at least 5,000 to begin with. At the end almost 60,000 sandbags would be delivered for use in the defenses of the village. In many instances the number of wagons needed to bring up supplies had to be increased, in some cases making two trips each night to carry all of the materials required.

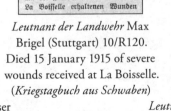

Brigel
Leutnant d. L. im Reserve-Inf.-Regt. 120 (Rechtsanwalt), gestorben am 15. Januar 1915 an den bei La Boisselle erhaltenen Wunden

Leutnant der Landwehr Max Brigel (Stuttgart) 10/R120. Died 15 January 1915 of severe wounds received at La Boisselle. (*Kriegstagbuch aus Schwaben*)

Gaiser
Leutn. d. R. i. Res.-Inf.-Regt. 120, gefallen am 18. Januar 1915 bei la Boisselle

Leutnant der Reserve Julius Gaiser (Rottweil) 12/R120. Killed in action 18 January 1915 at the *Granathof.* (*Kriegstagbuch aus Schwaben*)

Leutn. d. R. Haußer
gef. bei La Boisselle 18. 1. 1915

Leutnant der Reserve Max Hausser RIR 120. Killed in action 18 January 1915 at the *Granathof.* (*Kriegstagbuch aus Schwaben*)

With the large number of trips each night it was not long before the supply horses were fatigued to the point where they could no longer be used. The solution was to draft the artillery horses into use despite the objections of the artillery commander.

The frantic pace of construction proved to be too much of a strain on the Bavarian *Pionier Hauptmann* Theocharis. He was replaced by *Pionier Hauptmann* Kuprion, who was able to complete the task. The infantry and pioneers worked side by side, night after night to finish the work. While some worked on the trenches and strongpoints above ground an extensive mine system was also being constructed under the ground and several mines were being driven forward toward the enemy line as quickly as the conditions allowed.

The problem in the production of the immense amount of wood required was solved when a motor driven sawmill was set up at Martinpuich. Craftsmen from the regiments performed all of the work at the depots. They produced frameworks, loopholes, observation mirrors, cartridge boxes for the machine guns, road signboards, mine trucks to carry the spoil from mining operations and other items needed for the trenches. Assault bridges were constructed in large quantities and placed in each company sector ready for use. Collapsible wooden sentry posts were created. Approximately 200 candles were produced each day for each regiment.

When French trench mortar fire caused extensive damage to the trenches more concrete and mined dug-outs were constructed. Toward the end of March electric power plants were being installed to supply electricity to as many areas of the front as possible.

During the fortification of La Boisselle the village and trenches were as dangerous as they had been before the attack on 18 January despite the lack of any offensive action by either side. French artillery and machine guns fired constantly at night in order to prevent another surprise attack like the one made on the 18th. When German observers noted a large concentration of French troops near the *Granathof* the artillery fired an unusually large number of shells on this target. The French were observed strengthening

Battery horses returning to their stalls – RFAR 29. (Author's collection)

the wire entanglements on the following day, apparently in expectation of a German attack, though none was planned.

Fromm was a regular visitor to the front at La Boisselle and he toured the lines on a daily basis to view the progress being made. He would often stop to talk to the men and at night he would crawl to areas that were unsafe to visit in daylight due to French fire. He carried cigars in his bag and other small gifts that were distributed to the sentries who admonished him for taking too many risks.

Von Soden also paid weekly visits to the positions at La Boisselle where he would talk to the men and give advice where he felt it was needed. The visits made by regimental, brigade and division staff members did much to maintain the morale of the men at the front as well as providing first-hand information about the conditions at the front to the senior commanders.

The XIV Reserve Corps continued to receive a large number of visitors from Germany who wanted to see the trenches. They were unwelcome by the men who did everything in their power to make the visit as uncomfortable as possible. One of the popular methods was to take the visitor near an area where the men knew the French guns would fire at a certain time each day. While the men knew that they were safe from danger in the trench the visitor invariably felt that the shell was heading directly toward him. The actions of the soldiers did little to change this opinion; in fact, it did much to reinforce the feeling of doom experienced by the visitor. The method was successful in many cases in reducing the number and frequency of sightseers to the front line.

On 7 February the 1/R120 set off a mine near the *Granathof.* The location of the new crater was in an unfavorable position and had to be occupied immediately before the French took advantage of it. RIR 120 sent a small detachment to man the crater and the French attacked shortly afterward. 1 officer and 9 men were killed, 5 men were wounded while 19 men were able to escape and make their way back to the German lines. During the following days several more mine explosions took place in the vicinity of La Boisselle on both sides but no appreciable gains were made.

When RIR 120 was relieved from the trenches at La Boisselle the sector was taken over by RIR 119. Just as the relief ended the French attacked. At 9 a.m. on 10 March the French detonated a mine at the northeast corner of the *Granathof* and French infantry advanced through the crater against the 7/R119. The sentries were able to hold off the attackers until reinforcements arrived and then occupied the French crater. The attackers were eventually driven back to their original line.

There was a similar attack by the French on 26 March with the same results. In response to the second attack the German batteries bombarded the cemetery in the afternoon. At 5.30 p.m. another mine was set off in front of the 12/R119. It turned out to be a ruse. When the 12th Coy occupied the crater in anticipation of an attack the French set off a second mine. The resulting fallout caused numerous casualties among the men of the 12th Coy. The French attack that followed the second mine was quickly repelled using hand grenades and many of the enemy dead were observed to be wearing the new Horizon Blue uniform.

There was one last duty performed by the men of RIR 120 once the fighting around La Boisselle had died down, a debt owed to the many that had fallen.

Kaißer
Leutnant d. R. im Res.-Inf.-Regt.
120 (stud. math.), gefallen am
7. Februar 1915 bei La Boiselle

Leutnant der Reserve Karl Kaiser
(Wäschenbeuren) 1/R120. Killed in
action 7 February 1915 at la Boiselle.
(*Kriegstagbuch aus Schwaben*)

Haupt
Leutnant d. R. im Inf.-Regt. 120
(Diplom-Ingenieur), gefallen am
14. Februar 1915 in La Boiselle.

Leutnant der Reserve Anton Haupt
(Ulm-Söflingen) 3/R120. Killed in
action 14 February 1915 at La Boisselle.
(*Kriegstagbuch aus Schwaben*)

They gave up the idea of taking away La Boisselle and concentrated their efforts on erasing everything that was left over the ground and in this they succeeded. La Boisselle was soon a desert of shell holes and we had to take our dead back to Pozières as their graves would be dug up again and again by shells. Considering the fact that they numbered over a thousand it was no small job. A monument had been cut for our dead in Courcelette and mounted at the entrance to the village opposite headquarters. This monument would sometimes lie on one side or stand upside down and more of it was shot away every day until finally one day it stopped a big one and was reduced to gravel. Hans Ludwig, 6/R120 [31]

The concept of mined dug-outs was eventually copied throughout the sector held by the XIV Reserve Corps. Trenches were being extended and improved, new strong points were created: *Krauses Ecke* in the first line, *Landwehrstellung, Grallsburg, Feste Alt-Württemberg, Hansastellung, Feste Schwaben* (Schwaben Redoubt) and the *Wundtwerk* in the reserve positions. Preparations were also being made to create a third line of trenches along the line Puisieux-Pozières.

It seems the men had not lost their sense of humor amidst the continuous construction and daily French fire. One comedian in La Boisselle placed a small tombstone next to a dud shell with the inscription:

Here lies the virgin shell,
It rests in the lap of the earth,
It perished, how it lived so insipidly,
Because it never went off.[32]

Trench near Thiepval, sign points to the left to the Stalactite
Cave, 72 Shrapnel Lane. (Lawrence Brown)

The men also gave humorous names to their trenches and dug-outs; Louse Avenue, Rubber Road because of the tenacious clay that stuck to the boots like rubber overshoes, Villa Badger House, *Erholungsheim* (Convalescent home), *Tropfsteinhöhle* (Stalactite cave) as a few examples. Some dug-outs had Dante-like verses over the entrances such as 'abandon all hope ye who enter here' among others.

Work on the trenches included constructing additional telephone stations in almost every company sector. In the case of RIR 99 each company had two and in some cases three separate telephone stations. The telephone lines were exposed with the wires being placed on pegs at the upper edge of the trench while in some regimental sectors the lines ran along the trench walls at knee height. Every sector of the front was connected in this manner while steel cables set 20 centimeters under the trench floor led back to the battle headquarters.

The telephone system gave the companies contact with battalion headquarters, battalion with regimental headquarters and finally to the artillery in the rear where support fire could be requested at any time subject to availability of ammunition. The telephone wires were often broken by French fire as well as from general use of the trenches because of their exposed position. The wires also became obstacles when the trenches were damaged by artillery fire. The men in the Telephone detachments often suffered losses while under fire as they were employed patching broken wires instead of simply sitting in a dug-out servicing the apparatus as most of the men thought.

Field kitchen – RIR 40. (*Das Reserve-Infanterie-Regiment Nr. 40 im Weltkrieg*)

A major development came when the telephone system was improved throughout the command. One platoon from Reserve Telephone *Abteilung* 14 was assigned to each division and assisted in the expansion of telephonic communication. Prior to this point some of the regiments were still relying on nothing more than individual pack telephones.

Bringing warm food to the trenches each night was still very dangerous due to random French fire so over time more food began to be cooked directly at the front. The Fricourt sector was one of the first to construct kitchen facilities close to the front. Hot food could now be delivered safely through communication trenches.

The battalion holding the left sector of Fricourt had a kitchen set up in a large cellar in the village, the right sector had a facility constructed in *Foureaux* Wood (High Wood) that grew in size and importance in a short time. It was named the *Edinger Dorf* after the officer who was in charge of construction. A deep tunnel had been driven into the hillside north of the copse. A spacious medical dug-out was located here and acted as the main dressing station for the regimental sector and housing for the medical staff. The tunnel complex included a kitchen, storerooms for ammunition, a horse stall and eventually a generator room where electricity was supplied for lighting and other uses.

The new kitchen facilities required additional supplies of smoke-free cooking fuel to be supplied to the trenches. The newly-formed Charcoal Burning Detachments furnished this. These detachments were sent out into the surrounding forests to produce sufficient charcoal for use by the men at the front as well as for the field kitchens in the rear. RIR 109 initially formed a charcoal burning detachment consisting of 24 men who worked daily in Bazentin Wood. These detachments were later increased in size, as the need for additional fuel grew.

Even with all of the improvements being made the lines were still far from complete and it was not uncommon for men to become lost and disoriented in the dark nights. Two men from RIR 40, Peter Schmitt and August Schilling, left the line in order to search for food one night. They quickly became lost in the dark night and wandered about for hours

Kitchen dug-out – food preparation. (*Das Reserve-Infanterie-Regiment Nr. 111 im Weltkrieg 1914 bis 1918*)

until they came across a trench. The men were unable to determine if it was occupied by German or French troops.

The two terrified men sat huddled in a nearby shell hole trying to decide what to do next. They heard voices that appeared to be speaking German and when they finally got up the nerve to approach the trench they were relieved to find it was the same one they had left hours earlier.

Most contact with the French during the first three months of 1915 occurred during nightly patrols and the occasional raid. The patrols were sent out every night to obtain intelligence concerning the layout of the French positions, location of sentries, identification of French units, attempts to overhear enemy conversations, identifying locations where entrenching or mining was taking place and to capture prisoners whenever possible.

Some men took to this new style of warfare quite easily while others were just as content to remain behind in the comparative safety of the trenches. Each regiment sent out patrols along the front after darkness had fallen. The early attempts to obtain prisoners were unsuccessful and more often than not the men returned only with various pieces of booty that had little military value. One patrol from the 5/R99 returned with a captured French flag taken from a burned mill in No Man's Land while another patrol brought back a steel breast shield it had stumbled across.

One patrol discovered that the French were experimenting with new ideas on how to breach the German wire entanglements. The patrol came across two bundles of explosives; each contained from 150-200 explosive charges that had been positioned against the wire in front of the 14/R99.

An attempt to capture a prisoner almost succeeded on 31 January. A patrol under *Unteroffizier* Löseckie and 8 men from the 7/R99 penetrated into a French trench while throwing hand grenades at the occupants. Simultaneously *Hauptmann* Ebelt and 12 men advanced further into the French lines. Artillery fire forced the small raiding party to withdraw bringing back two blood stained rifles left behind by the fleeing sentries. The French army report later stated that a German attack had been 'bloodily repelled' when in actuality the patrol had not lost a single man.

Despite the large number of patrols sent out each night it was rare to have two opposing patrols come into contact. One patrol clash did occur on 23 February. *Unteroffizier* Böcker, 6/R110 and four men accidentally bumped into an opposing patrol in the dense morning fog. Four enemy soldiers were killed in the ensuing fight and one wounded man was taken prisoner.

In one instance it was a matter of being at the right place at the right time. Emil Goebelbecker, 9/R109:

> At night they asked for volunteers to go on patrols out in No Man's Land. I went many a time. Well, one night I went out with a friend of mine. All of a sudden we saw two men coming and we thought, 'Oh, two Frenchmen.' We could see their red trousers sticking out. One was a little guy and the other was of regular build. They didn't notice us because they were walking straight ahead. We lay down and let them pass by and then we ran up and hollered 'Halt!' They got all excited but the big one lay down on the ground and then the other one did too. We took them to company headquarters. Later we found out that they had lost their way.[33]

In February a listening post of the 1/R40 observed a light flashing in front of the second set of wire entanglements. Several light rockets were launched and a French patrol was sighted in their glare. The company commander ordered a patrol to go out to find out what the French were up to. The patrol led by *Unteroffizier* Kuhn left the trenches and proceeded to the area but was not able to find any sign of the enemy.

They did not want to return to the trenches empty-handed so it was decided to proceed toward the French lines, 300-400 meters away. The patrol utilized a well-traveled path in the dark night when shots suddenly rang out in the darkness. At first it was a scattering of fire and then it grew into volley fire.

The men fell to the ground and lay as flat as possible in the mud. The French had apparently not seen the group but the cone of fire came uncomfortably close at times. Once the fire died down they decided it was time to withdraw.

The problem was that they had become disoriented in the darkness and from the enemy fire and did not know the way back to the German lines. The patrol wandered aimlessly for over two hours, at times moving quickly, at times dropping down into the mud. Eventually they came across wire entanglements and soon heard voices that were believed to be German.

Kuhn was the first one who climbed over the wire. Barely a minute later he was grabbed and dragged into the trench, a French trench. The trench garrison opened fire into the darkness. The second man, *Kriegsfreiwilliger* Häfele, was literally riddled with bullets and fell dead into the wire; his death had protected the third man, *Landwehrmann* Kunz. The fourth man in the patrol, Krummel, was lying on the ground further to the rear and attempted to squirm through the tangle of wire for several minutes:

I had to laboriously work through under the barbed wire. The strap of my Model 98 remained hanging in the wire. The Browning with the safety catch released was my last comfort and after all gave me a modest feeling of security. Finally I was through. Now I crawled upon all fours. Any increase in the height of my person could betray me. New evil threatened! The morning dawned. A saving thought kindled in me; I could spend the coming day motionless in a shell hole and make my way back to my line in the next night. However I first needed to find a promising lucky crater! Jump up, run! run! The enemy followed my shadow like a hound, like frightened game. I ran quickly. The bullets whistled around me. I succeeded in reaching my own trench with the exertion of all my strength. Helpful hands pulled me in. They showered me with questions. My voice failed. Gradually my tense nerves were able to calm down.[34]

Not all incidents at night had such an unpleasant ending. Also, not all of the noises heard at night were the result of enemy patrols or raiding parties. *Unteroffizier* Schultz, 2/R40:

It happened on a rainy night when a sentry suddenly heard a scrape and clinking sound at the wire entanglements and he alerted the company. A patrol composed of volunteers was sent in the direction of the sounds. Everyone awaited their return under a general tension. The 'piece of loot' however was only an old umbrella that was likely used by a listening post as protection against the rain. However it had become driven into the entanglements by a gust of wind.[35]

Many men in the XIV Reserve Corps held the view of 'live and let live' and hoped that the French would do the same. However, the men soon came to realize that the enemy must be harmed whenever possible. This was made possible with the introduction and refinement of numerous close-range weapons. Rifle grenades, hand grenades, throwing machines, *minenwerfers* and *erdmörsers*'[36] were becoming the weapons of choice. Many of these weapons were being manufactured locally in Péronne by pioneer units. All required careful handling and the men had to be trained in their use.

Many of the new inventions failed to live up to their potential; many had a large moral impact but little practical effect. Numerous casualties were associated with the early tests of the new weapons and the crews quickly learned to keep their distance when operating them.

The hand grenade was quickly becoming a favorite weapon among the men but the early varieties left much to be desired. The first hand grenades used by many of the men were generally homemade devices that had questionable value.

We invented hand grenades consisting of a small piece of board about 15 inches long and 3 inches wide on which we mounted with wire one or more packages of TNT and a fuse about 10 inches long. When it became necessary to throw one of these home made affairs, we had to go back to the doghouse, pull down the canvas, light a cigar and then go back again and hold the cigar to the end of the fuse until it started to spit sparks with a noise like a steam engine. Then we had to wait until it was burned halfway down before throwing it out. Once a quick-witted Frenchman had picked

Erdmörsers. (*Das Württembergische Reserve-Infanterie-Regiment Nr. 121 im Weltkrieg 1914-1918*)

one of them up and fired it right back. These fire crackers made more noise than anything else and I do not believe they did much damage as the burning of the fuse gave the French enough time to run as far as Honolulu. Hans Ludwig, 6/R120 [37]

The first crude hand grenades used extensively along the front consisted of nothing more than preserve cans filled with an explosive charge, nails and pieces of iron attached to a wooden handle.

The hand grenades that were manufactured in Germany required a great deal of maintenance as they suffered greatly in damp weather. Even when the well-known stick grenade was introduced where the fuze was located inside the hollow wooden handle it was subject to failing if it had become damp through improper storage rendering the black powder charge useless until it was dried out. There was also a great many injuries resulting when hand grenades exploded while being carried. The exposed string used to ignite the detonator often became caught on an obstruction inside the trench resulting in an explosion and resulting in death or wounds to the men in the surrounding area.

The rifle grenade was never very popular with the men at the front. RIR 121 had the opinion that they lost as many men to them as the enemy did. The *erdmörser* was a popular weapon and generally easy to construct, unfortunately it was not always the most reliable weapon. The tube was formed by sections of wood being bound together with wire and then placed in a fixed position. It fired a 25-kilogram projectile that was in the shape of a marmalade jar. When the projectile struck the target it went off with a huge explosion, or, as in many cases, not at all. Overall it was found to be a good weapon to use against fixed targets and they destroyed many French sniper and trench mortar positions.

Many of the new weapons required special emplacements as well as dug-outs to provide shelter for the crew and the ammunition and equipment needed to operate them. This required additional work by the pioneers attached to each division as well as the men who provided much of the physical labor of actually constructing the gun emplacements. Great care was taken to position the weapons where they could be used to their greatest advantage. Alternative emplacements also had to be constructed at the same time in case it was necessary to move the weapon if they were discovered.

The artillery emplacements were also greatly improved during the first three months of the year. The men and guns were protected in well-constructed emplacements so that when the French bombarded the positions they caused very little damage and loss of life. The gunners worked diligently digging stronger, deeper mined tunnels that could withstand even the heaviest fire from the French guns. The guns that were still exposed to the most French fire were the anti-aircraft guns. Those in the 26th Reserve Division were located at Beaucourt, Mouquet Farm and Pys.

The artillery units in the XIV Reserve Corps worked diligently to establish good working relationships with the infantry. However even the close cooperation between the artillery and the infantry could not prevent accidents from occurring. On 25 January a heavy mortar battery was firing at a group of houses near Fricourt. One shell fell short and penetrated a dug-out killing *Offizier Stellvertreter* Knappschneider, *Landwehrmann* Lehr and *Ersatz Reservist* Zipper.

The French artillery, superior in numbers and caliber, had become quite annoying with regular fire raids that caused damage to the German position. Even the division staff headquarters in the rear was not immune from the French railway guns. The lack of adequate shelters in the rear meant that enemy fire often resulted in casualties.

The French also held the advantage in the air in the number of aircraft and observation balloons. German aerial observers lacked adequate resources; there were too few aircraft and too few balloons. When a German pilot did make an appearance over the front it usually caused quite a stir among the men below. On the other hand French observation balloons stood at intervals along the entire front during moderately good weather and French aircraft seemed to be flying everywhere.

On at least one occasion in early 1915 the XIV Reserve Corps suffered losses due to friendly air activity. One night a German airship that was scheduled to bomb French positions near Doullens had apparently become confused in the darkness and dropped its bombs on Bapaume destroying two houses and the Field Post Office. The error also resulted in the death of one officer who was passing through the city. He was killed when a beam fell on him during the attack.

Apart from the airship attack life behind the lines had taken on more of a routine. Far behind the front line meant that the men could walk on the surface of the ground without the risk of certain death while taking a leisurely stroll through the countryside. Small items could actually be purchased in shops and stores in the virtually undamaged rear villages and towns. The men had the opportunity to purchase almost anything from cigars to writing paper or to purchase a meal or a drink at the local *estaminet*. It was a time when the men could rest and recuperate from their time at the front.

> Cambrai: so much life and active traffic prevail there. There are not many German soldiers there; on the other hand there are many young French people who could not escape because of the quick German advance. The female sex is a common sight to all due to its excessive clothing. Public houses and hotels are open; everywhere business goes on (besides the streetcars). In the canal lie the transportation vessels and on them the owners pass the time of their lives. German flags flew from the railway station and town hall. The cathedral and the church are worth seeing. Many schools and other public building, also two barracks are there. I spent the night in an *Auberge* (good economy inn) and a good night camp [bed]. I also ate there; in the evening soup, Beefsteak and *Pommes Frites*, butter, cheese and bread and a bottle of red wine. Midday: soup, a roast, potatoes; butter, cheese, bread, a bottle of white wine.

Luſt
Leutn. d. R. im Ref.-Inf.-Regt. 121
(Poſtaſſiſtent), gef. am 2. Febr. 1915
bei Thiepval

Joſenhans (Otto)
Leutn. d. L. im Ref.-Inf.-Regt. 121
(Betriebsleiter), geſt. am 24. Febr.
1915 a. d. bei Thiepval erh. Wunden

Leutnant der Reserve Eugen Lust (Ludwigsburg) RIR 121. Killed in action 2 February 1915 near Thiepval. (*Kriegstagbuch aus Schwaben*)

Leutnant der Landwehr Otto Josenhans (Stuttgart) RIR 121. Wounded in action near Thiepval, died 24 February 1915. (*Kriegstagbuch aus Schwaben*)

> Night meals and midday meals each 1 Mark, a bottle wine each 1 Mark, to spend the night 1 Mark, overall outlay 6 Marks. It was very beautiful. Karl Losch, 3/R119[38]

RIR 111 used the time allowed for rest to finally hold the Christmas celebration they had been denied the previous year. When the regiment was relieved from the front on 10-11 January the men celebrated the holiday with music, good food and gifts. Many warm woolen items of clothing from home were distributed among the men, which were the most needed at the time. The warm clothing from home was a welcome relief when the men took time to make a complete overhaul of their uniforms and equipment that had suffered considerably in the wet weather and mud.

For many men who did not receive packages their comrades either shared what they had received or made arrangements with friends and family at home to send them something to cheer them up.

> In our *Korporalschaft* is a *Wehrmann* named Hune, unmarried, who is also otherwise completely alone. In civilian life he is a shipyard worker and was a stoker on ships who already traveled far around the world. He is a decent person with great knowledge for his position. Since we have been in position here he has still not gotten a package; how about it if you would send him something if you want to, maybe a couple of *Peitschenstecken* [smoked and air-dried cured sausages] and some cigars? He would certainly be very happy. Address *Wehrmann* Karl Hune, otherwise the same as me. Karl Losch, 3/R119. [39]

While at rest the men were quartered in the villages in the rear. Most of these normally held only a small number of civilians before the war, now they were packed with hundreds

Improvised band. (*Die 26. Reserve Division 1914-1918*)

if not thousands of soldiers. Every available space was used to quarter the troops returning from the front, the line of communication troops as well from the artillery units, baggage train, etc. Overcrowded conditions resulted in numerous fires from homemade chimneys the men had created from materials lying about. The loss of even a few structures was a problem when trying to house all of the men in the Corps.

Long-range French fire and aircraft bombs continued to be a problem in some villages located behind the lines. Cellars were initially used as shelters against French fire but they proved to be unsafe against a direct hit so the construction of dug-outs in the rear areas was begun.

Several regiments used their time in the rear to form bands. In the case of Reserve *Jäger* Bn 14 the men formed a jazz band that consisted of two 'devil's fiddles', two harmonicas, one fife and two cook-pot lids.

> In peacetime Bapaume has almost 3,000 inhabitants, presently naturally many fewer live here as a result of the numerous soldiers. Yesterday the *Jäger* band played at the market place, Faidherbe place (who detained the Prussian advance in 1871, however afterward he was defeated). He has a beautiful monument. The duty is quite interesting, we have small battles that are conducted by any one of us and the others practice learning commands. One also sees a lot of finery; however we are no longer quite accustomed to it after trench life. Please send me a field grey handkerchief. Karl Losch, 3/R119 [40]

RIR 109 went one step further and established a full regimental band with the numerous musicians found in the regiment. The band was formed on 17 February under the leadership of *Unteroffizier* Ehrbrecht. The first rehearsal was held in the church in Martinpuich using instruments borrowed from RIR 111.

The 40 *Unteroffiziers* and Other Ranks chosen to play in the band were later given a rare furlough home in order to obtain their own instruments. Afterward the band

Regimental band – RIR 109. (*Das Reserve-Infanterie-Regiment Nr. 109 im Weltkrieg 1914 bis 1918*)

practiced in the church in Longueval and later in Martinpuich and played at funerals, church services, and parades and concerts.

During the time the men were not occupied with band duties they were trained as auxiliary stretcher-bearers. Life was fairly easy for the members of the band until one morning when the regimental commander showed up at their quarters for a surprise visit. He found the men still sound asleep long after they were supposed to have been awake and practicing. As a result of this visit the band members were ordered to report to the construction yard where they were put to work manufacturing footbridges and other items needed for the trenches.

Life in the rear was not all rest and leisure. The men were also expected to attend field training exercises, assault training that included storming fortified positions, rapid construction of mined shelters against artillery fire, guard duty, drilling, assemblies etc. Practice assault works were constructed behind the front at Martinpuich and Flers that were duplicates of the French and German trenches located at the front. The reserve battalions spent many hours working on storm tactics against these targets.

Karl Losch was among the many men sent to Bapaume on training courses that would hopefully lead to promotions. Karl had only been at the front for three months yet he could see just how different life was in the rear as opposed to being under enemy fire in the trenches. There was a widening gap between the men stationed at the front and those in comfortable billets in the rear.

We arrived in Bapaume today at noon. We have good quarters in a one-storey house – a large room with two big beds for 4 men. Sütterlin and I have gotten together again and will sleep in one bed. I only want to see if we are also still able to do so.

Now we are here for 4 weeks and will become further trained. We must begin at 7.30 in the morning and have the first hour for instruction and then field duty until 11.30 a.m. From 2-4 o'clock in the afternoon we have duty. Meanwhile we must primarily learn commands. It could become very interesting, but we are no longer accustomed to army discipline after three months of living in the trenches. You do not have any idea how many men are behind the front and who for the most part are loafing. And in the front there is a handful of men that hold the entire position. It is a terrific life in Bapaume. We slept splendidly in the last two nights. There are bedsprings and mattresses on the beds and for covering we have carpets. Naturally we cannot undress entirely, but it is however better to lie on a springy bed than on straw in the cellar or in our shelters where you feel it in your bones sometimes … a Frenchwoman sits opposite, with her there are also two more who are allowed to cook our lunch … Now we have some opportunities to perfect our poor French. However there is mostly gibberish spoken during the discussions, each knows only a scrap of French.

Today we are free from duty; however time goes past infuriatingly quickly, moreover if one has nice amusements - two young French women and a woman with a little child. There are all sorts of intrigues and one could easily learn some French. The French are gourmets of goodness first and cook beautifully … yesterday we had roast beef for lunch with cooked rice, similar to rice porridge and today cooked bacon with peas, mashed potatoes and cabbage that we had bought for about 40 Francs. Here you can get rid of your money if you really want to, for example, if you want a bottle of wine or to buy cheese and butter, because in the morning and in the evening we do not have much [to do] and also the mail still does not work right.

My billets are in the suburb St. Aubin; they are good quarters, approximately a brisk 5 minute walk from the market place. The French women are naturally nice and also funny in trafficking with us. For the billeting and food they receive nothing, however we give them bread from our rations and they get wood and cabbages that is very agreeable to them and sufficient compensation.

I was in the church today at noon and then in the city and have gotten many impressions. The church is beautiful and has a splendid organ. In front of and by the church there was an oratorio played from Handel and a symphony from Beethoven as well as something from the *Magic Flute*, simply wonderful.

Afterward it was more Catholic, the French going to church and there one could see the French women in their extravagant clothes. Bapaume is some ways is a smaller version of Paris, although in other ways it is like a very large town although it only has 3,000 inhabitants. Then a band played at the market place, with many soldiers and many officers standing about. 15 km behind the front! Is it possible? Some other times you have murderous inclinations; many men did not know how beautiful they have it behind the front at all. [41]

In addition to training many of the men were also used to cultivate the local farmland in order to supplement the food supply. The preparation and distribution of the massive amounts of fresh meat required by the Corps was centralized within the two divisions at this time. The 26th Reserve Division set up a slaughterhouse in Le Sars while the 28th Reserve Division set up a slaughterhouse in Le Transloy. Magazines, seltzer water factories and other manufacturing plants were established in Bapaume.

Zum christlichen Andenken im Gebete
an unfern lieben Sohn

Paul Thieringer

gedient beim Ref. Inf.-Reg. 110,
9. Komp. als Kriegsfreiwilliger,
und am 17. Januar 1915 im Alter
von 19 Jahren in Nordfrankreich
den Heldentod fürs Vaterland
gestorben.

19 year-old *Kriegsfreiwilliger* Paul Thieringer 9/R110. Killed
in action 17 January 1915. (Author's collection)

Presently we also have very beautiful weather, the trees bloom and the fields planted by the German army administration gradually turn green. The further one comes behind the front, the fewer one notices anything about the war. Karl Losch, 3/R119 [42]

Then there was the ever-present entrenching party. Up to one-third of the men who were officially at rest were taken to various parts of the line at the onset of darkness where they worked on constructing new positions, trenches and making repairs to existing defensive works. The duty normally ended just before dawn when the men were returned to the rear where they could try to get some rest after their arduous duties.

Sometimes nightly disturbances in the rest areas were not from enemy activity or entrenching duties. Sometimes it came from fellow soldiers. The men all lived in very close quarters and as a result if there was a disturbance it generally affected everyone sleeping in the room. Some of the men from Reserve *Jäger* Bn 14 were quartered in the home of a French civilian. One member of this group was a chronic snorer and the noise he made at night was so loud that it kept everyone else awake. His friends found that if they gave him snuff before going to sleep it kept the snoring down long enough for the others to fall asleep. Unfortunately it was not a cure for the condition and the snoring continued.

The culprit apparently had a colossal fear of rats so his friends conspired to imitate their presence in the hope he would remain awake long enough for the rest to fall asleep. When the lights were turned off one man rubbed a cork across a bottle to imitate a squeaking noise; another rustled paper on the floor and rummaged through a coal box. Still another man ran a wet piece of twine across the snorer's face to imitate a rat-tail or tickled his leg with a small stick. The ruse finally worked when the snorer jumped out of bed, lit his torch and remained perched on his bed shining his light around the room until 12 or 1 a.m. This allowed everyone else to be able to fall asleep first.

On the following morning the snorer demanded that the landlord plug up every hole and crack in the room with clay and lime despite repeated assurances from the elderly landlord that he did not have any rats in the house. The rat plan worked for several more

Officers billeted with the local populace in Mametz – RIR 111. (Author's collection)

nights without having to imitate the presence of the rodents. Once the offender began to fall asleep and snore again the 'rats' returned including a simulated nest under his pillow.

There were several special events held in the early part of 1915. Kaiser Wilhelm's birthday was observed on 27 January. The units celebrated the occasion as best they could under the circumstances. In the case of RIR 40 it was reported to be an enjoyable day in which each man received a ½ bottle of wine, 15 cigars, 12 cigarettes and 1 package of tobacco and sausage. There were always inspections in front of division and corps commanders.

> Because of the ban on letters I have completely forgotten to write about the details of the inspection. The commanding general was very content, we drilled some and then performed some battle practices. We 119th didn't come to the attention of the commander in front of loud Artillery *Leutnants* and *Offizier Stellvertreten* who had been promoted to Leutnants the day before. At the conclusion he gave one more little speech and said among other things: 'We are the young generation of officers, because so many active officers have fallen, and we must move into their positions when we hopefully advance soon.' For me I also hope to advance soon, because the stinking smell around behind the front does not suit us boys at all. Karl Losch, 3/R119[43]

The men of the 26th Reserve Division also celebrated the birthday of the King of Württemberg on 25 February with a bit more fanfare than usual. The trenches of the division were decorated with pennants and garlands while a red and black flag flew from a ruined house in La Boisselle. Two men had placed the flag on the house in the night on their own initiative. Six weeks earlier this would have attracted heavy French fire, now the enemy accepted it quietly.

Several other men in RIR 120 went even further to let the French know it was the King's birthday.

The morning of the day on which we were to celebrate the birthday of our King, a black and red flag, the colors of our country, were flying over the French trenches. Two of our men had put it there during the night. The French first tried to get it down but the flag was mounted on a piece of iron pipe and was flying in the wind all day. Not to be outdone the French brought over a Tricolor the next night and together with it marched back to Courcelette the same night. They had forgotten our outposts were waiting for such a thing to happen. That was the end of the French flag party. Hans Ludwig, 6/R120 [44]

The men of the 28th Reserve Division had a distinguished visitor early in 1915. The Grand Duke of Baden arrived in Martinpuich on 10 January where he met with the men. His visit must have attracted the attention of French observers as the village was briefly shelled. The only casualties consisted of 3 cows that were killed by the shellfire.

The visit also had a special significance as it marked the end of the association of Reserve *Jäger* Bn 8 with the 28th Reserve Division. The battalion was relieved from duty on 8 January and was transferred to Colmar in Alsace.

In February 1915 the German army in the field consisted of 51 Active divisions and 54 Reserve divisions. 22 of the Reserve divisions had been created since mobilization in October 1914 and February 1915. New plans for a possible summer offensive in Russia called for an additional increase in the number of divisions. The winter campaign and the

The King of Württemberg (3rd from left) visiting the 26th Reserve Division. (Author's collection)

Grand Duke Friedrich II of Baden speaking with *Wehrmann* Müller,
holder of the Iron Cross 1st Class and Iron Cross 2nd Class (*Das Reserve-
Infanterie-Regiment Nr. 109 im Weltkrieg 1914 bis 1918*)

recently-formed divisions had exhausted the 1914 Class of men and nearly the entire trained *Landsturm*. The 1915 Class of men was not available for use and there were insufficient numbers of trained men in the depots to form the new regiments needed.

However the increasing use of the artillery in a defense role and fewer men needed to garrison the trenches made it possible to reduce the infantry strength of the divisions. Plans were drawn up for the reduction of the basic division structure from four regiments to three. Three of the surplus regiments were then grouped together to form a new division. 19 new divisions were created in this manner in March and April.

The 26th and 28th Reserve Divisions were required to submit one regiment for the new formations. RIR 120 was relieved from the 26th Reserve Division on 13 March. In addition the division was required to turn over the 5th and 6th Batteries from the light field howitzer *Abteilung*, III/RFAR 26, which were transferred on 7 March to become part of the newly formed FAR 116. They were sent to Roulers where they became part of the Saxon-Württemberg 58th Division under General von Gersdorff. When RIR 120 left the association of the 26th Reserve Division General von Stein gave a farewell speech in which he praised the men for their devotion to duty in defending the village of La Boisselle since September 1914.

RIR 40 was relieved from the 28th Reserve Division on 29/30 March and was transported to Tournai to form part of the 115th Division. This meant that the XIV Reserve Corps had to defend the Corps sector with a total of seven regiments and one *Jäger* battalion where nine regiments and two *Jäger* battalions had once stood. Even with fewer men needed to garrison the trenches these losses placed greater responsibility and strain on the troops who remained behind.

The regiments remaining in the XIV Reserve Corps were still receiving the normal allotment of replacement troops. On 11 January RIR 109 received a draft of 208 replacements from Karlsruhe. The men arrived in Flers and consisted mainly of War Volunteers including one soldier who was only 17 years old. It was found that the replacements had not received sufficient training before arriving at the front so they were sent off for additional instruction before being distributed among the various companies.

The same problem confronted RIR 99 when 31 *Unteroffiziers* and 606 Other Ranks, mainly Thuringians, arrived on 8 February. The men had only received 13 weeks of training before arriving at the front. They were kept back in Irles and Miraumont where their training was completed.

The problem involving inadequately trained men being sent to the front was resolved in part by setting up special recruit depots as training areas behind the front for each division at Bertincourt, Barastre, Rocquigny and other locations. New replacements would automatically pass through these facilities in order to complete their training before being sent to front line companies. The system of Recruit Depots would provide a steady stream of replacements for the regiments at the front. It would also supply a labor pool, which could be used to work on the defenses in the rear. Construction work became part of the training regimen.

Some replacements were fully trained and ready for action when they arrived at the front. RIR 99 received a draft of men consisting of 4 officers, 15 *Unteroffiziers* and 65 Other Ranks who had been wounded earlier in the war and had just been sent back to rejoin their old regiment after recuperating.

RIR 99 also received a large draft of men on 7 March when 50 officers and 397 Other Ranks reported for duty. The officers and men had been on duty in an armored train detachment and had seen action in Belgium, France and even Russia for a short time. The armored train duty was apparently not very strenuous and the unit had suffered few losses. The men were returned to their original companies and by 11 March RIR 99 consisted of 69 officers, 13 officer Replacements, 3,314 Unteroffiziers and Other Ranks. With the additional men the regiment could now hold regular battalion rotations from the front in the same manner as the other regiments in the division. This was desperately needed because clothing and equipment were suffering badly in the wet clay and chalk and needed to be replaced or repaired.

Officers in the *Ersatz* Battalion RIR 119. (Author's collection)

The next three months would see many changes taking place along the front of the XIV Reserve Corps and the relatively quiet times at the front would be a thing of the past.

Chapter Notes

1. Losch, *Feldpost* letter dated 3 February 1915.
2. Losch, op cit, *Feldpost* letters dated 11 January and 26 January 1915.
3. Losch, op cit, *Feldpost* letters dated 1 February and 3 February 1915.
4. Losch, op cit, *Feldpost* letter dated 11 January 1915.
5. An intercepting mound erected in any fortification to protect the defenders from rear or ricochet fire. It was normally higher than the parapet so the men occupying the fire step were not outlined against the sky.
6. R. Baumgartner (Ed.), 'An der Somme, An interview with Soldat Emil Goebelbecker', *Der Angriff, A Journal of World War 1 History*, No. 3, p. 4.
7. *Feldpost* letter dated 22 March 1915 from *Gefreiter* Rudolf Siegele, 4th Battery, II/RFAR 29
8. H. Ludwig, Manuscript, 6th Company RIR 120, pp. 10-11.
9. Ludwig, op. cit., pp. 9-10.
10. Siegele, op. cit., Letter dated 3 March 1915.
11. W. Gallion, *Das Reserve-Infanterie-Regiment Nr. 40 im Weltkrieg*, p.60.
12. Ludwig: op. cit., pp. 20-21.
13. Ludwig, op. cit., p. 21.
14. *Donarit* was the name given to Trinitrotoluene (TNT).
15. Ludwig: op. cit., p. 21.
16. Ludwig, op. cit., pp. 21-22.
17. K. Metzger, *Vom Weltkrieg 1914/18. Selbsterlebnisse eines Frontsoldaten,* Metzger, op. cit., pp. 50-51. Gustav survived the war and returned to his position driving a beer wagon from Brewery Wulle in Stuttgart, the same position he held before the war.
18. Siegele, op. cit., letter dated 5 March 1915
19. Metzger, op. cit., pp. 9-11.
20. Losch, op cit, *Feldpost* letter dated 11 January 1915.
21. Fromm, *Das Württembergische Reserve-Infanterie-Regiment Nr. 120 im Weltkrieg 1914-1918,* p. 14.
22. Ludwig: op. cit., pp. 22-23.
23. Ludwig, op. cit., p. 23.
24. Ibid.
25. Ludwig, op. cit., p. 24.
26. Ibid.
27. Fromm, op. cit. p. 19.
28. Ibid.
29. Losch, op cit, *Feldpost* letter dated 26 January 1915. Official Reports of War Operations, France, *New York Times*, 19 January 1915, "Following the blowing up of an ammunition depot caused by the bursting of a shell, that part of the village of La Boisselle, (about twenty miles northeast of Amiens) occupied by our troops, was burned, and we were compelled to evacuate it. The evacuated territory was recaptured by us, however, in a vigorous counter-attack on the morning of the 18th."
30. Ludwig, op. cit., pp. 25-26.

31. Ludwig, op. cit., p. 24.
32. Fromm, op. cit., p. 15.
33. Baumgartner, No. 3, p. 4.
34. Gallion: op. cit., pp. 61-62
35. Gallion, op. cit., p. 60.
36. Literally 'Earth Mortar', generally of local manufacture and often partially buried in the ground in order to provide additional support to the mortar tube.
37. Ludwig: op. cit., p. 12.
38. Losch, op cit, *Feldpost* letter dated 26 April 1915
39. Losch, op cit, *Feldpost* letter dated 16 June 1915.
40. Losch, op cit, *Feldpost* letter dated 28 February 1915.
41. Losch, op cit, *Feldpost* letters dated 24 February, 26 February, 28 February, 8 March and 14 March 1915.
42. Losch, op cit, *Feldpost* letter dated 26 April 1915.
43. Losch, op cit, *Feldpost* letter dated 15 April 1915.
44. Ludwig, op. cit., p. 25.

6

April – June 1915

On 4 April *General der Infanterie* Fritz von Below assumed command of the Second Army from *Generalfeldmarschall* von Bülow. A new Army Group was formed at this time consisting of the 26th Reserve Division, 28th Reserve Division, 52nd Division and 2nd Guard Reserve Division. These divisions formed Group Stein within the Second Army. While the administrative details facing the new Army Group were being addressed life in the 26th and 28th Reserve Divisions did not change appreciably.

The sector held by the Corps continued to be improved and expanded. Entrenching continued on a large scale in order to expand and maintain the position. The end of the cold period brought warmer weather and heavy rain. On 4 May many positions were badly damaged by a severe cloudburst, in some places the trenches were covered in more than 1 meter of water. Numerous dug-outs had to be immediately evacuated by the garrison with the loss of all of their possessions. It took some time to pump out all of the excess water and repair the damage.

Additional chalk caves and mines found in many of the villages were uncovered and utilized whenever possible. The thick protective cover of soil provided excellent protection against French shells. Canteens were established in some of the mined dug-outs where men could obtain beer, wine, schnapps, coffee, sausages, oranges, knives, mirrors, combs, notepaper and pencils as well as sentimental postcards. Photographers were present throughout the front and were often called upon to take photographs of individuals, groups and even companies both in and behind the front line. These were printed as postcards and sent to friends and family at home. Many men also carried small pocket cameras and took photographs of the places they served and of their friends in the regiment. This practice was quite contrary to the rules of the French and British armies.

There were still areas where the opposing lines were a considerable distance from one another. In the area of Ovillers the trenches were still 900 meters apart and the distance needed to be shortened. The sapping method used to create new trenches was put to use once again. Thirteen saps were started from the existing front line; from right to left: *Koch, Klinkowström, Neumann-Cosel, Fölkersamb, Waldeck, Kronen, Kuhm, Leichen, Baum, Witwer, Krach, Weisshuhn and Friedhof.* When completed the sap heads were connected to form the new front line. The thirteen saps became communication trenches that provided safe access to the new front.

The village of Ovillers that had been in the front lines now became more of a rear stronghold. The village cemetery was integrated into the defensive line where the Dufour family crypt was cleared out and used as a dug-out. During the work the men pushed into the area that had seen considerable fighting in December 1914. Rain revealed the remains of French dead who had only been given a light covering of earth. Their trousers gleamed like red poppies in the green grass.

Drinking water was still extremely scarce on the Somme, especially at Ovillers. Several methods of transporting water to the front were tried including the use of donkeys and

Men from RIR 99 obtaining water from a well near Beaumont-Hamel. (Author's collection)

Body of dead French soldier lying out in No Man's Land. (*Das Reserve-Infanterie-Regiment Nr. 111 im Weltkrieg 1914 bis 1918*)

Postcard sent 2 May 1915 by a soldier in the 8/180: 'The one with the rifle is my sergeant, the other my *Unteroffizier*. He was killed in action at the same place one hour later.' *Unteroffizier* Gottlieb Steck 8/180. Killed in action 6 April 1915. (Author's collection)

barrels but none proved to be practical. Eventually several new wells were dug in the village and a water pipeline was installed from the village to the front line.

> Furthermore I ask you to send me a packet of ground coffee, because we have an excellent stove in our shelter and we even sometimes boil water that you must not drink (out of a very deep well). We still have very beautiful weather. This morning two French pilots circled very low over our positions, only the cuckoo knows what they wanted and intended. We have greatly reinforced our entanglement very much and now also created a second trench. Karl Losch, 3/R119 [1]

The remaining civilian population of the village of Ovillers was evacuated in June while the pioneers took down particularly tall houses that could serve as aiming points for French artillery observers.

French artillery fire was causing numerous losses to traffic in the village as well as to reserves lying in village cellars and damaging the wells, kitchens and supply depots. Orders were issued that the village should not to be used by the troops for most purposes. Separate dug-outs were constructed in the 2nd and 3rd lines to meet the requirements of the men.

While the opposing trench lines at Ovillers were still a reasonable distance from each other the situation in La Boisselle and other points along the line was the exact opposite.

In some locations the opposing trench sentries were a mere three paces from one another and every noise or movement made by either side could be heard.

Greater care was required when occupying these trenches and when the men were relieved. Trench relief needed to be carried out in strict silence. Talking and loud sounds were forbidden, as the sound would carry quite far. The men were not allowed to use cigars, cigarettes or pipes during the relief, nothing that would give them away to the enemy.

In a typical trench relief the replacement sentries were instructed on the habits and behavior of the opposing side, fire activity, the local terrain, trench layout - anything of importance. While the sentries were being instructed a large portion of the men were immediately put to work on entrenching and improving the wire entanglements. This would continue as long as it was dark. Nothing was allowed to interrupt the men who performed these duties. Additional troops were sent out into No Man's Land on patrol and to provide protection to the working parties.

> Tonight we were a trio (1 *Unteroffizier*, I and 1 man) on patrol from 9.30 p.m. until 00.30 a.m., however we observed nothing, only that the French had also improved their [wire] entanglement at individual positions. The French have a whole labyrinth of approach and fire trenches; we only have 1-2 fire trenches, but better developed. The patrol was easy to do, because the grass is very high and a field of clover lies between us and the French. We moved forward on all fours with fixed bayonets. The French rarely patrol; the 99th that were there before us had only one piece of advice - one naturally should not go too close in front of their position because they also have listening posts like us 100 meters in front of their position. From our listening post (our listening post in a sap) I have recently gotten the parachute of a French flare that the wind had driven across to us. The flare hangs underneath on the parachute and gradually burns from the heights from which they are fired, sinking to the ground, with rosy light. Our cartridge flares produce brighter light; they don't have any parachutes and are launched in a high arc. Karl Losch, 3/R119 [2]

Entrenching at night as well as carrying food and supplies became increasingly dangerous with the improved French flares. They produced longer lasting light than the standard German flare as they descended, increasing the possibility of being detected if caught in the open.

> Life in the trenches consisted of standing watch – *Posten* – for 4 hours in daytime, 2 hours nighttime. Others had to work to improve the trenches. The hardest job was getting food from the field kitchen near Contalmaison – about a 40-minute walk. One man carried hot food and bread for 4 men. When the lines were shot up, we had to go out at night and make repairs. That was dangerous. The French shot up flares that descended slowly with a parachute, lighting up a whole section at a time. We had many a close call. My partner was shot in the leg laying next to me. Emil Goebelbecker, 9/R109 [3]

The officers and non-commissioned officers would take inventory of the trench stores and dug-outs and keep the sentries alert through the night. Everything was done under strict silence, with an occasional rifle shot or machine gun burst heard in the distance.

Pioneers in the 4/Pioneer Bn 13, note light rail tracks. (Author's collection)

Now something about our life. At 8 o'clock in the evening on the 7th we marched out of Bapaume. At midday a cloudburst of rain came down. After several stops we arrived in Beaumont at 1.30 at night. The march went well, however as we had to ascend into Beaumont into the communication trench, this in part had collapsed and filled with water and mud, so that sometimes the mud nearly ran in over the top of our boots. The position of the 3rd Company is by the exit of the village of Beaumont along the road that runs north from Beaumont and merges with the larger Mailly-Serre-Puisieux road, therefore directly west. We wound our way through the communication trenches and came into our trench where we 17 men (also Sütterlin) were assigned a deep dug-out as a dwelling, about 3 meters under the earth. The deep dug-out is 1.50 meters high and 1 meter wide and quite long and has two entrances. Yesterday we spent our time more or less getting planks to cover the ground, and straw that we tied in our tent cloths to make a splendid bed. So far sleep is still an essential matter. Two hours of sleep, then stand guard and barely lay down again when there is a practice alarm or patrol or something else. Almost every hour of the night one must be out. Today sees the communication trenches impeccably clean again and the weather is beautiful. I sit beside the entrance to the deep dug-out, in which a ladder leads down and write this letter. So far we have not received any artillery fire, so that you could easily remain in the open. You can endure it quite easily with the splendid weather, in many ways it's like summer freshness and a carefree life. Cooking takes place in Beaumont - in the morning coffee, at noon rice, peas or else something with meat and in the evening coffee again. The food is brought to us in the trench. Karl Losch, 3/R119 [4]

Sontheimer
Leutnant d. R. i. Inf.-Regt. 180,
gefallen bei Irles
am 25. April 1916

Sommer
Leutn. d. L. im Ref.-Inf.-Regt. 121,
gefallen bei Serre
am 1. Juni 1916

Leutnant der Reserve Ludwig Sontheimer (Tübingen) 2/180. Accidentally killed 25 April 1915 near Irles. (*Kriegstagbuch aus Schwaben*)

Leutnant der Landwehr Heinrich Sommer (Hofstett) 2/R121. Killed in action 1 June 1915 near Serre. (*Kriegstagbuch aus Schwaben*)

Carrying parties would arrive at the front under cover of darkness with heavy loads of building materials, tools and other trench stores. By morning the carrying troops returned to the rear tired, soaked and muddy. The patrols came in from No Man's Land and the sentries were placed on increased alertness in the event of an enemy raid or attack.

Some relief from the seemingly endless fatigues came in the form of several light tramways that were constructed in May. The rail lines ran from Pozières and Martinpuich to the front and allowed supplies to be brought up using far fewer men and horses.

The mornings were normally quiet with both sides resting from the work done during the previous night, infantry and artillery fire would start later in the day. The troops took advantage of this time to relax, read letters or newspapers.

> For amusement we played cards, wrote letters, one man played the harmonica and we sang. Emil Goebelbecker, 9/R109 [5]

Some took to carving souvenirs to send home, such as chalk frames for photographs, paperweights decorated with the Iron Cross, letter openers, ashtrays, rings and other items made from the copper drive bands of shells and from empty rifle cartridges or shell casings. One industrious *Jäger* made a beautiful model of Cologne cathedral out of chalk. Others painted French shell fragments with scenes of the Fricourt Château or similar landmarks.

> I am sending you two copper drive bands from French shrapnel shells. You are able to make very beautiful bracelets out of these and these clearly form a very much-loved adornment. You can let some of them be gilded; hinge, lock and small chain are fastened on it. I know Lachenmager prepared many. The bracelets are approximately

6 Marks. The brighter rings are the most beautiful; you could give away the second one if you want, maybe to Helene Fanghaeuel. I naturally assume in advance that they are also allowed to have such a bracelet. Herr Sütterlin had one made for his daughter, who was confirmed this year, who was very pleased. Karl Losch, 3/R119 [6]

When weather permitted the men sunbathed in protected areas. When daylight faded the field grey climbed out of the trenches again to start the same routine once more.

During the most beautiful weather we sit in the trench or lie in the grass behind, protected by the earth piled up high, and let the sun shine on us and read or sleep. Karl Losch, 3/R119 [7]

The boredom of trench life was interrupted from time to time due to enemy activity. The number of deep, mined dug-outs continued to increase along the front and proved effective against artillery fire. At first many men feared being trapped inside the new dug-outs but soon forgot their concerns when the dug-outs survived even the heaviest bombardment.

However the new dug-outs, some 7-8 meters deep, still experienced high humidity most of the time. The chalk soil allowed water to continuously drip down from the ceilings where it was caught in empty food cans. Before the installation of wire bed frames the men slept on the bare floor, covered with straw if available, using old sacks as pillows and a woolen blanket for warmth. The men also shared their quarters with a variety of insect and animal life including the ever-present rats and lice that seemed to infest every item of clothing. Whenever the men were relieved one of the first stops made was to the 'Lausoloeum' in Flers or Bapaume. However the relief from the lice was short-lived as

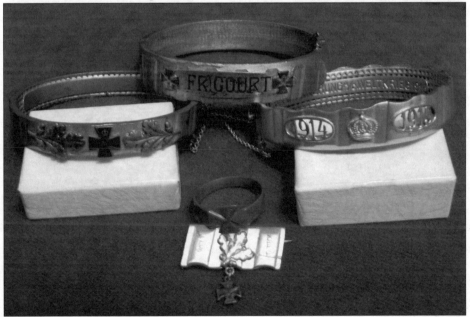

Examples of trench art. (Author's collection)

they soon returned. One soldier, Karl Losch, requested help from home, 'Please send me some fennel oil for prevention against *Flieger*, that is lice.' [8]

The French became very active in early April along the front held by the XIV Reserve Corps despite the Easter holiday. Heavy artillery fire fell on Maundy Thursday and Good Friday (1 and 2 April). The damage to the position was severe; many of the trenches were leveled and French shells penetrated a number of older dug-outs and even one or two of the newer design. This only resulted in several cases of shell shock, otherwise losses were low thanks to the well-constructed position.

Reserve *Jäger* Bn 14 estimated the battalion sector was receiving 200 shells each day in addition to numerous trench mortar bombs and rifle grenades. During the night the trenches were restored with help from the pioneers. They did not fear the French rifle grenades as during the day they could be observed coming over like small black balls and at night they could be seen by the glowing fuze. The top of the trench was often covered with a wire fence in order to intercept the rifle grenades.

The *Jägers* were approximately 50-100 meters distant from the French in most places but on their right wing the lines were much closer, approximately three paces from the enemy. The sentries used slits in steel shields to observe the opposing lines but rarely glimpsed any French soldiers. The *Jägers* were good shots and took great pride in their marksmanship. They picked a suitable spot and set up a rifle range and carefully observed part of the French lines approximately 800 meters away. Each hit made on an enemy soldier by a *Jäger* was carefully marked on a chalkboard and before too long the number had grown quite large.

With the departure of RIR 120 the sector of La Boisselle was taken over by RIR 109. The trenches occupied by the regiment ran from the southwest corner of Ovillers to

Hunting lice in the trenches, RIR 121. (Author's collection)

the western edge of La Boisselle to the hollow running east from Bécourt. As with many of the regiments the troops taking over a new position always considered the previous occupants to be slovenly and the position poorly developed, however it was soon brought into impeccable order according to the men in RIR 109.

La Boisselle was subjected to heavy bombardments by artillery and trench mortar fire in early April. Many older dug-outs with only 2½ meters of earth overhead collapsed. Work on deep mined dug-outs was accelerated in order to avoid future losses of this type. The failure to provide an adequate number of deep mined dug-outs resulted in higher losses than expected. Friedrich Thomas, 2/R109:

> Who should place demands on the living if death lurks nearby? Because! ... even if a shell hits in the neighboring area! ... the beams of the roof of the dug-out shatter like matches, and the layer of earth over it buries the occupants. Comrades quickly try to dig out those that are buried with their hands. It is too late: Grenadiers Hermann II, Halter II, Mosbacher II, Regenscheid, Sehlbach, War Volunteers Schäuble and Weber have paid for their fidelity with their lives. Another dug-out was destroyed not far from this position, in that four men are buried. Reservist Renkert of the 2nd Company comes upon it immediately afterward and tries to save the unlucky men. He succeeds in digging out two living comrades while both of the others had been killed. He was awarded the Iron Cross II Class for his brave behavior.
>
> It was no less bad in the foremost trench. Five sentries had been killed there through direct hits and it was not possible for the support groups to come forward through the very sharp artillery fire. *Unteroffizier* Klemm and *Gefreiter* Seekircher of the 2nd Company moved into the position of the fallen men and carried on as sentries from 10 o'clock in the morning until 10 o'clock in the evening.[9]

The men remarked that the view of the ruins of La Boisselle in the glow of French flares provided a frightening appearance. Aside from some wall remnants among which the church was still recognizable, the entire village consisted of a sea of smashed houses and tree stumps. No trees, no shrubs, just a fertile green plain crisscrossed by white chalk trenches and shell craters. The sector occupied by the 2/R109 near the *Granathof* was still a particularly dangerous location, even more so on Good Friday. Friedrich Thomas:

> Our sentries were in the fire trench at the exit of the village. A few steps in front of them was a destroyed farmstead, we called it the *Granathof*; the French called it the 'Blockhouse'. There was a roar over there by the enemy at regular intervals, and every time a few seconds later a shell smashed into the ruins. A geyser [rose] from the already hundred-fold disintegrated rubble! The sentries ducked and a hail of iron splinters rustled above them.
>
> You know the enemy battery that holds the farmyard continually under fire although one cannot see it. One only suspected that its position is on the road that leads toward the enemy. However this battery does not always fire alone, often it is several batteries that participate in the fire raids. Then the thunder rolls non-stop and the fire comes from different directions. A deeper sound mingles in the clear sound of the field guns. It is followed by a hollow bang that sounds above everything else. It was the exploding projectiles that were fired out of the heavy fortress guns that

were brought here installed on railway carriages and long barreled guns standing on the railway to Arras. Then again short sounds, followed by white cloudlets, out of which an iron hail falls to the earth. That is the shattering shrapnel whose balls spread far over the earth. The *Granathof* became like hell. No living being could exist there. The sentries have thrown themselves on the bottom of the trench. The iron hail covers the walls and tries to bury the men under the ruins.

The remaining trench garrison sits in niches and excavations. They have comfortably furnished these nooks and decorated them with memories of home. The comrades lie nestled closely together and look for sleep that does not want to come at all today. Each knew that the 'Frog' could begin an attack in the next moment. A weak light struggles with the darkness of the night. A layer of tallow was poured into an old preserved food can. A piece of twine in the end formed the wick. One will have to be content with this in the fire trench! [10]

The heavy artillery fire continued throughout the day and night along with rifle and machine gun fire that forced the trench garrison to remain on high alert in the event of a French attack. Despite these concerns no attack ever materializes. Friedrich Thomas:

Rifle fire patters continuously. One clearly hears the rattle of the machine guns. As the morning dawned the *Granathof* was quiet and forsaken. The following night made itself as noteworthy as the first. Here also we mourned the loss of faithful comrades. The 2nd Company suffered most under the prolonged shelling and constant alarm readiness and so the company leader, *Oberleutnant der Reserve* von der Ahe decided to ask the regiment about an early relief that was approved so that the 2nd and 4th Companies traded positions. The comrades of the replacement 4th Company cursed loudly; however we are glad to finally be able to escape this hell for a short time. In truth, the awful memory of Good Friday had been quite suitable as a day of mourning for us.….For every comrade that had experienced that terrifying night, it remains in their memory forever.[11]

The few days spent in La Boisselle made quite an impression on the men from RIR 119, especially Karl Losch:

It is also quite different in La Boisselle than in Ovillers. 1. Shell fire 2. Mine throwers. 3. Hand and rifle grenades. 4. Undermining. Our pioneers have dug tunnels of about 50 meters long and 7-8 meters under the ground with side corridors that run parallel to the position, to neutralize the French tunnels. Almost no day passes that the French do not set off an explosion, however often with little success; also they have already removed the tamped explosive charge from the back of the tunnel and once our pioneers removed the explosive charge from it they struck upon the French galleries.

In part we are only 30-50 meters distant, so that you are never sure when you might fly into the air. However we lie 4-6 meters under the ground in great caves dressed up with wood and plank floor covering and railroad ties for the ceiling, sometimes two layers, everything is well protected. No house stands any more, here and there a wall, and a couple of beams that still stick up rigidly in the air. All of La Boisselle is passed through with deep communication trenches, a huge earthen fortress

Gefreiter Sommer and *Gefreiter* Guberan 4/R121 standing with *Hauptmann* Frhr von
Ziegesar after receiving the Iron Cross 1st Class for daring, successful patrol activity. *Gefreiter*
Sommer was killed in action on 1 July 1916. (*Die 26. Reserve Division 1914-1918*)

that however on the French side opposite is an almost similarly strong position. The
4 days in La Boisselle were quite nice, we have seen much, only no French. What
are in the French reports are baseless lies. You could never determine what success
they have achieved; everything is in such an unbelievable form. [12]

The practice of sending out reconnaissance patrols was still the accepted method
used to maintain the offensive spirit of the men. However headquarters now decided to
send out larger patrols more frequently and to make small-scale raids against the French
lines. One of the largest raids planned in this period was set to take place on the night of
10/11 April by Reserve Infantry Brigade 51 with the objective of identifying the opposing
French units.

The raid was set to take place simultaneously at two locations starting at 2 a.m. on
11 April. The main raiding party would consist of the III/180 under Major Scupin that
would proceed against the French lines in Thiepval Wood near the Chapel while the 7/R99
under *Hauptmann* Ebelt would proceed against the village of Hamel in a diversionary role.

The decision to hold the raid had not been taken until late in the afternoon of 10
April. General von Wundt ordered the commanders of the II/180, 7/R99 and RFAR 26 to
assemble in Grandcourt. The meeting was held in the Estaminet called the '*Frontschwein*',
a popular spot where the officers would normally stop for a pint of beer.

This meeting was something more serious than a drink with friends when von Wundt
greeted Major Scupin with '*Morituri te Salutant*'.[13] The plan was quickly laid out before the
assembled officers. The purpose of the raid was to take prisoners and it would be carried
out without artillery preparation fire. The division artillery would provide support once
the raiding parties had entered the French lines at 2 a.m.

Chapel in Thiepval Park. Dug-out entrance on left side of the
building. (*Die 26. Reserve Division 1914-1918*)

After the meeting ended the officers returned to their commands to prepare for the undertaking. The troops were moved into position as quietly as possible while the artillerymen checked their guns and set the sights using the light from their lanterns. It was a mild spring night and it was unusually quiet.

The main body would consist of the 9th and 11/180 accompanied by groups from the 4/Pioneer Bn 13 and 2/Bavarian Pioneer Regiment. The target of the raid was the French line at the northern tip of Thiepval Wood opposite St Pierre-Division.

The signal for the start of the raid was a single rifle shot fired at 1.55 a.m. Both companies were able to get up to the French wire without any opposition. The 9th Coy found the wire was too thick and the trench garrison spotted the raiding party and opened a fierce flanking fire into them.

Five minutes after the infantry had advanced the field guns and howitzers opened a fire that was described by one soldier as if hell had been unleashed. French reserves were quickly assembled and rushed to the threatened area only to run into a wall of German artillery fire blocking every approach route.

The 11th Coy succeeded in entering the French trenches at the corner of the forest where the men quickly captured 9 prisoners and 1 machine gun with ammunition. The company commander wanted to go deeper into the forest but was overruled by Major Scupin who felt their task had been completed. The signal to return to the German lines was given and both companies withdrew. By 3 a.m. the raid was over and the front grew silent once more.

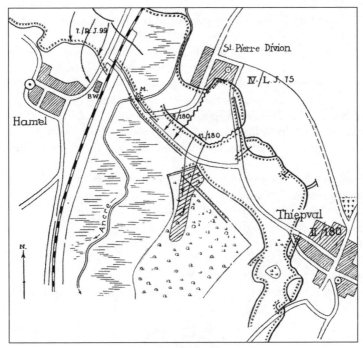

11 April 1915 trench raid.

The diversionary attack conducted by the 7/R99 took place in Sector J7 near the village of Hamel. This company had been chosen because the men had conducted numerous patrols in this area and were very familiar with the terrain.

There were a number of obstacles to overcome. The area in front of the French trenches consisted of a small, deep valley near the Ancre where strong wire obstacles had been constructed between the valley and the trenches. The terrain sloped steeply down to the Ancre on the eastern side of the position into an area consisting of marsh, water and trees.

Just before the infantry was scheduled to advance the pioneers cut four assault alleys through the German wire. *Leutnant* Schulten commanded the 1st Platoon on the right; *Offizier Stellvertreter* Lex would attack the center with the 2nd Platoon while *Leutnant* Thom took the 3rd Platoon by the embankment alongside the Beaumont-Hamel road to attack from the left flank. A detachment was instructed to block French reinforcements advancing from Hamel.

The 160 men of the 7th Coy left their trenches at 1.30 a.m. and took up position on the hillside in front of the small valley on a front of 200 meters. The infantry were accompanied by groups of pioneers who were equipped with wire cutters and hand grenades.

At exactly 2 a.m. the German artillery opened fire on the French lines for 5 minutes according to plan. At the same moment the men of the 7th Coy rushed up to the wire obstacles where the pioneers began to cut lanes leading to the French trench. It seemed to the men that the pioneers were taking forever to cut through the thick wire. *Leutnant* Schulten and his men decided not to wait and some crawled under the wire that was fortunately smooth and not barbed or jumped on top of it in order to flatten it down. The 1st Platoon entered the French trenches without losing a man and in the subsequent hand-to-hand fighting drove the French out of the main position and the adjoining communication trench.

The retreating French garrison ran into the fire of the 2nd Platoon that had also been able to get into the trench. The 3rd Platoon entered the French position and pressed the trench garrison toward the center. Some of the defenders managed to escape through a communication trench that lead toward the Beaumont-Hamel road while the remainder were forced back in hand-to-hand fighting until they also ended up in the fire of the 2nd Platoon, who fired down into the trench from above. The fire grew too much for the garrison and several men attempted to escape by going out through their own wire into No Man's Land.

The three assault platoons continued to fan out through the maze of trenches and advanced approximately 100 meters where they met with strong French reserves coming from the rear. A spotlight suddenly illuminated the terrain until a shot managed to knock it out. At the same time the company leader, *Hauptmann* Ebelt fell to the ground severely wounded. His servant Hans Wennemuth attempted to retrieve his body but he was also shot down.

At this point the men assigned to obstruct French reserves advancing from Hamel began to withdraw in front of superior forces. When the recall signal given by Major

Veil (Viktor)
Leutn. d. R. i. d. 4. Pionier-Komp.,
gefallen bei Beaumont-Hamel
am 11. April 1915

Kirn
Leutnant d. L. im Inf.-Regt. 180,
gefallen bei Hébuterne
am 8. Juni 1915

Arlan
Leutnant d. R. im Inf.-Regt. 180
(Lehrer), gefallen am 8. Juni 1915
bei Hébuterne

Leutnant der Reserve Viktor Veil (Schorndorf) 4/Pioneer Bn 13. Killed in action near Beaumont-Hamel 11 April 1915 during a trench raid. (*Kriegstagbuch aus Schwaben*)

Leutnant der Landwehr Richard Kirn (Horb) 9/180. Killed in action 8 June 1915. (*Kriegstagbuch aus Schwaben*)

Leutnant der Reserve Egbert Arsan (Villenbach, Bavaria) 10/180. Killed in action 8 June 1915. (*Kriegstagbuch aus Schwaben*)

Scupin sounded the men began to pull back. Since the valley in front of the French position was under heavy flanking fire the 7th Coy withdrew using the route alongside the Ancre valley near the road embankment and then to the German lines. French artillery fire on the slope in front of the wire entanglements cut off 15 men from the raiding party. They dug in on the hillside for cover and waited until it was safe to return the following night.

When the raiding party returned it was found that 3 men had been killed and 5 were missing including the company commander. 20 were wounded but all had been safely brought back to the rear. The pioneers had lost 1 *Offizier Stellvertreter* and 1 man killed, 6 men wounded and 1 officer and 1 man missing. Several other companies in RIR 99 had also suffered losses in the raid. French fire had resulted in 5 men killed and 25 men wounded in the regiment.

All three battalions of IR 180 had suffered losses either as participants of the raid or for providing demonstrations that were designed to draw enemy fire; a total of 55 officers and men.

The 7/R99 had captured 51 prisoners that belonged to several regiments in the French XI Corp. These results combined with the prisoners and weapons captured by IR 180 resulted in a very successful raid.

RIR 111 and Reserve *Jäger* Bn 14 executed an undertaking on the same night. The target was the position known as the *Besenhecke* near La Boisselle where the French had created an advanced post and armed it with machine guns.

The raiding party had managed to enter the French position but was unable to take any prisoners. *Leutnant* Magniessen, 4/*Jäger* Bn 14 with his platoon cut through the French wire and overran a sentry post. The guard was shot down and his cap and shoulder straps were cut off and brought back to the German lines, which established that the *118e Régiment d'Infanterie* occupied the line. The raiding party had not suffered any losses.

A similar attempt made by RIR 110 through a crater near Fricourt resulted in a hand grenade fight with the French defenders. The enemy lost several men during the fighting that allowed the regiment to determine that the French *410e Régiment d'Infanterie* occupied the line opposite their regiment.

The French had their revenge on the following day when there was particularly active shelling of division and regimental headquarters to which the German guns responded by bombarding Mailly. The gunners in RFAR 26 remarked 'that it was only fair that the French fired into the headquarters in the rear at times.'[14] One French shrapnel shell that fell near Thiepval on 13 April was made into a lamp for Anton von Borowsky, commanding IR 180, as a souvenir of this period. [15]

At 10 a.m. on 12 April the French artillery opened fire with shells and mines on the quarry near Fricourt. The strength of the bombardment caused RIR 110 to anticipate an attack would follow. As a result the 3/R110 was ordered to man their position at the quarry.

At 11 a.m. an enormous detonation took place under the position held by the 3/R110. The explosion destroyed part of the *Pionier Graben* and buried the entrance to Mine No. I. When the dirt and debris settled a crater had formed approximately 20 meters in diameter and 8 meters deep. The French infantry attempted to occupy the newly-formed crater but were expelled by the surviving members of the 3rd Coy using hand grenades.

The I Battalion *Arzt*, Dr. Niedenthal, who had been walking though the battalion sector that morning, witnessed the mine explosion:

French prisoners from XI Corps captured in raid of 10/11 April 1915 against Hamel and Thiepval Wood. Tallest officer in center is *Leutnant* General von Wundt, commander of the 51st Reserve Infantry Brigade. (*Die 26. Reserve Division 1914-1918*)

Coming back into my dug-out the clock indicated it was almost 10 [sic.] a.m. Suddenly, a roar, a hiss, a bellow, a noise that placed all of the sounds of fighting of the preceding days in its shadow arose in the air. Suddenly the hill was caused to shake and to sway, the covering of the dug-out fell. Everyone hurried into the open despite the impacting shells. The French had set off their mine explosion before ours. The weeklong product of the laborious work by our brave infantrymen and pioneers was destroyed, and with this the lives of more than 15 very courageous men. The earth no longer gave them up. The hail of shells started so suddenly, likewise it suddenly ceased. It was the highest call of duty.

However the approach trenches, communication trenches were all buried. The route to the top led across the open field. And there, what devastation, what woe, what misery! The crater exploded by the French was in the middle of the quarry; the mine had collapsed the largest dug-out and buried 12 reservists, the sergeant and the platoon leader. The men worked without pause to rescue their comrades despite the strong fire from the French. The first one that we found during our digging work was the platoon leader *Leutnant der Reserve* Weymann. He could be seen staring with dead eyes which bore the fear of death by asphyxiation. Above him lay the sergeant, dead. When it was then possible for us to advance into the depths we were happy at first, because the 12 reservists were huddled peacefully by the wall as if they slept. Yes, they slept the eternal sleep. They were sleeping across each other without agony.[16]

Work was started immediately to restore the quarry position while at the same time the crater was searched for wounded men. The explosive effect of the mine was so great that one sentry, *Reservist* Schindler, who was at his post at the moment of the detonation

Soldier in II/180 sending a photograph home displaying his newly-
won Iron Cross 2nd Class. (Author's collection)

was thrown out of the trench by the force of the blast and was buried up to his chest under a mass of earth and rock.

Landwehrmann Koger, 3/R110, spotted his comrade lying helpless in No Man's Land barely 20 meters from the French lines and tried to rescue him. Koger climbed out of the trench and ran up to Schindler and began to dig him out using his entrenching shovel. Koger was spotted by the French who opened fire and forced him to return to the German lines. Koger then improvised a leash out of two rifle slings and crawled back to Schindler despite the heavy fire. He was able to place the slings under Schindler's arms, free him from the loose soil and dragged him back to the German trench. Unfortunately Schindler had been hit at least 7 times by French fire and died the following day in the company position. Koger was awarded the Iron Cross II Class for his act of bravery.

The 3/R110 had suffered heavy losses on the 12th; one officer, one *Vizefeldwebel* and 19 men had been killed; 6 men had been severely wounded. Most of the losses resulted from the company being ordered to occupy the trenches in force in anticipation of an attack. Immediate steps were taken to prevent similar losses in the future. The subsequent change in tactics was to reduce casualties considerably.

The front line trench would be occupied only with a few sentries. The main defensive position and the majority of the men were to be positioned in the second trench. If the enemy was able to penetrate into the first trench after a mine explosion then he could be expelled with hand grenades by the main body of defenders from the rear.

The XIV Reserve Corps retaliated for the mine explosion by setting off Mine No. II on 13 April. Mine No. III was detonated on 21 April in order to head off a French mine that was thought to be ready to detonate. The resulting mine craters had become so numerous they had to be given designations. The mine set off on 12 April by the French became crater 'A', while the mines set off on the 13th and the 21st became craters 'B' and 'C'. Future mine explosions followed suit.

RIR 110 continued to undermine the French line in earnest and advanced a gallery toward the enemy trench once again. Throughout the period of March to June 1915 mine warfare continued to increase on both sides of the line and became a serious threat to the safety of the troops. Pioneer Bn 13 reported numerous losses of men killed by French mines that collapsed mine galleries and dug-outs. Position work in the Ovillers-La Boisselle sector was disrupted on average every 8 days due to a mine explosion.

Every effort was made to listen for enemy mining activity and to take appropriate counter measures but there was no way to determine the exact location of a mine or the date it was to be set off. From April 1915 through January 1916 the La Boisselle sector saw 61 separate mines detonated with charges ranging from 20,000 to 25,000 kilograms of explosives.

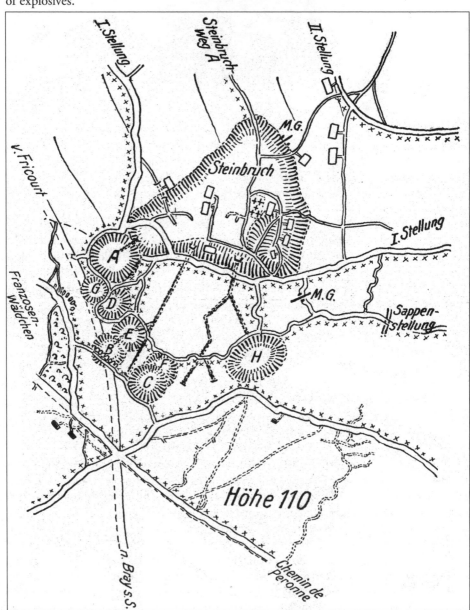

Mine craters on Hill 110.

Mine warfare resulted in changes being made to dug-out construction. Since the danger existed that a mine explosion could collapse the entrance, every dug-out was required to have at least two exits following the same rules being applied to the new mined dug-outs. These alterations called for additional entrenching work that seemed to never end in the opinion of the men. This additional burden was relieved somewhat when two labor companies consisting of over 700 men were assigned to the sector of RIR 109 in order to deepen the rear lines and construct dug-outs.

Daily patrols sent out from both sides of the wire also served to increase the strain on the men's nerves. The French became increasingly aggressive in patrolling No Man's Land and several times attempted to advance up to the wire in the gap between the 26th and 28th Reserve Divisions between Ovillers and La Boisselle. However, each time they were repelled by the alert sentries of RIR 111.

The 28th Reserve Division had still not been able to capture any enemy soldiers despite all of their attempts. A new idea was being tried out near Bécourt. It was decided to trick the French into leaving their trench so that prisoners could be taken once the trap was sprung. A patrol from the 11/R111 placed a straw dummy dressed in a German uniform close in front of the French wire obstacles. The plan called for the French to send out a patrol to inspect the 'fallen man'. RIR 111 would then ambush the patrol and hopefully take a prisoner. The scheme failed, it seems the dummy did not attract any attention from the French troops.

The 'fallen man' was left where he was and the plan was altered to have the artillery damage the French wire obstacles. The damaged obstacles and the body of a German soldier would surely attract the attention of the French this time. Still no one came out of the enemy lines to inspect the damage or the body and again no prisoners were taken. Finally, one patrol returned with an envelope found on the body of an enemy soldier that established that the *293e Régiment d'Infanterie* occupied the position.

Personal valor and pluck was still held in high esteem and one method in which a soldier could obtain recognition was through a daring deed. As such *Kriegsfreiwilliger* Eder, 1/R109, was promoted to *Gefreiter* for going up to the French lines at night and removing a French flag that had been put up on a pole.

The German forces in the west had been further reduced in the first half of 1915 in order to provide additional troops for General August von Mackensen's attempt to breakthrough on the Galician front. The Allies realized that they could not supply guns or troops to help the Russians. What they could do was to attack the Germans in France and Flanders thereby detaining German reserves in the West and hopefully break the trench stalemate at the same time.

General Joffre decided to attack the German lines around Vimy Ridge, the key to the Douai plain beyond. The ridge could then be used as a staging point for a future offensive. The French attacks would be combined with attacks made by British forces further to the north at Festubert and Aubers Ridge.

The French attack would be undertaken by the Tenth Army under General Victor d'Urbal that was familiar with the terrain around Vimy Ridge. It was reinforced with additional men and guns in the weeks prior to the attack.

Preparation fire started on 4 May and continued until the morning of 9 May. The initial French attack broke through the German lines and advanced up to the village of Neuville-St Vaast. The advance slowed considerably following the early success in part due to the lack of fresh reserves and stiffening German resistance in the hours following the attack. However, heavy losses required additional reserves if the German line was to hold. The sounds of the fighting in the north on 9 May could be clearly heard by the men in the 26th Reserve Division.

On 13 May RIR 99 received unexpected orders to prepare the regiment to march. The II, III and IV/R99 marched to Bapaume where the men were loaded on trains and transported to a location near Arras. The men had suspected that this was their destination due to the sounds of heavy fighting heard over the last few days.

RIR 99 reached the new front on the evening of the 13th and was made subordinate to the 1st Bavarian Reserve Division in the I Bavarian Corps commanded by *General der Infanterie Ritter* von Fasbender. The three battalions from RIR 99 were assigned to the Neuville-St. Vaast-Roclincourt-Thelus sector.

When the battalions were withdrawn from the XIV Reserve Corps the remaining regiments were forced to extend their lines in order to provide adequate coverage along the front. The line was now spread very thin and there were no reserves available. Marksmen equipped with telescopic sights were positioned at strategic locations along the front and were used to provide additional support.

RIR 99 was thrown into the heaviest part of the fighting on 14 May when they relieved Prussian and Bavarian units holding the ruined village of Neuville St Vaast. The position was surrounded by French troops on three sides and the fighting was fierce, many times coming down to hand-to-hand combat.

The journey to the village was through a narrow communication trench filled with wounded and exhausted men. Many soldiers who became buried by enemy fire had to be dug out along the route. The village was in chaos. Wagons barricaded some streets, many of the houses were in ruins and the only usable part was the strong stone cellars. The gardens were destroyed, half-charred corpses lay everywhere. The entire village was filled with bodies or pieces of bodies. There were no latrines. The air had a foul smell and constant downpours made the entire situation even worse. Food could only be brought up at night with great effort. Heavy French mines were fired at the German positions constantly adding to the general destruction of the village.

RIR 99 held several houses where the remaining window and door openings were barricaded with stones and sandbags. The French held the houses next door and across the street and had also barricaded the openings. The fighting was continuous all day long mainly with hand grenades, rifle grenades and heavy trench mortars. Men were buried during the day and were dug out at night. A large number of weapons were buried or destroyed in the heavy volume of fire.

It was fortunate for the men of RIR 99 that many of the heavy French trench mortar bombs (25cm) were duds as well as were many 28cm and *Rhimaillo* howitzer shells. The fighting continued for days on end with neither side gaining the advantage. The cellars soon became filled with suffocating smoke, walls were blown down and beams cracked under the strain.

The troops continued to defend the position even as exterior walls collapsed about them. They dug subterranean tunnels from one cellar to the next, worked on dug-outs and in some cases mass graves where the bodies of the fallen could be laid to rest. The latter needed to be done as the smell of the corpses was becoming overwhelming.

O
Herr
gib ihm
die
ewige
Ruhe!

Und
das
ewige
Licht
leuchte
ihm!

Zur frommen Erinnerung
an unsern lieben Sohn, und Bruder
Karl Roth
von Greut bei Waldburg
Pionier im 2. Pionierbatl. 13, 2. Komp.
gestorben den Heldentod fürs Vaterland am
2. Mai 1915 bei Fricourt (Nordfrankreich) im
Alter von 26 Jahren.

Pionier Karl Roth 2/Pioneer Bn 13. Killed in action 2
May 1915 near Fricourt. (Author's collection)

The men were allowed short periods of rest in the rear whenever possible where they enjoyed listening to the regimental bands, drinking Bavarian beer and participating in games and gymnastic events. Still there was the ever-present French aircraft and the occasional bomb plus the rain of shell splinters from German anti-aircraft shells.

Finally, on 29/30 June RIR 99 was relieved and returned to the 26th Reserve Division. The battalions had suffered heavy losses: 7 officers, 178 men killed; 8 officers, 480 men wounded; 52 men missing and 7 officers, 120 men sick.

The survivors of the regiment returned with a wealth of experience. The men had learned many important lessons from their time at Arras. Their experience was soon shared with the rest of the units within the Corps as RIR 99 lectured on their experiences, provided practical demonstrations of counterattacks, trench clearing and especially the use of hand grenades. The latter was practiced diligently but not without unfortunate losses resulting from accidents.

The men were also allowed to rest after their ordeal. They held target practice, route marches, determining range by sight, physical training and arms inspections. They were able to make repairs to their tattered clothing and equipment. The horses and men were given medical exams and many felt it was like peacetime service but without the fatigues.

The XIV Reserve Corps had to contend with further reductions in strength in May that stretched the Corps resources to the limit. Six Württemberg replacement companies that were being trained for the 26th Reserve Division were used for the formation of a new regiment. The companies became part of the III/Bavarian IR 25 being formed in Achiet le Petit, which was then used to form the core of the newly raised RIR 122 later in the month.[17]

Large numbers of active officers were also taken from the division and placed with new formations, especially the 54th (Württemberg) Reserve Division. The loss of so many veteran officers resulted in a drop in the efficiency of the division. Many of the losses were quickly made up with replacement officers and from non-commissioned officers being trained as probationary or aspirant officers behind the front.

The 28th Reserve Division also lost more men at this time. On 14 May RIR 109 turned over 3 officers, 1 officer replacement and 345 non-commissioned officers and men for the establishment of a Corps reserve. A short time later these men became part of the newly formed Baden IR 185 along with men taken from other regiments as well as new recruits.[17] Later in the month another company from RIR 109 was turned over to IR 185 as well. The loss of two companies was eventually made up from new replacement troops. The common practice was to integrate new replacements with veteran soldiers when the battalions were sent to the rear for rest. This allowed the new men to obtain additional instruction on trench warfare and the art of staying alive in the trenches.

The last *Jäger* Bn in the 28th Reserve Division was withdrawn from the division in May. Reserve *Jäger* Bn 14 was relieved and ordered to proceed to the Italian front. The XIV Reserve Corps was at its lowest point in regard to actual troop strength since the start of the war.

Shortly after RIR 99 left for Arras there were ominous signs that something unusual was happening along the Somme front. Toward the end of May it was becoming evident that the French were up to something, in particular in front of the 52nd Division.[19] Aerial photographs revealed the French had constructed at least five new communication trenches. The trenches were opposite the southern sector of the 52nd Division near Toutvent Farm.

The Toutvent Farm position had been created by the Guard Corps during the fighting in autumn 1914. The final line reached by the Guard Corps formed a salient jutting out into the French lines near Hébuterne almost 2,800 meters wide with a depth of over 900 meters. The salient had been extensively developed in the last seven months and the farm had been turned into a stronghold where the Germans had an excellent view of the Hébuterne-Colincamps Plain.

Infantry and artillery observers made note of the sound of wagons coming from the vicinity of Auchonvillers during the night. Observers in RIR 119 near Beaumont also noticed a growing restlessness in the French trenches and rear areas. Wagons and other vehicles could be seen moving back and forth, there was heavy train traffic between Albert and Auchonvillers. New saps were being driven forward from the French lines and more communication trenches began to appear. German aerial photographs confirmed these reports and gave the army time to plan for countermeasures against the expected attack. Cyclists brought rumors of a French attack that were also circulating among the remaining civilian population. It seemed that the name of Joffre was on everyone's lips and hope for liberation was growing rapidly.

French aircraft began to appear in large numbers along the front in early June. No part of the Somme front was safe from French bombers and fighters.

> On one day our German and French pilots circled in the air and pursued each other, something like Sven Hedin described it. In his book however he sometimes exaggerated quite strongly. For men, who are not in the war, it is written correctly; for us however his writing makes no such impression. (Much fiddle-faddle prevails in the war, but only behind the front. The girlish French also contribute their part). A pilot always appeared over Bapaume for the last three days and dropped bombs. He has already caused some wounded and dead (also French). One time the bomb ignited a large pile of straw by the railway station, and he was seen by the 4 guns

that put up a defense and always fired proficiently with shrapnel, so far unfortunately without success.

Already two times at night we noticed two airships; one of them dropped 3 bombs in Bapaume each 43kg., as reported in the newspapers, and the first hit the post office, the second striking into the garden of the house where General von Stein, the 14th Army Corps commander lives. The third did not explode. For different reasons one suspects that subterranean cables could still exist, for example from out of Cambrai or St. Quentin. The French behind our front enjoy too much freedom; they are interested in all troop movements and know fairly exactly the course of our positions. It was then no secret for example that we were going to Beaumont. Karl Losch, 3/R119 [20]

New enemy batteries appeared on the right of the 26th Reserve Division. The volume of artillery fire began to swell along the front of the 52nd Division as well as against the right flank of the 26th Reserve Division. The fire increased in strength and larger caliber guns appeared almost daily. It grew to such intensity that the staff of RIR 121 took the precaution of moving into the regimental battle headquarters. The days that followed provided the first experience of the effect of concentrated artillery fire on even the best-prepared defenses.

The connection between the two divisions had always been tenuous at best. Only a shallow communication trench connected the right wing of RIR 119 with the left wing of IR 170. This route could barely be traveled during the day. No attempts were made to improve the position until May when a deeper trench was started near the Serre-Mailly road. The trench was not completed before the French attack.

The III/R119 had a front row seat for the French assault. They watched the French gunners send shell after shell into the terrain from dawn until dusk. The artillerymen would use the services of aerial observation during the lunch hour in order to make corrections to their fire. The intense bombardment shredded wire obstacles and shattered the recently constructed trenches in the regimental sector. The right wing of the regiment suffered heavily in this fire.

The increased French activity was indeed the precursor of an attack. The French army was determined to eliminate the Toutvent Farm salient and capture the village of Serre. With Serre in their possession they could dominate the Ancre Valley and threaten the German lines further south. At the same time the French would create a diversion from the sector in the north around Arras where heavy fighting had been going on since May at the Lorette Spur and Vimy Ridge. Hopefully this would also force the Germans to withdraw men from the Arras front or at the very least tie up German reserves along the Somme front.

The forces that were involved by Serre were part of the French Second Army under General de Castelnau. The plan called for a period of preparation fire against the German lines after which the attack would take place on 7 June. Three regiments of infantry would take part in the initial attack, the *65e, 93e* and *137e Régiments d'Infanterie* on a front almost 2,000 meters wide. The French High Command expected that at least two German trench lines and Toutvent Farm would be captured within the first 10 minutes of the attack.

Serre before the Somme Offensive. (Author's collection)

The XIV Reserve Corps commander, von Stein, anticipated the attack would come shortly and fall mainly against the 52nd Division. He ordered the division to take all steps necessary to prepare for the attack. Von Stein also directed the 26th Reserve Division to provide support. Four battalions of infantry were immediately available in the event of an attack, the I/R99, II/R121, I and III/180. Additional reinforcements were available from the 28th Reserve Division, the II/R109 and III/R111. A new ammunition depot was established in Irles, communications between units was tested and the total number of communication officers was increased. The connections between the 26th Reserve Division and 52nd Division were constantly being tested. While all of the preparations were occurring the infantry could not quite believe it was going to happen, it was such a beautiful month.

The artillery units in the 26th Reserve Division regrouped to provide reinforcement batteries. Two new howitzer battery positions were established near the ruined mill of Pozières in a short period of time. The gun positions were carefully constructed and protected against aerial observation, not even tracks leading to the position were allowed to betray them. Further camouflage was used in the manner of tree branches that were hard to detect even at close range.

From 2 June to 4 June the 7th and 9/RFAR 26, light field howitzer batteries, moved from the left wing of the 26th Reserve Division and went into position at the mill, where the guns were registered. One further section of field artillery was placed behind Hill 143 and the newly arrived 10cm Battery Rickel was positioned east of the howitzers and behind the field gun section. The artillery was ready.

IR 180 sent out a patrol in the night of 4/5 June near the Chapel of Thiepval in an attempt to discover the enemy intentions. Unfortunately the patrol suffered a number of casualties and did not succeed in learning anything new

Reserves moving toward Serre, June 1915 – XIV Reserve Corps. (Author's collection)

During the first days of June French fire varied in intensity, it even died down for several days. Reports filtered through that heavy artillery and trench mortars had continuously bombarded the trenches in the Toutvent Farm-Beaucourt Sector. The trenches had been almost completely leveled and communications had been severely disrupted. On 6 June the fire increased in intensity and the trenches on both sides of Toutvent Farm suffered heavily and the wire obstacles became virtually torn apart.

On the same day the 52nd Division reported the French were cutting gaps in their wire obstacles, an attack was expected at any moment. However it did not materialize on the 6th. Instead French artillery fire against the 52nd Division and right wing of the 26th Reserve Division increased to an intensity never seen before by the troops. Certainly an attack could not be far off.

Several of the reserve battalions were moved closer to the anticipated battle zone. At 6.30 p.m. the III/180 was placed on alert and moved to Miraumont while earlier in the morning the III/R111 made preparations to move. Ammunition supplies were replenished; iron rations and bandage packets were inspected. The battalion was ready to leave at a moment's notice.

At 3 a.m. on 7 June a message arrived at the 26th Reserve Division during a lull in the French bombardment. It was dated 6 June and had been sent by the 52nd Division and read: 'Trenches completely buried. Attack expected in the morning, artillery support requested.'[21] The 26th and 28th Reserve Divisions immediately began to shift more men to the threatened area and alerted the artillery. The III/180 was sent to the hollow east of Puiseux, the I/R99 was sent to Hill 143 northeast of Beaumont while RIR 119 sent reserves behind Hill 143. Two companies from the II/R121 were sent to the artillery hollow east of Hill 143; the other two companies from this battalion were sent to Grandcourt. At 4 a.m. the III/R111 marched toward Beauregard in the dense morning fog. The battalion reached its destination and found shelter in old trenches and in folds in the ground that provided protection against artillery fire and aerial observation. The men soon discovered that their battalion was positioned alongside a number of batteries. This would prove to be an uncomfortable position as the day progressed and the batteries drew French fire that came closer and closer.

At 4 a.m. the French fire that had been silent for several hours suddenly grew to great intensity. Field guns covered the position of RIR 119 with numerous shells. 30 minutes later enemy infantry opened a lively fire against the regimental position. The men in RIR 119 stood ready to receive the French but still no attack came and shortly after 5 a.m. the rifle fire stopped. Afterward, heavy fire could be heard coming from their right, followed by an eerie silence. No one knew what was happening as the entire area was shrouded in fog and smoke and all telephone lines had been cut. The regiment informed division headquarters by runner while the men restored the buried trenches to a defensible state again and again. RIR 119 also reported that all contact with the 52nd Division had been lost and the right wing was hanging in the air; Sector S6 south of the Serre-Mailly road was holding.

In order to determine what was happening with the 52nd Division *Unteroffizier* Wenz and 4 men made a reconnaissance and reported their findings. They advanced toward the positions that had been held by IR 170 using all available cover. The patrol had to cross 400 meters of open ground up to a wide hollow in full sight of the French, cross the hollow and proceed another 200 meters over a hill where a French trench was located. The men jumped from shell hole to shell hole as they made their journey toward the hill and finally disappeared from view. 15 minutes later the five men were observed

Reserves moving forward, men from RIR 121 marching
toward the front. (*Zwischen Arras und Péronne*)

at the crest of the hill with French shells falling all around them. Eventually all 5 men in the patrol returned safely; the entire journey took five hours to accomplish and the men were exhausted.

Patrol Wenz reported the French had taken Toutvent Farm and threatened to envelop the left wing of IR 170. They brought back a rough sketch of the situation that was immediately sent to headquarters. Later in the evening Wenz guided reinforcements along the same path they had taken earlier in the day.

Many hours passed before any other messages arrived from the 52nd Division. The next message confirmed the report that the French had broken through the line at Toutvent Farm in the dense fog and were advancing toward Sector Serre-East. The advance had been stopped but Toutvent Farm was thought to be lost.

The French had quickly captured nearly 1,400 meters of trenches in the first rush but not the sought-after Toutvent Farm. The garrison of the farm held their ground at first but after continued French pressure the farm was eventually overrun. Once the initial assault was over the French began to consolidate their gains and prepare to meet any German counterattacks. Smaller attacks continued against pockets of German resistance.

The fog lifted sufficiently by 9 a.m. to allow the artillery observers in the 26th Reserve Division to determine the limits of the French advance. It appeared that the enemy had penetrated the width of nearly one-kilometer north of the Serre-Mailly road. Once visual contact had been established the gunners in the 26th Reserve Division provided valuable assistance to the hard-pressed men in the 52nd Division. Artillery Group Bornemann in Beaucourt directed the fire of two howitzer batteries and the 8/Foot Artillery Regiment 10 against the French.

Observers could see French reinforcements swarming in and behind the position like ants. Men could be seen carrying ammunition and entrenching tools as they moved into the newly-captured terrain.

At 7 a.m. the III/180 was at the exit of Puisieux ready to march. A short time later the battalion moved to a hollow at the southeastern exit of the village and created shallow emplacements for protection against artillery fire. At noon the battalion was ordered to recapture Sector S3 between La Louviere Farm and Toutvent Farm and then expand their gains out from La Louviere Farm. The men proceeded to Copse 125 and dropped their packs and picked up hand grenades and entrenching tools. The heat was oppressive and the men were under sporadic artillery fire. 18 men suffered from heat stroke and had to be left behind in the copse.

When the III/180 reached Sector S3 it was discovered that units from IR 170 and IR 66 had already recaptured most of the sector so it was decided to attack Sector S4 instead. The battalion advanced and after a brief fight occupied the sector and began to dig in.

Additional support troops were rapidly moving toward Serre. After receiving reports that the French had captured 1,800 meters of trenches between the Serre-Hébuterne and Serre-Mailly roads the II/R109 was immediately ordered to proceed toward Miraumont. Later in the evening the battalion moved west of the railway embankment at the Beaucourt-Puisieux au Mont-Miraumont road and came under heavy shellfire.

The artillery support from the 26th Reserve Division was critical on the first day of the French attacks and subsequent fighting. Group Bornemann provided covering fire to the 52nd Division with flanking fire from three field gun batteries and Section Mühlen. Two light field howitzer batteries at the mill under *Hauptmann* Graf von Preysing fired

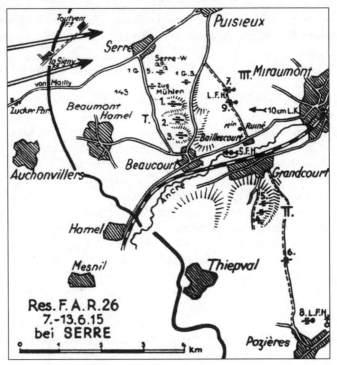

26th Reserve Division artillery positions near Serre, June 1915.

into the new French positions while *Hauptmann* Nickel in Puisieux directed the fire from his 10cm guns into the columns behind the French lines. Battery Köhler (15cm) directed its fire against La Signy Farm and the nearby sugar factory. The II/RFAR 26 under Major Stump and the left wing howitzer batteries at Pozières helped to paralyze French movement.

French guns searched for the annoying artillery throughout the day, aided by aerial observation. The German gunners maintained their fire in the hot June weather with shrapnel balls whistling about them almost non-stop. The 1st Battery, RFAR 26, alone, fired 1,350 shells on 7 June.

Toward midday French infantry advanced against Battalion Scupin (IR 180) over open fields; they were quickly brought to a halt. At 1 p.m. the III/R111 was ordered to Puisieux and marched toward the village under sporadic artillery fire. When the battalion reached the village the men found that it was still inhabited by old women and children, who felt that they would be safe behind the closed shutters of their homes. Afterward the III/R111 was ordered to support IR 170 at Serre. The battalion advanced toward the village using houses and badly damaged communication trenches for protection against enemy observation and fire.

Once darkness had fallen the light ammunition columns drove up to the batteries and replenished the ammunition supply while French guns continuously maintained a lively searching fire. The field kitchens also came up but the men barely had time to eat under the harassment fire that was kept up throughout the night. Counterattacks planned for the night of 7/8 June had to be cancelled because of the immense difficulties getting orders to the battalions scattered along the front and with the impossible task of trying to coordinate the attacks with such short notice.

8 June

The French offensive continued at 3 a.m. on the 8th. This time the attacks took place near La Louviere Farm using the *75e* and *14e Régiments d'Infanterie*. The 8th and 11/180 provided support for IR 170 and IR 66 in Sector S3 and prevented the French advancing from Toutvent Farm. At 4.15 a.m. forward units of the 10/180 counterattacked the portion of Sector S3 still held by the French by crossing over open fields. The 10th Coy was able to recapture the trench and took 40 prisoners in hand to hand fighting. The 9th and 11/180 advanced in support and assisted in taking the remainder of Sector S3 and 50 prisoners.

Just before 10:30 a.m. the French attacked in four consecutive lines that were completely shattered in the fire from the German batteries before they were able to reach their objective. During this time the 9th and 10/180 successfully forced down a French plane close behind enemy lines.

The French renewed their attacks at 11:30 a.m. during a violent thunderstorm. The attack was repelled once again with infantry and artillery fire. During the fighting two non-commissioned officers in IR 180 advanced with hand grenades and drove a number

Kielwein
Leutnant b. R. im Inf.-Regt. 180
(stud. mach.), gef. am 8. Juni 1915
bei Hébuterne

Mörike
Leutnant b. R. im Inf.-Regt. 180,
gefallen am 8. Juni 1915
bei Hébuterne

Autenrieth
Leutn. b. R. i.Res.-Feldart.-Reg. 26,
gefallen bei Beaucourt sur Ancre
am 9. Juni 1915

Leutnant der Reserve Friedrich Kielwein (Tübingen) 11/180. Killed in action 8 June 1915. (*Kriegstagbuch aus Schwaben*)

Leutnant der Reserve Paul Mörike (Nordhausen) 10/180. Killed in action 8 June 1915. (*Kriegstagbuch aus Schwaben*)

Vizefeldwebel/Leutnant der Reserve Ernst Autenrieth Staff I/RFAR 26. Killed in action 9 June 1915. (*Das Württembergisches Reserve-Feldartillerie Regiment Nr. 26 im Weltkrieg 1914-1918*)

of French troops in Sector S3 into the fire of the 9/180 where they were effectively cut off. They agreed to surrender after being promised good treatment; a total of 3 corporals and 34 privates were taken into captivity.

A number of French attacks were made during the day that were preceded by more than an hour of heavy bombardment - all failed in the heavy defensive fire. However the German trenches were also being slowly destroyed in each consecutive attack and by the end of the day they did not afford much protection.

The exhausted German defenders received some welcome relief at night in the form of two fresh companies from IR 66, who replaced two companies from IR 180. The I/190 also arrived at La Louvière Farm at midnight.

Detachment Hullesem (I/R99 and II/R121) received orders to prevent a breakthrough between Serre and Beaumont from Hill 143. At the same time Oberst Krause (I and II/185) along with the II/R109 were positioned east of Serre and the I/190 was located at Puisieux. These units were to throw the French out of Serre in the event the village was captured. The II/R109 moved 1 kilometer north of Beaucourt where the men were housed in stalls constructed out of planks in a hillside and nearby sunken road. They took cover in these crude shelters from the continuous French artillery bombardment.

The III/R111 reached the village of Serre at 5 a.m. on the 8th after suffering losses from shellfire along the route. The battalion found the existing defenses of Serre had been completely shattered by artillery fire; there were no deep dug-outs or wire obstacles. All they found was a badly damaged shallow trench and shell hole next to shell hole. The men quickly got their shovels out and began to deepen the trench, connect the shell holes and scraped crude shelters into the front wall of the trench.

The men of RIR 111 remained under heavy French fire from morning until evening. Whatever cover they had managed to create in the short time available to them was virtually leveled. Many men had become buried during the day and were dug out by their comrades only to be buried again a short time later. Every pause in the enemy fire was immediately used to restore the trenches to some order. The French fire increased at night and losses began to climb. Wounded men were treated in dressing stations located in the cellars of badly damaged houses. The men were thirsty and hungry and were forced to eat their iron rations.

In order for the German artillery to place effective fire against the new French positions they first needed to know the extent of the breakthrough. A patrol from RIR 119 under *Unteroffizier* Wenz was sent out again to plant signal flags on both sides of the breakthrough position for that purpose. Patrols were also sent out from RIR 111 to determine where the opposing lines were located.

French fire was still directed toward RIR 119 but still no infantry attacks followed. All the time this was going on fresh reserves were flowing into the area from the direction of Beaumont that formed two prongs ready to advance against the French along the Serre-Mailly road. Bombing parties stood guard at the trench barricades, many of whom were young recruits and volunteers with only a few weeks of experience in the trenches. A number of small French attacks all failed in the heavy defensive fire and the defenders were even able to retake some of the lost terrain in local counterattacks. Losses in RIR 119 and RIR 121 were low on this day.

Henßler

Haupt.mann im Ref.-Inf.-Reg. 119,
gefallen am 13. Juni 1915
bei Beaumont

Hauptmann Rudolf Henssler
(Stuttgart) 4/R119. Wounded
in action 13 June 1915, died
the same day at the main
dressing station, Miraumont.
(*Kriegstagbuch aus Schwaben*)

Hornberger

Hauptm. d. R. i. Ref.-Inf.-Reg. 121
(Finanzamtmann), gef. am 13. Juni
1915 bei Serre

Hauptmann der Reserve Gustav
Hornberger (Baiersbronn) 5/R121.
Killed in action 13 June 1915.
(*Kriegstagbuch aus Schwaben*)

Nagel

Hauptmann im Ref.-Inf.-Regt. 121,
gefallen am 13. Juni 1915
bei Serre

Hauptmann Guido Nagel
(Ludwigsburg) 7/R121. Killed
in action 13 June 1915.
(*Kriegstagbuch aus Schwaben*)

9 June

De Castelnau now changed the focus of his attacks to the south near the Serre-Mailly
Maillet road near La Signy Farm. Three fresh regiments would make the attack. The
243e and 347e Régiments would make the actual attack while the *233e Régiment* would
follow in reserve.

Heavy fog delayed the preparation bombardment and the attacks did not begin until
5 p.m. The main attack was broken up in the heavy defensive fire and from newly laid
belts of wire entanglements but the French persevered and forced back the units of the
52nd Division to the second line.

> In both of the last days the greatest possible hellish noise prevailed on the right of
> us. The mutual artillery fired furiously day and night. The French have attacked
> and occupied a forward trench. If they are still in there now I do not know. Huge
> reserves of infantry and artillery lie behind us. They still have not bombarded our
> position, I suppose however [they have] that of the 1st and 2nd Companies. We
> don't know if they will also attack us. We are on guard and ready to receive them
> warmly. Karl Losch, 3/R119 [22]

La Louvière farm. (*Die 26. Reserve Division 1914-1918*)

The flank of the I/R119 was exposed so reinforcements were sent as support consisting of the 6th and 8/R121, 1/180 and part of the I/R99. An attempt was made to establish a connection with the 1/170 during a hand grenade fight against the French but failed. Several unsuccessful French attacks took place against the position held by RIR 99 and RIR 121 in the early morning fog.

Two companies from RIR 121 were sent to *Feste* Soden near the southern extent of the French advance. They were ordered to close the gap between RIR 119 and IR 170 at the point where the new trench lines formed a distinct projection from the German lines.

Reinforcements from RIR 109 and RIR 111 remained in their positions in the event of further French advances toward Serre. RIR 109 was in an exposed position in a small hollow where 12cm shells impacted that resulted in only 7 men wounded. Conflicting orders arrived throughout the day. Instructions arrived to dig entrenchments but were then cancelled. Orders to prepare for a counterattack arrived and were also suddenly cancelled without explanation.

The III/R111 sent out several patrols to clarify the situation along their front. The battalion watched as several French attacks were broken up by infantry and artillery fire. By late evening it was possible to bring up the field kitchens and distribute warm food to the men.

The regimental adjutant worked feverishly to obtain sufficient building materials for the III/R111 in order to construct adequate shelters. In just a few days the battalion had constructed 50 shellproof dug-outs. The skills learned through hard work in quiet periods had paid off substantially and helped to reduce casualties considerably.

The heavy fighting had disrupted many of the connections between the different units. Patrols sent by the III/R111 toward Toutvent Farm established that the French had advanced to the '*Wisengrunde*' 700 meters west of Serre and had entrenched. A 3-man patrol sent from the right in order to establish a connection with IR 66 suddenly bumped into French soldiers behind a traverse. The patrol threw hand grenades and the enemy

Restoration work on the front line trench north of Beaumont following the
fighting at Serre, RIR 119. (*Die 26. Reserve Division 1914-1918*)

fled leaving 2 prisoners behind. The men in the patrol realized they could not advance
any further without knowing the strength and position of the French and they withdrew
with their prisoners and reported to headquarters.

The III/180 attacked on the right wing and ejected the French located near La Louviere
Farm. IR 180 continued to advance and eventually established a connection with IR 66.
100 prisoners were taken during the advance that belonged to the French 21st Division,
XI Corps and from several infantry and heavy artillery units from the XIV Army Corps.

10 June

French attacks continued throughout the 10th on the left wing by Beaucourt. At 4 p.m.
French artillery fired upon the weak remnants of IR 170 in Sector S6. The infantry assault
followed after one hour of fire but quickly suffered serious losses in the heavy defensive
fire from the 1/180 and 8/R121; however some enemy units continued to attack. The 8/
R121 was forced to withdraw before the company could be fully enveloped and withdrew
to Hill 143 by sections.

The 1/180 ran out of ammunition during the attack and the 12/R111 discovered
their predicament. The 12th Coy gathered all of the ammunition they could locate and
dragged it over to the 1/180, losing several men along the way to artillery fire.

When RIR 111 arrived they discovered the 1/180 had lost all of its officers and non-
commissioned officers in the heavy fighting. *Vizefeldwebel* Kessler took command and
several other non-commissioned officers assisted him in organizing the defenses.

Kessler sent several men toward Serre to request reinforcements. The French continued
to press the attack and threatened to overrun the small garrison when Kessler grabbed a
bugle and jumped up onto the parapet and sounded the call 'do not send reinforcements
here'. He was shot through the head and died instantly but his actions helped to hold
back the French and warn off any German reinforcements that might follow. When the
fighting died down almost everyone defending the sector had been killed or wounded.

This left the right wing of RIR 119 exposed once again. Two companies from the II/R121 were sent as support and the line was secure once more. French artillery continued to pound the German lines throughout the day.

Several small-scale counterattacks all failed to recover any lost ground; the attempts had not been coordinated and did not have sufficient forces needed to succeed. Larger counterattacks by the I/R99 and II/R109 did not take place at all due to the same difficulties in coordinating the actions of the separate units.

Sector S3 on the right wing was still in danger of being overrun from a hollow located to the south where the French could move troops against La Louvière Farm without being observed. This threat was overcome by shifting men from the I/190 and III/180 into new defensive positions during the night of 9/10 June and during the morning of the 10th.

All of the French attacks on this day had failed to shift the line but some of the defending units were forced to withdraw a short distance. The defenders received much needed support with the arrival of two battalions from the I Bavarian Army Corps that had just arrived on the field.

The heavy German artillery fire being employed from three directions stopped many of the French attacks. The night was put to good use repairing the badly damaged trenches and installing wire entanglements. Serre and the surrounding sectors were now officially assigned to the 26th Reserve Division.

11 June

The day was quiet and the defenders made use of this time to improve the trenches and accomplish some well-deserved relief of units that had been fighting since the start of the French attacks. Great care was taken to prevent French aircraft or balloons from observing any unusual foot traffic. It was believed that the battalion headquarters dug-out for the III/R111 was betrayed in this manner. Shell after shell landed in the vicinity of the dug-out until it was destroyed by two direct hits. Several runners and two orderlies were killed and the battalion staff was scattered.

RIR 111 started to dig a new front line west of the village of Serre. This activity drew the attention of French observers and resulted in an increase in French artillery fire that continued throughout the night into the 12th.

Plans were put into motion on the morning of the 11th for a counterattack against the French in Sector S6 by the Serre-Mailly road. The attack would be made by Regiment Krause (I and II/185), Regiment Heiden (II/R109 and I/186) and one battalion from Bavarian RIR 15. The instructions were distributed to the battalion and company leaders.

At 1.30 a.m. the men formed for the attack at the western edge of Serre. The 7th and 8/R109 were chosen as assault companies. The first wave would penetrate the enemy lines and hold the position. The second wave would clear the saps and trenches in the main line while the third wave would carry entrenching tools and prepare the captured trenches for defense. In order to avoid heavy losses there was a 20-meter spacing between the first and second waves, 30 meters between the second and third waves.

The assault began at 2 a.m. Numerous flares and searchlights slowed the advance when the men came under heavy machine gun and rifle fire, especially on the right flank. The first trench was reached but it was found to be unoccupied. The assault companies came to the conclusion that the French had withdrawn when the attack was discovered.

Just at the moment a hand grenade fight broke out between the opposing sides two red flares were fired from the French lines that signaled the start of a bombardment by light and heavy guns that lasted an hour.

The assault companies continued to advance into the maze of trenches but quickly became confused when the trench configuration did not match the crude maps they had been given before the advance. It was not feasible to continue under these circumstances.

The men withdrew toward Beaucourt with one platoon from the 6/R109 being left behind in order to establish a connection with the many missing men in case they showed up afterward. This platoon was also given instructions to establish a connection between the trenches south of the Serre-Mailly road with the trenches west of Serre. French fire prevented the platoon from accomplishing this last goal. A second attack was ordered for the early morning of 12 June with the men advancing at intervals in order to avoid unnecessary losses; however the second attack was also unsuccessful.

Hauptmann Nagel was in command of Sector S6. A decision was made to dig a new switch line that would close the existing gap at the right wing of the 26th Reserve Division by the Serre-Mailly road up to the area southwest of La Louvière Farm, a distance of 2.5 kilometers. Entrenching began immediately on what became designated the *Henssler Graben*.

Early on 13 June the French made one last attempt to capture Serre and the important heights controlled by the village. The *327e Régiment* along with the remnants of the *233e* and *243e Régiments* would make the attack that started shortly after 4 a.m. with two waves of infantry followed by assault columns.

The French attacked the German lines north of the Serre-Mailly road. The III/R121 holding the right flank was forced back by the onslaught. A number of prisoners were taken from the regiment but the bulk of the line held and the French were prevented from making any further headway. The II/R121 south of the road held its ground and many of the French troops were cut down 150 meters in front of the position by the fire of the support battalions.

The 4/R119 alongside RIR 121 repelled each attack upon its position while the flames from the burning Serre farmyard lit up the sky. The doctors and stretcher-bearers were busy rescuing the wounded men from the burning farm cellar during the fighting.

After the initial attack had failed the French made a few weak attempts to advance but by 8 a.m. the fighting was over. The men could clearly see the enemy flooding back toward La Signy Farm; there were no further attacks. The III/R121 had taken the brunt of the French attack on 13 June and had lost 314 officers and men.

As no additional reserves were required to repel the latest French attack IR 180 and RIR 99 were occupied constructing new trenches, wire obstacles and dug-outs in the Serre sector and in the vicinity of La Louviere Farm.

The French attempted a huge and desperate breakthrough, they succeeded in at most occupying 1 or 2 German trenches without any problem, but they did not get through any further. In the Frankfurt newspaper came a portrayal of the fighting at Arras and Neuve Chapelle from May 9th until the start of June. The fighting there seems to have become severe again. Maybe the attack at Hébuterne was an attempted diversion, so that we would move troops away from Arras. Today the

French artillery has still not fired many shots; maybe the fighting will gradually calm down. Karl Losch, 3/R119 [23]

Once the attacks were finally finished a projection had formed out of the isolated *Hennsler* and *Bayern* trenches created by IR 185 and Regiment Heiden. The position later received the designation '*Heidenkopf*'.[24]

French artillery fire continued to be heavy for much of the day. It eventually diminished and the infantry and artillery were observed moving off toward the south. In the days and weeks that followed there was a noticeable reduction in French forces along the Serre front.

The next few weeks saw extensive work on the new trench line running just west of Serre. The heavy damage caused during the French attacks had to be repaired and the front needed to be as strong as possible in order to withstand any future attacks. Much of the work was done under sporadic French fire and in some cases the men worked within 30 meters of the enemy.

This morning a small shell splinter flew in the fire trench and hit me on the little finger of my right hand that I had on my head, and caused a small flesh wound. I went to the doctor, there they brushed on iodine and made a plaster around it. Therefore not dangerous and however I mercifully remained protected ... Meanwhile

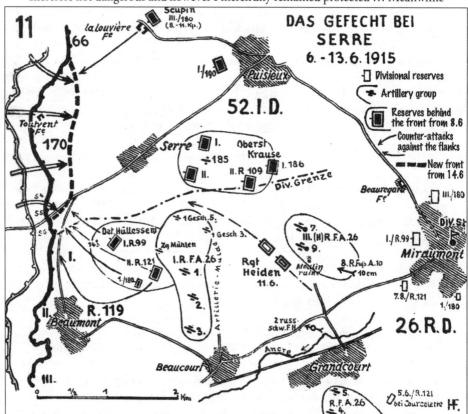

XIV Reserve Corps troop dispositions near Serre, June 1915.

Postcard sent by *Schützen* Poessel MG Coy/R119 on 27 June 1915. '… as you probably have heard we had much trouble here in the past but we were lucky…' (Author's collection)

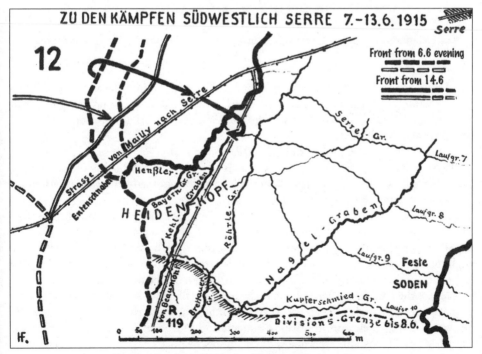

Formation of the *Heidenkopf* and new line near Serre.

Men from IR 180 in Serre after the June fighting. (Author's collection)

at Hébuterne it appears the thing has died down. The French artillery doesn't shoot much, ours somewhat more. Karl Losch, 3/R119 [25]

Losch kept his parents and siblings up to date on his wound. In a letter dated late June he wrote 'My finger is almost healed, the shell exploded far away and the splinter had lost its force.' Finally, in early July 1915 he wrote: 'The splinter has fallen on the ground and my finger has healed.' [26]

On 27/28 June two groups from the 4/R99 captured a listening post directly south of the Serre-Mailly, Serre-Beaumont crossroads while IR 185 captured another listening post north of the Serre-Mailly road. When this was accomplished it allowed a continuous front line trench to finally be completed.

All of the units that had been sent to the Serre sector were slowly returned to their regiments as fresh troops became available. The III/R111 had perhaps the longest march ahead of it as it returned to the 28th Reserve Division. The battalion was relieved on the night of 22/23 June and the men were assembled in Miraumont where they were met by the regimental band that had been sent to escort them on the march to Le Sars.

When the battalion reached Le Sars the road was lined with men from the regiment as if attending a parade. The weary III Battalion marched into the village at dawn while the band played. Their uniforms were disintegrating and covered in clay and chalk, their faces had a wild look and everyone sported a heavy beard.

2R/Pioneer Bn 13 on Hill 110 near Fricourt displaying their equipment. (Author's collection)

By the end of the month the tedious existence of trench warfare had returned. The German command came to the conclusion that the French attacks were not an attempt to break through the German lines; instead it was a diversion and a means to improve their position.

The lessons learned in the last few weeks were reviewed by the staff of the XIV Reserve Corps. Despite the precautions taken by the 52nd Division and the preparations made by the 26th Reserve Division the French were still able to advance on a 2.5-kilometer front using artillery and trench mortars to prepare the way. German counterattacks were found to be less than successful in retaking the lost ground. While the latter was considered to be a serious setback by the German command it also provided practical experience for the future. The conclusion was that more men and longer artillery preparation would be needed if the counterattacks were to be successful. They realized that men serving under unfamiliar leadership was no guarantee that even with the appropriate orders being issued they would actually be executed, particularly at night. Finally the German command realized that other than the moral effect of retaking the old line it would not bring them any other benefits.

The German artillery had provided effective fire throughout the fighting. Many French assaults were broken up by heavy fire where up to 1,800 shells were fired daily by each battery. Much of the success was due to the foresight of the leadership providing reinforcements for the artillery on the right wing of the 26th Reserve Division. Special measures were taken in providing reconnaissance and registration fire prior to the attacks. Ample supplies of ammunition were kept at hand in shellproof armories where thousands of rounds could be stored. When supplies were being used up replacements were brought up in a timely manner each night.

During the fighting the French artillery had paid special attention to the gun positions located in the Artillery Hollow at Beaucourt using observation aircraft and balloons. There was considerable ammunition expenditure with conspicuously little effect. Some of the equipment was damaged in the shelling but the men were perfectly safe inside their deep dug-outs and tunnels. The greatest discomfort occurred when the ground trembled and quivered under the heavy impacts or when the occasional entrance was blown in

Overall, the lessons learned in the heavy fighting at Serre were to be put to good use in the following months and years. It was important that defensive artillery fire should be deployed quickly and accurately on all sectors of the front that were in range. Every attempt possible would be made to increase the depth of the effective range of the guns

Trench memorial to the loss of 40 brave comrades, 7/R121. See Appendix II – Jakob Hönes and Albert Thielecke, the subjects of this Appendix, were two of these men. (Author's collection)

to the front as well as on both flanks in order to guarantee the fastest fire readiness day and night. Collaboration with artillery units in neighboring divisions was painstakingly cultivated to provide mutual support. Firing with the aid of aircraft and balloons was preferred but increasingly prevented by enemy air superiority. Artillery liaison officers worked tirelessly with the infantry in order that each branch understood the needs and limitations of the other and the use and effectiveness of the different weapons. Registration fire for all targets was to be transmitted to senior commands using an extensive telephone network system that would enable artillery fire to be employed when and where needed.

The human cost of the fighting at Serre was high. The 26th Reserve Division alone lost many good officers including several at battalion level in the fighting. Overall the division lost some 900 officers and men killed or wounded. It is estimated that the French had lost some 2,000 killed and approximately 9,000 wounded.

Neither the attack on Vimy Ridge nor the subsequent fighting at Serre had the desired results the French expected. The German reserves were not tied down in the West, in fact two divisions had actually been sent to the East to help the German offensive in Galicia.

The fighting at Serre did not force the recall of the three battalions from RIR 99 fighting in Neuville St Vaast and failed to take the strategic village of Serre. The new French position was gained at a very high cost in killed, wounded and missing. During this period the 26th Reserve Division had received only one battalion as temporary reinforcements, the IV Battalion of Bremen *Landwehr* Regiment 75. The battalion was eventually withdrawn after only two months with the division.

The French had attempted to divert attention away from the fighting at Serre by setting off mines at various intervals along the front. Many of these were accompanied by small-scale attacks that were easily repelled. One subsequent attack took place against RIR 110 on 18 June. The infantry attack was repelled leaving behind 4 dead that were identified as belonging to the *403e Régiment*.

On 28 June the French set off a mine on Hill 110 and then attacked. This time the French utilized an especially heavy trench mortar with a shell that exploded with a loud crash. The men called the shells 'sauerkraut barrels' after their shape. The new trench mortar was found to have only a small physical and moral effect despite the large size of the missile.

The XIV Reserve Corps introduced a new weapon to counter French mining activity. Medium Minenwerfer Platoon 138 was installed in the sector of RIR 109 and used to bombard tunnel entrances using 17cm shells.

The following months would bring major changes to the front held by the XIV Reserve Corps. All of the experiences and hard work performed up until this point in the war would be repaid with interest in the following year.

Chapter notes

1. Losch, op cit, *Feldpost* letter dated 30 May 1915.
2. Ibid.
3. R. Baumgartner (Ed.), 'An der Somme, An interview with Soldat Emil Goebelbecker', *Der Angriff, A Journal of World War 1 History*, No. 3, p. 4.
4. Losch, op cit, *Feldpost* letter dated 14 May 1915.
5. R. Baumgartner (Ed.), 'An der Somme, An interview with Soldat Emil Goebelbecker', *Der Angriff, A Journal of World War 1 History*, No. 3, p. 5.
6. Losch, op cit, *Feldpost* letter dated 29 April 1915.
7. Losch, op cit, *Feldpost* letter dated 23 May 1915.
8. Losch, op cit, *Feldpost* letter dated 24 June 1915.
9. G. Frisch, *Das Reserve-Infanterie-Regiment Nr. 109 im Weltkrieg 1914 bis 1918*, p. 57.
10. Frisch, op. cit. p. 56.
11. Frisch, op. cit., pp. 57-58.
12. Losch, op cit, *Feldpost* letter dated 3 April 1915.
13. 'We who are about to die salute you'.
14. M. Klaus, *Das Württembergisches Reserve-Feldartillerie-Regiment Nr. 26 im Weltkrieg 1914-1918*, p. 31.
15. The lamp still functions and has the original red markings and copper drive band. There is a small aluminum tag indicating the date and location where the shell fell. It sits on the desk of the author.
16. Greiner, *Reserve-Infanterie-Regiment Nr. 110 im Weltkrieg 1914-1918*, pp. 73-74.
17. RIR 122 was part of the 183rd Division, formed in Cambrai in May 1915.
18. IR 185 was part of the 185th Division formed in May 1915.

19. The 52nd Division was formed in March/April 1915 and consisted of IR 66 (Magdeburg), IR 169 and IR 170. (Baden regiments). It was positioned on the right of the 26th Reserve Division and held the line between Serre and Gommecourt.
20. Losch, op cit, *Feldpost* letters dated 3 April and 2 June 1915.
21. Soden, *Die 26. (Württembergische) Reserve-Division im Weltkrieg 1914-1918,* p.82.
22. Losch, op cit, *Feldpost* letter dated 9 June 1915.
23. Losch, op cit, *Feldpost* letter dated 14 June 1915.
24. Quadrilateral Redoubt.
25. Losch, op cit, *Feldpost* letter dated 16 June 1915.
26. Losch, op cit, *Feldpost* letter dated 29 June and 4 July 1915.

7

The 'English' arrive

A period of calm followed the intense fighting around Serre in June. The overall decrease in enemy activity was put to good use by the entire Corps to work on a well thought-out, integrated plan for the extension of the position. Wire obstacles were reinforced throughout the sector, fire and communication trenches were improved and new ones were constructed while work continued on the second and third lines. The 26th and 28th Reserve Divisions were to be used primarily as labor divisions for the next six months as the men were kept busy preparing for the attack that was always expected. Each division held approximately 12 kilometers of front and the work on the trenches was often tiresome and there was always the inevitable daily losses from random fire.

Every available man was put to work on improving and extending the position of the XIV Reserve Corps. The Serre Sector took on a particular importance after the old front line had been pushed back almost to the edge of the village in the June fighting. It was imperative that a strong line was established at Serre in order to prevent any further enemy gains. Regiment Krause (I and II/185) had completed the switch line on both sides of the Serre-Mailly road by the middle of July and were then withdrawn in order to

Dug-outs and tunnels created by the 3/R99 including French
artillery shell vases and decorations. (Author's collection)

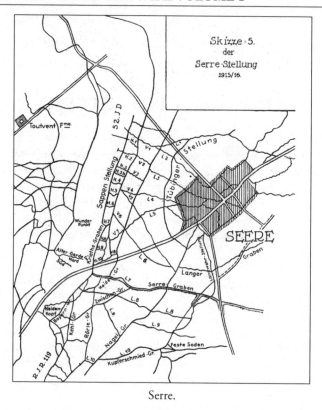

Serre.

complete their training, leaving the bulk of the remaining work to fall upon the regiments of the 26th Reserve Division.

IR 180 was assigned to the Serre Sector with the task of developing the defenses in accordance with the lessons learned from the recent fighting and all of the experience the regiment had obtained while at Thiepval. The position at Serre needed to be bolstered to withstand all of the newest fighting methods and weapons and to be resistant against any attack. Weapons had improved on both sides of the wire seemingly from month to month. In particular the caliber, range and penetrating force of the artillery were constantly increasing. Miners from RIR 99 assisted IR 180 by working diligently upon deep dug-outs in the Serre Hollow that were constructed with two or more exits. RIR 99 also dug saps, mined tunnels and helped to expand the depth of the wire obstacles.

The Serre Sector was slowly transformed from what was once a quiet rear area with minimal defenses into a virtual fortress. A new front line was established by sapping until a unified trench could be formed. The position by Serre would not change substantially for almost two years.

In early July the Second Army Commander, His Excellency General Fritz von Below, visited the positions held by the XIV Reserve Corps including Serre. The Corps commander, division and brigade commanders accompanied him on his tour of the front. After viewing the work completed by Regiment Krause, IR 180 and RIR 99 AOK 2 von Below[1] declared Serre a model position and invited other commands to visit the area in order to familiarize themselves on its construction.

Men from 2R/*Pionier* Bn 13 in the trenches with shovels,
flare gun and rifle. (Author's collection)

To obtain some idea of the amount of materials needed to create a new position or just to maintain an existing position one needs only look at the amount of supplies used by RIR 109 in the period from April 1915 through January 1916.

The regiment was provided with 2,560 sortie ladders; 9,819 beams; 1,544 beds; 13,049 planks; 41,276 boards; 20,574 hurdles; 10,160 slats; 26,340 mine frames, complete; 6,146 frame side sections; 2,426 riflemen's mirrors; 38,010 duck boards; 9,239 fascines; 3,634 *Brunsche* obstacles; 3,806 knife rests; 13,394 barbed wire balls and coils; 3,309 rolls of barbed wire; 13,212 parados facings; 3,349 railroad rails; 816 iron plates; 27,452 iron rods; 153 rifle racks; 28 sentry posts, complete; 212,965 sandbags; 379 armored shields; 2,900 girders; 10,933 pieces of angle iron; 27,060 wooden posts; 179 *Lochmann* entanglements[2]; 25,175 pounds of nails and 29 mirror poles. The other regiments of the XIV Reserve Corps consumed similar quantities of materials during the same period.[3]

Numerous mined dug-outs had been created up to 8 meters deep with two or more exits throughout the lines. Most dug-outs were also interconnected with tunnels as another means of escape in case of attack or if any part of one dug-out became damaged from enemy fire. In some areas not even pioneers were needed as the men had become quite proficient in mining techniques over time. The extension of the lines was helped with the arrival of the 6/Pioneer Bn 13, which was attached to the 26th Reserve Division. Now both divisions had two pioneer companies permanently assigned to them.

The business consists mainly of standing guard, mining what are called tunnels into the earth, digging up to 6 meters deep; the steps go gradually down and underneath being dug further to the right and to the left. Our 2nd position is completely undermined – above runs the trench, underneath tunnel to tunnel, which are connected to each other, which is obviously a huge undertaking in the chalk rock. Countless have been started there these days. Karl Losch, 3/R119 [4]

Labor companies were established during this period. The new units were formed from men who were no longer capable of field service in the trenches. These soldiers helped prepare new positions in the rear such as the trench that ran east from Pozières to the Copse at Bazentin then along to Longueval. These units were called 'shovelers' by the rest of the troops. A new trench line was constructed running south from the Beaucourt Château and a new battle headquarters was constructed for the 26th Reserve Division on Hill 131 south of Miraumont.

So the day before yesterday we had to carry 6 pieces of railroad rails three meters long that neatly pressed down on the shoulder and with that one has back-breaking work in the narrow trench. Today each group of 8 men must carry 30 sacks of gravel into the position. In reality I had only 4 men in my possession, and like the rails these are used for a small sentry booth. The booth is covered with the rails and upon it comes the gravel that is processed into concrete. Everything prepared becomes very badly shot up. Then you have to create the deep cover again or must work in the trench. However we do not overwork ourselves, you make it as comfortable as possible. As an *Unteroffizier* I have an advantage that I am not always needed to work, but you can always helps and that makes a good impression on the Other Ranks. Karl Losch, 3/R119 [5]

General von Soden and staff talking to men from RIR 119. (Author's collection)

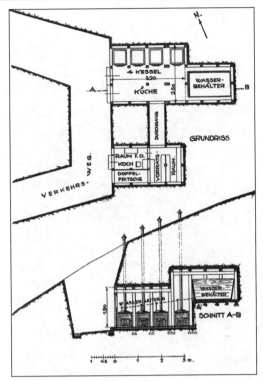

Sketch of bombproof kitchen facilities. (*Das 1. Badische Leib-Grenadier-Regiment Nr. 109 im Weltkrieg 1914-1918*)

All of the trenches were given designations and marked with signposts to make them easier to use. Each man was required to memorize the various communication trenches that led from the rear to the front so that troops could be moved in the fastest possible manner in the event of an emergency. Ammunition storage recesses were cut into the forward trench walls. Every so often the men created small cooking recesses where they could prepare warm food. Stoves were manufactured out of chalk that used wood shavings as fuel. As soon as it was possible additional shellproof kitchens were constructed in the rear trenches of each sector so that hot food could be quickly brought to the men. New sources of drinking water were located utilizing an ancient technique, divining rods. Surprisingly enough the success rate was quite good.

The company commander's dug-out was centrally located in each sector to provide easy access. Daily orders and reports were posted outside the dug-out entrance on a bulletin board along with anything else the men needed to know. Additional canteens were installed that provided for the needs of the men for a nominal fee.

The trenches continued to suffer extensive damage from daily artillery and trench mortar fire. The fire was usually directed towards a specific target utilizing aerial observation for maximum accuracy. Brushwood was now the material of choice to restore trenches and hold up the trench walls. This method required a great deal of materials and maintenance in order for it to be effective.

Trench sentry near Mametz – RIR 109. (*Das Reserve-Infanterie-Regiment Nr. 109 im Weltkrieg 1914 bis 1918*)

Individual sections of the line that were particularly exposed to enemy fire such as the *Heidenkopf* near Beaumont, finally became so ravaged by shells and the earth became so pulverized that brushwood no longer had any effect and the soil began to slide into the trenches, particularly in rainy weather. These positions would remain in poor condition until dry weather made it possible to bring the trenches into repair once again.

Of course life in the trenches was not all hard work and danger. There were many occasions where men were able to relax and enjoy the summer weather. Music and laughter could be heard along the line as troops took advantage of quiet periods. Many could be found sitting on the fire step talking to friends while hunting for lice. Others could be found cleaning their rifles or equipment, reading a letter or newspaper or simply enjoying a box of delicacies that had just been delivered by the Field Post.

We could have butter from our cyclists, who ride to Bapaume daily. The fact is that a large part of the Other Ranks have it better than in civilian life. I also feel it is so. In the morning I eat black coffee, bread and butter with preserves. That is what I would have at home, I never imagined it. Depending upon the situation this lasts up to 10 o'clock. At 12 o'clock comes lunch, the length of the course is not as good as at home and also you do not get as much; it is just to have something warm. At six o'clock in the evening there's coffee again, by which it would be a good evening again. In civilian life I have eaten more bread than sausage etc.; now it is vice versa.

Field kitchen staff from the Construction company – RIR 110. (Author's collection)

The men seem all good and strong; for many it is better than in civilian life. They can also buy beer, (I drink very rarely) and they also have sufficient cigars. Karl Losch, 3/R119[6]

This period of calm was rudely shattered at 10 a.m. on 10 July when the French suddenly placed heavy mortar fire into the quarry position near Fricourt held by RIR 110. The shelling lasted six hours until most of the trenches were destroyed. However the garrison of the quarry was safe inside their dug-outs, many of which were located five meters or more underground. The only losses suffered in the heavy fire were 2 men killed and 3 men wounded; numbers that amply demonstrated the effectiveness of the deep dug-outs.

The heavy mortar fire was followed by an infantry attack that was easily repelled resulting in numerous French losses. RIR 110 lost an additional 3 dead and 5 wounded as a result of the attack. Some of the wounded men needed to be rescued when their dug-out partially collapsed due to a heavy shell. Once the infantry assault was over the French artillery opened fire again.

On 19 July the French attempted a second attack against the quarry. The ground was covered with numerous craters from the shells, many times crater overlapped crater. The fire was being directed against the German minefield where 20 tunnels extended out towards the French. These tunnels were located between 10 to 20 meters below the surface and were connected to one another through long galleries.

Aerial photograph of the crater field on Hill 110 near Fricourt. (*Reserve-Infanterie Regiment Nr. 110 im Weltkrieg 1914-1918*)

The artillery fire started at 9 a.m. and included 28cm shells with delayed impact fuzes directed at the rear of the quarry. *Leutnant der Reserve* Hibschenberger and the Artillery Liaison Officer *Leutnant* Meyer were photographing the explosion of the shells. When the smoke became too thick to continue the two officers moved into a nearby dug-out. Within 5 minutes Hibschenberger was called away to take a telephone call from battalion headquarters. Just as he went toward the telephone dug-out a French shell smashed in front of the dug-out entrance smashing the telephone equipment. Hibschenberger and his servant then made their way into tunnel No. 1 where they took cover from the heavy fire.

Shortly before 10 a.m. several reports were received from observers who saw at least five French detachments approaching Hill 110 that were not being taken under fire. At 10 a.m. the bombardment increased to a continual rolling and continued at this level of intensity for the next ten hours with short pauses from time to time.

According to German estimates the French had fired 23,000 shells of every caliber and 3,000 trench mortar bombs of all types on a front 200 meters wide. Observation aircraft and balloons continued to direct the fire. The heaviest caliber shells fell upon the Pioneer Village and the second position from the quarry up to Sap 2. Mined dug-outs that were less than 5 meters deep under the earth collapsed one by one and numerous men were buried inside of them. During the heaviest part of the bombardment a direct hit caused a gallery between two dug-outs to collapse killing 5 pioneers. Other pioneers were wounded and dazed from the gas caused by the shell explosions.

However the tunnel system lying far underground was completely intact during the heavy fire so that officers and men were able to move to the different parts of the position, orders were able to be transmitted and supplies could be distributed where needed.

At 2 p.m. the fire noticeably decreased so that all dug-outs in the Second Position between the quarry and Sap 2 that were still intact were evacuated. The French troops spotted four hours earlier had already entered the quarry and the defenders took steps to counterattack and expel them from the German lines. The machine gun located in the eastern corner of the quarry was still intact despite the heavy fire and provided valuable fire support.

Artillery fire increased dramatically upon the German positions once French aircraft spotted the German counterattack. At this time the German guns were also firing into the opposing trenches in an attempt to disrupt enemy reinforcements; it was a hellish spectacle according to one observer.

Shortly after 7 p.m. French fire was transferred to the German rear positions, a sign that the infantry attack was imminent. An officer in the 1/R110 in reserve in the *Herzberggraben* described the scene:

The sight of Hill 110 under the drumfire was marvelous. The summit was shrouded in dense dark and bright drifts of smoke from the deepest black dazzled with white. Huge fountains of earth sprayed forth from the heavy impacts and beams were hurled into the air. The communication trench located at the rear slope of the hill was marked by an almost non-stop series of renewing puffs of bursting shells and shrapnel. So it went on for hours. Strange! Only the hill and communication trench were under fire, silence prevailed everywhere else around so that the support company at Fricourt-West in the *Herzberggraben* could look at the drama in all 'comfort'. And it would have been a pleasure had one not been anxious about the fate of their comrades under the hail of fire.

Then – about 7 o'clock in the evening – suddenly total silence, then the enemy placed fire upon the approach trenches and the shout 'they're coming!' sounded through the *Herzberggraben*. One could see the grey-blue chaps running high over the lime white crater walls, first a pair, then rank after rank. They dive down into the crater ground, coming up again on this side. Will they take the hill? Then our machine gun from the village of Fricourt also barks and takes them in the flank. Where is our artillery?

Yet not a minute has passed when invisible swarms rustle toward them, the 15's[7] strike into the ranks of the attackers placing a death-bringing barrier in front of the enemy position that is immediately shrouded in black smoke. 'Cheers' run through the *Herzberggraben* again. The grey-blue figures flood back, many remain lying on the ground then there is a crash of hand grenades. The attack has failed.

Our 'heavies' ceaselessly crash here and into the ranks of the fleeing men. The artillery did not have any difficulty because the attack position was limited and our batteries fired exquisitely. God knows why the adversary made it so easy for us and did not attempt the least distraction! When the support company from the right battalion in the *Trockengraben* moved forward the quarry was long ago free from the enemy again.[8]

Once the artillery had lifted off of the main German line the machine guns of RIR 110 immediately opened fire. 13 French soldiers did manage to penetrate the German lines up to the tunnel entrances however they were driven out using hand grenades.

The attackers were able to make their way into Crater 'A' and advance up to *Thuringian* Sap until several groups from the 10/R110 threw them back in a counterattack. After

Landwehrmann Leopold Scheu 9/R111. Killed in action 27 July 1915. (Author's collection)

hours of bitter fighting the position was finally clear of all French troops. The damage to the German surface position was considerable but the underground mine system was completely intact.

The 10/R110 had lost 9 men killed and 25 wounded, most of whom were seriously wounded. The known French losses were 1 officer, 1 officer aspirant, 32 men killed; 4 seriously wounded men were taken prisoner. All of the French casualties belonged to the 6th and 7th Coy, *403e Régiment d'Infanterie*. The number of French dead lying between the lines was impossible to determine but it was thought to be considerable.

The night was very stressful as the position was cleared of the dead and the wounded were taken to the rear. The trenches were reorganized once again and the men remained on alert expecting further French attacks. During the cleanup of the position the body of *Leutnant* Meyer was discovered sitting at a table completely buried up to his chest in earth and debris. The shell that had exploded outside his dug-out in the afternoon had also caused the dug-out roof to collapse on top of him.

Something was taking place in the enemy lines opposite the XIV Reserve Corps in late July 1915. Listening posts, trench sentries and patrols from every regiment in the Corps reported unusual activity in and behind the French trenches.

RIR 111 observed marching columns of men on the hills between Bouzencourt and Millencourt as well as heavy wagon and railroad traffic behind the lines. Further to the north RIR 121 reported similar traffic on the roads in the French rear. Batteries of 4 and 6 guns could be seen driving up to the front as well as leaving the lines. Motor vehicles were observed traveling on the road from Bray to Corbie, from Engelbelmer to Hédauville, Hédauville to Mailly as well numerous baggage wagons and vehicles of every type. On 2 August no fewer than 170 vehicles were counted.

Columns of up to 50 vehicles began to be seen while enemy aircraft suddenly appeared in larger numbers, sometimes in groups up to 16 aircraft, and at a much higher altitude than usual.

A couple of days ago we also saw a French airplane squadron of 16 pilots fly by the position. They were supposed to drop bombs on Cambrai. According to the French reports the pilots had it in for the Royal palace and railway station. Yes, they would be quite safe in the cellars. Naturally the artillerymen have not brought any down, the same thing with us at the front also. On the other hand our fighter pilots are tremendous. We saw such a French pilot shot down in Miraumont. Karl Losch, 3/ R119 [9]

Large bodies of troops were also observed; company, battalion and regimental strength as well as large bodies of cavalry. Everything pointed to a significant change occurring in the French lines, but what?

Towards the end of the month clues were provided to explain the sudden flurry of activity. The enemy artillery started to change its firing habits. Before this time the men knew when to expect the French artillery to fire their morning and evening 'blessings' as well as knowing what their favorite targets were. Now the guns actively fired during the day – as if the guns were being registered once again. The men of XIV Reserve Corps were puzzled by the sudden increase of shrapnel clouds floating high in the air. The guns also made a different sound than before.

New batteries started firing from the flank and something new was added; incendiary shells. On 12 August St. Pierre-Divion was shelled for the first time. The French gunners had previously spared this small village along the Ancre.

Shell splinters were collected and examined and the men discovered they were thicker than they had been the previous month. One day RIR 119 discovered a blown-out shell and the regimental souvenir hunters wanted to save the driving band. They quickly realized that the band was wider than previous shells found and the shell casing was much thicker and the caliber was 8.7cm and not the 7.5cm normally found. When they attempted to

Captured enemy aircraft being inspected by officers from
the XIV Reserve Corps. (Author's collection)

Men from the 2/R119 relaxing while showing off captured French
caps. They would soon face a new enemy. (Author's collection)

remove the driving band the chisel became damaged because the shell was apparently
manufactured from drawn steel. The marks found on the base of the shell indicated that it
was manufactured in England. Empty shrapnel cases were found from new, larger caliber
guns including 11.4cm, something not seen before this time.

Other regiments soon discovered additional shell fragments and duds that clearly
indicated that British artillery had replaced the French. The shell fragments and duds
clearly bore the marks of English manufacturers as well as several with the mark Bethlehem
Steel Corporation, an American manufacturer.

While it had become accepted that the British artillery had taken over from the French
the question still lingered 'What about the infantry?' Was a new French attack division
taking over the line? Did the British have the numbers of men required to take over such
a large area? The trench and dug-out strategists were having trouble determining where
the British would find the men needed to take over the lines from the French. These
questions needed to be answered as quickly as possible.

There were noticeable changes in the behavior of the opposing infantry. There was
less patrol activity in No Man's Land. Machine guns and infantry fired more often and
at shorter intervals than before indicating a general nervousness on their part, especially
at night. The familiar slow 'tack-tack' of the French machine gun had changed as well.
Normally there was a pause after 25 rounds had been fired as the gun crew inserted a

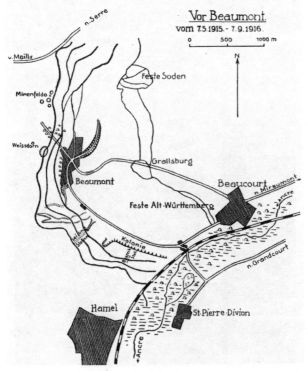

North of the Ancre.

new strip of cartridges. Now the machine guns fired longer bursts spraying the terrain with a wide cone of fire.

On 3 August RIR 109, RIR 110 and RIR 121 observed men wearing flat caps among the enemy trenches while observers from RIR 111 reported seeing different color enemy uniforms among the familiar French horizon blue. Rifle bullets were also different. Up until this time bullets were copper coated; now they had a steel jacket. The enemy was more careless than usual and was often exposed. This provided an increased number of targets for German snipers.

Some observers reported seeing enemy soldiers wearing the round flat forage cap that had not been used in the British army since the 19th Century. It was the same manner in which so many German magazines and newspapers of the period portrayed British soldiers.

At least one observer in RIR 121 reported seeing Indian troops in the middle of August. Many of the men believed the front would become dangerous when this new enemy would sneak over in the darkness with their sharp knives and silently cut down sentries. No contact was ever made with these exotic troops, no patrols observed, only the sound of coughing from the British lines. After a few weeks all observations of Indian troops ceased.

Some patrols returned with conflicting information. RIR 99 reported hearing English spoken in the enemy trench while on 4 August a patrol from RIR 121 heard French being spoken and the trench garrison singing *Sambre et Meuse*, the Alsatian Marseillaise.

RIR 111. *Granathof* Stellung. Tr = Crater. (Author's collection)

On the same day another patrol from RIR 121 reported seeing a man wearing a round, stiff, sandy colored cap with visor and a brown uniform. A *Feldwebel Leutnant* who had taken part in the China Campaign shot down an adversary in front of Thiepval who had exposed himself from the knees up. He clearly recognized that the man was wearing an British uniform gray-green in color with breast pockets and pleated tunic

On 5 August RIR 121 reported the enemy trench garrison was wearing brown uniforms and carrying short rifles and the new troops relieving the line were definitely wearing British uniforms. They could also clearly hear the sound of wood and iron rails being unloaded that indicated the trenches were actively being developed.

However, a short time later an officer's patrol from RIR 99 near Hamel approached the enemy wire and clearly heard French being spoken as well as the French national anthem being sung. There was no clear idea of what was taking place in the opposing lines.

The German command surmised at first that British forces were training with the French XI Corps, possibly the first of the new Kitchener Divisions. The only way to determine this with any accuracy would be to take prisoners. It became a matter of honor to be the first regiment to capture a British soldier.

One of the first opportunities to take a prisoner took place in the night of 4 August. A patrol from RIR 119 damaged the enemy wire and then waited in ambush for a repair party to appear. An officer and several men were observed inspecting the wire entanglements and in the ensuing firefight the officer was struck and mortally wounded. His body was

Private William McCorist 6th Black Watch [AKA William Nicholson] (*The People's Journal*)

left where he had fallen and in the following night they returned and were able to place a rope around the body and pull it into their trench.

The body turned out to be a French officer, Lieutenant Dechoz of the *62e Régiment d'Infanterie.*[10] The papers found on his body were useful to the German command but they did not shed any light on the presence of British troops.

Night after night patrols were sent into No Man's Land where the men would lurk in vain waiting for an enemy patrol to come by. The patrols did report that the opposing trenches were loud and noisy and that the sound of wood and rails being unloaded could clearly be heard along with the sounds of construction.

On 6 August RIR 111 decided to send out a patrol to observe the enemy lines in the vicinity of the *Kronenwerk* on the Ovillers-Authuille road, approximately 400 meters from the German lines. *Leutnant* Sigel worked his way through the grass until he was in a position to be able to observe the trenches. He concealed his telescope with grass and watched British soldiers entrenching and performing sentry duty. After approximately 30 minutes Sigel noticed a patrol approaching his position with hand grenades, apparently he had been spotted. He quickly withdrew back to the German lines and reported his observations. They still had no idea of who was facing them. This mystery was to be resolved on 9 August.

RIR 109 made preparations to send out a patrol from the 10th Coy under *Vizefeldwebel* Adler with 6 men whose only objective was to capture a prisoner. The patrol was going to enter the line by the *Granathof* in front of La Boisselle where the trenches were only 40 meters distant from each other. The area between the opposing trenches contained a mine crater from an earlier explosion. The patrol would go forth under cover of several nearby mine explosions and take advantage of the confusion caused by the blasts.

The mines were set off at the pre-arranged time with a great deal of noise and the patrol left their trench along a lane that had been cut through the wire obstacles earlier. They made their way along the old crater edge towards the enemy position. Machine guns fired at random, however the patrol succeeded in arriving at the so-called sandbag position without any losses where a steep embankment offered some cover.

The patrol quickly cut through the wire entanglements and climbed up the steep slope where they reached the trench. Adler carefully reconnoitered the trench and noticed several sentries in close proximity. He threw a hand grenade at them and they all ran off except for one. Adler called to the man in French and asked him to surrender. The sentry started to come closer to the patrol but suddenly turned and ran off.

Adler chased after the man, fired his pistol and struck him in the thigh just as he ran into a nearby dug-out. The remaining men from the patrol blocked off the trench on both sides while Adler threw a hand grenade into the dug-out. After the explosion he proceeded inside and discovered the wounded sentry lying on the floor. Adler grabbed the man and brought him back to the trench where the patrol fashioned a makeshift stretcher from a blanket placed between two rifles. While the wounded sentry was being lifted over the parapet a three-man British detachment approached the raiding party. Adler called out to the men, which apparently startled them. They turned and ran off followed by Adler who fired a few shots at them before turning to follow the rest of the patrol.

The patrol managed to get the prisoner over the parapet and through the wire entanglements. They slid down the slope towards the crater and hurried toward their own trench. The return journey was difficult because so many explosions had turned the soil into a fine powder so that it gave at every step. Several Very lights were launched causing the men to lie on the ground each time until the light faded. They finally reached the German trench by exerting all of their strength.

The entire patrol had taken only twenty minutes from start to finish and the mission was successful. The wounded prisoner was identified as Private William Nicholson, 6th Royal Highlanders, 153rd Brigade, 51st Highland Division – a Scottish Highlander from a Territorial battalion of the 'Black Watch' regiment in full battle gear. [11]

The participants of the patrol were rewarded for their efforts; the leader received the Iron Cross 1st Class while the men with him received the Iron Cross 2nd Class. Each man received a 10-day furlough (exclusive of travel time) and 100 Marks as spending money from the Army Commander. Each man was also given 10 Marks as travel expenses while one married man in the patrol received an additional 30 Marks for his children. The regimental commander was very pleased with the performance of his men.

The men who participated in successful raids and patrols were singled out for their actions and were used as an example to inspire others to achieve the same recognition for their bravery. The men would be publicly praised in a Corps Order of the Day as well as receiving a certificate of achievement signed by the Corps Commander. In addition most men involved in successful raids would receive the Iron Cross 1st or 2nd Class as well as monetary rewards and furloughs. Everything was being done to instill a desire for the men to undertake these dangerous undertakings voluntarily.

Two members of the 15/R99, Infantrymen Fuchs and Hirsch, captured the second prisoner taken on 9 August under completely different circumstances. A British corporal from the 1st East Lancashire Regiment on wiring duty had become lost in the fog during the night and wandered into the German lines along the swampy Ancre ground near the 'Biber Kolonie' where he was taken prisoner[12]. The result of these two events provided valuable information to the German High Command on what enemy units were opposite the XIV Reserve Corps. At least two British divisions had been identified, the 4th (Regular) and the 51st (Territorial) divisions. Active reconnaissance in the Ancre valley by RIR 99 confirmed that 'the English and short-skirted Scotsmen had replaced the Frogs'.[12]

The enemy was very cooperative in providing additional evidence that the British Army now faced the XIV Reserve Corps. On 10 August an enemy patrol threw several British newspapers into the trench held by the 2R/Pioneer Bn 13 as a friendly gesture. This only confirmed the recent findings that the British had taken over the trenches from the French along the Somme.

Corporal Stevenson, 1st Royal Irish Fusiliers and captors, 13 August 1915. (*Die 26. Reserve Division 1914-1918*)

Yesterday was now the third time we were at the French entanglements; the patrol was 12 men strong. It was necessary to determine who lies opposite us. To that, one man yesterday could hear English spoken, for example: 'If you will'. On the left of us they have caught a prisoner. However nobody moved outside the trench, also no patrols, we only heard the sentries in the trench speaking and coughing. Karl Losch, 3/R119 [13]

During the night of 13 August a patrol from RIR 119 ran into a British officer's patrol by Redan Ridge. An officer and a corporal were wounded in the subsequent fighting and were taken prisoner.

Last night the 2nd Company was successful in shooting an enemy patrol, in fact a British officer and NCO. It is therefore actually a couple of days since the British were opposite us. Both British were taken prisoner, both wounded. Karl Losch, 3/R119 [14]

The officer was badly wounded and immediately brought into the German trenches while the corporal was brought in later with less serious wounds. Both men were found to belong to the 1st Battalion Royal Irish Fusiliers, 4th (Regular) Division and were identified as Lieutenant Hugh Warnock and Corporal Stevenson. The prisoners related their regiment had suffered heavy losses at Ypres and had been sent to the Somme for a few days of rest. The prisoners apparently did not speak highly of the French and complained about the poor condition of the trenches.[15] Captain H.A. MacMullen, C Coy 1/RIF wrote:

Infantryman – RIR 119. (Author's collection)

This patrol under Lt Warnock went out to patrol the front from left to right at about 10pm. The patrol started off from no.1 on the left and went out right-handed. They returned to the same place having seen nothing. They then proceeded along our barbed wire to point 2. Here they left the wire to make another right handed loop. I told them should await them at the listening post 3 and in order to give the direction would send up flares in the direction of B. I had been there about 20 minutes when Lt. Low joined me. Soon after a volley was heard in the direction of X and we heard excited talking. General sniping began in that part of the German lines. About 3 minutes later a party of about 6 men were seen walking up to our wire at point 4. Our sentry knowing our patrol was about challenged twice in a very loud voice. The party began to scatter so he opened rapid fire as did the sentry with him. Nothing more was heard until about 2.30am when news was brought to me that one of the patrol had been brought in badly wounded on the right of our line.

As far as I could gather from his version of the affair the patrol was suddenly confronted by about 9 Germans who at once opened fire on them. Warnock shot one and Corporal Murray two – of our patrol all were hit but none was killed. Lt. Warnock was incapable of crawling or running whilst Corporal Stevenson, as Corporal Murray put it, 'seemed to go mad' and ran straight into the Germans. As the Germans advanced at Corporal Murray [he] crawled away. He does not know how he got to the place he was eventually picked up at. I think the Germans who came up at point 4 must have been searching for Corporal Murray.[16]

Of course not every attempt to capture a prisoner succeeded. One patrol sent out in the night of 3 August from RIR 111 commanded by *Gefreiter* Hager became lost in the dense fog and ended up being fired upon by the sentries of the neighboring regiment who considered them to be the enemy. They hid in a turnip field until the firing died down. Two men sent out to capture the 'enemy' were surprised when Hager identified himself.

In some cases it was the Germans who ended up being taken prisoner. *Leutnant* Schaef and 3 men from the III/R111 went out on patrol but failed to return at the appointed time. On the next night a second patrol was sent out to try and determine their fate. They came across a section of grass that gave clear indications that the patrol had been overpowered in hand to hand fighting. There was no sign of the missing men.

Everything possible was done to prevent any member of the XIV Reserve Corps from being taken prisoner. This included men who were killed while out in No Man's Land whose bodies were recovered whenever possible. On 22 September *Kriegsfreiwilliger* Jehle, 9/R109, discovered the badly decomposed body of a member of RIR 109 lying out in No Man's Land. He was first identified as belonging to the regiment by his shoulder straps. Jehle went back to the body and was able to obtain the identity disc that positively identified the body as *Landwehrmann* Notheis, 10/R109, who had been killed in action on 30 September 1914. Jehle and two other men made three attempts to recover the body before they were successful. Notheis was finally given a decent burial in the regimental cemetery.

Additional British prisoners were taken over time in raids and patrol fights that provided a clear picture of the forces opposite the XIV Reserve Corps. For now the new foe behaved in a quiet manner. The British tended to send out less patrols at night than the French but they were often larger in size and well protected on the flanks and in the rear.

RIR 110 initially thought that the new opponents were not as aggressive as the French. The 110th sent out numerous patrols in order to capture a prisoner but all were unsuccessful. They reported that the British soldiers did not venture far from their strong positions and did not even try to occupy the numerous mine craters lying between the lines.

Within a short time British patrols became increasingly active and bold. Opposing patrols would occasionally clash in short, vicious fights in No Man's Land. The mill located along the Ancre near Hamel was a constant point of contention. The location of the mill made it impossible for either side to hold it securely and it often changed hands or was the scene of intense fighting.

On 1 September 1915 a patrol from RIR 99 attacked the mill and forced a British outpost to withdraw. However the following day the men from RIR 99 were forced to withdraw as well when the mill came under heavy and accurate artillery fire. Only a short time later, on 10 September, another group from RIR 99 attacked the mill on their own initiative and forced out approximately 60 British troops who had reoccupied the building and installed a machine gun in the ruins. The back and forth fighting at the mill would continue for many months to come.

One patrol from RIR 119 collided with a British patrol on the night of 6 September. There was a short exchange of hand grenades between the opposing forces and the British patrol was forced to retire. One man could be heard wailing loudly as the enemy returned to his lines.

By September the British patrols had started to make small attacks against the German trenches at several locations. Certain areas seemed to attract more than their

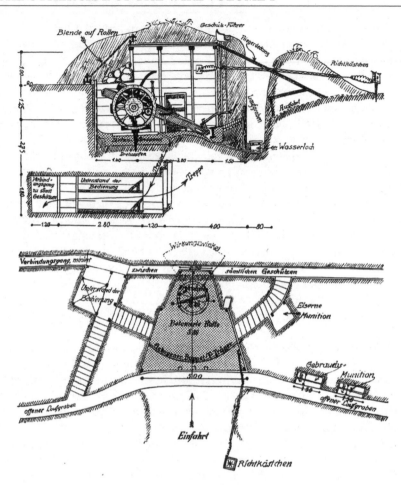

10.5cm Light Field Howitzer emplacement - RFAR 26. (*Das Württembergisches Reserve-Feldartillerie Regiment Nr. 26 im Weltkrieg 1914-1918*)

share of patrol activity such as the sunken road near Beaumont and the mill by Hamel, which made them quite dangerous at times.

While the enemy infantry at first were prone to nervous firing at night and appeared more timid than their predecessors the Germans quickly learned to fear the British snipers who were quite good at their trade. In general the Germans considered the trenches to be safer than when the French were opposite them. This opinion would begin to change with time.

In autumn of 1915 I had been detached as an artillery observer and corporal commanding 12 men in an observation post on Hill 153. This was in our third trench line at a place called *Feste Staufen*, or 'Stuff Redoubt' as it was named by the British. Day and night we had to observe the sound and flashes of the British guns in order to fix their positions and other movements behind the front. For this purpose we had periscopes, for to raise your head out of the trench would invite certain death by a British sniper. Felix Kircher, RFAR 26.[17]

The men in the field artillery regiments assigned to the XIV Reserve Corps were also not sorry to see the French leave. No tears were shed as the 'malignant' French departed. The new opponents were regarded as more distinguished and calmer. The relative inexperience of the British artillery was a welcome relief to the gunners in the XIV Reserve Corps. Much of their fire was directed towards areas where 'neither man nor beast lived', in many cases in open fields.

To many it seemed as if the enemy artillery was using the German infantry for target practice until they became proficient in their trade. The strict observance of Sunday rest by the British gunners was especially agreeable. This allowed the men to relax and not feel as if they were in any real danger while sunbathing or hunting lice inside a trench.

The recent fighting at Serre had demonstrated the need to make improvements in several critical areas involving the use of artillery. Special attention was to be given to fire command exercises with the artillery commanders of the neighboring divisions. Special attention was also paid to expand training for artillery liaison officers.

Despite the British advantage in both the number and caliber of guns RFAR 26 was ordered to send three sections of guns from the I *Abteilung* to Württemberg *Landwehr* FAR 2 (2nd *Landwehr* Division) in July. This reduction in firepower was offset to some degree by the introduction of the first assault guns that were assigned to several infantry regiments within the Corps.

The battery personnel continued to dig and mine continuously during this period. The final result was a labyrinth of deeply-mined tunnels that connected all of the guns in each battery. The men could easily move from one gun to the next without having the need to go above ground. The ammunition rooms, storage, kitchens and billets formed part of a vast subterranean complex. The exits to each position were skillfully constructed and heavily reinforced in order to prevent them from being buried by enemy fire.

Thousands of rounds of ammunition were painstakingly stored in chambers near the guns and were overseen by the regimental armourer. Entrenching and construction materials, telephone equipment and other supplies were stored throughout the complex of tunnels as well as sufficient supplies of food and water. Everything needed for the guns and the gun crews was carefully stored in chambers similar to those found in homes in Germany.

The tunnels and chambers were also infested with uninvited guests, rats. These creatures were found in great quantity and were unusually large in size. Attempts were made to control these unwanted pests but no matter what methods were used the rats were always present. It became extremely annoying at night when a rat ran across their body or occasionally when a tail ended up in the mouth of a snoring comrade and suddenly awakened the sleeping man. Boots were thrown at the pests and the audible sounds of the squeaking rodents could be heard among the curses of the men as the rats scurried away from these makeshift missiles.

In addition to the development of the gun positions that were already occupied the men eagerly worked on reinforcement battery positions throughout the Corps area. Entrenching parties were brought up each night from the Light Ammunition Column and were used to construct new battery positions under the expert leadership of the battery and pioneer officers. These new positions were skillfully integrated into the overall defensive system and provided safe locations for the batteries in case they were forced to change their position as well as providing immediate cover for any reinforcement batteries. Great care was shown in hiding all new construction from the prying eyes of the British observers.

Enemy aircraft had become increasingly annoying. Each morning sentries sounded sirens alerting the men to the presence of British observation aircraft. The gunners would cease all activities on the surface and were only able to watch the aircraft from the relative safety of their tunnel and dug-out entrances. Any movement on the ground resulted in artillery fire or bombs dropped from planes. Great care also had to be taken that neither foot traffic or wagon tracks betrayed the location of the guns or the tunnel entrances.

One of the most important changes made in the artillery establishment of the XIV Reserve Corps was the establishment of Artillery Survey Sections. The section assigned to the 26th Reserve Division was under the command of *Leutnant der Reserve* Grieshaber. The new unit arrived at the headquarters of RFAR 26 in Miraumont where they set up their equipment that included a large drawing board, compasses, rulers, telephone equipment and all sorts of measuring devices. The work performed with this equipment would eventually allow the artillery to fire accurately on any target within range of the guns at a moments notice, or so Grieshaber claimed. At first he was treated with skepticism by the gunners who felt that the technical methods being applied would be of little value, they would shortly change their minds.

The first step of the new artillery plan was to have each artillery piece fire at clearly visible targets. The battery commanders would conscientiously list all details on the range, any plus or minus of the impact in relation to the target, the gun elevation and position.

Artillerie Messtrupp No. 2 (Artillery Survey Section No. 2). (*Das Württembergisches Reserve-Feldartillerie Regiment Nr. 26 im Weltkrieg 1914-1918*)

'Heroes' cellar, dug-out in Grandcourt on the road toward Thiepval. (Author's collection)

The information was passed by phone by the Artillery Plan observers to the Artillery Plan station where the numbers were plotted on the larger map. With each shell fired the angles passed quickly over the paper as shot after shot was fixed on the map. Each impact became exactly determined mathematically in its relation to the target. The effects of wind and air density were also calculated into the firing formula. This not only was a valuable supplement to firing by direct observation; it also provided valuable information on the performance of each gun.

The next step was to check the accuracy of the overall plan. This was accomplished by firing at targets only using the plan information. The results were so good that even the skeptics were quickly converted. Eventually every battery eagerly promoted firing according to the Artillery Plan.

The next step was to use the plan for firing upon concealed targets, important traffic points and above all on enemy artillery positions that had betrayed their location through night firing. The German guns would fire shrapnel shells according to the plan, usually quite high above the target and therefore harmless. The location of the shrapnel cloud was mathematically determined in relation to the concealed target and plotted on the plan. The new coordinates were transmitted to the artillery. The next shots fired were generally directly above the proposed target and the exact impacts were confirmed through aerial observation from aircraft and balloons.

Fire results were quite satisfactory with the help of the new Artillery Survey Plan and the number of direct hits upon concealed targets was substantially increased. This allowed the artillery to pay back the superior enemy artillery with compound interest. The German forces were able to maintain parity with the British artillery despite the gradual loss of aerial superiority and the increased number of enemy batteries arrayed against the XIV Reserve Corps.

The Artillery Survey Plan was also useful for other purposes. The survey stations were positioned at high points along the lines including the ruined mill near Hamel, *Feste Staufen* and the Mill of Pozières. The observers kept a close eye on the British lines and rear areas as well as on their own lines in their sector. They conscientiously made note of any unusual changes in the enemy lines, they reported the activity of the British artillery with the direction of the fire, the number of shots fired and caliber if possible. They also made note of the time and place of the flare signals fired by the British as well as their own. The Survey Plan leader was committed to training the personnel assigned to his unit in order to have them as proficient as possible in handling the duties needed for the position.

The artillery plan observations complemented the infantry observations and were sent to a central location. Intelligence officers used the detailed information to provide assessments of enemy troops, positions and activities that then were forwarded to the division and Corps commanders.

One advantage the British possessed was guns of heavier caliber and longer range than their predecessors had available and these guns made their presence felt in the German rear areas more and more. The heavy guns often bombarded the occupied villages lying far in the rear; something the French artillery had not done very often. Observers also noted that the French population in the British rear areas was being evacuated along the

Heinzmann

Leutnant in der 4. Pionier-Komp.
gefallen am 12. Juli 1915
bei Courcelette

Leutnant Heinzmann 4/Pioneer Bn
13. Killed by his own hand grenade
12 July 1915 near Courcelette.
(*Kriegstagbuch aus Schwaben*)

Steudle

Leutn. d. L. im Res.-Inf.-Regt. 119
(Kaufmann), gest. am 28. Juli 1915
an den bei Bapaume erhalt. Wunden

Leutnant der Landwehr Karl Steudle
(Reutlingen) 5/R119. Wounded in
action 24 July 1915, died 28 July
1915 in Field Hospital 1, Bapaume.
(*Kriegstagbuch aus Schwaben*)

front and civilians could be seen walking away from the lines heavily loaded with their possessions. It seemed to the many of the men of the XIV Reserve Corps that the British soldiers needed more room for their comfort than their French counterparts. Many German soldiers compared the different perceptions of the removal of the French civilians. 'When the British are involved it is considered the necessity of war, if the Germans are involved it was considered barbarism.'[18]

Large numbers of observation aircraft flew over the position of the XIV Reserve Corps on a daily basis taking photographs of every part of the defensive lines. The aircraft were usually followed by severe artillery fire from enemy batteries on the positions that had been photographed.

Bomber aircraft also appeared in larger numbers and paid special attention to the field railways and main rail lines at Le Sars and Bapaume. The increased bomber activity as well as new long-range artillery fire into the rear areas resulted in an increase in the number of dug-outs being constructed in the villages behind the front. These so-called 'heroes' cellars' were used as a refuge by the troops as well as any civilians that still lived in the area. On 29 July British aircraft bombed the *Edinger Dorf* and also dropped aerial darts, not seen since 1914.

The few observation aircraft available to the XIV Reserve Corps could not hope to compete with the increasing number of enemy fighters and observation aircraft. British fighters increasingly threatened even the tethered observation balloon located in the Grove of Grevillers. The only aerial assistance the Corps received at this time was the arrival of *Feld Luftschiff Abteilung 2*.

Anti-aircraft defenses were still quite primitive. 7.7cm Field guns and the older 9cm guns had been jury-rigged to allow them to fire at aircraft but their efforts were not very effective. 3.7cm quick firing pom-pom guns[19] were introduced but proved to be ineffective as well. The rapid-fire guns proved to be quite dangerous to the German troops on the

Machine gun training – IR 180. The instructor standing in doorway near the sign is wearing a Machine Gun Marksman sleeve badge. (Author's collection)

ground as unexploded shells often dropped among the men to the point that they were considered almost useless by many.

New, close range weapons were introduced by both sides during this period. Ball mines ('Plum Puddings')[20] made an unpleasant appearance and resulted in many casualties and a great deal of damage to the trenches. The British utilized a throwing machine from which bundles of hand grenades, up to 18 at one time, were being thrown toward the German trenches. They also showed particular aptitude in the use of rifle grenades.

Light *minenwerfers* were installed along the line of the XIV Reserve Corps while *Minenwerfer* Company 226 was now equipped with the new medium *minenwerfer*. Hand grenades were being improved in design and effectiveness. However they were still subject to damage from damp conditions and needed to be stored in a dry location. The hand grenades were also troubled with defective fuzes and several accidents occurred in July. On 7 July *Leutnant der Reserve* Gehring, 2R/Pioneer Bn 13 was killed when his hand grenade exploded prematurely. On 12 July *Leutnant* Heinzmann, 4/Pioneer Bn 13 was also killed while handling a hand grenade.

The heavy machine gun continued to demonstrate its reliability in the defense of the position. The recent fighting at Serre and the experiences of RIR 99 near Arras provided valuable information on the most effective methods of deploying the guns.

It was found that machine guns located in the front line trenches were often quickly destroyed by artillery fire thereby reducing the ability of the men to successfully hold the line in case of attack. The most effective way to deploy the guns was to provide flanking fire against any attacking force and to provide an interlocking field of fire between two or more guns.

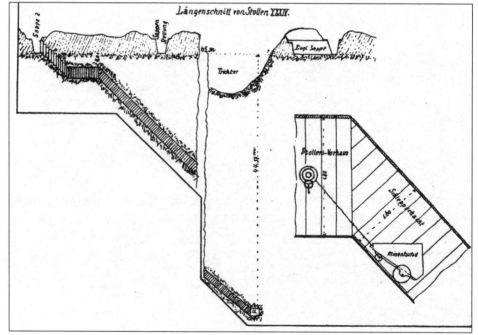

Cutaway drawing of Mine XXXIV under the British lines near Fricourt. (*Das Württembergische Pionier Bataillon Nr. 13 im Weltkrieg 1914-1918*)

Men from 4/Pioneer Bn 13 posing in front of mine entrance. (Author's collection)

The machine gun officers in the XIV Reserve Corps were kept busy locating new sites to position their guns. Once the locations were determined the men were put to work driving tunnels from nearby dug-outs located in the second and third trenches of the first line. The gun positions were made as inconspicuous and as shellproof as possible. The new machine gun posts could then provide cover for the main battle trench from elevated positions in the rear. In addition to the new machine gun posts the 26th Reserve Division also started construction on an armored machine gun tower located near the left wing of the division at the edge of the village of Pozières.[21]

Additional machine guns were acquired in order to increase the available firepower of the Corps. Captured French, Russian and Belgian guns were provided to both divisions and integrated into the line. One Belgian gun was positioned in the Ovillers cemetery while a Russian gun was placed inside the Schwaben Redoubt.

Possibly the most innovative improvement made during this period was the expansion of electricity into the trenches and dug-outs for lighting purposes. Electricity was already being used in limited form near Beaucourt and Beaumont. Now the positions near La Boisselle could enjoy the use of electric lighting as well. The work was begun in July when the foundation for the generator was laid in a mined machine house located inside the Regimental Crater. The machinery was installed by 16 August while the wiring of all nearby facilities, all dug-outs, kitchens, etc. at the regimental crater as well as in the positions of the right-hand battalion was completed by 29 August.

The regimental battle headquarters of RIR 109 would eventually be connected to the generator, as were all of the dug-outs along the *Trichtergraben*, *Alt Jäger Stellung* and *Steinmanngraben*. Maintaining power required a great deal of effort and maintenance by the men assigned to electrical duty. Poor fuel supplies often plagued the equipment and as a result the average daily illumination was restricted to 14 hours. One benefit of having electric lighting at La Boisselle and in locations along the 26th Reserve Division front was the illumination of the mine tunnels. The use of electric lights lessened the danger of running out of breathable air while working far under the ground.

Mine warfare continued to be active on both sides during the period from July to September. Fortunately it did not result in a large number of casualties, however it did result in high levels of tension and stress caused by the almost non-stop explosions of British mines.

When considering the number of mines started on both sides it was inevitable that the two sides would meet underground one day. This occurred on 8 July when 3 pioneers from the 2R/Pioneer Bn 13 penetrated an old French mine tunnel while they were digging. The men obtained explosives and planted charges by the tunnel entrance. The resulting explosion collapsed the mine tunnel and caused considerable damage to the enemy trench.

Whenever fresh piles of earth were observed in the opposing lines it was assumed that mining activity was taking place. The normal procedure would be to order a countermine to be constructed by the pioneers. While countermining was started immediately it could take some time to see a result depending upon what mining activity was already taking place in the sector.

When RIR 110 observed fresh piles of earth in the trenches opposite Fricourt the 28th Reserve Division ordered the suspected mine entrance to be bombarded by a 21cm heavy

Early gas protection equipment – RIR 121. (Author's collection)

Header of second edition of new trench newspaper of the XIV
Reserve Corps: *Der Schützengraben*. (*Der Schützengraben*)

howitzer battery using a large quantity of shells equipped with delayed impact fuzes. The endangered part of the German line adjacent to the bombardment area was evacuated beforehand to prevent unnecessary casualties. The heavy howitzers fired accurately but it was suspected that they accomplished very little to stop the mining activity.

Once the British arrived they took over the French galleries and continued to mine under the German lines. The first British attempts at mining were not handled in a skillful manner in the opinion of the German pioneers and many of the mine explosions were unsuccessful in causing any damage to the German lines. The British would slowly improve their mining techniques over time. A new minefield was started outside of Fricourt and the XIV Reserve Corps set off its first mine on 28 August after it had been determined that the British were placing explosive charges in a nearby mine chamber. The first recorded British mine was detonated on 1 September near Beaumont.

The use of poison gas increased during this period. Gas was delivered in one of two methods, the first blown across the ground by the prevailing winds, secondly by the use of gas shells. The men of the XIV Reserve Corps only had crude anti-gas protective measures available to them. The first anti-gas device was nothing more than cotton wadding soaked in a special liquid, which was then held over the nose and mouth. Later devices consisted of a gas pad with nose clamps. The pioneers were kept very busy creating and improving gas protective devices in the second half of 1915. The pioneers were also busy providing training in gas warfare to every unit in the Corps. The men eventually received the rubber coated *Gummi* gas mask[22] and later in the war an oiled leather version that was distributed when rubber was in short supply.

Toward the end of September the British divisions facing the XIV Reserve Corps appeared to become restless. Their artillery increased its fire upon the German lines and numerous aircraft made daily appearances above the lines. The artillery fire increased in intensity on 25 September and the Corps expected an attack to follow, but none occurred.

The reason for the sudden increase in enemy activity was quickly determined to be diversionary tactics for the joint British-French offensives in Artois, Champagne, Vimy Ridge and Loos under the overall control of General Joffre. After it was concluded that

Denkmal gefallener deutscher Helden
auf dem Friedhof
in Bapaume, Nordfrankreich

XIV Reserve Corps cemetery monument – Bapaume. (Author's collection)

there was no danger of an attack along the front of the Corps it allowed General von Below to send much needed reinforcements to the north.

The Machine Gun Company from RIR 99 under *Leutnant* Schöpfer as well as the I and II/R99 were sent to the Arras front where they were joined by the III/116 to form Regiment von Franconia.[23] The men would spend the next three months fighting near Arras in almost the same location they had fought in during spring 1915. The III and IV/R99 remained behind on the Somme and were joined by the IV/*Landwehr* Regiment 75.

In the days following 25 September the British artillery provided renewed bursts of fire along the front that were often accompanied by cheers and shouts for victory.[24] The men of the XIV Reserve Corps could only guess at the reasons for these sudden outbursts. One theory put forward was that the British probably wanted their young soldiers to become accustomed to 'battle commotion' and cried out to encourage them.

Life in the rear areas had not changed much in the last few months aside from the increase in artillery fire. One aspect that did change was the introduction of a corps newspaper called '*Der Schützengraben*' that was generally published bi-weekly. In addition to providing news of the war it also provided personal accounts of the men in the XIV Reserve Corps as well as interesting historical articles on the villages on the Somme, tasty trench recipes, advertisements for uniforms, cigarettes and other items for sale. It also listed the dates and times of local concerts and plays for the men stationed in the rear areas. The humorous cartoons and articles provided some relief to the men at the front and helped them pass the time.

'Furlough' – Soldier from RIR 109 with family. (Author's collection)

In early August the XIV Reserve Corps made arrangements to honor the dead of both divisions in a formal ceremony scheduled to take place on the one-year anniversary of the start of the war. A new cemetery was placed near the statue of General Faidherbe located in the market place of Bapaume.[25]

The monument was constructed out of limestone cement and formed from two pyramid-shaped sections crowned with a large globe. It carried an inscription written by the Corps commander General von Stein:

We pay homage to our dead,
Who gave up their lives loyally and without fear,
Their mortal remains we have here laid to rest,
Their spirits, released, have gone home.

The monument was placed in the center of the cemetery that was laid out in the shape of a circle. The graves were grouped by state, with men from Württemberg and Baden in the first line, Prussians, Bavarians and others in the next lines extending further out from the center. Even the bodies of enemy soldiers who had died in captivity were buried among the men from the XIV Reserve Corps. A hedge of beeches surrounded the entire site. A linden avenue ran through the cemetery in the shape of a cross. It was not the first time German soldiers had been buried in Bapaume; one grave belonged to a Prussian officer of the Guards killed in 1871.

Officer in RFAR 26 with wife at the front. (Sebastian Laudan)

The ceremony was held on a grey overcast day that threatened rain at any time. The area surrounding the new cemetery was decorated with small pennons and flags that the dignitaries and visitors would pass in order to get to the new monument. Many officers and men of the XIV Reserve Corps as well as the Grand Duke of Baden, Prince August Wilhelm, the Württemberg Adjutant General von Graevenitz and a number of representatives from the other Federal states, attended the dedication.[26] Following the ceremony the Grand Duke of Baden spent several days visiting his countrymen in the 28th Reserve Division in the villages behind the front.

Visitors continued to arrive at the front, both civilian and military. They included the Württemberg War Minister von Marchtaler who was accompanied by Adjutant General von Graevenitz, Major General von Mageries and *Rittmeister der Reserve* Federer. Whenever possible the visitors were given the opportunity to experience the front line at first hand. Until the arrival of the British these visits to the front were often quite dangerous or made to seem so by the troops but since the French had departed the front had become noticeably safer. This was especially true along the front from St. Pierre-Divion to Thiepval.

This sector had changed considerably since the days of September 1914 when IR 180 had taken possession of the village. Over the past year artillery fire had changed the landscape drastically. The village had been shelled into one large ruin. The larger stone cellars were being utilized as dug-outs and only a few wall remnants marked the location of the once-resplendent château. The large underground cellars of the château were covered with a large amount of debris under which many men lived. The soldiers appreciated living so close to the location where they were stationed. However it was safe as long as the enemy did not employ heavy artillery.

There were a few live trees here and there and some of the old village gardens still had green patches among the rubble. Flowers would appear through the debris adding some color to the scene. A few birds even nested among the old park trees. However it was different at the *Granatloch* where the heavy concentration of fire had erased all vestiges of vegetation and completely destroyed every tree in the area.

Among the advantages of the decrease in overall activity along the front held by the XIV Reserve Corps were furloughs. By September it was decided to send home up to 5% of the regimental strength. This meant that from between 10 and 12 men from each company were able to visit family and friends for a period of two weeks at one time. It was the first time leave could be issued to the officers and men since they left for the war over one year earlier. Von Soden was among those able to take advantage of the program and visited his family on a 14-day furlough, his first leave in 13 months. Still, many had to wait for their turn.

> There is still home leave, but in our company there are many more older and married men, who want home leave. Maybe it is possible later. Karl Losch, 3/R119 [27]

While many of the men looked forward to seeing their families once again most felt that the time at home was far too short and that the second parting from loved ones was even more difficult than when they had left at the outbreak of war. Still, it was a time to get away from the front and recall what life in civilian areas felt like again.

There was also a growing resentment among the men about the civilians at home.

> Pilots have now also dropped bombs on Stuttgart. Was it very scary? So really how is the mood among the Other Ranks? They say that it does no harm that they also know what war was like in Stuttgart, because they had to duck down etc. and their fraud continues on and on. That for example there are theater performances, a large part of the Other Ranks could not comprehend, because they also have none. They also did not have much to lose if they come home again, because they have already been ruined for the most part. The farmers grumble over the requisition of grain and everyone over the officers' high salaries, especially if they are still state officials. One could hardly do anything to counter this mood. One hardly finds enlightened points of view. For example they will not withdraw one red Pfennig for war bonds. We have heard that so far it is twelve and a half billion. The men always say the war will last so long until we have no men and no more money. The war already lasts too long. Karl Losch, 3/R119 [28]

On rare occasions some officers were fortunate to have their wives visit the front for a short period. This was not very common but still a most welcome change to the normal routine of the front line. However it was confined to officers as the Other Ranks could not take advantage of this possibility.

Chapter notes

1. AOK 2 von Below = 2nd Army Headquarters von Below.
2. A special portable obstacle, the Lochmann entanglement, was sometimes used. It consisted of a net of barbed wire, about 13 feet wide and 180 feet long, which was unrolled and then erected on two-legged iron pickets, placed by men who crawled under the wire and pegged it down at the sides.
3. G. Frisch, *Das Reserve-Infanterie-Regiment Nr. 109 im Weltkrieg 1914 bis 1918*, p. 98.
4. Losch, op cit, *Feldpost* letter dated 29 June 1915.
5. Losch, op cit, *Feldpost* letter dated 11 July 1915.
6. Losch, op cit, 29 June 1916.
7. 15cm heavy field howitzer shells.
8. Greiner, *Reserve-Infanterie-Regiment Nr. 110 im Weltkrieg 1914-1918*, p. 82.
9. Losch, op cit, *Feldpost* letter dated 29 September 1915.
10. Lieutenant Dechoz was reported to have behaved well in front of La Boisselle in earlier fighting. He received the military cross for his actions. The German patrol thought it was shameful that such an officer should have been left behind by his men to die and for the body to remain in No Man's Land all of the next day.
11. Private William Nicholson, 6th Royal Highlanders – Perthshire, 153rd Brigade, 51st Highland Division. Born in Crieff, Perthshire, a Confectioner (Pastry Chef) by trade. Despite being severely wounded he was confident of eventual British victory. He actually enlisted under an alias. His real name was William McCorist, son of John and Ann McCorist, 61 East High Street, Crieff, Perthshire. He died of his wounds on 12 August 1915 and is buried in the AIF Burial Grounds, Flers. 6th Black Watch War diary 8/8/15: "10.50pm Germans exploded mine at NE corner of Îlot. Exploded into gallery of French counter mine & did little damage. 11.45pm another mine blown up. Whole front wrecked. Parapets leveled. Two dug-outs demolished & garrisons buried. – No. 3 Coy. Parties working all night repairing damage & digging out men. Enemy made no attempt to attack. Crater shelled by enemy's trench mortars, rifle grenades and aerial torpedoes. Casualties – 1 man killed, 1 missing, 14 wounded or crushed."
12. The prisoner provided detailed information during his interrogation including the size of his draft, his Company commander's name, his division and brigade among other facts.
13. Losch, op cit, *Feldpost* letter dated 11 August 1915.
14. Losch, op cit, *Feldpost* letter dated 14 August 1915.
15. P. Müller, *Geschichte des Reserve-Infanterie-Regiment Nr. 99*, p. 81.
16. PRO W095/1482, 1st Battalion Royal Irish Fusilier diaries.
17. R. Baumgartner (Ed.), 'The Somme 1 July 1916', *Der Angriff, A Journal of World War 1 History*, No. 13, p. 5.
18. G. Holtz, *Das Württembergische Reserve-Infanterie-Regiment Nr. 121 im Weltkrieg 1914-1918,* p. 24.
19. 3.7cm *Maschinen Flak.* Used in defense of torpedo boats and adapted to anti-aircraft duties. The tracer ammunition used for aiming purposes received the nickname 'Flaming Onions' from British airmen.
20. 'Plum Pudding' was the common term for the British 2-inch Medium Trench Mortar shells

21. This reinforced concrete strongpoint called 'Gibraltar' was to figure prominently in the defense of the village during the fighting in July 1916 when Australian troops were attacking Pozières. The remains of the strongpoint can still be seen today.

22. An early gas mask that was constructed of rubberized fabric.

23. The regiment was named after the new commander of RIR 99, *Oberstleutnant* von Franconia und Proschlitz. He was the former Chief of Staff of the Turkish Army and a member of the German Military Mission to Turkey. He had taken over RIR 99 when *Oberst* Grall became ill and was forced to return to Germany for treatment.

24. The Allied offensives in the Artois and Champagne included the Second Battle of Champagne, Third Battle of Artois, Second Battle of Vimy Ridge and the Battle of Loos. The fighting raged from 25 September – 6 November without any appreciable gains by the Allied armies.

25. The statue of General Faidherbe was erected to commemorate the Battle of Bapaume, 3 January 1871.

26. This is one of the few German memorials from the war that has survived to the present time. The monument was moved from Bapaume after the war and can now be seen at the German military cemetery at Villers au Flos.

27. Losch, op cit, *Feldpost* letter dated 18 August 1915.

28. Losch, op cit, *Feldpost* letter dated 26 September 1915.

8

October–December 1915

While the majority of the men in the XIV Reserve Corps were not involved in any large-scale fighting during the last three months of the year for the two battalions of RIR 99 that had been sent north to Arras this time would be an experience the men would not soon forget. The I and II/R99 were to spend the last months of 1915 in almost constant fighting against the French at Arras. They were first deployed near the village of Thelus, later at *Hörner* Sap south of Neuville-St. Vaast, a vast labyrinth of trenches. The regiment was positioned to prevent any further French breakthrough between Loos and Arras. The composite regiment served under several different commands in the 12th Division as well as Bavarian Division von Hartz. The troops were subjected to daily artillery fire and the threat of underground mine explosions was constant.

On 26 October RIR 99 suffered a particularly heavy loss from French mine activity. The enemy detonated a large mine near the Lille-Arras road that completely destroyed three dug-outs of the regiment. One officer and 32 men from the 1/R99 were buried in the explosion and could not be saved despite heroic attempts to dig them out. An attack that followed the explosion resulted in even more losses.

Day after day fire or heavy rain destroyed the parapets. Night after night the men rebuilt those once again using sandbags. The troops often stood knee deep in mud and

Infantry group – RIR 99. (Author's collection)

clay in the trenches. They had to be on constant alert, as snipers were particularly active and effective.

Large rats scurried though the trenches and around the feet of the men while mice rustled about in the musty dug-outs with their moist clay walls. The misery caused by the enemy, the elements and the vermin was amplified when the sound of French miners could clearly be heard underground. However no one knew the location of the new mine tunnel or when it might suddenly explode under their feet.

Finally, on 20 December, the two battalions were ordered back to the 26th Reserve Division. As a result of the fighting near Arras the regimental commander *Oberstleutnant* von Franconia und Proschlitz received the Iron Cross 1st Class while 60 other members of the regiment received the Iron Cross 2nd Class. RIR 99 suffered considerable losses while at Arras: 98 men had been killed including 1 officer. 203 men were wounded including 2 officers while 276 men had reported sick. The men who were ill showed quick improvement once they had been returned to their old division and many returned to duty within a short time.

The troops brought back invaluable experiences from nearly three months of heavy fighting. The regiment would use this experience and knowledge to improve their own position and much of what they had learned was incorporated into training bulletins that were sent to every unit within the XIV Reserve Corps. RIR 99 also held practical demonstrations for the other regiments.

The overall defensive system of the XIV Reserve Corps continued to be developed in the last quarter of the year. A number of strongpoints had been developed in the third trench of the 1st Line continued to be strengthened and improved: *Feste Soden*, the *Grallsburg*, *Feste Alt Württemberg*, *Feste Schwaben* and Mouquet Farm.

The 2nd Line, Puisieux – Grandcourt – Pozières Windmill, contained the *Alte Garde Stellung*, strongpoints at the western edge of Grandcourt, north and south of Hill 151 as well as the *Staufen* and *Zollernfeste*. The 3rd Line, Achiet le Petit, Irles, Pys, Le Sars, had been surveyed and the line had been chosen, a total distance of 10 kilometers along the front held by the 26th Reserve Division alone. In order to complete such a major project outside help was needed.

All of the recruit companies found in both divisions were being used to entrench as part of their daily routine. However this work seriously hampered their training in modern trench warfare. The IV/*Landwehr* Regiment 75 had also been put to work creating new positions and was responsible for creating the strongpoint *Feste Alt Württemberg*, a model of which was created in Stuttgart and was featured in a war exhibition. The IV/*Landwehr* 75 was then withdrawn from the XIV Reserve Corps on 4 December. Two additional replacement battalions were then obtained from the XVIII Army Corps to help dig, the III/115 and II/117 and later the III/117.

Every able man was combed from the Corps to help with the endless digging. On 8 December 100 men from Württemberg Reserve Dragoon Regiment 8 were sent to help RIR 109 dig and maintain the trenches in good order. Several of the regiments in the Corps formed additional construction companies. Men who had been miners and engineers were the most sought after:

> Incidentally it is often nicer to be in the fire trench than in reserve, where you must entrench every second night, as our 2nd Battalion does presently. Karl Losch, 3/R119 [1]

Officer with Iron Cross 1st Class - RIR 121. (Author's collection)

RIR 110 formed a Construction Company that consisted of 2 officers, three Groups from each company to act as laborers, 24 masons, 43 men attached to the regimental Pioneer Corps to work with the electrical detachment, 12 woodcutters and 2 men to work on the wells.

Despite the increased difficulties in training new recruits every attempt was made to provide the men with the latest information and techniques of trench warfare in order to maintain their efficiency. The practical demonstrations provided by RIR 99 were of great help to the newer men.

Expanded training programs were developed for the troops resting in the rear especially the art of throwing hand grenades. Events were held along the lines of a sports outing where the men competed for distance and accuracy. This would yield great benefits in the months that followed. Other training activities included how to quickly dam up trenches with sandbags as well as the distribution of new gas masks and how to use them, all of which had practical application when the men were sent to the front.

The months of fighting had taken a serious toll on the pre-war officer Corps. Many officers with long service had been killed, wounded or transferred to other units. At the outbreak of the war a typical infantry company in the Corps was commanded by a *Hauptmann*. Now, typically a *Leutnant der Reserve* commanded a company.

The replacements, while good officers, lacked the experience their predecessors had obtained from years of service. Training schools for replacement officers and company leaders were expanded behind the front that provided some much-needed instruction for

Field Kitchen – Irles, RIR 121. (*Das Württembergische Reserve-Infanterie-Regiment Nr. 119 im Weltkrieg 1914-1918*)

the new officers that could also be put to good use in the trenches. Despite the increased need of officers the old pre-war attitudes were difficult to overcome.

According to a decree from War Minister von Marchtaler the demand for young reserve officers was covered. No consideration is taken of the occupation, family situation etc. because it has occurred that sons of bakers, butchers etc. are '*Reserve Offizier Aspirants*' or even *Leutnants* and that certainly does not pass with the German Army or Prussian militarism. According to the statements by the Prussian training officers the Württemberg Aspirants are good soldiers generally, individually however they are lacking pluck and presence (Swabian = Gob). The Württemberger were simply dismissed by the Prussians.

The beauty is that *Vizefeldwebel* etc. from Germany are still coming into the field and to the company, although we already have enough. So 2 *Vize* came to us recently, of which one was already in the field, the other not (first inducted in November or December). They stink around in Germany, until they are shown the way out and we, who were with the company since December shall have to suffer. Well enough of it. Karl Losch, 3/R119 [2]

Supplying sufficient food for an entire army Corps was a daunting task at the best of times. While centralized facilities had been established to provide fresh meat and bottled seltzer water for the men and hay and fodder for the horses each regiment supplemented the official rations during the summer months by planting extensive vegetable gardens. With the onset of winter quickly approaching additional resources were required to maintain the nutrition level required by the physical labor of entrenching and by spending a great deal of time exposed to inclement weather.

Hares, rabbits and hens, which were abundant in the area, were hunted extensively during this period and this provided a pleasant interruption in the monotony of position warfare for senior staffs during the winter. The game that was shot was used to augment the nutritional needs of the troops.

We had one hot meal a day. It consisted of beans, peas, lentils and dehydrated vegetables. These were cooked with meat and tasted very good. We also had bread with marmalade and made coffee and tea in the trenches. We also had emergency rations – canned meat, bottled water and first aid supplies. Emil Goebelbecker, 9/R109 [3]

Heavy downpours marked November and December and the trenches and dug-outs soon filled with water. The weather was simply described as being repulsive. Trench walls began to collapse; water seeped through the ground and accumulated in the dug-outs, mainly by dripping from the ceilings. Many of the communication trenches leading to the rear were soon impassable as they were transformed into muddy brooks. The lines were kept open only by great exertion and to the detriment of all other needed work.

The ceaseless rain quickly accumulated in the mined dug-outs, craters and trenches to the point that pumps were needed in order to keep them clear. Duckboards with raised legs were tried in some of the worst areas but this meant that the men were required to walk bent over otherwise they would present an easy target for snipers.

The troops were constantly wet for weeks at a time; their clothing soaked through by the mud and rain. Two labor companies and an armament company were used to keep the trenches clear in RIR 110 but despite their best efforts the men were often in the positions in water up to their stomachs. One man in communication trench 'A' in the regimental sector had to be pulled from the mud several times in one day as he became stuck in the mud over and over again. The grey mass of mud on the men's boots resembled elephant's feet according to the troops and could only be cleaned off using knives or pieces of wood.

Don't let it be said that the 26th Reserve Division headquarters did not have a sense of humor during the worst of the weather. One morning report sent out from headquarters during this period quoted Psalm 69, verses 1-2:

Save me O God, for the waters are come in, even unto my soul. I stick fast in the deep mire where there is no ground; I am come into deep waters, so that the flood runs over me. [4]

The troops at the front were not the only ones to suffer the misery of the bottomless mire. The thick mud was experienced by many of the higher-ranking officers including division and corps commanders. The commanding officer of the 28th Reserve Division General von Pavel, personally learned about the difficult conditions facing the troops while visiting the lines of RIR 110 on Hill 110. The general was touring the front accompanied by several officers, orderlies and acting regimental commander Gandenberger von Moisy. During the walk through the trenches two of the orderlies had to support von Pavel when he lost his footing and on a number of occasions they had to physically extract him from the mud.

At one point the regimental commander lost his balance and fell into a deep hole where the water was over his hips and began to pour into his trousers. At the same time an aide, *Hauptmann* Humricht, slipped and fell flat on his stomach with outstretched hands and ended up covered in a thick coating of mud.

The small party continued their journey until another aide had a mishap. While leading the group through a particularly bad section of trench *Hauptmann* Steiner's

Blank

Leutnant im Infanterie-Regt. 180,
gefallen bei Serre am
8. Oktober 1915

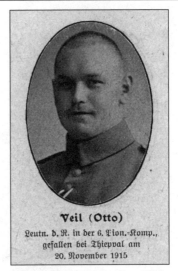

Veil (Otto)

Leutn. d. R. in der 6. Pion.-Komp.,
gefallen bei Thiepval am
20. November 1915

Leutnant Josef Blank (Landshut, Bavaria)
5/180. Killed in action 8 October 1915
near Serre. (*Kriegstagbuch aus Schwaben*)

Leutnant der Reserve Otto Veil
(Heidenheim) 6/Pioneer Bn 13. Killed
in action 20 November 1915 near
Thiepval. (*Kriegstagbuch aus Schwaben*)

boot became stuck in the mud and when he pulled his leg out of the thick slime the boot remained stuck fast. He continued to walk until his second boot became stuck as well and was pulled off his foot.

Steiner continued to walk in his socks and they provided some protection from the mud until they too were pulled off in the sticky morass. He walked barefoot until an orderly took pity on him and carried the *Hauptmann* to the rear on his shoulders. A second orderly followed carrying the muddy boots. Half an hour later the mud-covered officers were sitting in front of a warm stove where Humricht sat with his legs stretched out, his muddy brown feet drying by the fire while orderlies went to fetch clean water. During the entire time the division commander sat nearby with a broad smile on his face.

Not long afterward von Pavel became ill and was forced to leave the division to seek treatment. His replacement, General von Hahn, had formerly been the Adjutant General of His Royal Highness the Grand Duke of Hesse.

The period of heavy rain was followed by a cold spell and the ground finally froze bringing much needed respite from the mud. Everyone breathed a sigh of relief but it was short-lived. The frost broke and the ground turned into a sea of mud once more and every effort was required to maintain the trenches in a passable state.

The Birthday of Her Highness, Queen Charlotte of Württemberg was solemnly celebrated on 10 October. The different regiments and friends of the 26th Reserve Division created a fund for the war wounded and war survivors and called it the Queen Charlotte Foundation. The initial donations to the fund came to an impressive 10,000 Marks.[5]

The months of October and November passed quietly on the front of the XIV Reserve Corps. Only the enemy artillery appeared to have been strengthened during this period. There were numerous bombardments of villages and headquarters by mobile and railroad guns.

Communication trench in the village of Fricourt – RIR 111. (Author's collection)

'All Souls' Day ceremony, 26th Reserve Division cemetery monument in
Miraumont, 2 November 1915. (*Die 26. Reserve Division 1914-1918*)

The 26th Reserve Division headquarters had been located on Hill 131 south of
Miraumont since 5 October 1914. The commanding general now wanted to move his
headquarters as well as the headquarters of the artillery commander to Grevillers due to the
increase in artillery fire. The only drawback of this move was a longer journey to the front.

The British maintained air superiority and the XIV Reserve Corps estimated that at
least 40 aircraft were stationed at the Marieux airfield at Doullens. In order to provide
sufficient warning to the different regiments in the Corps when enemy aircraft were

active an aerial barrier was formed. A series of observers reported any sightings of aircraft through the use of wireless radios and sirens.

Aerial observation of the German lines increased from month to month by British aircraft. Occasionally observation planes were brought down by ground fire including one near RIR 111. The aircraft crashed into the British lines where the German artillery bombarded the wreckage and set it on fire.

On 6 November a lone British plane flew over the quarry position of RIR 110 and attempted to bomb it. Fortunately for the men in the quarry the pilot miscalculated the trajectory of the bomb and it ended up landing in the British lines where it exploded. The British did not attempt to bomb the quarry after this.

Intelligence officers had determined that little had changed with the British forces facing the Corps. The 36th (Ulster) Division that had been reported disembarking in Boulogne and Le Havre at the beginning of October was now identified as being opposite the 26th Reserve Division. The 48th Division faced the 52nd Division and the 5th and 18th Divisions faced the 28th Reserve Division.

Detailed interrogations of prisoners captured by patrols and on raids provided precise details of the order of battle of the four British divisions. Observers noted the increased use of steel helmets in place of the familiar soft caps formerly worn by British troops.

New units arrived to bolster the defensive strength of the XIV Reserve Corps. On 14 October *Minenwerfer Abteilung* 130 arrived in the sector held by RIR 109 and on the same day the regiment formed a second machine gun company from Fortress Machine Gun *Abteilung* Diedenhofen.

The British were observed reinforcing the wire entanglements in front of their trenches and this was interpreted as meaning they had no intentions of attacking the German lines in the near future. The British were also observed to be eagerly working on their lines near Ovillers. The observers in RIR 111 reported the numerous trenches gave the

Crashed plane and pilot. (Author's collection)

appearance of a honeycomb. Kitchen facilities were identified and heavy traffic could be seen moving to and from these locations. The observation posts even reported seeing a football matches being played in the areas just behind the lines.

At the same time the British were actively sapping towards La Boisselle on the left wing of RIR 111. The dense autumn fog was aiding their work by concealing their activities.

Patrol frequency increased on both sides of the wire in the latter part of 1915. In many cases the success or failure of a patrol was a matter of luck. A veteran patrol leader in 12/R 119, *Unteroffizier* Mathias Dirr, sent one graphic account of a patrol as a *Feldpost* letter to his family:

> My love! How are you? I am well; I am still healthy and lively, although I may thank God that I am still in the world. We had bad luck on our patrol, so did Theodor; who also received a grazing shot two days ago when we were over there again with the Englishmen, naturally in the fog, in the immediate vicinity, approximately 5-10 meters from the English trench. However it only grazed his cap and ripped it, but he carried away an indentation on his head and it was slightly burned because the bullet was broiling hot. He is with me alive and well. I gave a good report, where I made an impeccable sketch of the enemy trench, of the sap, of the wire-obstacles, of the enemy advanced sentries and altogether of the whole terrain.
>
> All of this naturally went to the battalion. A few days previously we, I and Theodor, and five more men, ones that one could absolutely rely upon, bloodily repelled an enemy hand-grenade attack on our listening post. I must still point out that the British are greatly superior to us. My patrol with me is seven men strong, while we were attacked by two patrols each with eight men. As we attacked the forward patrol, we were attacked by the second in the rear of us. They threw some hand-grenades at us, which were well thrown, but nevertheless no one was hit. We paid them back, four men fired on the run and we others threw hand grenades, in a moment nine were thrown and only the splinters, the fire, smoke and powder vapor rumbled. Soon one saw nothing more and the flares fired by us gave off only gloomy light as with thick fog.
>
> As said, we knew however we could not go forward without everyone being stabbed or hit with a rifle butt on the head and everyone still fired at what they could see in front of them and then it was as if you had a tankard smashed against your head because the second patrol threw hand grenades into the rear of us and delivered rapid fire from the turnip field. Shortly and safely, we moved back so that we always had the enemy in front of us. However we had shown him the way home, and we had given him a sore nose because it made him turn around and disappear into the darkness of the night. Each of us was well and I was happy that all had gone so smoothly. After a half hour were we relieved and after this – in my opinion interesting incident – we could then quietly have a good sleep. Of course, all was directly reported and everything went to the Battalion again with the names of my men from the patrol. Yesterday and the course of the previous night were very quiet. An airship went over the position.
>
> Now I called my men together, I reported to the duty officer and went on patrol at 6.45 o'clock. Immediately following another patrol, patrol Müller, also went quickly under the protection of the fog ... . We went forth with hand grenades and

armed with a few belts of cartridges. Immediately at the start we observed a few Englishmen, who worked on the entanglements. We changed our course and were not seen. We came unseen until we were at the English entanglements. The other patrol stalked around in the area behind us. Theodor, I and one more of my trusted men worked forward into the wire entanglements. Our wire cutters functioned perfectly. Everything was cut. In an area of approximately 30 meters there were only bare posts in a short time. We came closer to the trench; we had cut ourselves a large gap. Behind us on the right was the enemy advanced listening post that we have so far already come across. In front of us on the right also ran the communication trench that connected the listening post with the English fire trench and through that naturally the sentries were also relieved. We forged ahead as noiselessly as possible on hands and knees, however to all appearances the patrol behind us allowed itself to be seen. Confirmation of the fact was that the English listening post sentries alarmed the entire position. A volley cracked suddenly, completely unexpected. Instinctively the patrol lay down. The leader, Müller, and his best friend Gehring (both had the Silver Medal for Merit and only two days ago received the Iron Cross) were still indecisive and remained standing to orient themselves in the terrain as to where that volley came from, and this single moment in their life, this single moment cost two loving, faithful souls their lives. In this moment the second volley crashed; this volley was accurate, as was also no wonder, because the wind had blown away the fog and suddenly it became lighter and it was bright. In broad daylight one can easily hit two men in true size from a distance of 100 meters. As said, when the second volley cracked Gehring fell back, he had been shot in the head, it went in at the ear and out the rear of the head. It tore his head apart.

These miserable low down convicts, this cowardly and mean class of men had again used explosive Dum Dum bullets, so that Gehring, his brain, his sinews and fibers were hanging out of the head, and the leader Müller had at the same time received a shot in the right thigh. This explosive bullet nearly tore the thigh apart. There was a hole that one could put a fist in. The bullet had hit the artery and the bright red blood shot out like a river, like a fountain. A scream and he was unconscious. We lay still in front in the wire entanglements for what seemed the longest time, [then] we had to go back. When the Englishmen realized the fact that we had two severely wounded men, who were being carried by a third man (we slid everyone back with the greatest effort), they came out of the trench and fired at our movements, standing on the trench like savages. We were the foolish ones and if we did not have all the luck again then it might have turned out completely different because we had to go back through a route in the English entanglements approximately 40 meters long. We crawled back like the snakes on the ground, and we used all of our strength, we came out unseen from the wire entanglements. At one time all of the fire was directed at my patrol because as I said the Englishmen came out of their trench. I believed they wanted to capture us and this would have been dealt with in a life and death struggle. We strained greatly, with the right hand convulsively grasping the rifle, in the left twitched the hand grenade, but we felt they were content to remain and only watch us. We used each tuft of grass, each thistle and each turnip stem as cover, naturally only from being seen, [and] we crept back nestled close to the ground. Even when only a turnip stem moved the equivalent of a dozen bullets flew at it. Only when we were half way could we relax again, relieved and draw a deep breath and give a small sigh. We now helped to carry in the wounded. Unfortunately both died. Müller died from loss of blood and Gehring from the shot in the head. Both were placed into coffins and were buried in the cemetery by the church in Miraumont. My patrol has returned intact and lucky again. If we ever have a favorable opportunity then we will bitterly avenge our two dear comrades. The matter is reported and my patrol has presumably distinguished everyone in the battalion. Shortly afterward Theodor received the Iron Cross. Cordial greetings to all! Your Heifi.[6]

Karl Losch also ran into the British while out on patrol one night in October:

The night of the day before yesterday I had a little adventure on patrol. We went forward against a grove for the third time that was located approximately between our position and the English position. We kneeled 10 to 15 meters in front of the grove in order to observe and to listen. Immediately thereafter we heard a noise and saw after a couple of shapes moving along the grove. We sat quiet as mice and allowed the 2 or 3 in front creep up until they were about 10 meters from us (3 or 4 others were still at the grove), then 3 hand grenades flew against 1, 2, 3 of the Englishmen. The Englishmen threw a hand grenade at us that exploded 4-5 meters in front of us, on which one of us threw a fourth one across at them. There was just a crash. We started to fire our rifles and heard the Englishmen running away while we slightly withdrew. Afterwards the pair of us (Storch and I) remained lying there while Emhardt fetched some hand grenades from the sap. Immediately following him came another 3 men and then we 6 examined the terrain, by which one (Weiching) found a rifle that an Englishman had left lying on the ground (maybe the one who had thrown the hand grenade). Hereupon we turned back and yesterday morning I had to carry the rifle to the battalion. Our *Hauptmann Freiherr* von Hirschberg congratulated me, as did the Battalion Adjutant (*Leutnant* Sattelmager). There was an Englishman, who was very close to the advanced position; however we did not bring him back, still it is good we escaped so well and that is the most important thing.[7]

Despite these clashes in No Man's Land many of the companies still had not brought in an enemy prisoner, alive or dead. When this finally occurred there was a sense of accomplishment in the regiment.

It is still calm by us, except the day before yesterday there was a patrol battle again (I was not there) and at 8 o'clock this evening today's patrol found a dead Englishman at the location of the fight (shot in the breast) that the patrol brought back. Now the company also has the joy of procuring the long-awaited dead or alive Englishman. *Unteroffizier* Schiedel was the patrol leader. Karl Losch, 3/R119 [8]

In spite of the events described by Dirr and Losch it still seemed that many of the British patrols did not venture far from their trenches. New methods were needed to entice the British out of their lines in order to obtain information regarding unit identification and other intelligence. RIR 119 and RFAR 26 developed a plan by which the artillery would damage the wire entanglements at a specific location. This would bring the enemy out of his trench in order to make repairs where he could then be taken prisoner in an ambush.

Sector B7 near Hamel was chosen as the test case for this new idea. A deep cut separated the opposing lines and it seemed to be the ideal location. On 12 October the guns of RFAR 26 and *Minenwerfer* Coy 226 shelled the British wire entanglements resulting in a large gap being formed. The enemy would hopefully feel the strong urge to make immediate repairs. A wiring party was indeed sent out as soon as darkness had fallen however they were unaware of the patrol from RIR 119 lurking nearby.

While the enemy was occupied in repairing the wire a German machine gun previously sited on the gap opened fire into their ranks scattering the men. A short time later the patrol moved in and discovered a dead British soldier who was quickly taken back to the German lines. In light of the success the same method was quickly applied to several other locations along the front including Serre and the forest of Authuille.

RIR 121 made use of this method to obtain intelligence concerning the units opposing the regiment. On 29 October the artillery, *minenwerfers* and *erdmörsers* fired on the British wire and opened a 50-meter wide gap in the defenses. The 12/R121 sent out a patrol to intercept any soldiers sent out to repair the damage. They came across 3 men and quickly attacked them. One man escaped the trap while a second was killed and left behind. The third man was severely wounded and brought back to the German lines. He died within 30 minutes of being brought in. He was identified as belonging to the 4th Lancashire Regiment (154th Brigade, 51st Division).

A similar attempt made by the II/R121 near the *Granatloch* failed completely. The same methods were employed but the enemy did not rise to take the bait on this occasion and no wiring parties were observed. Later in the day the German lines were covered in fire from light and heavy guns, apparently in revenge for the attempted ambush.

Men (and dog) in the trenches – RIR 121. (Author's collection)

la Boiselle, 28. 11. 15.

Oberst Ley and Adjutant shortly before British machine gun fire caused them to
squat down when the bullets came uncomfortably close. (Author's collection)

It was evident that the British had caught on to the ploy and new methods would be
needed to entice them out of their trenches. In fact the British copied the very method
on several occasions. During the night of 17/18 November a strong enemy bombardment
badly damaged the wire entanglements in front of RIR 109. Several men volunteered
to make the necessary repairs. The enemy fired a Very light that illuminated the area.
A machine gun opened fire simultaneously and one man, a soldier named Rupp, was
severely wounded. His friend, *Kriegsfreiwilliger* Köhler braved the heavy fire and brought
him to safety.

On the night of 28 November RIR 111 attempted to use the same ruse against their
opponents one last time. Artillery fire severely damaged the British wire in the vicinity
of the *Hoheneck*. The regimental commander *Oberst* Ley and his adjutant watched the
bombardment from a forward trench and were forced to quickly learn how to squat down
as British machine gun fire came uncomfortably close in response to the artillery fire.

Leutnant Ritter and 18 men from the II/R111 entered No Man's Land at the onset of
darkness in order to ambush any British working party that should be sent out to make
repairs. The German patrol was provided with additional protection consisting of two
smaller detachments sent out on each flank.

When the British did not show as expected several members of the main patrol crept
closer to the enemy trenches where they found a subterranean listening gallery that had

Deep trench at the 'Minefield' near Beaumont, RIR 119. (*Das Württembergische Reserve-Infanterie-Regiment Nr. 119 im Weltkrieg 1914-1918*)

been destroyed by a direct hit, but it was unoccupied. The patrol was finally forced to withdraw without having achieved their purpose.

Several days' later two men attempted to enter the British lines through the damaged listening post but were detected by alert sentries and fired upon. RIR 111 continued to send out patrols in order to take prisoners but in each case they were unsuccessful. In the night of 1/2 December an officer and a non-commissioned officer managed to enter the British trenches but were disappointed to only find deep water and mud, not an enemy in sight.

While the patrols from RIR 111 were unsuccessful in capturing a prisoner they did provide valuable observations regarding the opposing lines and activities of the trench sentries. *Leutnant* Riemer, III/R111, had discovered an unused trench approximately 50 meters distant in front of the British wire entanglements. The trench had apparently been abandoned and had become used as a drainage ditch. *Leutnants* Riemer and Clouth would often settle in to the disused trench and observe the British lines throughout the day. Their observations provided valuable details concerning the placement of machine guns, the types of wire entanglements, the behavior of sentries, troop relief and other important details.

A particularly active patrol area was located along the front held by RIR 119. The sector included the mine crater field, the sunken road near Beaumont-Hamel as well as the road leading toward Auchonvillers where the *Weissdorn* shrub stood.[9]

Each side sent patrols into this area and there were frequent clashes in the darkness of No Man's Land where it was often a matter of luck which side came out on top. One such patrol took place on the night of 22 October when five men from the 9/R119 set out near *Weissdorn Höhe* where the British were known to also send out patrols. It was considered a good place to lurk in ambush in the hope of obtaining a prisoner.

Unteroffizier Meiser accompanied by *Ersatz Reservists* Bitzer and Hähnle, *Reservist* Knies and *Kriegsfreiwilliger* Baun left their trench shortly after 7 p.m. The patrol made its way toward the enemy lines through the foggy night where they could clearly hear the sounds of clanking wagons and shovels and picks being used in the British trenches.

While the patrol moved carefully from crater to crater due to bright moonlight that came through the cloud cover at times they often stopped to listen before proceeding. Suddenly the patrol spotted five shapes sneaking toward the German lines. It was decided almost immediately to attempt to take the men prisoner therefore the patrol members laid flat on the ground and allowed the enemy to pass. As the British patrol approached Patrol Meiser realized they were actually facing up to 20 enemy soldiers and were now cut off from their own trenches.

Meiser immediately called for his men to throw their hand grenades and attack the superior enemy force. The grenades exploded among the startled British soldiers and several fell wounded. The 5 man German patrol then advanced with their rifle butts raised over their heads and began to strike their opponents down. Just as Meiser struck one man in the head he was shot from out of the darkness. The night was filled with the sounds of crashing grenades, rifle shots and close quarter fighting.

The British patrol had no idea of the size of their opponent's force and quickly withdrew to their lines carrying their dead and wounded while being fired at by the remaining members of Patrol Meiser. Additional troops rushed from the German lines to assist their comrades and opened fire on the fleeing enemy.

Expecting a possible reprisal raid the 9th Coy sent out an entire platoon into No Man's Land to wait in ambush for any unsuspecting British patrol early on 23 October. A short time later, approximately 40 enemy soldiers were observed working toward the German lines. A firefight broke out between the two groups, the dark night again being lit up by rifle fire and exploding hand grenades.

The British were withdrawing when a figure rose up from a shell hole behind the German patrol. Apparently one member of the British patrol had become disoriented in the darkness and confusion and had ended up between them and the German trenches. He was quickly taken prisoner and turned out to be a Second Lieutenant of the South Lancashire Regiment. Similar clashes occurred along the entire front held by the XIV Reserve Corps as each side attempted to gain supremacy over No Man's Land.

Mining activity on both sides continued to expand in the last part of 1915. Mines set off by the opposing sides caused a number of casualties among the infantry holding the line but in many cases it was the pioneers who suffered the most.

On 25 October the largest mine yet was set off, the explosion formed a crater 25 meters in diameter. An even larger explosion took place on 21 November; it left a crater with a depth of 27.2 meters. It was formed using 15,000 kilograms of explosives. It was estimated that all British tunnels and lines were damaged within a radius of 30 meters based upon similar findings from damage to the German lines after a mine explosion. RIR 109 alone experienced 11 mine explosions in the month of December – 5 British and 6 German.

On 9 December *Pionier* Maier became trapped under a fallen support beam in his listening post due to a mine detonation. *Pioniers* Schmiederer, Kastler, Kieninger and

Mine crater 'A', Hill 110. (*Reserve-Infanterie Regiment Nr. 110 im Weltkrieg 1914-1918*)

Schulze quickly rushed in and were killed in an attempt to rescue their friend. They had forgotten the basic danger of gas poisoning following an explosion.

The British started to actively mine in the vicinity of Fricourt. They were thought to have an advantage over the German miners because of the type of high explosives they employed in the soft chalk soil and the use of drills and explosive charges in the mining process. The explosives quickly filled the entire mine system and nearby tunnels with poisonous gases. As a result the Germans were forced to evacuate the dug-outs near the minefield and those to the north of it.

The second Christmas in the field was quickly approaching. This time the holiday did not have the same meaning as in 1914 and the festivities were kept to a minimum. The landscape was not covered in white snow; there was mud and filth everywhere. Most of the men spent Christmas Eve in their dug-outs or in a rear area billet thinking quietly about their families and home.

> Today I want to be able to surprise you with something that you surely didn't think was conceivable; today I have received the Iron Cross II Class with both of my other patrol party [members]. Our *Hauptmann* pinned it on us today at noon. We received it for the patrol fighting in October. At the beginning of November I was recommended, but could not be considered for it. Now the *Hauptmann* has proposed the 3 of us again. That is a Christmas gift! Naturally I could only think of you in my joy that was hard to describe. You could let it be printed in the Stuttgart daily paper so: Losch, Karl *Kriegsfreiwilliger Vizefeldwebel* in Res. Inf. Reg. 119; Son of the--.[10]

In fact Karl's promotion to *Vizefeldwebel* was also due in part to his patrol activity. Just a short time earlier he wrote:

> So far we have always been lucky on our patrols. In part I owe them thanks for my promotion to *Vizefeldwebel* that has come out today. I was naturally very happy. The Englishmen had all sorts of papers with them.[11]

Losch's parents and friends were very generous when it came to gifts throughout the year but in particular at Christmas time:

> I got your Christmas package that filled me with undiminished joy for all of the beautiful and good things. You have fulfilled my tastes perfectly, Cognac, cigars, *Schnitzbrot*, gingerbread etc.
>
> Yesterday evening we were relieved from the front line and came into a rear position, called the *Gralsburg*. Here I guarded the old abandoned regimental dugout together with Richard Seeger, where we had a very beautiful opportunity to celebrate Christmas. We are in possession of a large space and above us is where 20 men live in the tunnel. All sorts of precautions arrived from the company about the correct way to celebrate Christmas. We are not lacking a Christmas tree. It promises to be very nice.
>
> We have celebrated a very beautiful Christmas. We had a lighted Christmas tree in our dug-out and under this we sang Christmas songs with the Other Ranks. It was a very pleasant celebration, a memory that I would not want to have missed. [12]

There was no attempt to fraternize with the enemy during this Christmas. The lines near Thiepval were pounded by approximately 1,500 shells up to 24cm in caliber on 24 December, a noticeable difference from the previous year.

The acting commander of RIR 121, *Oberstleutnant* Kündinger (Dragoon Regiment 25) went on a tour of the regimental trenches on Christmas Eve accompanied by his Adjutant *Hauptmann* Reischle. Both men wanted reassurance that the trench garrison was prepared in case of an attack.

Kündinger decided to set off an alarm bell – no response. He shouted 'alarm!' down the dark steps of a nearby dug-out, again no response. Finally the two officers heard a voice coming from the depths that 'greeted him in good Swabian and in a manner not to be misunderstood that he did not want his rest to be disturbed.'[13] After several similar experiences from different dug-outs the two officers were convinced that the men still had their nerves and they continued to walk their rounds.

The men decorated their quarters with small Christmas trees and as in the previous year a large quantity of gifts had arrived in the Field Mail. The regimental bands played holiday music in the rear areas but the mood was still somber. One of the few celebrations held on this Christmas took place in the sector of RIR 99 where a small church was decorated with evergreens and a majestic Christmas tree lit up the room:

> It was Christmas Eve 1915. The small church had been quickly decorated with evergreens as with magical hands. A majestic Christmas tree beamed in gleaming brilliance in the sanctuary and in the evening the Field Grey, head next to head, filled the place of worship. Were these the same men who lurked at the crater edge with cold blood and hard eyes and sent death out with iron fists that there were so childlike and devout, whose hard working hands were folded? No, the eyes of children shone toward the ancient lighted wonder of the Christmas tree, and all of the fondness of the German child's heart vibrated in the sounds of the Christmas song, with, as now out of many hundreds of soldier's throats over candle flames and the odor of fir, the German melody sounded toward heaven, solemn and consecrated

through the French church: Silent Night, Holy Night! And while the brave men, that never flinched in view of death sang gloriously with prayerful faces, many a drop that rolled from the eyelashes mirrored in the candle light! Nobody was ashamed of that in the consecration of the hour.[14]

The regiment marked the end of 1915 with a tattoo and torch parade in the village of Marcoing.

1915 would not end peacefully for some on both sides of the wire; instead it would bring fear and death. Neither side saw fit to take a break from the war during this period. Patrols were constantly being sent out into No Man's Land in order to capture a prisoner or bring back pieces of uniforms with identifying marks. One patrol from RIR 110 returned with several British caps that had the words Gibraltar and Northamptonshire on the cap badges. Another came across a dead British soldier who had been shot earlier in the evening. Several attempts were made to bring the body back to the German lines but all were unsuccessful. It was not finally brought in until the following night.

The patrols had not been as successful in obtaining detailed information about the enemy units opposite the 28th Reserve Division as had been expected. It was decided to send a large patrol, a raiding party, against the enemy lines instead. Division headquarters ordered RIR 110 to plan and carry out the raid against a small farmstead occupied by the British known as 'Häusergruppe Fricourt'. RIR 110 was to bring in as many prisoners as possible. The only restriction set for the undertaking was that it would take place before the end of 1915. The regiment started its preparations immediately.

Three officers were selected to command the raiding party, *Leutnants der Reserve* Partenheimer, Vulpius and Weiss. Numerous men from the regiment volunteered to participate in the raid of which 45 men as well as pioneers were chosen. Practice for the raid took place in Bazentin where an accurate model of the British position had been created by the pioneers. The volunteers practiced the plan of attack, throwing hand grenades, jumping over trenches, climbing up embankments and many other tasks that might be needed on the actual raid.

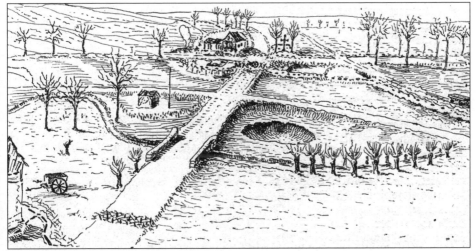

Sketch of 'House Group Fricourt'. (*Reserve-Infanterie Regiment Nr. 110 im Weltkrieg 1914-1918*)

Leutnant Vulpius and *Leutnant* Weiss. (*Reserve-Infanterie Regiment Nr. 110 im Weltkrieg 1914-1918*)

The training sessions were designed to accomplish two goals. First: to ensure the men were in top physical condition for the raid. Second: So that the men would become familiar with one another and the officers since they came from every company in the regiment and had never served together before.

When not training the men attended lectures and viewed up-to-date models of the British position. They were provided with the latest intelligence information regarding the condition and quality of the British lines, the type and structure of the wire entanglements including the direction of the entanglements and trenches. When practice was finished the men were given lectures on gas warfare and the latest methods of using the new anti-gas protection mask. The *Gummi* mask had only been issued a month earlier and had already proven to be more efficient than the makeshift masks currently in use. When the new equipment was distributed it marked the end of the thick beards worn by many of the men. In order to maintain a secure airtight seal around the mask each soldier was required be clean-shaven.

Detailed preparations were being worked out for the supporting arms: artillery, *minenwerfers* and regimental machine guns. The plan called for the use of three field howitzer batteries (one 155mm, one 12cm and one 9cm), two field artillery batteries (1st and 2/RFAR 29), two heavy and four medium *minenwerfers* and a light *minenwerfer* section, finally six heavy machine guns from the 1st Machine Gun Coy.

At 5:15 p.m. the heavy field howitzers would open fire upon 'House Group Fricourt' and the nearby Fricourt railway station with K-Projectiles[15] as well as on access routes leading to Hill 110 and other targets further to the rear. At 5.45 p.m. the field guns, heavy and medium *minenwerfers* would fire on the wire obstacles and barricades in front of the British position while the light *minenwerfers* fired on the trenches in the group of houses. Five minutes before the raiding parties were to attack the six machine guns were to spread their fire on the communication trenches and adjoining positions.

During the preparation period the British were becoming increasingly active, especially with the use of artillery fire along the entire line. On 26 December Sector Fricourt West was subjected to a particularly strong artillery bombardment. 11 men were killed or injured when their cellar collapsed from a direct hit from a heavy shell. This incident resulted in orders being issued that cellars were no longer to be used as shelters.

A special command post for the officer commanding the light and heavy field howitzers was set up in a forward position. A second command post was established at the exit of Fricourt facing Bray for the *minenwerfer* commander.

The infantry and pioneers had been divided into three equal groups consisting of one officer and 15 men. Patrol Partenheimer was assigned to advance from the *Lehmgrubenhöhe* to the west. Patrol Vulpius would advance toward Hill 110 from the east and attack the farmstead and roll up the enemy trench from the right to the left. Patrol Weiss would act as support and had a small detachment of stretcher-bearers assigned to it. Most of the men were armed with rifles while some were given pistols and knives. Almost everyone carried hand grenades and all were equipped with gas masks.

In order that the raiding parties could identify friend from foe the men wore a white bandage on the left arm. All caps, shoulder straps and any other piece of equipment that might give away their identity were to be left behind. The raid was scheduled to take place at 5 p.m. on 29 December. It was one of the first raids on the Somme where gas shells would be used in large numbers.

On 27 December a patrol was sent against 'House Group Fricourt' to make sure that the target was actually occupied. The men proceeded toward a gravel pit and the line keeper's house located by the target area when a fierce hand grenade fight broke out with enemy sentries. In the course of the fighting the patrol leader, *Leutnant* Weiss, and 4 men became wounded. During the return journey to the German lines it was discovered that one of the men was missing. The remainder of the patrol volunteered to look for the missing man. They were successful and were back in the German lines a short time later. Now Weiss was unable to participate in the main raid due to his injuries.

In the afternoon of 29 December the men were marched up to the dug-outs assigned to them. Patrol Vulpius was assigned to the last dug-out in the *Strassen Sap* by the poplar-lined Mametz – Albert road. The men were to be kept out of sight until just before the raid was to start. While they waited for the signal to begin many had the distinct impression that their comrades viewed them as guinea pigs.

Every watch had been synchronized; all there was left to do was wait. The weather up until the date of the raid was wet and miserable. Worst of all the wind had maintained a steady westerly direction and was unfavorable for the use of gas. However on 29 December the wind changed and was blowing in the right direction for the attack to begin.

At exactly 5.15 p.m. the artillery opened fire and the men on sentry duty could see the fiery trails of the shells as they whizzed overhead and impacted in the British lines. *Leutnant* Vulpius described the scene:

> The twitching fire trails of the shells look like a wild army of shooting stars and over there the great work of destruction begins. Section after section of the house group became covered with every caliber shell. Mighty fountains of earth sprayed up and fell back with a clap, intermingled with large beams that whirled through the air.[16]

The bombardment would last for three-quarters of an hour and then increase to a continual roar or 'drum fire' while the men in the raiding parties watched the spectacle from the safety of their trenches. At 5.50 p.m. the order to advance was given. The raiding parties ran forward until they were 50 meters from the British position where they were ordered to lie down. The heavy *minenwerfers* were still firing at the group of houses and the men could easily see their path through the air as the trench mortar bombs dropped into the enemy lines. The shells exploded with a paralyzing noise followed by a sheaf of fire climbing up into the dark night with millions of small sparks raining down to the ground.

Vulpius looked at his watch until the time approached 6 p.m. when he gave the order 'Up, at the double!' Just as the men rose up a heavy trench mortar bomb came across the sky and headed toward the British trenches. Vulpius gave the order for the men to lie down again but the explosion caught them in mid-stride. The splinters from the bomb whizzed by them, hitting one man who was sent to the rear for medical treatment.

The rest of the party advanced toward the British trench and reached it in just 5 seconds. The trench mortar bombs had flattened the obstacles but the damaged wire still ripped at the boots and shoes of the men. The caustic odor of gas was still in the air and they were ordered to don their gas masks. Within a few moments the order was given to remove their masks as the gas was quickly dissipating and the masks were cumbersome to wear.

The British trench was entered and a small detachment took up position to protect the main body and to keep alert for enemy activity. The rest of the patrol moved forward into the farmstead while the support fire was directed further to the rear.

The explosions and rocket flares were giving off sufficient light so that the men could see where they are going. One building had the entire roof blown off and it lay a short distance from the shattered walls. Vulpius attempted to cross the damaged roof and both legs became trapped when it gave way beneath his weight. While his men helped to free him a second covering party remained behind at the mouth of a nearby trench.

British dead could be seen inside of a smashed dug-out and pistol shots were heard coming from the other side of the house group where the second raiding party should be located. Vulpius was finally freed and his detachment of four men proceeded toward the sounds of the pistol shots. They stopped when they reached the corner of the building and looked cautiously around the edge. A pitch-black cellar opening gaped before them.

Vulpius shouted the password '*Gandenburger*' down into the dark opening because he felt it was possible that members of Patrol Partenheimer might have already gone down inside of it. The voices he heard were definitely English so he decided to throw a hand grenade into the entrance. Within a few seconds there was a loud noise of the explosion followed by smoke drifting up from below and the sounds of men crying out could be heard.

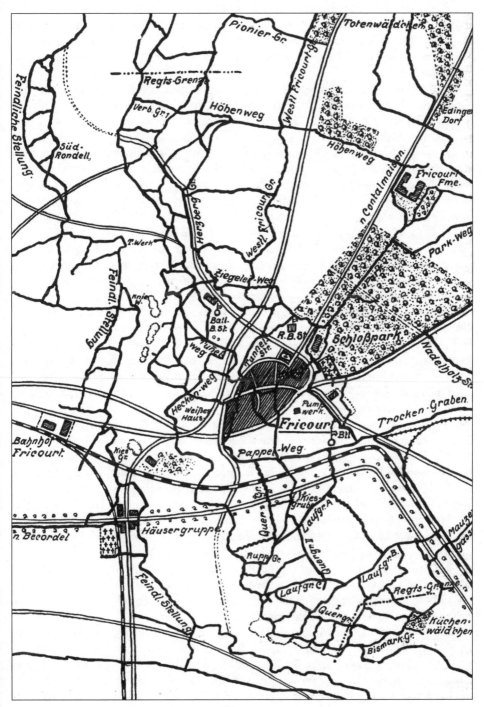

Fricourt.

Live prisoners were needed so it was decided not to throw a second hand grenade into the cellar. While Vulpius directed two of his men to secure the mouth of a nearby communication trench he attempted to get the enemy out of the dug-out using what little English he knew: 'Discard your weapons, come up immediately!' It was only answered by the sound of wounded men. 'Are you wounded?' 'Yes, yes' was the reply but still no one appeared.[17]

'You will be treated well if you come out immediately' but still the occupants refused to come out. Vulpius noticed rocket flares climbing into the sky, the signal for the raiding parties to return. He made one last attempt to obtain the surrender of the men inside the dug-out. 'Either you come up or you get a second hand grenade'. That finally worked. Unarmed British soldiers, 'Boys, audacious looking lads from the London suburbs' according to Vulpius, began to emerge from their dug-out in single file with their arms raised above their heads, their faces distorted with fear. 13 non-commissioned officers and men finally stood out in the open. It was later determined that the lieutenant of this group had gone on leave the previous day.[18]

Vulpius warned his prisoners 'If anyone moves he is a dead man'. He looked over prisoners with his hand torch while six of his men prepared to bring them back to the German lines. 'If the British attempted a counterattack at this moment through a nearby communication trench we would be finished but fortunately nothing happened.' There was no other activity so the raiding parties returned to the German lines.

The prisoners were directed toward a lane bordered by tall poplars that could be seen in the flash of the shells. They were warned not to attempt to escape, as they would be shot if they tried. One man who had been badly wounded in the stomach by the hand grenade was carried by two of his comrades at the end of the line of prisoners. The German artillery was still firing at the British lines while scattered British fire struck around the area.

During the journey back Vulpius was surprised to see one of the prisoners lighting a cigarette for his guard and himself. Several of the prisoners did attempt to escape from the line in the darkness and confusion but a quick prick of a bayonet soon brought them back into order. When the German trench was reached each man was helped down into the trench with a swing of an arm from a large German sentry.

The wounded man was carefully carried into the trench and into a nearby dug-out. The prisoner was made as comfortable as possible and given some water. His wounds were considered to be fatal and he died a short time later. Vulpius made a head count of his men and found that everyone had returned unharmed. He also learned that *Leutnant* Partenheimer had also been successful and had taken seven prisoners making the total 20 non-commissioned officers and enlisted men captured in the raid.

The prisoners were assembled for the march back to Bazentin with one man standing between two German guards. When the column approached the village the men were surprised to see the entire garrison lined up on both sides of the road greeting the raiding party by signaling with their hand torches.

The prisoners were assembled inside the village church where they would remain until arrangements could be made to transport them further to the rear. The British soldiers seemed to be relieved at the good behavior they were receiving from their German captors. One man was reported to have taken off his cap badge and given it to one of the men in the raiding party. When asked why he did this he replied 'because you have not killed me'.[19]

Interrogation of prisoners, 6th (Service) Bn Northamptonshire Regiment
in the church at Bazentin le Petit. (Author's collection)

The men came from the 6th (Service) Battalion of the Northamptonshire Regiment who had only been in France since July. During the bombardment the men had sought shelter in a cellar. A total of 20 men had been captured of which one died from his wounds, 2 others were killed and 3 wounded.[20]

Explosions could be heard coming from the ruined houses the following day. Vulpius wrote:

That was not difficult to explain as the Englishmen opposite us had proceeded to attack the farmstead that we had abandoned for some time since in the assumption that it was still occupied by us. How we laughed![21]

The raid was a complete success. The only German casualty was the man wounded by the *minenwerfer* shell splinter at the start of the raid, everyone else returned without an injury.

The total British casualties were never fully established but it was estimated that a considerable number had been killed or wounded during the heavy fire deployed during the raid. The two officers, Vulpius and Partenheimer were awarded the Iron Cross 1st Class while all other members of the raiding party were awarded the Iron Cross 2nd Class. Everyone was also to receive a furlough home. The entire incident had provided RIR 110 with a morale boost by showing that it could not only take the enemy position by storm it could also overpower the garrison.

The year had finally come to an end with little fanfare or celebration for most. Still, some men managed to mark the end of another year. The artillery on both sides of the wire played their part in the celebration.

Yesterday evening we came from the *Gralsburg* to Miraumont. From 12 o'clock ours and the English artillery fired for the New Year, which was quite a unique sound, the

Trench periscope near the Carnoy Mulde between Mametz
and Montauban – RIR 111. (Author's collection)

heavy discharges and impacts, which rattled the window panes. The Other Ranks
fired their rifles into the air. It was really great in part. But I have never celebrated
New Year's Eve so dry. That happened anyway because last night we had nothing

2/R121 in the trenches near the *Heidenkopf*. (Author's collection)

left. It was quite something at Christmas; there was wine, beer and punch. Karl Losch, 3/R119 [22]

The final act of the year involved the last mine fired on the front held by the XIV Reserve Corps. On 31 December the English detonated a mine opposite Beaucourt that buried and suffocated 3 pioneers.

The last 12 months had been witness to many changes along the front held by the XIV Reserve Corps. What had started as a single trench in many places had been developed over time into a veritable fortress. The main defensive line consisted of three to four consecutive trenches protected by large belts of barbed wire. Numerous communication trenches allowed easy access to every part of the line including some that were several kilometers long leading to the rear areas.

A second line of trenches similar to the main line was already well under construction approximately one kilometer to the rear and a third was marked out and under construction in many locations. The pioneer commander estimated that the 26th Reserve Division sector alone contained 150 kilometers of trenches without counting traverses and over 200 kilometers if the traverses were included. The actual front line facing the enemy for the division amounted to approximately 11 kilometers.

By the beginning of 1916 the 26th Reserve Division had approximately 1,500 mined dug-outs and 150 shellproof observation posts, almost as many in the sector of the 28th Reserve Division. The sector was considered to be one of the best defensive sites on the Western Front.

The trenches were well constructed and deep while the trench floor was covered in wooden duckboards. *Minenwerfer* positions signal stations and extensive drainage facilities were constructed throughout the lines.

Men from 4/Pioneer Bn 13 relaxing at a makeshift canteen and music hall. (Author's collection)

Mined listening posts, shell-proof sentry posts, artillery observation posts and machine gun positions had been constructed using concrete and iron rails whenever possible. Numerous artillery emplacements had been constructed to safely house the guns and artillerymen who manned them. The amount of wood and iron needed to construct this elaborate defensive system was immense. Trench construction and the large number of sandbags being used could be wearing on the men. Felix Kircher, RFAR 26:

> Our principal work was to fortify our guns, to make dug-outs, observation points, trenches and fill sandbags, always sandbags. It was said that the war would only be over when the whole of France was filled with sandbags.[23]

Procuring the vast amount of material and equipment needed to construct and maintain such a trench system required a great deal of work and organization. Numerous Pioneer parks had been established that were provided with light rail connections and large sawmills. Specialty units had been formed as needed with men drawn from the different regiments of the Corps. In this manner the regiments could send back men who because of age or illness were no longer suited to the rigors of trench life and could be put to better use working in the rear. At the same time many proficient craftsmen were also assigned to the Pioneer depots and workshops where their talents were put to good use. While many considered life in the rear to be easier and safer than the front it can also be said that the troops laboring in the rear had substantially more work to do on a daily basis than the infantryman at the front.

Workshops for blacksmiths and wagoners were set up with the baggage areas in order to care for the large number of horses and transport required for each division. Medical facilities including regimental sick rooms, dressing stations, medical dug-outs and hospitals

Reading room, Villers-au-Flos. (*Zwischen Arras und Péronne*)

Sick room, 26th Reserve Division. (*Die 26. Reserve Division 1914-1918*)

were established in a network that was designed to provide the greatest benefit to men who were wounded or sick. Bathing stations were established; water pipes were set up to supply the entire sector with drinking water. Canteens where men could purchase luxury items were constructed, reading rooms were designated where the men could relax and keep current with the world around them or have a peaceful place in order to write to their family.

1916 was to be a year of great change as well for the XIV Reserve Corps as the signs of the enemy offensive began to grow. When it came all of the hard work performed by the men would finally be put to the test.

Chapter notes

1. Losch, op cit, *Feldpost* letter dated 2 August 1915.
2. Losch, op cit, *Feldpost* letter dated 29 September 1915.
3. R. Baumgartner (Ed.), 'An der Somme, An interview with Soldat Emil Goebelbecker', *Der Angriff, A Journal of World War 1 History*, No. 3, p. 5.
4. M. Gerster, *Das Württembergische Reserve-Infanterie-Regiment Nr. 119 im Weltkrieg 1914-1918*, p. 40.
5. The Queen Charlotte Foundation continued to grow in size until it contained 400,000 Marks in 1918. Unfortunately post-war inflation destroyed any value the fund might have had and in 1923 the remnants of the fund, some 3,000,000 Marks, were transferred to the Government in Berlin by order of the Federal Ministry of Labor.
6. 'Feldpostbrief für das Kriegstagbuch', *Kriegstagbuch aus Schwaben*, pp. 815-816.
7. Losch, op cit, *Feldpost* letter dated 5 October 1915
8. Losch, op cit, *Feldpost* letter dated 11 October 1915.
9. The Weissdorn shrub was known in English as the Hawthorn, hence the name given to the location by the British troops, Hawthorn Ridge.
10. Losch, op cit, *Feldpost* letter dated 18 October 1915.

11. Losch, op cit, *Feldpost* letter dated 20 October 1915.

12. Losch, op cit, *Feldpost* letters dated 18, 23 and 26 December 1915.

13. G. Holtz, *Das Württembergische Reserve-Infanterie-Regiment Nr. 121 im Weltkrieg 1914-1918*, p. 25.

14 P. Müller, *Geschichte des Reserve-Infanterie-Regiment Nr. 99*, p. 83.

15. Asphyxiating gas shells.

16. Greiner, *Reserve-Infanterie-Regiment Nr. 110 im Weltkrieg 1914-1918*, p. 91.

17. Greiner, op. cit., 92.

18. Ibid.

19. Greiner, op. cit., p. 93.

20. The men captured on 29 December were: 13480, Lance Corporal W.J. Truss; 13911 Lance Corporal F.J. Trassler; 14763 Private P. Harris; 15167 Private P. Inns; 13862 Private J.F. Jordan; 15920 Private E.W. Preston; 13193 Private G. Trusler; 13940 Private E. Tyler; 13741 Private P. Wallis; 17089 Private T. Warboys; 15065 Private A.E. Winter; 17946 Private H. Stock; 18095 Private W. Rice; 14423 Private F.G. Worrall; 14663 Private A. Pratt; 14562 Private W. Underwood; 13889 Private A.E. Wrigley; 13171 Private J.H. Thompson; 14392 Private W. Tinkler; 10690, Private J.L. Chamberlain. *Peterborough Advertiser*, 16 February 1916.

21. Greiner, op. cit., p. 93.

22. Losch, *Feldpost* letter dated 1 January 1916.

23. R. Baumgartner (Ed.), 'The Somme 1 July 1916', *Der Angriff, A Journal of World War 1 History*, No. 13, p. 5.

9

January – March 1916

The XIV Reserve Corps was faced with a dilemma at the beginning of 1916. The Corps staff wanted to accomplish several tasks but did not have the manpower to implement all of their ideas at the same time. Further extension of the second and third lines of trenches along the front was crucial if the Corps was going to be successful in stopping any possible Allied attack. At the same time the men had been working around the clock for many months and desperately needed a period of rest, recuperation and training in the newest methods of trench fighting. The decision was made to sacrifice the extension of the position and instead concentrate upon training.

Orders were issued in January that would allow entire regiments to be relieved from the front at one time to be sent back to rest areas that were out of range of enemy artillery. While the regiments were in the rear the men would be given detailed instructions in the newest lessons and techniques of trench warfare, participate in large-scale training maneuvers as well as have time to rest, and make repairs to their uniforms and equipment. Gas masks were tested in gas chambers set up behind the front. Training included new innovations in offensive tactics such as advancing in loose waves instead of in dense rows as they had in 1914. Instructions were given to platoon, company and battalion-sized units.

The Other Ranks were not the only ones who received training during the first quarter of 1916; additional classes were set up for adjutants and company leaders. Courses were provided with the latest developments regarding gas protection, use and placement of machine guns, combat lessons taken from recent British trench raids and more. A covered riding school was even built in Miraumont in order to instruct officers on horsemanship.

I arrived here in Bapaume yesterday and live with a watchmaker's wife with a little 5 year old boy. She is a genuine Frenchwoman from Brittany (Madame Collet), however it is just for them to get by. You make yourself as comfortable as possible; I also have a very pleasant bed….The little one became 5 years old the day before yesterday and since yesterday goes to school. For his birthday I have given him a bar of chocolate. He is a very nice chap. We are not so secluded from the French; sometimes there exists very friendly traffic. The training is exactly like army regulations, at eight o'clock in the morning we move out until half past 12 o'clock. At one o'clock lunch in a so-called Food Group with about 25 men, then midday classes. Mornings, the time is very long; at 7 o'clock we grab some coffee. You can send me chocolate sometimes … Karl Losch, 3/R119 [1]

The troops that remained behind to garrison the trenches while the regiments were rotated out of the front now had the increased burden of extending their lines to cover the sectors left vacant by the missing units. The 26th Reserve Division still had the luxury of having four regiments instead of the normal three found in most divisions.

This allowed the XIV Reserve Corps to loan RIR 99 to the 28th Reserve Division when RIR 110 was relieved.

The 28th Reserve Division shifted the regiments to occupy different sectors as they were returned to the front line. RIR 99 was sent to Fricourt to replace RIR 110 on 14-15 January after being inspected by the leaders of both divisions. They found their new home was far different to the extensively developed front they had just vacated. The distance between the opposing lines varied from several hundred to as little as 40-60 meters with an extensive minefield containing three large craters.

After inspecting their new quarters the regiment felt that while the communication trenches were in good condition the rest of the sector left much to be desired. Work was begun immediately on extending the trenches, enlarging the wire entanglements and improving the dug-outs and other facilities.

The regiment was given additional support in the form of several Russian machine guns as well as Bavarian Pioneer Company Nr. 104. Losses due to enemy fire remained low due to the diligence of the men and the improvements to the position. Baths, delousing and the new issues of clothing increased the spirit and the fighting value of the men of the regiment.

The time spent in the rear for units such as RIR 110 was very beneficial. The regiment had spent the last 17 months holding the front near Fricourt without the entire regiment ever being withdrawn from the battle trenches at any one time.

Once the men were safely in their new billets they were able to receive the retraining they desperately needed. This was particularly important considering the influx of new replacement troops who had received minimal instruction before being sent to the regiment. RIR 110 also took this time to form a regimental band, most of the members having been musicians in civilian life. The bandsmen were trained as auxiliary stretcher-bearers and when not on duty in either capacity they were required to work in the regimental construction yard.

Regimental band – RIR 110. (*Reserve-Infanterie Regiment Nr. 110 im Weltkrieg 1914-1918*)

For troops accustomed to life at the front the experience of walking in daylight in the open without drawing enemy fire was a great relief. As each regiment was withdrawn from the front the men had access to many diversions. The larger rest areas such as Bapaume included cinemas, concerts, visiting the local airfield at Vélu, canteens, estaminets, cafes and shops where the men could still purchase civilian goods. The officer's mess was considered to be quite pleasant.

Later, in March, the men were given the opportunity to attend concerts and shows put on by members of the Royal Stuttgart Opera as part of a program to entertain the troops. For some these amenities were a new experience.

> The duty is not too strict. From 8-12 drills etc. At 1 o'clock we eat lunch and then we drink coffee with a cigar. From 3-5 drills again, at 6 o'clock dinner; in the evening we drink beer and sit together or go to the cinema or take an evening stroll. Sometimes a band concert also occurs in the market place. There is a concert in the church on Sunday and once a week a Bapaume artist evening occurs: that is a string concert or song recital by German artists … When you sit together speaking of this and that, of literature, of music etc. remember I have not read much literature, always only for school … Then, I was never in the theater, never been to a concert, never at a major event, and in the short time I have lived it has been very restrictive and I lead a very closed life, to which the *Treubund* is largely at fault. Karl Losch, 3/R119[2]

Band concert by statue of General Faidherbe, Bapaume. (*An der Somme*)

The King of Württemberg reviewing the troops – RIR 99. (Author's collection)

Fresh supplies of beer began to arrive from home much to the enjoyment of the men. Athletic competitions were held once the weather improved, which the men enjoyed after a long period of relative inactivity.

On 27 January all of the regiments celebrated the Kaiser's birthday in the most joyous manner possible depending upon their current situation. Just a few days later the King of Württemberg arrived at the 26th Reserve Division for his third visit to the division since the beginning of the war. The men who were positioned in the rear were paraded in front of the king in each regimental sector. He took the time to speak to the soldiers in each unit, and he reviewed and then distributed medals to those who had been recommended for bravery in the field. Afterward the royal entourage was taken to an exhibition of captured British equipment on display in the town hall of Grevillers.

When the King arrived at the headquarters of RFAR 26 he expressed a strong desire to visit the batteries in their firing positions. The arrangements were made but not without worried glances towards the British positions at Mesnil and Auchonvillers. The King and his aides drove from division headquarters in Miraumont toward the Ancre valley. The

The King of Württemberg (S.M.) visiting the 5/RFAR 26. (Author's collection)

vehicles passed through Grandcourt and proceeded south along the *Stumpweg*, a steep road that was in full sight of the British. Fortunately the royal party was not fired upon.

His Royal Highness visited the 4th and 5th Batteries and surveyed the battlefield for a long time. While at the 5th Battery he was taken on a tour of the artillery emplacements. He was shown the guns that were carefully camouflaged against aerial observation and then he was taken down some 20 steps into the twilight-like tunnels deep under the ground. During the tour the King would often stop and talk to the gunners he met. The division staff and his personal aides were quite relieved when he finally left for the rear and was safely out of danger.

RIR 109 was the next regiment relieved from the position at La Boisselle by RIR 110 after being at the front since 1 April 1915 and was made acting Army Reserve. The men looked forward to a long period of rest and training while in the rear. The regimental strength at this time consisted of 60 officers, 6 officer replacements, 3,208 men (2,701 rifles), one Machine Gun Company (7 machine guns) and one field machine gun section (3 machine guns).

During this time the regiment received news about the former 12th Coy, now designated as the 1/185. Their old company had participated in a successful advance in the Champagne region in which 300 French soldiers had been taken prisoner. Sadly many of their old friends had been killed and wounded in the heavy fighting.

Despite concentrating upon training the defensive works of the XIV Reserve Corps continued to be improved and expanded albeit at a much slower pace than in previous months. The field railway line running past Puisieux and then to the east past Serre through the Ancre Valley beyond Beaumont was completed and was particularly helpful in improving and expanding the defensive system. A second railway line was completed in the sector of the 28th Reserve Division. This line ran through Mametz Wood and ended just to the east of Fricourt. These small gauge railways made it much easier to bring up large quantities of supplies and building materials with the minimum use of manpower or horses.

With the temporary loss of RIR 99 the 26th Reserve Division received much needed assistance in the form of one battalion each from RIR 202 and RIR 204 (43rd Reserve Division) that were put to work on the extension of the second and third lines in the division sector.

This was followed by a guard detachment arriving from Württemberg that was designed to relieve the front line troops of much of the sentry duty they had performed until then. This new unit consisted of men who were only deemed fit for garrison duty.

RIR 111 was the last regiment of the 28th Reserve Division to be relieved from the front line, being replaced by RIR 109 in the Ovillers Sector. When the men of RIR 109 took over the trenches in this sector they found them in poor condition due to the rainy weather. The men were set to work reinforcing the wire entanglements in front of the main line. New fire steps were created to allow more of the trenches to be used in defense against an attack. The *Konstanzer*, *Stockacher* and *Schwarzwaldgraben* were extended and widened so that they connected to the 2nd and 3rd trenches.

New positions were created for light and flag signal posts. Weather stations and emplacements for heavy *minenwerfers* were constructed. Additional dug-outs were mined deep under the ground while older, shallow dug-outs were reinforced as much as possible. The 2nd, 3rd and 4th trenches were furnished for defense. New observation posts were

Field Railway Pioneer Park Irles-Miraumont-Beaumont. (*Die 26. Reserve Division 1914-1918*)

installed, additional machine gun posts were set up and the telephone lines were transferred into the trenches where the wires were buried deep under the floor of the trench. Covered Russian saps were extended into No Man's Land.

The men in RIR 109 were fortunate that they had expert help in the regiment when constructing their dug-outs.

> We had good ones [dug-outs] as we had men of Polish descent in our outfit who had been mineworkers in Germany in the Ruhr. They built them like mineshafts with heavy beams and 12 steps down. [There were] two entrances. Inside there were bunk beds along the walls for 8 to 14 men to sleep, also a table with benches. Emil Goebelbecker, 9/R109[3]

After completing their training the men of RIR 111 returned to the front where the regiment was assigned to the Fricourt/Hill 110 Sector. RIR 99 could now be returned to the 26th Reserve Division.

The regiment continued the work started by RIR 99 of improving the depth of the wire entanglements that protected its sector. Trenches were deepened and new mined dug-outs were added to the front and support trenches that allowed them to abandon many of the older, dangerous shelters that were too shallow. A layer of earth up to 8 meters thick now protected the new dug-outs. Much of this work could only be accomplished by the formation of a new construction squad that took men from the rest battalions in the rear as well as labor soldiers from *Landwehr Brigade Ersatz Battalion 55*.

When RIR 99 was relieved by RIR 111 the regiment took over the Thiepval Sector, from St. Pierre-Division in the north to the *Granatloch* in the south. RIR 99 would remain in this sector until the British attack on 1 July. RIR 111 now had new neighbors on the left flank, IR 23, Silesians from the 12th Division that had been recently posted to the

Somme front and that had replaced the Bavarian troops that had been positioned next to the XIV Reserve Corps since the fighting in September 1914. .

When RIR 110 returned to the front on 4 February the regiment was assigned to the La Boisselle Sector. The regimental strength at this time consisted of 81 officers and 2,979 Other Ranks. RIR 110 felt that the La Boisselle Sector was well-developed and consisted of three strong trench systems labeled 'Blue', 'Green' and 'Brown'. The entire village lay in ruins and little was left that could be identified. It consisted of piles of rubble, splintered tree trunks and an occasional red tile wall remnant pierced by enemy shell and shrapnel fire. There was a large white mound that was identified as being the former church; everything was absolutely barren and desolate.

The sector was divided into two parts, the *Schwabenhöhe* to the south and the *Lehmgrubenhöhe* to the north. The southern sector was considered to be quieter than the north by the men in the regiment.

The elevated *Kirchstellung* was located in the middle of the village while the *Granathof Stellung* formed the projecting tip of the sector and as such was very exposed to flanking fire. A large crater field lay in front of the entire position.

The *Granathof Stellung* was cut deep into the ground but because of the frequent shelling and mine activity it was only possible to maintain the trench by using wood, wire mesh and sandbags to hold back the crumbling walls. The revetment material hopelessly blocked the trenches after each bombardment and all movement inside of it was greatly hindered. Consideration was given to the idea of withdrawing from the *Granathof* position once and for all. However, all of the mining activity started in the *Granathof Stellung* and it would be impossible to abandon the position. It was continuously reinforced and eventually made into a self-contained defensive work.

Ruins of La Boisselle. (Author's collection)

Ruins of the Mill of Pozières. (*Die 26. Reserve Division 1914-1918*)

The regimental machine guns were placed throughout the two sub-sectors where the guns would have the best possible field of fire. A machine gun emplacement from the neighboring RIR 111 helped to protect the left wing. This gun was to prove invaluable in the heavy fighting on 1 July.

The large crater designated as the 'Regimental Crater' contained kitchen facilities, a military hospital, physician's quarters, a pioneer depot and most importantly a large water basin that was filled each night from Martinpuich. The men in RIR 110 started to dig a new sap running to the north from the *Granathof Stellung* that was designated the *Blinddarm*.

La Boisselle continued to be hard hit by enemy fire. The *Kirchstellung*, the National Road, the newly constructed *Blinddarm* and other nearby locations appeared to be targeted on a regular basis. The two machine gun posts, the *minenwerfer* and *erdmörser* positions in the village all required extensive repairs. Still the garrison did not suffer heavy losses due to the deep mined dug-outs.

Prolonged bad weather had transformed many of the trenches into an almost bottomless morass, especially those leading toward the *Lehmgrubenhöhe*. Alternating frost and thaws caused considerable damage that required nightly entrenching work. The British artillery was becoming increasingly active and accurate in 1916 and the constant shelling not only caused more damage to the trench system it also disrupted the repair work being performed at night.

The response to this fire was generally restricted due to the ongoing need to conserve ammunition. Many times the only answer the Germans could give consisted of patrol activity, sniper, *minenwerfer* and scattering machine gun fire into the British trenches.

Most special projects planned, such as a new water pipeline to the front, were postponed until the weather improved and men could be taken away from maintenance and repair work. Drinking water was always a problem on the Somme. The number of existing wells never kept pace with the need for fresh water for an entire Corps. When RIR 109 returned to the front to the Ovillers Sector the regiment was determined to solve the water issue once and for all. The men started several new wells until the regiment had a total of seven that produced 20,000 liters of water each day.

Familiar landmarks were slowly being destroyed one by one by enemy fire. A 23cm shell destroyed the well-known mill of Pozières. The artillery staff and battle headquarters located below the mill were forced to find new accommodations.

The inclement weather also had an effect upon the health of the men in the trenches. RIR 99 reported over 200 men had to be transferred into military hospitals in the month of January because of influenza, colds, intestinal disturbances and leg cramps. Many others were treated in the field barracks room and were returned to duty in a short period of time.

Poor weather conditions and heavy fire did not prevent the pioneers on both sides of the wire from tunneling under each other's trenches and detonating their newly completed mines. The first mine tunnel set off in 1916 occurred on 2 January. Pioneers attached to RIR 119 set off an explosion in the minefield in front of Beaumont that left behind a crater 15 meters in diameter.

At approximately 4 p.m. on 2 January the British set off their first mine in 1916 in front of La Boisselle. It was followed a few minutes later by a second mine located close by. Both mines were the largest yet seen along the front and had created two gigantic craters. Fortunately there was no damage to the German positions and only one casualty. A pioneer had gone into a subterranean listening post in order to check for damage after the first mine explosion. He was trapped in the listening gallery by falling timbers as a result of the second explosion. However he was eventually removed with minor injuries and sent to the hospital in the rear. German pioneer officers estimated that the two mines had been charged with between 20,000 and 25,000 kilograms of explosives each.

Mine explosions and *camouflets* were being set off constantly in the minefield at Beaumont in the days and weeks that followed. Two German mines were set off on 8 and 9 January, followed by three British mine explosions on the 16th, 17th and 18th. The last three caused 15 meters of a German mine tunnel to collapse. However the pioneers had evacuated the position before the explosion and there were no casualties. German and British miners alternated mine explosions on 24 January, 4, 13, 14, 21 and 25 February without any notable damage to either side.

For several days at the end of February and the beginning of March the German listening posts could clearly hear British mining activity near Beaumont. On 2 March the pioneers and the men of RIR 119 decided to beat the British to the punch and began to place explosive charges into a partially completed mine.

The men dragged heavy chest after heavy chest of explosives into the tunnel that slowly began to fill. Work was stopped at intervals in order to listen to any enemy underground activity. The Germans had almost completely filled the mine chamber with explosives when all sounds coming from the British mine ceased.

The question arose whether the British had discontinued the work on their mine or had they completed it and started to load the explosive charge? The German pioneers used sensitive listening devices in order to hear any noise coming from the British mine. They could clearly hear the sound of men hastily running back and forth under the ground. It had now become a race to see which side would finish first.

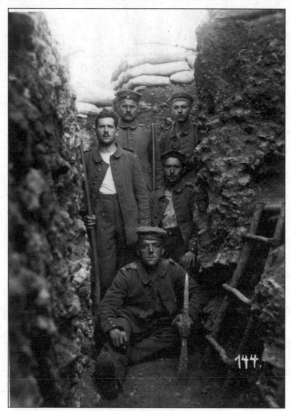

Never-ending trench construction – RIR 119. (Author's collection)

The German mine was completely loaded a short time later and the detonators were inserted into the charge. Electrical lines leading to the detonator box were then attached and the wire was run back into the main mine gallery.

Now the tamping began. The tunnel was filled with alternate layers of sandbags and wood beams for a length of 20 meters behind the explosive charge. This had to be done carefully, as the power of the explosion was so great that if the tamping was not done properly the explosive force could be blown back into their own mine system and trenches causing considerable damage and loss of life.

As night fell work continued at a feverish pace. Just before midnight the mine was finally ready for detonation. The infantry had taken up their positions. The *minenwerfers* and artillery had been notified of the time of the explosion and were ready to open fire.

A pioneer officer connected the electrical lead to the detonator box while the men made sure that the mineshaft and mine galleries were clear of any workers. The mine was scheduled to be detonated at midnight. At the stroke of 12 the plunger was depressed and the dug-out began to stagger and threatened to collapse as the earth began to shake and roll from the explosion. The ground above the mine raised and lowered like a wave, a smoke cloud appeared to hover above it. Suddenly blue flames flickered upward from the ground then suddenly shot up into the dark sky. A few seconds passed then two bluish flames were seen flickering among the British trenches and then the view of No Man's Land faded in the dying light of the explosion.

The only response consisted of several rifle shots and machine gun bursts coming from different points along the British trenches. When it was completely dark again the horizon behind the German front lit up brightly as the artillery and *minenwerfers* fired simultaneously. The shells could be seen crossing the sky from the glow of the fuzes likes the paths of meteors through the black sky. The shells crashed into the British lines for five minutes and then it suddenly became quiet once again.

It was later determined that the second sighting of the bluish flames following the first explosion must have come from the British mine that had also been set off by the blast. The minefield at Beaumont remained silent for the next two weeks following this event. Eventually further British and German mines were set off on 17, 22 and 31 March and 1 April. A number of pioneers from the 2R/Pioneer Bn 13 were killed or gassed as a result of the explosions but in general losses were very low due to the presence of a defensive gallery running at a right angle at the end of the mine tunnels. The gallery formed a buffer that effectively separated the mine tunnels from the main defensive position.

One problem facing both sides from the extensive use of mines was the damage being done to the ground. Numerous explosions coupled with frequent artillery bombardments had pulverized the soil in the areas near Beaumont, La Boisselle and Fricourt to the point where it was collapsing when the miners tried to dig through it. The fine soil also allowed the gases from the explosions to escape through the ground and often caused the men positioned in trenches nearby to become dazed and confused. The numerous mine explosions also required a great deal of physical and mental strength. Still, many of the men had become accustomed to mining and frequent explosions and it was looked upon as just another daily occurrence.

The amount of effort needed to work on the position, provide labor to assist the pioneers in digging mines and to make up for the men who had been withdrawn for training soon became almost too much to bear for the remaining troops. Some sort of help was needed. Much-needed assistance did arrive in January when electric lighting was expanded into all of the mine tunnels and galleries in the Corps as well as the introduction of electric boring machinery. These machines made the task of advancing the tunnels under the British lines much easier than simply using a pick and shovel. Now every sector in the XIV Reserve Corps could have illumination in the long mine tunnels without using up precious oxygen that was consumed by candles and carbide lamps.

The British troops opposite the men of the XIV Reserve Corps had started the year quietly. This period of calm was quickly destroyed on 4 January when the guns of RFAR 26 and *Minenwerfer* Coy 226 concentrated their fire upon the British trenches at Hamel in 'revenge fire' as payback for the mine explosion on New Year's Eve. However British artillery batteries soon became increasingly active and continued to exhibit larger caliber guns. Movement behind the British lines also noticeably increased in January and continued to grow through February and March.

Gathering intelligence about the opposing army was always a high priority objective. An excellent method of obtaining details about enemy activity was through aerial observation and aerial photography. However the number of captive balloons deployed by the 26th and 28th Reserve Divisions was small and their field of vision was limited in some cases due to the nature of the terrain. Aerial photography was used as often as possible

Electrical generation for the trenches. (*Reserve-Infanterie Regiment Nr. 110 im Weltkrieg 1914-1918*)

and every aspect of the British line was photographed during suitable flying weather. The photographs were so detailed that there were very few secrets about the British positions and facilities. These photographs also provided invaluable information for the artillery in plotting any action being taken against the enemy positions.

British aerial superiority continued to grow in the early part of 1916 and it became harder and harder for the German observation and spotter aircraft to operate over the British lines. British aircraft also increased the unpleasant and effective practice of dropping bombs on German positions. Different forms of camouflage were tried to counter this problem but most proved ineffective. It was assumed that the enemy also had detailed photographs of the entire German position that could be seen above ground.

Sentries, observation posts, artillery survey posts and listening posts all provided valuable details about activities in and behind the British front line. All of the information gathered from these sources was reviewed in each division headquarters in order to build a picture of the enemy forces opposing the XIV Reserve Corps.

One of the most effective methods of obtaining detailed information was from the Moritz stations set up in subterranean galleries driven out toward the British lines. The Moritz stations were distributed along the entire front of the XIV Reserve Corps by early 1916. Great effort was made in training the operators in the latest techniques of eavesdropping and the result was an effective method of obtaining details concerning enemy intentions, daily activities, etc. The Moritz devices were found to be extremely sensitive and utilized the conductivity of the ground and had an effective range of 1 kilometer. As long as the British were unaware of the new equipment the German listening posts were able to intercept almost every phone conversation being made by them. Soon the Germans had a detailed collection of every order issued by their opponents as well as knowing the name of every company commander in every battalion facing the Corps.

Since it was believed that the British would have similar listening apparatus great care was used when operating the telephone network. Pseudonyms were to be used for any necessary communication whenever possible in order to deceive the enemy.

Nightly patrols in No Man's Land were still one of the more useful methods of obtaining detailed information about enemy activities, trench system and wire obstacles. Poor weather conditions made nightly patrol activity very difficult, as many times it was virtually impossible to move through the dense mud found in No Man's Land. The crater field near Beaumont was a particularly dangerous area in bad weather when the heavy rain filled the craters with water. If a man slipped on the slick edge of a crater and fell into the deep water he was almost sure to be lost and could not be saved.

Despite the dangers both sides still sent out patrols all along the line whenever possible. Opposing patrols continued to clash in No Man's Land in brief, violent fights. Generally one side or the other would quickly take the upper hand and drive off their opponents.

Men from RIR 121 bumped into British patrols twice in January and February near Thiepval. On both occasions they were able to overpower their counterparts and recover the bodies of the patrol leaders. One was a lieutenant, the other a corporal from a Scottish regiment.

The following month the 5/R119 had successfully driven off a British patrol near the sunken road in front of Beaumont. This route was regularly used by British patrols so the 5th Coy decided to lay an ambush the next night.

The trap was set and within a short time at least 20 British soldiers could be seen occupying the sunken road. The signal was given and the 5th Coy opened fire with rifles and threw hand grenades into the ranks of the enemy below, scattering their opponents in every direction.

The British losses were assumed to be heavy but the survivors put up a good defense against their unseen foe. The 5th Coy brought up reinforcements from the 3/R119 who were able to round up four prisoners from the pitch-black night and recover the body of another fallen soldier. The German patrol suffered only two men wounded in the short fight.

One group from RIR 109 had a rather unfortunate incident. The patrol was sent out in the night of 5/6 January near La Boisselle. The men approached a point in the British lines known to the Germans as the *Besenhecke* when the men met with disaster. They had become entangled in an area containing contact mines. Two men were severely wounded when several mines were set off. One of the men was safely brought back to the German lines but second man was missing. Later the surviving patrol members returned to the area where the mines had been encountered and located the body of the second man. He was also brought back to the German lines despite heavy fire.

One detachment from RIR 119 planned to observe the British lines during an artillery fire raid against positions north of Beaumont. The artillery fire was scheduled to take place at 10 p.m. on 18 January. Four men from the regiment crawled to within close proximity of a group of British soldiers that were entrenching. They watched as the first shells and trench mortar bombs struck into the middle of the group causing them to scatter. Their observations were cut short when they were spotted by the opposing garrison and fired upon. While withdrawing from the area the unfortunate patrol members also found themselves in danger from several friendly shells landing too close for comfort.

The men of RIR 119 still badly wanted to take a prisoner. The 6/R119 had noted that their opponents had placed a sentry post inside a large crater located in the minefield. At

9 p.m. on 20 January *Vizefeldwebel* Walzer led a small patrol through the crater field to where the British sentry was observing the foreground from the entrance of a dug-out. Two other soldiers were observed on guard inside the shelter.

Walzer began his attack by throwing two hand grenades at the sentries. Two rolled down the slope into the muddy water, dead. The third man was taken prisoner by Walzer and his men and brought back into the German lines where he soon succumbed to his wounds.

Events on the Somme and elsewhere on the front now called for something larger than patrols and small raids. Well-planned raids consisting of a large group of men were to become a regular occurrence throughout the next six months as both sides hurtled toward the climatic battle of the Somme in July 1916.

The first German offensive on the Western Front since the attack against Ypres in April 1915 was in the planning stages in the latter part of 1915. The attack would be directed against the French fortresses at Verdun. Many details needed to be worked out for such a massive undertaking and part of the overall offensive plan called for smaller diversionary attacks to take place at other locations on the front. These were designed to distract the enemy's attention from the real threat.

On 26 December 1915 the 28th Reserve Division was ordered to plan and execute such a raid. The attack would take place by 31 January 1916 and RIR 109 was given the responsibility of carrying it out. The attack goal was the *Besenhecke*, a spot in the opposing line well known to the men in the regiment.

A considerable force of artillery would support the raid. Artillery participation was in the hands of the 1/RFAR 29. Besides the guns belonging to the 28th Reserve Division the raiding party would have the support of the guns from the *Ersatz Abteilung* FAR 76, the heavy howitzer battery of the 26th Reserve Division and two *minenwerfer* platoons.

The artillery support consisted of one section of 21cm mortars, two batteries of heavy field howitzers, one battery of 12cm field howitzers, one section of 155mm field howitzers, ten detachments of 9cm field howitzers, two light field howitzer batteries and six field gun batteries. 300 'T' and 'K' gas shells[4] were to be used in the bombardment. Four medium and one heavy *minenwerfer* would flatten the wire obstacles and afterward form a defensive ring about the target area in the British trenches where the patrol was operating in order to prevent reinforcements from moving forward. In order to deceive the British about the location of the raid a mine explosion was scheduled to take place at La Boisselle as well as artillery bombardments of different targets along the British lines.

The raiding party was to proceed through the sunken road leading out of a sap and break into the British lines approximately 150 meters northwest of the *Besenhecke*. Once inside the British trench the raiding parties would split up and proceed along the trench to the right and the left as well as into the intermediate line.

The members of the raiding party consisted of volunteers under the leadership of *Leutnant der Reserve* Hofmann. The patrol was divided into three separate detachments and included a connection detachment that would ensure the safe return to the German lines as well as a reserve group inside the sunken road. The patrol strength consisted of 3 officers, 1 *Fähnrich*, 9 *Feldwebels* and 75 *Unteroffiziers* and Other Ranks.

A model of the British trenches being attacked was constructed at Martinpuich. It was made as accurately as possible using the most updated aerial photographs. The men practiced on the model on a daily basis until they knew their tasks precisely. The

(L to R) *Leutnant* Weiss, *Leutnant* Lazarus, *Fähnrich* Ludwig, *Leutnant* Hofmann – RIR 109. (*Das Reserve-Infanterie-Regiment Nr. 109 im Weltkrieg 1914 bis 1918*)

members of the patrol also used all of the experiences learned by a neighboring regiment in an earlier raid. The troops practiced firing pistols as well as running and firing while wearing gas masks.

Additional work was performed at the point where the patrol would leave the German trenches. The steep part of the sunken road toward the enemy was marked out for the men and deepened. The nearby listening post was widened and the corners of the emplacement were rounded for easier access.

Specific dug-outs were designated for use by the patrol as well as for the medical service all of which became connected with the regimental command post by telephone. An additional telephone connection was established inside the listening sap.

Arrangements were made to record the names of the men who returned after the raid and report the names of those who were missing. A double sentry post inside of the listening sap would also count the men as they left for the raid and when they returned.

One dug-out was designated for any British prisoners that were taken. In the event the men returning could not find the route through the sunken road in the darkness the wire obstacles were opened at specific locations along the front line that were well known to the men and were marked with white flags on the night of the raid.

The artillery fire plan was worked out with the same level of detail. Almost all of the guns were able to operate from their existing positions with the exception of one heavy field howitzer battery that needed to be brought forward. The artillery began registration fire on 17 January.

The actual date of the raid depended upon the weather and the direction of the wind as gas was being used in the opening bombardment. The raid had to be postponed from 19 January through the 23rd because the wind was unfavorable. The weather reports issued from the weather station at St. Quentin indicated the wind had altered to a favorable direction and the patrol was ordered into position.

The raid had to be cancelled on the 24th because the wind changed to an unfavorable direction once again. Conditions were right on the 29th when the wind suddenly altered direction. There was some concern when a dense fog arose on the morning of the 30th but it soon dissipated and the preliminary artillery fire could begin.

The British had been quiet until the 29th. They suddenly began to reinforce the wire obstacles northwest of the *Besenhecke* and actively fired upon the German front lines except for the area around the sunken road and listening sap on this day. Despite the increased activity the artillery and *minenwerfers* began to fire punctually according to plan. The mine at La Boisselle was detonated and a powder barrel was exploded at a different location.

At 6.10 a.m. 30 January the men moved out of their dug-outs and were in place at the listening sap by 6.17 when a shell suddenly exploded in the sunken road coming from the direction of Bécourt Wood accompanied by machine gun fire coming from the British trenches. Hofmann seized the moment when there was a pause in the British fire and moved his men into the sunken road and begin to advance at 6.22 a.m.

The British trenches were reached in a few moments at the run. When the patrol arrived they found that the wire obstacles were still intact at the projected entry point. Fortunately a gap was discovered some 20 meters further to the west where the wire was completely flattened.

During the short time the patrol was delayed looking for an opening in the wire 20 to 30 British soldiers were observed coming out of their dug-outs into the front line trench. When they saw the patrol many of them were reported to have tried to escape by taking cover in nearby shell holes and trenches while a small group began to fire at the approaching German soldiers. Most of the men attempting to escape ended up running into the German barrage fire and were either killed or wounded according to the after action report from the raiding party.

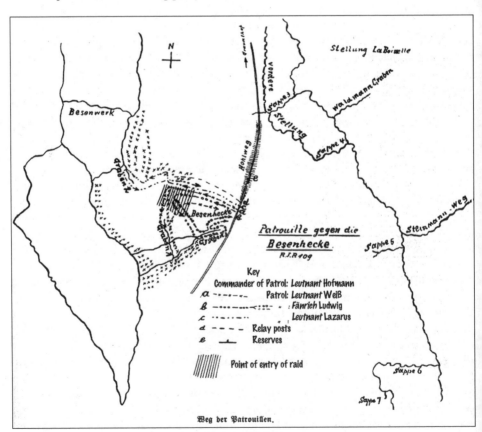

Besenhecke Raid, RIR 109.

Once the British line was entered the right-hand detachment moved deeper into the trench assigned to it. After approximately 10 steps the men came upon a 10-meter long unoccupied sap and after a few steps further a machine gun post equipped with steel plates and covered with iron rails that had been completely destroyed. The men looked for the machine gun but could not locate it.

30 meters further along the trench the detachment came upon a badly damaged dug-out from which legs of several men protruded from the debris. The patrol made several attempts to free the buried soldiers but had to abandon their efforts, as the destruction was too great. They had also called into the damaged dug-out but did not receive any response. Then they came upon three undamaged fire steps where they discovered a number of rifles with fixed bayonets, these were gathered up and the advance continued.

Just behind the next traverse the patrol came upon two British soldiers who were wearing gas masks. The soldiers opened fire on the patrol, which promptly returned fire. One British soldier turned and escaped while the second man attempted to flee over the open ground where he was struck by a shell and killed. In the meantime another British soldier came upon the patrol and was taken prisoner.

The middle patrol under *Leutnant* Weiss accompanied by Hofmann pushed forward into the intermediate line. After about 20 steps they came upon a collapsed dug-out and after another 30 meters came upon another out of which voices could be heard. The main exit of this dug-out had completely collapsed however there was an emergency exit just outside of the trench. The patrol fired several shots into this exit and then threw in a hand grenade. The Germans called to the occupants to come out but no one appeared at first. A short time afterward two soldiers did appear at the exit and were taken prisoner. A third soldier attempted to fight back against the raiders but was also overpowered and taken prisoner.

The left-hand patrol spotted 4 British soldiers withdrawing from a trench further to the rear from where the first group of enemy soldiers had been observed. The detachment penetrated into the British trench through a gap in the wire obstacles along the route assigned to them and captured 3 men almost immediately. Another member of the patrol went past a dug-out from which shots were fired. After returning fire the Germans shouted toward the dug-out for the men to come out and surrender. Several men exited and were taken prisoner. A small detachment from the patrol advanced into the *Besenhecke* Sap that had been covered in a dense belt of wire. They advanced to the end of the sap only to find it was unoccupied.

When Hofmann was convinced that all three detachments had been successful and had taken prisoners he gave the order for the bugle call to be sounded that signaled the men to return to the sunken road. Once inside sunken road Hofmann allowed a green flare to be fired, the pre-arranged signal that indicated the raid was finished. He remained with the reserve until everyone had returned. Once Hoffmann was satisfied everyone had been accounted for he ordered the wire obstacles to be closed.

During the entire time of the raid the British artillery fired shrapnel into the terrain west of the sunken road although the fire was weak. The enemy also maintained light infantry fire coming from the third trench but nothing that affected the raid.

The raid was a complete success. By 6.25 a.m., 5 minutes after the raid began, the first British prisoners had already been sent back to the German lines. By 6.33 the signal

RIR 109 raiding party and prisoners – 10th Essex Battalion 31 January 1916.
(*Das Reserve-Infanterie-Regiment Nr. 109 im Weltkrieg 1914 bis 1918*)

XIV. Reservekorps
Generalkommando
Nr. 4242.

K. H. Q., 20. 2. 16.

Korps-Tagesbefehl.

Ib IIa 1.   Bei einer Patrouillen-Unternehmung am 31. 1. 16 haben sich besonders ausgezeichnet:
R. I. R. 1o9.

   1. Führer des Ganzen: Leutnant d. Res. Hofmann, bei ihm Vizefeldwebel Steinmann, Wœrner und Kriegsfreiwilliger Frey, 2. Komp.

   2. Patrouille Lazarus (rechter Flügel): Leutnant d. L. Lazarus, Vizefeldwebel Hauck, Rüdiger, Schuhmann.
   · Wehrmann Fross, Kriegsfreiw. Strecker 4. Komp.; Grenadier Schuhmacher 5. Komp.; Grenadier Herschel, Gefreiter Würz 6. Komp.; Kriegsfreiw. Nagel, Musketiere Herter, Glatt, Gefreiter Maier 9. Komp.; Untffz. Romeik 10. Komp.; Gefreiter Bühler 11. Komp.; Gefreiter Kallmann, Fischer, Ers. Res. Schmidt, Untffz. Angst 12. Komp.

   3. Patrouille Weiss (Mitte): Leutnant d. Res. Weiss, Vizefeldwebel Schuler.
   Gefreiter Eder, Schuster, Kriegsfreiw. Hallwachs, Ers. Res. Dürrholder 1. Komp.; Gefr. Kauss 2. Komp., Gefreiter Kammerer Kriegsfr. Bogner 3. Komp.; Untffz. Moskopp Grenadier Nebgen 5. Komp.; Gefreiter Ratzel, Quitz, Landsturmmann Krikow 7. Komp.; Kriegsfreiw. Gartner II., Grenadier Grimm 8. Komp.; Ers. Res. Korn, Musketier Willer 10. Komp.; Gefr. Gumpel, Kriegsfreiw. Kessler, Maute 11. Komp.; Untffz. Graf 12. Komp.

   4. Patrouille Ludwig (linker Flügel): Fähnrich Ludwig.
   Reservist Mellert 2. Komp.; Reservist Miebach 6. Komp.; Landsturmmann Schulz 5. Komp.; Gefr. Bœckle 7. Komp.; Untffz. Steinle, Gefr. Rummel, Mangelsdorf 9. Komp.; Kriegsfreiw. Bossart 11. Kompagnie.

   Die sorgfæltig vorbereitete und schneidig durchgeführte Unternehmung hat zu einem vollen Erfolg ohne eigene Verluste geführt. Zwœlf Gefangene, viele Waffen und Ausrüstungsstücke wurden eingebracht.
   Ich spreche allen an der Unternehmung beteiligten Dienststellen und Truppenteilen meine volle Anerkennung aus und wünsche ihnen Glück zu dem schœnen Erfolge.

Der kommandierende General:
v. Stein.

Notiz.   Dienstag, den 22. 2. 16 6 und 9 Uhr Nachm. Vortragsabend des Vizew. Gebühr im Rathaussaal zu Bapaume. (Rezitation und Lieder zur Laute.)

V. s. d. G. K.
v. Kleist.

XIV Reserve Corps Daily Order No. 4242 for raid of 31 January 1916. (Author's collection)

to return had been given and by 6.45 all of the patrol participants were back in the German trenches.

12 prisoners had been taken in the raid including 1 sergeant and 2 lance corporals. 3 of the prisoners were slightly wounded and 1 was severely wounded. In addition to the prisoners 14 rifles, 10 bayonets, 7 gas masks, belts, steel helmets, shovel picks, letters, pocketknives, identity discs, etc. were brought back. RIR 109 did not lose a single man during the attack.

The prisoners belonged to the 10th Essex Battalion, 53rd Brigade, 18th Kitchener Division. They were interrogated and provided a wide variety of information. They stated that the normal size of their companies was 250 men but due to strong German artillery fire and trench mortar bomb explosions they had been reduced to between 160 and 180 men that were divided into four platoons. The prisoners alleged that the battalion had only entered the lines on the afternoon of the raid and that they were normally billeted in houses requisitioned from the citizens of Albert. There were no cooking facilities in the front line. All food was prepared in Bécourt Wood and brought up to the front three times a day where it was distributed to the sergeants of each platoon. The breakdown of the Essex Battalions was the following: No. 1 to 3 in the Regular Army; No. 4 to 8 in the Territorial Army; No. 9 to 14 in the Kitchener Army.

The raiders also reported on the condition and makeup of the British lines. The captives stated that the pioneers were responsible for the construction of the wire obstacles while

Iron Cross 2nd Class award for *Gefreiter* Otto Würz 6/R109
for raid of 31 January 1916. (Author's collection)

the infantry companies were used for sentry duty and for defense. The members of the raiding party reported that the trenches were well developed, at least 1.8 meters deep but smaller than the ones found in the German lines. The trenches lacked duckboards and the traverses were found to be only 2 ½ meters wide. The parapets and fire steps were constructed with sandbags and had sandbag loopholes.

The dug-outs located in the foremost trench were not mined. They were shallow and covered with tree trunks and earth and could house from between 6 to 12 men each. The dug-outs were parallel to the trench and had two entrances. The distance from the main dug-out to the trench was through a corridor between 1 and 2 meters long. On a personal matter almost all of the prisoners explained that they had become soldiers because they had been urged to do so by their friends at home, especially their female acquaintances.

A much smaller undertaking in the sector held by RIR 111 followed this raid almost immediately. Patrols had already established the presence of a British listening post located near the *Kronenwerk*. The main object of this undertaking was to take prisoners.

According to the plan a strong patrol under the command of *Oberleutnant* Haug, 5/R111 would sneak up to the listening post and wait for a pre-arranged signal before attacking. At 12.30 a battery fired three shells at the *Kronenwerk* in order to suppress a known machine gun post; this was the signal for the attack. Two hand grenades were thrown into the listening post and immediately after they exploded the raiding party jumped into the trench.

One sentry ran off at the sight of the Germans while the second put up a fight until he was disabled by a pistol shot and a knife thrust. The wounded sentry was quickly grabbed and taken back to the German lines for interrogation. Unfortunately the prisoner succumbed to his wounds a short time later. He was the first British prisoner taken by RIR 111. His name was Joseph Tait, a private in the 16th Battalion Highland Light Infantry, 97th Brigade, 32nd Division.[5]

This was to be the last raid against the *Kronenwerk* for the time being. A larger assault was being planned for the same area and the senior commanders wanted to make sure the British were complacent first. The larger raid was scheduled to take place in February on a date when the wind was favorable for the use of gas shells.

The men who volunteered for this raid spent their time practicing all of the details of the attack at a model of the enemy position constructed between Le Sars and Eaucourt l'Abbaye. The details of the artillery preparation and support during the raid were completed. The guns began registration fire on the *Kronenwerk* as inconspicuously as possible at the beginning of February in order to prepare the trenches for the attack. At the time of the actual raid the guns would hold down the opposing artillery, block off all enemy flanking positions and access routes for reinforcements. When the raid was almost complete the guns would provide covering fire along the route the raiding party would travel to get back to their own lines. All that was needed was a favorable wind for the gas. The *minenwerfers* were being used primarily to blow apart the enemy wire and create gaps that the infantry could exploit.

On the afternoon of 9 February the wind direction was ideal for using gas ammunition. *Oberst* Ley ordered the bombardment to begin at 6 p.m. At 6.30, when it was growing dark, the raiding party left the German lines through a passage previously prepared under the German wire. 5 minutes later the last shell fell and the raiding party lying in front of the British wire immediately penetrated into the trenches at the *Kronenwerk*.

wegen ausgezeichneter Leistungen im Patrouillendienst
für den

Gefreiten **Würz**

6.Komp. Res. Inf. Regt. 109 .

Den 20.Februar 1916.

Der kommandierende General des XIV. Reservekorps :

v. Stein

Trench raid certificate issued to *Gefreiter* Otto Würz for the
successful raid of 31 January 1916. (Author's collection)

Initial resistance was reported to be light, possibly as a result of the use of gas. The poisonous vapors still lingered in the British trenches, forcing the German soldiers to wear their gas masks. Despite this inconvenience the target trenches were quickly rolled up and all resistance was overcome. All dug-outs in the area were then smoked out using hand grenades.

When the first British prisoners were sent back to the German lines the escort could not locate the support party that was supposed to be positioned in between the two lines. It was later discovered that this detachment had decided to abandon their position and duties and join in on the raid and enter the British lines. Fortunately this did not have any negative affect on the overall undertaking.

At 6.45 the signal was given for the men to return – a blow on a whistle and launching a green flare. 10 minutes later Ley received a message that the raiding party had returned to the German lines without suffering any casualties. The undertaking was successful in that 15 prisoners were captured who belonged to the 2nd Battalion King's Own Yorkshire Light Infantry, 97th Brigade, 32nd Division. The raiding party also brought back arms and equipment along with one machine gun.

2nd King's Own Yorkshire Light Infantry and captors, RIR 111. (*Das Reserve-Infanterie-Regiment Nr. 111 im Weltkrieg 1914 bis 1918*)

The British were quite busy raiding the German lines during this period as well. One such attack occurred on the sector held by RIR 119 in the pre-dawn hours of 11 February.

At 6 a.m. a German soldier appeared out of a subterranean corridor that led to a nearby listening post. He jumped up onto the fire step and peered out into the foreground. Two men getting coffee nearby asked him 'What is it?' he replied in a whisper 'Englishmen are in front of the listening post!' Others heard his warning and figures silently emerged from their dug-outs and manned the fire steps. Soon 50 pairs of eyes were peering intently into the darkness in front of the trench.[6]

Several men returned to the listening post and went through a subterranean corridor that emptied into a crater situated just in front of the post followed by a third man. The last man climbed up the narrow chute while a sentry positioned above him called 'come up and listen'. He answered that he could still not make anything out in the darkness. Finally he climbed higher and saw two shadowy forms sneaking about. The shapes had come out of a nearby shell hole. A voice came from the darkness speaking in German 'Is there a sap here?' The sentry suspected a ruse so he raised his rifle, aimed at the dark figures and fired while other members of the garrison in the trench also fired into the black night. The shadowy figures were suddenly gone.[7]

The sentries proceeded into the crater to see if they had hit anything. The men could not see in the darkness but the sound of running feet was quite audible. Suddenly a figure was seen against the horizon at the crater edge trying to climb up and flee.

The sentries ran up and quickly grabbed the struggling man and dragged him back to the German lines in spite of British machine gun fire being sprayed across the terrain. Their prisoner was reported to be a dockworker from Dublin. He had been struck 5 times by German fire but his wounds were only minor. The prisoner was armed with hand grenades and a club studded with iron spikes. He told his captors that they had intended to capture the German sentries located inside the listening post. The British returned night after night with the same intent but each time the patrols were driven off.

The British did have some success a few nights later when they ambushed a German detachment being led by a veteran patrol leader. *Unteroffizier* Dirr had already led over 200 successful patrols into No Man's Land when he set off on 14 February in a dark night. His men exited the German lines through a corridor that led to a path through the minefield. Just as the men exited a mined sap through the narrow opening a number of hand grenades dropped around them thrown from a nearby crater.

Dirr was killed instantly and grenade fragments wounded two other men. The fourth man in the patrol fired in the direction of the unseen enemy in an effort to keep them away. Once his last cartridge was fired he helped two wounded men to safety with the help of a comrade. Every attempt to recover the body of the dead patrol leader failed as the British would throw hand grenades to drive the rescuers off.

The survivors of the patrol watched from the saphead as the rest of the garrison fired at the British in order to prevent them from taking Dirr's body. Hand grenades were thrown back and forth from both sides. Finally the company commander called for *minenwerfer* and *erdmörser* fire against the British patrol and within a few seconds, massive explosions ripped through the misty rain. During the bombardment an intrepid soldier suddenly ran out from the German lines, grabbed the fallen leader and dragged the body back to the trench through the narrow passage leading to the sap.

Dirr was 18 years old when he joined RIR 119 and in spite of his age he had achieved the recognition of a brave and fearless patrol leader. The following is an excerpt of the letter of condolence sent to his father by his company commander:

> The death of this good boy touches my heart as if he was related to me. We all appreciated and loved him. Just a few days ago he behaved splendidly and at the next opportunity he would certainly be given the Iron Cross 1 Class. For his last action he had been recommended for the Silver medal of Merit. Unfortunately he can no longer experience the gratification. I lose one of my best boys in him and my most proficient patrol leader. Also a promotion to *Vizefeldwebel* was expected. Now unfortunately all hopes are shattered.[8]

Within a month another veteran patrol leader was dead. *Vizefeldwebel Offizier Aspirant* Pfund, 8/R119 was killed near the British wire while on patrol on 12 March. His body was not discovered and his men were able to recover his remains the following day.

Now it was the turn of IR 180. The raid was scheduled for 7 p.m. on 19 February at the *Wunden Punkt*, located just north of the Serre-Mailly road in the sector Serre-North.

The raid was to be carried out by volunteers from the regiment along with support from the 4/Pioneer Bn 13 that were divided into two groups: Detachment North: consisted of 1 officer, 9 non-commissioned officers, 52 men. Detachment South: consisted of 1 officer, 11 non-commissioned officers, and 52 men.

The artillery planners realized that many of the old methods used to support raids were no longer effective against the British. New ideas were needed in order to guarantee some level of success in obtaining prisoners.

The artillery survey plan calculations were critical for this type of raid. The guns needed to fire accurately on all known enemy artillery and infantry positions without prior registration of the guns. The artillery planners also wanted to deceive the enemy regarding the location and type of raid being planned.

The wire obstacles were destroyed at several locations along the front in the days before the attack. Concentrated bursts of fire were then employed each night supposedly in the hope of catching the repair parties by surprise thereby giving the British the idea that the Germans were up to their old tricks.

On the night of the raid every artillery piece in the 26th Reserve Division and a large part of the 52nd Division opened fire and tore alleys through the British wire at locations ranging from Toutvent Farm to Hamel. The British returned fire but their effectiveness was reduced because of the numerous possibilities offered for the location of the actual raid.

The attack took place at the appointed time. The Northern Detachment found the British trench fully occupied at individual positions whilst at others the entire garrison had been killed by the artillery preparation fire. The trench was entered and several prisoners were quickly taken and were back in the German lines by 7.07 p.m. The trenches the raiders now encountered were so filled with mud it was no longer possible to advance any further. An idea of the conditions was expressed afterward by one of the raiders.

> Several men pursued two Englishmen into the trenches. One man struck down an
> Englishman who immediately sank down into the mud. There was nothing more
> to see of him. Thereupon the other Englishmen surrendered.[9]

The patrol leader decided to return to the German lines as he felt enough prisoners had been taken. The signal was given and by 7.20 p.m. Detachment North was back in their trenches.

Detachment South reached the British lines and found what little was left of the British trench unoccupied. The Germans could only find traces of the position in their search; everything was filled with mud and buried from the preliminary bombardment.

2nd Lancashire Fusiliers and captors, IR 180, marching through Grevillers. (Author's collection)

The ground was pock marked with shell hole next to shell hole with an occasional mine crater with a diameter of over 5 meters and at least 3 meters deep.

Detachment South received weak infantry fire coming from the direction of the British rear but nothing that would cause alarm. When the signal was given for the patrol to return, Detachment South broke off their search and quickly returned to the German lines without finding a single British soldier.

The two detachments had captured 1 slightly wounded Second Lieutenant, 10 unwounded privates and 1 dead soldier that belonged to the Lancashire Fusiliers, 4th Division. In addition to the prisoners, 4 rifles and numerous pieces of equipment and letters as well as an excellent aerial photograph of the German position were brought back. The prisoners stated that their trenches were in a muddy condition, which had been amply supported by the reports of the participants of the raid. IR 180 lost 2 men killed, 3 men badly wounded, 7 slightly wounded and 1 man missing.

The last major raid held in February 1916 took place on 22 February when men from the 7/R99, Field Pioneer Coy 104 and the 2R/Pioneer Bn 13 participated in an attack against the *Kniewerk* near La Boisselle.

RIR 99 received orders to undertake an offensive raid against the British lines in an attempt to learn more about movements being observed behind the enemy trenches. The volunteers were given several weeks to practice at a model of the position that had been constructed in Flers. During this period the schedule for all support units was laid down.

The day of the raid was cold and damp. Snow had fallen on the surrounding terrain for several hours and had only ended in the afternoon when the skies finally cleared. At 6.16 p.m. the artillery and *minenwerfers* opened fire on the *Kniewerk* and on different locations meant to deceive the British about the true location of the attack. The German guns and mortars fired thousands of rounds of ammunition against the British lines including a high concentration of gas shells. The British response was swift. White Very

2nd Lancashire Fusiliers and captors, IR 180. (Author's collection)

British prisoners after treatment by German medics – RIR 99. (Author's collection)

lights were seen being fired into the air calling for the British guns to open a heavy barrage fire along the German front.

At 7 p.m. 120 men left the German lines in several groups in the face of rifle and machine gun fire. Several of the detachments arrived at the British wire where they found it had not been cut according to plan. The medium *minenwerfers* had been assigned the task of destroying the wire entanglements at three locations but apparently failed.

The detachment on the right approached the wire only to find that it was intact. While looking for a possible route to enter the trench the leader of this detachment became wounded. The British rifle and machine gun fire was increasing in strength when suddenly the enemy artillery transferred its fire back onto the British front line adding to the heavy defensive fire.

The situation did not appear to be very good for the raiders. Just as the company commander gave the order 'back' with his megaphone the wounded leader of the right hand detachment crawled over to report that his men had discovered a wide gap in the British wire further to their left. The attackers had used this gap to enter the shattered enemy trenches. They came upon a dug-out from which shots were fired. The Germans quickly threw hand grenades into the entrance and later found approximately ten dead British soldiers.

The attackers continued to roll up the trenches to the east, bombing every dug-out they passed until they came upon the group of *Leutnant* Beyler who had also found a path into the British lines. Beyler's detachment had suffered heavy losses in the advance from the German lines and had also found the wire intact and was initially unable to enter the British lines.

Beyler and several men returned to the German lines by running along the northern edge of a mine crater where they obtained much-needed reinforcements. The men returned to the British lines and had literally forced their way through the wire until they were inside the trench with torn uniforms and bleeding from numerous cuts to their hands and legs.

Once inside the trench the detachment proceeded along the route assigned to them. They threw hand grenades into every dug-out they encountered. Afterward the detachment returned to the German lines by exploiting the cover provided by a nearby crater. Beyler's group returned with several pieces of equipment and details concerning the British lines, no prisoners had been taken.

The southern detachment under *Leutnant* Willegerod was able to enter the British trench though the only lane where the wire had been flattened by *minenwerfer* fire. The trench had apparently been evacuated. This detachment proceeded along its designated route and within a short time a hand grenade fight broke out between the raiding party and the British defenders.

After a brief fight the detachment was able to capture nine British soldiers from among the dug-outs they had passed. The dug-outs and tunnels were then destroyed using hand grenades and explosive charges carried by the pioneers. After 15 minutes the southern detachment also returned with their prisoners.

Upon returning to the German lines the patrol discovered that one of their officers was missing. Several men volunteered to look for him. His body was discovered by the British wire and was carried back to the German lines with the help of an officer from the 1st Machine Gun Coy whose machine gun had been placed out of action by two direct hits. This officer spent the rest of his time searching No Man's Land for wounded and missing men. He was able to recover four more wounded before he was forced to stop by enemy fire.

Funeral procession for men killed in the raid of 22 February
1916 – RIR 99. (Author's collection)

RIR 99 and pioneers had suffered heavy losses during this undertaking. The 7/R99 lost 1 officer 2 non-commissioned officers and 2 men killed. One *Feldwebel Leutnant*, 2 non-commissioned officers and 9 men were wounded, 2 non-commissioned officers and 6 men missing. The pioneer companies lost 1 killed, 6 wounded and 3 missing. On the next day all of the missing men were accounted for except for 3 who were later listed as having been killed during the raid. The days following the raid saw a noticeable increase in the volume of British artillery and trench mortar fire as well as rifle grenades.

At the beginning of March it was quite obvious to all of the German units in the XIV Reserve Corps that enemy activity was increasingly from week to week. Trench mortar and artillery fire seemed to increase almost on a daily basis. RIR 121 reported that at the end of March it was not unusual for the regiment to receive over 500 heavy and over 1,000 light and medium shells in one day. On top of this 30 to 40 heavy spherical trench mortar bombs and just as many lighter ones of different designs were fired. The British were sending up more and more captive balloons and observation aircraft. According to the men of RIR 121 it was not anything like the quiet times in the summer of 1915.

A number of different methods were tried by the XIV Reserve Corps to counter the increase in British artillery activity. The pioneer units attempted to deceive enemy observers by using discharge lamps to simulate the flash of artillery fire. New dummy parks and camps were established in order to divide the effect of the artillery fire.

By far the best method to deal with the enemy artillery was counter-battery fire by the Corps field guns and howitzers. A major drawback of the use of the German guns was the huge consumption of ammunition. Nightly artillery battles broke out where literally thousands of shells were fired by each side. In addition the artillery was supporting the numerous infantry raids and all of these actions required larger ammunition consumption than expected. A typical trench raid would consume up to 10,000 shells.

Last Rights of the men killed in the raid of 22 February 1916 – RIR 99 (Author's collection)

The replacement of ammunition from supply depots was limited and the physical delivery of the shells to the individual battery positions was extremely difficult. The Light Ammunition Columns were kept busy day and night. During the day the men prepared the wagons and horses for the nightly journey then spent each night moving from battery to battery dropping off their load.

If the artillery was used on a daily basis, especially at night, the fire provided valuable information to the British artillery observers who directed heavy fire into the suspected German gun positions. The number and caliber of guns available to the XIV Reserve Corps was limited so any loss of a gun was to be avoided at all cost. Night firing was reduced dramatically by March 1916 in order to protect the gun positions.

While the artillery continued to provide much-needed support during daylight hours it was also directed to avoid firing whenever possible and allow the close range weapons, the *minenwerfers* and auxiliary trench mortars, to take over more and more of these duties. The numbers and variety of close range weapons had increased dramatically since the early days of the war. *Minenwerfer* Coy 226 was brought up to strength with 2 heavy, 4 medium and 6 light *minenwerfers* and numerous auxiliary trench mortars and *erdmörsers*.

The pioneer companies provided the crews for most close range weapons at this time. The 2R/Pioneer Bn 13 operated 9 *Albrecht* mortars, 3 *erdmörsers*, 7 *Lanz minenwerfers*, 1 *Mauser minenwerfer*, 5 *Priesterwerfer*, 7 rifle grenade stands and 2 *Bosch* throwing machines in the sector occupied by the 28th Reserve Division. This company was also responsible for the maintenance and upkeep of the hand grenade stock of the division. The hand grenades had suffered greatly from the winter weather and had to be inspected for defects. All of the *erdmörser*, *minenwerfer* and *Priesterwerfer* positions also had to be constantly maintained and kept in good working condition.

'Literally forced their way through the wire until they were inside the trench with torn uniforms and bleeding from numerous cuts to their hands and legs.' Group of men showing off their wounds, torn uniforms and Iron Cross awards after a successful raid. (Author's collection)

At the same time the British close range weapons were increasing in numbers and effectiveness. According to RIR 99 the enemy had demonstrated remarkable accuracy with rifle grenades. Everything possible was done to counter this threat. Each regiment was provided with a complement of close range weapons in their sector. Additional weapons were installed whenever possible such as on 11 March when two new *Albrecht* mortars were installed on the *Schwabenhöhe* south of La Boiselle.

The increased use of close range weapons had a positive effect on the daily lives of the men. RIR 111 reported that in the time before their installation, from 10 to 17 March, the regiment suffered losses of 9 men killed and 34 wounded, mainly from trench mortars and rifle grenades. In the period following the installation and use of close range weapons the losses suffered by the regiment were dramatically reduced. In the period from 18 to 31 March the regiment lost only 1 man killed and 16 men wounded. Much of the improvement in losses was attributed to the close range weapons effectiveness against similar enemy weapons as well as snipers.[10]

The German ability to react to enemy fire was seriously reduced in early March when the 8/Reserve Foot Artillery Regiment 10 (Köhler) was relieved from the 26th Reserve Division. The loss of this heavy battery would eventually be made up with the introduction of 12cm and 15cm heavy batteries into the division, but not until a later date.

The artillery used for counter-battery work relied heavily upon the Artillery Survey Plan as well as the Artillery Liaison Officers (AVO[11]) positioned in the front lines. The AVO had developed a high level of cooperation between the artillery, infantry and trench mortars. This was critical for the success of many raids against enemy lines, counter-battery work and general artillery fire against targets of value.

It was normally quite difficult to locate the position of an enemy trench mortar. The AVO was given a great deal of credit when they were able to discover such a location. Preparations were made to destroy the suspected emplacement but the overall success was usually limited. Most of the time the trench mortars were moved into a new firing position and the search for it began again.

The damage caused to the position by British trench mortar bombs was considerable but the losses to the garrison were light. If a bomb did happen to fall into a trench the men were usually safe due to its depth and construction. Still, the repairs to the damaged trench and the terrifying noise of the trench mortar bombs exploding were getting on the nerves of the troops.

The month of March saw an increase in offensive patrols and trench raids on both sides of the wire. The increased enemy activity was a cause of alarm for the men of the XIV Reserve Corps and there was a greater need to obtain intelligence concerning the British positions, identity of the opposing units and the need to maintain the upper hand in controlling No Man's Land. The size and frequency of the raids went hand in hand with the increase in activity behind the British lines.

Several regiments in the Corps received orders in late February to make preparations for raids in their sectors in March. On 3 March RIR 109 sent a proposal to brigade headquarters for a raid against the British lines. The regiment had considered several sites as good possibilities for an attack and they were carefully studied.

The *Kronenwerk* was eventually chosen as the new target. Several reconnaissance patrols were sent out toward the enemy works in order to obtain the latest information about the position, the wire entanglements and sentry posts. The regiment sent out reconnaissance patrols to report on the second choice of the raid, the *Hoheneck*. Due to circumstances beyond their control the regiment was forced to postpone the raid for the time being.

The first large-scale German raid carried out in March took place near Thiepval Wood, and was undertaken by RIR 121 on the 11th. The preparation fire as well as artillery support during the attack would be supplied by the artillery of the 26th Reserve Division, and part of the artillery complement of the neighboring 52nd Division.

Preparations for the raid included reconnaissance of the enemy position by ground patrols as well as observer aircraft, registration fire by the artillery, patrol rehearsals at special exercise works behind the front and the effort needed to bring up the *minenwerfer* and ammunition supplies, construction of telephone lines and special arrangements with the medical services. Everything needed to be completed and checked before the attack could take place.

At the time of the raid all available guns and *minenwerfer* fired at a given point in the British lines for 30 minutes. At the appointed time the fire was shifted to the rear and flanks of the target area and a patrol from the 11/R121 under *Leutnant der Reserve* Reichert penetrated into the British lines and brought back 8 prisoners – 1 officer and 7 Other Ranks.

The British had responded quickly once the German guns opened fire with artillery and machine-gun fire. During the preparation fire one dashing Tommy ran toward the German lines and split a German soldier through the head with his spade and then quickly returned to his trench. Actually the soldier was a straw-filled dummy meant to deceive the enemy and draw his fire – it had apparently worked.

Not every German casualty was a dummy however:

> In the hand-to-hand fighting with the Germans in the trench, there was a German caught in the wire and a fellow from Cookstown called Ned Anderson tried to send up a flare. Well it caught the German on the wire. Now whether or not the fellow was alive or dead I don't know but we could smell him burning as the fire blazed up. It fair turned your insides but we had to fight on until the Germans went back... They tried to bomb a dug-out we had at a cross-trench but one of our men had the presence of mind to throw across the main trench a couple of rolls of wire and we sniped at them every time they tried to force their way across. [12]

Once the raid was over the surviving members of the enemy garrison had further ample proof of the fierce hand-to-hand fighting that had taken place in front of the entrance of the Company Sergeant-Major's store in a front line dug-out as the ground was littered with blood stained caps and equipment. Private J. Hughes, 16th Lancashire Fusiliers left an account of the German bombardment:

> They started bombarding us at 11 p.m., and kept it up until 12.30 a.m., and I don't think there has been anything worse for the time being in any part of the line. I should think we had 2,000 shells all about our little place. The flare from the shells so illuminated the place that we thought the village was on fire...We had to sit in our cellar, with no help for ourselves and trust to luck. We expected a shell dropping in every second. The noise of the bursting shells, especially the big ones, was deafening, and as they came through the air they sounded like engines coming along. We dare

not venture out, as shrapnel was bursting in front of us, and there were holes all around where shells had dropped. One of these holes is about 16 feet in circumference and on what is left of the walls are marks where they were struck by the shells. Men said their prayers who, perhaps, had never said them before. I can tell you that we are most exceptionally lucky fellows, and we congratulated ourselves later when we sat down to breakfast. The Huns also shelled the trenches, and I assure you they found their billets. The trenches and the dug-outs were blown up. I am sorry to say that from what I hear the casualty list will be a large one.[13]

The losses had indeed been heavy in the Fusiliers. 1 officer and 12 men had been killed, 4 officers and 31 men had been wounded, 1 officer and 7 men were missing and 16 men were listed as being in shock. 1 officer and 2 men died from their wounds in the next two days. While the raid was a relatively small affair the preparation fire and heavy ammunition consumption needed to counter the British artillery was enormous and placed great strain on the Corps artillery.

The British were quite active in March as well. The 1st Dorsets holding the line in front of La Boisselle had been preparing for a raid against the German trenches at a spot known as the 'Y' Sap (*Blinddarm*) for a number of days. The attack was scheduled to take place in the early morning hours of 27 March in order to test the German defenses, obtain prisoners and identify the regiment holding the village of La Boisselle.

The British had taken every precaution to keep the Germans in the dark regarding the raid. This included holding practice attacks on a model representing the German trenches located at Millencourt.

There were some telltale signs that the Germans actually knew what was being planned. The German artillery had registered fire on the British lines opposite the village for several days. On the night of the raid the German lines were conspicuously silent with just occasional machine gun fire and flares being fired into the air above La Boisselle. It did not bode well for the men who had volunteered for the raiding party. Charles Douie, 1st Dorsets, watched as the men moved into position:

> The broken posts and wire which marked the boundaries of No Man's Land and the white chalk of the mine craters were agleam in the moonlight, and it was so clear I could discern the ruins and broken tree stumps of the village. Yet no shot was fired while a hundred men crawled through our wire into shell holes in front. Behind them the trenches were lined with men, for the 'Stand-to-Arms' had been passed down. The deathly silence did not augur well, and as the Colonel passed down the line I noticed grave anxiety on his face.[14]

The attack began with the detonation of three small mines under the German lines, all set off 5 minutes too early. Many of the men in the raiding party were still not in position, yet the attack took place as scheduled. The British guns opened a devastating fire onto the German lines and the night was lit up with their flashes. Almost immediately the German counter-barrage fell upon the British lines.

> The mine exploded. It seemed to me a very small mine. The earth throbbed. Then again, but for one moment only, there was an unearthly stillness. This was succeeded

View of Ovillers from the *Blinddarm* (Y Sap). (Author's collection)

by a weird sound like rustling leaves for a fraction of a second; then with the noise of a hurricane the shells passed, and the whole outline of the German position was seared with the appalling lightning and thunder of our artillery. There were a thousand flashes, and a lurid light spread over the battlefield, the light only seen in the most dreadful spectacle, a night bombardment. The thunder of the guns was such that speech was impossible. But there was no time to observe the scene, as in an inferno of flashes and explosions the German counter-barrage broke on our line.

The intensity of the counter-barrage showed beyond a doubt that the German batteries had been standing to their guns and that every detail of our attack was known. The craters and trenches of La Boisselle were evacuated and full of wire in which those of our men who got through the entanglements were at once caught and impaled. Of Germans there were none to be seen, until their bombers closed in from each side. From end to end of 'No Man's Land' a hell of machine gun fire was raging; the trenches were quite untenable.[15]

The raiding parties proceeded to their objectives under intensive rifle and machine gun fire. Sergeant-Major Shephard, 1st Dorsets noted:

We 'stood to arms' at 12.15 a.m., the mines went up at 12.25 a.m. (5 minutes too soon). They were feeble, and did very little damage. Our artillery opened up a heavy bombardment on enemy 2nd, 3rd, and reserve lines. Enemy very much awake, they opened up an intensive volume of fire in very short time. Heavy artillery on Albert, USNA Redoubt, and counter attack trench, whizz-bangs, trench mortars, bombs, machine gun fire, etc., on our front trenches and intervening ground over which our attacking party of 80 were moving. It was a fine sight for outsiders. I felt uncomfortable, as the enemy could not have retaliated quicker had they known of our plans, of which we came to the conclusion later they must have been fully aware. In Redoubt we were so heavily shelled that we finally 'stood to' in dug-outs, anxiously waiting news by phone.[16]

A few of the men were able to enter the German trenches at 'Y' Sap only to find them abandoned. The Germans had apparently deepened the trenches and placed barbed wire throughout. Many of the men became entangled in the wire and were unable to extricate themselves.

The trapped men suddenly came under fire from German *minenwerfers* while hand grenades rained down upon them. They could not advance into their own barrage fire and to stay would be suicide. At 12.45 a.m. the signal to retreat was given and the raiders tried to make their way back. Shephard:

> Fighting continued fiercely. At 1.30 a.m. we heard that the attack was over, but no prisoners could be got. Only 20 had returned, although the Strombos horn had sounded for the party to return. Later we got fuller details. In first place the REs blew the mines 5 minutes too soon, before our party was properly in position. The party, on arrival at enemy position, found on dropping into it that it was 15 foot deep and wired inside, also the enemy immediately started dropping trench mortars and whizz-bangs in it. This was quite unexpected and proves the enemy knew and had prepared for the attack. Bombs, machine gun and rifle fire was fully expected, but not to find such a deep trench, wired, and enemy dropping trench mortars and whizz-bangs into his own trench at such short notice.
>
> Not a German in the trench, naturally. Apparently it had been deepened, wired, and evacuated for the occasion and would have proved a deadly trap to less experienced soldiers. No use trying to push on to the enemy second line, as our artillery were shelling it, order to retire sounded, terrible job to get disentangled from wire and all under severe grueling from trench mortars, whizz-bangs, etc. At 2.00 40 were still missing. At 2.30 am the bombardment had lessened a good deal, and search patrols, stretcher-bearers went out to find and bring in remainder. Four were found dead in enemy trench, hopelessly tangled in wire, and impossible to move owing to heavy bombing. Wounded were got in, remainder of party got back to USNA at 3.00 am. and were issued with rum and tea. Their clothing was torn to shreds. They returned to Millencourt at 5.00 am. Great efforts were made until dawn to get in dead and find missing.[17]

The sight that greeted the observers the following morning was dreadful:

> Dawn came at last. The ruins of the village and the surrounding trench lines became distinct, and it was day. On the German wire there were dark specks, among them the dead subaltern and my faithful orderly. Behind me lay a city of the dead, before me men, my friends, who yesterday had been so full of life and now lay silent and unheeding in death.[18]

Shephard was correct in that the Germans did know the raid was coming. On 26 March the Moritz listening post at La Boisselle intercepted a telephone transmission that indicated a raid was going to take place imminently.

RIR 110 was ordered to be on increased alert status starting from 9 p.m. that evening. Part of the position known as the *Blinddarm* (Y Sap) appeared to be the goal of the raiding party and was evacuated in preparation for the anticipated attack. Pioneers then placed contact mines inside the dug-outs and strung barbed wire inside the trenches. Once the final preparations were completed the garrison waited for the Dorsets to come.

The regiment reported that at 1.25 a.m. on 27 March the British attacked the *Kanzel* and *Blinddarm* sector after a short period of fierce bombardment on the surrounding areas. Mine explosions accompanied the start of the assault. When the garrison saw the British soldiers appear in front of their parapet they called for barrage fire by launching 10 red flares.

The defenders opened fire with rifles and machine guns and proceeded to drive the British off but not before at least 4 enemy soldiers had managed to enter the *Kanzel* and *Blinddarm* only to become hopelessly entangled in the new wire obstacles. When the firing died down the Germans discovered that the raiding party was gone and had left behind several rifles and about 20 sacks of hand grenades. The British fire ceased about 2 a.m., afterward RIR 110 sent out patrols into No Man's Land.

One patrol came back with a severely wounded officer who had been found tangled in the wire near the *Blinddarm*; he died shortly after being brought in. The same patrol also brought in the body of a dead non-commissioned officer who had also been found entangled in the wire obstacles. Another patrol brought in a wounded man from the area of the *Blinddarm* while a second wounded man was brought in on the following evening by a patrol from the 7/R110.

The prisoners told their captors that the raid was made in order to take prisoners and to establish the identification of the regiment opposite their lines. They mentioned that the raiding party did not have any specific training for the raid beforehand, as the men had not been chosen to participate in the assault until 25 March. This was a deceitful story as the raiding party had practiced at Millencourt some time before the actual raid.

The German trenches had been badly damaged during the preparation fire and the men of RIR 110 started their repair work immediately. While working a sign appeared in front of the British trenches on 31 March, it read: 'How is Lieutenant Blakeway, captured on March 27th?' RIR 110 sent a response in the same manner on the following day advising the Dorsets that he had died from his wounds.[19]

Considering all of the recent events the question that started to be asked throughout the Corps was when would the British attack? It was only a matter of time.

Chapter notes

1. Losch, *Feldpost* letter 2 March 1916 and 10 March 1916. His new address: *Vizefeldwebel* Losch 14th Res. AK 9th Training Company.
2. Ibid, *Feldpost* letter dated 10 April 1916.
3. Baumgartner, op cit, No. 3, p. 4.
4. 'K' Gas shells were filled with asphyxiating gas. 'T' Gas shells were filled with lachrymatory gas.
5. Private 15192 Joseph Drysdale Tait, age 23. C Coy., 16th Battalion Highland Light Infantry. Son of Annie Green (formerly Tait) of 36, Willowbank Street, Glasgow and the late John Tait. AIF Burial Ground Flers, Somme, France. Memorial 2.
6. Gerster, op. cit., p. 44.

7. Ibid.
8. 'Feldpostbrief für das Kriegstagbuch', *Kriegstagbuch aus Schwaben,* p. 816.
9. Vischer, *Das 10.Württembergische Infanterie-Regiment Nr. 180 im Weltkrieg 1914-1918,* p. 30.
10. 28th Reserve Division Report 1 April 1916.
11. Artillery Liaison Officer = *Artillerie Verbindungs Offizier* (AVO).
12. P. Orr, *The Road to the Somme,* P. 135.
13. Stedman, *Salford Pals,* p. 79.
14. Douie, *The Weary Road,* pp. 126-127.
15. Ibid, pp. 127-128.
16. Shephard, *A Sergeant-Major's War.* p. 92.
17. Ibid, pp. 92-93.
18. Douie, p. 129.
19. Second Lieutenant Noel Blakeway, 1st Battalion, Dorsetshire Regiment. Noel Carleton Blakeway, son of George Sheffield Blakeway and Florence Blakeway, of Staniforth, Tuffley, Gloucester. Age 20, Buried in Grave A. 17, Martinpuich British Cemetery, Pas de Calais, France.

10

The Impending Attack
April – June 1916

L ife in the rear went on in the XIV Reserve Corps as it had for almost two years. Living conditions in the small villages were generally comfortable. New deep dug-outs provided protection against the increasing long-range artillery fire and aircraft bombs.

The 26th Reserve Division had just completed the construction of a second divisional cemetery located at the northwestern edge of Miraumont that had a small Brenner chapel. The commemorative monument planned for the cemetery was being constructed and would be finished by June. Work on a new cinema in the same village was almost completed. The opening day for both was set for the morning of 24 June.

The health of the men was good overall. Food was not as plentiful as it had been at the beginning of the war but it was sufficient to meet the needs of the troops even considering the heavy labor they were performing. The meat ration actually increased for the men assigned to the front, they now received 288 grams in their rations. Warm, sunny days in May helped to improve the health of the soldiers and made much of the hard work tolerable.

DEUTSCHES THEATER IN
HAVRINCOURT

Gastspiele einer erstklassigen deutschen Schauspielertruppe

SPIELPLAN

Freitag, den 28. April 1916:

Ein herrschaftlicher Diener wird gesucht

Samstag, den 29. April 1916:
Die spanische Fliege

Sonntag, den 30. April 1916:
Thoma - Abend (I. Klasse usw.)

Beginn der Vorstellungen an allen drei Tagen 7³⁰ Uhr abends :: Dauer 2—2 ½ Stunden :: Die 150 Plätze in den vordersten Reihen kosten **2.50** Mark, die 550 weiteren Plätze **1.**— Mark :: Platzbestellungen bis möglichst 24. April abends an die Ortskommandantur Havrincourt erbeten
Für Besucher von der Front ist Zugverbindung vorhanden :: Næheres Programm folgt

Theater notice. (*Der Schützengraben*)

Stuttgart Theater Group. (*Die 26. Reserve Division 1914-1918*)

The division clergymen looked after the spiritual health of the men. They made regular visits to the front as well as holding weekly services in the rear areas and billets. The priests and ministers assigned to the divisions were flexible in the manner in which they provided religious services. Many were held at the front inside medical and regimental dug-outs where small groups could assemble, safe from British fire.

Concerts and plays continued to be favorite pastimes among the troops while in the rear. A small theatre was set up in a barn in Bihucourt where comedies written by Ludwig Thoma such as *Lotchen's Birthday*, *First Class* and *The Spanish Fly* were presented.

At the beginning of June the Stuttgart Traveling Theatre came to the Somme for a second visit and presented concerts and artist evenings in Bapaume and Pys. The players also provided a number of operettas and melodramas that the men enjoyed immensely.

Vizefeldwebel Karl Losch was still enjoying life in the rear while attending his training course. He also took advantage of the many diversions that Bapaume offered the men. Over time he apparently grew closer to the French family he was billeted with:

> I have also celebrated another birthday yesterday, in fact that of Madame Collet, my housewife. We drank wine in the evening with one another and also ate cake. Little Robert liked the way it tasted, and [did] what Fritzi would have done on this event; he sat on my lap. Madame Collet is now 30 years old......she already can speak some German and in the evening we carry on speaking together in German and French for ¾ of an hour. She has good pronunciation and also learns quickly.
>
> Thank you for the Easter rabbit, it has pleased me very much … I have also given it away to little Robert, who naturally was very happy. Incidentally we are still here over Easter; the course became extended until the 26th instant … I have managed with my pay, there are probably some who still have to send money home because they have led a life of debauchery. Admittedly the little one sometimes reminds me of Fritzi, he also chatters the whole time. Incidentally Madame Collet has the idea

to possibly make a trip to Württemberg after the war with her husband where they have been invited by some Aspirants she has already lived with.

The French admittedly also know something of the Easter rabbit, however not so much in the war. Madame Collet knows nothing definite of her husband, but he still seems to be alive, which they learned from a third party. On Easter Sunday morning I was in a well-known Estaminet where we drank our coffee and brandy and ate 3 fried eggs and on Monday we made ourselves pancake with jam and wine in Treiber's quarters. What do you notice of the war there? We live like Gods in France.[1]

Visitors continued to show up at the XIV Reserve Corps, from artists to authors to royalty. *Leutnant* Bruno Affolter, RIR 109, had a visit from an old friend and schoolmate whom he took on a tour of Ovillers. *Leutnant Zur See* Killinger considered the position to be immaculately developed and appreciated all of the hard work the men had performed. He had the chance to observe the inner workings of a dug-out when the two officers were forced to take cover during a fire raid.

On 14 April Prince von Hohenzollern visited several regiments in the XIV Reserve Corps where he met with his fellow countrymen. He passed out medals to those who had been recognized for bravery including three men in RIR 109. On 9 June His Highness the Duke of Saxony-Meiningen also visited RIR 109 and met with 76 of his countrymen in Barastre where he passed out awards for bravery.

Throughout the months of April, May and June indications of an impending British attack on the Somme front increased weekly. During this period there was corresponding activity in the extension of the German position. By this time few officers and men in the Corps wondered if the British would attack, the only question was when?

RIR 99 received a new commanding officer on 15 April. Major Hans von Fabeck assumed command of the regiment when his predecessor *Oberstleutnant* von Frankenberg-

Pozières windmill drawn by visiting artist. (Author's collection)

Proschlitz was appointed Chief of Staff of the XII Reserve Corps. Von Fabeck had previously commanded the Guard *Jäger* Bn and had seen extensive fighting in the Vosges from April 1915 to April 1916.

Upon arriving at Corps Headquarters von Fabeck met with von Stein who advised the new regimental commander that 'a great attack by the English was expected on the Corps front in the foreseeable future.'[2] He was convinced that the Major and the regiment would do their duty to the fullest.

After the meeting von Fabeck joined RIR 99 and toured the regimental sector. He issued a series of orders that would have far-reaching consequences in the coming battle. Fighting in the mountainous Vosges region had taught him that the only way troops could stand at the breastworks and receive an attack was if they were intact after the enemy's annihilation fire. He felt that if his men could withstand the first onslaught and defend their sector, then, once the attack was broken they could destroy the British through counter-attacks.

In order to achieve this goal the men would require bombproof dug-outs a minimum of 7 meters under the ground. In order to ensure that the troops could quickly exit the dug-outs at the time of the attack he issued further orders that each dug-out would have three exits and that galleries would connect every three dug-outs. By the end of June more than 140 of these dug-outs existed in the German 1st Trench in the Thiepval Sector. All of his specifications met or exceeded any orders already issued by Corps headquarters.

Von Fabeck ordered the immediate construction of two massive underground complexes. The first was positioned under the ruins of Mouquet Farm. The depth of the dug-out varied from 8 to 10 meters and it would be large enough to accommodate the regimental battle headquarters, a field hospital, telephone exchange, storage areas and accommodations for at least 300 men. The second dug-out was a tunnel complex built into the slope of the hill above the Ancre by St. Pierre-Division. It would have sufficient space for a medical staff, storage areas, staff quarters and room to accommodate 1,000 men safely; both projects were started immediately. The men of RIR 99 were quite familiar with this type of construction and were quickly making headway on completing the complexes in the shortest possible time.

Even limited aerial reconnaissance was particularly useful in detecting and identifying British activity through May and June. The photographs clearly showed recently-constructed approach routes; new field railroad lines, freshly dug assembly trenches, huts and other buildings that were being erected along the entire British front. Numerous trees were being felled in the local forests indicating a massive need for lumber. The trench observers reported that gaps were being cut in the wire obstacles in different places and considerable road traffic could be observed behind the front. Several reports indicated the possibility of French artillery units being involved in the daily bombardments while at least one observer in the 26th Reserve Division reported seeing two companies of Russian soldiers at the front, an account that was never confirmed through any other source.

Much of the British activity took place at night under cover of darkness but whenever there was a favorable wind the men in the German trenches could clearly hear the sound of wagons and field railways rumbling behind the front, unloading wood and iron accompanied by knocking and hammering.

The use of German reconnaissance aircraft was increasingly becoming restricted because of British aerial superiority. Numerous British planes swarmed above the front

Well-constructed dressing station, I/R99, St. Pierre-Divion. (Author's collection)

that disrupted nearly all ground traffic while fighter aircraft prevented most German observation aircraft from crossing the British lines. The Second Army did not possess enough fighter aircraft needed to expel British observation aircraft or prevent their free reign over the German lines and was unable to obtain sufficient numbers of anti-aircraft guns or motorized guns to help keep aircraft at a distance.

At the beginning of June 1916 the activity of the English began to be vivid. We observed new positions of artillery and shellfire increased dramatically. The English shelled the villages and crossroads behind our front, and their airmen shot down our captive balloons. The English fliers were in such superiority that our own fliers could not penetrate over our trenches. Felix Kircher, RFAR 26 [3]

Because of the German weakness in the air the British pilots grew more and more impudent, in some cases flying as low as 100 meters above the German positions. Large numbers of British observation balloons appeared along the line that kept a sharp watch on the German positions and virtually paralyzed the activity of the German artillery in order that the guns not give away their positions.

However, the low-flying British aircraft were not immune to German defensive fire. On 27 May an observation aircraft was shot down by an anti-aircraft gun and reportedly crashed south of Mesnil. This was the second plane shot down in as many days at the same location. Just the day before *Unteroffizier* Michalski, 3/R99, fired at a British plane using a telescopic sight and K-ammunition. The aircraft was seen to waver and go down behind a hill south of Mesnil.

Abgeschossenes Feindl. Flugzeug zwischen den Feindl. Linien gelandet und von der 7. Komp. Res. Regt. 99 geborgen

Patrol from 7/R99 with the wreckage of a BE 2c in No Man's Land. (Author's collection)

Enemy aircraft were not the only thing flying across the Somme. For some time the men of RIR 99 noticed that carrier pigeons were flying over their lines traveling from east to west. Marksmen were successful in bringing down many of the birds and in doing so deprived the British of vital information.

Without adequate aerial observation the artillery units in the XIV Reserve Corps were unable to fire using aircraft control and direction. The batteries were forced to rely almost solely upon the Artillery Survey Section and captive observation balloons.

British artillery activity increased dramatically over the course of April, May and June. Guns appeared to be registering fire upon every part of the German line. Numerous trench mortar bombs, aerial and torpedo mines were becoming a common occurrence. The British artillery that the Germans had once laughed at had learned to shoot very well and copied many of the German tactics with well-placed fire and the destruction of obstacles.

RIR 121 reported shells from 24cm to 38cm were falling upon the trenches near Beaumont resulting in considerable damage to the defensive works. Even the deep dug-outs were not safe against the heavier shells and would often collapse if they received a direct hit despite all of the precautions being taken. The *Heidenkopf* suffered especially heavy damage under the concentrated artillery and trench mortar fire; it appeared to be a favorite target of enemy guns.

RIR 99 reported that artillery fire against the Thiepval Sector grew in strength each month. The regiment reported that it was not unusual for the sector to receive an average of 1,000 shrapnel and light high explosive shells as well as about 100 shells, 50-70 trench mortar bombs and 20-30 small caliber rounds each day. By May the British were actively targeting specific trench sections with concentrated fire. On one occasion a heavy shell penetrated the medical dug-out by Sectors C1 and C2 causing considerable damage to the dug-out and the surrounding trench system.

British artillery and trench mortar fire eventually took on a pattern that seemed to indicate something important was being planned. Concentrated artillery fire increased

Well-developed trenches, Thiepval North. (*Die 26. Reserve Division 1914-1918*)

to a daily occurrence along the entire line, no area in the sector of the Corps was ignored. Important trench junctions, communication trenches and similar targets received numerous shells. The forward trenches were covered with light caliber shells and shrapnel while heavier shells fell on the rear trenches and strong points. However the bombardments did not result in permanent damage to the position and much of what did take place could be repaired. If there was something the men of the XIV Reserve Corps knew it was how to dig. At times the shelling grew so heavy that alarms were sounded in the expectation of an attack but none occurred.

The nights were no longer peaceful as the British used this time to scatter artillery and machine gun fire over the German lines. The British now started to systematically destroy any close range weapons they discovered. When such a weapon was located the emplacement was subjected to a concentrated bombardment by numerous batteries and trench mortars.

A reserve *minenwerfer* emplacement located near the *Waldeck* Sap in the sector of RIR 109 was the object of such an attack on the evening of 27 May. The dug-out located near the *minenwerfer* was covered with 3 meters of earth but still collapsed under the heavy fire. Fortunately the occupants had previously recognized the danger of remaining inside the dug-out and had evacuated it.

The *minenwerfer* crew and several men from the 7th Coy spent the following night digging out the *minenwerfer*, telephone equipment, stores and other items of personal equipment and clothing from under the debris.

Albrecht *Mörser*. The tube was wrapped with wire to provide support when fired. It was not a particularly accurate weapon but the size and explosive force of the shells could be devastating. (*Das Württembergische Reserve-Infanterie-Regiment Nr. 121 im Weltkrieg 1914-1918*)

The position of the close range weapon was most vulnerable during firing if the British were able to locate the gun by the discharge of the shell. Any fire from the *erdmörsers* or *Albrecht* trench mortars would invariably trigger enemy counter-battery fire. The Ovillers Sector was particularly hard hit by enemy revenge fire. Any trench mortar activity in the vicinity of Ovillers would bring forth heavy retaliatory fire in the form of 23.4 to 24cm caliber shells falling on the hollow between *Klimkowström* and *Waldeck* Saps, *Kuhm* and *Leichen* Saps, *Baumallee* and *Wittwer* Saps, *Quergraben II* and *Hauggraben* and the area surrounding the church of Ovillers. A great deal of effort was required to reopen these important routes leading toward the front. Losses were kept low due to the depth and design of the trenches. In one instance numerous heavy shells resulted in only 2 dead and 5 wounded in the regiment.

At the beginning of April many of the regiments assigned one man from each company to serve on the crew of an *Albrecht* trench mortar or an *erdmörser*. This was to prove almost as dangerous as enemy shellfire. Loading and firing these weapons took great care and many men had been killed or wounded due to barrels bursting while being fired or in some cases from the premature explosion of the shell.

The headquarters staff of the Second Army and the XIV Reserve Corps had come to the conclusion long ago that the Somme front was to be the scene of a major enemy attack.

General von Soden visiting the front line – RIR 119. (*Die 26. Reserve Division 1914-1918*)

The date and scope of the attack was still unknown but considering all of the evidence accumulated through 1 June it appeared that a large attack would be taking shape shortly.

The concern over what preparations were needed to meet the threat had to be tempered with the physical restrictions placed upon the army due to the allocation of reserves and resources to other parts of the front and to other theatres.

On 15 May the IV/R99 returned to the regiment after being temporarily assigned to the 2nd Guard Reserve Division. Even the arrival of a single battalion was seen as a welcome addition. At the end of May the division sectors were shifted in response to the British buildup. The Serre Sector was taken over by IR 66 and IR 169 from the 52nd Division. This allowed IR 180 to be withdrawn from the front on 23 May and sent to the rear to rest. While in the rear the men played sports, held drills, rifle, and pistol and hand grenade practice among other duties.

In conjunction with training courses being held in the rear the men holding the front held daily alarm practice. As a result the alarm readiness of the men was brought to the highest level ever. The men were reminded to use caution in the use of telephones so that the enemy would not be able to listen in on any conversations and obtain valuable intelligence.

Morale was maintained at a high level, in part with frequent visits by senior commanders to the front. The high ranking officers toured the front line on a weekly basis to encourage the men to maintain their vigilance and to assure them that everything possible was being done to prepare for the big attack. These visits continued to allow senior commanders to maintain a connection with the actual events taking place at the front and not to solely rely upon reports from subordinates.

In May 1916 the XIV Reserve Corps printed a booklet outlining all of the principles of trench warfare the Corps had established to this point in time. It was a highly detailed manual that covered every aspect of modern warfare regarding infantry positions, alarms, infantry combat and artillery. It was designed to provide a uniform approach to the Corps front and was distributed to every command.[4]

Deep communication trench, not yet prepared for defense as outlined
by the Principles of Trench Warfare issued by the XIV Reserve Corps.
(*Reserve-Infanterie Regiment Nr. 110 im Weltkrieg 1914-1918*)

The manual required every trench to be used as a fire trench including communication trenches that would allow the men to fire from either side. The troops should be able to climb out of every trench either through sortie steps or ladders otherwise the trench could become a trap for anyone caught inside. The Corps stressed that every man possible should fire his rifle over the parapet.

The 1st Line Position would consist of at least three separate lines of trenches; each was to be protected by two rows of wire entanglements in front of each trench whenever possible. Each company sector should have at least two communication trenches that connected the 1st trench to the 3rd trench but the points where the communication trenches entered and left the 2nd trench should not be opposite one another. Every battalion sector should have at least two communication trenches that connected the 1st Line to the rear. One of these should be designated for men coming toward the front, the other for men leaving the front. The trenches should be marked accordingly and the troops should be advised of their special use beforehand.

Each company sector should have a sufficient number of dug-outs that could house the trench garrison needed to repel an attack. The work on any sector requiring additional dug-outs should be concentrated on the 1st trench then the 2nd and 3rd as needed.

The front line trenches of each company were to be marked with a board 20 inches square divided by a diagonal line. One half of the side facing to the rear was to be painted red, the other white. The reverse side facing the enemy was to be made as inconspicuous as possible. These markers were to be placed on the parapet or parados so that the artillery could locate the line occupied by friendly troops.

It was felt that sufficient food, water and lighting requirements should be available for a three-day period and stored in the dug-outs of the 1st trench in the 1st Line Position. The food would consist of iron rations, coffee, salt, sugar, rum or its equivalent and cigars. Water should be stored in barrels and bottled mineral water. Lighting equipment would include electric lighting whenever possible, paraffin or acetylene lamps and candles.

The Intermediate and 2nd Line Positions would be constructed in the same manner as the 1st Line Position but only needed to consist of two lines of trenches. The 3rd Line Position was still under construction and was actively worked on when recruits were being given training.

Dug-out construction had undergone numerous changes and improvements since the mined dug-out was developed in early 1915. Reports from the different regiments were reviewed in order to provide a guideline for the best designs used in creating new shelters or in upgrading existing ones. The ground cover above each dug-out in the main defensive lines needed to be sufficiently thick in order to protect the men against the heaviest artillery shells. Between 6 and 7 meters of earth was deemed sufficient for this purpose and this was applied to any new dug-out constructed at this time.

It was not considered feasible to place the dug-outs any deeper otherwise the men might not be able to react to an attack in sufficient time in order to repel them. Every dug-out, new or old, was to have at least two exits. A large number of dug-outs constructed in the last year already had two exits but in many cases the exits were too close together to be of any practical use and had to be corrected.

Revetment of trench walls was covered in detail. From past experience the use of fascines, wire netting or corrugated iron as revetment material was forbidden. Whenever

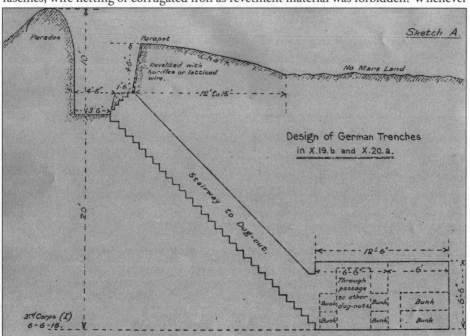

German deep dug-out sketch made after a raid on 5 June
1916 by British III Corps. (PRO W0157/171)

a trench utilized these materials and was subsequently damaged the materials being used acted as obstacles in their own right and made it difficult to clear the obstruction. However it was found that brushwood held in place by pickets and pegged into the trench walls did not cause any problems if damaged and therefore was allowed. Accordingly the XIV Reserve Corps Pioneer Commander was ordered to provide as much brushwood and as many pickets as he possibly could.

Wire entanglements were to be used whenever possible. Special attention was directed to the 2nd Line Position where passages were to be left in the belts of wire that could be easily closed off in case of an emergency. These lanes would be used to allow troops to advance toward the front or retire as needed. Points where roads crossed trench lines were to be left open but also easily closed off when needed.

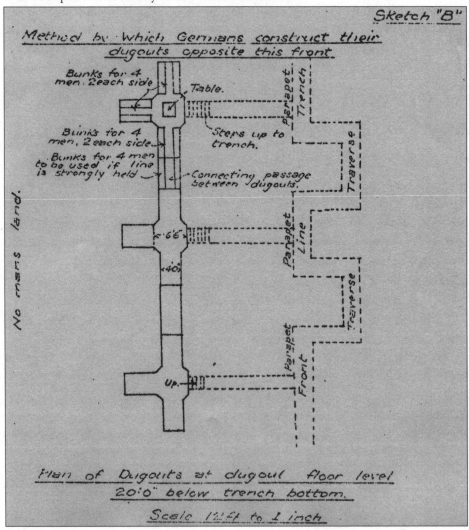

Plan of German dug-out complex made after raid on 5 June
1916 by British III Corps. (PRO W0157/171)

12/R121 in the trenches. The knife rest on the parapet behind the men was
used to block off trenches in an emergency. (Author's collection)

Every possible improvement required by Corps headquarters was being made to the
trenches in the greatest possible speed. Two labor companies worked diligently on the
extension of the 2nd Line. They were provided valuable assistance by several battalions
from the RIR 15 and Bavarian RIR 8 (2nd Guard Reserve Division and 10th Bavarian
Division respectively).

A special concrete construction company was kept busy installing reinforced concrete
observation posts in the Intermediate and 2nd Line positions. All existing wire obstacles
were strengthened, mined tunnels were extended and enlarged and the telephone network
was improved with additional lines and by burying the new cables deep under the floor
of the trenches.

RIR 99 had taken the initiative to bury all existing telephone lines at least 2 meters
under the ground when laid in the open and at least 1 meter or more under the floor of
the trench. Adjutant Dall was provided with a daily work force of 100 men in order to
accomplish this task

The number of Moritz listening stations was increased in order to be able to intercept
as many telephone messages as possible. The Moritz station located in the *Leiling Stollen*
provided important intelligence information on enemy activity and this information was
used to issue alerts and warnings about imminent enemy raids.

New regulations were issued that alarms used for defense against gas attacks would
be different than alarms sounded for infantry attacks. Church bells, sirens and gongs

388 THE OTHER SIDE OF THE WIRE VOLUME 1

in areas that were in the fire zone that would warn the men, transport and packhorse personnel in case of gas. Shouting, police whistles, foghorn and other devices would provide notice of an infantry attack.

Large numbers of shellproof ammunition depots were constructed in the front line and hand grenade reserves were established in the zone of fire. New kitchen and medical facilities were established. All of the experiences gained from the fighting in Arras, Champagne and Verdun and almost two years on the Somme were applied to the sector held by the XIV Reserve Corps. All of the facilities in the rear were improved as far as possible and adapted to resist a large enemy attack. Part of this included making preparations to remove the last of the civilian population from the rear areas.

Improvements were made in the paths, tracks and roads leading to the front. The field railway network was extended into additional areas. New wells were constructed and water pipes were laid down wherever possible. Electric lighting was expanded into every area possible in part by installing accumulators in dug-outs. Much of this work, especially the water pipes and the new electric lines leading up to Thiepval were not expected to survive a heavy bombardment or infantry attack but it was decided that the benefits would be useful as long as the facilities continued to function.

All of the work required by these improvements and other projects placed such a huge demand upon the men that all further infantry training was cancelled. By June all leave was cancelled as well, every man was needed at the front. Time off was granted for agricultural needs and only when sufficient replacements had arrived to cover any loss of manpower.

The XIV Reserve Corps placed great emphasis on the proper use of sentries who were considered to be the cornerstone of any successful defense against an attack.

III. The Infantry Combat

12. **Sentries.** Our entire system of defense depends on the trustworthiness of the sentries in advanced listening posts and in the fire trenches. Sentries must, in most cases, remain in the listening posts even during a heavy bombardment. The sentries in the fire trenches must clearly understand that on a dark night they must not rely on the sentries in the listening posts or on patrols sent out in front. Every sentry must be convinced that the safety of the position and of his comrades depends on *his* vigilance and *his* endurance. His task will present great difficulties under an intense bombardment, when he will frequently be forced to take cover. With regard to the latter point, he must be given definite instructions as to whether he should stand at the entrance to the dug-out, whether he should lie down, etc. In no circumstances may observation of the front suffer interruption. There will nevertheless be casualties among the sentries. For this reason, the garrison of the trenches concerned must be in a state of instant readiness in the dug-outs, and the commander will immediately replace any sentry who falls. Sentries will carry the gas mask hung on the chest, or in the box, with the slings of the mask and of the box round the neck.[5]

The guidelines continue regarding the defense of the position by the trench garrison.

13. **Garrison of the trenches.** The garrison of the 1st Trench of the 1st Line Position should be strong enough to repulse the enemy's attack, assuming that the men

reach the parapet in time, but no stronger. The better the 1st Trench is defended by flanking fire, especially that of machine guns, the more can the infantry garrison be reduced. To man the parapet promptly requires constant observation, good alarm arrangements, suitable construction of the entrances to the dug-outs, practice of the alarm in the form of a regular drill, and most important of all, observation of the fall of the enemy's artillery fire (lift of barrage).

Above all, every group commander and every man must realize that the success or failure of an assault depends on his timely appearance at the parapet. It must be made clear to the men that, once in the trench, the enemy will throw hand grenades into the dug-outs. Everything depends, therefore, even when the alarm signal is not heard, on not missing the instant at which the enemy's fire lifts, and immediately hurrying to the firing line. Experience has justified the practice of posting sentries, armed with hand grenades, at the entrance to the dug-outs, to deny approach to the enemy and to facilitate the task of ejecting him.

Machine guns, which are left in breastworks or trenches during the enemy's intense bombardment, will be destroyed, unless they are covered by very strong concrete emplacements. It will generally be impossible to erect such concrete structures in the 1st Trench. Machine guns must, as a rule, be kept in the dug-outs of their crews until the enemy assaults, and must then be placed rapidly in position at suitable points on the parapet without making use of the sledges, as these are too heavy for trench warfare. It is taken for granted that the crews are trained in firing without the sledge, on a pedestal built up of sand bags. This method of firing must be learnt. The resulting dispersion, which is known to be the disadvantage of this method, is of no account at assaulting distance.

In order to make the enemy disperse his fire and prevent him locating the positions really employed for flanking fire, the latter must be masked and a number of dummy positions constructed.

14. Supports. The 2nd Trench of the 1st Line Position is garrisoned by the Supports, one portion of which is specially detailed to defend the trench itself and in particular the entrances to the communication trenches, while the other portion consists of strong, specially formed bombing parties, which are held in readiness to rush forward at once to the support of the foremost trench. This manoeuver must be practiced as if it were a regular drill. Local conditions may make it necessary to station part of the Supports in the 3rd Trench.

15. Sector Reserves. The fighting strength of both the front trenches would be soon exhausted if the Sector Reserves were not put in. They must therefore be brought close up in good time, either into the 3rd Trench or into special reserve trenches. In case of an attack, they should be moved forward into the 2nd (or 3rd) Trench, to replace the reinforcements, which have already gone forward (the Supports) and continue the task allotted to the latter. Should the enemy's fire permit of an advance across the open, this is always preferable to an advance along the communication trenches.

The Sector Reserves must not therefore be saved up too long, but must be thrown in early. Otherwise they will arrive too late. Every battle has shown that

Württemberg Reserve Dragoons in a trench at *Feste Alt Württemberg*
near Beaucourt. (*Die 26. Reserve Division 1914-1918*)

trenches which are either lost or in dispute may be comparatively easily cleared or
recaptured, when this is undertaken immediately. I expect leaders to show the greatest
determination and initiative in such cases.[6]

The heavy fighting at Serre in June 1915 had already demonstrated that sending troops
into action in an unfamiliar area under foreign command often lead to confusion. In order
to prevent this from happening again each division assigned guides that would lead any
reinforcements to the location where they were needed. The reinforcements would follow
routes designated for this purpose and would avoid any direct path through a village due
to the constant enemy shelling of these locations. The Württemberg Reserve Dragoon
Regiment provided guides for the 26th Reserve Division.

At the end of May the Württemberg War Ministry issued orders for the formation of
a new field artillery regiment. It was designated RFAR 27 and would be attached to the
26th Reserve Division. The regiment was created by combining parts of FAR 29, FAR 65
with guns taken from RFAR 26 as well as from *Ersatz Abteilung* 29 and 65.

Hauptmann Wiedtmann, formerly in FAR 65 took command of the I *Abteilung* while
Major Reininger; FAR 29 became the new regimental commander. The 28th Reserve
Division was also equipped with a second artillery regiment, RFAR 29 that was combined
with RFAR 28 into the newly formed Reserve Field Artillery Brigade 28.

The month of June saw the largest increase in the number of guns assigned to the 26th
Reserve Division since the beginning of the war. Twelve reinforcement batteries arrived
including three field howitzer batteries from Bavarian Foot Artillery Regiment 20 (10th
Bavarian Division), the I *Abteilung* RFAR 12 (12th Division) and the I *Abteilung* FAR 104
(52nd Division). Additional heavy batteries were brought into position bringing the total
artillery compliment of the 26th Reserve Division to 28½ field gun batteries (including

7.7cm field gun emplacement near Fricourt – RFAR 29. (Author's collection)

older 9cm batteries) and 10½ heavy batteries, a total of 39 batteries and the accompanying ammunition columns that would all be in place in time for the expected British attack.

The 28th Reserve Division was provided with additional artillery support in the form of the 2nd and 3/FAR 57 (12th Division), 4(F)/FAR 21 (12th Division) and 1/Bavarian Foot Artillery Bn 10 (10th Bavarian Division).

Registration fire for the new batteries had to be completed as quickly as possible. Registration was not considered complete until at least two salvos of shells had fallen on target. Each gun was provided with the coordinates and ranges of every known target the gun could reach and by the end of June every gun in the Corps was ready for action.

The newly-formed RFAR 27 moved into prepared battery positions in the 26th Reserve Division starting 11 and 12 June. The regiment consisted of the I *Abteilung* that had three 4-gun batteries that were equipped with the Field Gun M. 96, new model as well as the II *Abteilung* consisting of three light field howitzer batteries, each armed with four M. 98/09 10.5cm howitzers.

With the arrival of the new regiment the artillery of the 26th Reserve Division was completely reorganized on 12 June with the formation of Reserve Field Artillery Brigade 26 under the command of *Generalmajor* Maur whose headquarters was located in Grevillers.

When the commander of the new regiment reported to *General der Artillerie* von Stein that his batteries were in position he received the response:

It is good that the regiment is here, we expect an enemy attack in the next few days and therefore with the shortage of artillery your arrival was urgently desired.[7]

The batteries were positioned near Courcelette, Miraumont and Pozières.[8] The next few weeks were taken up with adjustment fire, with special attention being paid to flanking fire. The men were put to work on further extension of the battery positions and the new

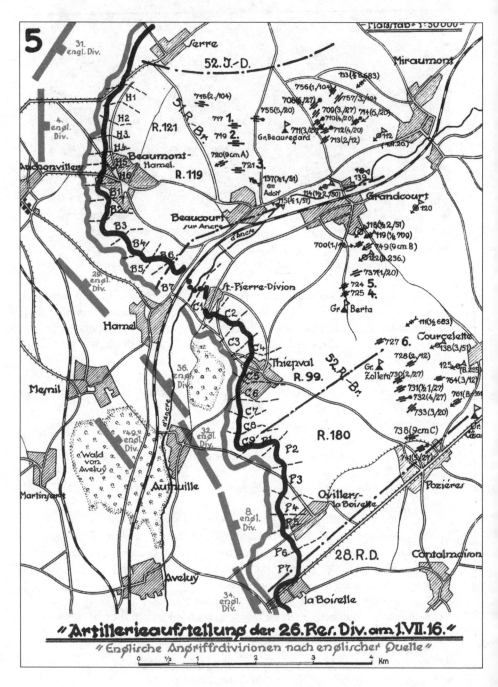

Artillery emplacements, 26th Reserve Division.

10cm Ring cannon. (*Die 26. Reserve Division 1914-1918*)

artillery observers were provided with an orientation of the artillery plan and the terrain they would be covering.

In June the artillery of the 26th Reserve Division was divided into two Groups: Group Miraumont consisting of Sub-Groups Adolf and Beauregard and Group Pys consisting of Sub-Groups Zollern, Caesar and Berta.

The 26th Reserve Division artillery contingent consisted of seventy-two 7.7cm field guns, twenty-four 10.5cm light field howitzers, and twenty 9cm guns. In addition there were thirty-eight heavy guns (Russian, Belgian and older German models) of which twelve were flat trajectory guns, twenty-six were steep trajectory guns, mostly older models. A total of 154 guns positioned along the 11-kilometer front of the division. In addition to the increase in artillery a Bavarian *minenwerfer* Company reinforced *minenwerfer* Coy 226.

While this may have seemed like a considerable amount of artillery there were a number of hidden drawbacks. Only the 7.7cm field guns and 10.5cm light field howitzers were modern weapons. The others were older, obsolete models. The Russian heavy field howitzers were temperamental and prone to breakdown after being fired for only a short time while the 9cm guns lacked any recoil system. Still the artillery complement would provide effective support in the event of an attack.

In addition to the normal number of artillery rounds needed for daily firing each battery would have an 'iron ration' of shells to be used to repel any attack. Each battery was issued 9 rounds of case shot to be used against approaching enemy infantry and each 9cm gun would be issued 5 case shot.[9] For the most part the guns had considerably more ammunition stored in shellproof dug-outs awaiting the start of the attack.

Demolition explosives were kept near the older model guns for which there were no limber teams available and the gun crews were instructed in their use. If the gun crew found it impossible to withdraw a gun during the enemy advance it would be destroyed. If it were not possible to destroy the gun then the ammunition and gun would be rendered harmless by unscrewing and removing the fuzes and removing the breechblocks.

Field Gun Battery	2,000 Rounds
Light Field Howitzer Battery	1,500 Rounds
10cm Battery	1,000 Rounds
Heavy Field Howitzer Battery	1,000 Rounds
21cm Mortar Battery	100 Rounds
German 12cm Battery	800 Rounds
German 15cm Battery	800 Rounds
Russian 15cm Battery	800 Rounds
Belgian 8.7cm gun	80 Rounds
9cm gun	180 Rounds

The artillerymen were kept very busy during the months of April, May and June. Detailed instructions had been given to every artillery commander in anticipation of the expected British offensive. Reserve Field Artillery Brigade 26 established new barrage fire regulations. The gun crews worked on individual gun emplacements making sure everything was in good working order. The batteries practiced fire control on a daily basis during which the method of identifying targets and the transmission of orders was thoroughly tested and refined so that the guns could be accurately fired in the shortest possible time. Every battery was required to practice the rapid concentration of fire on the enemy's point of assembly in every detail.

The batteries were to practice every possible scenario of attack the British might employ. Exact records were kept of fire distribution, overall results, and target details among other requirements. In order to check the accuracy of each battery engaged in such a drill one gun would fire a shell at the target sector at the end of the practice session and the results would be noted.

A battery position would not be considered complete until it had observation posts, a concealed gun position, a sufficient number of mined dug-outs to protect the gun crew and to safely store the thousands of rounds of ammunition needed for each gun. Each battery position was to be protected against an infantry attack with a belt of wire entanglements as well as having a stock of at least 50 hand grenades. All of the gun crews were given training in the proper storage and use of the hand grenades in case of an emergency.

Accurate observation was critical for the effective use of artillery. Each battery was required to have at least two observation posts. The main observation post would be positioned as close to the battery as possible depending upon the local conditions. The second or auxiliary post would be situated in or close behind the infantry positions.

All observation posts were to be made shell proof and their location was to be kept concealed from enemy view. Any movement or foot traffic should not betray its location. Notice boards were to be placed on all paths leading to the posts pointing out the necessity for proceeding with caution. All Artillery Liaison officers attached to infantry units were to be located at the infantry commander's battle headquarters or in the immediate vicinity.

In order for artillery observers to be effective they needed to be able to convey their information to the battery commanders in the shortest possible time. Telephone

Vizefeldwebel Friedrich Gakenstein 4/R121 (and friend) in the trenches. A sign on the left points the direction to a listening post. The tree to the upper left is covered with carved initials indicating former occupation by IR 180. (Author's collection)

communications were considered the fastest method of relaying information to the batteries but this was not always possible if enemy fire damaged the telephone lines. Alternate methods of relaying the information would then be used that included lamp and flag signaling, colored pyrotechnic light signals and runners. If the telephone lines remained intact the messages 'Barrage Fire' and 'Gas Attack' were to take priority over all other messages.

In order to reduce the time needed to identify a target designation the entire enemy position had been numbered and divided into sectors that were transferred to a map. Target Sector 30 up to 75 covered the area from Serre to La Boisselle. The maps consisted of one-kilometer squares that were numbered in sequence from north to south and from east to west. Each square was then divided even further into 25 numbered squares and each of these was divided into four lettered areas. Each lettered square represented an area with sides of 100 meters. This system allowed the guns to identify enemy targets and direct fire upon them in the shortest possible time. It was similar to the manner by which the British guns identified targets.

Each regimental sector was divided into areas corresponding to letters or numbers. The Serre Sector was designated with the letter 'S', the Heidenkopf Sector was designated as H1 through H6 while the Beaumont Sector received the designation letter 'B' (B1 through B6). Thiepval: C1 through C9, Ovillers P1 through P7. The other sectors were designated in a similar manner.

Every battery position received a number. The field gun and field howitzer battery positions were numbered starting from 700 while heavier caliber guns received designations starting at 100 and up.

The German guns were registered on all known British artillery positions and every target within range of the particular battery. If a British battery was taken under fire it was not simply to silence it, the aim was to destroy it. The XIV Reserve Corps estimated that it would take about 150 rounds from a 15cm heavy field howitzer or 100 rounds from a 21cm mortar to accomplish this goal.

With an attack expected at any time the prompt deployment of the artillery available to the XIV Reserve Corps was critical and nothing should interfere with the guns opening fire at the proper time. Specific orders were issued to ensure that this was the case:

> 32. **Method of engaging the enemy's infantry.** When an infantry attack is threatening, intense artillery fire will be directed on the enemy's trenches (Corps Orders, Ia 693, Secret, of 12/5/16, para. 7).

> When the assault is launched, barrage fire will be opened (Corps Orders, Ia 693, Secret, of 12/5/16, para. 7)[10]

The use of flare signals and other methods to contact the artillery during an attack were covered in detail. Different color and style flares were designed to relay critical messages when other methods failed. Initially the artillery designated the cartridges that produced a red light that broke into pearls for the start of barrage fire. In the event the fire was too short a cartridge where the light was green and broke into pearls would be used to lengthen the range.

Each company on trench duty and in the support lines was issued 100 red and 70 green flare signal cartridges. Great care was needed to ensure these cartridges remained dry and proper storage was stressed. Additional supplies were kept in division stores along with sufficient white flares used to illuminate No Man's Land at night. There were concerns that the sentries were not making enough use of flares during dark nights so additional flare pistols were distributed along with instructions to use them frequently in order to prevent enemy raiding parties from approaching the line unseen.

The British quickly established the color designation used by the artillery and at times attempted to trick the German batteries into opening fire in order to identify individual gun positions for counter-battery fire. This forced the XIV Reserve Corps to alter the colors used for the various artillery commands from time to time.

Another problem with the flare cartridges arose when RIR 99 discovered that the color of the light did not always match the color code on the cartridge due to poor manufacturing controls. The potential disaster that could arise from using the wrong color light had to be avoided at all cost. This was only solved by regularly testing the cartridges before use.

The XIV Reserve Corps instructions regarding the use of artillery stressed that in cases where communication from the front was impossible the artillery commanders should not wait to act:

The artillery should never delay in opening fire when the intensity of the enemy's artillery fire leads to the supposition that an attack is imminent. When the artillery fire in any particular sector is already fairly heavy, the right moment may easily be missed, in such cases, the artillery, so far from waiting for flare signals or telephone messages from the infantry (both means of communication may fail), should shell the enemy's trenches with an intensity increasing in proportion to the enemy's fire, in order to prevent his infantry from leaving its trenches. Immediately it becomes evident, from the enemy's artillery fire, at what point he intends to break through, the fire of every battery, with the exception of the (21cm) mortars, will be directed on to the portion of the enemy's front line trench which is opposite the sector threatened. Battery commanders have necessarily to act on their own initiative in this matter. The (21cm) mortars will shell the enemy's assembly trenches which have been previously located. Should the enemy launch an assault, barrage fire will be opened.[11]

Due to ammunition restrictions and the need to prevent the British from locating the gun emplacements many requests for artillery fire from the front line infantry were increasingly directed to the *minenwerfers* and *erdmörsers*. Still there were times when artillery fire was necessary and the guns responded to the call for aid.

If a British trench mortar position was discovered the artillery often fired at the target until it was destroyed. In June observers along the front of RIR 99 noted 12 motor lorries bringing up supplies in Sector 54 near Thiepval. The target was too tempting so the artillery was notified. After a short period of fire from the field guns all of the lorries were burning heaps of twisted metal.

Patrol activity continued to increase on both sides in the months before 1 July. These often led to short, vicious fights in the darkness between opposing patrols and the losses from these actions continued to grow. The number of raids launched from both sides seemed to keep pace with the activity related to the impending offensive and were increasing in size. The men of the XIV Reserve Corps were determined not to let the British rest.

In late March the 28th Reserve Division instructed RIR 110 to plan and conduct a raid against the British lines in order to bring in prisoners, equipment and intelligence information. The date, time and location of the raid were left up to the regiment to decide.

Several points along the British lines were considered good places to hold the raid, and in the end it was decided to attack the section of trench called the *Spion* that was opposite Sap 3. The decision was made to execute the raid on 11 April.

Several regiments along the front including RIR 119 were planning similar raids. At the beginning of April the German High Command had ascertained that the British 29th Division had left Egypt and wanted to know where it had gone. Raids were ordered along the front in the hopes that prisoners could be taken that would provide an answer. The location of the 29th Division was quickly established when a patrol from RIR 119 captured an officer from the division in front of their lines; the 29th Division was on the Somme in front of the XIV Reserve Corps.

On the night of 6/7 April RIR 119 sent out four patrols from the II Battalion against Mary Redan in Sector 47 opposite the *Leiling Schlucht*. The raiding parties consisted of 3 officers and 78 Other Ranks. Extensive planning went into the raid covering all aspects of the different objectives assigned to each group, the timetables for artillery, minenwerfer and machine gun fire as well as diversionary tactics.

The patrols were housed in the *Leiling Mulde* on the day of the raid. Each man had a white cloth stitched to his uniform jacket on each arm for identification in the darkness. The men were warned against taking any documents or equipment that could provide intelligence to the enemy in the event of their capture or death. All shoulder straps were removed, no identity discs were worn and each man would wear his *Feldmütze* only.

The raiding parties were armed in part with rifles while the majority were equipped with pistols and trench knives. Each man would carry 2 bandage packets, 6 hand grenades and were to leave their gas masks behind. 4 men in each patrol carried wire cutters, 2 had rolled tent halves, 2 had axes and 2 had sharpened trench shovels.

C Coy, 2nd South Wales Borderers occupied Mary Redan on the night of 6 April. It was their first time in the trenches and they had only been in the line for the last 3 days. It was to be an experience the men would not soon forget.

Just prior to the start of the preparation fire *Vizefeldwebel* Böcker and 4 men from the 6/R119 approached a listening post in the neighboring sector (Rooney's Sap) and threw approximately 20 hand grenades at the occupants before withdrawing. It had the desired effect of taking some of the enemy attention away from the actual target sector.

The preliminary bombardment was very effective as entire sections of wire entanglements were destroyed, dug-outs were smashed in, telephone lines were cut and much of the front line trench was blown in. At the appointed time the artillery and mine fire was shifted further to the rear to block off the target sector, it was time for the patrols to move forward.

Three patrols moved into the British trenches as planned while the fourth remained to the rear as protection and to supply support as needed. The raid lasted no more than

Example of a raiding party, 10/R247 taken in June 1916. Note the identifying white cloths on each man, sharpened trench shovels, rifles, wire cutters, rolled tent halves and pistols. (Author's collection)

Patrol Böcker, 6/R119 on slope close to the enemy position north of Hamel. (*Die 26. Reserve Division 1914-1918*)

15 minutes and the result was the capture of 19 prisoners from the 2nd South Wales Borderers who had become trapped inside a dug-out due to the intense bombardment. The successful raid was a hard lesson for the South Wales Border Battalion:

> At 10.30 p.m. the bombardment suddenly ceased and the battalion could reoccupy the front trench and set about investigating and repairing the damage. This had been considerable. It was 'a terrible shambles', one officer writes, 'bay after bay being blown in and killed and wounded being buried under the blown-in trenches.' Not only the front line but the communication trenches were badly knocked about, the wire had been practically completely demolished, and the Borders and the Inniskillings had to send up working parties to help reconstruct the parapet and clear away the debris.[12]

The bombardment of the British lines completely smashed the front line trenches, the barbed wire and communication trenches. Besides prisoners the raiding party brought back a large quantity of weapons and materials verifying the presence of the new division. The total casualties suffered by the 29th Division amounted to 112 officers and men: 1 officer, 33 Other Ranks killed, 8 officers, 42 Other Ranks wounded and 28 Other Ranks missing.

> Altogether it was a dismal opening to the battalion's career on the Western Front. It was pure bad luck to have been holding a sector which had evidently been marked down as the victim of a carefully prepared and organized raid; the weight of the bombardment – about 8,000 shells, mainly high-explosive, were calculated to have fallen on the area bombarded – would have tried any defences.[13]

Prisoners from 2nd South Wales Borderers receiving rations after being
captured 7 April 1916. (*Die 26. Reserve Division 1914-1918*)

The losses to the raiding party amounted to 3 men killed and 1 man severely wounded from enemy hand grenades in the 5th Company: *Unteroffizier* Otto Bruchlacher, *Musketier* Maximilian Bigiel, *Musketier* Karl Stapf killed and Christian Walker severely wounded.[14]

Vizefeldwebel Böcker's illustrious patrol record was to come to an untimely end only three days later. On 9 April Captain Streater, 1st Border Regiment, shot Böcker in an ambush. He was fatally wounded and died shortly after returning to the German lines.

RIR 109 continued to send reconnaissance patrols toward the *Hoheneck*. On the night of 8 April a patrol sent out by the 2nd Coy under *Leutnant der Reserve* Risse obtained valuable information concerning the position and wire obstacles. The patrol spent some time in front of the trenches and observed British soldiers entrenching at close range.

Additional patrols were sent out against the *Kronenwerk*. It was decided to see just how effective the *minenwerfer* could be in destroying British wire entanglements. The 6/R109 sent out a patrol under *Vizefeldwebel* Weigele to determine how wide the gaps were in the wire after a bombardment. They reported their findings and a raid was planned under the code name 'Stiftungsfest'. Sortie gaps were cut in the German wire, the actions of the artillery and close range weapons were coordinated and everything appeared ready for the raid to proceed. Unfortunately it had to be postponed due to a shortage of men.

RIR 111 still had not taken a single live prisoner. The night of 7/8 April would be no different. During the night a patrol from the 9th Coy found itself in a hand grenade fight with a British patrol. During the brief encounter the enemy was forced to withdraw leaving behind a fallen man.

The body lay in No Man's Land the following day and the British were prevented from recovering him by occasional bursts of fire. Later, after darkness had fallen, another patrol was sent out and was able to recover the body. It turned out to be a sergeant from the 20th Manchester Battalion, 22nd Brigade, 7th Division.

The undertaking being planned by RIR 110 was quickly taking form under the leadership of *Hauptmann* Wagener. He was assigned *Leutnants der Landwehr* Erb and Boening to assist in the planning and execution of the raid. *Leutnants der Reserve* Stradtmann, Freund, Dumas and Böhlefeld were to command the different raiding parties. The detachment was complete when the services of *Oberarzt* Dr. Wisser, one bugler and four stretcher-bearers were added. The men making up the raiding parties came from volunteers from several companies. The total strength of the undertaking was set at 50 infantrymen and 4 pioneers.

The final preparations were made for the undertaking including an elaborate ruse designed to deceive the British as to the actual location of the raid. The British line north of the La Boisselle cemetery was chosen as the location of the feint attack. This part of the British trench would be bombarded by artillery fire while the wire obstacles were systematically destroyed using *minenwerfer*. The preparation fire against the deception location continued throughout the day and night preceding the actual attack.

At the appointed time the artillery would fire on the actual target for 15 minutes before shifting to the rear trenches cutting off the front from reinforcements. A shallow tunnel was prepared for detonation and at the time fixed for the attack it would be blown. Straw-filled dummies were set up in the German lines near the *Blinddarm* in La Boisselle so that they had the appearance of German assault detachments moving out into No Man's Land. The dummies would appear in several places then vanish again and were set up at different locations in order to confuse the British.

While the deception was taking place the actual raid would enter the British lines and take as many prisoners as possible. The men were divided into four groups: Group Stradtmann 10 men, Group Dumas 10 men, Group Böhlefeld 10 men and Group Freund 24 men. Boening, Erb, Dr. Wisser and the stretcher-bearers remained with the patrol leader.

2nd South Wales Borderers and captors – RIR 119. (Author's collection)

Each participant wore a white canvas triangle attached to their chest as an identification mark so that they could recognize one another in the dark.

The British almost stumbled upon clues that would have provided information that a raid was going to take place and to prepare accordingly. Lieut. G.H.P. Whitfield, No. 1 Platoon, A Coy, 1st Royal Irish Rifles:

> In the evening, when we were having dinner and things had gotten quieter, Sgt D'Arcy came in and reported to ffrench-Mullen that he thought the Germans were cutting the wire opposite his platoon front which was on the left of mine. We were amazed at the idea but went up with Sgt D'Arcy to have a look. We could see nothing so returned. Sgt D'Arcy was right as we afterwards found out to our cost.[15]

At 4 o'clock in the afternoon of 11 April the patrol members marched from Martinpuich via Pozières, through the *Lattorfgraben*, the Regimental Crater and the *Krebsgraben* into the dug-outs designated for the undertaking on the left of Sap 3.

At 8 p.m. the artillery preparation fire began. Within minutes the British position was shrouded in a grey-white smoke that was quickly blown across the lines over Sap 3 and into the German trenches. The smoke eventually became so bad that the raiding party was forced to put on their gasmasks.

At 8.20 p.m. the four patrols exited the dug-outs and proceeded into the nearby sunken road in the order: Stradtmann, Dumas, Böhlefeld and Freund. The patrols were assembled in the sunken road by 8.25 p.m.

The gas and smoke clouds formed by the heavy fire completely obstructed all view of the British lines and the men could not tell whether the artillery fire still fell along the front line or if it had shifted to the rear. Despite the lack of visibility the patrols were ordered forward. Patrol Stradtmann advanced at 8.27 followed closely by Boening and the stretcher-bearers who formed a human chain behind Patrol Stradtmann and who were visible to men in the rear by the use of red signal lamps that were blocked off to the rear and sides. These men would direct the remaining raiding parties as they advanced across No Man's Land as well as guide them back upon their return.

At 8.28 Patrols Dumas and Böhlefeld began to cross over to the British trenches. By the time the line of stretcher-bearers reached the point of entry into the British lines Patrol Stradtmann had already captured a 15-meter stretch of trench and taken 3 prisoners.

Patrol Dumas turned left upon entering the British trench and almost immediately came upon a badly damaged machine gun post. One man from Patrol Stradtmann, Reservist Nadolny, had already been assigned to dig out the gun so Patrol Dumas continued to advance through the trench.

They reached a communication trench that led back toward a spot the Germans called the *Weisse Steinmauer*. The patrol came across a dug-out that had apparently been destroyed by a direct hit. Dumas sent three of his men forward with orders to attack the next trench line from the rear. This trench was approximately 10 meters behind the first one. While this was happening several British soldiers came out of the second trench with the apparent idea of escaping the German blocking fire by going into the front line. The 'Englishmen' were taken by surprise and bayoneted.

Patrol Dumas then advanced up to the next communication trench where they came across another large dug-out from which dead bodies could be seen. Before the patrol had a chance to explore the shelter they came under attack from British soldiers advancing along another communication trench and along side of it. After a brief fight that consisted of hand grenades, rifles and pistols the enemy soldiers were forced to withdraw after suffering a number of casualties. Those who remained behind were forced to surrender or were killed.

Meantime Patrol Böhlefeld advanced to the right from the point of penetration and came upon three dug-outs. One dug-out was filled with dead and wounded while the garrisons of the other two came out with their hands up when *Leutnant* Böhlefeld demanded their surrender. He sent the prisoners to the rear under escort and had the dug-outs searched and cleared using most of his remaining men while he stayed behind to cover the trench with two men in order to provide protection.

No noise was coming from the break-in location at 8.30 p.m. or on the right where Patrol Böhlefeld was located. However rifle fire and hand grenade explosions could be heard coming from the left, approximately 60 meters away. Wagener ordered *Vizefeldwebel* Elb to take five men and reinforce Patrol Dumas on the left. The regimental adjutant *Leutnant* Erb joined them.

A short time later all sounds of fighting on the left also ceased and the first prisoners were seen being sent back under escort. Wagener came to the conclusion that the raiding parties had full control of their areas so he decided to fully exploit the situation using the last patrol group under Freund.

Freund was ordered to advance further into the British lines with fifteen men. *Vizefeldwebel* Wölfle was ordered to take four men from the Patrol Freund and reinforce Patrol Böhlefeld on the right and to attack the *Spion* from the rear while Wagener remained at the point of penetration with the remaining men in support.

Patrol Freund advanced over the first trench and followed the terrain to the right until they came to a communication trench that intersected the front line. They came upon a group of British soldiers and after bayoneting several that had put up a defense the rest, 10 men, were taken prisoner almost without a struggle. Several tried to escape and had to be shot down.

Freiwilliger Herrmann discovered an improvised trench mortar. They tried to carry it back to their own lines but it was too firmly set in the emplacement. *Vizefeldwebel* Wölfle then destroyed the weapon as best he could with hand grenades and pistol shots.

Patrol Freund met up with Patrol Böhlefeld and the combined force continued to advance into the British trenches. They discovered 3 to 4 dug-outs that were filled with enemy dead. When individual British soldiers were encountered in the trench they were either killed or taken prisoner.

It was estimated that 25 to 30 British soldiers had managed to withdraw from the front line either during the preliminary bombardment or since the German patrols broke into the line. It was surmised that these men had attempted to find safety at the *Weisse Steinmauer* however the German box barrage drove them back toward the front.

This group was observed approaching the break-in position by members of Patrol Stradtmann who believed it was a counterattack. Several members of the patrol stormed forth out of the trench with fixed bayonets. Two men were bayoneted and the rest of the enemy who did not surrender were killed in this fight and added to the growing number already sent to the rear.

Erb and his men had quickly come upon Patrol Dumas and joined in the fight against any small pockets of enemy resistance. There was an almost constant sound of rifle and pistol fire occasionally interrupted by the bursting of hand grenades as almost every enemy soldier encountered offered resistance. .

Patrol Dumas had attempted to advance further into the British lines but constantly came across small groups of British soldiers who were putting up a strong defense. The Germans had the advantage of numbers and surprise and in most cases were able to kill or wound the defenders. It was estimated that more than 20 British soldiers had been killed and more wounded during the fighting. Patrol Dumas had only had one man slightly wounded from the fighting.

While Patrol Dumas was occupied with these small actions the remainder of the raiding parties assembled at the break-in position and successfully returned to the sunken road in No Man's Land. When Wagener realized that he was missing one of the patrols Boening and Stradtmann accompanied by several men returned to the British trenches in order to find them.

They came upon Patrol Dumas in a short time and ordered them to return to the sunken road. By 8.50 p.m. the last of the men from the patrol were in the sunken road and a short time later the men were safely inside their dug-outs. At 8.51 the first British shells fell into the German front line trench near Sap 3 and by 8.57 p.m. the artillery commander was given the message that the artillery fire could be broken off slowly.

The total British losses from this raid were reported to be: 2nd Lieut. P.M. Harte-Maxwell and nine men killed, 39 wounded and 28 men missing. Only one member of Patrol Dumas had been slightly wounded in the forehead by a splinter from a hand grenade. He was treated and quickly returned to his company.

Patrol Wagener had several additional casualties from the raid. Several men were slightly wounded and one soldier, Josef Winkler, 3rd Coy who was reported missing was later found to have died of wounds as a British Prisoner of War.

1st Royal Irish Rifles and captors – RIR 110. (*Reserve-Infanterie Regiment Nr. 110 im Weltkrieg 1914-1918*)

The feint attacks near La Boisselle had apparently fulfilled their objectives by keeping the British guessing as to the location of the raid. The dummies had been joined together in groups of three using wooden slats. They could be operated from the safety of the dug-outs by the use of strings. In this manner the operators would be protected from enemy shellfire.

At 8.15 the preparatory bombardment was lifted off of the British trenches and 30 seconds later the first dummies appeared at the parapet of the *Blinddarm*. One set of dummies had to be quickly repaired when it became badly damaged by a shell but was quickly set in place once again. The groups of dummies immediately came under heavy artillery and machine gun fire once they became visible to the British. After a few minutes the operators caused them to disappear from view, waited a short time and then raised them up once again.

They continued this ruse while the actual patrol was taking place. When it was over the dummies were inspected and each one was found to have suffered considerable damage from enemy fire, five being hit by rifle and machine gun fire while nearly all suffered damage from shell splinters and stone fragments. The idea of using dummies was as successful as the men of RIR 110 could have hoped for.

The raiding party had brought in a total of 24 unwounded and 5 wounded British prisoners.[16] In addition to the prisoners they had brought back one Lewis Gun, a rifle with a telescopic sight, 20 rifles and numerous pieces of equipment. The prisoners belonged to the 1st Royal Irish Rifles, (25th Brigade, 8th Division) and gave an excellent impression to their captors.

The loss of the Lewis gun was grounds for a Court of Enquiry. 2nd Lieut. W.V.C. Lake:

> As we were getting ready for 'Stand To' one evening, they laid on a heavy artillery barrage, under which a strong raiding party appeared in the front line. The wire was breached and the communication trenches were filled with broken chalk.
>
> Four of us were just putting on our equipment when it all started, and immediately our exit was plugged with heaps of chalk in the dug-out doorway, jamming the door. Shells came thick and fast and the sacking on the windows blew in at every explosion. All we could do was lie low and wait for the end. Our orders had been that in the event of an attack we were to rush up to the front line with all speed. But how was this to be done? It does sometimes happen that orders cannot be obeyed.
>
> I had been appointed Lewis Gun Officer by this time and the Germans had captured one of my guns, together with the crew. I had to face a Court of Enquiry because of this, but the Court accepted my account of the raid and I was not punished.[17]

The prisoners were interrogated and provided an insight into the raid from the enemy point of view. Some of the prisoners stated that 'in essence the impressions during the fighting were horrible.' By the morning of 10 April, during the adjustment fire by the *minenwerfer* and heavy artillery A Coy had already suffered approximately 20 killed and wounded.

The 1st Royal Irish Rifles had expected a German attack during the night of 10 April as a result of the heavy fire however when nothing occurred the men were reported to be in a good mood and on 11 April any thought of a raid had been completely forgotten.

When German shellfire fell on the British lines at 8 p.m. it took them by surprise and coincided with the relief of two platoons of D Coy from the front. When questioned about an upcoming British offensive the prisoners claimed to know nothing about it.

The British were not slow to retaliate for the successful German raid. Artillery fire was increased along the front held by RIR 110. The *Schwäbenhöhe* and *Lehmgrubenhöhe* came under particularly heavy artillery fire with shells up to 20.5cm.

The British fire increased noticeably for several days. At 10.30 p.m. on 22 April it increased to the level of drumfire on the positions held by the 8/R110, *Schwäbenhöhe* and the right-hand battalion. At 10.50 the heavy fire was extended to include the 5/R110 and right wing of the 6/R110.

At 11.20 the machine gun post in the 5th Coy sector observed an enemy patrol of approximately 20 men directly in front of the wire obstacles. The alarm was sounded and almost immediately infantry and machine gun fire opened up. The raiding party was forced to withdraw leaving behind a dead non-commissioned officer who had been killed by a pistol shot fired from a sentry.

A second patrol in front of the left wing of the 8th Coy was also spotted and driven back with heavy fire. The patrol in front of the 8th Coy had been predicted in part from intelligence gathered from the Moritz listening station located by La Boisselle and the men were placed on alert accordingly. The following day the Moritz station reported the fury and helplessness of the British commander about the failure of the patrols and the 'Damned Germans.'[18]

The British attempted several raids along the front held by the XIV Reserve Corps on the night of 22/23 April, Easter Sunday. One of these was directed against RIR 99 at Thiepval. At 10.20 in the evening Sector C7 Thiepval-South was covered in heavy fire just as the III Battalion was relieving the I/R99. Shortly after 11 p.m. the fire lifted off of the trenches and the sentries reported that a powerful patrol was just in front of the wire entanglements.

The raiding party broke into the German lines after passing through the partially damaged wire and proceeded to throw bombs into dug-out entrances. The men who were able to exit their dug-outs met the attackers and the dark night was filled with the sounds of crashing hand grenades and hand-to-hand fighting. A short time later the raiding party withdrew and returned to the British lines.

When the fighting was over RIR 99 discovered 4 enemy dead inside the trenches as well as a canvas bag containing hand grenades, a rifle and a trench club studded with nails. The III/R99 had lost a total of 22 men during the raid. 9 men were wounded including 2 *Schützen* from the 2nd Machine Gun Coy; 13 were missing and had been apparently dragged off as prisoners. Once the raid was over the German batteries covered the British lines with heavy fire in retaliation.

RIR 99 sent out numerous patrols each night in an attempt to capture an enemy soldier. On the night of 30 April several patrols were sent to investigate a sap that had been advanced into No Man's Land. The occupants were attacked with hand grenades and rifle fire and were driven back to the main British line leaving behind one man who

Assorted weapons and equipment recovered after failed British
raid 30 April 1916. (*Die 26. Reserve Division 1914-1918*)

fell into the hands of RIR 99. He belonged to the Lancashire Fusilier Regiment (96th
Brigade, 32nd Division).

The British attempted to raid the trenches held by RIR 119 and RIR 121 on the
same day but were spotted by alert sentries. They were successfully driven off by rifle,
machine gun and artillery fire leaving behind a number of dead and wounded men and
their equipment.

> Seeger and Sütterlin were also involved in the patrol; as the hand grenades fell
> they were hurrying to assist and helped 'handle' the English. In the night of 30th
> April the English made a raid on the left of us, by the 1st Company, after artillery
> preparation; however they were thrashed. Immediately as the first English artillery
> shells fell, our artillery opened up and fired into the English trenches opposite using
> what they heard and saw going on. During the following night the patrol of the 1st
> Company brought in 5 dead Englishmen who lay in front of the wire entanglements.
> Karl Losch 3/R119 [19]

The British were successful in talking several prisoners during a raid against RIR 109
near Ovillers. The 15th Lancashire Fusiliers (1st Salford Pals) raided the trenches held
by this regiment and in the course of the attack killed a number of the defenders and
dragged off several prisoners.

RIR 111 was forced to abort a raid planned for the evening of the 30th. Detailed
preparations had been made for a raid against the *Weisse Steinmauer* and the *Häusergruppe*
southwest of Fricourt. The date, 30 April, had been chosen as the British generally behaved
very quietly on this day, Sunday. Part of the preparations called for several deception
raids along the front.

Shortly after 3 a.m. on 30 April the artillery opened fire on the British lines. Thirty
minutes later the 2nd Bavarian Pioneer Coy broke into the trenches located at the *Kniewerk*
just after a mine had been detonated at the western edge of Fricourt.

The pioneers threw hand grenades and explosive charges into a mine tunnel they discovered and destroyed it. The pioneers encountered weak resistance and returned to their lines shortly afterward without any prisoners. This attack was designed to throw off any enemy suspicions about an attack later the same day.

RIR 110 was supplying support for RIR 111 by using close range weapons along the western edge of Fricourt. Disaster struck two of the *Albrecht* mortars in Communication Trench II that were being fired by means of an electric lead from nearby dug-outs. British artillery responded to the mortar fire and after the second shot from the *Albrecht* mortars a direct hit on the ammunition storage caused a gigantic explosion that hurled both mortars 15 meters away and smashed them beyond use.

Several mines were detonated at La Boisselle, by Fricourt and on Hill 110 to deceive the British of the actual location of the raid. Straw dummies were set up in the trenches in the *Blinddarm* once again. Some enemy fire was directed against the dummies but the heaviest concentration of fire remained in front of Fricourt and was expanded until the fire reached past Hill 110.

With the majority of the British fire falling on the area that was to be used by the raiding party *Oberst* Ley ordered the undertaking to be cancelled at 9 p.m. He felt that any success they might have could only be achieved with heavy losses. In spite of the volume of British shells only two men were wounded in RIR 111, however the trenches were badly damaged and required a great deal of repair.

On the night of 6 May the 5th, 11th and 10/R109 holding the center of the regimental sector came under heavy shellfire starting at 2 a.m. The fire on the front line lasted two hours and the position was severely damaged, in places completely leveled.

The bombardment had been so heavy it was decided that it would be pointless to sacrifice the lives of the sentries so they were withdrawn into the dug-out entrances where they could jump out into the trench at intervals and observe the foreground for enemy activity.

The volume of fire indicated an attack or raid would follow. In order to be prepared to meet any advance the trench garrison was placed on alert and stood ready on the dug-out steps waiting for the moment when the fire was transferred to the rear indicating infantry were approaching.

AVO *Leutnant* Pein sent a message to the artillery for support and the guns opened fire on target areas in front of the three German companies. The 2nd Machine Gun Coy joined in and held the hollow running in front of the position as well as the British trenches opposite the right wing company under heavy fire. The volume of German fire apparently held several raiding parties in check but not all.

Large groups of British soldiers had used the protection of the bombardment to work up to the edge of the German wire. Utilizing a new method to cross the German wire one raiding party was able to penetrate the lines held by the 5th Coy without being observed by the trench sentries.

The raiders approached several dug-outs whose occupants had been prevented from exiting due to the partial collapse of the entrances. The men could only get out be crawling through a narrow opening one by one. As they exited the men were either taken prisoner or killed by the waiting British soldiers.

The enemy penetration had been so swift that in one case a platoon leader was in the process of exiting his dug-out with two men after hearing the alarm cry of a sentry when two hand grenades were thrown at his feet and exploded. The platoon leader was severely wounded on each leg, one arm and the right side of his stomach while a man behind him was slightly wounded.

The raiding party attacked a total of four dug-outs. 2 occupants were killed, 6 were wounded and 4 were later reported missing. During the attack several occupants of dug-out No. 17 attempted to crawl through a narrow chute that connected it to dug-out No. 16. One *Landsturmmann* was too slow and was grabbed by the legs and captured. Another man, *Landsturmmann* Faller fought off his attackers with a revolver and was eventually able to make it to safety.

The garrison of dug-out No. 15 managed to reach dug-out No. 14 through the connecting emergency exit and alerted the garrison inside of the attack. The men quickly exited the dug-out and proceeded to man the fire step with hand grenades at the ready. However the raiding party had already left, taking several prisoners with them.

Following the British raid of Easter Sunday the staff of RIR 99 worked out the details of a larger trench raid against the British position in Sector 54 scheduled for 7 May. The participants of the raiding party came from volunteers from the 2/R99, commanded by *Hauptmann* Lingke and the 6/Pioneer Bn 13. The three raiding parties would consist of 102 officers and men.

The artillery preparation was assigned to the III *Abteilung*, RFAR 26, consisting of the 7th, 8th and 9th batteries. Additional artillery support was provided as well as *minenwerfers* and *erdmörsers*. Both regimental machine gun companies would be used to provide suppression fire during the attack.

The section of trench chosen for the raid was located between Hammerhead Sap and Maison Grise Sap. The site was well situated for a trench raid due to its proximity to the German trenches and the distance between the lines that varied between 200 and 250 meters. Several small wooded areas provided excellent cover for the attackers. The largest copse was located just outside of Thiepval and extended into No Man's Land almost up to the British trench at Hammerhead Sap. Known as the 'Park' by the men of RIR 99, this wood effectively screened the main German trench and the sunken road that ran from Thiepval to Hamel along its northern edge.

During the night of 6 May the 1st Dorsets (14th Brigade) relieved the 16th Lancashire Fusiliers (96th Brigade) from this portion of the line. The Dorsets held the front with three platoons from each company in the firing line and one platoon in support. The 19th Lancashire Fusiliers were on their right, the 10th Inniskilling Fusiliers, (109th Brigade, 36th Division), were on their left.

When the Dorsets took over the line four sergeants accompanied them from the 17th Northumberland Fusiliers. They had been sent to the front in order to learn trench routine and upon their return they would pass along their knowledge to their companies.

7 May began raw and chilly when the 1st Dorsets 'Stood to Arms' at 2:45 a.m. The Germans shelled the Dorset trenches several times on the 7th otherwise it was fairly quiet. A slight rain began to fall at 7 p.m., adding to the discomfort of the men.

7 May happened to be the same day the 36th Division planned to hold the first large-scale raid planned by the Ulstermen; the attack was scheduled for midnight. The raid was to be carried out by six officers and 84 men from the 9th Inniskilling Fusiliers (the 'Tyrones'). They were under the command of Major Peacocke. The Inniskillings notified all nearby battalions about the raid and advised them to seek cover from the inevitable

German retaliatory fire. In response Major Shute, C.O. 1st Dorsets, issued orders to his company commanders to cease all wiring at 10:45 p.m. All men were to take cover in their dug-outs, except for trench sentries.

While the British preparations were being completed, the officers and men of the 2/R99 and 6/Pioneer Bn 13 moved into their positions in No Man's Land opposite the Dorset trenches. The raiders split into three groups, each consisting of about 32 men. Two groups (A and C) would advance and hold the flanks of the target area, while the center group (B) was designated as the break in portion of the patrol. The men waited for the signal to advance.

At 10 p.m. von Fabeck met with his Adjutant, *Oberleutnant der Reserve* Dall, and his Ordnance Officer, *Leutnant der Reserve* Arnold, in the front line trench in order to watch the attack. The 9th Inniskillings raiding party took up their positions along the sunken road at the same time and waited.

At precisely 11 o'clock the German artillery, *minenwerfers* and *erdmörsers* opened fire simultaneously. To deceive the British as to the location of the raid, German shellfire was directed against the trenches surrounding the target area and Sectors 47 and 70, north and south of Thiepval.

When the shelling began the 19th Lancashire Fusiliers did not treat it seriously. The 1st Dorsets reported that trench mortars and 'oil cans' were directed against the front line trench while gunfire was directed on the support and communication trenches. Sergeant-Major Shephard, B Coy 1st Dorsets, remarked in his diary: 'At 10 P.M. [sic] the enemy situated artillery fire on our F.G.1 and F.G.2 trenches (A and my company).'[20]

When the heavy fire continued Major Shute called for artillery support and batteries C161 and B168 soon opened fire. It was some time before battery C164 was able to assist as their guns were registered to support the raid by the Inniskillings. Trench Mortar Battery Y32 provided additional support. Shephard wrote:

> Gradually they (Germans) worked up into a very intensive bombardment, and after a time they switched fire on to C and D (holding outskirts of Thiepval).[21]

Major Shute telephoned each of his companies at 11:10 and ordered them to 'Stand To'. Shortly after this call all telephone lines to the forward companies were cut with the exception of C Coy.

The fire of the German howitzer batteries was very accurate and all communication and support trenches leading to the forward line of the 1st Dorsets were effectively closed while the medium and heavy *minenwerfers* blasted whole sections of trenches, destroyed wire obstacles and crushed dug-outs.

The German fire continued to shift north until it covered the trenches from R.25.9 to Union Street including all of the support and communication trenches to the rear. The volume of fire was devastating, the 1st Dorsets reported:

> The whole of that portion of the line occupied by D Coy. (extreme left of the Battn.) was practically demolished by trench mortar bombs and artillery fire before the enemy raided.[22]

At 11:30 the Dorsets noticed the fire directed on their trenches lifted slightly, and the shelling concentrated on the communication trenches; Sauchiehall Street, Buchanan Ave., Govan Street, Queens Cross Roads and the northeast section of Paisley Ave. At the same time the machine guns of RIR 99 opened fire on the right and left center companies (B and C), as well as on the communication trenches.

The men of RIR 99 had been waiting for the fire to lift so they could begin their attack. The first group (A) came from the direction of Diamond Wood towards trench R.25.7. Shephard recalled their approach:

> We opened up a rapid fire, although it was exceedingly difficult, the shells were so thick it seems a marvel how we lived through it.[23]

The Germans in Group 'A' stopped their advance when they encountered the heavy fire and moved right, further towards the line held by D Coy. Shute suspected this attack had been a feint, as the Germans did not appear to be very determined. Shephard felt differently:

> The enemy raiding party in first place headed for my (B Coy) trenches, (this would be about the time we started rapid fire). Evidently they were convinced we were on the 'qui vive' and they swung over to D Coy trenches, on outskirts of wood.[24]

The Germans in Group 'A' did report receiving violent machine gun and heavy rifle fire as they approached the Dorset trench. They decided to break off their assault and move right in support Group 'B'. They felt their adversary proved to be very alert possibly as a result of recent attacks on neighboring positions.

Group 'C' approached the British trenches at R.25.14, just north of Hammerhead Sap. This group used the cover provided by the sunken road and the 'Park' to approach the British lines unseen. They broke into the forward British trench to cover the right wing of the raiding party. The center group, (B), commanded by *Leutnant* Metzmacher, *Vizefeldwebel* Pflug, *Vizefeldwebel* Hebestreit and *Unteroffizier* Loos, approached the British trenches from the direction of Oblong Wood. As they came up to the shattered trenches they received weak infantry fire from the defenders. Passing through the remnants of the wire entanglements Metzmacher and his men entered the Dorset trenches with little difficulty at R.25.12.

Metzmacher and his men moved through the trench, towards group C. Armed with rifles, bayonets, clubs and hand grenades they overcame any pockets of resistance and rounded up prisoners as they proceeded. Despite the intensity of the bombardment small groups of men still offered fierce opposition from their dug-outs, firing rifles and throwing hand grenades at the raiders.

Near Hammerhead Sap the raiding party came up behind a machine gun post. They grabbed the gun crew and an officer and dragged them out of the trench as prisoners. One man, Corporal Miller, 10th Inniskillings, and the officer struggled with their captors forcing the raiders to kill them.[25] The raiders began their withdrawal a short time later.

Within a few minutes the British artillery opened fire on the German lines as Peacocke and his men raided the German trenches. They broke into the trenches but the men of RIR 99 were on the alert and no prisoners were taken. RIR 99 showed fight according to

Peacocke, firing up the steps of their deep dug-outs. The 'Tyrones' bombed six dug-outs until all sounds of life below had ceased and they destroyed a machine gun. The 'Tyrones' had lost only one man killed and two wounded when they left the German trenches. However during the withdrawal they came under heavy machine gun fire as well as heavy German barrage fire. Peacocke and his men were forced to wait two hours in the sunken road while under fire and suffered a number of casualties. The raiding party felt that their artillery should have covered the German machine guns, which would have reduced their casualties. However the batteries were busy repelling the raid by RIR 99.

Shortly after midnight Metzmacher and his men returned to their lines with 26 prisoners. The prisoners consisted of 1 sergeant, 3 corporals, 3 lance corporals, and 16 privates of the 1st Dorsets, 1 sergeant of the 17th Northumberland Fusiliers and 2 privates from the 109th Brigade.

Von Fabeck questioned the prisoners who for the most part were candid about the damage and casualties caused by the bombardment and the raid. They did clear up one thing that had puzzled the Germans. Just before the raid German observers noted that the British lines were unusually quiet. They now knew that this was due to the preparations for the raid by the 9th Inniskillings. When von Fabeck questioned one of the sergeants, he 'desired not to consent to give information.'[26] The sergeant was praised by von Fabeck and was not questioned any further. The officers thought he made an excellent military impression.

Artillery fire continued until 2:30 a.m. when the situation returned to normal. Shephard gave an account of the aftermath of the raid:

> Our trenches were smashed up badly at a number of places. A Coy on my right had no casualties. C Coy on my left had several wounded in trenches, and nearly

1st Dorset prisoners and captors – RIR 99 – being interrogated by the division commander General von Soden. (Author's collection)

THE IMPENDING ATTACK APRIL – JUNE 1916   413

a platoon killed and wounded in support dug-outs in Johnson Post. I went down there at 4:30 A.M. There were 8 N.C.O.s and men in one dug-out killed by a high explosive shell. Several men were lying dead along the roadway, killed by machine gun fire. This platoon could neither get up to the firing line or get back by roadway so fierce was the enemy 'barrage of fire'. I went from the post through Buchanan Ave. to D Coy. Their firing line was in a terrible state, almost leveled to the ground; trees rooted up and flung across trenches, dug-outs blown to atoms. Most of the dead have been removed when I got there, but there were several men buried under the debris, some headless, others smashed like pulp.[27]

The men in the raiding party received the praise of the staff of RIR 99. They had carried out a successful raid, inflicted serious casualties on the enemy, and sustained minimal casualties in the process. When the roll was called after the raid they found two men had been wounded and one man was missing. The missing man had been killed; he was twenty-three year-old Johannes Herb, a *Pionier* in the 6/Pioneer Bn 13. The Germans estimated that the British had suffered 40-50 casualties in addition to the prisoners. The number was actually much higher, a total of 124 officers and men.

The Dorsets lost: 1 officer, 13 men killed; 1 officer, 30 men wounded; 2 men gassed; 6 men shell-shocked; 23 men missing. The 19th Lancashire Fusiliers lost: 1 officer, 31 men killed and wounded; the 10th Inniskillings lost 10 men. Of the 4 sergeants from the 17th Northumberland Fusiliers, 2 were wounded and 1, 17/158 Sergeant James Spencely, D Coy, was missing. The 2 privates from the 109th Brigade and Corporal Miller were members of the Machine Gun Corps.

RFAR 26 was praised by the division commander for supporting the raid and then almost instantly switching to defensive fire thanks to the alert artillery observers and by using the artillery survey plan. More than 10,000 shells were fired in the course of the

1st Dorset prisoners and captors – RIR 99. (Author's collection)

evening. Following the raid RIR 99 noted an increase in British attentiveness along the front, which made patrol activity more difficult.

The British also bombarded the sector held by RIR 109 in the first weeks of May with shells of every caliber. Shrapnel and trench mortar fire continued undiminished in the days following the raid. The level of fire concerned headquarters who fully expected another enemy raid. As a result the regiment was kept on alert up until 9 May when the fire diminished slightly.

The following day brought new concerns that another British raid was going to take place. British pilots flew low over the regimental sector many times during the morning hours and continued on and off the entire day. The British artillery held the right sector of the regiment under heavy fire, especially the 2nd and 3rd line as well as the communication trenches north of the hollow. However no attack took place.

RIR 109 decided to send out a patrol in the early morning hours of 12 May in order to determine exactly what the British were up to. At 2.15 a.m. *Vizefeldwebel* Pfister and seven men from the 2nd Coy advanced toward the British wire entanglements at the southern edge of the line designated as the *Marmorpalastes* (Marble Palace) in order to explore new obstacles and the purpose of a nearby sap.

Pfister and two men remained behind in a crater to act as support for the rest of the patrol and maintain contact with the company commander if necessary. At 3.05 the flank guard of the patrol reported seeing a small British patrol disappear into the hollow that led towards the village of La Boisselle.

Meanwhile *Unteroffizier* Franzischack had crawled to within 10 meters of the sap and observed a sentry standing guard. A short time later he heard the sounds of large detachments of men inside the trench followed by the sound of a patrol in front of the British wire.

A commotion arose on the left of the German patrol in the direction of the *Hoheneck*. A strong party of British soldiers could be seen climbing out of their trench. At first Franzischack thought they might be a wiring party until he observed them spread apart and lay flat on the ground.

At 3.55 a.m. four British mines were detonated near the German front and strong shellfire fell on the German trenches. The British patrol observed by Franzischack, some 60-70 men, rose up and advanced bent over toward the German trenches. Whenever a German sentry fired a light flare that illuminated the foreground the enemy soldiers would immediately lie down. Once the light from the flare had faded they continued to crawl closer to the barbed wire.

Patrol Pfister-Franzischack opened fire on the British raiding party, thus immediately alerting the German trench garrison. The artillery was notified and as a result of the flanking fire from the patrol and the bombardment the British raiding party was forced to retreat.

The patrol from RIR 109 returned to their trenches suffering only two casualties; *Ersatz Reservist* Roth who was reported missing and *Vizefeldwebel* Pfister who was killed by a shrapnel ball at the moment he was jumping from the parapet into the trench.

Once the men had returned *Leutnant* Risse observed ten red barrage flares launched by the British to his left. He hurried there with six men and joined two groups that had already opened fire upon the withdrawing British raiding party.

No man's land was searched after the front had become quiet and a number of steel helmets were recovered along with hand grenades, trench clubs, rifles and other equipment left behind by the British including two dead soldiers found close to the wire entanglements. Everything seemed to indicate a hasty withdrawal. It was thought that additional casualties were inflicted on them from the artillery fire but the men were unable to verify this assumption. The days following the raids were generally quiet on both sides of the line; however the British continued to maintain active artillery and trench mortar fire against the German lines.

The Germans maintained their vigilance along the entire front. On 15 May Lieutenant Mansel-Pleydell, the intelligence officer of the 1st Dorsets, went into No Man's Land and brought back some steel plates belonging to RIR 99. On 17 May Mansel-Pleydell and Captain Algeo went out into No Man's Land from Hammerhead Sap and entered the wooded area of the 'Park'. These were seen as attempts to raise the morale and offensive spirit of the men after their recent brushes with the Germans.

Witnesses saw the officers by the edge of the wood when Mansel-Pleydell was seen to beckon, and both officers ran into the wood. There was a commotion and Algeo was heard shouting, 'hands up, hands up, put it down'. A volley of rifle fire and revolver shots followed, then a scream, then silence.

Later, two sergeants, Goodwillie and Rogers, went out from Hammerhead Sap to investigate the fate of the missing officers. After entering the woods the sounds of revolver fire could be heard.

Rogers returned alone a half hour later. He reported they had found no signs of the officers and that Goodwillie had pressed on too quickly. Rogers heard a lot of voices and firing, and then returned to his own lines. Later in the day it was discovered that RIR 99 had placed a line of wire entanglements just inside the edge of the wood.

Algeo and Mansel-Pleydell had apparently been killed by a German patrol. Goodwillie stumbled onto the same patrol in his eagerness and was also shot down. RIR 99 brought the bodies of the officers and Sergeant Goodwillie back to their lines. They were buried in Courcelette with full military honors.[28]

Any chance of a successful defense against a raid depended upon how alert the sentries were. At 4.15 a.m. on the night of 14 May *Landsturmmann* Strobel, 11/R111, heard sounds by the wire entanglements in front of his trench near Fricourt. He noticed two dim shapes attempting to place some kind of mat over the wire and he sounded the alarm.

The garrison opened fire and drove off the shadowy figures. Once darkness had fallen a patrol was sent out to investigate. It was determined that a large force had been preparing to raid their trench when they were discovered. Pieces of equipment; rifles, helmets, rolled mats to cross the German wire were brought in along with the body of what was suspected to be the patrol leader. It was an officer who had been killed by rifle fire despite wearing steel armor. He was given a decent burial in the rear.[29] A telephone line was discovered that led back toward the British lines, which was destroyed.

May had been a busy month for patrols including those from RIR 119 north of the Ancre. Small clashes occurred frequently; 7 May: a hand grenade fight between patrols, 10 May, British prisoner taken, 18 May fierce patrol clashes in front of 7th Coy after which a dead British officer was brought in. On 19 May the regiment suffered the loss of a veteran patrol leader, *Vizefeldwebel* Lehmann.

Gefreiter Paul Selg 6/R110, taken near Fricourt. Selg was wounded
in action on 27 May 1916. (Author's collection)

On the night of 19 May Lehmann and two men went out on patrol and were ambushed by the British. Lehmann was killed by a pistol shot and his companions barely escaped being taken prisoner. When the 7th Coy sent out a larger patrol to recover the fallen leader they became embroiled in a fierce hand-to-hand fight with a large British patrol and was forced to return without the body.

On the following day the company put up a sign asking about the fate of Lehmann. When it was light the British answered that he had been buried and described the grave to them. Not long after another patrol from RIR 119 was sent out and tried to enter the sunken road but instead came across a large British patrol that occupied the position. The men returned and relayed the information to the I *Abteilung* RFAR 26 that fired on the sunken road and drove the British out.

Several smaller raids were attempted at the end of May including one by the 2/R121 that had disastrous results. The raiding party reported that it had come under friendly fire from shells fired from German batteries that were providing support fire. They suffered losses and were forced to return without completing the attack. Intercepted telephone messages afterward indicated that the British had suffered losses of several killed, 46 wounded and 2 men missing as a result of the artillery and trench mortar fire.

At the end of May RIR 110 made preparations for a large raid against the *Besenhecke* in the Bécourt Hollow. *Hauptmann* Wagener was again chosen as the leader of the raid.

This time 200 volunteers were called for and the men who volunteered were housed in Eaucourt-L'Abbaye.

The British position was reproduced at a practice work on the slope of the hill south of Eaucourt according to information obtained from aerial photographs. The men worked hard each day at the practice trenches until everyone knew his part of the raid by heart. The remainder of the time was spent relaxing and enjoying life in the small village. During the practice period arrangements were made in assembling the large force of artillery needed and to coordinate their efforts with the artillery, *minenwerfers* and machine guns using all of the experiences gained up until that time.

Two patrols from the 11/R110 were sent out in the night of 21/22 May to inspect the area of the *Besenhecke* in preparations for the raid. They reported that there were extraordinarily well-maintained belts of wire in front of the position. The obstacles consisted of two separate belts 5-8 meters wide each. The area between the two was filled with trip wires.

The patrol had to be cut short when two of the men were discovered in the second British trench and a hand grenade fight broke out. After a brief exchange of fire the patrol withdrew with 2 wounded. As a result of the clash the patrols reported that the *Besenhecke* appeared to be occupied and the main opposition line was the third trench. The raiders returned with a crate of hand grenades as proof that they had indeed entered the British lines. The date for the raid was set for 4 June.

The volunteers were divided into ten teams, each with a specific task. The raid would be supported by a total of 22 batteries of heavy and light guns. Access lanes were cut through the German wire in a zigzag pattern several days before and in the following night they were marked with white linen tape.

When the artillery preparation fire began all of the patrols would assemble at their appointed location in Bécourt Hollow that was marked by a red lantern shielded from enemy view. The lantern would be located with the lead patrol under *Feldwebel Leutnant* Aullen.

Immediately after the artillery fire had ended the lead patrol would advance at the double to reach the break-in position at the southern extension point of the projecting *Besenhecke*. The plan was to roll up the British trenches on both sides of this point and bring back as many prisoners as possible.

The sunken road that led past the tip of the *Besenhecke* toward the *Schwabenhöhe* would be the return route to the German lines. The area north, south and behind the target trenches would be kept under strong artillery and machine gun fire during the entire undertaking. The nearby *Nordrondell* would be kept under gas bombardment during the raid. The patrols did not bring along any gas masks so success depended upon the lead patrol finding the right path.

At 2.45 a.m. on 4 June the men took up their positions along the salient formed near the *Schwabenhöhe*. The night was pitch black; they could not see their hands in front of their faces.

The patrols left their dug-outs just as the first shells fell upon the British trenches. The night was so dark however the patrols could not locate the tape and the alleys cut through the wire. While the men were trying to locate their exit points British machine guns fired randomly along the German lines until they were silenced by the bombardment but not before wounding two men. One man had been severely wounded in the stomach and died several days later in a military hospital.

Some of the troops located the lanes and proceeded to exit the trenches while others simply forced their way through the wire, tearing their hands and shredding their uniforms in the process. Once the raiding parties reassembled they waited for the bombardment to end. The noise coming from hundreds of shells impacting on the British trench with the clatter of the machine guns was indescribable according to the men. The patrol leader had to shout his orders as loudly as possible directly into the ear of the neighboring man in order to be heard at all.

After 10 minutes of heavy fire the red lantern was waved to and fro, this was the signal for the advance. Wagener ordered each patrol forward into the darkness and the men started to run past at the double one by one with each man staying close to the person in front.

The raiders continued to run toward the British trenches far longer than they had expected. Suddenly they realized the 5th patrol had gone astray in the dark night and had shifted too far south.

The 5th Patrol and those following approached the British lines that were lit up in glaring brightness from the impacts of shells while machine gun bullets whizzed past them from the rear. They hesitated and the men in front kneeled down in the remnants of wire entanglements in order to become oriented.

The British trench was visible in the glow of the heavy fire and there was the odor of bitter almonds in the air; gas! The men had no doubt that they were lost and were actually in front of the *Nordrondell* that was under heavy artillery, gas and machine gun suppression fire. Without gas protection they realized they could not remain in this location but did not know what to do.

The leader of the patrol entered the trench and opened fire but the men would not follow him through the support fire. It was finally decided it was useless to carry the attack forward at the wrong location in unfamiliar trenches with German shells bursting all around them. It was in conflict with the original plan of attack. The connection to the rear had been broken and no new orders had arrived.

The men hesitated several moments longer until *Vizefeldwebel* Elb showed signs of being completely dazed by the gas and several men began to vomit and complain that their eyes burned. One of the officers shouted 'Everyone who can hear my command must go back with us.'[30]

The orders were repeated and the men began to retrace their steps in order to reach the German lines. The patrols used the flashes of the German guns to determine the direction of their trenches but decided against trying to pass in front of the *Besenhecke* because it had not been under fire for the last ten minutes and the garrison was probably intact and alert.

The withdrawal took place though Bécourt Hollow under German machine gun fire. Not everyone was able to follow the main body and several groups strayed off the path and had to find their own way back. Soon the lime white of the German trenches marked with wide belts of wire came into view. The returning men now came under British barrage fire that had started in response to the raid. They were sprayed with shrapnel fire and had to lie prone every few feet. Once the fire grew lighter the men rose up and forced their way through the obstacles once again between shrapnel shells and finally made their way into the German trenches but not before a number of men were hit.

The troops were reassembled and it was discovered that a large number of them had been wounded and five men were listed as missing.[31] It turned out that all of the patrols had become disoriented in the darkness and had failed to enter the British trenches at all. By dawn the survivors of the raiding party were returned to their quarters on wagons. There was a general feeling of dejection among the men for failing in their task.

The survivors reported to Wagener who advised the volunteers that a new plan was already being drawn up for another try at the *Besenhecke*. Corps Headquarters gave orders that the new raid would take place on the same day, later that night.

This raid would be a scaled-down version of the previous undertaking. Only 75 men would form the raiding party and there would only be 5 minutes of preparation fire using a fraction of the ammunition consumed in the previous attack.

A sortie gallery from the *Schwabenhöhe* was chosen as the starting point. The patrols would then move along the sunken road to the head of the *Besenhecke* where the first patrol would remain as support while the remainder would enter the British trenches at the break-in location designated for the previous raid.

The men were excited over the news and the gloomy mood disappeared. Everyone capable of taking part in the raid had volunteered to go. 'Everyone wanted to be part of the revenge match. The Englishmen should not get the wrong idea of the 110th.'[32]

The new instructions were passed out and in the evening the 75 volunteers entered the dug-outs on the *Schwabenhöhe* where they were given nothing stronger than soda water to drink. Each man stood ready, heavily armed with pistols, rifles, daggers and hand grenades.

At 10.55 p.m. the bombardment began and the ground shook beneath their feet. At 11 o'clock the men exited the dug-outs into the clear night with the sounds of clanking equipment. Suddenly there were shouts from the front, 'the howitzers are firing too short!' 'We have dead and wounded!'[33]

Funeral for fallen British soldier who died from his wounds after being taken prisoner in a raid dated 4 June 1916. (*Reserve-Infanterie Regiment Nr. 110 im Weltkrieg 1914-1918*)

The artillery liaison officer quickly corrected the fire by telephone and the raid continued:

> We reached the break-in position, my patrol, as the third had to clear the foremost trench from there to the head of the Besenhecke. I ran along above, *Unteroffizier* Blohm behind me, another in the trench and behind them. We shouted our battle cry as if possessed [however] that only betrays us and after a couple of steps we come across four, five chaps with flat helmets. I wanted to fire, at the same time I felt a strong blow against my right side, my raised arm sank down numb and I landed on the ground. The brave Blohm kneeled down next to me and fired at the Tommies. They now put their 'hands up' because in the meanwhile my men approached; there is no help for them anymore. *Unteroffizier* Blohm led the patrol further; I went back into the dug-out where my friend Petzold, the assistant surgeon, held office.[34]

The prisoners belonged to 34th Division that consisted almost entirely of Kitchener men, 'therefore well-trained Other Ranks'. The prisoners reported they were completely unnerved by the terrible fire of the last two operations that had also caused heavy losses. They made statements that their unit had practiced attacking but that they knew nothing of any pending attack.

The men appeared to be surprised by the good treatment they received from the Germans. On the following day several of them attended a funeral of one of their comrades who had died from his wounds. They were deeply moved by the solemnity of the occasion and the respect paid to the deceased by their foe.

Just a few days later it was the enemy's turn. At 1 a.m. on 6 June the right battalion sector of RIR 110 was under strong fire. The trenches between the *Ratten* and *Grenadierweg* were covered by trench mortar fire and shells up to 24cm in size that blocked off the surrounding areas.

The British fire was transferred to the rear on several occasions as if to deceive the defenders into thinking the attack was imminent however there was no sign of infantry. The 6/R110 commander and the sentries used these pauses to go out into the badly damaged trench and observe the British position.

Between 2 and 3 o'clock several British soldiers appeared in the German trenches during one of the pauses and began to throw hand grenades at the sentries as they exited their dug-outs. The trench became a scene of confusion and shouting men as hand grenades exploded, pistols and rifles were fired at close range and the men engaged in hand-to-hand fighting.

The raiders were slowly forced back by increasing numbers of defenders who were converging on the threatened trench. One man stood out for his actions that night, *Gefreiter* Müder. During the fighting he fired his last cartridge at close range and hurried into the mouth of a nearby dug-out in order to reload. The British came up to the entrance and demanded his surrender upon which he shouted 'no' and at the same time fired his rifle out of the entrance. The raiders then threw a hand grenade into the dug-out and wounded two men coming up to help Müder.

Once the raid had been repelled the men scanned the foreground but saw nothing in the darkness. A pioneer patrol was sent out on the following day and found that the British had abandoned a footbridge made of bamboo poles with canvas stretched between them, which they had used to cross the wire obstacles; it was still in good condition. RIR 110 suffered a loss of 2 dead, 3 slightly wounded and 5 men listed as gas sick. The latter had been inside a dug-out that received a direct hit from a 24cm shell. The local Moritz listening station reported that the British had suffered losses totaling 41 men as a result of the raid and the subsequent German artillery bombardment.

British patrol activity increased noticeably in the month of June with more reports coming in of men being spotted in front of the trenches. On the night of 3/4 June *Ersatz Reservist* Köhninger, 12/R109 shot and killed a man from the 2nd Yorks & Lancs close to the wire entanglements.

On the night of 3/4 June the British appeared to hold a rehearsal for the expected attack. The British artillery fired on the German lines from Serre to the Ancre for one hour followed by patrols at several locations. Every attempt was stopped by defensive artillery barrage fire and heavy infantry fire and was prevented from entering the German lines except for one patrol that did manage to penetrate the trenches of the 8/R119 for a brief time before being expelled.

Between 5.30 and 6.30 on the night of 5 June a 30 meter wide lane was opened in the wire entanglements near the *Krach* Sap by British trench mortar and artillery fire. The garrison was placed on alert and told to expect an attack at any time but nothing occurred. Then, at 1.05 a.m. on 6 June the positions between *Weisshuhn*, *Krach* and *Wittwer* Saps were taken under heavy fire and again an attack was expected. The garrison called for artillery support fire from the batteries in the rear but the British never came. The men assumed that the attack had been 'nipped in the bud' by the heavy defensive fire.

> Presently something is going on almost every night, either that the English make a raid or make one on the right or on the left of us. The artillery activity is also mentioned in the English reports … Geiger probably became wounded during the raid the English recently made. They succeeded in penetrating into the trench at one position. Karl Losch, 3/R119 [35]

A larger raid against the *Biber Graben* near the Ancre followed this shortly afterward on 6 June. The British destroyed the wire entanglements by using tubes of explosives (Bangalore torpedoes). Once inside the trench they threw hand grenades and explosive charges into the dug-outs. They were finally expelled without being able to take any prisoners. RIR 119 reported that British aggressiveness suddenly seemed to die down along their portion of the front after this last raid.

The lack of aggressive action did not apply to the men of RIR 119 however. On 10 June a patrol from the regiment set up an ambush in No Man's Land and attacked a four man British patrol. Two of the opponents were killed in the fighting, one of which was an officer. The third man was captured while the fourth man managed to escape. British reinforcements were driven off by fire from the German trenches while the patrol brought in their captives, alive and dead. The result of this night's work meant that the patrols from RIR 119 had brought back a total of eleven English officers, dead and alive, since August 1915.

Another raid attempted on 11 June near Hamel suffered the same fate as the patrol from RIR 121 in late May. The III/R119 advanced toward the British lines as planned until several short rounds from the German batteries fell among the men and the undertaking

Dr. Kallenberger

Stabsarzt d. 2. im Ref.-Feldart.-
Regt. 29, gefallen bei Pozières
am 5. Juni 1916

Stabsarzt der Landwehr Dr. Kalenberger RFAR 29. Killed near
Pozières 5 June 1916. (*Kriegstagbuch aus Schwaben*)

was called off. In the words of the division commander it was not unexpected and that losses from friendly fire had to be considered and could not be completely avoided.

The British had also raided the German lines on the same night, in the sector lying between Fricourt and Hill 110. Fortunately the raiding party was discovered by an alert sentry and driven off by rifle and machine gun fire. Later in the evening a patrol succeeded in recovering the body of a sergeant from the Royal Irish Rifles (12581 Sergeant J. Boyd, 8/Royal Irish Rifles).

Large quantities of ammunition including gas shells were consumed with every raid. Losses occurred to friend and foe alike and the positions suffered considerable damage. The frequency and size of the raids was starting to have a negative effect on the men and often unsettled the garrisons involved. Each action also increased tension for the leaders who needed to remain calm under very trying circumstances and still make sound decisions to meet every contingency.

By the latter half of June the divisions of the XIV Reserve Corps were as ready as they would be for the inevitable British offensive. The limited reserves placed at the disposal of the Corps meant that the coverage of the front line was not as strong as hoped for. The XIV Reserve Corps was responsible for a front that extended 45 kilometers from Gommecourt to Mametz and the troops at hand were barely enough to adequately garrison the trenches.[36]At the beginning of June the 26th Reserve Division held a front 11 kilometers long with 13 battalions of infantry.

The 1st Line of the 26th and 28th Reserve Divisions was improved and extended with feverish activity. The men worked on the 2nd and 3rd Line, especially the *Grallsburg* and *Schwaben* Redoubt as much as possible. The barrier across the Ancre valley was strengthened. New positions with switch lines and communication trenches were planned and completed in the shortest time possible. Two labor companies worked on the extension of the 2nd Line with the assistance of several battalions from the Bavarian RIR 8 and RIR 15 in the sector of the 26th Reserve Division. Numerous battery positions were completed for reinforcement batteries that were expected to arrive in the future. The Corps headquarters staff located in Bapaume made arrangements to transfer all Corps activities to Louverval, 12 kilometers northeast of Bapaume.

Each division had a small reserve, in the case of the 26th Reserve Division it consisted of the Reserve Dragoon Regiment and six recruit companies currently being trained for duty at the front. The Corps was provided with additional reserves that consisted of the 10th Bavarian Division as well as one regiment each from the 2nd Guard Reserve Division and the 12th Division. However the troops from these units could not be used to man the existing line and were kept in the rear where they were kept busy digging entrenchments.

The pioneers assigned to the 26th Reserve Division consisted of the 4th and 6/Pioneer Bn 13 as well as detachments from the Bavarian Pioneer Regiment. The 28th Reserve Division had the 1st and 2nd Reserve Companies of Pioneer Bn 13 plus additional pioneers from the Bavarian Pioneer Regiment.

The infantry battalions in the Corps had an average strength between 850 and 900 men each. The 28th Reserve Division received a welcome increase in firepower on 15 April when RIR 111 received a second machine gun company that was formed by combining Machine Gun Platoons 55 and 95.

Some regiments were fortunate in having more guns than called for in army regulations. RIR 99 holding the Thiepval Sector was one such regiment. Instead of the normal twelve guns plus two reserve guns distributed in two machine gun companies the regiment actually had 26 German heavy machine guns as well as one captured British and one captured Russian machine gun.

Now each infantry regiment had over two machine gun companies each. The normal allotment of machine guns had been supplemented along the front with the addition of 9 captured Russian guns and 12 Belgian guns. Fortress Machine Gun *Abteilung* Fasbender

4/Pioneer Bn 13. (Author's collection)

had recently arrived with 6 additional machine guns. Each division had the added firepower of one *Musketen* Battalion that was distributed along the front. At the start of the British attack the 26th Reserve Division would have a total of 90 heavy machine guns and 30 *Musketen*.[37]

The role played by the regimental machine guns had always been important in the past and would be a critical factor in the approaching attack. The troops manning the machine guns had been carefully trained and could be relied upon in any situation.

Each gun crew was responsible for keeping the machine gun in working order as well as maintaining the spare stores that included three extra barrels, water and oil. Each gun crew maintained an individual target and range card that would prove invaluable in the coming battle. The use of range cards, the 2½ power Goerz prismatic sight and the constant training made the machine gun crews formidable foes.

Each gun had a standard complement of six men, each one being capable of assuming the duties of any member of the team in case someone was placed out of action. Part of the training machine gunners went through included firing at targets at various ranges and one of the requirements was that each man was able to hit the target with the first rounds fired and not 'walk' the bullets to the target. Most of the machine gunners in the 26th and 28th Reserve Divisions had the advantage of being stationed in the same area for months at a time and therefore every target, every location within range of the gun was noted and registered accordingly.

The value of the machine gun rose with the reduction in use of the artillery. Machine guns were used to harass the enemy working on the wire entanglements or bringing up stores. Guns would often be moved to a temporary location at night where they would open fire on a particular target without giving their original position away.

Ready for action – Machine Gun Company IR 180. (Author's collection)

The relief of enemy troops often brought down machine gun fire. Much of this was due to the careless manner in which the British troops behaved, who talked and made a great deal of other noise.

Indirect fire was used as often as possible. Known communication trench positions, tracks and other targets that were out of direct view were plotted and came under bursts of machine gun fire in the hope of causing losses.

Each regimental machine gun officer had been given the responsibility of finding the best sites for their guns in order to provide the greatest firepower against enemy infantry. Each gun was also given alternate sites in the event they were needed during an attack.

Every available gun would be needed in the defense of the German lines. *Hauptmann* Wagener of RIR 110 was placed in charge of the machine guns in the regiment as well as the guns from *Landwehr Brigade Ersatz* Bn 55. He diligently searched for positions that would provide the greatest flanking field of fire against enemy infantry.

The regimental machine gun officers had known that placing machine guns in the 1st trench of the 1st Line Position was not a good idea. The guns were often damaged or destroyed by enemy fire and in some cases overrun and captured before their firepower could be put to good use. Despite this general rule some guns were still positioned in the front line trench if the situation called for it.

All of the lessons learned from fighting on the Somme as well as those brought back primarily by RIR 99 from experiences obtained on the Arras front enabled the XIV Reserve Corps to provide guidelines on the use of machine guns on the Corps front:

18. **Machine Guns.** When the ground permits the use of machine guns being employed on commanding points in the 2nd and 3rd Trenches, with a view to firing over the 1st Trench, every advantage should be taken of it. It is advisable to employ the bulk of the machine guns not in, but behind the 1st Trench. When fixing their site, the possibility of delivering both frontal and flanking fire must not be forgotten.

Used as an emergency garrison for the Intermediate or 2nd Line Position, they may prevent a break through if the enemy succeeds in overrunning the 1st Line Position.

Machine gun units are particularly suitable for employment as a commander's mobile reserve.[38]

Corps orders called for each regiment to maintain an adequate ammunition supply for each machine gun. The ideal amount was considered to be 5,000 rounds in belts and 5,000 rounds loose in reserve for each gun.

The cumbersome *minenwerfers* would still be a valuable asset in the event of an attack and every effort was to be made to ensure their safety and proper use. In the event an attack was considered imminent the *minenwerfer* would be removed from the 1st trench of the 1st Line Position and placed in prepared positions in the 2nd and 3rd trenches of the 1st Line. The light 7.6cm *minenwerfers* were placed where their full range and mobility could be used. They were to bring fire down on any location where the enemy could be expected to concentrate, which should be flanking fire whenever possible.

Ammunition would be a critical component in any attack, especially if the defending regiments had insufficient stocks available. The XIV Reserve Corps sent out orders that all small arms ammunition stocks must be kept full at all times. Each infantryman would

Medium *minenwerfer* ready to fire – XIV Reserve Corps. (*Die 26. Reserve Division 1914-1918*)

carry the normal 150 rounds of ammunition in his cartridge boxes while at the same time an additional 150 rounds per man would be available in each battalion sector. In the case of RIR 99 the total number of rounds available at the front at the time of the British assault was 1,500,000, more than adequate to provide a solid defense for several days, possibly more if supplies could not be brought forward. An adequate supply of hand grenades was also an issue addressed by the Corps:

> **20. Hand grenades.** Training in grenade fighting will be carried to the point of thoroughly instructing all officers, N.C.O.'s and men of the infantry and pioneers, *minenwerfer* companies, searchlight sections, gunners and observers of the field and foot artillery, as well as those detachments of cavalry which take their turn in the trenches, and the field companies of ammunition columns and trains. Officers and N.C.O.'s must, in addition, know how hand grenades should be tested and stored. Our hand grenades are not weather-proof and in this respect their design leaves much to be desired. When storing them, particular stress must therefore be laid on protection against wet. Corps H.Q. will endeavor to maintain the stocks of hand grenades with the units of the Reserve Corps on the scale:[39]

Infantry Regiment	8,000
Ind. Infantry Battalions (including IV/R99)	3,000
Pioneer Coy	750
Battery	50
Division Reserve	8,000

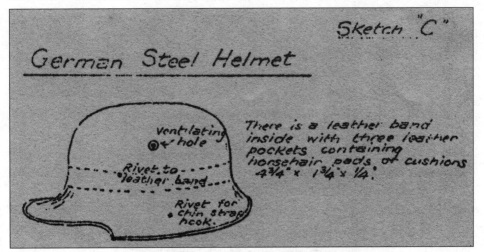

Sketch of new German steel helmet encountered in raid on 5
June 1916 by British III Corps. (PRO W0157/171)

Corps Reserve	80,000

A piece of equipment was being slowly introduced at this time that would change the look of the German soldier. Several regiments had received the newest piece of field equipment, the steel helmet. Supplies of the new helmet were still quite low so for the time being they were only issued to sentries in order to reduce the number of head wounds being suffered. It would take time before all of the men could be issued a steel helmet and it would take time for the men to become accustomed to the different shape and weight of the new equipment. Some men wanted to test the helmets and see how bulletproof they really were:

When they took the pickelhaube from us and gave us the steel helmet, we didn't believe you could shoot through that thing. We took one and hooked it up on a (pig) tail by the wire. I took my rifle (and fired) and the bullet went through it but it was sticking in the leather inside, hanging on the pad. They had a special plate that could be put over (the helmet) when I was on *Posten*, but I took it off.

So we had to account for that. We brought (the helmet) back and they said,' How did it get that hole?' I said, 'We don't know. It was just laying there and there was a shot.' They wrote in their report, 'Unexplained.' Emil Goebelbecker, 9/R109.[40]

The Army High Command received word in early June that a large British/French attack was expected in the foreseeable future. The information was based upon the numerous intelligence reports received by the General Staff from many sources including the foreign press. The reports were passed along to the different commands on the Second Army front along the Somme but it was not new information. It only confirmed what the men had already assumed from watching the enemy build-up. The only question left was when would the attack begin?

All activities related to repairing and improving the lines were accelerated as much as possible given the exhausting pace of work the men were currently under. The troops

Machine gun position near Ovillers – RIR 109. (*Das Reserve-Infanterie-Regiment Nr. 109 im Weltkrieg 1914 bis 1918*)

were already being worked to the limit of their abilities in order to be ready to meet the inevitable attack. The 28th Reserve Division headquarters issued orders to all units that they should continue to develop the position as strongly as they could in order to withstand an attack with new forces constantly being introduced for a period of one week.

Many of the units took the warning in earnest and in the last few weeks before the attack drilled new wells, created additional medical dug-outs. Ammunition depots and provision warehouses were created and ammunition, surgical bandages, durable provisions and mineral water were laid down in large quantities. The trenches and defensive positions required a great deal of repairs as a result of daily British fire and every available man was put to work. In early June the sectors assigned to the regiments of the 28th Reserve Division were shifted once again to meet the expected attack and each regiment was placed into a new part of the front.

In the middle of June RIR 109 was relieved from Ovillers and sent to occupy the line Carnoy – Montauban road – Bernafay – Trones – Longueval – Sugar Factory – Ginchy-Lesboeufs that was formerly occupied by RIR 110. The men of RIR 109 were quite frustrated at handing over the Ovillers sector to another regiment after having done considerable work in improving the position.

One officer felt that a position is like a dwelling; that everyone decorates to their own taste when they move in. One rumor circulating at the time was that the regiment was moved to the new location as punishment because their officers had constructed a new mess at Le Sars without receiving official approval.

They were even more upset when they occupied the new sector. They came to the conclusion that the sector had not been involved in any serious fighting such as they had

Keeping weapons in good order – IR 180. (*Das 10.Württembergische Infanterie-Regiment Nr. 180 im Weltkrieg 1914-1918*)

experienced at Ovillers and La Boisselle. The new line was not ready to meet an enemy offensive. There was a considerable lack of telephone lines and equipment throughout the sector. The right battalion sector only had one telephone wire leading to one company. There were no iron rations or ammunition depots in the front lines. The wire was inadequate and the number and depth of the dug-outs left much to be desired and was not considered fit to resist artillery fire.

Evidently the previous occupants had not paid any attention to the orders and directives issued from Corps headquarters in the past few months. Work was started immediately to improve the position but it was felt that given all indications they would not have enough time to make any significant improvements before the big attack came.

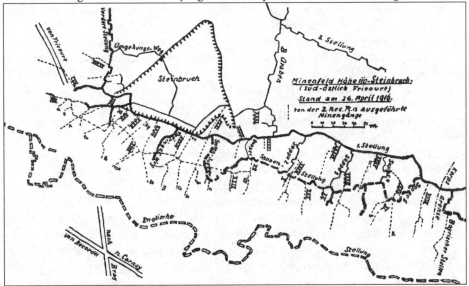

Minefield, Hill 110.

On the other hand RIR 110 was quite pleased with the conditions found in the La Boisselle sector. While the regiment felt the sector did require a little more work the majority of the time was spent on making repairs caused by the daily bombardments. The field railway line between Pozières and the regimental crater that was currently under construction was diligently worked on so that it could be put to use at the earliest possible time.

There were numerous indications that the British were planning a massive mine against the *Schwabenhöhe* and had driven a gallery to within 50 meters of the foremost German trench. Listening posts reported hearing definite sounds of mining within 10 meters of the *Blinddarm*. The sap was immediately evacuated and only occupied by sentries and occasional patrols.

All of these findings spurred the men on to complete their work even faster. In an attempt to counter the British mines the 28th Reserve Division ordered the pioneers and 70 men from *Landwehr Brigade Ersatz* Bn 55 to expedite the completion of three mine tunnels to be used against the British.

Large sandbag barricades appeared on the British side of Hill 110 and it was thought they concealed new mine tunnels. Every means possible was used to destroy these potential threats. Several different types of mortars were used to shell the sandbag walls but the British persisted and made good use of numerous trench mortar and artillery fire to counter the German actions.

Overall the German machine guns, close range weapons and artillery made the enemy's life as miserable as possible as often as possible. Any damage that could be inflicted upon the British might prove valuable in the battle that was fast approaching. In May a German shell struck into the ruins of the Fricourt railway station that resulted in an enormous secondary explosion. It was assumed that it was either a hand grenade or ammunition depot.

Perhaps one of the most telling signs of the approaching attack were the numerous reports that the British were not repairing their wire entanglements, which were in part badly damaged and in some areas almost obliterated. The division headquarters immediately ordered reinforcement artillery batteries to take up position nearby.

The British apprenticeship was a thing of the past. Their behavior was more systematic, the infantry and artillery actions were more coordinated, there were numerous planes in the air and there was little the XIV Reserve Corps could do about it.

One British pilot circled above the trenches of RIR 110 for nearly an hour and fired numerous times into the trenches near the *Granathof* before flying off. RIR 109 reported that between 18 and 23 June British artillery fired daily against the railway station hollow, Mametz, communication trenches, the *Staubwassergraben, Jaminwerk*. Montauban had to be abandoned at times because of the fierce fire but it was still not considered to fall into the category of systematic destructive fire.

The British artillery fire took on the characteristics of 'drumfire' or a continual barrage more and more and in some cases leveled a section of the front. The guns started to fire with precision, especially on the crossroads, the *Parkweg* near the Fricourt Château, the *Trockengraben* and the Doctor's House and this greatly impeded all movement. The *Trockengraben* had to be closed at times and when the repair work was started it was destroyed once again by batteries being directed by aerial observation. Low-flying aircraft

Group of non-commissioned officers, June 1916 – RIR 111. (Author's collection)

fired machine guns at trench sentries and fatigue parties disrupting work on many parts of the line.

The number of British observation balloons along the horizon began to increase rapidly. Rest areas in the rear such as Bazentin-le-Petit, Flers, and Martinpuich were regularly being shelled by long-range guns. Aircraft were also used to register much of the long-range fire such as on the evening of 23 June when one directed heavy fire into Longueval. Fortunately the damage was not serious and casualties were light.

Listening posts were being slowly destroyed along the front whenever the British identified one. Listening Post No. 2 in the right battalion sector of RIR 109 must have presented a particular threat to the enemy as it was completely buried and destroyed by artillery fire. In the days following several nearby listening posts suffered similar fates.

IR 180 returned to the line in early June and occupied the Ovillers Sector formerly held by RIR 109. The regiment felt that the 109th had done a good job in developing the sector but there were urgent improvements needed.

The wire obstacles were not considered to be sufficient in size and depth and work was started immediately to reinforce them. Additional dug-outs were installed across the entire sector to provide secure housing for the trench garrison. New communication trenches were constructed in order to provide easier access to the front line. New phone lines were installed in each company sector to ensure undisrupted communication to the rear.

The largest project undertaken by IR 180 was the construction of a new regimental battle headquarters. The existing one was located in a rather deeply mined dug-out. However the dug-out was very close behind the 3rd trench and in the extreme left wing of the sector. It was not considered a favorable location due to the proximity to the 1st trench as well as the poor observation it had over the other sectors of the regiment.

A new battle headquarters was started immediately located on both sides of the *Stockacher Graben*, approximately 250 meters south of the Pozières-Thiepval road. Another important project was the construction of an intermediate position running from Pozières to Mouquet Farm. This was the responsibility of a labor detachment of the II/180. Work on the new battle headquarters was often disrupted by British fire but was soon completed. Both sides of the facility connected to the *Stichgräben*, each had two stairway tunnels leading down to the headquarters however there was no mutual connection between the sections underground.

By the last week of the month it became obvious to all that the attack was imminent. RIR 121 received orders to occupy the positions in depth. Special reserves for counterattacks were established. Rest battalions were moved forward to *Feste Soden* and the *Grallsburg*.

On 23 June the situation had become so acute that the 26th Reserve Division ordered all regimental and brigade commanders to occupy their battle headquarters. Division headquarters was located in the Biefvillers Château. A chalk cave located in the courtyard had been expanded and put to use as a shelter and housing area where the division staff could remain safe from British fire.

General von Auwärter occupied his battle headquarters in *Feste Zollern* on Hill 153 west of Courcelette. General von Wundt immediately moved into his battle headquarters in the *Alte-Garde Stellung* west of Beauregard Farm. The regimental staff of IR 180 moved into the new battle headquarters on 23 June. It was a peaceful and restful day because there was almost no enemy activity. At 11 p.m. IR 180 decided to move the regimental reserves closer and ordered the 6/180 from Le Sars to occupy dug-outs in the *Quergraben* II between the *Folkersamb* Sap and the *Konstanzer Graben*.

Von Soden visited the front on 23 June, the last time before the attack and during his stop in the Thiepval Sector he spoke to Major von Fabeck. He wished the men 'good luck in the approaching battle of life and death'.[41] Von Fabeck reported that the two underground complexes started by RIR 99 under Mouquet Farm and by St. Pierre-Divion in early April had been completed that morning. At 9 a.m. von Fabeck and his staff moved into their new quarters; now it was only a matter of waiting.

Chapter notes

1. Losch, *Feldpost* letters from 14 April 1916, 22 April 1916 and 4 May 1916.
2. P. Müller, *Geschichte des Reserve-Infanterie-Regiment Nr. 99*, p. 89.
3. Baumgartner, (Ed.), 'An der Somme, An interview with Soldat Emil Goebelbecker', *Der Angriff, A Journal of World War 1 History*, No. 3, p. 5.
4. The Principles in Trench Warfare as laid down in the XIV Reserve Corps, 19th May 1916. Document S.S. 490, Ia/13590.
5. The Principles in Trench Warfare, op. cit., p. 4.
6. The Principles in Trench Warfare, op. cit., pp. 4-5.
7. E. Moos, *Das Württembergische Res.-Feld-Artillerie Regiment Nr. 27 im Weltkrieg 1916-1918*, p. 2.
8. The 1st Battery position 731/765 southwest of Courcelette, 2nd Battery position 730 southwest of Courcelette, 3rd Battery position 709/711 west of Miraumont at the mill ruins, 4th Battery position 732 southwest of Courcelette, 5th Battery position 745 northern edge of Pozières and the 6th Battery position 708 at the mill ruins west of Miraumont.
9. Case shot was a shell filled with lead balls as in a shrapnel shell and had a fuze that was almost instantaneous. The gun in effect would become a large shotgun and quite effective against infantry in the open.

10. The Principles in Trench Warfare, op. cit., p. 7.
11. The Principles in Trench Warfare, op. cit., p. 8.
12. C.T. Atkinson, *The History of the South Wales Borderers 1914-1918,* p. 220.
13. Ibid.
14. Württemberg *Verlustlisten* No. 377, 3 May 1916, p. 12, 305.
15. J. Taylor, *The 1st Royal Irish Rifles in the Great War,* p. 71.
16. There are no records of the names of the prisoners and why the German report shows one man more than the British reports.
17. Taylor, op. cit., p. 72.
18. Greiner, *Reserve-Infanterie-Regiment Nr. 110 im Weltkrieg 1914-1918,* p. 111.
19. Losch, *Feldpost* letter 4 May 1916.
20. E. Shephard, Unpublished Diary, entry dated 'Sunday, 7th'.
21. Ibid.
22. PRO WO95/2389 1st Dorset Report to C.O. 14th Brigade.
23. Shephard, op. cit., entry dated 'Sunday, 7th'.
24. Shephard, op. cit., entry dated 'Monday, 8th'.
25. *The Londonderry Sentinel,* 20 May 1916, 'Derry Volunteer prefers Death to Yielding'.
26. P. Müller, *Geschichte des Reserve-Infanterie-Regiment Nr. 99,* p. 94.
27. Shephard: op. cit., entry dated 'Monday, 8th'.
28. Confirmation of the death of Captain Algeo and Lieutenant Mansel-Pleydell came to the regiment on 25 June. Copies of their identity discs and reports of their death were sent to the War Office through the U.S. Embassy. Sgt. Goodwillie is buried in the Miraumont Commonwealth Cemetery.
29. It is believed that the officer was 2nd Lieutenant Roger Vernon, 8th Somerset Light Infantry, age 23, reported as Killed in Action 14 May 1916, buried in Cabaret Rouge Military Cemetery, Souchez, France. Grave No. XXX A 38. Son of the Rev. F.W. Vernon, sometime Vicar of Rangeworthy, Glos., and Edith S.H. Vernon, of Weatheroak, Alvechurch, Birmingham.
30. Greiner, op. cit., p. 114.
31. One of the missing men, Reservist Robert Kirchstetter, 3/R110, was captured on the night of the raid. He was interrogated by Captain W.W.T. Tork, General Staff, III Corps: His interrogation was thorough and a great deal of information was obtained regarding RIR 110 as well as details on the raid, composition of the companies, officers, machine guns, systems of relief, location of dumps, water and food supplies and method of holding the line. Kirchstetter claimed that most of the dug-outs were connected with one another so that it is possible to get along the whole battalion front underground and that the dug-outs often have 6 meters of earth on top of them. He also advised that they have been frequently warned during the last month to hold themselves in readiness to repel an attack from the British. Much of the information obtained from Kirchstetter confirmed the evidence of another prisoner, George Roth, RIR 109.
32. Greiner, op. cit., p. 114.
33. Ibid.
34. Greiner: op. cit., p. 114.
35. Losch, *Feldpost* letters 6 June 1916 & 13 June 1916.

36. The XIV Reserve Corps consisted of the 2nd Guard Reserve Division, 52nd Division, 26th Reserve Division and 28th Reserve Division. For the sake of this account only the two original divisions were used: the 26th and 28th Reserve Divisions.

37. *Musketen*: The Danish Madsen Light machine Gun, top-fed 25-round magazine. The gun was air cooled and utilized a bipod support. They were usually paired together and fired alternately so one gun did not become overheated.

38. The Principles in Trench Warfare, op. cit., p. 5.

39. Ibid, pp. 5-6.

40. R. Baumgartner (Ed.), 'An der Somme, An interview with Soldat Emil Goebelbecker', *Der Angriff, A Journal of World War 1 History*, No. 3, p. 5.

41. Müller, op. cit., p. 97.

11

Bombardment

Day 1: Saturday, 24 June 1916

Just as the sun was about to rise on a new day there was a thunderous sound as hundreds of artillery pieces opened fire on the German lines from Gommecourt in the north to Vermandovillers in the south. To the Germans in the XIV Reserve Corps it seemed as if every British artillery piece – from field guns to 38cm howitzers – were ranged on their small section of trench.

At first the bombardment was considered by many officers in the Corps simply to be a fire raid and it would soon pass. However, when the barrage continued throughout the morning hours and into the afternoon it soon became generally accepted that this was the preparation for a full-scale attack. The uncertainty regarding the date of the British/French offensive was over; the Battle of the Somme had begun.

The firing soon took on a pattern with shrapnel and trench mortar fire falling on the frontline trenches and adjoining communication trenches. The heavier shells fell along the rear areas near villages, division and Corps headquarters. The fire was heavy at times and often reached a crescendo before dying down. Windows rattled and doors were twisted off their hinges in even the furthest rear areas of the Corps sector.

Some frontline companies reported receiving between 150 and 300 trench mortar bombs on the first day of the bombardment. Most shrapnel fire was ineffective and caused little damage to the trenches and very few casualties among the men. The trench mortar fire however was having an effect on the position by destroying earthworks, tearing apart wire entanglements and causing an occasional casualty among the sentries who were standing at their posts. Once the heavy fire had started the German garrison took shelter in the deep dug-outs that existed along the front.

The front held by the XIV Reserve Corps was a model defensive position. Every advantage was used during the construction of the trench lines; every fold in the ground and every commanding point had been utilized to the utmost. Particular attention had been paid to the selection of the command posts for the regiments. The command positions of the sub-sector commanders, the battalion leaders, lay mostly in the 2nd or 3rd trench of the 1st Line Position in deep mined dug-outs that were well-equipped with a telephone network. The sector commanders, the regimental leaders, were positioned behind the 1st Line Position and the brigade command areas behind them. Similar steps had been taken with the artillery commanders and sub-group commands.

Each command post was connected to the companies in the front lines as well as to the rear and neighboring units through an immense network of telephone lines. In the event the telephone lines failed there were numerous backup systems including carrier pigeons, messenger dogs, alarm bells, wireless transmitters, runners and flag and light signaling stations.

Comfortable deep mined dug-outs withstood most of the week-long
bombardment – RIR 99. (*Geschichte des Reserve-Infanterie-Regiment Nr. 99*)

Many sentries used a system that employed mirrors, which allowed the men to stand
in the relative safety of the trench or dug-out entrance and observe the British. Wilhelm
Lange, RIR 99:

> Behind our trench we had a mirror mounted on a post so that we could see over No
> Man's Land. During the bombardment we had one sentry on duty in the trench at
> all times watching the mirror. The ground was shaking as though the end of the
> world was coming, and the mirror was quivering but it never broke.[1]

Unteroffizier Hinkel, 7/R99 also made use of a mirror to watch the British:

> It was a wonderful way to make observations of the enemy trenches from the stairs
> of the smashed entrances to our dug-outs despite the violent fire on our position.[2]

Certain areas of the front were subject to bombardment with heavy shells. The British
had obviously located and targeted key points along the German front, in particular
battalion and regimental command posts.

One battalion dug-out in the *Sigelgraben* in RIR 110 came under fire at 6 a.m. from
heavy shells and the men reported seeing fountains of earth as high as a house accompanied
by huge detonations. The same regiment also reported that the battle headquarters was
under fire from at least three batteries of 24cm guns and one battery of 28cm guns, the
ground literally shook under the massive impacts.

Even the best-prepared positions could not withstand the ferocity of the bombardment.
The roof of regimental battle headquarters of RIR 121 received a direct hit from a heavy
shell and was severely damaged despite being constructed out of steel reinforced concrete.

Numerous aircraft flew low over the positions that were observing the heavy fire and
in many instances directing and making corrections as needed. The XIV Reserve Corps
was helpless in preventing this. There were too few German planes available to counter
the problem and the anti-aircraft gunners, few as there were, had to seek cover from the
clouds of shrapnel balls and earth-rending detonations of high explosive shells.

Well-protected battalion headquarters – I/R99. (*Geschichte des Reserve-Infanterie-Regiment Nr. 99*)

Heavy damage to the regimental battle headquarters RIR 121. (*Die 26. Reserve Division 1914-1918*)

Medium and heavy caliber duds. (Author's collection)

The artillery batteries of the two divisions reacted quite differently to the bombardment. This difference would have a major impact on the outcome of the fighting when the infantry attack finally took place.

The guns with the 26th Reserve Division had been under strict orders for some time to conserve ammunition in anticipation of the expected offensive. The batteries had also been withholding fire for a considerable period of time in order to prevent the British from locating their positions. This was especially true at night when the muzzle flashes could give the position away.

Still, the guns of the division were not completely silent during the opening phase of the bombardment. The forward artillery observers manned their observation posts despite the heavy fire and stayed in contact with the batteries as long as the telephone lines remained intact. When the lines were broken, which was often, runners and flag signals were used to transmit reports to the battery commanders while telephone repair squads ventured out in the heavy fire in order to mend the line.

Artillery fire was directed against British targets where troop concentrations could be seen. The observers also still called for fire whenever possible when an annoying trench mortar was located.

The German artillery positions would naturally be a priority target for many of the British guns on the 24th. However the situation differed greatly depending upon the part of the line being looked at. The men of RFAR 26 watched as shells burst all around the

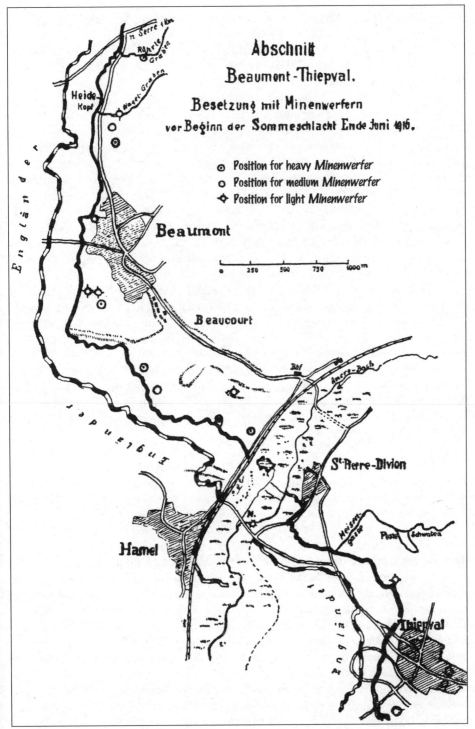

Minenwerfer positions, 26th Reserve Division.

gun positions sending up huge clouds of smoke and fumes while shrapnel clouds appeared almost everywhere in the blue sky above.

Large caliber shells burst in front of and behind the guns while the area in between was covered with 12cm shells. Damage to the positions and equipment was very light despite the immense number and size of shells being used.

Fortunately for the defenders many of the heavier shells were duds and failed to explode on impact. A popular photograph sent home at this time was the immense size of many of these shells. The cause apparently lay in the fuzes either from faulty manufacturing or corrosion damage from the long sea voyage from the United States. In any case this undoubtedly aided the German soldier by reducing the overall effect of the bombardment.

However with the large volume of shells being fired it was not long before some damage did occur. Individual gun positions in Beaucourt Hollow (Sub-Group Adolf) and near the ruined mill (Sub-Group Beauregard) received direct hits and the positions caught fire and were burned out resulting in a total loss of the emplacement and any equipment it contained. Guns from the 4th and 5th Batteries in the *Stumpweg* were literally hurled out of the position onto the road. Thanks to the well-developed gun emplacements the dug-outs holding the men and ammunition were still intact.

The battery positions of RFAR 27 also watched the heavy British fire fall nearby but for some reason the gun positions and artillery billets remained free from any shelling. The guns of RFAR 27 also responded to the British fire in a limited manner as the orders to restrict fire were still in place. The batteries applied short bursts of fire on the British lines, especially on rear trenches as well as on Thiepval Wood, Aveluy Wood and Authuille Wood.

The guns of the neighboring 28th Reserve Division were being subjected to artillery fire but the majority of the shells seemed to be directed towards the infantry positions. The officers of RFAR 28 did not think much of the bombardment at first and stuck to their normal routine that included holding a gas mask inspection in the gas chamber in Pozières that was scheduled for 6 a.m.

Reinforcement batteries continued to arrive in the Corps area when the British bombardment began. One battery, the 7/RFAR 12, had been traveling toward the Somme most of the night. By the time it had reached Martinpuich the men had already traveled 20 kilometers. Unfortunately the sun had also risen and the battery was in danger of being observed by the numerous British aircraft flying overhead.

The commander of the regiment, *Oberst* Pawlowski, requested permission to wait until dark before attempting to place the guns in the battery position located near Contalmaison. His request was turned down and the guns were ordered forward in full light.

The guns were directed to their new position under the guidance of men from the 6/RFAR 28. The teams were driven up as if it was still peacetime and the guns were put into position, all the time under direct aerial observation but without any interference. The 7/RFAR 12 began to register the guns with the assistance of the 6/RFAR 28 when both batteries came under heavy fire from large caliber shells. The counter-battery fire lasted for some time and at the end of the bombardment one gun from the 7/RFAR 28 had been rendered unserviceable while another gun was damaged. The two damaged guns were removed and the registration fire continued for the remaining pieces.

Artillery fire against the northern part of the 26th Reserve Division between the Ancre and Serre did not start until 7 a.m. The soldiers of RIR 119 positioned near Beaumont and the *Leiling Schlucht* had just gotten their coffee at the kitchens in the early morning

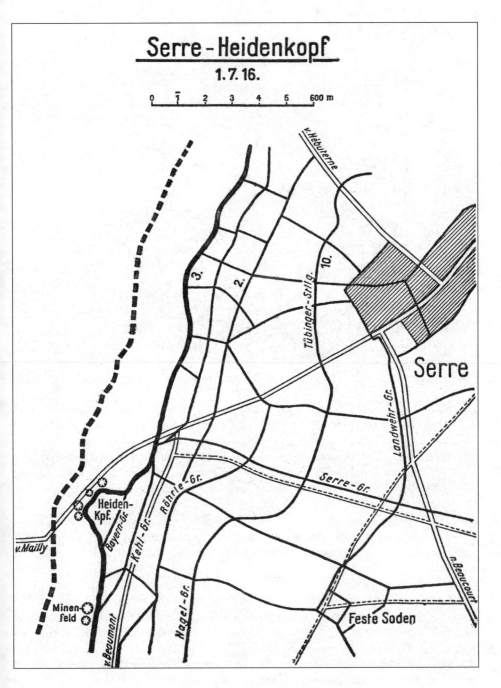

Serre-*Heidenkopf* sector.

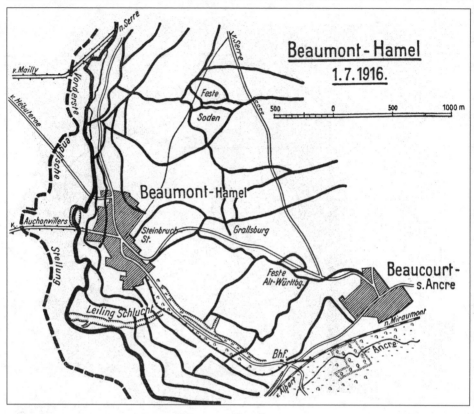

Beaumont-Hamel sector.

light, it promised to be a warm, sunny day. The men were heading to work on mining in the position when the bombardment started. At first it only consisted of light shells and shrapnel directed against the front lines.

White shrapnel shell clouds filled the blue sky and the hail of lead balls whistled through the air shredding the foliage off of the trees and striking the remnants of the village buildings. The shelling continued throughout the day but caused little damage to the position and virtually no losses to the regiment.

> There could be no doubt that the big attack that had been expected for a long time would now follow. It was actually a relief when one finally knew that it was going to happen.[3]

Once it had become evident that this was the start of the offensive and not simply a large fire raid the contingency plans were immediately placed into action. The baggage and light columns were redeployed further to the rear; additional ammunition, food and water reserves needed to be laid down in the front line so the men would not have to resort to eating their iron rations. The Intermediate and Second lines were occupied by recruit and labor companies as security garrisons. Commanders were appointed for the intermediate positions and a new switch line was started behind *Feste Schwaben*. The

The village of Beaumont, heavily damaged by the
bombardment. (*Die 26. Reserve Division 1914-1918*)

regiments issued orders for alarm and battle preparedness to the companies and battalions
under their command. The entire German line was manned and ready for action by 2 p.m.

One Grenadier in RIR 109 reacted in a rather odd manner to the opening
bombardment:

> When the British shelling started, one of our Grenadiers put on his best uniform,
> went to the company commander and asked indignantly, 'Who has started this silly
> shelling? In God's name, someone is going to get hurt'.[4]

Mametz railway station. The trench running across the center is the *Zeppelin Graben*,
the village of Mametz is located at the upper right. (Author's collection)

Hauptmann von Neuenstein with officers and men visiting the trenches near Ovillers
– RIR 111. (*Das Reserve-Infanterie-Regiment Nr. 111 im Weltkrieg 1914 bis 1918*)

A problem facing all of the regiments of the XIV Reserve Corps was the disruption to their communications as many of the well-placed telephone lines were damaged. The initial bombardment had cut most but not all of the lines leading toward the front. This required the telephone repair units to continuously go out into the heavy fire to restore service. It seemed that as fast as one line was repaired another was torn apart by a shell. Numerous telephone repair troops were killed or wounded as they worked in the open at the height of the bombardment.

In some areas the telephone lines remained intact despite the heavy fire. The main telephone line from La Boisselle to the rear as well as to the Moritz listening station located deep under the ground in front of the village designated 'Moritz 28 North' continued to work throughout the day. Shellfire had already damaged or destroyed most of the telephone lines in the sector occupied by IR 180 before 24 June. However many of the lines running from RIR 99 battle headquarters under Mouquet Farm to the rear as well as to the neighboring IR 180 were intact and that enabled the commanders to report on the conditions of their sectors and call for artillery support fire if needed. Adjutant Dall and his telephone operators had been receiving and transmitting up to 1,000 calls per day that allowed them to control the flow of reinforcements, ammunition, supplies and artillery fire.

It was time to make final preparations to meet the attack. Bavarian RIR 8 was moved to Pys, Irles and Warlencourt to support the 26th Reserve Division. The men could still only be used as laborers and it was not yet time to put them closer to the front. The 1st *Musketen* Bn was moved forward in the event its services were required.

The fire lasted throughout the morning and into the afternoon with varying strength but never coming to a complete stop. It was described as being a continuous rolling,

The badly damaged mill near Beaucourt. (*Die 26. Reserve Division 1914-1918*)

cracking and rumbling where every now and then a heavy shell could be heard striking nearby from among the general commotion.

The shelling continued in varying strength until 6 p.m. when the level surged and the full force of 'drumfire' returned. At 8 p.m. it suddenly dropped off dramatically and stopped in some areas altogether. The lull in shelling was seen as a perfect time to bring up much needed supplies of food, water, construction materials and ammunition.

At 10 p.m. the British guns opened fire once again but this time most of the fire fell on the rear areas, approach routes, villages and roads while the front lines received only light shrapnel fire.

Most approach routes were covered with a wall of impenetrable fire. It was not possible for the men of RIR 119 to travel to Beaucourt, Beaucourt Railroad station or Grandcourt nor were they able to bring up supplies by rail or wagon. Most supply columns were forced to turn back. Any materials brought to the front would need to be hauled by carrying troops drawn from the baggage train or reinforcement troops. RIR 110 reported Martinpuich was under such heavy fire that all of the horses and transport had to be withdrawn to Ligny-Thilloy and Le Transloy.

It was now the turn of the rear area and villages to fall under the British bombardment. The villages that had not suffered much in the last two years of war were now systematically reduced to rubble. One 24cm shell tore through the roof of the church belfry in Miraumont and caused considerable damage including destroying the rear wall. The Black Eagle hotel in Pys was destroyed and the entire village of Irles was virtually leveled.

The National road near the Pozières-Courcelette sugar factory received especially heavy fire at night. Exploding shells all the way to Corps headquarters in Bapaume illuminated the darkness. British aircraft carried the destruction even further to the rear as bombs rained down from the air. Miraumont became a particular target during the night with the village being covered by 24cm shells.

Officers in RIR 111 standing in front of building used as an air raid shelter
(sign to left of door provides directions to shelter). (Author's collection)

The exact date of the infantry attack was still a mystery. However the defenders of Gommecourt had captured a soldier, Private Victor Wheat, from the 5th North Staffordshire Regiment, 46th Division who had been part of a wiring party and had been wounded by machine gun fire. He became lost and wandered into the German lines in the early hours of 25 June. The prisoner was reported to have stated:

> A great attack will come at the latest in 2 or 3 days. It will begin with 4 up to 5 days of artillery fire. Then the infantry would advance. The frontage amounted to 48 kilometers. Our southern neighbors advance first. Then next comes the 56th Division. Gas would not be used on the entire front but would be released at some positions.[5]

This was valuable information since the Moritz station located with the 2nd Guard Reserve Division near Gommecourt had broken down and was no longer capable of eavesdropping on British telephone communications. Only time would tell if the information provided was correct.

Day 2: Sunday, 25 June 1916

The bombardment started promptly at 6 a.m. The well-constructed trenches and defensive positions endured the fire relatively well. Dug-outs remained intact and traffic through the trenches was maintained by making use of every fire pause to clear damaged sections and make quick repairs. There were some reports that the wire entanglements were suffering from the fire, in particular from trench mortar fire. IR 180 reported much of their wire obstacles had been badly damaged, especially in front of Sector Ovillers-South. RIR 110 reported the trenches of the 8th Coy located in the *Sigel Graben* and *Frühlings Graben* had almost been leveled and that the wire obstacles were heavily damaged.

In order to be closer to the regimental position *Oberstleutnant* von Baumbach and headquarters staff of RIR 109 moved into the I Battalion command post located at the northern edge of Montauban near the road toward Mametz. The I Battalion staff transferred their command post to a secure dug-out located in the *Bismarck Graben* just west of the entrance to the *Zeppelin Graben*.

The British seemed to be concentrating their attention more on the villages along the front on the second day of the bombardment. RFAR 27 observed several heavy bursts of fire at midday from at least 12 British batteries falling upon Pozières, Bazentin, Contalmaison and other villages. The fire on Pozières lasted only 15 minutes and was described as a veritable firestorm of the heaviest type; the entire village was in ruins.

The men of IR 180 observed the heavy fire placed upon Pozières and Contalmaison from the relative safety of their deep trenches.

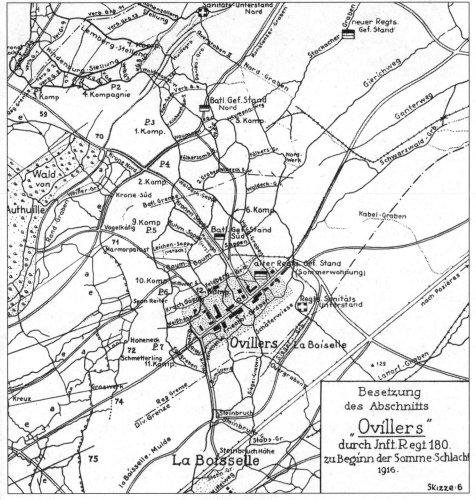

Ovillers Sector.

Civilians being evacuated as a result of the heavy bombardment. (*Das Reserve-Infanterie-Regiment Nr. 109 im Weltkrieg 1914 bis 1918*)

We could see the smoke and masses of earth flying up like a shroud into the air above them and the incessant flashes of the shrapnel shells was like being in the mouth of Hell.[6]

RFAR 28 also observed the heavy fire falling upon Pozières, Contalmaison, Martinpuich and Flers. The batteries of the regiment were ordered to shell Albert in retaliation using the code name '*Budenzauber*'. The revenge fire lasted from 11 a.m. to noon and was repeated later in the evening.

The British guns particularly targeted the former headquarters of the 26th Reserve Division in Miraumont. The obelisk erected to commemorate the division's dead was badly damaged by a direct hit along with the church and the cinema that was to open 24 June. Beaumont, Irles, Courcelette and Le Sars were soon reduced to a pile of ruins.

Many villages in the rear still had a civilian population, mainly the very old or the very young, and it became necessary to evacuate them to safer areas. Soldiers in the XIV Reserve Corps noted the pitiful scene of the refugees as they fled the destruction of their homes during lulls in the fire. The old men, women and children fled along the roads to the rear with enormous piles of clothing and other possessions piled precariously on handcarts of every type. It was a heart-rending sight for many of the German troops who must have thought about their own families as the wretched procession meandered into the distance.

Many German guns stopped firing because the need to conserve ammunition for the expected infantry attack took priority over everything else. The number of shells fired daily by RFAR 28 in the last two days had severely depleted the ammunition stockpiles and the drain continued throughout the day.

The destruction of German artillery emplacements continued to be a high priority of the British gunners. British artillery observers made note of any German gun that fired and in this manner identified 102 guns, mainly along the front of the VIII and X Corps.

The 5/RFAR 27 emplacements were heavily damaged on the 25th and a number of guns were damaged and the positions were destroyed. However the deep mined dug-outs continued to provide adequate protection to the gun crews and the men remained safe in the heavy fire. The 2/RFAR 27 was hard hit on this day and the battery lost one gun and all of its ammunition to a direct hit.

Guns in the 28th Reserve Division continued to fire at any target that presented itself. The 6/RFAR 28 was observed by British aircraft while firing and came under counter-battery fire. The well-constructed emplacements prevented any serious losses and only 2 men were wounded in the heavy fire.

12cm shells damaged two dug-out corridors in this battery and required extensive effort to keep them clear. At the same time a shell struck the trail of the second gun in the battery and it required field repairs before it was operable again. There was no further damage from the shelling. The forward artillery observers that were still in phone contact with the batteries tried to give ample warning if they observed any fire being directed toward the guns in order to allow the men to take shelter in the deep dug-outs.

Much of the damage to the guns of the 26th Reserve Division was repaired by the battery Armourer and blacksmiths located in Grevillers. The restored guns were quickly put back into action.

Low-flying aircraft circled above the German lines directing fire on every trench, access road and battery position and directing fire upon individual dug-out entrances. Two-thirds of the dug-outs located in the front line of the 2/R109 had already been buried by heavy trench mortar bombs and were unusable. The men were being squeezed into the few remaining intact dug-outs in their sector for as long as they lasted.

The 2/R109 was concerned that the trench garrison was no longer evenly distributed along the entire front and that the large numbers of men occupying the limited number of dug-outs would prevent them from quickly exiting the dug-outs and manning the front in case of an attack.

Most of the wire obstacles in front of RIR 109 had been destroyed or seriously damaged primarily due to trench mortar fire. The volume of fire effectively prevented any repairs from being undertaken. The regimental sector came under heavy fire at 11 p.m. and was quickly answered by support batteries in the rear. RIR 111 reported that *minenwerfer* positions were being destroyed one by one by artillery and trench mortar fire under the accurate guidance of low-flying aircraft.

Between 4 and 5 o'clock on Sunday afternoon German observation balloons fell from the sky along the front of the XIV Reserve Corps. The British were attempting to further reduce the German's ability to accurately observe their lines. The 26th Reserve Division balloon was located in the Grove of Grevillers and became one of the victims of this attack. British aircraft firing incendiary ammunition attacked the balloon and it quickly caught fire and crashed to the ground in flames.

The balloon had two occupants, *Vizewachtmeister* Auchter and *Leutnant der Reserve* Welte. Auchter was killed during the attack while Welte survived the initial attack only to die of his wounds on the journey to the hospital in Bapaume.

Frhr. v. Ziegesar

Hauptmann i. Res.-Inf.-Regt. 121,
gestorben am 27. Juni 1916 an
den bei Serre erhaltenen Wunden

Leutn. d. R. Welte

gef. bei Bapaume als Ballon-
beobachter 25. 6. 1916

Hauptmann Frhr Eberhard von Ziegesar RIR 121 (Stuttgart). Wounded 27 June 1916, died later that day. (*Kriegstagbuch aus Schwaben*)

Leutnant der Reserve Eugen Welte 3/RFAR 26. He died while being transported to the hospital from wounds received when his observation balloon was shot down in flames 25 June 1916. (*Das Württembergisches Reserve-Feldartillerie-Regiment Nr. 26 im Weltkrieg 1914-1918*)

British aircraft using incendiary rockets also destroyed the 28th Reserve Division balloon at Geuedecourt. While the German balloons were being destroyed one by one the British balloons seemed to be everywhere across No Man's Land. Up to 11 balloons floated in the summer breeze by Fricourt; many more were reported all along the front. The German Air Force was helpless in the face of British aerial superiority and while the aerial eyes of the XIV Reserve Corps were closed the British floated high above the battlefield undisturbed.

At night the British fire fell mostly on rear areas. The main road from Miraumont to Beaucourt became impassable once again and severely limited the ability of the men to bring supplies to the front. A pioneer in the 2R/Pioneer Bn 13 wrote:

Sunday 25th. An intense artillery bombardment by guns of all calibers began. Several shells fell in the yard of the company and surroundings. The stables were hit and 4 horses were killed…

The bombardment in the early morning lasted about half an hour then only single shots came over. This continued throughout the whole of Sunday and Monday and the following night. Tonight as well shells are falling from time to time into the village. The damage to the houses in the whole village is very big, the living rooms and stables being badly knocked about. The surrounding villages Eaucourt L'Abbaye, Le Sars, Courcelette, Longueval, Flers, etc. are also being heavily shelled. Four men wounded in this Coy, one man killed and two men badly wounded. Wagons and horses have been taken further back.[7]

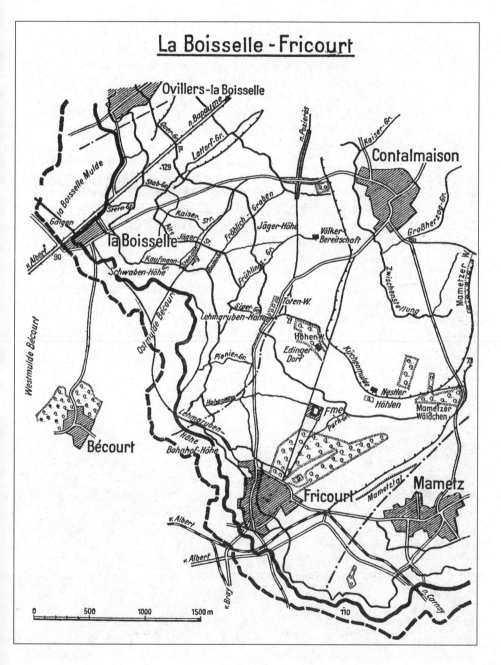

La Boisselle-Fricourt sector.

Soldiers such as *Freiwilliger* Eversmann, transferred to the 3/R99 from IR 143 now found himself sitting in the *Wundtwerk* under heavy shellfire wondered just how long it could continue. Any pause in the enemy fire was utilized to bring up essential supplies such as coffee and bread. Eversmann estimated that at least 60,000 shells had fallen near his position in the last 12 hours alone. The biggest question was when the attack would actually take place; no one seemed to know.

The ammunition columns showed great skill and courage bringing their wagons up to the gun positions in the darkness while traveling along paths that were in poor condition and under constant shellfire. The men unloaded their cargo of shells as quickly as possible and raced to the relative safety of the rear.

The field railways were all destroyed by direct hits on the tracks in the first two days of the bombardment. Wagons could only travel so far along the roads until they too were forced to stop due to continuous shellfire.

Food and ammunition-carrying parties had a difficult time getting to the front while under fire. Their journey was made even harder when the troops were required to wear gasmasks and make repairs to the road by bridging the numerous shell craters. They were short of breath, their eyepieces fogged over and their bodies dripped with sweat as they carried their vital loads or performed the work of navvies. The strength and endurance of the men was being stretched to the limit.

The journey to the front now took hours. The approach routes to Mametz and Montauban were held under heavy fire resulting in numerous losses to men and horses as supplies were carried to the front. Telephone repair crews redoubled their efforts until nearly all of the lines were in working order once more only to see them destroyed a short time later.

The ruins of Beaucourt. (Author's Collection)

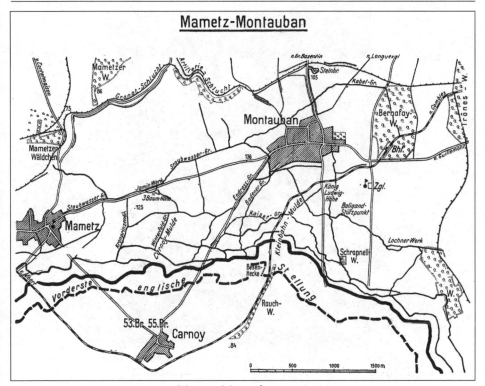

Mametz-Montauban sector.

Food and water supplies that had been stockpiled by the regiments in the Corps were considered adequate at the start of the bombardment. Now, just two days later food began to run out and mineral water was being used up surprisingly fast.

> 25.6.16. Bombardment continued all day, impossible to fetch rations. After dark a party hurried up to the church and brought back some stew.[8]

All of the wells along the front had become unusable. The heat of the sun and the whirling dust and smoke intensified the men's thirst. Fresh supplies needed to be brought up as soon as possible. Every lull in the bombardment was put to good use by the troops. Food, water and construction materials were brought up as well as ammunition. RIR 110 reported the regiment could not replenish supplies of hand grenades or flare cartridges since the magazine in Martinpuich had been blown up from a direct hit in what became a spectacular display of colored lights and numerous smaller explosions as the flames reached the boxes of hand grenades.

While the artillery fire died down somewhat at night it never truly ended. RIR 99 estimated the regimental sector had received up to 10,000 shells in the previous 24 hours. The damaged barbed wire was repaired with pre-made obstacles that had been prepared for such an emergency. However the majority of the men simply waited for the attack to begin in tense excitement.

Family memorial to *Ersatz* Reservist Jakob Haman 1/R119. Wounded in action 25 June 1916 near Beaumont, he died 27 June 1916 at Reserve Field Hospital 1, Bapaume. 'God in His wisdom has ordained that we must part from those that are dearest to our heart'. (Author's Collection)

Day 3: Monday, 26 June 1916

The bombardment had entered the third day without any signs of an infantry attack or any reduction in the numbers of shells being fired. A new danger existed for the German trench garrison when several trench raids were undertaken in the early morning hours of the 26th. At 1 a.m. RIR 110 noticed a patrol in the obstacles between *Ratten* and *Sodenweg*. The 11/R110 opened fire and drove the raiding party back.

Reports from RIR 121 stated the British had made several attempts to enter their lines. Each time they were spotted by alert trench sentries who stood inside the dug-out entrances and would jump out in order to take a quick look into No Man's Land. The patrols in front of RIR 121 were also repelled by heavy infantry and machine gun fire.

IR 180 reported that shortly after midnight Sectors P5, P6 and part of P7 were already under heavy artillery fire. It was later determined that the heavy fire was in support of a raiding party advancing toward Sector P5.

The 9/180 held Sector P5 and in accordance with standard trench procedures had sent out small patrols into No Man's Land in order to observe enemy activity. One group heard noises coming from in front of the wire obstacles. While trying to determine the cause of the commotion the men could clearly hear commands being given in English and saw approximately 40-50 soldiers climbing out of the British trench.

This patrol quickly returned to the German lines and reported their observations to the trench duty officer who immediately alerted the garrison. The raiding party was allowed to come almost up to the wire entanglements when the 9/180 opened fire. Red flares were fired into the air and were answered almost immediately by accurate barrage fire from batteries lying in the rear.

The majority of the raiding party was quickly destroyed in the accurate artillery fire and forced to retreat but not before gaining access to a portion of the German trenches. One sentry, *Infanterist* Fetzer 9/180, was standing guard while his comrades alerted the garrison nearby when he was attacked by three soldiers who struck him several times in the head. He was able to get off a shot at one of the soldiers who sank to the ground with a cry. The two remaining opponents then attempted to drag Fetzer out of the trench using a contraption that was described as being a pitchfork with bent prongs. He put up a fierce struggle against his would be captors and they eventually let him go and were last seen withdrawing into the darkness carrying their wounded friend with them.

Once the artillery fire had ceased on both sides another patrol was sent out from the 9th Coy to check for enemy activity and casualties. They came back with a variety of equipment left behind by the raiding party, including 2 rifles with fixed bayonets. Each rifle had a tube-shaped hand torch affixed to the forward end with an elastic band. The front end of the torch had an oval piece of glass and a bulb; a string was used to turn on the light. The men of the 180th assumed it was a device that would allow the enemy to blind their opponent and then shoot them in safety. The patrol also brought back 5 steel helmets, one with an officer's insignia and one with a non-commissioned officer's insignia, 2 wire cutters, 2 trench clubs similar to a mace, 3 pitchforks with straight prongs, 2 hand grenades, 1 tent square and a very sharp dagger made out of a raw piece of iron that had been attached to a wooden handle and placed in a scabbard.

Soldiers in IR 180 felt it necessary to comment on the last piece of booty that had been recovered:

> The latter vividly recalls the expeditions of the British nation against wild tribes, although they haughtily claim to fight for humanity and true culture. The Englishmen even have a special standard as the events of Baralong also demonstrated.[9] Nonetheless they call us 'Huns' and accuse us of the most shameful atrocities.[10]

One of the ten raids made by the British against the German lines in the early morning hours of 26 June was directed against RIR 99 in the Thiepval Sector by members of the 13th Royal Irish Rifles (Down Volunteers), 36th (Ulster) Division. The raiding party was able to penetrate the German lines and after a brief period of hand-to-hand fighting captured one officer and twelve men from RIR 99. The prisoners, along with others taken from IR 180 and RIR 111 were interrogated:

EXTRACTS FROM FOURTH ARMY SUMMARY
Examination of prisoners. Prisoners belonging to the 111th Res. Inf. Regt. State that owing to movement seen behind our line they were expecting some local attacks. In consequence of this they have recently brought their formations up from rest billets to the support and reserve trenches, and now hold the line with two battalions in front and one battalion in reserve trenches. Some Labour Battalions are in rear of these again.

This information corresponds with that given by the prisoners belonging to the 180th Regt. captured yesterday.

The prisoner thought that the 2nd Guard R. Division went away some time in May.

His own Regt. was resting in BAPAUME at Easter about April 23rd.

The prisoners belonging to the 99th Reserve Inf. Regt. were not expecting an attack, but were on the lookout for raids. They knew nothing of any Bavarian troops being in the neighborhood nor had they heard of any artillery having been brought up.[11]

The prisoners had been questioned about the effects of gas that had been released before the raid but they denied any knowledge of gas and their respirators did not smell of it.

Although the prisoners were cowed and glad to surrender, at many places the resistance was stout. The interrogation of prisoners however, seemed to show only local attacks were expected.[12]

One member of the 13th Royal Irish Rifles who took part in the raid left an impression of the hand-to-hand fighting that took place that night:

When you shoot a man you never see his face and it is as easy as shooting a fox. A few days before we went into the big battle we raided the German lines. It was the first time I had to kill a man at close range and I did it with a fixed bayonet. It was not very light and he was a shadow but as I twisted the bayonet clear he squealed like a stuck pig. It was not till I was on my way back that I started to shake and I shook like a leaf on a tree for the rest of the night.[13]

Dieterich
Leutnant d. R. i. Res.-Feldart.-
Regt. 27, gefallen bei Pozières am
26. Juni 1916

Leutnant der Reserve Dietrich RFAR
27. Killed near Pozières 26 June 1916.
(*Kriegstagbuch aus Schwaben*)

Stöckle
Leutnant d. R. i. Inf.-Regt. 180,
gefallen bei Ovillers la Boisselle
am 27. Juni 1916

Leutnant der Reserve Hermann Stöckle
(Sindringen) 9/180. Killed in action 27
June 1916. (*Kriegstagbuch aus Schwaben*)

Dr. Amels and staff – RIR 99. (*Geschichte des Reserve-Infanterie-Regiment Nr. 99*)

The artillery battle continued to rage; the few remaining intact telephone lines were slowly being destroying despite the heroic attempts by telephone repair units to keep them open. Even when repairs were successful the lines were only working for a few minutes.

RFAR 28 was fortunate that the main telephone line running from the batteries to the rear remained intact, however the lines leading to the observers at the front were constantly being cut. The losses among the telephone repair teams were so high it was finally decided to abandon all repair attempts on lines leading to the front and instead concentrate on keeping communications open to the rear. All messages between the guns and the observers would be handled by flag signals when possible or by runners.

A large quantity of gas was used along the entire front on the third day of the bombardment, mostly in the form of gas clouds. The forward artillery observers were able to provide ample warning to the batteries in the rear so the gunners could take all necessary precautions.

The trench sentries provided ample warning to the garrison when gas clouds were observed coming from the British lines. In some cases the gas clouds were so weak that it seemed they barely left the opposing trenches, other times the clouds went straight up into the air. When a gas cloud did roll across toward the German lines months of training took over and every precaution possible was used to counter the effect of the poisonous mist.

Shortly before noon RIR 119 noted that the British artillery suddenly went silent and at least nine separate gas clouds were observed rolling toward the Sector Beaumont-North. Gas masks were donned and the men manned the trench in the event of an assault. No attack took place; instead the British artillery opened fire once more in an attempt to destroy the German trench garrison while in an exposed location. The men quickly took cover once more in their deep dug-outs while alert sentries stood guard.

The British tried this tactic one further time between 3 and 4 o'clock in the afternoon at Sector Beaumont-South. Fortunately the gas clouds moved through the hollow in No

Landsturmmann Franz Schitterer 4/R111. Killed in action 26
June 1916 near Fricourt. (Author's Collection)

Man's Land toward the Ancre and never reached the German lines. Overall the gas attacks that took place on the 26th caused minimal losses among the defenders.

Still, the medical dug-outs were becoming filled with wounded and sick men as it had become impossible to transport them to the rear once the horse-drawn ambulances could no longer make the journey safely. The problem was solved when motorized ambulances were sent to the front and evacuated the men to hospitals.

The defenses were starting to show signs of damage that was beyond the ability of the men to repair during the occasional lull in the shelling. Light shrapnel and occasional high explosive shell falling along the front caused little loss of life or damage to the defensive works By far the greatest damage done to the front line trenches was still due to trench mortar fire.

At times heavy shells did penetrate dug-outs with up to 7 meters of earth overhead. The command post of the II/R111 was destroyed in this manner. The battalion commander *Hauptmann von* Neuenstein, *Stabsarzt* Dr. Krauss and the communication trench officer *Leutnant* Jansen were killed, many others were wounded.

The front line trench held by the 4/R111 near the *Lehmgrubenhöhe* had to be abandoned when all of the dug-outs were crushed because they were not constructed deep enough due to the nature of the ground. A few sentries who remained behind to keep watch occupied the trench.

RIR 121 reported the overall regimental sector was heavily damaged and many of the wire obstacles were nearly destroyed in some places. Entire stretches of trenches had

In the trenches – RIR 119. (Author's Collection)

been leveled and many dug-outs had collapsed or became heavily damaged and had been evacuated.

RIR 119 reported the sector held by the 9th Coy had suffered particularly heavy damage from spherical trench mortar bombs. The men especially feared these objects and it appeared that no dug-out, no matter how deep, could resist their terrible explosive force.

The right wing of RIR 119 was hardest hit of all. The trenches were located on a hillside that descended toward Auchonvillers and could be seen by British observers. One trench mortar bomb fell after another along the length of this trench leaving behind craters 3 meters deep and up to 5 meters across. Almost in a sense of irony the regimental history stated that strangely enough the garrison always came away from there frightened. One soldier noted:

26.6.16. All night long it was never quiet for a moment. The enemy bombards dug-out after dug-out until they give way. Up to the present six slightly wounded.[14]

Heavy fire on the German rear areas was also taking a large toll on the men and equipment and making life harder for the men located at the front. The ruins of Mametz suffered even more under the impacts of heavy shells. One field kitchen located in Mametz had already been destroyed the previous day, now three more were blown apart in the heavy fire. The loss of the kitchens now required a longer journey by the food carriers and a greater danger of loss of life from the searching artillery fire.

Machine gun Marksman gun crew. (Author's Collection)

Heavy shells continued to impact in the villages in the rear causing heavy damage to many buildings that had survived almost two years of warfare. A heavy shell struck the beautiful church at Miraumont and completely destroyed the interior. Another shell struck the newly constructed cinema that burned fiercely for some time afterward.

Incendiary shells struck the home of Notary Turlot setting the home on fire. This inferno also destroyed the magnificent library taken from the Beaucourt Château and all of the possessions of the Turlot family. The library had been stored in the house for safekeeping by the 26th Reserve Division after the château had been badly damaged in 1914.

The 28th Reserve Division received much-needed support on the 26th with the arrival of the Machine Gun Marksman Detachment 132 that was attached to RIR 109. On the same day RIR 111 was reinforced with the arrival of Machine Gun Marksman Detachments 131 and 161, giving the regiment the equivalent of more than three machine gun companies. The regiment also received two Bavarian Pioneer companies, a detachment from the 2R/Pioneer Bn 13 and a medium *minenwerfer* platoon from *Minenwerfer* Company 28 representing a substantial increase in firepower for the regiment.

Morale was still very high among the troops and they had great confidence that their hard work and diligence would stand the test of battle. The German position had been subjected to a ferocious rain of steel and high explosives for the last 72 hours. Yet, there was still no sign of an attack and the shellfire went on, and on. Nerves were beginning to fray and many men were suffering from headaches, lack of sleep and mental exhaustion. However, the Kaiser's men, in the main, remained stoical.

The 26th Reserve Division headquarters issued the following message regarding the anticipated attack:

The effort and work in the course of the last two years that were made in the extension of our positions, may already have to endure a powerful test in the next days. Now it requires everyone to be firm, to courageously persist, to do your duty, to shun no sacrifice and no exertion, so that the enemy is refused victory. And everyone must be conscious that it is necessary that we hold the bloody embattled ground and that no Englishman or Frenchman who penetrates into our lines might remain unpunished. I know that I am united in these convictions with the entire division and I look forward to the coming events with full confidence. Our watchwords are With God, for King and the Fatherland!   Frhr. von Soden.[15]

Day 4: Tuesday, 27 June 1916

The day passed much in the same manner as the previous ones; trench mortar fire and shrapnel along the front line, heavier shells in the rear and occasional gas clouds being released along the front.

It was four days into the bombardment. Pauses in the heavy fire were used to fetch additional supplies of coffee and bread but these trips were becoming more difficult by the day. The constant shelling, noise and dust were causing the men to have headaches and an increase in thirst. Many could not believe that the enemy had such quantities of ammunition and felt that they must run out soon, anything to end this horrible experience.

The British attempted a number of early morning raids at different points along the front line that were repelled in strong defensive fire but not before six men from the 7/R111 were captured from a dug-out and taken back to British lines. Several prisoners were also taken from the raiding parties who provided conflicting information about the date of the British attack.

Another strong raid was directed against the 9/R119. The trench officer *Leutnant der Reserve* Breitmeier and the sentries on duty had remained alert throughout the heavy bombardment. They observed the patrol approaching the wire entanglements and quickly alerted the garrison while firing red flares to call up barrage fire from the artillery.

The patrol was caught in the heavy fire but held their ground while throwing hand grenades into the German trenches. They were finally forced to withdraw because of the large volume of fire they were subjected to.

The men of RIR 119 spent the remainder of the day under the worst bombardment they had experienced yet. The shelling was interspersed with gas and smoke cloud attacks against different points of the line. The village of Beaumont lay under the heaviest fire yet seen. For the first time the men were experiencing the destructive force of 38cm shells. The soldiers could hear the heavy guns being fired far in the rear and the shells traveling through the air before impacting into the village with a sound of thunder while throwing up huge fountains of earth and debris.

The *Leilingstollen* received the concentrated fire of batteries firing 23cm shells that were being directed by several observation aircraft circling above the target. Soon all of the entrances to the dug-outs and tunnels were buried and the men were required to clear them over and over again.

There were several early morning gas attacks against Ovillers and IR 180, some of which were blown back into the British lines. At other times the gas clouds completely enveloped parts of the main trench where the gas masks proved to be very effective against

Heavy damage to German trenches west of Beaumont after British shelling. (*Die 26. Reserve Division 1914-1918*)

the poisonous fumes. Forward observers noted some type of smoke bomb or smoke machines also being used to produce the smoke and gas.

On one occasion a cloud approached Sectors P3 and P4 that was so thick it completely concealed the British lines. The gas attacks often coincided with the cessation of all artillery fire almost as if the enemy was trying to fool the defenders into thinking an attack was going to take place, although no attack came.

Much of the gas dissipated long before reaching the artillery emplacements. Gas was the least harmful in the morning where the damp high grass and humidity caused the gas to lose almost all of its effectiveness. In some instances the thick gas clouds benefited the defenders and were used by the artillerymen to replenish ammunition supplies.

The third gas cloud of the day completely covered the Pozières valley. RFAR 28 used the cover provided by the dense cloud to bring up the ammunition wagons in daylight. The 6/RFAR 28 reported it received 232 rounds of ammunition and before the gas dispersed four ammunition wagons were safely under cover behind Flers after dropping off their loads.

Despite the dangers of giving away their positions the artillery of the 28th Reserve Division continued to fire and reply as often as possible to calls for support directly from the front line infantry. The division artillery batteries were beginning to suffer losses due to British fire and breakdowns from heavy use. The loss of even a few guns would have a disastrous effect in the coming battle.

The men were already noticing the reduction in the volume of support fire. *Leutnant* Lazarus, 9/R109:

> I have the impression that the artillery could not give sufficient support. Enemy *minenwerfer* have been systematically firing at each of our dug-outs with the aid of aerial observation. (Less so to-day) They have been able to handle their *minenwerfer* as if on parade and have not been engaged at all by our artillery. I also noticed today

Beaumont after 6 days of bombardment. (*Die 26. Reserve Division 1914-1918*)

that when artillery fire was called for on our left the artillery reply was late and, in comparison to the enemy fire, weak.[16]

Welcome reinforcements arrived this day in the form of six Musketen from *Musketen Bn 1*. Two guns each were distributed in the *Staubwassergraben, Ostring* and *Zeppelingraben* in the sector held by RIR 109.

During the night the rear areas, communication trenches and traffic routes received extraordinarily heavy fire. Courcelette was particularly targeted with gas shells so that the food wagons were not able to drive through the village, which disrupted the food supplies for at least half a day.

Once darkness had fallen the men took every opportunity to make as many repairs as possible to the trenches dug-outs and wire entanglements. Much of the damage could not be repaired as many stretches of trenches had been leveled and in some areas the wire entanglements had been blown apart.

Many of the dug-outs had suffered damage, in particular the entrances were constantly being blown in. Heavy shells and trench mortar bombs caused many of the dug-outs, especially the older ones, to collapse. Repairs were made whenever possible in order to ensure that there was sufficient protection for the trench garrison. If a dug-out was rendered useless the affected occupants were placed into nearby shelters. In some areas the overcrowding of the existing dug-outs was becoming a problem. The Moritz tunnel under La Boisselle was often used to house surplus troops when needed.

The men constantly took to their spades and cleared the debris away from the dug-out entrances. They tried to keep the trenches open and used pre-prepared wire entanglements to block off any openings in the wire but any real attempt to make extensive repairs often resulted in further casualties. These losses could still be made up by taking men from the reserve companies lying further to the rear.

Bringing up rations and water continued to be a problem because of the heavy enemy fire:

27.6.16. No letters arriving, and we are lucky to get anything to eat as it is very difficult to fetch rations owing to barrage fire. Nothing comes up during the day.[17]

Day 5: Wednesday, 28 June 1916

The bombardment continued without a let up. It was something the men had never experienced and many continued to wonder where the enemy was getting all of the ammunition they were using.

British aircraft roamed above the German front with impunity. It seems there were so many aircraft in the sky they could even give their full attention to a lone soldier, *Feldwebel* Felix Kircher, RFAR 26:

> Three days before the battle started I was fetching something from Miraumont to Grandcourt when an English aeroplane chased me for about ten minutes. I escaped by dodging among the willow trees along the Ancre.[18]

Reinforcements continued to arrive and were distributed between the different units. The 6/FAR 50 arrived and was directed into several unfinished positions near the 6/RFAR 28. Once in position the guns began their registration following the fire from the 6/RFAR 28. Each battery alternated firing at specific targets in range of the guns.

The registration fire did not take place without consequences. The British had observed the batteries firing and covered the area with heavy shells. Two guns were destroyed by direct hits and placed out of action. The 6/FAR 50 was reduced in strength by half before the battle even started.

The 6/RFAR 28 received less attention with only occasional heavy bursts of fire. The 3/RFAR 28 (Battery Fröhlich) suffered the worst losses in the regiment so far, 6 dead from direct hits on the gun positions.

The village of Pozières was covered with heavy fire for the fifth straight day and was completely shattered. Apparently the British were searching for German batteries reported to be in the village and wanted to completely destroy them using gas and 38cm shells. The village did contain German guns, four batteries in all. The 2/RFAR 28 (Leinenkugel) and the 3/RFAR 28 (Metzger) were located near the village exit facing Ovillers. A light field howitzer battery (Burg) from RFAR 26 and a Bavarian battery of 15cm Belgian guns were inside the village proper.

The exploding shells formed white clouds in the humid weather and the village was soon shrouded in a milky veil of haze. Several men located nearby noticed how the different shells sounded upon impact noting that the gas shells did not make as much noise as the high explosive shells.

The number of casualties from gas continued to remain quite small. Much of this was due to the extensive gas warfare training, good equipment and gas discipline among the men. The dug-outs were kept free of gas by hanging damp cloths over the entrances and setting fires to draw the poisonous fumes up into the air.

Communications between the regiments and the rear was quite difficult after five days of shelling. Runners now carried almost every message. The light signal station codenamed 'Sonne' on Hill 110 was a great aid in calling for artillery fire if the signal rockets could not be seen due to the smoke and haze. Unfortunately even the light signal

Street scene in Mametz. (Author's Collection)

stations were useless at times due to the hazy conditions and the large amount of dust and debris in the air.

The atmosphere began to clear somewhat on the 28th when thunderstorms came through the region. The weather had been quite sunny and warm until this point, now the days and nights were filled with storms while the sky remained hazy.

The heavy fire on the rear had continued to threaten Corps headquarters in Bapaume and many urged the commander to move further back. However von Stein decided to stay and direct the fighting from his old headquarters instead of trying to move and possibly cause even more of a disruption in communications than the British shells had accomplished.

The day had started with raids against different locations of the front as the British probed the German lines for weaknesses, each time they were driven off before any real damage could be done. A number of prisoners were taken by RIR 119 belonging to the 29th Division gave dates for the start of the attack. Other prisoners were taken by RIR 111 gave conflicting dates of the main attack as the 28th, 29th and 30th of June.

The Moritz stations had been intercepting numerous telephone messages and passing the details to headquarters for review. The Moritz station at La Boisselle sent back one report that stated the British troops appeared to be drunk and making a great deal of noise in the trenches opposite the village. The report further stated that one message gave the time and date of an attack as 2.30 a.m. on the 29th. All possible precautions were taken in the event it was true.

Losses due to artillery fire continued to grow among the trench sentries, runners and carrying parties. Stretcher-bearers, including the band members of each regiment, moved through the position searching for wounded and bringing them to the nearest aid station. The dead were also brought into shelters where the bodies of the fallen were prepared for burial further in the rear.

British fire continued to wreak havoc on the well-constructed position but could not completely obliterate the extensive defenses. Additional dug-outs collapsed under the relentless artillery bombardment but many of the deeper ones remained intact.

Leutnant der Reserve Stahlhofer, a platoon commander in 2/8th Bavarian RIR was positioned in support south of the Ancre. His regiment would play a key role in the coming battle. Now, he was more interested in staying alive during the height of the bombardment. While standing in a badly damaged trench he reminisced about the time before the bombardment:

> The trench of the second position was quite shallow; it barely covered us up to the hip. The mud poured over our boots like soft dough, in parts it reached up to the knee. The terrain dropped off to the left, in front of us was the valley of the Ancre brook; high on the far edge was Beaucourt that once must have been a delightful nest. During the time we worked in the vicinity of Beaucourt, I had looked at the sad remains of this village, the soldier's graveyard that lay upon the heights, with the beautiful monuments, also the remains of the little St. Pierre-Divion, as well as the dug-outs positioned on the steep hillside by the Württembergers, where canteens and shops were accommodated, such that everything looked like a charming garden suburb to me.[19]

Now, as the British pounded the German lines with artillery fire all he could do was act as a spectator as Beaucourt was slowly destroyed:

> We saw the interesting picture, how the 'thirty eights' smashed in Beaucourt, how the clouds of red tile dust and the splinters flew up to us and we were a good one and a half kilometers distant from it.[20]

Soldiers' Cemetery at Beaumont, battalion dug-outs in the rear. (Author's Collection)

Close range weapon emplacements were constantly being cleared of dirt and debris thrown up from the shells and made ready for action. In one instance *Unteroffizier* Gross, 12/R111 and six men dug out a machine gun and crew from Machine Gun Sharpshooter Detachment 161 that had been buried by shellfire. Their quick action allowed the gun to be put back into action in a short period of time.

While many of the men felt the strain of the constant bombardment and the uncertainty about the date and time of the attack that was sure to follow the overall mood of the troops manning the German trenches was one of confidence and resolve. Morale among the men was high even after experiencing over 100 hours of enemy gas attacks and shellfire. The men sitting inside the deep dug-outs waited for the time when the bombardment would lift and they could come to grips with the enemy. Until that time they could only wait and reflect on the events of each day.

Obtaining rations from the rear was a deadly affair and many men who attempted it were either killed or wounded in the heavy fire. Many men were wondering just how long they could survive under these conditions such as *Freiwilliger* Eversmann sitting in the *Wundtwerk*. Still, despite the intense bombardment mail was still being delivered to the men at the front and letters were being sent home by the men.

> I received both packets from the 20th instant. Many thanks. The mail really has a great many difficulties … You will have gotten the card, where I confirmed the receipt of both packets from the 20th instant. Package mail has difficulty coming into the position at this time because the roads are closed. Letter mail still comes. Even sending mail back is difficult. You must put up with this. I am still well, likewise Sütterlin. The English take their offensive seriously. We do not know if they will come at us. Our positions lie under artillery fire. They have also discharged gas; however it did not come up to our trenches. We are all in good spirits and will just thrash them when they come. Warmest greetings and kisses from your grateful Karl. Sigle became severely wounded (in the face) 4 or 5 days ago. Karl Losch, 3/R119 [20]

The physical misery was keeping pace with the mental stress. The men complained of lack of sleep, lack of food and being so dry that the tongue would stick to the roof of their mouth.

There was a growing feeling of despair of being cut off from all contact with the rear and with family. While some mail was getting through there were times when the letters were delayed or in some cases lost during the bombardment. The concerns of the men were magnified by having to worry about their families and how they were reacting to the news of the bombardment. In this matter it is doubtful the friends and family at home had any idea of the conditions their loved ones faced. Casualty reports for this period would not be in print for almost a month and little news was being printed about the events as they unfolded. It would be a matter of days or weeks before any information would be available to those sitting at home about the terrible conditions on the Somme.

One German soldier gave a personal view of the bombardment in a letter to his wife that was found on the battlefield:

> Thank God I reached my company in safety after going through heavy artillery fire. Since Saturday 24th, the whole 6th Company front has been bombarded without

stopping. Everything is in pieces and houses burning. Two chums badly wounded. It looks terrible here, five days and nights the artillery fire continues – for 10 kilometers behind the trenches everything blown to bits; the English want to crush us with artillery fire. Some of the dug-outs blown in and very many have been buried in the dug-outs. Do not write again until I tell you, letters are now being stopped. We are not safe for one hour, something might happen any moment.[21]

Several diaries discovered during the battle also gave some idea of the ordeal faced by the defenders after five days of continuous shelling: [22]

Every one of us in these five days has become years older. We hardly know ourselves. Bechtel said that in these five days he lost 10 pounds. Hunger and thirst have also contributed their share to that. Hunger would be easily borne but the thirst made one almost mad. Luckily, it rained yesterday and the water in the shell-holes, mixed with the yellow shell sulphur tasted as good as a bottle of beer. Today we got something to eat. It was impossible before to bring food into the front line under the violent curtain fire of the enemy. We have had no letters since the 23rd.

An unknown author in the vicinity of Fricourt-Mametz wrote the following:

… they had to move out, as shells were falling there. The villages are burning almost day and night; terrible to see. You can imagine the misfortune – there were many tears, the people were crying, very hard for them and specially the little children. Perhaps one day I will be able to tell you more about it. Our artillery are also kept going, as you can think. We must stand firm; that is the main thing…Tonight we must relieve the 63rd in the front line, as they have been now five days in the intense bombardment and have had a good many losses. Everyone is now very 'fed up' with this nonsense and then after all you may get one over the head. There is never any peace…we cannot get our food regularly, sometimes not for days together…We are also having pretty rotten weather, which does not exactly help things; it has been raining cats and dogs the whole day and night. No wonder that we cannot get our food. Perhaps we shall be able to beat off the attack, which we hope will be the last. The enemy are straining everything in their power…In Combles they blew up an ammunition depot, as they continually fired incendiary shells into the place – we were about half an hour away. You should have seen it, it was at night and all the sky was lit up …

Day 6: Thursday, 29 June 1916

Day six of the bombardment, and there appeared to be no end to the torment. The listening posts had picked up information through an intercepted telephone message that an attack was going to take place against RIR 110 at La Boisselle.

It seemed that the British were preparing to launch a raid against La Boiselle with a detachment consisting of men from four battalions of infantry. The attackers were going to approach the German lines on both sides of the National road and assault the trenches located at the southwest corner of the village. The time of the attack was set for 2.30

a.m. on the 29th. The British were reported to be using six platoons from the different battalions for the assault.

RIR 110 was ordered to occupy the *Alte Jäger Stellung* at the onset of darkness. The supporting batteries of RFAR 28 were given orders to open fire on the British assembly trenches precisely at 2.25 a.m. for a period of 5 minutes, there was no response. The guns remained silent for slightly more than one hour before opening fire on the suspected assembly trenches once again. The guns covered the British trenches with heavy fire at 2.25 and at 3.45 a.m. No infantry attack took place so it was assumed that the prompt response to the threat had effectively prevented the attack from taking place at all.

The only enemy activity in the La Boisselle Sector at the time of the proposed attack was a fire raid against the regimental headquarters by heavy caliber shells that ended at 2.20 a.m., otherwise the opposing front was very quiet.

While the fire from RFAR 28 may or may not have prevented a local attack against RIR 110 other portions of the line were not as fortunate. RIR 119 reported a raid that took place against the 10th, 11th and 2nd Coy was repelled by heavy infantry and artillery defensive fire.

However the flash from the artillery being fired in the darkness also gave away the battery positions to the enemy. The British reported identifying 57 German batteries in action during the 29th.

The 2/23 from the 12th Division arrived at the front early on the morning of the 29th, a welcome sight for the men of the 28th Reserve Division. The men of IR 23 were exhausted after their long march to the front. As no dug-outs or rations were available for the men the company was moved to a safe location where they could rest and recover from their journey.

It was the sixth day of the bombardment and most of the men had become accustomed to the daily fire routine. So far the 6/RFAR 28 was fortunate in that the battery had only suffered a few wounded up until this point, no one killed so far. The men played *Skat* to pass the time using matches and slips of paper in place of money. The game was often disrupted when the battery opened fire in retaliation for the heavy shelling.

The luck of the battery was to come to an end on this date. *Fahrer* Bobre became the first man in the unit to be killed. He was acting as a runner and telephone operator during the bombardment. Observation Post 34 had received a direct hit and was destroyed and Bobre was part of a small group of men that were attempting to salvage equipment and documents from the tangled wreckage that included a range finder and important documents regarding targets. While in the observation post another direct hit crushed the roof and killed Bobre and an *Unteroffizier* from the 1/RFAR 28 (Battery Teufel).

At 6.30 p.m. the regimental commander of RIR 110 ordered the artillery to begin a fire raid upon the British trenches. As a result the British batteries shifted their fire from the German trenches and concentrated on counter-battery work. The regimental commander of RIR 109 also ordered his support batteries in Group Leinenkugel and Group Gericke to take enemy positions under fire for 20 minutes where British reserves were suspected of being assembled. Afterward British shellfire and gas attacks increased in size and frequency.

At 7 p.m. gas clouds were observed heading towards the German lines at several locations. In some places the gas was blown back into the British trenches due to a

38cm dud in trench near Thiepval. (*Die 26. Reserve Division 1914-1918*)

shifting wind. In the areas where the cloud continued to drift over the German lines it had dissipated by the time it reached the battery positions so that it had become harmless.

The British were continuing to concentrate their fire upon key points along the German lines, especially regimental and battalion command posts that must have betrayed their location by the amount of foot traffic observed going to and fro. The regimental battle headquarters of RIR 110 was particularly targeted on the 29th with one hour of concentrated artillery fire. All six entrances were destroyed and the regimental staff was buried and trapped underground.

The runners and orderlies on the regimental staff worked non-stop for 8 hours using oxygen bottles on hand for such an emergency. The men were successful in tunneling 5 meters to an adjacent dug-out where the officers and men on the staff were able to evacuate the headquarters.

The division commander approved the request to move the battle headquarters of RIR 110 to Contalmaison on the evening of 30 June because all of the telephone lines and telephone equipment in the former headquarters had been completely destroyed. During this time runners maintained contact with the battalions. Telephone communications to division headquarters were still intact from the new location.

The headquarters dug-out of the II/RFAR 27 located at the sugar factory at Courcelette also came under concentrated fire on the 29th and within a short time had been destroyed. The staff moved into another dug-out located in a concrete blockhouse in front of the western exit of Courcelette. The British did not detect the new location and the staff of the II *Abteilung* did not come under any further fire during the next few days or during the infantry attack on 1 July. This would prove to be very useful when orders and fire control could be achieved without interference.

While some sectors received heavy fire, others almost appeared to have been forgotten. IR 180 holding the line from the right flank of the *Granatloch* to Ovillers reported that

View of Ovillers cemetery from a covered position at La Boisselle. (Author's Collection)

it was very quiet from dawn to 5 p.m. Only individual shells or trench mortar bombs fell in the sector during this time. However at 5 p.m. the sector was covered in heavy fire that lasted two hours before it died down to sporadic shelling.

The regiment sent a report to brigade headquarters on the condition of the trenches:

P1. Completely destroyed by shelling. All dug-outs entrances in the southern half of the sub-sector had collapsed or were severely damaged.
P2. Leveled only in stretches, protected traffic was not possible.
P3. In good condition.
P4. The first trench and the *Fölkersamb* Sap were leveled.

In Sector Ovillers-South the first and second trenches were leveled for the greater part. The wire obstacles were shot up almost everywhere. The dug-outs that had been buried by the bombardment were cleared over and over again in order to keep them open. The remaining dug-outs were still in very good condition otherwise.[23]

The regiment reported that the rear trenches were subjected to the heaviest shells, up to 24cm. The area around the regimental command post was in bad condition, the northern entrance was buried and the entire dug-out trembled and shook under the continuous impacts of shells; however it remained intact despite the heavy fire. Particular locations

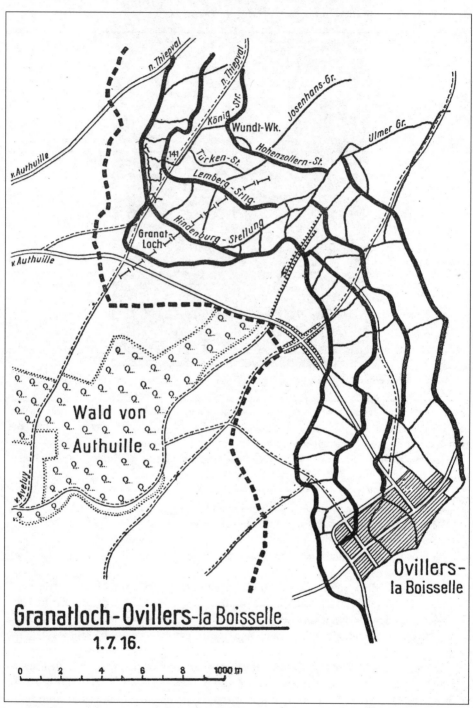

Granatloch-Ovillers-La Boisselle sector.

received numerous heavy shells using delayed impact fuzes in the hopes of reaching the deep targets.

The British enjoyed the use of numerous observation balloons as well as aircraft when the weather permitted flying. RIR 109 reported at least 15 observation balloons along the front while the only German observation balloon still in the sector was shot down in flames on this day leaving a dark smoke trail as it descended to the ground. The men's nerves were starting to become extremely tense under the constant watchful eye of the enemy observers and continuous shelling. One officer in RIR 111 wrote:

> You cannot imagine what our former nice clean trenches look like. Our losses are, however, very small as we have such deep dug-outs that they do not get quite destroyed. But the effect on the nerves! [24]

Unteroffizier Hinkel, 7/R99 agreed with the last point:

> The torment and the fatigue, not to mention the strain on the nerves, were indescribable. There was just one single heart-felt prayer on our lips: 'Oh God, free us from this ordeal; give us release through battle, grant us victory; Lord God! Just let them come!' and this determination increased with the fall of each shell. [25]

The six-day bombardment had taken a toll on the strength of the trench garrisons. The I/R109 reported a total of 12 dead, 32 wounded in the period of 24 June through 29 June. The battalion also reported that the companies holding the front had been reduced by at least one-third from their strength before 24 June by men killed, wounded or reporting sick. The battle strength of the 1st Coy was down to 164 men, the 2nd Coy 151 men and the 4th Coy 142 men.

The enemy fire was having an increasing effect on disrupting the re-supply of the front line especially water. All of the water pipelines had been destroyed and most wells had been rendered useless as had been expected. The heat and dust made the men very thirsty and water became a great concern. Every attempt was made to ensure an adequate supply of potable drinking water at the front. According to one soldier 'our thirst is terrible. We hunt for, and drink the water in shell holes.'[26]

Day 7: Friday, 30 June 1916

It was the seventh day of the bombardment and the men's nerves were stretched to the breaking point. The fact that the men had been able to endure the heavy fire at all was attributed to the deep, mined dug-outs that had been prepared in the months before the attack.

The day started off with the inevitable raiding parties trying to penetrate the German lines by RIR 121, RIR 110 and others. The 5/R110 reported that a skirmish line of approximately 200 men had been spotted approaching their trench on the *Schwabenhöhe*. Infantry and artillery fire drove them off before being able to reach the German trenches.

British batteries had opened a hurricane of fire on many sectors of the front. IR 180 was targeted by 18cm steel-tipped shells that collapsed two deep dug-outs in Sector P6. Heavy trench mortar bombs reached up to the third trench while the first trench continued to receive lively shrapnel fire.

Deep, well constructed trench near Thiepval. (Author's collection)

At least one German deserter brought mixed news to his captors:

> A deserter from the 109th Reserve Regiment stationed near Mametz stated that no
> warning of an impending attack had been received, but that the men expected one
> and wished it would come and be over; no supplies had reached them for three days,
> and contrary to orders they had eaten their iron rations.[27]

RIR 121 reported that the regimental position looked dreadful; wire obstacles were
destroyed or swept away by shrapnel and spherical trench mortar bombs. The trenches
had been almost leveled in many places and were scarcely shallow hollows in the ground.
Crater rim touched crater rim and half buried holes indicated where the dug-out entrances
were located.

The front line held by the 9/R121 had suffered the most. All of the dug-outs within
the company sector had collapsed due to the explosive force of the heavy trench mortar
bombs fired by the British. Only a few wall remnants still existed of the small village of
Beaumont. The soldiers' graveyard had been devastated, the monument was destroyed and
the field railway was torn up and useless. Shattered wagons littered the road leading to
the railroad station. Dead horses and scattered material was everywhere. All of the trees
had been knocked down and the shattered branches covered the ground.

'Convent farm' at Serre. (*Die 26. Reserve Division 1914-1918*)

The Thiepval Sector held by RIR 99 was described as having the appearance of a graveyard; the ground was covered with hundreds of white chalk markers. No house, tree or shrub remained; all were leveled by the shellfire. The terrain was barren and devoid of life. Every bird, dog and horse that once occupied the area had disappeared as a result of the shells and gas.

Leutnant Kassel, 1/R99 from Darmstadt recalled the terrible conditions the men faced under the hail of shrapnel and high explosives. Many of the men detailed to fetch food came back empty-handed and the field kitchens could not come anywhere near the lines so the men would not have any warm food again.

After many days of heavy fire the trenches were uncomfortable and quite dangerous with all of the metal and debris flying through the air. The men were becoming exhausted from the non-stop shelling that prevented the men from falling asleep. Kassel felt that their very lives were in the hands of the sentries who stood watch at the top of the dug-out steps looking for signs when the enemy fire was lifted from the trenches and placed further to the rear. Then the infantry attack would take place.

In the periods where there were lulls in the fire the sentries could make a quick dash to the parapet and look out across No Man's Land to see if there was any enemy activity. Since the sentries were only human it required the officers to make periodic checks of the sentries to make sure they were all still alert and standing at their posts.

From time to time different sections of the trenches were targeted by the heaviest caliber guns. Kassel felt that the English were being very cautious and that not a single German would be left alive once the attack began.

While the men sat helpless inside their deep dug-outs they often wondered 'Where is our artillery fire?' Why did the guns remain silent? Why did they allow the British guns to fire without challenging them?

What they did not know was that their guns had not been silent during this time. Von Stein submitted a report of the average daily expenditure of ammunition of his batteries in the Corps from 24 June to 30 June: Field Gun Batteries: 1,500 rounds. Light Field

Thiepval Château after the bombardment. (*Die 26. Reserve Division 1914-1918*)

Howitzer Batteries: 1,050 rounds. Heavy Field Howitzer Batteries: 520 rounds. 21cm Mortar Batteries: 200 rounds.

The greatest number of rounds fired seemed to come from the guns of the 28th Reserve Division, mainly RFAR 28 and RFAR 29. The 6/RFAR 28 reported firing 5,132 rounds during the seven-day period.[28]

Even the limited fire from the German guns could have devastating effects upon the British. On 28 June a single German shell fell amidst No. 11 Platoon and the Battalion Headquarters Staff, 13th Royal Irish Rifles, as they were about to march during a relief of the front line. The battalion suffered 14 killed, including the second in command, Major R. P. Maxwell and the Adjutant, Captain Wright.

German artillery observers were severely hampered by the loss of their captive balloons and the lack of observation aircraft. Many of the observation posts prepared before 24 June had been damaged or destroyed and improvised observation posts could be extremely dangerous as *Unteroffizier* Felix Kircher, RFAR 26, discovered while using the church tower of Pozières for this purpose.

> The village lay straight opposite Albert on the highest point of the region. With great difficulty we reached the church and ascended the church tower. Here we saw an overwhelming panorama of the battle. While most soldiers of the First World War heard around them the noises of battle, very few saw the events from down in their trenches. Up here we could see columns of English infantry marching to their trenches, hundreds of guns firing and aeroplanes taking off and landing.
>
> But we did not have much time to observe this spectacle. Our 'colleagues' over on the other side discovered us, probably from the church tower of the cathedral in Albert with its famous hanging Virgin. Suddenly a shell rushed over our heads and burst on the altar of the church. Seconds later another shell hit the ground near the tower and destroyed the staircase. We were trapped and each moment feared the tower would be next. In mortal fear we threw down the bell ropes and glided to the earth in the greatest hurry. A second later the tower crashed, but we were saved.[29]

Pozières Church. (Author's collection)

Despite the loss of aerial observation and constant British counter-battery work the German guns would continue to fire at intervals almost up to the point when the British attacked on 1 July. Sergeant-Major Shephard, B Coy, 1st Dorsets, noted in his diary on 1 July that they came under heavy shelling and shrapnel while in Authuille Wood in the hours before 4 a.m. One shell killed ten men and set some supplies on fire, causing two men from the 2nd King's Own Yorkshire Light Infantry to be burnt to death.

Despite the duration and weight of fire the men experienced the mood among the defenders was still generally quite good. Overall losses amounted to about 900 men killed, wounded and missing in each division, quite small considering the immense number of shells being fired at them. Diaries and letters from this period are rare but the ones that have survived provide an insight into the mood of the men just before the great attack. Felix Kircher:

> On June 24 thousands of guns opened fire on our trenches, dug-outs, communication trenches, artillery positions and roads. We could not get any supplies from behind, no ammunition, no food, no water. The bearers of such things had to carry them three to five kilometers and had to jump from shell hole to shell hole. If they arrived at all it was well past midnight and they only had about one-tenth left in their kettles.
>
> The telephone lines constantly were cut from the artillery fire so we had no communication with the staffs. We suffered terribly from hunger, thirst and lack of sleep. Observation was impossible.[30]

A diary found near Fricourt from a soldier in RIR 111:

> We are quite shut off from the rest of the world; nothing comes up to us, no letters. The English keep such a barrage on all the approaches; it's terrible. Tomorrow

morning it will be seven days since this bombardment began; we cannot hold out much longer; everything is shot to pieces.[31]

From a letter written by an optimistic man in the I/R111 to a friend who worked in the 28th Reserve Division Post Office in Bapaume:

Heavy fire since 24th inst. Our casualties are, I am glad to say, quite small. In our company, for example, there have been no killed. No attack so far; anyway we are prepared. Our artillery is doing splendidly. If the shellfire does not drive you out of Bapaume there is no need to move on account of the English; they won't get as far as that.[32]

Extract taken from a captured diary, name and unit unknown:

A dug-out was destroyed and four men poisoned by the fumes of the explosion, one man suffocated. The strain on my nerves is terrible and I cannot write any more of what I have gone through.[33]

Regarding the problem of supplies and thirst, a report to the 9/R109:

Unable to send [anyone] to fetch the coffee. Will the Company Commander please make efforts to get the Battalion to send down some water – the men are suffering very much from thirst.[34]

Extract taken from a letter:

For eight days [sic.] now intense artillery activity and in all probability there are bad times in store for us. What the English are going to do, we do not know.[35]

Extracts taken from captured diaries, names and units unknown:

Dear Wife, We are in a beastly hole. The English have been shooting day and night since Saturday 24th. They started at seven o'clock in the morning, simply terrible, the whole front, not only at us, we hear it up at Arras where they wanted to attack. They have already been driven back once or twice by our neighboring regiments. They sent gas over at us three times this morning, we have no rest day and night. Sleep is quite a secondary thing. As regards food, that is the same, we do not get anything except a little coffee …Yesterday evening my N.C.O. and the other men came back, they had missed their way. Yesterday, at night, they went off again to get some food and came back this morning at seven o'clock with some coffee. I managed to get a cup full, and then the man who was carrying it fell down the dug-out steps and we had to drink it there. Now we must wait again until tomorrow morning until we can get some more. If the 'push' had not come, we were to have been relieved on the 28th and now we have to stick it out. They have been shooting for 144 hours now this morning and are continuing, let us hope it will stop soon. We heard they were going to shoot for a week.

We came into the front line ten days ago. During these ten days I have suffered more than any time during the last two years. The dug-outs are damaged in places, but the trenches are completely destroyed.[36]

Leutnant der Reserve Kassel also waited for the end of the shelling sitting in his dug-out near the village of Thiepval. The men had lived with the thundering crash of the shells and the constant movement of the earth around them. They were becoming dull and apathetic as they waited in their dug-outs for the bombardment to stop. They may have been cut off from everything and everyone they knew but they were still ready to defend their positions to the end. The desire to get back at the enemy for the long suffering grew daily and they would defend themselves whatever the cost.

The British continued to use gas along the entire front whenever the conditions were favorable. RIR 111 described some of the gas being whitish in color while at other times a bluish color. Everything was covered in a fog with a bittersweet smell. Soon the grass and other foliage assumed a yellowish wilted appearance and all dogs and cats had disappeared and happily, for the time being, so did all of the rats.

A few men from RIR 109 reported being slightly sick from the gas. This was only after the men had used their gas masks frequently in the last week and had been unable to obtain replacement filters.

For the last week the transport wagons traveled to and from the front in the heavy fire. The transport drivers paid dearly for the many quiet times of the past as the shells killed and wounded many among their ranks.

In spite of the constant shelling some soldiers attempted to take advantage of any opportunity presented to them. *Leutnant der Reserve* Stahlhofer and his servant Schiele happened upon an unexpected treat:

> I had abundant time to devote myself to the redcurrant and gooseberry stand that displayed the fullest profusion of fruit. It was so alluring to nibble on these things that the fire that was on this place did not keep me away. However I once have the pleasure to spoil the chaps. My servant Schiele and I took a walk to the battalion and with it passed a garden that was filled with fruit-laden gooseberry bushes. On the return route I said to Schiele: 'I say, it would almost be a sin if we let these beautiful things spoil.'…We had picked a while when suddenly pieces of earth and wood pattered above us, and the stinking black powder smoke tickled us in our noses and palates. A heavy shell smashed not 10 meters from us. It was unfortunate now about the berries that had to spoil because our appetites were gone.[37]

After watching the German lines being shelled for a week, just what did the British soldier feel about the approaching battle? Many must have felt that no German soldier could have survived the massive bombardment, much of the barbed wire had been destroyed, trenches leveled or reduced to a series of shell holes. Dug-outs must have collapsed, machine gun and observation posts been destroyed and life in the batteries and rear areas made intolerable.

> As one watched the shells bursting, sending up huge columns of earth, day after day, it appeared as if no life could continue in that tortured and blasted area.[38]

View of Thiepval Wood from the Park at Thiepval. (Lawrence Brown)

The men of the 16th Northumberland Fusiliers (Newcastle Commercials) had been given the impression that the attack would be easy. The men were assured that the artillery preparations would be so effective that no German would be left alive in the front line and that not even a rat could survive the shelling. All the men had to do was to follow the barrage and then consolidate. While all of this sounded reassuring the men were realistic and expected some sort of opposition but even with their reservations the men expected an easy time of it. Some even joked about having lunch in Contalmaison.

Private William H. Batty, 20th Manchesters watched the German lines being pounded thinking that the Germans were really getting a pasting this time. Private W.H. Hunt of the 9th Devonshires had similar thoughts. After watching the bombardment of the German lines he thought that no one could have lived through it, it was as if there was a wall of fire.

The forward observers opposite Thiepval did not share this optimistic point of view. From their observation posts the German wire in front of Thiepval appeared to be nearly intact and very thick. Artillery observers from the 36th Division on Mesnil Ridge noted that there were up to sixteen belts of wire guarding the front line south of the River Ancre, and an average of five belts along the second line.

The damage caused to the German lines in the vicinity of the *Lehmgrubenhöhe* near La Boisselle was reaching a critical point. Losses in RIR 110 had been small considering the number of shells fired at the regimental sector. The hardest hit company was the 8/R110 located on the *Lehmgrubenhöhe*. The position had suffered serious damage due to trench mortar fire and there were few dug-outs that could still be occupied. The company had numerous losses and was down to 80 effectives, about one-third of the original company strength.

Because the 8/R110 was so understrength a gap arose between RIR 110 and the neighboring RIR 111. The reserve company, the 2/R110, was moved into position to close this gap from the rear using infantry fire as needed and the company was given the use of a machine gun for added firepower. The final placements were finished by midnight. RIR 111 also moved several groups in order to close the gap from their side.

Final preparations

The night of 30 June/1 July was conspicuously quiet; did this indicate the attack was coming? The gunners in the XIV Reserve Corps were ready for the next move of the British. Every artillery battery had at least 2,000 rounds of ammunition on hand for the start of the attack. Each howitzer battery was supplied with 1,500 rounds while each heavy howitzer battery had 1,000 rounds ready for use. RFAR 26 went far beyond the Corps requirements as the regiment had already placed 4,500 shells for immediate use with each field gun battery in the event of an attack

However not everyone saw the reduction in enemy activity and fire in the same manner. The officers of the 6/RFAR 28 were confused by the sudden decrease in activity. After all, they had fired for a week and still no attack. They felt that the British should have already attacked by now and many of the officers felt that nothing was going to happen at all.

Others along the front knew something was going to happen, but when?

> The seven-day bombardment of the English did not cause us many losses. Our battalion occupied a three-line trench system and had built very strong and deep dug-outs. They were eight to 10 meters deep and had been strengthened with heavy wooden beams and railroad ties. Luckily for us this provided a quite adequate shelter. But several days before 1 July we had heard underground digging and knew a mine was being dug and prepared. *Musketier* Walter Peeck, 12/R119[39]

The infantry sitting inside the crowded dug-outs waited for the inevitable attack, many even longed for it in order to give the enemy a dose of what they had lived through for the past week. Two of the regiments had been scheduled for relief at this time but this was cancelled because of the impending attack. RIR 99 at Thiepval had expected to be relieved by Bavarian IR 16 while RIR 109 had been scheduled for relief by IR 23 on the night of 30 June/1 July.

Most telephone lines had been cut in numerous places and had been rendered useless. However several key lines were still intact and would become extremely valuable in the coming battle. The telephone line buried 2 meters under the ground in the sector held by RIR 110 remained in use until the 29th allowing headquarters to remain in contact with all three battalions. The buried line leading from the regimental headquarters to the Moritz listening post deep under the ground at the tip of La Boisselle would remain in use throughout the week-long bombardment and transmitted numerous important messages to division and Corps headquarters.

The Moritz stations were constantly intercepting reports concerning enemy events and orders. In one instance one Moritz station had learned that the British had evacuated their front line trench on which the majority of German destructive fire was being placed. *Oberst von* Vietinghoff, commander of RIR 110 then sent orders to the sector commander of the supporting artillery to cease fire on this trench.

A new plan was drawn up whereby the artillery would employ strong fire raids for a period of 30 minutes to 1 hour each, known as annihilation fire waves, on the concept

Beaumont South along the Ancre before the bombardment. (Author's collection)

Beaumont South along the Ancre after the bombardment. (Author's collection)

that the infantry regiment should have full control over the artillery fire in order to inflict maximum losses on the enemy.

Subsequent intercepted messages gave indications that one of these fire events resulted in the wounding of two high ranking British officers who had been meeting, one of whom was supposed to be a battalion commander.

The signal stations were still in good working order and were used when telephone communication was disrupted and when the use of colored flares was not effective in contacting the supporting artillery batteries.

A collection of French and English duds. (*Das 10.Württembergische
Infanterie-Regiment Nr. 180 im Weltkrieg 1914-1918*)

Reinforcements were on the move in the early morning hours to spots that were
considered vital. *Leutnant der Reserve* Stahlhofer was on his way to the 4th Coy located
in *Feste Schwaben*. He turned 23 years old on 1 July.

The heavy fire of the last 7 days had damaged much of the German position but the
remaining defenses were still formidable obstacles to any attacking force. Few machine
guns in any of the regiments had been damaged in the British fire and were ready for use.
The machine gun *Schützen* had been kept busy cleaning and oiling their guns, making
sure the ammunition was in good order and waiting for the moment when the guns
could be brought up out of the dug-outs and put into action. *Musketen* Bn Nr. 1 and the
additional *minenwerfer* companies were ready for the moment the British would attack.

A message was received from the King of Württemberg on 30 June amidst the feverish
activity of the 26th Reserve Division headquarters in Biefvillers:

> If the attack finally came now it would be desired and greeted by the troops with
> great pleasure. We feel confident that the same will be bloodily repelled. The current
> situation of perseverance in the heavy enemy artillery fire places the highest demands
> on the troops.[40]

In the early morning hours of 1 July the 9/R110 reported seeing enemy soldiers at the
Galgen placing tape from the British lines toward the La Boisselle Hollow in a northeastern
direction. Listening post Moritz 28 sent in a report at 2 a.m. on 1 July that the British
Fourth Army had issued orders that the attack would take place at 8 a.m. News of the
attack time was quickly sent to division headquarters, the neighboring regiments and
batteries by cyclist messengers. Everyone would be ready for the attack.

All that was left to do was to wait. The great attack was about to take place and all
of the training and hard work by the men of the XIV Reserve Corps was about to be put
to the ultimate test. The sun rose on the morning of 1 July and it looked as if it would be
a beautiful day of sunshine and warm weather.

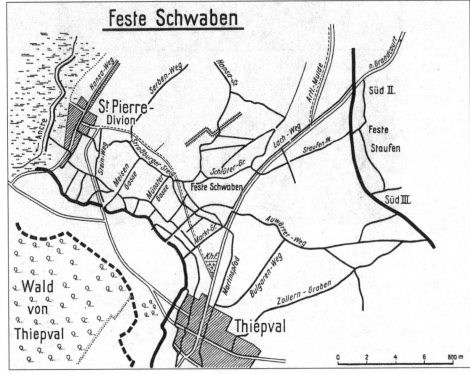

Feste Schwaben sector.

Chapter notes

1. M. Middlebrook, *First Day on the Somme*, pp. 80-81.
2. P. Müller, *Geschichte des Reserve-Infanterie-Regiment Nr. 99*, p. 107.
3. Middlebrook, op. cit., p. 80.
4. G. Holtz, *Das Württembergische Reserve-Infanterie-Regiment Nr. 121 im Weltkrieg 1914-1918*, p. 32.
5. Soden, *Die 26. (Württembergische) Reserve-Division im Weltkrieg 1914-1918*, p. 107.
6. A. Vischer, *Das 10.Württembergische Infanterie-Regiment Nr. 180 im Weltkrieg 1914-1918*, p. 33.
7. PRO W0157/171 4th Army Intelligence Summaries, June 1916.
8. Ibid.
9. The HMS *Baralong*, a Q-ship commanded by Lt. Cdr. Godfrey Herbert, sank U-27 and shot the survivors in the water. Some of the Germans, including SM U-27's captain, *Kapitanleutnant*. Bernhard Wegener, sought refuge aboard the SS *Nicosian*, which had been abandoned by its crew and was still afloat. Herbert sent marines aboard the *Nicosian* who hunted down and killed the remaining German survivors. The deed would have gone unreported except that among the *Nicosian's* crew were several Americans who told the story to the American press when they got home. The British response was to claim 'operational necessity' based on the possibility that the Germans might have armed themselves and escaped aboard the *Nicosian*.
10. Vischer, op. cit., p. 33.

11. W. Turner, *Accrington Pals*, p. 135. VIII Corps Daily Summary No. 86 (from 6 a.m. 26/6/16 to 6 a.m. 27/6/16).

12. J. Edmonds, *History of the Great War. Military Operations France and Belgium 1916. Sir Douglas Haig's Command to the 1st July: Battle of the Somme*, p. 304.

13. Orr, *The Road to the Somme*, p. 155.

14. PRO W0157/171 op. cit. Diary of an unknown German soldier believed to have been found near Fricourt.

15. Soden, op. cit., p. 108.

16. PRO W0157/171 op. cit. Report of Platoon Commander *Leutnant* Lazarus to Commanding Officer 9th Coy, RIR 109 dated 27 June 1916.

17. PRO W0157/171 op. cit.

18. Middlebrook, op. cit., p. 81.

19. H. Wurmb, *Das K. B. Reserve-Infanterie-Regiment Nr. 8*, p. 148.

20. Losch, op cit, *Feldpost* letters dated 28 June 1916 and 30 June 1916.

21. Wurmb, op. cit., p. 149.

22. PRO W0157/171 op. cit.

23. Ibid.

24. Vischer, op. cit., p. 34.

25. PRO W0157/171 op. cit.

26. Müller, op. cit., p. 107.

27. PRO W0157/171, op. cit.

28. Edmonds, op. cit., p. 306.

29. A. Frick, *Erlebnisse in den Ersten Tagen der Somme-Schlacht (24 Juni bis 7 Juli 1916)*. 24 June: 509 rounds; 25 June: 568 rounds; 26 June: 1,036 rounds; 27 June: 517 rounds; 28 June: 581 rounds; 29 June: 865 rounds; 30 June: 1,076 rounds.

30. R. Baumgartner (Ed.), 'The Somme 1 July 1916', *Der Angriff, A Journal of World War 1 History*, No. 13, p. 9.

31. Ibid.

32. PRO W0157/171 op. cit.

33. Ibid.

34. Ibid.

35. Ibid.

36. Ibid.

37. Ibid.

38. Wurmb, op. cit., p. 149.

39. C. Falls, *History of the 36th Division*, p. 47.

40. Baumgartner, op. cit., No. 13, p. 11.

41. Soden, op. cit., p. 108.

Appendix I

Orders of Battle
XIV Reserve Corps

August 1914

Commanding General: *General der Artillerie* von Schubert
Chief of Staff:*Oberstleutnant* Bronsart von Schellendorf
26th Reserve Division: *General der Infanterie Frhr.* von Soden
    51st Reserve Infantry Brigade: *Generalleutnant* von Wundt
        IR 180: *Oberst* von Linck
        RIR 121: *Oberstleutnant* von Josenhans
    52nd Reserve Infantry Brigade: *Generalleutnant* von Auwärter
        RIR 119: *Oberstleutnant Frhr.* von Ziegesar
        RIR 120: *Oberstleutnant* Neumann
    Württemberg Reserve Dragoon Regiment: *Major* Kündinger
    Reserve Field Artillery Regiment 26: *Oberstleutnant* Erlenbusch
    4th Pioneer Company 13th Pioneer Battalion
    Reserve Division Bridging Train 26
    Württemberg Reserve *Sanitäts* Company 26

28th Reserve Division: *Generalleutnant* von Pavel
    55th Reserve Infantry Brigade: *Generalleutnant* von Sieg
        RIR 40: *Oberstleutnant* John von Freynd
        RIR 109: *Oberstleutnant* von Baumbach
        Reserve *Jäger* Battalion 8

Staff of the 28th Reserve Division. (*Reserve-Infanterie Regiment Nr. 110 im Weltkrieg 1914-1918*)

56th Reserve Infantry Brigade: *General Major* von Hammerstein-Equord
    RIR 110: *Oberstleutnant Frhr.* von Vietinghoff
    RIR 111: *Oberstleutnant* von Ley
    Reserve *Jäger* Battalion 14
Reserve Dragoon Regiment 8: *Major* von Bresler
Reserve Field Artillery Regiment 29: *Oberstleutnant* von Deimling
1st and 2nd Reserve Pioneer Companies 13th Pioneer Battalion
Reserve Division Bridging Train 28
Reserve *Sanitäts* Company 14

Corps Troops
    Reserve Telephone *Abteilung* 14
    Reserve Ammunition Column and Trains: *Major* Ingenohl
    Since 19 August 1914 RIR 99: *Oberstleutnant* Rayle, assigned to 26th Reserve Division
    6th Battery Reserve Foot Artillery Regiment 10: *Hauptmann* Berlin
    8th Battery Reserve Foot Artillery Regiment 10: *Hauptmann* Koehler

30 June 1916

(The corps was comprised of five divisions at this time, 2nd Guard Reserve Division, 52nd Division, 26th Reserve Division, 28th Reserve Division and 12th Division. This chart will only address the 26th and 28th Reserve Divisions)

Commanding General: *Generalleutnant* von Stein
Chief of Staff: *Major* Kirch
26th Reserve Division: *General der Infanterie Frhr.* von Soden
    51st Reserve Infantry Brigade
        IR 180 with two machine gun companies
        RIR 121 with one machine gun company, Machine Gun Company Fassbender and Machine Gun Marksman Detachment 198
    52nd Reserve Infantry Brigade
        RIR 119 with two machine gun companies
        RIR 99 with two machine gun companies
    Württemberg Reserve Dragoon Regiment
    26th Reserve Field Artillery Brigade
        Reserve Field Artillery Regiment 26
        Reserve Field Artillery Regiment 27
        Flak Detachment 137
    Württemberg Cyclist Company 2
    4th and 6th Reserve Pioneer Companies 13th Pioneer Battalion
    Spotlight Detachment 256
    Minenwerfer Company 226
    Reserve Division Bridging Train 26
    Reserve *Sanitäts* Company 26
    Medical Ambulance Column 5
    Field Recruit Depot

Attached units:

    Bavarian RIR 8 with one machine gun company, Machine Gun Marksman Detachment 45 and Machine Gun Marksman Detachment 89 (10th Bavarian Infantry Division)

    Bavarian Field Artillery Regiment 20 (10th Bavarian Infantry Division)

    Bavarian *Minenwerfer* Company 10 (10th Bavarian Infantry Division)

    I/Field Artillery Regiment 104 (52nd Division)

    I/Reserve Field Artillery Regiment 12 (12th Reserve Division)

Attached Corps units:

    Staff, 1st, 2nd and 3rd Batteries Foot Artillery Battalion 51

    Foot Artillery Battery 749 (From Foot Artillery Battalion 229)

Attached Army units:

    Four Belgian 5.7cm Cannon

    Foot Artillery Battery 471

    Foot Artillery Battery 551

    ½ 7th Battery 2nd Guard Foot Artillery Regiment

    ½ Foot Artillery Battery 550

    Foot Artillery Battery 683

    Foot Artillery Battery 709

    Foot Artillery Batteries 235 and 236

    1/Foot Artillery Regiment 20

    M. Fr. 43

    Fortress Signal Troop 46 and 47

    2 Motorized Spotlights from Corps Headquarters

    1/ *Musketen* Battalion 1

    Bavarian Pioneer Company 5 (Mining)

    5/*Armierung* Battalion 31

28th Reserve Division: *General Leutnant* von Hahn

    56th Reserve Infantry Brigade

        RIR 109 with two machine gun companies and Machine Gun Marksman Detachment 131

        RIR 110 with two machine gun companies and Machine Gun marksman Detachment 161

        RIR 111 with two machine gun companies

    28th Reserve Field Artillery Brigade

        Reserve Field Artillery Regiment 28

        Reserve Field Artillery Regiment 29

        Flak Detachment 33

    1st and 2nd Reserve Pioneer Companies 13th Pioneer Battalion

    Minenwerfer Company 228

    Reserve Division Bridging Train 28

    Reserve *Sanitäts* Company 14

    Field Recruit Depot

Attached Army units:

IR 23 with one machine gun company and Machine Gun Marksman
    Detachment 132 (12th Division)

Staff, I, 2nd and 3/Field Artillery Regiment 57 (12th Division)

4(F)/Field Artillery Regiment 21 (12th Division)[1]

Staff and I/Bavarian Foot Artillery Battalion 10 (10th Bavarian Division)

Attached Corps units:

Staff, 2nd and 3/Foot Artillery Battalion 229 (Batteries 750 and 751

Attached Army units:

Landwehr Brigade Ersatz Battalion 55 with one machine gun company

2/*Musketen* Battalion 1

II(F)/Field Artillery Regiment 39 with Staff, 5th(F) and 6th(F)/Field Artillery
Regiment 39 and 6th(F)/Field Artillery Regiment 50

III(F)/Field Artillery Regiment 12 (12th Division)

Two Belgian 5.7cm cannon

½ Foot Artillery Battery 550

⅔ Bavarian Foot Artillery Battery 468

½ Foot Artillery Battery 473

Foot Artillery Battery 377

Foot Artillery Battery 718

Foot Artillery Battery 11

4/Foot Artillery Regiment 7

Foot Artillery Battery 381

½ Foot Artillery Battery 473

1st and 3/Foot Artillery Battery 44

7/Reserve Foot Artillery Regiment 12

K *Flak* 72

M Fr 122

1st Reserve and 2/Bavarian Pioneer Regiment

Saxon Pioneer Company 323 (Mining)

1st and 4/*Armierungs* Battalion 64; 2/Bavarian *Armierungs* Battalion 5

---

1 (F) after a battery designation indicates the battery is made up of howitzers.

Appendix II

The discovery and identification of *Landwehrmann* Jakob Hönes

In October 2003 a team of experts, 'No Man's Land', a Great War Archaeological Group, was on a dig that was searching for a dug-out once used by Wilfred Owen in 1917 and that featured prominently in the poem *The Sentry*. During the course of the excavation a large portion of the German front line trenches were discovered along with numerous artifacts but most importantly the remains of three soldiers – two German and one British.

'No Man's Land' is made up of people with different areas of expertise – trained archaeologists, forensic experts, explosive ordnance disposal experts and historians who often double as laborers on site. 'No Man's Land' uses the expertise of each member in order to provide the most accurate depiction of any finds the group makes during the course of a dig.

Once found the human remains took precedence over all other concerns. The archaeologists and forensic experts carefully uncovered the remains and preserved all findings, from the presence of insect larvae to the artifacts discovered in context with the body in the hope of not only identifying the regiment each man served in but to also have the opportunity to identify the men by name.

The finds discovered with each body would have a great impact on this process. The items uncovered could be compared to known information on the fighting that took place in the vicinity of the dig and the historians of the group could attempt to piece together their identities and the details of events the soldiers experienced at the time of their death.

In the case of the lone British soldier items discovered with the remains provided clues to his regiment, the 1st King's Own (Royal Lancaster) Regiment. From the study of the historical records and the condition of the remains it appears most likely that this soldier was killed by shellfire sometime on 1 July 1916 on the opening day of the Battle of the Somme. Unfortunately there was not enough information discovered with the soldier to indicate his identification but the search goes on. His remains were buried in the Serre Road No. 2 Cemetery, a fitting location as it is adjacent to the spot where he fell in 1916.

German No. 1 was found lying in a shallow depression just outside the excavated trench. He was apparently wearing most of his equipment but lacked a helmet and his rifle. The head of the body had been destroyed by deep plowing, something relatively new to the area. He was discovered with full ammunition pouches and his bread bag. Most importantly he was discovered with a personal souvenir, a pot lid from a German department store in Stuttgart and a partially corroded identity disc.

The disc gave some tantalizing clues to his possible identity. It was a single piece disc, the 1915 model as opposed to the two-part perforated disc issued from 1916 to the end of the war. The 1915 disc would provide his unit information but the name of the soldier would normally be missing.

Skeletal remains of Jakob Hönes. ('No Man's Land' Great War Archaeological Group)

Skeletal remains of Albert Thielecke. ('No Man's Land' Great War Archaeological Group)

In this case however the soldier had apparently scratched his name and possibly his hometown on the reverse side so there were additional clues to his identity. A team of historians from England, Germany and the United States reviewed the information and came to the conclusion that the best possibility of matching a regiment to the body was Reserve Infantry Regiment No. 121, more specifically the 7th Company according to the information found on the disc.

This regiment had been active in the area of the dig in 1915 and 1916. Several team members labored over the almost illegible scratches on the reverse side of the disc while the third reviewed the list of possible matches with the known casualties of this company and regiment.

What appeared to be a town or village name starting with 'Mün....' As well as a last name 'Hines' and a first name 'Jak..' was compared to the casualty list without any match. After looking at the last name in greater detail it was discovered that the name was actually 'Hönes' and when looking at the casualty list there was a match: *Landwehrmann* Jakob Hönes, killed in action on 13 June 1915 during the French attacks against Serre. Further confirmation was found when reviewing the hometown listed for Jakob – it turned out to be Münchingen.

The official record of his death found in the Stuttgart Archives reads simply: 'On 13th June killed in action at Serre near Albert, Northern France, by rifle bullet, buried

Jakob Hönes, 1902. (Hönes – Rapp families)

close to the lines 1 km south of Serre. Courcelette, 18th June 1915, von Raben, captain and company commander.' His name appeared on the Württemberg *Verlustlisten* No. 226 dated 23 July 1915, page 7,797.

Subsequently 'No Man's Land' was able to locate the village historian of Münchingen who was able to supply valuable information on Jakob and his life in the small town. Most importantly he was able to locate the family of Jakob Hönes including one of his children, a son.

The family has been very helpful in providing further details on the life of Jakob and in providing the photographs showing him with his comrades in the period just before his death. It was a very satisfying result to a detailed search into the life and death of a German soldier.

The second German body found was to prove harder to identify. While uniform details and insignia provided clues that he was probably in the same regiment as Jakob as well as being a senior non-commissioned officer he was not found with his identity disc.

The remains were in a similar condition as that of Jakob. German No. 2 was wearing most of his equipment minus his helmet or rifle. His bread bag contained a Neolithic flint scraper that he could have very well found during the construction of the numerous trenches on the Somme.

He did however have a bundle of papers inside a packet in his bread bag that would provide key clues to his identity. The documents were in poor condition. being under the ground for the last 88 years. but there was hope that something could be discovered among the rotting paper. The papers did reveal one important clue; the packet was originally a bankbook cover from a private bank in Halberstadt named 'B.J. Bär'. It was hoped that the bank records might have survived all of these years as the bank was discovered to still be in existence in Switzerland. The trail stopped here as we discovered that it was a bank operated by a Jewish family and all records and bank operations were taken over by the German Reich in the 1930's when the owners fled to Switzerland.

The search continued for further clues as to his identity. In checking the casualty lists for RIR 121, in particular the 7th Company, we discovered a senior non-commissioned officer who was killed a few days earlier than Jakob and who was the only man who matched the rank found on the body and most importantly the only casualty who had a strong connection to Halberstadt; his birthplace. His name was *Vizefeldwebel* Albert Thielecke.

It appears that while Albert was serving in a Württemberg regiment he was actually born in Halberstadt and had started his military career in Infantry Regiment No. 27 'Prinz Louis Ferdinand von Preussen' (2nd Magdeburg). He was a career soldier who ended up in Heilbronn where he became part of RIR 121 at the outbreak of the war.

We have been fortunate in locating several relatives of Albert but they were not able to provide any photographs of him with the exception of one slightly damaged photo that could be the man we are looking for. Unfortunately the photograph is not identified. We do know that he was slightly taller than 5 feet 4 inches. He had fair hair and wore a moustache.

The official record of his death as reported by his company commander found in the Stuttgart Archives was: 'Fallen near Serre on 11.6.1915, shot in the head by rifle bullet at

7/R121 in early 1915, Jakob Hönes is far left first row. (Hönes – Rapp families)

7 a.m., buried next to the lines, 1 km south of Serre near Albert in Northern France. To testify to the above, Friedrich von Raben. Captain and Company commander.'

Albert's name originally appeared in Württemberg *Verlustlisten* No. 226 under the name Thidecke (23 July 1915, page 7,797). It later appeared in *Verlustlisten* No. 404 (20 June 1916, page 13,023) where the error was corrected.

The remains of both men were turned over to the *Volksbund Deutscher Kriegsgraberfursorge* for proper burial. The remains were taken to the Labry German Military Cemetery near Verdun where they were interred in a marked grave. A detachment of *Bundeswehr* Signals personnel were present tending the graves and they formed a guard of honor for the fallen men.

Based upon the historic review of the circumstances surrounding the death of both men I have pieced together a brief account of the events of that fateful month over 90 years ago.

The events of early June 1915 along the right flank of the 26th Reserve Division near Serre were chaotic. The French had launched an attack against the neighboring 52nd Division that had captured a large portion of the German front line in the Toutvent farm sector and threatened the right flank of the 26th Reserve Division. If Serre fell then the positions further south at Beaumont, Beaucourt and Thiepval would be threatened.

The 7/R121 was among the large number of units sent to the threatened sector in order to hold the French in check and to limit the gains made by the enemy. On 10 June the 7/R121 consisted of 2 officers, 1 *Offizier Stellvertreter* and 241 Other Ranks, most of whom were veterans of 9 months of trench warfare.

Jakob Hönes and friends, 7/R121. (Hönes – Rapp families)

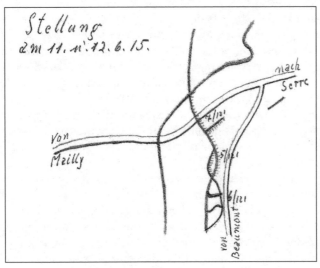

Position of the 7th Coy RIR 121 near Serre, June 1915.

The company arrived on Hill 143 at 9.30 p.m. on 10 June and was ordered to proceed to a section of trench between Hill 143 and Serre along with the 5th Company where they would expel a small force of French troops that had penetrated the German line between the 1/170 and 1/180 and to reinforce the line. A reconnaissance group discovered that the situation had already changed so both companies were now ordered to reinforce the right wing of RIR 119 and 1/170 located there.

The companies advanced under heavy shell fire and arrived in the position at 1 a.m. on the 11th, with the 7/R121 holding the right hand position and adjacent flanking trench, 180 meters north of the Serre-Mailly road. The 5/R121 and a small number of men from 1/170 were located nearby.

The II Battalion staff accompanied the 7/R121 and took up position where the flanking trench joined the main line. The position occupied by elements of the II/R121 was formerly the counter-attack position of IR 170. The position only contained 5 dug-outs for the 5th and 7/R121; there were no observation posts; the weak wire entanglements had been completely destroyed in the heavy artillery fire and most of the fire steps had been destroyed and in many locations the trench was completely leveled.

The flanking trench occupied by the 7/R121 was approximately 70 meters in length of which 60 meters were only knee deep and no fire steps existed at all. The men were put to work in an attempt to improve the position by deepening the trench and creating fire steps. Food could not be brought up because of the heavy fire and no men could be spared to carry the food forward. The hard work continued.

On 11 and 12 June the men were under constant artillery fire. The majority of the men took what cover they could find, mostly lying down in the shallow trench while a small number of men acted as sentries. The losses started to climb as men were buried by collapsing trench walls or being struck by shell splinters and rifle fire.

On 11 June one man, *Vizefeldwebel* Albert Thielecke, 7/R121 was shot through the head at 7 a.m. and killed instantly. There was no time to give him a proper burial so the body was wrapped in a ground sheet and dragged a short distance behind the trench where he was laid to rest on his left side in a shallow depression. The body was covered with a thin layer of soil. Albert was one of many men who became casualties on this day.

One platoon leader, *Leutnant der Landwehr* Stamm, was buried three times by shellfire and each time quickly dug out by the quick-thinking *Unteroffizier* Schick. Stamm remained with his men despite numerous painful contusions.

Everything the men had achieved through hard work during the night was destroyed over and over again during the day by French shellfire. There was no possibility of the men constructing dug-outs or putting up wire entanglements under the current conditions. These tasks were being handled by the 1st Platoon of Pioneer Company 185 under *Leutnant* Rudolf.

Two machine guns arrived on the 11th and were quickly set up in the trenches. Numerous French aircraft flew above the position at altitudes of 100-200 meters. Every attempt to drive them away with rifle and machine gun fire only resulted in more shelling.

In the night of 12/13 June the remnants of the 1/170 were withdrawn leaving only the companies of RIR 121 to hold the line. The French troops opposite them were acting in a restless manner during the night indicating a possible attack the following morning. Shellfire started at 3.30 a.m. that lasted for 2 hours and eliminated any doubts the men may have had.

The sentries of the 7th Company (Schauer and Fuldner) suddenly shouted 'The French are coming!' The French attack came with two waves of skirmishers followed by an assault column. The primary attack was directed toward the small trench held by the

Jakob and Albert's funeral, Labry, France. ('No Man's Land' Great War Archaeological Group)

7th Company and the French troops were supported through heavy flanking fire directed against the 7/R121.

Rifle and machine gun fire from the 7/R121 brought the two lines of skirmishers to a complete stop and they did not get any closer than 150 meters from the German line. The assault column was equally destroyed in the fire of the German artillery that covered the ground in rapid fire.

The French were able to capture a small piece of trench north of the Serre-Mailly road but every attempt to expand their gains was thwarted. Finally they ceased all attacks and were content to hold a small section. It appeared that the French had lost all desire to continue their attacks in the face of such stiff resistance.

Most of the losses suffered by the 7/R121, including *Landwehrmann* Hönes and *Hauptmann* Nagel, were probably the result of the French flanking fire. Jakob had been killed by a rifle shot and was reported to have been with his brother Christian at the time of his death. Christian Hönes survived the French attacks in June 1915 only to become fatally wounded in July 1916 during the Battle of the Somme.

It is suspected that Jakob was killed early on in the attack by the French as his ammunition pouches were almost completely filled, indicating he did not have much time to fire his weapon in defense, if at all.

The body, fully-equipped, was wrapped in a ground sheet and dragged to a nearby depression where he was buried by his comrades, his helmet probably marking his final resting place. When the 7th Company was relieved on 15 June 1915 the company consisted of 1 officer and 99 Other Ranks giving the company a loss of 2 officers, 1 *Offizier Stellvertreter* and 142 Other Ranks.

The fact that the Great War Archaeological Group 'No Man's Land' took such great care and respect of the human remains they discovered lying forgotten under the soil of a French field for almost 90 years allowed the positive identification of two of the three men. These actions allowed the three men to receive the burial they all deserved so long ago and to save them from anonymity.

While it will prove impossible to recover and identify most of the numerous dead from the Great War it does show that with the proper care and expertise the men killed so long ago can still be identified and given the respect long overdue.

The site of the dig and the men are commemorated on a plaque honoring their memory set up on the Serre-Mailly road not far from where the men were discovered near Serre Road No. 2 Cemetery.

Appendix III

Training in the use of hand grenades[1]

Translation of a German document, dated 28/2/16.

TRAINING in the use of HAND GRENADES

(Supplementary orders to those issued by the 180th Regt. No. 729 of 6/2/16.
In training men for grenade fighting the following points are to be noted:

1. During practice with dummy grenades the thrower must always act as if using live grenades and think of the timing, so that when using live grenades he is able to make the necessary pause; counting e.g. *'zwei und zwanzig'* (22), *'drei und zwanzig'* (23) *'vier und zwanzig'* (24), appears practical. These three numbers give the correct amount of pause approximately.

    As a general rule, the grenades are thrown too <u>soon</u>. It must be made clear to the bombers that this practice is quite wrong and can have disastrous results; for the enemy has time to avoid grenades or to throw them back or to one side as the case may be.

2. When the bombing squads of the platoons are fully trained, a second squad of each platoon is to be formed and trained. The first and chief bombing squads of platoons are, however, to be given further training every 14 days. *Leutnant* Helferich will report to me when he considers the bombing squads of the various companies fully trained. I shall then take steps to verify this.

3. The bombing squads and also the 1st squad of the Grenadier platoon are to be armed and equipped as follows:

    Nos. 1 to 4, Pistol, dagger and 6 grenades each.

    Nos. 5 to 8, Rifle, 6 grenades, and 25 sandbags each.

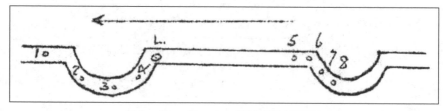

Taken from document PRO WO157/171.

4. Trench tactics will be practiced as shown below:

    No. 1 Thrower

    No. 2 Carrier

---

1   PRO WO157/171 op. cit.

No. 3 Thrower

No. 4 Carrier

L. Leader

Nos. 5 & 6 Carriers

Nos. 7 & 8 Spare men

It is essential to keep the men extended to facilitate freedom of action and enable them to dodge the enemy's grenades, but care must be taken that cohesion is not sacrificed in consequence.

Each squad must be trained that every man can take the place of any other in it. The leading man (No. 1) only will throw, the carrier (No. 2) will prepare the grenades.

Two cases may arise when Nos. 2 and 3 will also throw:

(a)   At the moment of making an attack in order to surprise and confuse the enemy with a sudden shower of grenades. As soon as the attack is in progress Nos. 2 and 3 will cease throwing.

(b)   When the resistance is too strong for the leading thrower to overcome it by himself.

5.   The sandbags carried by Nos. 5 – 8 serve for the rapid construction of a barricade which is held with rifles.

One man, by means of his haversack strap, can easily carry 25 sandbags on his back and, with rifle slung, experience little inconvenience.

6.   The greatest attention is to be paid to the instruction of the Leaders for they will have to act on their own initiative in most circumstances.

In the Grenadier Platoon the position of the Platoon Commander varies with the situation, but, as a general rule, the most suitable position would be with No. 3 Group.

7.   In trench fighting the Platoon Commander or Squad Leader must pay particular attention to the following points:

(a)   See that every man is provided with six grenades.

(b)   See that there is no crowding, in order to minimize the risk of casualties from a well-aimed enemy bomb. There is always danger of crowding during a check in the advance.

(c)   When the resistance of the enemy is not too great, the advance must always be continuous. Special attention must be paid to the supply of grenades.

(d)   As soon as a traverse has been taken No. 2 calls out 'Cleared' ('Geraumt'), the Squad Leader gives the command 'Advance' ('Vor'). Every section of the trench captured must be at once occupied by riflemen.

(e)   The Squad Leader must be provided with small white flags which he will place at intervals, on top of the traverses to mark the progress of the attack. This will prevent bombing parties which are working up the same trench in opposite directions from bombing each other by accident. Small white flags will be made and taken with the men when they carry out training.

(f)   Should the resistance of the enemy be so strong that further advance is impossible even with the help of numbers two and three, the construction of a barricade must be proceeded with at once. The Squad Leader will give the command 'Sandbags up' ('Sandsacke vor'). The Platoon Commander can then decide whether it is possible to relieve the bombing squad and continue the attack, or whether to call a halt in the operations.

The construction of a barricade at 'a1' will be scarcely possible, owing to the number of the enemy's grenades which are being thrown, more especially if our intention is known to him.

The barricade will, therefore, be built at 'a' and if possible the space a-b will be roofed over with stout planks as a protection against grenades.

Nos. 1 – 4 will hold back the enemy until the barricade is completed.

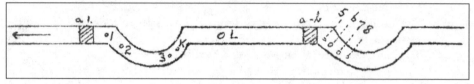

Taken from document PRO W0157/171.

  (g) Should it be necessary to block a communication trench a good thrower at 'a' will give the necessary protection to the remainder who will build the barricade at 'b'.

8. The question of the supply of hand grenades is of the utmost importance.

  (a) <u>Supply during an attack across the open</u>.

If the first wave of the assault has succeeded in entering the enemy's trench, communication to the rear must be kept up so that sandbags, containing about 6 grenades each can be passed forward continuously.

  (b) <u>Supply in the Trench</u>.

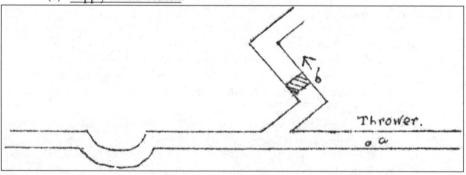

Taken from document PRO W0157/171.

<u>No</u>. 1 (Thrower) will only use the grenades which are passed up to him, never his own, which must be kept as a reserve for an emergency.

In Grenadier Platoons every squad, except the first, must be provided with a small box of grenades or with three or four sandbags each containing six grenades. The passing up of grenades should be thoroughly practiced.

(Signed) FISCHER

Appendix IV

Casualty lists (*Verlustlisten*)

Shortly after the arrival of the XIV Reserve Corps on the Somme and the start of trench warfare small cemeteries began to appear in the towns and villages behind the front due to the increasing numbers of men who had been killed in action, died from disease or injury. Later, when it was accepted that the XIV Reserve Corps would be positioned on the Somme for an extended period of time larger, well-planned cemeteries were created at Bapaume, Miraumont and other locations.

Whenever possible the dead were transported to one of the many cemeteries that dotted the countryside where they could receive a proper burial and marked grave. In times of stress it was not always possible to do this and many men were simply buried where they fell as in the case of Jakob Hönes and Albert Thielecke and their comrades who fell during the June fighting near Serre.

In the years following the war little research has been directed to the German casualties and in most cases they have remained anonymous. Recently, with the advent of the Internet and sites such as http://www.volksbund.de/ where anyone can look up details on the fatal casualties of the German army for both World Wars this research has been made easier. The unfortunate aspect of research into the men who served in the war is that it is far easier to locate information if the man was killed than if he survived.

The men shown in the lists below each represent a son, brother, father or uncle to a family in Germany. Their names until now have only been known to a few researchers and to some of their families. Many have become lost to history as their memories fade and the people who once knew them have passed away.

Most of the men listed below who gave their lives for what they believed in have no known grave. Some may have been buried in a cemetery during the war with a marked grave but many of these were destroyed during the fighting between July and November 1916 as well as in 1918 when the war returned to the Somme with all of its violence.

Some graves that survived the fighting were subsequently destroyed by the French population and government in the post-war years but the few that survived both the heavy fighting and anger of the returning population were consolidated into a few central cemeteries containing German war dead. Most of the burials are in mass graves and there are few marked graves in comparison to the numerous Allied cemeteries that dot the landscape.

Not every regiment in the XIV Reserve Corps is represented in the lists shown below. Much of the information needed to prepare similar lists for every unit does not exist, in some cases due to the destruction of German archives during WWII. While some materials do exist that could be used to reproduce a list of the fatal casualties they do not provide sufficient detail in order to create an accurate accounting without years of effort.

The regiments listed below, one artillery regiment and seven infantry regiments, will provide the reader with some idea of the scale of casualties suffered in these regiments.

While the lists only show fatal casualties the number of wounded, injured and captured from these regiments would be much higher.

As an example, in comparing the number of men killed to the number of men wounded for the period of time covered in the following charts for three of the regiments – RIR 119, RIR 121 and RIR 180 – I would have to add an additional 3,187 names to the list for these regiments alone for the same period.

In comparison to the number of British and cemeteries that appear virtually everywhere one looks on the Somme there are only a few German cemeteries one can visit that have any connection to the heavy fighting on the Somme from the 1914-1916 period. The largest is located Fricourt on the D-147 as one heads toward Contalmaison. This cemetery contains 17,027 German burials with the majority (11,970) located in four large mass graves. Other German cemeteries that can be visited by interested parties are at Sapignies opposite the church where there are 1,550 burials; Achiet-le-Petit (next to the village cemetery) with 1,314 burials; Villers-au-Flos lying north of the village with 2,449 burials; Rancourt on the D-20 southwest of the village where there are 11,422 burials in individual graves and mass graves; Bray-sur-Somme, located west of the village with 1,119 burials, and Proyart, 500 meters from the center of the village in the direction of Bray-sur-Somme and next to the village cemetery with 4,643 burials.

The cemeteries listed above cover both the French and British sectors of the Somme.

RIR 40 NAME	RANK	CO.	DATE OF DEATH	LOCATION	NOTES
Gaukel, Josef	Infantryman	4	27-Sep-1914	Fricourt	
Glasbrenner, Ludwig	Infantryman	6	27-Sep-1914	Fricourt	?
Liebscher, Richard	Infantryman	12	27-Sep-1914	Flers	Died in hospital.
Diez, Friedrich	Infantryman	2	28-Sep-1914	Fricourt	M.I.A., declared dead.
Braun, Josef	Infantryman	6	28-Sep-1914	Fricourt	
Seuss, Karl	Infantryman	6	28-Sep-1914	Fricourt	
Walker, Karl	Infantryman	6	28-Sep-1914	Fricourt	
Zimmer, Alfred	Oberleutnant der Reserve	9	28-Sep-1914	Fricourt	
Beltle, Gotthold	Infantryman	10	28-Sep-1914	Fricourt	
Fluhr, Friedrich	Infantryman	10	28-Sep-1914	Fricourt	
von Freynd, Richard John	Oberstleutnant	Regt. Staff	28-Sep-1914	Contalmaison	Killed by shrapnel shell
Glock, Franz	Infantryman	1	29-Sep-1914	Fricourt	M.I.A., declared dead.
Pahl, Josef	Infantryman	1	29-Sep-1914	Fricourt	
Fütterer, Karl	Unteroffizier	2	29-Sep-1914	Fricourt	
Kratzmüller, Franz	Infantryman	2	29-Sep-1914	Fricourt	
Geiss, Daniel	Infantryman	3	29-Sep-1914	Fricourt	
Buchhorn, Heinrich	Infantryman	4	29-Sep-1914	Fricourt	M.I.A., declared dead.
Kurtz, Karl	Infantryman	4	29-Sep-1914	Fricourt	
Maier, Franz	Unteroffizier	6	29-Sep-1914	Fricourt	

RIR 40 NAME	RANK	CO.	DATE OF DEATH	LOCATION	NOTES
Maier, Franz	Infantryman	6	29-Sep-1914	Fricourt	
von König, Walter	Unteroffizier	6	29-Sep-1914	Fricourt	
Dietz, Gottlieb	Infantryman	9	29-Sep-1914	Fricourt	
Gollub, Julius	Infantryman	9	29-Sep-1914	Fricourt	
Grosch, Ernst	Offizier Stellvertreter	9	29-Sep-1914	Fricourt	
Hemberger, Karl	Unteroffizier	9	29-Sep-1914	Fricourt	
Henke, Otto	Infantryman	9	29-Sep-1914	Fricourt	M.I.A., declared dead.
von Bergen, Ludwig	Unteroffizier	9	29-Sep-1914	Fricourt	
Balzer, Karl	Unteroffizier	10	29-Sep-1914	Fricourt	M.I.A., declared dead.
Klein, Otto	Infantryman	10	29-Sep-1914	Fricourt	
Kreh, Karl	Vizefeldwebel	10	29-Sep-1914	Fricourt	
Mehlin, Karl	Infantryman	10	29-Sep-1914	Fricourt	
Schwächler, Xaver	Infantryman	11	29-Sep-1914	Fricourt	
Brosch, August	Infantryman	12	29-Sep-1914	Fricourt	M.I.A., declared dead.
Dirkes, Hermann	Infantryman	12	29-Sep-1914	Bazentin	Died in hospital.
Schüdzick, Wilhelm	Infantryman	12	29-Sep-1914	Fricourt	M.I.A., declared dead.
Baumeister, August	Infantryman	9	30-Sep-1914	Fricourt	
Bose, Otto	Infantryman	9	30-Sep-1914	Fricourt	
Boulanger, Paul	Unteroffizier	10	30-Sep-1914	Fricourt	
Bewig, Heinrich	Gefreiter	11	30-Sep-1914	Fricourt	
Czarnecki, Ludwig	Infantryman	11	30-Sep-1914	Fricourt	
Hellmich, Ludwig	Infantryman	11	30-Sep-1914	Fricourt	
Herre, Karl	Infantryman	11	30-Sep-1914	Fricourt	
Kanzler, Adam	Infantryman	11	30-Sep-1914	Fricourt	
Kessler, Jakob	Infantryman	11	30-Sep-1914	Fricourt	
Lutz, Julius	Infantryman	11	30-Sep-1914	Fricourt	
Neudeck, Heinrich	Infantryman	11	30-Sep-1914	Fricourt	
Walter, Sigmund	Unteroffizier	11	30-Sep-1914	Combles	Died in hospital.
Hofheinz, Oskar	Infantryman	4	1-Oct-1914	Fricourt	
Müller, Friedrich	Gefreiter	7	1-Oct-1914	Fricourt	
Deuschle, Emil	Infantryman	8	1-Oct-1914	Longueval	Died in hospital.
Jung, Friedrich	Infantryman	8	1-Oct-1914	Combles	Died in hospital.
Epp, Hermann	Infantryman	10	1-Oct-1914	Flers	Died in hospital.
Jung, Heinrich	Unteroffizier	11	1-Oct-1914	Fricourt	
Münch, Johann	Infantryman	11	1-Oct-1914	Fricourt	M.I.A., declared dead.
Binder, Alfons	Infantryman	4	2-Oct-1914	Fricourt	

| RIR 40 | | | DATE OF | | |
NAME	RANK	CO.	DEATH	LOCATION	NOTES
Klink, Robert	Infantryman	4	2-Oct-1914	Fricourt	
Stein, Leonhard	Infantryman	5	2-Oct-1914	Flers	Died in hospital.
Becker, Adam	Infantryman	7	2-Oct-1914	Contalmaison	Died in hospital.
Dagenbach, Karl	Infantryman	11	2-Oct-1914	Fricourt	
Hess, Georg	Infantryman	7	3-Oct-1914	Fricourt	
Müller, Otto	Vizefeldwebel	8	3-Oct-1914	Fricourt	
Seiler, Ludwig	Unteroffizier	8	3-Oct-1914	Fricourt	
Soganger, Wilhelm	Infantryman	9	3-Oct-1914	Fricourt	
Kroner, Franz	Infantryman	10	3-Oct-1914	Fricourt	
Abele, Albert	Offizier Stellvertreter	2	4-Oct-1914	Fricourt	
Meckel, Arno	Infantryman	2	4-Oct-1914	Fricourt	
Müller, Andreas	Infantryman	2	4-Oct-1914	Fricourt	
Schaum, Gustav	Infantryman	2	4-Oct-1914	Fricourt	
Ulses, Heinrich	Infantryman	2	4-Oct-1914	Péronne	Died in hospital.
Lindekeit, Wilhelm	Unteroffizier	4	4-Oct-1914	Fricourt	M.I.A., declared dead.
Baier, Michael	Infantryman	8	4-Oct-1914	Flers	Died in hospital.
Hartle, Friedrich	Infantryman	10	4-Oct-1914	Fricourt	
Psiuk, Vinzenz	Gefreiter	10	4-Oct-1914	Fricourt	
Benz, Heinrich	Infantryman	2	5-Oct-1914	Flers	Died in hospital.
Fuhrer, Philipp	Infantryman	2	5-Oct-1914	Fricourt	
Metzger, August	Infantryman	2	5-Oct-1914	Flers	Died in hospital.
Schnatterer, Karl	Infantryman	2	5-Oct-1914	Fricourt	
Umhauer, Albert	Gefreiter	3	5-Oct-1914	Fricourt	
Rauch, Johannes	Infantryman	8	5-Oct-1914	Contalmaison	
Schilze, Albert	Unteroffizier	11	5-Oct-1914	Fricourt	
Henk, Alfons	Gefreiter	3	6-Oct-1914	Fricourt	
Hartmann, Johann	Infantryman	6	6-Oct-1914	Flers	Died in hospital.
Egler, Gustav	Infantryman	11	6-Oct-1914	Fricourt	
Scheurmann, Martin	Infantryman	1	7-Oct-1914	Fricourt	M.I.A., declared dead.
Eidel, Ambros	Infantryman	2	7-Oct-1914	Fricourt	
Schimper, Theodor	Gefreiter	2	7-Oct-1914	Bapaume	Died in hospital.
von Schmidt, Waldemar	Hauptmann	3	7-Oct-1914	Fricourt	
Bamberger, Franz	Infantryman	4	7-Oct-1914	Fricourt	M.I.A., declared dead.
Brenk, Philipp	Infantryman	4	7-Oct-1914	Fricourt	M.I.A., declared dead.
Gruber, Heinrich	Infantryman	4	7-Oct-1914	Fricourt	M.I.A., declared dead.
Härlin, Friedrich	Infantryman	4	7-Oct-1914	Fricourt	M.I.A., declared dead.
Kunkel, Karl	Infantryman	4	7-Oct-1914	Fricourt	M.I.A., declared dead.

RIR 40 NAME	RANK	CO.	DATE OF DEATH	LOCATION	NOTES
Liebmann, Johann	Infantryman	4	7-Oct-1914	Fricourt	M.I.A., declared dead.
Loeb, Mathias	Infantryman	4	7-Oct-1914	Fricourt	
Meistermann, Alois	Infantryman	4	7-Oct-1914	Fricourt	M.I.A., declared dead.
Metzger, Anton	Infantryman	4	7-Oct-1914	Fricourt	M.I.A., declared dead.
Meyer, Christian	Infantryman	4	7-Oct-1914	Fricourt	M.I.A., declared dead.
Nohe, Ludwig	Infantryman	4	7-Oct-1914	Fricourt	M.I.A., declared dead.
Rau, Gotthilf	Infantryman	4	7-Oct-1914	Fricourt	
Ruf, Camillo	Infantryman	4	7-Oct-1914	Fricourt	
Sauer, Anton	Unteroffizier	4	7-Oct-1914	Fricourt	M.I.A., declared dead.
Schäfer, Georg	Infantryman	4	7-Oct-1914	Fricourt	
Braun, Karl	Infantryman	1	8-Oct-1914	Fricourt	
Eisenhauer, Rudolf	Infantryman	1	8-Oct-1914	Fricourt	M.I.A., declared dead.
Kirsch, Philipp	Infantryman	1	8-Oct-1914	Fricourt	
Knapp, Bernhard	Infantryman	1	8-Oct-1914	Fricourt	M.I.A., declared dead.
Richels, Heinrich	Infantryman	1	8-Oct-1914	Fricourt	M.I.A., declared dead.
Kümmerle, Georg	Infantryman	3	8-Oct-1914	Fricourt	M.I.A., declared dead.
Fränznick, Josef	Infantryman	4	8-Oct-1914	Fricourt	M.I.A., declared dead.
Martin, Ludwig	Unteroffizier	4	8-Oct-1914	Fricourt	
Metzger, Philpp	Infantryman	4	8-Oct-1914	Fricourt	M.I.A., declared dead.
Kohler, Eugen	Infantryman	5	8-Oct-1914	Fricourt	
Berg, Philipp	Infantryman	11	8-Oct-1914	Fricourt	
Bergmauer, Johann	Infantryman	11	8-Oct-1914	Fricourt	
Hartmann, Ludwig	Infantryman	12	8-Oct-1914	Cambrai	Died in hospital.
Schmitt, Nikolaus	Infantryman	6	9-Oct-1914	Fricourt	
Popp, Ludwig	Infantryman	6	10-Oct-1914	Cambrai	Died in hospital.
Schelb, Emil	Infantryman	1	11-Oct-1914	Fricourt	Died in hospital.
Hedryk, Stanislaus	Infantryman	11	12-Oct-1914	Fricourt	
Meier, Albert	Infantryman	6	17-Oct-1914	Fricourt	
Roth, Wilhelm	Gefreiter	6	18-Oct-1914	Cambrai	Died in hospital.
Hörstchen, Paul	Gefreiter	10	18-Oct-1914	Fricourt	
Kleber, Friedrich	Unteroffizier	10	18-Oct-1914	Fricourt	
Stehle, Xaver	Unteroffizier	10	18-Oct-1914	Fricourt	
Demmerlein, Georg	Infantryman	2	19-Oct-1914	Fricourt	
Krüger, Heinrich	Infantryman	2	19-Oct-1914	Fricourt	
Manninger, Franz	Infantryman	4	19-Oct-1914	Fricourt	M.I.A., declared dead.
Beckmann, Johann	Unteroffizier	10	20-Oct-1914	Flers	Died in hospital.
Bach, Michael	Infantryman	2	21-Oct-1914	Fricourt	
Faltin, Josef	Infantryman	10	21-Oct-1914	Fricourt	

RIR 40 NAME	RANK	CO.	DATE OF DEATH	LOCATION	NOTES
Lenz, Ernst	Infantryman	4	25-Oct-1914	Flers	
Dressel, Oskar	Infantryman	5	26-Oct-1914	Flers	Died in hospital.
Factin, Gustav	Infantryman	12	31-Oct-1914	?	
Göddenhoff, Emil	Infantryman	M.G.	1-Nov-1914	Mametz	
Eberle, Wilhelm	Infantryman	6	3-Nov-1914	Flers	Died in hospital.
Fischer, Wilhelm	Infantryman	6	3-Nov-1914	Flers	Died in hospital.
Frank, August	Infantryman	8	8-Nov-1914	Mametz	
Woll, Johannes	Infantryman	7	16-Nov-1914	Mametz	
Brückner, Wilhelm	Infantryman	9	21-Nov-1914	St. Quentin	Died in hospital.
Müller, Christian	Unteroffizier	4	23-Nov-1914	Montauban	
Schischke, Wilhelm	Infantryman	10	23-Nov-1914	Mametz	
Bea, Albert	Unteroffizier	10	29-Nov-1914	St. Quentin	
Bamberger, Franz	Infantryman	11	30-Nov-1914	Montauban	
Geist, Mathäus	Infantryman	4	6-Dec-1914	Combles	Died in hospital.
Karg, Anton	Unteroffizier	12	6-Dec-1914	Flers	Died in hospital.
Ruck, Ludwig	Infantryman	9	8-Dec-1914	Montauban	
Hirschinger, Heinrich	Infantryman	8	13-Dec-1914	St. Quentin	Died in hospital.
Beer, August	Infantryman	7	14-Dec-1914	Flers	Died in hospital.
Metzgel, Johann	Infantryman	8	15-Dec-1914	Villers au Flos	Died in hospital.
Büttner, Josef	Infantryman	8	16-Dec-1914	Montauban	
Botz, August	Gefreiter	6	17-Dec-1914	Montauban	
Hecher, Max	Unteroffizier	6	17-Dec-1914	Montauban	
Urban, Adolf	Infantryman	6	17-Dec-1914	Montauban	
Conrad, Karl	Infantryman	9	17-Dec-1914	Mametz	
Dörtelmann, Heinrich	Gefreiter	9	17-Dec-1914	Mametz	
Brückmann, Johann	Infantryman	10	17-Dec-1914	Mametz	
Hage, Clemens	Infantryman	10	17-Dec-1914	Mametz	
Schäfenacker, Christof	Infantryman	10	17-Dec-1914	Mametz	
Knoch, Hermann	Infantryman	5	18-Dec-1914	Flers	Died in hospital.
Schmitt, Thoedor	Vizefeldwebel	5	18-Dec-1914	Montauban	
Senn, Julius	Infantryman	7	18-Dec-1914	Montauban	
Bernhardt, Emil	Infantryman	8	18-Dec-1914	St. Quentin	Died in hospital.
Weil, Wilhelm	Infantryman	8	18-Dec-1914	Flers	Died in hospital.
Hennegriff, Josef	Infantryman	11	18-Dec-1914	Montauban	
Thomann, Hermann	Hauptmann der Reserve	11	18-Dec-1914	Montauban	
Hennegriff, Karl	Infantryman	4	19-Dec-1914	Montauban	
Gautzsch, Wilhelm	Offizier Stellvertreter	11	19-Dec-1914	Montauban	

RIR 40 NAME	RANK	CO.	DATE OF DEATH	LOCATION	NOTES
Neubeck, Franz	Unteroffizier	11	19-Dec-1914	Montauban	
Altrieth, Gustav	Infantryman	12	19-Dec-1914	Flers	Died in hospital.
Eisenhauer, Wilhelm	Infantryman	M.G.	19-Dec-1914	Mametz	
Bassemir, Hermann	Unteroffizier	4	21-Dec-1914	St. Quentin	Died in hospital.
Georgi, Otto	Infantryman	6	21-Dec-1914	Montauban	
Fath, Nikolaus	Infantryman	8	21-Dec-1914	Montauban	
Hilty, Alfons	Infantryman	8	21-Dec-1914	Montauban	
Kraus, Fritz	Leutnant der Reserve	12	21-Dec-1914	Mametz	
Hannemann, Friedrich	Infantryman	8	22-Dec-1914	Montauban	
Becher, Franz	Infantryman	12	22-Dec-1914	Mametz	
Blaszczyk, Stanislaus	Infantryman	12	22-Dec-1914	Flers	
Ehmer, Adams	Gefreiter	6	24-Dec-1914	St. Quentin	
Schmalholz, Xaver	Infantryman	12	24-Dec-1914	St. Quentin	Died in hospital.
Wenzel, Alexander	Infantryman	2	25-Dec-1914	St. Quentin	Died in hospital.
Haas, Walter	Infantryman	2	26-Dec-1914	Flers	Died in hospital.
Bell, Irwin	Unteroffizier	12	28-Dec-1914	Flers	Died in field hospital.
Dürr, Max	Infantryman	12	28-Dec-1914	St. Quentin	Died in hospital.
Greiner, Johannes	Infantryman	1	29-Dec-1914	Mametz	
Jung, Valentin	Infantryman	1	29-Dec-1914	Mametz	
Schaum, Wilhelm	Infantryman	1	29-Dec-1914	Mametz	
Weicker, Karl	Infantryman	4	29-Dec-1914	Mametz	
Dressel, Albert	Infantryman	6	30-Dec-1914	Montauban	
Schuhr, Karl	Infantryman	10	1-Jan-1915	Montauban	
Drach, Jakob	Infantryman	11	2-Jan-1915	St. Quentin	Died in hospital.
Albicker, Adolf	Infantryman	11	3-Jan-1915	Mametz	
Zapp, Otto	Infantryman	6	5-Jan-1915	Montauban	
Fischer, Georg	Infantryman	3	6-Jan-1915	Montauban	
Lutz, Emil	Infantryman	5	8-Jan-1915	Montauban	
Kahlmeier, Michael	Infantryman	3	10-Jan-1915	Montauban	
Eckhardt, Emil	Unteroffizier	9	15-Jan-1915	Montauban	
Wörner, Alfred	Infantryman	10	17-Jan-1915	Montauban	
Schneider, Wilhelm	Infantryman	3	19-Jan-1915	Flers	Died in hospital.
Schnepf, Karl	Infantryman	12	20-Jan-1915	Flers	Died in hospital.
Luz, Ernst	Infantryman	7	26-Jan-1915	Mametz	
Fried, Josef	Infantryman	9	26-Jan-1915	Montauban	
Niemeyer, Karl	Infantryman	7	28-Jan-1915	Mametz	
Staudt, Georg	Infantryman	8	29-Jan-1915	Montauban	

RIR 40 NAME	RANK	CO.	DATE OF DEATH	LOCATION	NOTES
Breisch, Valentin	Infantryman	3	30-Jan-1915	Montauban	
Ertl, Xaver	Infantryman	7	30-Jan-1915	Mametz	
Hagner, Ernst	Vizefeldwebel	7	30-Jan-1915	Montauban	
Hildenbrand, Emil	Infantryman	7	30-Jan-1915	Mametz	
Kraft, Adam	Unteroffizier	7	30-Jan-1915	Montauban	
Mayer, Ludwig	Infantryman	7	30-Jan-1915	Mametz	
Wolf, Karl	Infantryman	7	30-Jan-1915	Mametz	
Wenzel, Friedrich	Gefreiter	5	1-Feb-1915	Mametz	
Grimm, Edwin	Infantryman	7	1-Feb-1915	Flers	
Zillesen, Heinrich	Infantryman	11	5-Feb-1915	Mametz	
Häfele, Koni	Infantryman	3	7-Feb-1915	Montauban	M.I.A., declared dead.
Kuhn, Hugo	Unteroffizier	3	7-Feb-1915	Montauban	M.I.A., declared dead.
Achtabowsty, Wojciek	Infantryman	9	10-Feb-1915	Mametz	
Beyer, Hermann	Infantryman	10	11-Feb-1915	Mametz	
Diehlmann, Hermann	Infantryman	11	13-Feb-1915	Mametz	
Pfisterer, Ludwig	Infantryman	5	17-Feb-1915	Montauban	
Hüster, Johann	Unteroffizier	11	18-Feb-1915	Mametz	
Möstle, Franz	Infantryman	4	20-Feb-1915	Mametz	
Harnist, Eugen	Infantryman	5	20-Feb-1915	Mametz	
Menges, Wilhelm	Infantryman	11	8-Mar-1915	Montauban	
Fuckel, Karl	Infantryman	5	12-Mar-1915	Mametz	
Reutter, Christof	Infantryman	5	12-Mar-1915	Mametz	
Weber, Josef	Infantryman	5	12-Mar-1915	Mametz	
Heitz, Franz	Gefreiter	2	14-Mar-1915	Montauban	
Winter, Friedrich	Infantryman	2	14-Mar-1915	Montauban	
Bloch, Paulus	Gefreiter	8	15-Mar-1915	Montauban	
Gauggel, Augustin	Unteroffizier	2	17-Mar-1915	Montauban	
Karcher, Karl	Infantryman	2	17-Mar-1915	Montauban	
Bölzner, Ernst	Unteroffizier	1	21-Mar-1915	Montauban	
Kaufmann, Karl	Infantryman	1	21-Mar-1915	Montauban	
Völkel, Josef	Infantryman	12	25-Mar-1915	Flers	
Weller, Ludwig	Gefreiter	4	22-May-1915	Mametz	
Bütterlin, Karl	Infantryman	5	22-May-1915	Mametz	M.I.A., declared dead.
Merkel, Theodor	Infantryman	5	16-Jun-1915	Beaumont	Died in hospital.

RIR 109

NAME	RANK	CO.	DATE OF DEATH	LOCATION	NOTES
Blum, Lorenz	Grenadier der Landwehr I	1	27-Sep-1914	Ligny	W.I.A., died 30-Sep-1914 at Bapaume.
Britsch, Rudolf	Gefreiter der Landwehr I	1	27-Sep-1914	Contalmaison	W.I.A., died in Bapaume
Konstandin, Gustav	Grenadier der Landwehr II	1	27-Sep-1914	Ligny	
Doser, August	Reservist	2	27-Sep-1914	Bapaume	
Kempter, Julius	Wehrmann	4	27-Sep-1914	Bapaume	
Knopf, Ludwig	Landwehrn-mann	12	27-Sep-1914	Bapaume	
Bickel, Josef	Grenadier der Landwehr I	1	28-Sep-1914	Contalmaison	
Hollander, Leonhard	Gefreiter der Reserve	1	28-Sep-1914	Contalmaison	W.I.A., died 30-Sep-1914 during transport from Bapaume to Cambrai.
Munz, Leopold	Grenadier der Landwehr II	1	28-Sep-1914	Contalmaison	
Schanzlin, Ernst	Grenadier der Landwehr I	1	28-Sep-1914	Contalmaison	
Schimpf, Albert	Grenadier	1	28-Sep-1914	Contalmaison	
Windbiel, Anton	Feldwebel	1	28-Sep-1914	Contalmaison	
Götz, Emil	Reservist	2	28-Sep-1914	Contalmaison	
Reiss, Emil	Reservist	2	28-Sep-1914	Contalmaison	W.I.A., died 8-Oct-1914 in Aachen.
Buntru, Josef	Wehrmann	3	28-Sep-1914	Contalmaison	

Soldiers' cemetery in Miraumont. (Author's collection)

RIR 109

NAME	RANK	CO.	DATE OF DEATH	LOCATION	NOTES
Hauber, Johann	Reservist	3	28-Sep-1914	Contalmaison	W.I.A., died 3-Oct-1914 in Field Hospital Contalmaison
Haug, Georg	Gefreiter	3	28-Sep-1914	Contalmaison	
Hauser, Josef	Gefreiter	3	28-Sep-1914	Contalmaison	
Kleiser, Augustin	Unteroffizier	3	28-Sep-1914	Contalmaison	
Möller I, Hermann	Gefreiter	3	28-Sep-1914	Contalmaison	
Paul, Jakob	Wehrmann	3	28-Sep-1914	Contalmaison	
Reinbold, Rudolf	Reservist	3	28-Sep-1914	Contalmaison	
Rich, Ernst	Wehrmann	3	28-Sep-1914	Fricourt	W.I.A., died 3-Oct-1914 at Field Hospital, Flers.
Schneider, Georg	Wehrmann	3	28-Sep-1914	Contalmaison	
Steinberger, Johann	Wehrmann	3	28-Sep-1914	Contalmaison	
Weiss I, Theopont	Gefreiter	3	28-Sep-1914	Contalmaison	
Bertsche, Eduard	Wehrmann	4	28-Sep-1914	Contalmaison	
Dörflinger, Alfred	Gefreiter	4	28-Sep-1914	Contalmaison	
Jenne, Karl	Wehrmann	4	28-Sep-1914	Contalmaison	W.I.A., died 4-Oct-1914 in Cambrai.
Knopf, Karl	Wehrmann	4	28-Sep-1914	Contalmaison	W.I.A., died 4-Oct-1914 in Flers.
Kornatz, Emil	Musketier	4	28-Sep-1914	Contalmaison	W.I.A., died 30-Sep-1914 in Flers.
Kubach, Wilhelm	Gefreiter	4	28-Sep-1914	Contalmaison	
Lortiz, Eduard	Wehrmann	4	28-Sep-1914	Contalmaison	W.I.A., died 1-Oct-1914 in Le Sars.
Maier III, Josef	Wehrmann	4	28-Sep-1914	Contalmaison	
Pfeiffer, Karl	Wehrmann	4	28-Sep-1914	Contalmaison	
Scholl, Peter	Wehrmann	4	28-Sep-1914	Contalmaison	
Steiger, Karl	Wehrmann	4	28-Sep-1914	Contalmaison	W.I.A., died 30-Sep-1914 in Flers.
Weimer, Ernst	Wehrmann	4	28-Sep-1914	Contalmaison	W.I.A., died 29-Sep-1914 in Flers.
Beck, Felix	Reservist	5	28-Sep-1914	Contalmaison	W.I.A., died 30-Sep-1914 in hospital in Contalmaison.
Jakubowsky, Johann	Reservist	5	28-Sep-1914	Contalmaison	
Nees, Ludwig	Landwehrmann	5	28-Sep-1914	Contalmaison	
Vogelbacher, Jakob	Reservist	5	28-Sep-1914	Contalmaison	
Korn, Friedrich	Wehrmann	7	28-Sep-1914	Contalmaison	W.I.A., died 10-Oct-1914, Contalmaison.
Thomann, Franz	Landwehrmann	7	28-Sep-1914	Fricourt	
Hummel, Rudolf	Reservist	8	28-Sep-1914	Contalmaison	
Braun, Berthold	Sanitäts Gefreiter	1	29-Sep-1914	Fricourt	W.I.A., died 9-Oct-1914 at Lüttich.
Maier, Otto	Grenadier der Reserve	1	29-Sep-1914	Fricourt	
Schmidt, Adolf	Vizefeldwebel der Landwehr II	1	29-Sep-1914	Fricourt	W.I.A., died 30Sep-1914.

RIR 109

NAME	RANK	CO.	DATE OF DEATH	LOCATION	NOTES
Seleger, Josef	Grenadier der Landwehr I	1	29-Sep-1914	Fricourt	
Haug, August	Reservist	2	29-Sep-1914	Fricourt	
Horrey, Friedrich	Wehrmann	2	29-Sep-1914	Fricourt	
Klebs, Ludwig	Vizefeldwebel der Reserve	2	29-Sep-1914	Fricourt	
Roth, Gottlieb	Gefreiter der Landwehr	2	29-Sep-1914	Fricourt	
Gretschmann, Karl	Wehrmann	3	29-Sep-1914	Fricourt	W.I.A. at Fricourt, died 30-Sep-1914 in Field Hospital Contalmaison.
Baumann, Franz	Wehrmann	4	29-Sep-1914	Fricourt	W.I.A., died 30-Sep-1914 in Flers.
Engelhardt, Jakob	Wehrmann	4	29-Sep-1914	Fricourt	
Kramer, Friedrich	Wehrmann	4	29-Sep-1914	Fricourt	
Mangold, Stephan	Wehrmann	4	29-Sep-1914	Fricourt	W.I.A., died 9-Oct-1914 in Bapaume.
Simon, Otto	Wehrmann	4	29-Sep-1914	Fricourt	
Bauchert, Christian	Gefreiter	5	29-Sep-1914	Fricourt	
Blänkle, Friedrich	Gefreiter	5	29-Sep-1914	Fricourt	
Engelhardt, Robert	Landwehrmann	5	29-Sep-1914	Fricourt	
Jung, Alfred	Reservist	5	29-Sep-1914	Fricourt	W.I.A., died 30-Oct-1914, Reserve Field Hospital II, Aachen.
Melchert, Friedrich	Gefreiter	5	29-Sep-1914	Fricourt	
Ebenberger, Julius	Wehrmann	6	29-Sep-1914	Fricourt	M.I.A.
Gansser, August	Gefreiter	6	29-Sep-1914	Contalmaison	
Göhringer, Otto	Wehrmann	6	29-Sep-1914	Fricourt	
Schenk, Emil	Wehrmann	6	29-Sep-1914	Fricourt	
Singler, Josef	Wehrmann	6	29-Sep-1914	Fricourt	
Boxberger, Heinrich	Reservist	7	29-Sep-1914	Fricourt	
Frank, Martin	Unteroffizier der Landwehr	7	29-Sep-1914	Fricourt	W.I.A., died 30-Oct-1914, Contalmaison.
Ganter, Karl	Unteroffizier der Reserve	7	29-Sep-1914	Fricourt	
Kammerer, Rudolf	Reservist	7	29-Sep-1914	Fricourt	
Krebiehl, Wilhelm	Gefreiter der Landwehr	7	29-Sep-1914	Fricourt	
Krüger, Karl	Reservist	7	29-Sep-1914	Fricourt	
Lauinger, Rudolf	Wehrmann	7	29-Sep-1914	Fricourt	
Laule, Heinrich	Reservist	7	29-Sep-1914	Fricourt	W.I.A., died 2-Oct-1914,Contalmaison.
Rohrbach, Simon	Reservist	7	29-Sep-1914	Fricourt	
Schmidt, Georg	Vizefeldwebel	7	29-Sep-1914	Fricourt	
Schnetz, Josef	Landwehrmann	7	29-Sep-1914	Fricourt	
Vonflie, Bernhard	Reservist	7	29-Sep-1914	Fricourt	
Nagel, August	Gefreiter	9	29-Sep-1914	Fricourt	
Brecht, Johann	Wehrmann	10	29-Sep-1914	Fricourt	

RIR 109

NAME	RANK	CO.	DATE OF DEATH	LOCATION	NOTES
Mornhinweg, Karl	Grenadier	10	29-Sep-1914	Fricourt	
Wicker, Leonhard	Wehrmann	10	29-Sep-1914	Fricourt	
Haffner, Karl	Gefreiter	11	29-Sep-1914	Fricourt	
Karst, Friedrich	Vizefeldwebel	11	29-Sep-1914	Fricourt	
Merz, Karl	Gefreiter	11	29-Sep-1914	Fricourt	
Schmidt, Karl	Gefreiter	11	29-Sep-1914	Fricourt	
Stricker, Josef	Landwehrnmann	11	29-Sep-1914	Fricourt	
Carl II, Friedrich	Reservist	12	29-Sep-1914	Fricourt	M.I.A., declared dead
Ledermann, Johann	Reservist	12	29-Sep-1914	Fricourt	
Schmid, Josef	Landwehrnmann	12	29-Sep-1914	Fricourt	W.I.A., died 4-Oct-1914, Military hospital, Cambrai.
Kox, Jakob	Gefreiter	1 M.G.	29-Sep-1914	Fricourt	
Pawaronschitz, Johann	Grenadier	1 M.G.	29-Sep-1914	Fricourt	W.I.A., died 10-Oct-1914, Infirmary Stat. 5, Aschersleben.
Essler, Wilhelm	Gefreiter der Landwehr II	1	30-Sep-1914	Fricourt	
Kraus, Karl	Vizefeldwebel	1	30-Sep-1914	Ovillers	
Fein, Georg	Wehrmann	3	30-Sep-1914	Fricourt	
Hahn, Josef	Gefreiter	3	30-Sep-1914	Fricourt	
Lang, Hermann	Reservist	3	30-Sep-1914	Fricourt	W.I.A., died 19-Oct-1914 at Reserve Hospital IV, Aachen.
Leier, Anton	Wehrmann	3	30-Sep-1914	Fricourt	W.I.A., died 22-Oct-1914 at St. Josefs Hospital, Cöln-Kalk.
Scherer, Josef	Wehrmann	3	30-Sep-1914	Fricourt	
Seifermann, Josef	Wehrmann	3	30-Sep-1914	Fricourt	W.I.A., died 4-Oct-1914 at Bavarian Field Hospital 7, Contalmaison.
Bechtel, Heinrich	Landwehrmann	5	30-Sep-1914	Fricourt	W.I.A., died 8-Oct-1914 in Fortress Hospital, Namur.
Behr, Eugen	Gefreiter	5	30-Sep-1914	Fricourt	
Egger, Karl	Reservist	5	30-Sep-1914	Fricourt	M.I.A., declared dead
Frenk, Wilhelm	Reservist	5	30-Sep-1914	Fricourt	
Gros, Gustav	Landwehrmann	5	30-Sep-1914	Fricourt	
Heck, Anton	Reservist	5	30-Sep-1914	Fricourt	
Hipp, Heinrich	Reservist	5	30-Sep-1914	Fricourt	
Huber I, Oskar	Reservist	5	30-Sep-1914	Fricourt	
Kurz, Adolf	Landwehrmann	5	30-Sep-1914	Fricourt	
Lang, Karl	Landwehrmann	5	30-Sep-1914	Fricourt	
Opalka, August	Reservist	5	30-Sep-1914	Fricourt	
Schnitt III, Friedrich	Reservist	5	30-Sep-1914	Fricourt	
Walter, Paul	Reservist	5	30-Sep-1914	Fricourt	W.I.A., died 4-Oct-1914, Military Hospital, I Army Corps, Cambrai.
Beller, Julius	Reservist	6	30-Sep-1914	Fricourt	
Hurst, August	Unteroffizier	6	30-Sep-1914	Fricourt	

RIR 109

NAME	RANK	CO.	DATE OF DEATH	LOCATION	NOTES
Rimmele, Johann	Wehrmann	6	30-Sep-1914	Fricourt	W.I.A., died 14-Oct-1914, Fricourt.
Göttler, Wilhelm	Wehrmann	7	30-Sep-1914	Fricourt	
Kutterer, Georg	Gefreiter der Landwehr	8	30-Sep-1914	Fricourt	
Speck, Leopold	Landwehrmann	8	30-Sep-1914	Fricourt	
Süss, Wilhelm	Landwehrmann	8	30-Sep-1914	Fricourt	
Appenzeller, Karl	Gefreiter	9	30-Sep-1914	Fricourt	
Böhme, Paul	Unteroffizier	9	30-Sep-1914	Fricourt	
Kreiner, Gustav	Gefreiter	9	30-Sep-1914	Fricourt	
Richter, Friedrich	Füsilier	9	30-Sep-1914	Fricourt	
Herrmann, Josef	Reservist	10	30-Sep-1914	Fricourt	W.I.A., died 26-Oct-1914, Oberhausen near Köln.
Kutterer, Anton	Wehrmann	10	30-Sep-1914	Fricourt	W.I.A., died 14-Oct-1914, Field hospital, Meppen.
Thomas, Erwin	Reservist	11	30-Sep-1914	Fricourt	W.I.A., died 16-Oct-1914, Düren.
Bechtold, Franz	Grenadier	1 M.G.	30-Sep-1914	Fricourt	
Boetsch, Leodegar	Grenadier	1 M.G.	30-Sep-1914	Fricourt	
Dais, Adam	Grenadier	1 M.G.	30-Sep-1914	Fricourt	
Jost, Karl	Gefreiter	1 M.G.	30-Sep-1914	Fricourt	
Kaucher, Jakob	Grenadier	1 M.G.	30-Sep-1914	Fricourt	W.I.A., 18-Oct-1914, Flers.
Korn, Josef	Grenadier	1 M.G.	30-Sep-1914	Fricourt	W.I.A., died 2-Oct-1914, auxiliary hospital Speyer.
Sauer, Jakob	Reservist	1 M.G.	30-Sep-1914	Fricourt	
Sommer, Emil	Gefreiter	1 M.G.	30-Sep-1914	Fricourt	
Spieler, Sebastian	Grenadier	1 M.G.	30-Sep-1914	Fricourt	
Sinner, Robert	Oberleutnant der Landwehr	III Bn.	30-Sep-1914	Fricourt	W.I.A., died 30-Sep-1914, Contalmaison. (III Battalion Adjutant)
Edrich, Wilhelm	Gefreiter	3	1-Oct-1914	Fricourt	W.I.A., died 2-Nov-1914 at Brussels.
Knamm, August	Wehrmann	3	1-Oct-1914	Fricourt	
Schmiedt, Karl	Wehrmann	3	1-Oct-1914	Fricourt	
Schmiedt, Xaver	Wehrmann	3	1-Oct-1914	Fricourt	
Büchel, Friedrich	Wehrmann	10	1-Oct-1914	Fricourt	M.I.A., declared dead
Daiber, August	Reservist	10	1-Oct-1914	Fricourt	M.I.A., declared dead
Heim, Ludwig	Wehrmann	10	1-Oct-1914	Fricourt	W.I.A., died 8-Oct-1914, hospital, Charleroi.
Leier, Johann	Unteroffizier	10	1-Oct-1914	Fricourt	
Loewert, Hieronymous	Wehrmann	10	1-Oct-1914	Fricourt	
Münch, Franz	Gefreiter	10	1-Oct-1914	Fricourt	
Munz, Albert	Wehrmann	10	1-Oct-1914	Fricourt	M.I.A., declared dead
Notheis, Peter	Wehrmann	10	1-Oct-1914	Fricourt	
Notheisen, Andreas	Wehrmann	10	1-Oct-1914	Fricourt	M.I.A., declared dead

RIR 109

NAME	RANK	CO.	DATE OF DEATH	LOCATION	NOTES
Simianer, Leopold	Wehrmann	10	1-Oct-1914	Fricourt	W.I.A., captured, died 8-Oct-1914, P.O.W. camp, Invisy-Triaz.
Müller, August	Reservist	11	1-Oct-1914	Fricourt	
Bitz, Friedrich	Gefreiter	12	1-Oct-1914	Fricourt	
Elsässer, August	Landwehrnmann	12	1-Oct-1914	Fricourt	
Roth, Karl	Offizier Stellvertreter	12	1-Oct-1914	Fricourt	
Wagner, Adam	Reservist	12	1-Oct-1914	Fricourt	
Walter, Karl	Reservist	2	2-Oct-1914	Fricourt	
Kümmerlin, Alfons	Reservist	9	2-Oct-1914	Fricourt	M.I.A., declared dead
Spindler, Josef	Wehrmann	10	2-Oct-1914	Fricourt	
Braun, Julius	Landwehrnmann	11	2-Oct-1914	Fricourt	
Kasprzat, Johann	Reservist	11	2-Oct-1914	Fricourt	
Paplack, Ignaz	Reservist	11	2-Oct-1914	Fricourt	W.I.A., died 13-Oct-1914, Catholic Hospital, Eickel.
Jais, Jakob	Landwehrnmann	12	2-Oct-1914	Fricourt	
Dürr, August II	Grenadier der Landwehr I	1	3-Oct-1914	Fricourt	Killed in the White House, Fricourt
Schmidt, Wilhelm	Grenadier der Landwehr II	1	3-Oct-1914	Fricourt Bahnhof	
Wohleb, Johann	Grenadier der Landwehr I	1	3-Oct-1914	Fricourt	W.I.A., died 22-Nov-1914 at Wandsbeck near Hamburg.
Berger, Reinhold	Gefreiter der Landwehr	2	3-Oct-1914	Fricourt	
Schäfer, Robert	Wehrmann	2	3-Oct-1914	Fricourt	
Siegrist, Adolf	Wehrmann	2	3-Oct-1914	Fricourt	
Möller, Heinz	Vizefeldwebel	3	3-Oct-1914	Fricourt	W.I.A., 7-Oct-1914
Glöckler, Johann	Wehrmann	4	3-Oct-1914	Fricourt	
Müller, Hugo	Wehrmann	4	3-Oct-1914	Fricourt	
Stoll, Adam	Wehrmann	4	3-Oct-1914	Fricourt	
Constantin, Karl	Unteroffizier der Reserve	8	3-Oct-1914	Fricourt	W.I.A., died 4-Oct-1914, Field Hospital, Flers.
Hübner, Karl	Reservist	8	3-Oct-1914	Fricourt	W.I.A., died 5-Oct-1914, Mons.
Joachim, Michael	Landsturmmann	8	3-Oct-1914	Fricourt	W.I.A., died 14-Oct-1914, Bapaume.
Joos, Theodor	Landwehrmann	8	3-Oct-1914	Fricourt	
Kühler, Karl	Reservist	8	3-Oct-1914	Fricourt	
Weschenfelder, Leopold	Landwehrmann	8	3-Oct-1914	Fricourt	W.I.A., died 4-Oct-1914, Field Hospital, Contalmaison.
Buri, Anton	Reservist	2	4-Oct-1914	Fricourt	
Hergt, Paul	Vizefeldwebel der Reserve	2	4-Oct-1914	Fricourt	
Zaum, Eugen	Wehrmann	2	4-Oct-1914	Fricourt	
Fleig, Josef	Reservist	3	4-Oct-1914	Fricourt	

RIR 109

NAME	RANK	CO.	DATE OF DEATH	LOCATION	NOTES
Fischer, Sebastian	Wehrmann	4	4-Oct-1914	Fricourt	W.I.A., died 6-Oct-1914 in Flers.
Hötzel, Friedrich	Wehrmann	4	4-Oct-1914	Fricourt	
Pesch, Jakob	Wehrmann	4	4-Oct-1914	Fricourt	
Wacker, Josef	Wehrmann	4	4-Oct-1914	Fricourt	
Maninger, Josef	Wehrmann	6	4-Oct-1914	Fricourt	
Waldmann, Wilhelm	Reservist	6	4-Oct-1914	Fricourt	
Zäpfel, Karl	Reservist	6	4-Oct-1914	Fricourt	W.I.A., died 17-Oct-1914 in auxiliary hospital, Academy Infirmary, Heidelberg.
Mackert, Franz	Wehrmann	7	4-Oct-1914	Fricourt	W.I.A., died 5-Oct-1914, Flers.
Menningen, Walter	Leutnant der Reserve	7	4-Oct-1914	Fricourt	
Erb, Hermann	Landwehrmann	8	4-Oct-1914	Fricourt	
Kiefer, Max	Landwehrmann	8	4-Oct-1914	Fricourt	W.I.A., died 6-Oct-1914, Military Hospital, Cambrai.
Burkhardt, Gottlieb	Reservist	10	4-Oct-1914	Fricourt	
Frank, Leopold	Wehrmann	10	4-Oct-1914	Fricourt	
Lang, Josef	Reservist	5	5-Oct-1914	Fricourt	
Meinzer, Christof	Wehrmann	6	5-Oct-1914	Fricourt	
Schätzle, Friedrich	Wehrmann	6	5-Oct-1914	Fricourt	
Windbiel, Franz	Wehrmann	6	5-Oct-1914	Fricourt	
Neubaus, Hermann	Musketier	4	7-Oct-1914	Contalmaison	
Rimmele, Alfred	Wehrmann	6	7-Oct-1914	Fricourt	
Gebhardt, Karl	Reservist	12	8-Oct-1914	Fricourt	W.I.A., died 9-Oct-1914, Military Hospital, 21st Army Corps.
Gross, Otto	Reservist	6	10-Oct-1914	Fricourt	
Kopf, Ludwig	Reservist	6	10-Oct-1914	Fricourt	M.I.A., declared dead
Obert, Florian	Gefreiter	11	10-Oct-1914	Fricourt	
Goll, Friedrich	Wehrmann	3	14-Oct-1914	Fricourt	
Krebs, Heinrich	Wehrmann	3	14-Oct-1914	Fricourt	W.I.A., died 19-Oct-1914 in Field Hospital in Flers.
Kazorek, Felix	Musketier	4	14-Oct-1914	Fricourt	
Kowalski, Adalbert	Musketier	4	14-Oct-1914	Fricourt	
Jenne, August	Grenadier der Reserve	1	17-Oct-1914	Fricourt	W.I.A., died in Württemberg Field Hospital Nr. 2 Flers.
Rapp, Hermann	Grenadier der Reserve	1	17-Oct-1914	Fricourt	
Schneider, Emil	Musketier der Landwehr I	1	17-Oct-1914	Fricourt	
Hähnle, Jakob	Landwehrnmann	12	17-Oct-1914	Fricourt	W.I.A., 29-Dec-1914, Reserve Hospital I, Heidelberg.
Schindler, Erwin	Kriegsfreiwilliger	2	25-Oct-1914	Fricourt	
Gerdon, Franz	Ersatz Reservist	6	25-Oct-1914	Fricourt	
Rohnacker, Albert	Sergeant	6	25-Oct-1914	Fricourt	

RIR 109

NAME	RANK	CO.	DATE OF DEATH	LOCATION	NOTES
Kienzler, Berthold	Grenadier der Landwehr I	1	28-Oct-1914	Fricourt	
Brütsch, Dominikus	Wehrmann	6	28-Oct-1914	Fricourt	
Flösser, Robert	Ersatz Reservist	6	29-Oct-1914	Fricourt	
Keller, Hubert	Landwehrnmann	12	30-Oct-1914	Fricourt	
Sieber, Karl	Reservist	8	1-Nov-1914	Mametz	
Zoller, Karl	Wehrmann	7	12-Nov-1914	St. Quentin	Died of illness, Military Hospital Nr. 7.
Wyrwohl, Georg	Kriegsfreiwilliger	9	8-Dec-1914	Fricourt	
Hofsäss, Ferdinand	Gefreiter der Landwehr I	1	17-Dec-1914	Fricourt	W.I.A., died 31-Dec-1914 at Reserve Hospital Bielefeld.
Erath, Richard	Gefreiter	3	17-Dec-1914	Mametz	
Müller, Friedrich	Wehrmann	3	17-Dec-1914	Mametz	
Mussgnug, Albert	Ersatz Reservist	3	17-Dec-1914	Mametz	
Schott, Heinrich	Offizier Stelvertreter	3	17-Dec-1914	Mametz	
Zanger, Nikolaus	Wehrmann	3	17-Dec-1914	Mametz	
Schrumpf, Konrad	Unteroffizier	10	17-Dec-1914	Mametz	
Utz, Adolf	Kriegsfreiwilliger	10	17-Dec-1914	Fricourt	W.I.A., died 19-Dec-1914, Bapaume.
Wachter, Franziskus	Wehrmann	10	17-Dec-1914	Mametz	
Bentz, Karl	Ersatz Reservist	3	18-Dec-1914	Mametz	
Höfel, Hermann	Wehrmann	3	18-Dec-1914	Mametz	
Jung, Robert	Unteroffizier	3	18-Dec-1914	Mametz	W.I.A., died 24-Dec-1914 in War Hospital Abteilung I, 7th Army Corps, St. Quentin
Kischko, August	Reservist	3	18-Dec-1914	Mametz	
Schlatter, Max	Wehrmann	3	18-Dec-1914	Mametz	
Steinhauser, Wilhelm	Reservist	3	18-Dec-1914	Mametz	W.I.A., died 20-Dec-1914 at Württemberg Reserve Field Hospital Nr. 1, Bapaume.
Breier, Richard	Wehrmann	9	18-Dec-1914	Fricourt	
Dürr, Karl	Wehrmann	9	18-Dec-1914	Fricourt	W.I.A., died 2-Jan-1915, Hospital, St. Quentin.
Mislin, Josef	Grenadier	1M.G.	18-Dec-1914	Fricourt	
Herth, Albert	Kriegsfreiwilliger	3	19-Dec-1914	Mametz	
Krauss, Georg	Gefreiter	9	20-Dec-1914	Fricourt	
Mohr, Wilhelm	Kriegsfreiwilliger	9	20-Dec-1914	Fricourt	
Volkenhoff, Johann	Reservist	9	20-Dec-1914	Fricourt	
Bauer, Christian	Kriegsfreiwilliger	11	20-Dec-1914	Fricourt	
Hermann, Otto	Gefreiter	11	20-Dec-1914	Fricourt	
Zimmermann, Wilhelm	Kriegsfreiwilliger	6	23-Dec-1914	Fricourt	
Scheuble, Jakob	Gefreiter	4	24-Dec-1914	Fricourt	
Harter, Valentin	Gefreiter	5	24-Dec-1914	Fricourt	
Dürr, Jakob	Hornist	6	24-Dec-1914	Fricourt	

RIR 109					
NAME	RANK	CO.	DATE OF DEATH	LOCATION	NOTES
Godelmann, Wilhelm	Ersatz Reservist	6	24-Dec-1914	Fricourt	
Härter, Erwin	Gefreiter	4	25-Dec-1914	Fricourt	
Rödel, Wilhelm	Wehrmann	4	25-Dec-1914	Fricourt	
Hofmann, Wilhelm	Ersatz Reservist	6	25-Dec-1914	Fricourt	W.I.A., died 27-Dec-1914, Miraumont.
Krambs, Michael	Unteroffizier der Landwehr	8	25-Dec-1914	Fricourt	
Demonges, Jakob	?	1	26-Dec-1914	Fricourt	W.I.A., died 28-Dec-1914 in Field Hospital Flers.
Höpfer, Jakob	Wehrmann	4	26-Dec-1914	Fricourt	
Wachter, Josef	Reservist	10	30-Dec-1914	Fricourt	
Goepfert, Gustav	Reservist	12	31-Dec-1914	Fricourt	W.I.A., died 1-Jan-1915, Reserve hospital, Flers.
Schmitt, Karl	Gefreiter	5	4-Jan-1915	Fricourt	
Voigt, Karl	Kriegsfreiwilliger	9	4-Jan-1915	Fricourt	
Rehmann, Fritz	Gefreiter	12	5-Jan-1915	Fricourt	W.I.A., died 6-Jan-1915, hospital, Flers.
Jansen, Gerhard	Kriegsfreiwilliger	6	6-Jan-1915	Fricourt	
Lahn, Paul	Kriegsfreiwilliger	1	8-Jan-1915	Fricourt	
Funk, Friedrich	Reservist	7	8-Jan-1915	Fricourt	W.I.A., died 9-Jan-1915, Flers.
Jozwiak, Kasimir	Reservist	9	12-Jan-1915	Fricourt	W.I.A., died 13-Jan-1915, Reserve Medical Company 14, Flers.
Wägele, Wilhelm	Kriegsfreiwilliger	12	12-Jan-1915	Fricourt	
Schmidt I, Josef	Wehrmann	6	14-Jan-1915	Fricourt	
Döhling, Josef	Grenadier der Landwehr I	1	15-Jan-1915	Fricourt	Buried.
Machauer, Franz	Kriegsfreiwilliger	1	15-Jan-1915	Fricourt	
Rösch, Ernst	Wehrmann	6	15-Jan-1915	Fricourt	
Koch, Friedrich	Gefreiter	9	15-Jan-1915	Fricourt	W.I.A., died 1-Jul-1916, Montauban.
Vollmer, Ferdinand	Wehrmann	3	22-Jan-1915	St. Quentin	Died of disease in Military Hospital Nr. 7, Army Corps Gruppe III.
Kölble, Anton	Kriegsfreiwilliger	1 M.G.	22-Jan-1915	Flers	W.I.A., died 23-Jan-1915, hospital, Flers.
Knappschneider, Adam	Offizier Stellvertreter	12	25-Jan-1915	Fricourt	Killed by German heavy howitzer shell striking his dug-out.
Lehr, Stefan	Landwehrnmann	12	25-Jan-1915	Fricourt	Killed by German heavy howitzer shell striking his dug-out.
Zipper, Ludwig	Ersatz Reservist	12	25-Jan-1915	Fricourt	Killed by German heavy howitzer shell striking his dug-out.
Deck, Karl	Kriegsfreiwilliger	12	30-Jan-1915	Fricourt	W.I.A., died 31-Jan-1915.
Gässler, Karl	Landwehrnmann	12	30-Jan-1915	Fricourt	W.I.A., died 31-Jan-1915.

RIR 109

NAME	RANK	CO.	DATE OF DEATH	LOCATION	NOTES
Kästel, Karl	Kriegsfreiwilliger	1	3-Feb-1915	Fricourt	
Neuberger, Albert	Grenadier der Landwehr I	1	11-Feb-1915	Fricourt	W.I.A., died 19-Feb-1915 at Military Hospital VII, near St. Quentin.
Lang, Julian	Reservist	6	12-Feb-1915	Mametz	Buried.
Eschbach, Friedrich	Landwehrmann	8	13-Feb-1915	Mametz	
Kuhn, Valentin	Reservist	8	13-Feb-1915	Mametz	
Steinebrunner, Wilhelm	Landwehrmann	8	13-Feb-1915	Mametz	
Wehrle, Markus	Landwehrmann	8	13-Feb-1915	Mametz	W.I.A., died 16-Feb-1915 Main Dressing Station, Flers.
Hesch, Adolf	Kriegsfreiwilliger	5	14-Feb-1915	Mametz	
Kröber, Karl	Unteroffizier der Landwehr	1	17-Feb-1915	Mametz	
Keilbach, Hermann	Unteroffizier	5	17-Feb-1915	Mametz	
Wang, Wilhelm	Kriegsfreiwilliger	4	19-Feb-1915		Left sick, died 10-Nov-1915 in Augsburg.
Faller, Johann	Wehrmann	4	20-Feb-1915	Mametz	W.I.A., died 28-Feb-1915 in Bapaume.
Karcher, Georg	Wehrmann	7	21-Feb-1915	Mametz	
Vogel, Johannes	Gefreiter	10	24-Feb-1915	Mametz	
Kleine, Josef	Reservist	11	25-Feb-1915	Mametz	W.I.A., died 11-Mar-1915, military hospital, Landry
Strümpfler, Karl	Gefreiter	5	27-Feb-1915	Mametz	W.I.A., died 1-Mar-1915 Hospital, Flers.
Küst, Friedrich	Ersatz Reservist	5	2-Mar-1915	Mametz	
Jung, Otto	Kriegsfreiwilliger	1	8-Mar-1915	Mametz	
Felger, Johann	Reservist	6	17-Mar-1915	Mametz	
Steinke, Hermann	Ersatz Reservist	6	19-Mar-1915	Mametz	W.I.A., died 22-Mar-1915 in hospital, Flers.
Ried, Ludwig	Gefreiter der Landwehr	2	22-Mar-1915	Mametz	W.I.A., died 30-Mar-1915 in Flers.
Appel, Georg	Wehrmann	4	22-Mar-1915	Mametz	
Lutz, Gottlieb	Ersatz Reservist	4	22-Mar-1915	Mametz	
Nowinski, Konstantin	Musketier	4	22-Mar-1915	Mametz	
Siebler, Hermann	Wehrmann	4	22-Mar-1915	Mametz	W.I.A., died 26-Mar-1915 in Flers.
Walter, Alois	Wehrmann	4	22-Mar-1915	Mametz	
Friedland, Arthur	Kriegsfreiwilliger	4	23-Mar-1915	Mametz	
Krischik, Ludwig	Grenadier	1 M.G.	29-Mar-1915	Mametz	W.I.A., died 2-Apr-1915.
Kaiser, Oskar	Landwehrnmann	12	30-Mar-1915	Fricourt	
Schäuble, Oskar	Gefreiter der Landwehr	2	1-Apr-1915	La Boisselle	Killed in collapse of 1st dug-out in the *Granathof* by French shelling.
Weber, Karl	Wehrmann	2	1-Apr-1915	La Boisselle	Killed in collapse of 1st dug-out in the *Granathof* by French shelling.

RIR 109

NAME	RANK	CO.	DATE OF DEATH	LOCATION	NOTES
Halter, Xaver	Reservist	2	2-Apr-1915	La Boisselle	Killed in collapse of 1st dug-out in the *Granathof* by French shelling.
Herrmann II, Josef	Reservist	2	2-Apr-1915	La Boisselle	Killed in collapse of 1st dug-out in the *Granathof* by French shelling.
Mosbacher II, Julius	Reservist	2	2-Apr-1915	La Boisselle	Killed in collapse of 1st dug-out in the *Granathof* by French shelling.
Regenscheid, Rudolf	Reservist	2	2-Apr-1915	La Boisselle	Killed in collapse of 1st dug-out in the *Granathof* by French shelling.
Sehlbach, Heinrich	Ersatz Reservist	2	2-Apr-1915	La Boisselle	Killed in collapse of 1st dug-out in the *Granathof* by French shelling.
Zimmermann, Georg	Gefreiter der Reserve	2	2-Apr-1915	La Boisselle	Killed in collapse of 2nd dug-out in the *Granathof* by French shelling.
Bodamer, August	Ersatz Reservist	3	2-Apr-1915	La Boisselle	Killed in collapse of 2nd dug-out in the *Granathof* by French shelling.
Willy, Gustav	Kriegsfreiwilliger	3	2-Apr-1915	La Boisselle	
Fritz, Karl	Wehrmann	3	3-Apr-1915	La Boisselle	
Killi, Christian	Wehrmann	3	3-Apr-1915	La Boisselle	
Glockner, Georg	Kriegsfreiwilliger	3	6-Apr-1915	La Boisselle	
Heger, Emil	Landwehrmann	5	10-Apr-1915	La Boisselle	W.I.A., died 17-Apr-1915, Field Hospital, Bapaume.
Vetter, Xaver	Gefreiter	8	15-Apr-1915	La Boisselle	
Holziegel, Julius	Gefreiter	10	16-Apr-1915	La Boisselle	
Stoll, Friedrich	Wehrmann	12	18-Apr-1915	La Boisselle	
Fies, Karl	Kriegsfreiwilliger	12	20-Apr-1915	Sachsenhausen	Died of illness, Reserve Hospital Nr. 5.
Spiess, Gottfried	Reservist	6	24-Apr-1915	La Boisselle	
Müll, Friedrich	Ersatz Reservist	7	24-Apr-1915	La Boisselle	
Hohenreuther, Hermann	Grenadier	1 M.G.	24-Apr-1915	La Boisselle	
Braun, Augustin	Unteroffizier	11	25-Apr-1915	La Boisselle	
Sutter, Appolina	Reservist	7	1-May-1915	La Boisselle	W.I.A., died 4-May-1915, Flers.
Bach, Johann	Reservist	6	2-May-1915	La Boisselle	
Kappler, Julius	Ersatz Reservist	1	4-May-1915	La Boisselle	
Körner, Markus	Ersatz Reservist	4	6-May-1915	La Boisselle	W.I.A., died 7-May-1915 in Flers.
Maier, Martin	Wehrmann	4	6-May-1915	La Boisselle	W.I.A., died 22-Nov-1915 in Augsburg.
Schlager, Karl	Unteroffizier	4	6-May-1915	La Boisselle	
Pfister, Franz	Ersatz Reservist	1	15-May-1915	La Boisselle	
Mild, Wilhelm	Wehrmann	9	16-May-1915	La Boisselle	W.I.A., died 15-Oct-1915, Infirmary, Augsburg.

RIR 109

NAME	RANK	CO.	DATE OF DEATH	LOCATION	NOTES
Kaiser, Franz	Kriegsfreiwilliger	12	21-May-1915	La Boisselle	
Berger, August	Unteroffizier	9	22-May-1915	La Boisselle	
Klingmann, Jakob	Ersatz Reservist	12	22-May-1915	La Boisselle	W.I.A., died 31-May-1915, Reserve field hospital I.
Haag, Emil	Unteroffizier der Reserve	7	25-May-1915	La Boisselle	W.I.A., died 23-May-1915, Flers.
Kunzelmann, Franz	Wehrmann	4	26-May-1915	La Boisselle	
Böhler, Karl	Reservist	3	28-May-1915	La Boisselle	W.I.A., died 31-May-1915 at Flers.
Seifer, Anselm	Unteroffizier	3	29-May-1915	La Boisselle	W.I.A., died 30-May-1915 in Flers.
Vogel, Ludwig	Kriegsfreiwilliger	12	30-May-1915	Villers au Flos	Died of illness, Reserve Field Hospital Nr. 55.
Huber, Wilhelm	Wehrmann	3	1-Jun-1915	La Boisselle	
Keller, Otto	Unteroffizier	4	1-Jun-1915	La Boisselle	
Schwab, Franz	Ersatz Reservist	4	1-Jun-1915	La Boisselle	
Kiefer II, Christoph	Wehrmann	2	2-Jun-1915	La Boisselle	
Zepp, Johann	Grenadier	5	4-Jun-1915	La Boisselle	W.I.A., died 5-Jun-1915, Reserve Field Hospital, Flers.
Hug, Fritz	Ersatz Reservist	3	7-Jun-1915	La Boisselle	
Klingelhöfer, Heinrich	Unteroffizier	4	7-Jun-1915	La Boisselle	
Gottschalk, Günther	Kriegsfreiwilliger	11	7-Jun-1915	La Boisselle	
Adler, Heinrich	Ersatz Reservist	4	8-Jun-1915	La Boisselle	
Härdter, Friedrich	Ersatz Reservist	4	8-Jun-1915	La Boisselle	
Seiler, Richard	Reservist	2	9-Jun-1915	La Boisselle	
Bender, Max	Kriegsfreiwilliger	5	12-Jun-1915	Serre	
Henkelmann, Ludwig	Landwehrmann	5	12-Jun-1915	Serre	
Heuchele, Emil	Ersatz Reservist	5	12-Jun-1915	Serre	
Kienle, Adolf	Landwehrmann	5	12-Jun-1915	Serre	W.I.A., died 13-Jun-1915, Reserve Field Hospital I, Bapaume.
Lauer, Karl	Grenadier	5	12-Jun-1915	Serre	
Roth, August	Landwehrmann	5	12-Jun-1915	Serre	
Rotheimer, Simon	Gefreiter	5	12-Jun-1915	Serre	
Schülz, Johann	Feldwebel	5	12-Jun-1915	Serre	
Wallner, Hermann	Kriegsfreiwilliger	5	12-Jun-1915	Serre	
Geng, Johann	Wehrmann	6	12-Jun-1915	Serre	
Münch, Georg	Unteroffizier	6	12-Jun-1915	Serre	
Schmelzinger, Martin	Wehrmann	6	12-Jun-1915	Serre	W.I.A., died 15-Jul-1915, Orphelinat.
Flum, Johann	Wehrmann	7	12-Jun-1915	Serre	W.I.A., died in P.O.W. camp.
Menzel, Berthold	Ersatz Reservist	7	12-Jun-1915	Serre	
Rink, Wilhelm	Kriegsfreiwilliger	7	12-Jun-1915	Serre	

RIR 109

NAME	RANK	CO.	DATE OF DEATH	LOCATION	NOTES
Simon, Wilhelm	Wehrmann	7	12-Jun-1915	Serre	W.I.A., died 14-Jun-1915, Field Hospital Nr. 1, Bapaume.
Weber, Johann	Wehrmann	7	12-Jun-1915	Serre	M.I.A., declared dead
Zankl, Josef	Wehrmann	7	12-Jun-1915	Serre	M.I.A., declared dead
Banschbach, Rudolf	Unteroffizier der Reserve	8	12-Jun-1915	Serre	
Eisele, Hermann	Landwehrmann	8	12-Jun-1915	Serre	W.I.A., died 21-Jun-1915, Military Hospital 7, Justice Palace, St. Quentin.
Gaa, Heinrich	Landwehrmann	8	12-Jun-1915	Serre	
Herr, Otto	Kriegsfreiwilliger	8	12-Jun-1915	Serre	
Kreiner, Friedrich	Kriegsfreiwilliger	8	12-Jun-1915	Serre	M.I.A., declared dead
Schleicher II, Karl	Reservist	8	12-Jun-1915	Serre	
Streit, Paul	Landwehrmann	8	12-Jun-1915	Serre	W.I.A., died 19-Jun-1915, Reserve Hospital, Aachen.
Sturn, Gustav	Landsturmmann	8	12-Jun-1915	Serre	
Clauss, Franz	Kriegsfreiwilliger	1	13-Jun-1915	La Boisselle	
Schaaf, Friedrich	Kriegsfreiwilliger	2	13-Jun-1915	La Boisselle	
Amann, Johann	Wehrmann	4	13-Jun-1915	La Boisselle	W.I.A., died 14-Jun-1915 at Flers.
Huber, Georg	Ersatz Reservist	4	16-Jun-1915	La Boisselle	W.I.A., died 17-Jun-1915 in Flers.
Kachler, Eduard	Reservist	11	19-Jun-1915	La Boisselle	
Fischer, Bapt.	Unteroffizier der Landwehr II	3	22-Jun-1915	La Boisselle	
Bickel, Friedrich	Grenadier	1M.G.	24-Jun-1915	La Boisselle	
Leonhard, Theodor	Kriegsfreiwilliger	6	11-Jul-1915	La Boisselle	W.I.A., died 12-Jul-1915 in hospital, Flers.
Siebert, Konrad	Ersatz Reservist	4	12-Jul-1915	La Boisselle	
Volk, Christian	Gefreiter	5	18-Jul-1915	La Boisselle	
Steinle, Ferdinand	Ersatz Reservist	8	21-Jul-1915	La Boisselle	
Faas, Gustav	Ersatz Reservist	11	23-Jul-1915	La Boisselle	
Hermann, Friedrich	Ersatz Reservist	3	27-Jul-1915	La Boisselle	
Joos, Alfred	Wehrmann	4	29-Jul-1915	La Boisselle	
Mangold, Paul	Ersatz Reservist	4	2-Aug-1915	La Boisselle	
Herr, Gottfried	Vizefeldwebel	11	4-Aug-1915	La Boisselle	
Kleistner, Ernst	Musketier	7	6-Aug-1915	La Boisselle	
Münkel, Theodor	Reservist	5	10-Aug-1915	La Boisselle	
Losinger, Albert	Leutnant der Reserve	7	11-Aug-1915	La Boisselle	
Braun, Philipp	Landwehrmann	7	13-Aug-1915	La Boisselle	W.I.A., died 14-Aug-1915, field hospital, Flers.
Kost, Albert	Ersatz Reservist	1	14-Aug-1915	La Boisselle	W.I.A., died 16-Aug-1915 at Flers.
Reinholz, Richard	Ersatz Reservist	2	18-Aug-1915	La Boisselle	
Schweizer, Markus	Ersatz Reservist	4	19-Aug-1915	La Boisselle	W.I.A., died 20-Aug-1915 in Flers.

RIR 109

NAME	RANK	CO.	DATE OF DEATH	LOCATION	NOTES
Becker, Ernst	Wehrmann	3	21-Aug-1915	La Boisselle	
Araaft, Eugen	Grenadier der Reserve	1	28-Aug-1915	La Boisselle	
Gür, Wilhelm	Ersatz Reservist	8	28-Aug-1915	La Boisselle	
Hanns, Bernhard	Unteroffizier der Landwehr	2	8-Sep-1915	La Boisselle	
Feger, Paul	Grenadier	1	17-Sep-1915	La Boisselle	
Dorer, Josef	Wehrmann	4	17-Sep-1915	La Boisselle	
Ender, Ernst	Musketier	4	17-Sep-1915	La Boisselle	
Fröhner, Karl	Landsturmmann	4	17-Sep-1915	La Boisselle	
Ender, Ernst	Reservist	11	17-Sep-1915	La Boisselle	
Höfer, Johann	Musketier der Landwehr I	1	23-Sep-1915	La Boisselle	
Büchling, Karl	Landsturmmann	10	25-Sep-1915	La Boisselle	W.I.A., died 26-Sep-1915, hospital, Flers.
Soulier, Heinrich	Kriegsfreiwilliger	9	30-Sep-1915	La Boisselle	
Bender, Ernst	Wehrmann I	1	8-Oct-1915	La Boisselle	W.I.A., died 14-Oct-1915 at Flers.
Grundler, Josef	Grenadier	9	10-Oct-1915	La Boisselle	
Rendler, Josef	Landsturmmann	7	12-Oct-1915	La Boisselle	W.I.A., died 14-Oct-1914, Württemberg Field Hospital I, Bapaume.
Sieferle, Franz	Wehrmann	2	14-Oct-1915	La Boisselle	W.I.A., died 28-Oct-1915 at Field Hospital 3 d, 52nd Infantry Division, Bapaume.
Fetzner, Hermann	Kriegsfreiwilliger	3	14-Oct-1915	La Boisselle	
Hock, Karl	Kriegsfreiwilliger	3	14-Oct-1915	La Boisselle	
Ehrenbieth, Leo	Landsturm Pfl.	1	18-Oct-1915	Martinpuich	
Wüst, Wilhelm	Ersatz Reservist	1	19-Oct-1915	La Boisselle	
Wipfler, Johann	Kriegsfreiwilliger	4	28-Oct-1915	Le Cateau	Left sick, died 25-Dec-1915 in Le Cateau.
Müller, Johann	Ersatz Reservist	1	31-Oct-1915	La Boisselle	W.I.A., died 1-Nov-1915 in Flers.
Völker, Richard	Unteroffizier der Landwehr	3	3-Nov-1915	Fricourt	
Papies, Gustav	Gefreiter	11	3-Nov-1915	Pozières	
Janzer, Hermann	Wehrmann	10	4-Nov-1915	La Boisselle	W.I.A., died 2-Jun-1916, auxiliary hospital Mainz.
Spiegel, Fritz	Kriegsfreiwilliger	1	6-Nov-1915	La Boisselle	W.I.A., died 2-Jan-1916 in Bruchsal.
Mann, Albert	Ersatz Reservist	10	7-Nov-1915	La Boisselle	W.I.A., died 7-Nov-1915.
Rupp, Emil	Landsturmm Recruit	1	18-Nov-1915	La Boisselle	
Faulner, Johann	Landsturmmann	3	19-Nov-1915	La Boisselle	
Pfeiffer, Hermann	Kriegsfreiwilliger	7	19-Nov-1915	Mametz	
Levistein, Berthold	Landsturmm Recruit	12	23-Nov-1915	La Boisselle	
Säubert, Longinus	Reservist	5	26-Nov-1915	La Boisselle	

RIR 109

NAME	RANK	CO.	DATE OF DEATH	LOCATION	NOTES
Sumser, Anselm	Landsturmmann	10	28-Nov-1915	La Boisselle	W.I.A., died 1-Dec-1915, military hospital, St. Quentin.
Dostmann, Nikolaus	Landsturmmann	9	3-Dec-1915	La Boisselle	
Lang, Heinrich	Wehrmann	9	3-Dec-1915	La Boisselle	W.I.A., died 4-Dec-1915, Flers.
Müller, Julius	Wehrmann	4	16-Dec-1915	La Boisselle	
Frank, Friedrich	Landsturmmann Recruit	2	18-Dec-1915	La Boisselle	W.I.A., died 20-Dec-1915 at Flers.
Bührer, Andreas	Ersatz Reservist	10	24-Dec-1915	La Boisselle	W.I.A., died 30-Dec-1915, hospital, Flers.
Gissler, Friedrich	Landwehrmann	8	31-Dec-1915	La Boisselle	
Englert, Michael	Ersatz Reservist	10	2-Jan-1916	La Boisselle	
Hummel, Friedrich	Ersatz Reservist	8	9-Jan-1916	La Boisselle	
Schuhmann, Heinrich	Grenadier	1 M.G.	10-Jan-1916	La Boisselle	
Wittner, Theodor	Ersatz Reservist	6	29-Jan-1916	Flers	
Reicheneder, Franz	Landsturmmann Pfl.	1	31-Jan-1916	La Boisselle	
Hofmann, Philipp	Ersatz Reservist	4	1-Feb-1916	La Boisselle	
Schmid, Norbert	Ersatz Reservist	4	1-Feb-1916	La Boisselle	
Steinkeller, Fritz	Unteroffizier der Landwehr	7	6-Feb-1916	Montauban	
Keller, Josef	Unteroffizier	9	29-Feb-1916	Ovillers	
Russ, Reinhold	Reservist	10	10-Mar-1916	Ovillers	
Müller, Georg	Ersatz Reservist	9	16-Mar-1916	Ovillers	
Schäfer II, Oskar	Wehrmann	3	27-Mar-1916	La Boisselle	
Schlegel, Josef	Ersatz Reservist	8	28-Mar-1916	Ovillers	
Schwall, Hugo	Kriegsfreiwilliger	7	30-Mar-1916	Ovillers	W.I.A., died 1-Apr-1916, Flers.
Schreiner, Nikolaus	Gefreiter	2 M.G.	6-Apr-1916	Ovillers	W.I.A., died 8-Apr-1915, Main dressing station, Flers.
Kast, Friedrich	Landsturmmann Pfl.	1	14-Apr-1916	Bazentin le Petit	
Morsch, Josef	Landsturm Recruit	6	22-Apr-1916	Ovillers	
Nagel, Arthur	Kriegsfreiwilliger	2	25-Apr-1916	Ovillers	
Miketta, Josef	Reservist	4	30-Apr-1916	Ovillers	W.I.A., died 1-May-1916 in Flers.
Ringwald, Ludwig	Wehrmann	10	30-Apr-1916	Thiepval	
Kühner, Heinrich	Ersatz Reservist	3	4-May-1916	La Boisselle	
Eckert, Wilhelm	Ersatz Reservist	5	6-May-1916	Ovillers	
Roth II, Anton	Unteroffizier	5	6-May-1916	Ovillers	W.I.A. Ovillers/Thiepval, died 8-May-1916, Field Hospital, Flers.
Sutter, Julius	Gefreiter der Landwehr II	5	6-May-1916	Ovillers	

RIR 109

NAME	RANK	CO.	DATE OF DEATH	LOCATION	NOTES
Weichold, Albert	Landsturmm Recruit	5	8-May-1916	Ovillers	W.I.A. Ovillers/Thiepval, died 10-May-1916, Field Hospital, Flers.
Pfister, August	Vizefeldwebel	2	11-May-1916	Ovillers	
Zoller, Friedrich	Gefreiter	3	11-May-1916	Ovillers	
Ruder, Adolf	Ersatz Reservist	2	12-May-1916	Ovillers	
Mungenast, Leopold	Landwehrmann	5	19-May-1916	Ovillers	
Kiefer, Hermann	Landsturmmann	9	21-May-1916	Ovillers	
Zipperer, Karl	Unteroffizier	7	24-May-1916	Ovillers	
Fuller, Karl	Landsturmmann	7	25-May-1916	Ovillers	W.I.A., died 27-May-1916, Flers.
Müller, Jakob	Ersatz Reservist	11	28-May-1916	La Boisselle	
Heiler, Jakob	Landsturmmann	10	6-Jun-1916	Ovillers	
Grimm, Ludwig	Ersatz Reservist	1	17-Jun-1916	Mametz	
Ihrig, Karl	Kriegsfreiwilliger	1	19-Jun-1916	Mametz	W.I.A., died 14-Jul-1916 in Military Hospital Le Cateau and buried nearby.
Franzischak, Martin	Unteroffizier	2	21-Jun-1916	Mametz	
Barth, Jakob	Landsturmmann	10	23-Jun-1916	Montauban	
Gramlich, Karl	Landsturmmann	10	23-Jun-1916	Montauban	
Schmieder, Moritz	Ersatz Reservist	2	24-Jun-1916	Mametz	
Küchly, Luzian	Ersatz Reservist	12	24-Jun-1916	Montauban	
Stengel, Heinrich	Wehrmann	2	25-Jun-1916	Mametz	
Kilian, Martin	Landsturmmann	4	25-Jun-1916	Mametz	
Kallmann, Friedrich	Gefreiter	12	25-Jun-1916	Montauban	
Anderer, Wendelin	Ersatz Reservist	4	26-Jun-1916	Mametz	
Müller, Wilhelm	Ersatz Reservist	4	26-Jun-1916	Mametz	
Schäfer, Wilhelm	Kriegsfreiwilliger	4	26-Jun-1916	Mametz	
Kulot, Karl	Gefreiter	8	26-Jun-1916	Montauban	
Günther, Hermann	Reservist	9	26-Jun-1916	Montauban	W.I.A., died 27-Jun-1916, Field Hospital Nr. 9, 12th Infantry Division.
Kopf, Wilhelm	Musketier	9	26-Jun-1916	Montauban	
Köhler, Berthold	Wehrmann	10	26-Jun-1916	Montauban	
Kruss, Ludwig	Ersatz Reservist	10	26-Jun-1916	Montauban	
Roster, Gustav	Kriegsfreiwilliger	10	26-Jun-1916	Montauban	W.I.A., died 17-Jan-1917, reserve hospital, Karlsruhe.
Bäumlin, August	Landwehrmann I	11	26-Jun-1916	Mametz	
Becker, Goswin	Ersatz Reservist	11	26-Jun-1916	Mametz	
Buchmann, August	Landwehrmann	11	26-Jun-1916	Mametz	
Dörr, Pius	Landsturmann	11	26-Jun-1916	Mametz	
Herm, Otto	Unteroffizier	11	26-Jun-1916	Mametz	
Mächtel, Leander	Landwehrmann	11	26-Jun-1916	Mametz	
Merx, Ludwig	Reservist	11	26-Jun-1916	Mametz	
Seufert, Karl	Landwehrmann	11	26-Jun-1916	Mametz	
Stisi, Karl	Grenadier	1M.G.	26-Jun-1916	Montauban	

RIR 109 NAME	RANK	CO.	DATE OF DEATH	LOCATION	NOTES
Trautz, Karl	Leutnant der Reserve	1 M.G.	26-Jun-1916	Montauban	W.I.A., died 27-Jun-1916 at Field Hospital Nr. 9, 12th Infantry Division
Wille, Johann	Unteroffizier	2 M.G.	26-Jun-1916	Montauban	
Mussler, Hermann	Kriegsfreiwilliger	1	27-Jun-1916	Mametz	
Herger, Josef	Ersatz Reservist	2	27-Jun-1916	Longueval	
Oetzel, Josef	Unteroffizier der Landwehr I	2	27-Jun-1916	Mametz	W.I.A., died 23-Sep-1916 Reserve Hospital II Abteilung Sick House, Forst-Aachen
Senger, Emil	Wehrmann	7	27-Jun-1916	Montauban	W.I.A., died 17-Jul-1916 at Reserve hospital Nr. 1 Aachen
Regenscheit, Karl	Reservist	8	27-Jun-1916	Montauban	
Buntrock, Otto	Ersatz Reservist	9	27-Jun-1916	Montauban	
Eppel, Ludwig	Ersatz Reservist	9	27-Jun-1916	Montauban	
Sytzki, Wilhelm	9/6/1887	9	27-Jun-1916	Montauban	
Bauer, Eugen	Kriegsfreiwilliger	10	27-Jun-1916	Montauban	
Gerber, Fritz	Freiwilliger	10	27-Jun-1916	Montauban	
Zendel, Karl	Kriegsfreiwilliger	10	27-Jun-1916	Montauban	
Utz, George	Ersatz Reservist	11	27-Jun-1916	Mametz	
Hollwedel, Karl	Landsturmm Recruit	12	27-Jun-1916	Montauban	
Müller, Ernst	Grenadier	1 M.G.	27-Jun-1916	Montauban	
Armbruster, Friedrich	Unteroffizier	2 M.G.	27-Jun-1916	Thilloy	
Köhler, Heinrich	Unteroffizier	2 M.G.	27-Jun-1916	Montauban	
Gutknecht, Eugen	Grenadier der Reserve	1	28-Jun-1916	Mametz	
Ebner I, Wilhelm	Reservist	2	28-Jun-1916	Longueval	
Mussgnug, Gustav	Gefreiter	2	28-Jun-1916	Mametz	
Ondrusch, Alois	Reservist	2	28-Jun-1916	Mametz	
Weis, Albert	Ersatz Recruit	2	28-Jun-1916	Mametz	
Wollensack, Wilhelm Ludwig	Wehrmann	3	28-Jun-1916	Longueval	
Bernauer, Fridolin	Landsturmmann	4	28-Jun-1916	Mametz	W.I.A., died 29-Jun-1916 at Longueval
Fischer, Ludwig	Landsturmmann	4	28-Jun-1916	Mametz	W.I.A., died 11-Jul-1916 at Barreux
Lavori, Johann	Unteroffizier	6	28-Jun-1916	Mametz	W.I.A., died 8-Jul-1916 Reserve Field Hospital Nr. 57
Trefzer, Reinhard	Reservist	6	28-Jun-1916	Mametz	W.I.A. died 7-Jul-1916 Reserve Field hospital Bertincourt
Benslein, Lorenz	Ersatz Reservist	7	28-Jun-1916	Montauban	W.I.A., died 4-Jul-1916 Reserve Field hospital Nr. 57 Bertincourt
Straub, Heinrich	Landsturmmann	9	28-Jun-1916	Montauban	

RIR 109

NAME	RANK	CO.	DATE OF DEATH	LOCATION	NOTES
Gauss, Heinrich	Unteroffizier	12	28-Jun-1916	Montauban	
Zachow, Ernst	Landsturmmann Pfl.	1	29-Jun-1916	Mametz	
Kattermann, Friedrich	Kriegsfreiwilliger	2	29-Jun-1916	Mametz	W.I.A., died 1-Jul-1916 in Field Hospital, Bertincourt.
Erbe, Ernst	Unteroffizier	4	29-Jun-1916	Mametz	W.I.A., died 7-Jul-1916 at Bertincourt
Müller, Benedikt	Wehrmann	4	29-Jun-1916	Mametz	
Fitz, Hermann	Landsturmm Recruit	5	29-Jun-1916	Mametz	
Rabiger II, Wilhelm	Landsturmm Recruit	5	29-Jun-1916	Mametz	
Dillenkofer, Karl	Ersatz Reservist	6	29-Jun-1916	Mametz	
Glatt, Karl	Recruit	9	29-Jun-1916	Montauban	
Rudorf, Walter	Vizefeldwebel	11	29-Jun-1916	Mametz	
Riedlinger, Johann	Landsturmm Recruit	2	30-Jun-1916	Mametz	
Kissling, Ludwig	Landsturmmann	9	30-Jun-1916	Montauban	W.I.A., died 1-Jul-1916, Field Hospital Nr. 2, 52nd Infantry Division.
Gropp, Hermann	Landwehrnmann	11	30-Jun-1916	Mametz	W.I.A., died 18-Jul-1916 in Field Hospital Nr. 57.
Huber, Karl	Kriegsfreiwilliger	11	30-Jun-1916	Mametz	W.I.A., died 1-Jul-1916 Reserve Field hospital Nr. 57.
Kramer, Karl	Landsturmann	11	30-Jun-1916	Mametz	

26th Reserve Division cemetery near Miraumont. (Author's collection)

Grave photograph of the brother-in-law of the man on the right, sent
home to the family – RIR 110. (Author's collection)

RIR 110

NAME	RANK	CO.	DATE OF DEATH	LOCATION	NOTES
Gabler,	Unteroffizier	5	28-Sep-1914	?	M.I.A.
Zippert, Julius	Infantryman	5	29-Sep-1914	Fricourt	
Warzewsky, Friedrich	Infantryman	6	30-Sep-1914	?	Died from wounds
Fütterer, Otto	Infantryman	7	30-Sep-1914	Courcelette	
Hilzinger, Wilhelm	Infantryman	7	30-Sep-1914	Courcelette	
Gilbert, Karl	Infantryman	7	1-Oct-1914	Courcelette	
Hauser, Karl	Infantryman	7	1-Oct-1914	Courcelette	
Meisterlein, Georg	Infantryman	7	1-Oct-1914	Beaumont	
Wawrock, Jakob	Gefreiter	7	1-Oct-1914	Courcelette	
Geisel, Hermann	Infantryman	3	2-Oct-1914	?	Died from wounds
Kern I, Wilhelm	Infantryman	7	3-Oct-1914	Courcelette	
Luyken, Friedrich	Hauptmann	7	4-Oct-1914	Beaumont	
Burgert, Albert	Infantryman	6	5-Oct-1914	Beaumont	
Hüller, Camill	Unteroffizier	6	5-Oct-1914	Beaumont	
Kopp, Karl	Infantryman	6	5-Oct-1914	Beaumont	
Pabst, Johann	Infantryman	6	5-Oct-1914	Beaumont	
Schaub, Karl	Infantryman	6	5-Oct-1914	Beaumont	
Seger, Heinrich	Infantryman	6	5-Oct-1914	Beaumont	
Seiler, Franz	Unteroffizier	6	5-Oct-1914	Beaumont	
Strinkau, Andreas	Infantryman	6	5-Oct-1914	Beaumont	
Stumpf, Gustav Josef	Infantryman	6	5-Oct-1914	Beaumont	
Wein, August	Infantryman	6	5-Oct-1914	Beaumont	
Deck, Michael	Infantryman	7	5-Oct-1914	Beaumont	
Dinger, Gottlieb	Infantryman	7	5-Oct-1914	Beaumont	
Grün II, Johann	Infantryman	7	5-Oct-1914	Beaumont	

RIR 110

NAME	RANK	CO.	DATE OF DEATH	LOCATION	NOTES
Hennig, Hermann	Infantryman	7	5-Oct-1914	Beaumont	
Reis, Jakob	Unteroffizier	7	5-Oct-1914	Beaumont	
Rimmelspacher, Albert	Infantryman	7	5-Oct-1914	Beaumont	
Schneckenburger, August	Infantryman	7	5-Oct-1914	Beaumont	
Streier, Heinrich	Infantryman	7	5-Oct-1914	Beaucourt	
Stuckmann, Emil	Infantryman	7	5-Oct-1914	Beaucourt	
Tilger, Karl	Unteroffizier	7	5-Oct-1914	Beaucourt	
Witte, Wilhelm	Infantryman	7	5-Oct-1914	Beaucourt	
Breunig, Johann	Infantryman	9	5-Oct-1914	Beaumont	
Flesch, Edmund	Infantryman	9	5-Oct-1914	Beaumont	M.I.A.
Hess, Wittilo	Infantryman	9	5-Oct-1914	Beaumont	
Heuer, Georg	Gefreiter	9	5-Oct-1914	Beaumont	
Koch, Oskar	Gefreiter	9	5-Oct-1914	Beaumont	
Moritz, Ludwig	Infantryman	9	5-Oct-1914	Beaumont	
Nonnenmacher, Christian	Infantryman	9	5-Oct-1914	Beaumont	
Nord, Ludwig	Infantryman	9	5-Oct-1914	Beaumont	
Wankmüller, Max	Infantryman	9	5-Oct-1914	Beaumont	
Weber, Adolf	Infantryman	9	5-Oct-1914	Beaumont	
Culmbacher, Otto	Infantryman	10	5-Oct-1914	Beaumont	
Ludwig, Georg	Gefreiter	10	5-Oct-1914	Beaumont	
Müller, Traugott	Infantryman	10	5-Oct-1914	Beaumont	
Rauenbühler, Johann	Infantryman	10	5-Oct-1914	Beaumont	
Schmidt II, Johann	Gefreiter	10	5-Oct-1914	Beaumont	
Wild, Wilhelm	Infantryman	10	5-Oct-1914	Beaumont	M.I.A.
. . . .	Infantryman	11	5-Oct-1914	Beaumont	
Fischer, Hermann	Infantryman	11	5-Oct-1914	Beaumont	
Kleinschrot, Emil	Infantryman	11	5-Oct-1914	Beaumont	
Kohler, Karl	Infantryman	11	5-Oct-1914	Beaumont	
Pahl, Hermann	Infantryman	11	5-Oct-1914	Beaumont	
Scheller, Friedrich	Gefreiter	11	5-Oct-1914	Beaumont	
Spitzmüller, Josef	Gefreiter	11	5-Oct-1914	Beaumont	
Ehmer, Konrad	Infantryman	12	5-Oct-1914	Beaumont	
Lehmann, Emil	Infantryman	12	5-Oct-1914	Beaumont	
Reich, Karl	Infantryman	12	5-Oct-1914	Beaumont	
Walter, Friedrich	Gefreiter	12	5-Oct-1914	Beaumont	
Schwendemann, Xaver	Infantryman	5	6-Oct-1914	Thiepval	
Szay, Franz	Infantryman	6	6-Oct-1914	Beaumont	Died from wounds
Lehmann, Wilhelm	Unteroffizier	8	6-Oct-1914	Beaumont	
Schollenberger, Adam	Infantryman	8	6-Oct-1914	Beaumont	
Benz, Oskar	Infantryman	9	6-Oct-1914	Beaumont	
Sinniger, Alfons	Infantryman	12	6-Oct-1914	Beaumont	Died from wounds

RIR 110

NAME	RANK	CO.	DATE OF DEATH	LOCATION	NOTES
Meusel, Walter	Infantryman	12	7-Oct-1914	Beaumont	
Basler, Josef	Infantryman	6	8-Oct-1914	Beaumont	
Hauber, Karl	Infantryman	6	8-Oct-1914	Beaumont	
Martus, Josef	Infantryman	6	8-Oct-1914	Beaumont	
Schröder, Peter	Infantryman	7	8-Oct-1914	Beaumont	
Ziemann, Friedrich	Infantryman	7	8-Oct-1914	Beaucourt	
Zimmer, Friedrich	Infantryman	7	8-Oct-1914	Beaucourt	
Balcevzak, Bartholomäus	Infantryman	10	8-Oct-1914	Beaumont	Died from wounds
Bühler, Friedrich	Infantryman	11	8-Oct-1914	Beaumont	
Machniski, Josef	Infantryman	11	8-Oct-1914	Beaumont	
Schmelting, Heinrich	Infantryman	6	9-Oct-1914	Beaumont	Died from wounds
Schmidt, Ernst	Infantryman	8	9-Oct-1914	Grandcourt	
Grün, Gottlieb	Infantryman	9	11-Oct-1914	Beaumont	
Kressig, Anton	Infantryman	9	11-Oct-1914	Beaumont	
Schindler, Josef	Infantryman	9	11-Oct-1914	Beaumont	
Binder, Gottlob	Infantryman	2	13-Oct-1914	Beaumont	
Boschert, Josef	Infantryman	2	13-Oct-1914	Beaumont	
Kleehammer, Xaver	Infantryman	11	13-Oct-1914	Beaumont	
Kirchenlohr, Ludwig	Offizier-Stellvertreter	12	13-Oct-1914	Beaumont	
Lohmann, Ernst	Offizier-Stellvertreter	12	13-Oct-1914	Beaumont	
Moritz, Adolf	Leutnant der Reserve	7	14-Oct-1914	Somme	
Lenz, Emil	Infantryman	6	15-Oct-1914	Beaumont	
Gossenberger, Wilhelm	Infantryman	7	15-Oct-1914	Beaumont	
Behringer, Friedrich	Vizefeldwebel	12	15-Oct-1914	Beaumont	
Kormann, Karl Fr.	Infantryman	7	16-Oct-1914	?	Died from wounds
Leutner, Gustav	Infantryman	7	16-Oct-1914	?	Died from wounds
Wiese, Karl	Infantryman	12	16-Oct-1914	?	Died from wounds
Jordan, Albert	Infantryman	2	17-Oct-1914	?	Died from wounds
Ehrhardt,	Leutnant der Reserve	1 M.G. Co.	17-Oct-1914	Beaumont	
Martz, Josef	Schützen	1 M.G. Co.	17-Oct-1914	Beaumont	
Schäfer, Franz	Schützen	1 M.G. Co.	17-Oct-1914	Beaumont	
Jakoby, Christian	Gefreiter	6	18-Oct-1914	Beaumont	Died from wounds
Nelder, Wilhelm	Infantryman	6	18-Oct-1914	Beaumont	
Sedlmaier, Hermann	Schützen	1 M.G. Co.	18-Oct-1914	Beaumont	Died from wounds
Leckebusch, Hermann	Infantryman	10	19-Oct-1914	?	Died from wounds
Rönicke, Paul	Infantryman	12	19-Oct-1914	?	Died from wounds

RIR 110

NAME	RANK	CO.	DATE OF DEATH	LOCATION	NOTES
Meyer, Jakob	Infantryman	2	20-Oct-1914	?	Died from wounds
Burger, Gustav	Infantryman	9	20-Oct-1914	Flers	
Behringer, Wilhelm	Vizefeldwebel	12	21-Oct-1914	Miraumont	
Strack, Franz	Infantryman	4	24-Oct-1914	Guillemont	
Weinrich, Josef	Infantryman	4	24-Oct-1914	Guillemont	
Bitzer, Gottlob	Infantryman	7	26-Oct-1914	?	Died from wounds
Krawczynski, Anton	Infantryman	11	27-Oct-1914	?	
Barth, Friedrich	Infantryman	6	28-Oct-1914	?	Died from illness
Ochs, Kamill	Infantryman	1	2-Nov-1914	?	M.I.A.
Graf, Fritz	Infantryman	4	3-Nov-1914	?	Died from illness
Lang, Wilhelm	Infantryman	4	3-Nov-1914	Fricourt	
Barthlot, Karl	Infantryman	7	4-Nov-1914	Fricourt	
Schäfer I, Leo	Infantryman	7	4-Nov-1914	Fricourt	
Oberle II, Georg Fr.	Infantryman	6	5-Nov-1914	Fricourt	
Hildinger, Eugen	Gefreiter	3	8-Nov-1914	Fricourt	
Schindler, Mathias	Infantryman	Rad-fahrer	9-Nov-1914	La Boisselle	Died from wounds
Kirchhofer, Eugen	Infantryman	11	12-Nov-1914	Strassburg	Died in hospital of illness
Lang, Franz	Infantryman	4	13-Nov-1914	?	Died from illness
Federer, Hermann	Infantryman	9	16-Nov-1914	?	Died from wounds
Kuttler, Konrad	Infantryman	1	17-Nov-1914	Fricourt	
Werner, Karl	Unteroffizier	3	20-Nov-1914	?	Died from wounds
Weber, Hans	Unteroffizier	9	21-Nov-1914	Fricourt	
Herp, Josef	Infantryman	11	21-Nov-1914	Fricourt	
Volz, Wilhelm	Infantryman	11	21-Nov-1914	Fricourt	
Krieg, Franz	Infantryman	4	25-Nov-1914	?	Died from illness
Fiedler, Johann Robert	Infantryman	6	26-Nov-1914	Fricourt	
Kiefer, Ernst	Infantryman	8	28-Nov-1914	?	Died from wounds
Kimmer, Karl	Infantryman	2	8-Dec-1914	Fricourt	
Baas, Michael	Infantryman	4	8-Dec-1914	?	Died from wounds
Brohammer, Friedrich	Ersatz Reservist	2	10-Dec-1914	Arnsdorf	
Bühler, Julius	Infantryman	7	13-Dec-1914	Fricourt	
Lehmann, Anton	Infantryman	12	16-Dec-1914	?	Died from wounds
Zipse, Wilhelm	Infantryman	8	18-Dec-1914	Mametz	
Wiegert, Lorenz	Infantryman	11	18-Dec-1914	Mametz	
Rettkowski, Gustav	Infantryman	8	20-Dec-1914	Mametz	Died from wounds
Dreher, Johann	Infantryman	11	20-Dec-1914	Mametz	
Foltzer, Eugen	Infantryman	11	21-Dec-1914	Mametz	
Rolli, Oskar	Infantryman	11	21-Dec-1914	Mametz	
Neureither, Johann	Infantryman	1	24-Dec-1914	Mametz	
Schäfer, Georg	Infantryman	1	24-Dec-1914	Mametz	
Stockert, Wilhelm	Infantryman	1	24-Dec-1914	Mametz	
Huber, Adolf	Infantryman	1	28-Dec-1914	Mametz	Died from wounds

RIR 110

NAME	RANK	CO.	DATE OF DEATH	LOCATION	NOTES
Kirrstädter, Hermann	Infantryman	11	4-Jan-1915	Mametz	Died from wounds
Makamull, Max	Infantryman	11	6-Jan-1915	Mametz	Died from wounds
Rückert, Otto	Infantryman	10	13-Jan-1915	Mametz	
Gebhardt, Heinrich	Infantryman	9	15-Jan-1915	Mametz	
Wunsch, Markus	Infantryman	11	16-Jan-1915	Mametz	
Koch, Karl	Infantryman	4	17-Jan-1915	?	Died from wounds
Beck, Heinrich	Infantryman	9	17-Jan-1915	Mametz	
Frauenfeld, Georg	Unteroffizier	9	17-Jan-1915	Mametz	
Schmerber, Albert	Infantryman	9	17-Jan-1915	Mametz	
Thieringer, Paul	Kriegs-frei-williger	9	17-Jan-1915	Mametz	
Kolb, Ludwig	Infantryman	11	17-Jan-1915	Mametz	
Ross, Jakob	Infantryman	11	20-Jan-1915	Mametz	
Merkel, Anton	Unteroffizier	4	21-Jan-1915	Mametz	
Doll, Josef	Infantryman	2	22-Jan-1915	Flers	
Bär, Hermann	Infantryman	7	22-Jan-1915	Mametz	
Bauerer, Emil	Infantryman	8	23-Jan-1915	Mametz	
Albert, Friedrich	Infantryman	12	23-Jan-1915	Mametz	
Link, Andreas	Infantryman	6	24-Jan-1915	Mametz	
Staroska, Adolf	Infantryman	6	27-Jan-1915	Mametz	
Siehl, Karl	Infantryman	9	27-Jan-1915	Mametz	
Keilbach, Hermann	Infantryman	10	31-Jan-1915	Mametz	Died from wounds
Kopp, Wilhelm	Infantryman	1	2-Feb-1915	Mametz	
Ehehalt, Friedrich	Infantryman	8	3-Feb-1915	Mametz	
Berndt, Friedrich Wilhelm	Infantryman	10	7-Feb-1915	Mametz	
Welte, Eugen	Infantryman	11	7-Feb-1915	Mametz	
Bogenschütz, Josef	Infantryman	12	7-Feb-1915	Mametz	
Beinert, Friedrich	Infantryman	2	9-Feb-1915	Mametz	
Späth, Friedrich	Infantryman	4	9-Feb-1915	Mametz	
Hüfner, Erich	Vizefeldwebel	1 M.G. Co.	9-Feb-1915	Fricourt	
Schillinger, Johannes	Infantryman	1	12-Feb-1915	Mametz	
Roll, Hermann	Infantryman	2	14-Feb-1915	Mametz	Died from wounds
Ebel, Johann	Infantryman	5	14-Feb-1915	Mametz	
Rohrauer, Wilhelm	Infantryman	5	15-Feb-1915	Mametz	
Rummelhardt, Desiere	Infantryman	8	16-Feb-1915	?	Died from illness
Breig, Reinhardt	Infantryman	4	19-Feb-1915	Mametz	Died from illness
König, Gustav	Infantryman	8	19-Feb-1915	Bapaume	
Steiert, Josef	Infantryman	11	19-Feb-1915	Fricourt	
Krug, Ludwig	Infantryman	10	21-Feb-1915	Fricourt	
Ochs, August	Infantryman	3	22-Feb-1915	Mametz	
Stehle, Hermann	Infantryman	10	25-Feb-1915	Fricourt	Died from wounds
Wessbecher, Franz	Infantryman	3	26-Feb-1915	Fricourt	

RIR 110

NAME	RANK	CO.	DATE OF DEATH	LOCATION	NOTES
Gredy, Eugen	Infantryman	4	26-Feb-1915	Mametz	M.I.A.
Jhmann, Max	Infantryman	6	26-Feb-1915	Mametz	
Kimmerle, Josef	Infantryman	6	26-Feb-1915	Fricourt	
Schulze, Wilhelm	Infantryman	6	26-Feb-1915	Fricourt	
Kilburg, Josef	Infantryman	6	27-Feb-1915	Fricourt	
Horn, Heinrich	Gefreiter	11	1-Mar-1915	Fricourt	
Eisele, Augustin	Infantryman	9	4-Mar-1915	Fricourt	
Trauzettel, Friedrich	Feldwebel	1	8-Mar-1915	?	Died from wounds
Menger, Ludwig	Infantryman	10	11-Mar-1915	Fricourt	
Stumpf, Friedrich	Infantryman	4	14-Mar-1915	Martinpuich	
Betsch, Emil	Unteroffizier	5	16-Mar-1915	Fricourt	
Dietrich, Albert	Infantryman	5	19-Mar-1915	Fricourt	Died from wounds
Erb, Max	Infantryman	5	21-Mar-1915	Fricourt	
Fluck, Wilhelm	Infantryman	9	21-Mar-1915	Fricourt	Died from wounds
Schwald, Karl	Gefreiter	12	24-Mar-1915	Mametz	Died from wounds
Eckert, Fridolin	Gefreiter	12	25-Mar-1915	Mametz	
Santo, Fritz	Leutnant der Reserve	12	25-Mar-1915	Mametz	
Schütterle, Karl	Infantryman	10	28-Mar-1915	Fricourt	
Wagner, Ludwig	Infantryman	1	29-Mar-1915	Auchy	
Birk, Josef	Infantryman	12	29-Mar-1915	Mametz	
Karl, Adolf	Schützen	1 M.G. Co.	1-Apr-1915	Fricourt	
Wagner, Franz	Infantryman	3	3-Apr-1915	Mametz	
Pawlak, Franz	Infantryman	4	5-Apr-1915	?	Died from wounds
Huber, Augustin	Infantryman	5	5-Apr-1915	Fricourt	
Geier, Oskar	Infantryman	10	9-Apr-1915	Fricourt	M.I.A.
Hülsenbrand, Hermann	Unteroffizier	5	10-Apr-1915	?	Died from wounds
Anselment, Karl	Infantryman	3	12-Apr-1915	Mametz	Died during enemy mine explosion.
Blum, Emil	Infantryman	3	12-Apr-1915	Mametz	Died during enemy mine explosion.
Feisst, Georg	Gefreiter	3	12-Apr-1915	Mametz	Died during enemy mine explosion.
Gerstner, Dominik	Infantryman	3	12-Apr-1915	Mametz	Died during enemy mine explosion.
Haas, Hermann	Unteroffizier	3	12-Apr-1915	Mametz	Died during enemy mine explosion.
Hartmann, Hermann	Gefreiter	3	12-Apr-1915	Mametz	Died during enemy mine explosion.
Jörger, Josef	Infantryman	3	12-Apr-1915	Mametz	Died during enemy mine explosion.
Jülg, Bernhard	Infantryman	3	12-Apr-1915	Mametz	Died during enemy mine explosion.
Klittich, Rudolf	Infantryman	3	12-Apr-1915	Mametz	Died during enemy mine explosion.

RIR 110

NAME	RANK	CO.	DATE OF DEATH	LOCATION	NOTES
Lang, Johannes	Infantryman	3	12-Apr-1915	Mametz	Died during enemy mine explosion.
Nock, Albert	Infantryman	3	12-Apr-1915	Mametz	Died during enemy mine explosion.
Peter, Wendelin	Infantryman	3	12-Apr-1915	Mametz	Died during enemy mine explosion.
Sailer, August	Infantryman	3	12-Apr-1915	Mametz	Died during enemy mine explosion.
Schaufler, Alois	Infantryman	3	12-Apr-1915	Mametz	Died during enemy mine explosion.
Vogel, Stefan	Gefreiter	3	12-Apr-1915	Mametz	Died during enemy mine explosion.
Weissenberger, Josef	Infantryman	3	12-Apr-1915	Mametz	Died during enemy mine explosion.
Weymann, Karl	Leutnant	3	12-Apr-1915	Mametz	Suffocated after being buried in mine explosion.
Wollrauch, David	Infantryman	3	12-Apr-1915	Mametz	Died during enemy mine explosion.
Weinle, Karl	Infantryman	4	12-Apr-1915	Mametz	
Zimmer, Augustin	Infantryman	4	12-Apr-1915	Mametz	
Steidle, Otto	Infantryman	2	13-Apr-1915	Mametz	
Schindler, August	Infantryman	3	13-Apr-1915	Mametz	Shot 7 times after mine explosion on 12-Apr-1915.
Cisewski, Johann	Schützen	1 M.G. Co.	14-Apr-1915	?	Died from illness
Liebis, Blasius	Infantryman	4	15-Apr-1915	Mametz	Died from wounds
Neumeier, Anton	Infantryman	4	16-Apr-1915	Mametz	
Lauer, Wilhelm	Infantryman	5	17-Apr-1915	?	Died from wounds
Sproll, August	Infantryman	3	22-Apr-1915	Mametz	
Soth, Georg	Infantryman	4	22-Apr-1915	?	Died from wounds, Military Hospital VII Army Corps
Seibel, Johann	Infantryman	11	22-Apr-1915	Fricourt	
Wieland, Alfred	Infantryman	11	24-Apr-1915	Fricourt	
Lutz, Adolf	Infantryman	6	28-Apr-1915	Fricourt	
Hermann, Lorenz	Infantryman	8	28-Apr-1915	Fricourt	
Klotz, Eugen	Infantryman	5	29-Apr-1915	Mametz	
Furtwängler, Karl	Infantryman	6	29-Apr-1915	Fricourt	
Oser, Karl	Infantryman	6	29-Apr-1915	Fricourt	
Grosshans, Georg	Infantryman	6	1-May-1915	Mametz	
Decker, Augustin	Infantryman	7	2-May-1915	Mametz	
Reith, Karl	Infantryman	7	2-May-1915	Mametz	
Manz, Adolf	Unteroffizier	8	5-May-1915	Fricourt	
With, Karl	Infantryman	8	5-May-1915	Fricourt	
Nass, Peter	Infantryman	6	7-May-1915	Mametz	
Ehrhardt, Lebrecht	Infantryman	2	14-May-1915	Mametz	M.I.A.
Schweighard, August	Unteroffizier	2	14-May-1915	Mametz	M.I.A.
Fuchs, Karl	Infantryman	10	14-May-1915	Fricourt	

RIR 110

NAME	RANK	CO.	DATE OF DEATH	LOCATION	NOTES
Frank, Nathan	Infantryman	7	15-May-1915	Mametz	
Stark, Karl	Gefreiter	7	15-May-1915	Mametz	
Kronauer, Friedrich	Infantryman	10	16-May-1915	Fricourt	Died from wounds
Schleh, August	Vizefeldwebel	1	20-May-1915	Mametz	
Hackl, Georg	Schützen	1 M.G. Co.	22-May-1915	Mametz	
Kummer, Richard	Infantryman	12	24-May-1915	Mametz	
Schewe, Friedrich	Infantryman	6	28-May-1915	?	Died from illness
Rutschmann, Rudolf	Infantryman	7	28-May-1915	Fricourt	
Kälble, Fiedrich	Infantryman	5	29-May-1915	Fricourt	
Werkmeister, Josef	Infantryman	3	1-Jun-1915	Mametz	Died from wounds
Hitzler, Josef	Infantryman	11	1-Jun-1915	Fricourt	
Kärcher, Stefan	Schützen	1 M.G. Co.	1-Jun-1915	Fricourt	
Mayer, Ludwig	Infantryman	6	2-Jun-1915	?	Died from wounds
Fischback, Markus	Infantryman	9	3-Jun-1915	Fricourt	
Weth, Otto (v.d.)	Infantryman	11	5-Jun-1915	?	Died from illness
Kupfer, Adolf	Infantryman	8	6-Jun-1915	Fricourt	
Burkhard, Ludwig	Infantryman	7	7-Jun-1915	Fricourt	
Ketterer, Xaver	Infantryman	7	7-Jun-1915	Flers	
Sommer, Karl	Infantryman	7	7-Jun-1915	Flers	
Hipp, Leo	Gefreiter	1 M.G. Co.	7-Jun-1915	?	Died from illness
Wittmann, Jakob	Infantryman	1	10-Jun-1915	Mametz	
Beetz, Friedrich	Infantryman	7	11-Jun-1915	Fricourt	
Schweitzer, Ludwig	Infantryman	7	11-Jun-1915	Fricourt	Died from wounds
Baudendistel, Franz	Infantryman	11	12-Jun-1915	Fricourt	Died from wounds
Veith, Stefan	Infantryman	1	13-Jun-1915	Mametz	
Weisser, Hermann	Infantryman	1	13-Jun-1915	Mametz	
Wawrocki, Josef	Infantryman	7	16-Jun-1915	Fricourt	
Sammer, Eugen	Infantryman	12	16-Jun-1915	Arras	
Ernst, Christian	Infantryman	3	18-Jun-1915	Mametz	
Fautz, Heinrich	Infantryman	1	20-Jun-1915	Mametz	
Herrmann, Heinrich	Infantryman	1	20-Jun-1915	Mametz	
Ohnemus, Leo	Infantryman	1	20-Jun-1915	Mametz	
Voigt, Ernst	Gefreiter	1	20-Jun-1915	Mametz	
Wick, Rudolf	Sergeant	1	20-Jun-1915	Mametz	
Gregan, Wilhelm	Infantryman	4	20-Jun-1915	Fricourt	
Noe, Adam	Infantryman	4	20-Jun-1915	Mametz	
Rüttenauer, Anselm	Infantryman	4	20-Jun-1915	Mametz	
Müller, August	Schützen	1 M.G. Co.	20-Jun-1915	Fricourt	
Lehmann, Friedrich	Infantryman	1	21-Jun-1915	Mametz	
Heizmann, Vinzenz	Infantryman	1	22-Jun-1915	Mametz	
Weber, Franz	Infantryman	6	7-Jul-1915	Fricourt	

RIR 110

NAME	RANK	CO.	DATE OF DEATH	LOCATION	NOTES
Lohrer, Josef	Infantryman	5	10-Jul-1915	Fricourt	
Schlachta, Valentin	Infantryman	5	10-Jul-1915	Fricourt	
Libis, Josef	Infantryman	9	10-Jul-1915	Fricourt	Died from wounds
Müller III, Ernst	Gefreiter	12	10-Jul-1915	Mametz	
Porth, Karl	Leutnant der Landwehr	5	17-Jul-1915	Fricourt	Died from wounds
Rost, Josef	Infantryman	2	19-Jul-1915	Mametz	
Bugger, Josef	Infantryman	4	19-Jul-1915	Mametz	
Talmon, Wilhelm	Infantryman	5	19-Jul-1915	Fricourt	
Stanislawski, Franz	Infantryman	7	19-Jul-1915	Fricourt	
Bauer, Wilhelm	Infantryman	10	19-Jul-1915	Fricourt	
Brückner, August	Infantryman	10	19-Jul-1915	Fricourt	
Gerold, Josef	Infantryman	10	19-Jul-1915	Fricourt	
Halder, Christian	Infantryman	10	19-Jul-1915	Fricourt	
Hanns, Josef	Infantryman	10	19-Jul-1915	Fricourt	
Johmann, Eugen	Infantryman	10	19-Jul-1915	Fricourt	
Meier, Hermann	Infantryman	10	19-Jul-1915	Fricourt	
Santer, Karl	Infantryman	10	19-Jul-1915	Fricourt	
Weber, Ernst	Infantryman	10	19-Jul-1915	Fricourt	
Ritter, Emil	Schützen	1 M.G. Co.	19-Jul-1915	Fricourt	
Herold, Peter	Infantryman	10	20-Jul-1915	Fricourt	Died from wounds
Niemeyer, Gottlieb	Infantryman	10	21-Jul-1915	Fricourt	
Streif, Fridolin	Infantryman	10	21-Jul-1915	Fricourt	
Grentz, Karl	Infantryman	11	26-Jul-1915	Fricourt	
Butscher, Albert	Unteroffizier	8	29-Jul-1915	Fricourt	
Konstantin, Karl	Infantryman	5	1-Aug-1915	Fricourt	Died from wounds
Kusch II, Peter	Infantryman	10	2-Aug-1915	Fricourt	
Arnold, Gustav	Infantryman	5	4-Aug-1915	Fricourt	
Stupfel, Franz	Infantryman	4	6-Aug-1915	?	Died from wounds
Mayer, Josef	Gefreiter	12	16-Aug-1915	?	Accidental death
Waldinger, Adam	Infantryman	12	18-Aug-1915	Fricourt	
Guhl, Julius	Infantryman	12	20-Aug-1915	Fricourt	
Ochler, Paul	Unteroffizier	2	23-Aug-1915	Mametz	
Buss, Karl	Infantryman	2	25-Aug-1915	Mametz	M.I.A.
Döringer, Johann	Infantryman	7	29-Aug-1915	Mametz	
Rahnenkamp, Wilhelm Heinrich	Infantryman	7	30-Aug-1915	Mametz	
Haungs, Adolf	Infantryman	2	2-Sep-1915	Mametz	
Kist, Albert	Gefreiter	9	4-Sep-1915	Fricourt	
Pawlack, Vinzenz	Infantryman	9	4-Sep-1915	Fricourt	
Reis, Nikolaus	Infantryman	8	5-Sep-1915	Fricourt	Died from wounds
Becker, Karl	Infantryman	8	7-Sep-1915	Fricourt	
Dietrich, Nikolaus	Infantryman	8	7-Sep-1915	Fricourt	
Ebenau, Julius	Unteroffizier	8	7-Sep-1915	Fricourt	
Eckert, Wilhelm	Infantryman	8	7-Sep-1915	Fricourt	

RIR 110

NAME	RANK	CO.	DATE OF DEATH	LOCATION	NOTES
Hess, Karl	Infantryman	8	7-Sep-1915	Fricourt	
Käfer, Robert	Infantryman	8	7-Sep-1915	Fricourt	
Keller, Rudolf	Infantryman	8	7-Sep-1915	Fricourt	
Maier, Wilhelm	Infantryman	8	7-Sep-1915	Fricourt	
Mossbrugger, Paul	Infantryman	8	7-Sep-1915	Fricourt	
Woydowski, Johann	Infantryman	8	7-Sep-1915	Fricourt	
Tepel, Friedrich	Infantryman	5	10-Sep-1915	Fricourt	
Wermelinger, Karl	Infantryman	4	16-Sep-1915	Fricourt	
Klauk, Wilhelm	Infantryman	7	27-Sep-1915	?	Died from wounds
Stoltz, Alois	Infantryman	12	27-Sep-1915	Fricourt	
Armbrust, Alois	Infantryman	12	29-Sep-1915	Fricourt	
Wurz, Robert	Infantryman	9	2-Oct-1915	Fricourt	
Freitag, Kaspar	Infantryman	1	6-Oct-1915	Mametz	
Braunbarth, Otto	Infantryman	5	6-Oct-1915	Fricourt	
Kerker, Michael	Infantryman	7	6-Oct-1915	Fricourt	
Lindenmaier, Karl	Unteroffizier	3	13-Oct-1915	Mametz	
Reinhartz, Wilhelm	Unteroffizier	7	13-Oct-1915	Fricourt	
Lepp, Johann	Infantryman	8	13-Oct-1915	Fricourt	
Späth, Franz	Infantryman	3	15-Oct-1915	Thiepval	
Ose, August	Infantryman	10	19-Oct-1915	Fricourt	
Pfundstein, Alfons	Infantryman	11	20-Oct-1915	Fricourt	
Brucks, Wilhelm	Infantryman	10	21-Oct-1915	Fricourt	M.I.A.
Oehrlein, August	Infantryman	12	27-Oct-1915	Fricourt	
Guckenhahn, Wilhelm	Infantryman	10	30-Oct-1915	Fricourt	
Huf, August	Infantryman	10	30-Oct-1915	Fricourt	
Beischler, Karl	Infantryman	6	1-Nov-1915	Fricourt	
Hubbuch, Philipp	Infantryman	6	1-Nov-1915	Fricourt	
Clements,	Leutnant der Reserve	4	3-Nov-1915	Fricourt	
Bluin, Anton	Infantryman	5	3-Nov-1915	Fricourt	
Clemens, Xaver	Leutnant der Reserve	6	3-Nov-1915	Fricourt	
Kemker, Karl	Infantryman	4	10-Nov-1915	Fricourt	
Roth, Ulrich	Infantryman	6	11-Nov-1915	Fricourt	
Stehlin, Ernst	Infantryman	7	13-Nov-1915	Fricourt	
Badura, Konstantin	Infantryman	5	15-Nov-1915	Fricourt	
Lipowski, Martin	Infantryman	6	16-Nov-1915	Fricourt	
Zucker, Josef	Infantryman	3	21-Nov-1915	Fricourt	
Tritt, karl	Infantryman	6	27-Nov-1915	Fricourt	
Weihrich, Karl	Infantryman	6	27-Nov-1915	Fricourt	
Bücheler, Paul	Infantryman	1	11-Dec-1915	Mametz	
Leibold, Johann	Infantryman	5	12-Dec-1915	Fricourt	
Hotz, Ludwig	Infantryman	4	15-Dec-1915	Fricourt	
Ummenhofer, Wilhelm	Infantryman	9	24-Dec-1915	?	Died from wounds

RIR 110

NAME	RANK	CO.	DATE OF DEATH	LOCATION	NOTES
Leitzig, Franz	Infantryman	2	26-Dec-1915	Fricourt	
Bauer, Friedrich	Infantryman	4	26-Dec-1915	Fricourt	
Blum, Karl	Infantryman	4	26-Dec-1915	Fricourt	
Ruh, Reinhardt	Infantryman	4	26-Dec-1915	Fricourt	
Hender, Ernst	Infantryman	7	27-Dec-1915	?	M.I.A.
Schnebelin, Albert	Infantryman	8	27-Dec-1915	Fricourt	
Senft, Gustav	Infantryman	10	27-Dec-1915	Fricourt	
Hasel, Karl	Unteroffizier	3	28-Dec-1915	Fricourt	
Tröscher, Friedrich	Infantryman	4	28-Dec-1915	Fricourt	
Fischer, Heinrich	Infantryman	10	28-Dec-1915	Fricourt	Died from wounds
Wüstenberg, Albert	Infantryman	10	28-Dec-1915	Fricourt	Died from wounds
Hofstetter, Franz	Infantryman	12	29-Dec-1915	Fricourt	
Jennissen, Wilhelm	Infantryman	2	15-Jan-1916	?	Died from wounds
Griesbaum, Robert	Infantryman	10	5-Feb-1916	La Boisselle	
Kimmig, Josef	Infantryman	10	5-Feb-1916	La Boisselle	
Lipps, Wilhelm	Infantryman	1	13-Feb-1916	?	Died from wounds
Wacker, Franz	Infantryman	12	2-Mar-1916	?	M.I.A.
Spath, Wilhelm	Infantryman	1	4-Mar-1916	La Boisselle	
Huber, Josef	Infantryman	11	17-Mar-1916	La Boisselle	
Deger, Kilian	Infantryman	4	25-Mar-1916	La Boisselle	
Strzeczynski, Michael	Infantryman	7	26-Mar-1916	La Boisselle	
Schröder, Fritz	Infantryman	8	27-Mar-1916	La Boisselle	
Mäkel, Albert	Infantryman	5	2-Apr-1916	La Boisselle	
Fath, Heinrich	Infantryman	2	4-Apr-1916	La Boisselle	
Winkler, Josef	Infantryman	3	11-Apr-1916	?	Captured, died in British P.O.W. camp.
Felix, Paul	Infantryman	9	13-Apr-1916	La Boisselle	
Gemple, Wilhelm	Infantryman	5	20-Apr-1916	La Boisselle	
Seelig, August	Infantryman	4	22-Apr-1916	La Boisselle	
Zyburstki, Franz	Infantryman	8	22-Apr-1916	La Boisselle	
Wunsch, Ludwig	Infantryman	7	29-Apr-1916	La Boisselle	Died from illness
Maurer, Karl	Infantryman	3	2-May-1916	?	Captured, died in P.O.W. camp.
Wenk, Max	Infantryman	5	2-May-1916	La Boisselle	
Wernette, Julius	Infantryman	8	4-May-1916	La Boisselle	Died from wounds
Schorpp, Alois	Infantryman	1	18-May-1916	?	Died from wounds
Kleinteich, Franz	Gefreiter	9	20-May-1916	La Boisselle	Died from wounds
Smolnik, Friedrich	Infantryman	7	23-May-1916	La Boisselle	
Wiotrowski, Franz	Unteroffizier	7	23-May-1916	La Boisselle	
Wolf, Josef	Infantryman	7	25-May-1916	La Boisselle	
Gsell, Stefan	Infantryman	6	26-May-1916	La Boisselle	
Moser, Hugo	Infantryman	7	27-May-1916	La Boisselle	Died from illness
Burkard, Mathias	Infantryman	2	28-May-1916	La Boisselle	
Friedmann, Wendelin	Unteroffizier	2	28-May-1916	La Boisselle	

RIR 110

NAME	RANK	CO.	DATE OF DEATH	LOCATION	NOTES
Niklas, Johann	Schützen	1 M.G. Co.	1-Jun-1916	La Boisselle	
Müller, Adolf	Infantryman	8	2-Jun-1916	La Boisselle	
Eckerle, Friedrich	Schützen	1 M.G. Co.	3-Jun-1916	La Boisselle	
Bogner, Albert	Infantryman	3	4-Jun-1916	La Boisselle	
Ruf, Josef	Gefreiter	4	4-Jun-1916	La Boisselle	
Schubert, Max	Infantryman	6	4-Jun-1916	La Boisselle	M.I.A.
Metzger, Ludwig	Vizefeldwebel	11	4-Jun-1916	La Boisselle	
Naber, Andreas	Unteroffizier	1 M.G. Co.	6-Jun-1916	La Boisselle	
Schwarz, Wilhelm	Schützen	1 M.G. Co.	6-Jun-1916	La Boisselle	
Herrenknecht, Wilhelm	Unteroffizier	1	10-Jun-1916	La Boisselle	
Münzer, Reinhardt	Infantryman	4	10-Jun-1916	La Boisselle	
Bickel, Karl	Vizefeldwebel	4	11-Jun-1916	La Boisselle	
Boy, Adolf	Sergeant	12	16-Jun-1916	La Boisselle	Died from wounds
Schmitt, Peter	Infantryman	11	17-Jun-1916	La Boisselle	Died from wounds
Schlegel, Julius	Unteroffizier	11	21-Jun-1916	La Boisselle	
Boening, Wilhelm	Leutnant der Landwehr	Rgt. Staff	21-Jun-1916	La Boisselle	
Fritz, Severin	Unteroffizier	1	25-Jun-1916	Martinpuich	
Kohmann, Emil	Infantryman	1	25-Jun-1916	La Boisselle	
Echin, Karl	Gefreiter	4	25-Jun-1916	Martinpuich	
Schulz, Johann	Infantryman	6	25-Jun-1916	La Boisselle	
Hucher, Xaver	Infantryman	9	25-Jun-1916	Martinpuich	
Noe, Adam	Infantryman	12	25-Jun-1916	La Boisselle	
Wicker, Josef	Infantryman	1	26-Jun-1916	Martinpuich	
Henn, Oskar	Gefreiter	9	26-Jun-1916	La Boisselle	
Klöpfer, Karl	Vizefeldwebel	9	26-Jun-1916	La Boisselle	
Mehrer, Wilhelm	Infantryman	9	26-Jun-1916	La Boisselle	
Ziems, Richard	Infantryman	9	26-Jun-1916	La Boisselle	
Frank II, Martin	Infantryman	11	26-Jun-1916	La Boisselle	
Haas, Philipp	Infantryman	11	26-Jun-1916	La Boisselle	
Haessig, Adolf	Infantryman	11	26-Jun-1916	La Boisselle	
Kohlmeier, Friedrich	Infantryman	11	26-Jun-1916	La Boisselle	
Noch, Leopold	Infantryman	11	26-Jun-1916	La Boisselle	
Dick, Anton	Schützen	1 M.G. Co.	26-Jun-1916	La Boisselle	
Gottselig, Hermann	Schützen	1 M.G. Co.	26-Jun-1916	La Boisselle	
Baumann, Adalbert	Infantryman	2	27-Jun-1916	La Boisselle	
Strohmaier, Alois	Infantryman	5	27-Jun-1916	La Boisselle	
Sübeck, Hermann	Infantryman	5	27-Jun-1916	La Boisselle	
König, Bernhard	Gefreiter	6	27-Jun-1916	La Boisselle	
Neumeier, Erhard	Infantryman	6	27-Jun-1916	La Boisselle	Died from wounds

RIR 110

NAME	RANK	CO.	DATE OF DEATH	LOCATION	NOTES
Pöhl II, Gustav	Infantryman	6	27-Jun-1916	La Boisselle	
Wlodarczyki, Martin	Infantryman	8	27-Jun-1916	La Boisselle	Died from wounds
Wild, Josef	Infantryman	9	27-Jun-1916	La Boisselle	
Fehrenbach, Otto	Schützen		27-Jun-1916	Fricourt	
Issler, Heinrich	Unteroffizier		27-Jun-1916	Fricourt	
Kammerer I, Gottlieb	Gefreiter		27-Jun-1916	Fricourt	
Klostermaier, Gustav	Schützen		27-Jun-1916	Fricourt	
Schneider I, Otto	Schützen		27-Jun-1916	Fricourt	
Neumann II, Hermann	Infantryman	1	28-Jun-1916	La Boisselle	
Simon, Georg	Vizefeldwebel	7	28-Jun-1916	La Boisselle	
Ratayczak, Martin	Infantryman	8	28-Jun-1916	La Boisselle	
Schmid, Johann	Infantryman	8	28-Jun-1916	La Boisselle	
Wölfle, Hermengild	Leutnant der Reserve	8	28-Jun-1916	La Boisselle	
Wölfle, Hermengild	Leutnant der Reserve	8	28-Jun-1916	La Boisselle	
Bartler, Johann	Infantryman	9	28-Jun-1916	La Boisselle	
Kammerer, Johann	Infantryman	9	28-Jun-1916	La Boisselle	
Häffner, Hermann	Schützen	1 M.G. Co.	28-Jun-1916	La Boisselle	
Vogt, Kamill	Schützen	1 M.G. Co.	28-Jun-1916	La Boisselle	Died from wounds
Albiez, Theodor	Infantryman	Bau	28-Jun-1916	La Boisselle	Died from wounds
Weimer, Ernst	Infantryman	8	29-Jun-1916	La Boisselle	
Sollich, Emil	Unteroffizier	10	29-Jun-1916	Ovillers	
Stang, Josef	Infantryman	10	29-Jun-1916	Ovillers	
Walzer, Gustav	Gefreiter	11	29-Jun-1916	La Boisselle	
Götz, August	Schützen	1 M.G. Co.	30-Jun-1916	La Boisselle	
Kohler, Josef	Schützen	1 M.G. Co.	30-Jun-1916	La Boisselle	

RIR 111

NAME	RANK	CO.	DATE OF DEATH	LOCATION	NOTES
Halder, Joachim	Gefreiter	5	28-Sep-1914	Fricourt	Killed 28 or 29-Sep-1914.
Hublow, Richard	Offizier Stellvertreter	6	28-Sep-1914	Fricourt	
Lutz, Karl	Unteroffizier	6	28-Sep-1914	Fricourt	
Screiber, Johann Georg	Reservist	6	28-Sep-1914	Fricourt	
Wick, Albert	Wehrmann	9	28-Sep-1914	Fricourt	
Armbruster, Isidor	Wehrmann	9	28-Sep-1914	Fricourt	
Banhofer, Konrad	Reservist	9	28-Sep-1914	Fricourt	

RIR 111

NAME	RANK	CO.	DATE OF DEATH	LOCATION	NOTES
Betz, Franz Josef	Gefreiter	9	28-Sep-1914	Mametz/ Fricourt	
Blickle, Markarius	Landsturmmann	9	28-Sep-1914	Fricourt	
Höfflin, Andreas Gustav	Reservist	9	28-Sep-1914	Fricourt	
Mans, Johann Baptiste	Wehrmann	9	28-Sep-1914	Fricourt	
Meurer, August	Reservist	9	28-Sep-1914	Fricourt	
Türk, Konrad	Wehrmann	9	28-Sep-1914	Flers	
Wannemacher, Damian	Reservist	11	28-Sep-1914	Fricourt	
Hausmann, Sigmund	Wehrmann	11	28-Sep-1914	Fricourt	
Schweigert, Friedrich	Wehrmann	1	29-Sep-1914	Fricourt	
Binder, Meinrad	Reservist	1	29-Sep-1914	Fricourt	
Fink, Josef	Reservist	1	29-Sep-1914	Fricourt	
Meder, Josef	Wehrmann	1	29-Sep-1914	Fricourt	
Meyer, Jakob	Reservist	1	29-Sep-1914	Fricourt	
Neupold, Anton	Wehrmann	3	29-Sep-1914	Fricourt	
Kinzler, Friedrich	Gefreiter	4	29-Sep-1914	Fricourt	
Auth, Karl	Wehrmann	4	29-Sep-1914	Fricourt	
Hässig, Oswald	Wehrmann	4	29-Sep-1914	Fricourt	
Krettler, Eugen	Gefreiter	4	29-Sep-1914	Fricourt	
Lösselt, Paul	Reservist	4	29-Sep-1914	Fricourt	
Schmieder, Augustin	Gefreiter	4	29-Sep-1914	Fricourt	
Sperle, Georg	Gefreiter	5	29-Sep-1914	Fricourt	
Beil, Fridolin	Wehrmann	5	29-Sep-1914	Fricourt	
Breinlinger, Peter	Wehrmann	5	29-Sep-1914	Fricourt	
Buchegger, Johann	Wehrmann	5	29-Sep-1914	Fricourt	
Göggel, Hermann	Unteroffizier	5	29-Sep-1914	Fricourt	
Gönner, Severin	Wehrmann	5	29-Sep-1914	Fricourt	
Höbel, Friedrich		5	29-Sep-1914	Fricourt	
Stehle, Friedrich	Gefreiter	5	29-Sep-1914	Fricourt	
Weber, Josef	Wehrmann	5	29-Sep-1914	Fricourt	
Weigold, Mathias	Reservist	6	29-Sep-1914	Fricourt	
Keller, Martin	Unteroffizier	6	29-Sep-1914	Fricourt	
Straub, Hermann	Wehrmann	6	29-Sep-1914	Fricourt	
Strobel, Wilhelm	Unteroffizier	6	29-Sep-1914	Fricourt	
Wurtenberger, Wilhelm Maria	Reservist	7	29-Sep-1914	Fricourt	
Berner, Karl	Wehrmann	7	29-Sep-1914	Fricourt	
Dreher, Xaver	Wehrmann	7	29-Sep-1914	Fricourt	
Manner, Wilhelm	Wehrmann	7	29-Sep-1914	Fricourt	
Neidhart, Josef	Wehrmann	7	29-Sep-1914	Fricourt	
Schwarzmayer, Franz Josef	Unteroffizier	7	29-Sep-1914	Fricourt	

RIR 111

NAME	RANK	CO.	DATE OF DEATH	LOCATION	NOTES
Stocker, Franz	Wehrmann	8	29-Sep-1914	Fricourt	
Höllinger, Karl	Wehrmann	8	29-Sep-1914	Fricourt	
Hutz, Josef	Wehrmann	9	29-Sep-1914	Fricourt	
Kaiser, Martin	?	9	29-Sep-1914	Mametz	
Lauber, Lukas	Vizefeldwebel	9	29-Sep-1914	Mametz	
Merk, Theodor	Reservist	9	29-Sep-1914	Mametz	
Möhrle, Adolf	Gefreiter	9	29-Sep-1914	Mametz	
Riester, Fridolin	Wehrmann	9	29-Sep-1914	Fricourt	
Schoy, Pius	Wehrmann	9	29-Sep-1914	Mametz	
Staiger, Karl	Gefreiter	9	29-Sep-1914	Mametz	
Störk, Heinrich	Wehrmann	9	29-Sep-1914	Mametz	
Strobel, Leopold	Wehrmann	9	29-Sep-1914	Fricourt	
Tritsch, Kamill	Wehrmann	10	29-Sep-1914	Mametz	
Böhmann, Hermann	Wehrmann	10	29-Sep-1914	Mametz	
Gäng, Johann	Wehrmann	10	29-Sep-1914	Mametz	
Rist, Karl	Wehrmann	10	29-Sep-1914	Mametz	
Ross, Friedrich	Wehrmann	10	29-Sep-1914	Mametz	
Storz, Leopold	Gefreiter	10	29-Sep-1914	Mametz	
Tritschler, August	Wehrmann	10	29-Sep-1914	Mametz	
Weiss, Franz	Unteroffizier	11	29-Sep-1914	Fricourt	
Christmann, Heinrich	Wehrmann	11	29-Sep-1914	Fricourt	
Sänger, Friedrich	Wehrmann	11	29-Sep-1914	Fricourt	
Sonntag, Karl	Reservist	11	29-Sep-1914	Mametz	
Stöckel, Jakob	Wehrmann	12	29-Sep-1914	Mametz	
Gassmer, Josef	Wehrmann		29-Sep-1914	Fricourt	W.I.A., died 5-Oct-1914.
Schröder, Karl	Leutnant der Reserve	4	30-Sep-1914	Bazentin	C.I.A., W.I.A., died 13-Jul-1916, Dartford, England.
Schwarz, August	Wehrmann	5	30-Sep-1914	Contalmaison	
Benz, Xaver	Wehrmann	6	30-Sep-1914	Contalmaison	
Heinzelmann, Martin	Reservist	6	30-Sep-1914	Contalmaison	
Simonklein, Hieronimous Leodeg.	Reservist	7	30-Sep-1914	Fricourt	
Schülli, Alfons	Wehrmann	8	30-Sep-1914	Contalmaison	
Rabe, Karl	Unteroffizier	9	30-Sep-1914	Mametz	
Klötzlen, Josef		9	30-Sep-1914	Bazentin	
Lohr, Bernhard	Reservist	11	30-Sep-1914	Fricourt	
Müller, Anton	Wehrmann	11	30-Sep-1914	Fricourt	
Schiller, Engelbert	Wehrmann	11	30-Sep-1914	Bazentin	
Steinhard, Oskar	Gefreiter	12	30-Sep-1914	Mametz	
Schlude, Balthasar	Wehrmann		30-Sep-1914	Fricourt	
Freyhold von, Max	Hauptmann	1	1-Oct-1914	Fricourt	
Spinner, Karl	Reservist	6	1-Oct-1914	Fricourt	
Armbruster, Josef	Reservist	6	1-Oct-1914	Fricourt	

RIR 111

NAME	RANK	CO.	DATE OF DEATH	LOCATION	NOTES
Betz, Michael	Gefreiter	7	1-Oct-1914	Flers	
Fritz, Balthasar	Wehrmann	8	1-Oct-1914	Contalmaison	
Schmid I, Josef	Wehrmann	9	1-Oct-1914	Mametz	
Kost, Josef	Wehrmann	9	1-Oct-1914	Mametz	
Maier, Ottmar	Reservist	10	1-Oct-1914	Fricourt/Mametz	
Dreher, Kuno	Wehrmann	10	1-Oct-1914	Fricourt	
Gebhard, Karl	?	10	1-Oct-1914	Mametz	
Grosshans, Franz Josef	Wehrmann	10	1-Oct-1914	Mametz	
Stärk, Emil	Wehrmann	10	1-Oct-1914	Mametz	
Walter, Theodor	Wehrmann	12	1-Oct-1914	Flers	
Morath, Johann	Wehrmann	12	1-Oct-1914	Combles	
Oschwald, Josef	Wehrmann	1	2-Oct-1914	Fricourt	
Knoblauch, Fidel	?	1	2-Oct-1914	Fricourt	
Schnatter, Otto	Reservist	3	2-Oct-1914	Mametz	
Gebhard, Eugen	Reservist	6	2-Oct-1914	Flers	
Saile, Gustav	Unteroffizier	8	2-Oct-1914	Contalmaison	
Schöb, Josef	Wehrmann	8	2-Oct-1914	Flers	
Schuler, Friedrich	Unteroffizier	11	2-Oct-1914	Flers	
Schiller, Johann	Wehrmann	12	2-Oct-1914	Flers	
Lohren, Jakob	Reservist	5	3-Oct-1914	Contalmaison	
Ebe, Julius	Gefreiter	7	3-Oct-1914	Cambrai	
Kempter, Johann	Unteroffizier	7	3-Oct-1914	Mametz	
Ritter, Christian	Wehrmann	8	3-Oct-1914	Contalmaison	
Mayer, Lorenz	Gefreiter	12	3-Oct-1914	Mametz	
Klüss, Paul	Gefreiter	1	4-Oct-1914	Fricourt	
Breinlinger, Gerhard	Wehrmann	1	4-Oct-1914	Fricourt	
Fuchs, Georg	Wehrmann	4	4-Oct-1914	Fricourt	
Huber, Robert	Unteroffizier	7	4-Oct-1914	Fricourt	
Schulz, Willi Robert Max	Gefreiter	8	4-Oct-1914	Contalmaison	
Kreisner, Julius	Wehrmann	11	4-Oct-1914	Peronne	
Hagg, Erich	Wehrmann	12	4-Oct-1914	Flers	
Kohler, Otto	Wehrmann		4-Oct-1914	Fricourt	
Bömke, Walter	Oberleutnant der Reserve	10	5-Oct-1914	Mametz	
Hummel, Fridolin	?	12	5-Oct-1914	Mametz	
Säbele, Gustav	Wehrmann	12	5-Oct-1914	Mametz	
Steigert, Vinzenz	Wehrmann	12	5-Oct-1914	Mametz	
Wolber, Gottlieb	Wehrmann	2	6-Oct-1914	Fricourt	
Zimmer, Albert	Wehrmann	9	6-Oct-1914	Flers	
Bader, Peter	Wehrmann	11	6-Oct-1914	Bapaume	
Dorn, Gottlieb	Wehrmann	11	6-Oct-1914	Flers	
von Ow, August	Landsturmmann	11	6-Oct-1914	Combles	
Wälde, Karl	Wehrmann	12	6-Oct-1914	Cambrai	

RIR 111

NAME	RANK	CO.	DATE OF DEATH	LOCATION	NOTES
Steingruber, Otto	Sergeant	3	7-Oct-1914	Fricourt	
Seufer, Emil	Reservist	5	7-Oct-1914	Fricourt	
Sax, Karl	Reservist	5	7-Oct-1914	Fricourt	
Schenk, Marcellus	Reservist	5	7-Oct-1914	Fricourt	
Wäldin, Adolf	Unteroffizier	10	7-Oct-1914	Fricourt	
Vogler, Johann	Wehrmann	1	8-Oct-1914	Fricourt	
Lankenecker, Ignaz	Reservist	2	8-Oct-1914	Fricourt	
Grüb, Friedrich	?	5	8-Oct-1914	Fricourt	
Koch, Wilhelm	Reservist	5	8-Oct-1914	Bécourt	
Trinler, Friedrich Johann	Wehrmann	8	8-Oct-1914	Bécourt	
Gans, Ernst Josef	Reservist	8	8-Oct-1914	Bécourt	
Isak, Eduard	Wehrmann	8	8-Oct-1914	Fricourt	W.I.A., died in French P.O.W. camp, details unknown.
Löhle, Bernhard	Wehrmann	8	8-Oct-1914	Bécourt	
Schneider, Adolf	Wehrmann	8	8-Oct-1914	Bécourt	
Weidele, Leopold	Gefreiter	12	8-Oct-1914	Fricourt	
Grill, Friedrich	Wehrmann	12	8-Oct-1914	Fricourt	
Ill, Theodor	Wehrmann	12	8-Oct-1914	Fricourt	
Steiger, Heinrich	Musketier		8-Oct-1914	Bécourt	
Haas, Gustav	?	12	10-Oct-1914	Fricourt	
Schulz, Josef	Wehrmann	1	11-Oct-1914	Fricourt	W.I.A., died in Field Hospital
Junghans, Karl	Wehrmann	6	11-Oct-1914	Cambrai	
Rössler, Isidor	Reservist	1	12-Oct-1914	Fricourt	
Bernhard, Karl	Sergeant	1	12-Oct-1914	Fricourt	
Dürrhammer, Emil	Offizier Stellvertreter	1	12-Oct-1914	Fricourt	
Klingstein, Friedrich	Wehrmann	1	12-Oct-1914	Fricourt	
Spitz, Adolf	Wehrmann	4	12-Oct-1914	Fricourt	
Reutemann, Wilhelm	Wehrmann	4	12-Oct-1914	Fricourt	
Seiler, Wilhelm	Reservist	2	13-Oct-1914	Fricourt	
Andreas, Ludwig	Gefreiter	2	13-Oct-1914	Fricourt	
Hauser, Emil	Reservist	2	13-Oct-1914	Fricourt	
Höge, Anton	Wehrmann	2	13-Oct-1914	Fricourt	
Mattes, Johann	Reservist	2	13-Oct-1914	Fricourt	
Moll, Otto	Wehrmann	2	13-Oct-1914	Fricourt	
Schmid, Richard	Reservist	3	13-Oct-1914	Mametz	
Gehring, Karl	Tambour	11	13-Oct-1914	Fricourt	
Sommereisen, Dominik	Reservist	10	14-Oct-1914	St. Quentin	
Liebenguth, Emil	Wehrmann	10	15-Oct-1914	Mametz	
Wollani, Adolf	Wehrmann	11	15-Oct-1914	Fricourt	
Frey, Gustav	Wehrmann	1	16-Oct-1914	Münster	Died in hospital.
Märklen, Wilhelm	Wehrmann	9	16-Oct-1914	Peronne	
Hellstern, Valentin	Wehrmann	11	16-Oct-1914	Aachen	

RIR 111

NAME	RANK	CO.	DATE OF DEATH	LOCATION	NOTES
Gayer, Albert	Wehrmann	11	16-Oct-1914	Bapaume	
Wagner, Lorenz	Reservist	6	17-Oct-1914	Villers-Brettoneux	
Sickinger, Johann	Wehrmann	1	20-Oct-1914	Bapaume	
Müller, Adolf	Wehrmann	10	22-Oct-1914	Villers-au-Flos	
Theiler, Emil	Wehrmann	5	24-Oct-1914	Mametz	
Altenburg, Max	Reservist	10	24-Oct-1914	Mametz	
Manz, Johann	Wehrmann	10	24-Oct-1914	Mametz	
Schimansky, Michael	Wehrmann	12	24-Oct-1914	Fricourt	
Schmidt, Hermann	Unteroffizier	2	25-Oct-1914	Mametz	
Stark, Rupert	Wehrmann	9	25-Oct-1914	Mametz	
Stumpf, Wilhelm	Reservist	11	25-Oct-1914	Fricourt	
Rauch, Anton	Wehrmann	3	26-Oct-1914	Fricourt	
Kaiser II, Alfred	Reservist	7	26-Oct-1914	Fricourt	
Frank, Martin	Wehrmann	6	27-Oct-1914	Montauban	
Zuckschwerdt, Hugo	Reservist	7	27-Oct-1914	Flers	
Huckle, Ruppert	Wehrmann	11	27-Oct-1914	Fricourt	
Butterstein, Eugen	Reservist	3	28-Oct-1914	Mametz	
Dapp, August	Reservist	3	28-Oct-1914	Flers	
Heine, Augustin	Reservist	3	28-Oct-1914	Cambrai	
Huber, Heinrich	Gefreiter	3	28-Oct-1914	Fricourt	
Rappold, Franz	Gefreiter	M.G.	28-Oct-1914	Mametz	
Irion, Gotthilf Alb.	Reservist	12	29-Oct-1914	Fricourt	
Kaiser, Viktor	?	3	30-Oct-1914	Mametz	
Breithaupt, Kilian	Wehrmann	3	30-Oct-1914	Mametz	
Gantert, Ferdinand	?	3	31-Oct-1914	Mametz	
Bader, August	Reservist	3	31-Oct-1914	Mametz	
Baumgartner, Fidel	Reservist	3	31-Oct-1914	Mametz	
Harr, Adam Sg.	Reservist	3	31-Oct-1914	Cambrai	
Kaiser I, Josef	?	3	31-Oct-1914	Fricourt	
Kammerer, August	Wehrmann	3	31-Oct-1914	Ovillers	
Keller, Jakob	Wehrmann	3	31-Oct-1914	Fricourt	
Meyer, Alois	Gefreiter Hornist	3	1-Nov-1914	Flers	
Keininger, Philip Christian	Reservist	9	2-Nov-1914	Mametz	
Schmid, Josef	Wehrmann	10	2-Nov-1914	Mametz	
Behringer, Oswald	Tambour	11	2-Nov-1914	Strassburg	
Zimmermann, Johann	Wehrmann	12	2-Nov-1914	Fricourt	
Zeller, Karl	Wehrmann	12	5-Nov-1914	Fricourt	
Bauknecht, Friedrich	Wehrmann	7	6-Nov-1914	Fricourt	
Haas, Adolf	Wehrmann	10	6-Nov-1914	Péronne	
Auer, Eugen	Wehrmann	10	10-Nov-1914	Flers	
Eggert, Eugen	Wehrmann	9	11-Nov-1914	Mametz	

RIR 111

NAME	RANK	CO.	DATE OF DEATH	LOCATION	NOTES
Weschenmoser, Friedrich	Reservist	2	12-Nov-1914	Mametz	
Wagner, Theobald	Wehrmann	3	12-Nov-1914	Fricourt	
Wegele, Jakob Ernst	Offizier Stellver-treter	4	12-Nov-1914	Montauban	
Luttenauer, Emil	Reservist	10	12-Nov-1914	Mametz	
Bernauer, Fiedel	Wehrmann	11	14-Nov-1914	Fricourt	
Vouthron, Emil	Reservist	11	16-Nov-1914	Flers	
Bernhard, Karl	Reservist	M.G.	16-Nov-1914	Mametz	
Keller, Johann	Sanitäts Unterof-fizier	9	17-Nov-1914	Mametz	
Spindler, Wilhelm Friedrich	Gefreiter	10	17-Nov-1914	Mametz	
Knebel, Robert	Ersatz Reservist	3	19-Nov-1914	Fricourt	
Morath, Adolf	Reservist	6	26-Nov-1914	Flers	
Streit, Remigius	Reservist	12	29-Nov-1914	Fricourt	
Kirner, Josef	Wehrmann	10	1-Dec-1914	Mametz	
Fendrich, Franz	Wehrmann	7	3-Dec-1914	Fricourt	
Güntert, Hermann	Ersatz Reservist	8	4-Dec-1914	Flers	
Schreiber, Fridolin	Wehrmann	11	4-Dec-1914	Fricourt	
Sauer, Franz	Reservist	6	7-Dec-1914	Mametz	
Allgaier, Hugo	Ersatz Reservist	11	7-Dec-1914	Mametz	
Strich, Xaver	Reservist	8	10-Dec-1914	Mametz	
Schmid, Alfred	Gefreiter	10	11-Dec-1914	St. Quentin	
Back, Max	Wehrmann	1	13-Dec-1914	Mametz	
Konz, Karl	Wehrmann	2	15-Dec-1914	Flers	
Schütze, Wilhelm Heinrich	Reservist	1	16-Dec-1914	Mametz	
Fantz, Hermann	Vizefeldwebel	3	17-Dec-1914	Fricourt	
Schäuble, Leo Josef	Reservist	5	17-Dec-1914	Mametz	
Joist, Mathias	Leutnant der Reserve	6	17-Dec-1914	Mametz	
Bischoff, Max	Wehrmann	6	17-Dec-1914	Mametz	
Häring, Josef	Reservist	6	17-Dec-1914	Mametz	
Krug, Josef	Wehrmann	6	17-Dec-1914	Mametz	
Madach, Robert	Wehrmann	6	17-Dec-1914	Mametz	
Rebstein, Albert	Gefreiter	6	17-Dec-1914	Mametz	
Reger, Otto	Reservist	6	17-Dec-1914	Mametz	
Strobel, August	Wehrmann	6	17-Dec-1914	Mametz	
Wild, Josef	Wehrmann	8	17-Dec-1914	Fricourt	
Dorn, Johann	Landsturmmann	8	17-Dec-1914	Mametz	
Jäkle, Friedrich	Unteroffizier	8	17-Dec-1914	Mametz	
Willibald, Franz	Wehrmann	8	17-Dec-1914	Mametz	
Wöhrle, Otto	Offizier Stellver-treter	2	18-Dec-1914	Mametz	
Diemunsch, Josef	Reservist	2	18-Dec-1914	Mametz	

RIR 111

NAME	RANK	CO.	DATE OF DEATH	LOCATION	NOTES
Montag, Franz	Füselier	5	18-Dec-1914	Mametz	
Graf, Emil	Wehrmann	5	18-Dec-1914	Mametz	
Heuberger, Friedrich	Wehrmann	5	18-Dec-1914	Mametz	
Obermann, Johann	Reservist	7	18-Dec-1914	Fricourt	
Jecker, Albert	Wehrmann	7	18-Dec-1914	Fricourt	
Karle, Franz	Wehrmann	7	18-Dec-1914	Fricourt	
Mack, Marcus	Wehrmann	7	18-Dec-1914	Fricourt	
Riede, Friedrich	Reservist	7	18-Dec-1914	Mametz	
Schäffer, Otto Wilhelm	Reservist	7	18-Dec-1914	Mametz	
Schöpf, Emil	Reservist	7	18-Dec-1914	Fricourt	
Zimmermann, Emil	Unteroffizier	8	18-Dec-1914	Mametz	
Graf, Konrad	Wehrmann	8	18-Dec-1914	Mametz	
Pontzen, Josef	Landsturmmann	10	18-Dec-1914	Mametz	
Giesser, Karl	Hauptmann	10	18-Dec-1914	Mametz	
Stotzka, Michael	Reservist	10	18-Dec-1914	Mametz	
Wick, Albert	Gefreiter	12	18-Dec-1914	Flers	
Kempf, Robert	Reservist	12	18-Dec-1914	Mametz	
Weber, Karl	Oberleutnant der Reserve	?	18-Dec-1914	Mametz	
Zingler von, Bodo	Hauptmann	6	19-Dec-1914	Mametz	
Schmid, Julian	Ersatz Reservist	8	19-Dec-1914	St. Quentin	
Seiz, Hermann	Vizefeldwebel	10	19-Dec-1914	Mametz	
Grimm, Josef	Unteroffizier	10	19-Dec-1914	Mametz	
Honold, Emil	Wehrmann	10	19-Dec-1914	Mametz	
Ley, Max	Wehrmann	10	19-Dec-1914	Mametz	
Nimrich, Emil	Wehrmann	10	19-Dec-1914	Mametz	
Stamm, Anton	Unteroffizier	10	19-Dec-1914	Mametz	
Stöckle, Julius	Wehrmann	7	20-Dec-1914	Flers	
Rieder, Johann	Wehrmann	11	20-Dec-1914	Montauban	
Böhni, Johann	Unteroffizier	11	20-Dec-1914	Montauban	
Burgath, Georg	Wehrmann	2	21-Dec-1914	Mametz	
Meier, Fabian	Wehrmann	2	21-Dec-1914	Mametz	
Reiser, Paul	Wehrmann	2	21-Dec-1914	Mametz	
Schmitz, Johann	Ldw. Herm. Reservist	5	21-Dec-1914	Mametz	
Hirt, Friedrich	Wehrmann	6	21-Dec-1914	Mametz	
Berenbold, Paul	Wehrmann	6	21-Dec-1914	Mametz	
Deutschle, Paul	Wehrmann	6	21-Dec-1914	Mametz	
Haug, Otto	Wehrmann	6	21-Dec-1914	Mametz	
Herzog, Karl	Wehrmann	6	21-Dec-1914	Mametz	
Kaplan, Friedrich	Wehrmann	6	21-Dec-1914	Mametz	
Käsler, Franz Georg	Reservist	6	21-Dec-1914	Mametz	
Muschania, Sebastian	Wehrmann	6	21-Dec-1914	Mametz	

RIR 111

NAME	RANK	CO.	DATE OF DEATH	LOCATION	NOTES
Specker, Karl	Wehrmann	7	21-Dec-1914	Mametz	
Dietner, Franz Xaver	Wehrmann	8	21-Dec-1914	Mametz	
Glöckler, Wilhelm	?	11	21-Dec-1914	Montauban	
Rauter, Paul	Unteroffizier	11	21-Dec-1914	Montauban	
Wörz, Johann	Wehrmann	12	21-Dec-1914	Mametz	
Amann, Johann	Wehrmann	12	21-Dec-1914	Mametz	
Hegle, Karl	Reservist	12	21-Dec-1914	Mametz	
Morgen, Richard	Wehrmann	12	21-Dec-1914	Mametz	
Siebenhaller, August	Reservist	1	22-Dec-1914	St. Quentin	
Oesterle, Martin	Wehrmann	5	22-Dec-1914	St. Quentin	
Kott, Erich	Vizefeldwebel	7	22-Dec-1914	Flers	
Häuptle, Eugen	Wehrmann	4	24-Dec-1914	Mametz	
Mattes, Christian	Wehrmann	5	27-Dec-1914	Mametz	
Handschuh, Josef	Wehrmann	7	27-Dec-1914	Flers	
Nesensohn, Johann	Ersatz Reservist	10	29-Dec-1914	Mametz	
Loos, Gustav	Reservist	10	30-Dec-1914	St. Quentin	
Stump, Johann	Wehrmann	5	31-Dec-1914	Mametz	
Hellstern, Bernhard	Reservist	6	31-Dec-1914	St. Quentin	
Zweifel, Karl	Gefreiter	5	3-Jan-1915	Mametz	
Meyer, Hermann	Wehrmann	12	3-Jan-1915	Strassburg	
Lübbemann, August Heinrich	Musketier	4	4-Jan-1915	Mametz	
Bautle, Franz	Reservist	4	4-Jan-1915	Mametz	
Reinold, Ernst	Kriegsfreiwilliger	6	4-Jan-1915	Flers	
Hummel, Jacob	Wehrmann	9	4-Jan-1915	Mametz	
Mayer, Edwin	Wehrmann	8	5-Jan-1915	Mametz	
Matt, Johann Adolf	Reservist	9	5-Jan-1915	Ovillers/La Boisselle	
Störk, Josef	Wehrmann	12	7-Jan-1915	Mametz	
Osswald, Josef	Wehrmann	2	8-Jan-1915	Mametz	
Lehmann, Leopold	Wehrmann	11	10-Jan-1915	Fricourt	
Dillberger, Johann	Musketier	6	12-Jan-1915	Aachen	
Mast, Rudolf	Ersatz Reservist	5	13-Jan-1915	Mametz	
Weber, August	Musketier	11	14-Jan-1915	St. Quentin	
Tröndle, Leo	Unteroffizier	12	14-Jan-1915	Flers	
Kalble, Josef	Gefreiter	M.G.	16-Jan-1915	Flers	
Wessinger, Wilhelm	Musketier	2	19-Jan-1915	Bapaume	Died in field hospital.
Peter, Rudolf	Wehrmann	3	19-Jan-1915	Fricourt	
Probst, Otto	Reservist	12	29-Jan-1915	?	Died in Field Hospital 10.
Häseke, Adolf	Reservist	12	30-Jan-1915	Flers	
Welde, Arman	Kriegsfreiwilliger	6	31-Jan-1915	Fricourt	
Morath, Gottlieb	Ersatz Reservist	12	5-Feb-1915	Fricourt	
Willibald, Eugen	Vizefeldwebel	1	6-Feb-1915	Offenburg	Died of illness.
Hüber, Andreas	Reservist	12	7-Feb-1915	Fricourt	

RIR 111

NAME	RANK	CO.	DATE OF DEATH	LOCATION	NOTES
Kuchler, Karl	Ersatz Reservist	9	8-Feb-1915	Fricourt	
Schuhmacher, Friedrich	Reservist	12	8-Feb-1915	Flers	
Müller, Emil	Kriegsfreiwilliger	12	8-Feb-1915	Fricourt	
Wolf, Josef	Wehrmann	12	9-Feb-1915	Fricourt	
Münchenbach, Benedikt	Wehrmann	12	9-Feb-1915	Flers	
Ritzi, Jonas	Gefreiter	1	15-Feb-1915	Contalmaison	
Schwab, Otto	Reservist	3	16-Feb-1915	Fricourt	
Schreiber, Maximilian	Gefreiter	11	16-Feb-1915	St. Quentin	
Golly, Leo	Wehrmann	1	17-Feb-1915	?	Died in Field Hospital.
Dreher, Albert	Wehrmann	M.G.	17-Feb-1915	Flers	
Simmendinger, Thomas	Ersatz Reservist	12	18-Feb-1915	Fricourt	
Vogt, Oskar	Kriegsfreiwilliger	5	18-Feb-1915	Fricourt	
Hangarter, Emil	?	3	20-Feb-1915	Mametz	
Beil, Jakob	Wehrmann	5	20-Feb-1915	Fricourt	
Kaupp, Friedrich	Reservist	8	21-Feb-1915	Fricourt	
Weinhart, Gottlieb	Wehrmann	8	21-Feb-1915	Fricourt	
Zimmermann, Josef	Wehrmann	5	23-Feb-1915	Flers	
Ammersin, Xaver	Reservist	8	25-Feb-1915	Fricourt	
Straub, Philipp Gottlieb	Wehrmann	7	27-Feb-1915	Fricourt	
Seyfried, Adolf	Ersatz Reservist	9	27-Feb-1915	Ovillers/La Boisselle	
Gamel, Wilhelm	?	6	7-Mar-1915	Fricourt	
Hupfer, Hilarius	Reservist	10	9-Mar-1915	Contalmaison	
Möhrle, Emil	Wehrmann	3	13-Mar-1915	Fricourt	
Morath, Otto	Reservist	4	21-Mar-1915	Villers au Flos	
Dees, Hugo	1 Year Kriegsfreiwilliger	3	25-Mar-1915	Mametz	
Helken, Alois	Reservist	7	29-Mar-1915	Flers	
Elsässer, Johann Baptiste	Ersatz Reservist	2	30-Mar-1915	Fricourt	
Hoher, Josef	Ersatz Reservist	4	30-Mar-1915	Fricourt	
Pfister, Josef	Ersatz Reservist	6	30-Mar-1915	Fricourt	
Pickenhagen, Karl August W.	Reservist	9	31-Mar-1915	Contalmaison	
Elser, Johann Georg	Reservist	9	31-Mar-1915	Fricourt	
Jehl, Michael	Reservist	M.G.	3-Apr-1915	Fricourt	
Imhof, Georg	Musketier	M.G.	6-Apr-1915	Manancourt	
Blödt, Anton	Schütze	12	10-Apr-1915	Fricourt	
Hausmann, Johann	Ersatz Reservist	10	15-Apr-1915	Fricourt	
Schilling, Adolf	Ersatz Reservist	1	23-Apr-1915	La Boisselle	
Ritter, Hermann	Ersatz Reservist	8	24-Apr-1915	Fricourt	

RIR 111

NAME	RANK	CO.	DATE OF DEATH	LOCATION	NOTES
Schwendemann, Josef	Ersatz Reservist	6	28-Apr-1915	Fricourt	
Häsele, Willibald	Unteroffizier	9	1-May-1915	Flers	
Kesel, Bernhard	Ersatz Reservist	4	2-May-1915	Ovillers	
Reinhard, Gregor	Ersatz Reservist	5	2-May-1915	Fricourt	
Späth, Michael	Ersatz Reservist	10	3-May-1915	La Boisselle	
Kempter, August	Ersatz Reservist	8	4-May-1915	Flers	
Messner, Emil	Kriegsfreiwilliger	8	4-May-1915	Fricourt	
Oster, Wilhelm	Reservist	8	6-May-1915	Fricourt	
Braun, Peter	Ersatz Reservist	8	6-May-1915	Fricourt	
Schilling, Friedrich	Wehrmann	11	8-May-1915	Serre	
Weiss, Augustin	Gefreiter	11	9-May-1915	Fricourt	
Reichert, Georg	Kriegsfreiwilliger	6	10-May-1915	Fricourt	
Hahn, August	Ersatz Reservist	1	13-May-1915	Flers	
Hildenbrand, Franz Karl	Ersatz Reservist	5	15-May-1915	Fricourt	
Amann, Eduard	Wehrmann	3	24-May-1915	Fricourt	
Willoth, Franz Xaver	Hornist	5	1-Jun-1915	Flers	
Halder, Anton	Unteroffizier	4	2-Jun-1915	Flers	
Mall, Albert	Ersatz Reservist	5	6-Jun-1915	Mametz	
Wiest, Philipp	Reservist	12	7-Jun-1915	Serre	
Baumann, Paul	Tambour	12	7-Jun-1915	Flers	
Einhart, Richard	Wehrmann	9	8-Jun-1915	Serre	
Lorenz, Josef	Kriegsfreiwilliger	9	8-Jun-1915	Serre	
Schmid, Martin	Kriegsfreiwilliger	9	9-Jun-1915	Serre	
Huggle, Rudolf	Gefreiter	10	9-Jun-1915	Serre	
Balzer, August	Ersatz Reservist	10	9-Jun-1915	Serre	
Ehret, Karl	Wehrmann	10	9-Jun-1915	Serre	
Fellhauer, Hermann	Ersatz Reservist	10	9-Jun-1915	Serre	
Raufer, Gustav	Unteroffizier	10	9-Jun-1915	Serre	
Wagner, Josef Anton	Unteroffizier		9-Jun-1915	Serre	
Kebe, Rudolf	Leutnant der Landwehr II	6	10-Jun-1915	Ovillers/La Boisselle	
Böhler, Jacob	Ersatz Reservist	9	10-Jun-1915	Serre	
Link, Christian	Wehrmann	10	10-Jun-1915	Serre	
Dünkel, August	Ersatz Reservist	10	10-Jun-1915	Serre	
Häusler, Wilhelm August	Reservist	10	10-Jun-1915	Serre	
Kessler, Emil	Reservist	11	10-Jun-1915	Serre	
Danzeisen, Karl	Musketier	11	10-Jun-1915	Serre	
Ganter, Adolf Karl	Musketier	11	10-Jun-1915	Serre	
Gassert, Karl Friedrich	Wehrmann	12	10-Jun-1915	Serre	
Kessler, Ernst	Vizefeldwebel	12	10-Jun-1915	Serre	
Seufert, Oskar Karl	Ersatz Reservist	11	12-Jun-1915	Aachen	Reserve Hospital

RIR 111

NAME	RANK	CO.	DATE OF DEATH	LOCATION	NOTES
Beck, Johann Adam	Wehrmann	11	12-Jun-1915	Serre	
Eger, Josef	Unteroffizier	11	12-Jun-1915	Serre	
Schlander, Hermann	Gefreiter	12	12-Jun-1915	Serre	
Gehri, Hermann	Wehrmann	12	12-Jun-1915	Serre	
Vetter, Eugen	Unteroffizier	6	13-Jun-1915	Serre	
Osswald, Friedrich	Wehrmann	9	13-Jun-1915	Serre	Battalion drummer.
Herdecker, Anton	Unteroffizier	9	13-Jun-1915	Serre	
Müller, Josef	Reservist	10	13-Jun-1915	Serre	
Hertrich, Theodor	Ersatz Reservist	11	13-Jun-1915	Serre	
Heinrich, Karl	Kriegsfreiwilliger	11	13-Jun-1915	Serre	
Held, Burkart	Musketier	11	13-Jun-1915	Serre	
Person, Eugen	Musketier	11	13-Jun-1915	Serre	
Schäffler, Wilhelm	Wehrmann	11	13-Jun-1915	Serre	
Sillman, Georg Hermann	Musketier	11	13-Jun-1915	Serre	
Spitznagel, karl	Reservist	11	13-Jun-1915	Serre	
Wunderle, Joahnn	Reservist	12	13-Jun-1915	Serre	
Mongel, Julis	Reservist	12	13-Jun-1915	Serre	
Stützle, Karl	Wehrmann	9	14-Jun-1915	Bapaume	
Stäbler, Johann	Reservist	11	16-Jun-1915	Serre	
Riedesser, Franz Josef	Wehrmann	12	16-Jun-1915	Ottenstein	
Waidele, Anton	Wehrmann	9	20-Jun-1915	Mametz	
Höfler, Fritz	Ersatz Reservist	7	26-Jun-1915	Ovillers	
Gengenbach, Ernst August	Ersatz Reservist	4	30-Jun-1915	Bapaume	
Merz, Joseph	Gefreiter	11	10-Jul-1915	Flers	
Bregenzer, Johann	?	12	12-Jul-1915	Ovillers/La Boisselle	
Buck, Karl	Wehrmann	11	16-Jul-1915	Ovillers/La Boisselle	
Bähr, Jakob	Reservist	8	18-Jul-1915	?	Died in French P.O.W. camp.
Bensinger, Rudolf	Wehrmann	9	18-Jul-1915	Ovillers/La Boisselle	
Hähnert, Karl	Wehrmann	9	18-Jul-1915	Ovillers/La Boisselle	
Klingenstein, Karl	Unteroffizier	11	18-Jul-1915	Ovillers/La Boisselle	
Briekmayer, Karl	Wehrmann	11	27-Jul-1915	Ovillers/La Boisselle	
Roth, Hugo	Wehrmann	10	29-Jul-1915	Serre	
Forster, Friedrich	Wehrmann	9	1-Aug-1915	Ovillers/La Boisselle	
Wittmann, Anton	Musketier	12	1-Aug-1915	Bayreuth	
Berger, Karl Wilhelm	Ersatz Reservist	9	11-Aug-1915	Ovillers/La Boisselle	

RIR 111

NAME	RANK	CO.	DATE OF DEATH	LOCATION	NOTES
Krampf, Wilhelm	Musketier	8	14-Aug-1915	Ovillers	
Stoll, Jakob	Unteroffizier	8	19-Aug-1915	La Boisselle	
Stumböck, Xaver	Musketier	2	28-Aug-1915	Villers au Flos	
Gentner, Christian Hermann	Wehrmann	4	30-Aug-1915	Ovillers	
Bernhard, Michael	Wehrmann	8	2-Sep-1915	Mons	
Schröder, Karl	Offizier Stellvertreter	9	5-Sep-1915	Ovillers/La Boisselle	
Freis, Wilhelm	Musketier	6	10-Sep-1915	Ovillers	
Geiger, Emil	Ersatz Reservist	7	10-Sep-1915	Ovillers	
Gluns, Friedrich	Gefreiter	2	22-Sep-1915	Flers	
Dörr, Karl Gottfried	Ersatz Reservist	5	22-Sep-1915	Ovillers/La Boisselle	
Stadel, Friedrich	Wehrmann	3	25-Sep-1915	Fricourt	
Schroff, Anton Josef	Kriegsfreiwilliger	8	25-Sep-1915	Mametz	
Huber, Karl	Wehrmann	2	29-Sep-1915	Ovillers	
Spitz, Franciscus	Reservist	5	29-Sep-1915	Flers	
Maier, Josef	Wehrmann	6	4-Oct-1915	Belle-Ile	
Schnibbe, Barthold Martin	Offizier Stellvertreter	6	5-Oct-1915	Mametz	
Egle, Eugen	Musketier		7-Oct-1915	Mametz	Killed on Hill 110.
Fischer, Otto	Leutnant	1	15-Oct-1915	Bapaume	
Amend, Heinrich	Kriegsfreiwilliger	M.G.	19-Oct-1915	Flers	
Runswinkel, Gerhard	Gefreiter	7	22-Oct-1915	Mametz	
Zintgraf, Bernhard	Landsturmmann	6	23-Oct-1915	Mametz	
Bayer, Franz	Ersatz Reservist	7	23-Oct-1915	Mametz	
Schilling I, Josef	Landsturmmann	4	8-Nov-1915	Cambrai	
Sauret, Heinrich Josef	Musketier	M.G.	9-Nov-1915	Flers	
Gotthilf, Adolf	Grenadier		15-Nov-1915	Ovillers/La Boisselle	
Kah, Bernhard	Leutnant der Reserve	11	21-Nov-1915	Ovillers/La Boisselle	
Wagner, Otto Wilhelm	Ersatz Reservist	9	23-Nov-1915	Ovillers/La Boisselle	
Munk, Bernhard Max	Landsturmmann	8	28-Nov-1915	Ovillers	
Behne, Wilhelm	Unteroffizier	M.G.	28-Nov-1915	Fricourt	
Schur, Hugo Reinhard	Unteroffizier	12	29-Nov-1915	Ovillers/La Boisselle	
Bachmann, Josef	Reservist	6	30-Nov-1915	Ovillers	
Fischer, Franz	Musketier	11	3-Dec-1915	Flers	
Restle, Ferdinand	Ersatz Reservist	6	18-Dec-1915	Mametz	
Krautter, Christian Friedrich	Reservist	11	9-Jan-1916	Flers	
Pfaff, Franz Josef	Musketier	12	10-Jan-1916	Flers	

RIR 111

NAME	RANK	CO.	DATE OF DEATH	LOCATION	NOTES
Wehrle, Karl Friedrich	Ersatz Reservist	4	17-Jan-1916	Le Sars	
Buhler, Josef	Gefreiter	4	17-Jan-1916	Le Sars	
Fröhlich, Oskar	Musketier	4	17-Jan-1916	Le Sars	
Strobel, Otto	Kriegsfreiwilliger	4	17-Jan-1916	Le Sars	
Würges, Philip	Musketier	8	19-Jan-1916	Ovillers	
Löffler, Augustin	Gefreiter	9	26-Jan-1916	Ovillers-La Boisselle	
Fechter, Weinrad	Wehrmann	M.G.	28-Jan-1916	Ovillers/La Boisselle	
Hertner, Hermann	Musketier	10	30-Jan-1916	Ovillers/La Boisselle	
Deusser, Ottmar	Vizefeldwebel	7	1-Feb-1916	Ovillers	
Lang, Friedrich	Landsturmmann	M.G.	10-Feb-1916	St. Quentin	
Salitz, Georg	Musketier	M.G.	15-Mar-1916	Fricourt	
Gäng, Franz Xaver	Musketier	2	21-Mar-1916	Fricourt	
Scwemmburger, Gustav	Reservist	3	23-Mar-1916	Fricourt	
Stumpf, Bernhard	Ersatz Reservist	4	23-Mar-1916	Fricourt	
Habicht, Gustav Conrad	Ersatz Reservist	1	26-Mar-1916	Fricourt	Died from wounds.
Beckert, Oskar	Landsturmmann	1	28-Mar-1916	Fricourt	
Kunle, Josef Anton	Ersatz Reservist	12	4-Apr-1916	Fricourt	
Mauch, Ferdinand	Wehrmann	2	6-Apr-1916	Fricourt	
Friedrich, Andreas Johann	Ersatz Reservist	2	6-Apr-1916	Fricourt	
Geoetz II, Franz Josef	Musketier	7	8-Apr-1916	Fricourt	
Ockle, Otto	Gefreiter	1	9-Apr-1916	Fricourt	Died from wounds.
Kempf, Georg	Landsturmmann	4	12-Apr-1916	Fricourt	Died from wounds by Reserve Medical Company 14.
Zimmermaann, August	Musketier	M.G.	12-Apr-1916	Fricourt	
Krauth,Martin	Gefreiter	8	22-Apr-1916	Fricourt	
Weiland, Alfred	Landsturmmann	2	26-Apr-1916	Fricourt	
Schneider, Johann	Reservist	2	27-Apr-1916	Fricourt	
Decker, Karl	Gefreiter	2	27-Apr-1916	Fricourt	
Hohenadel, Franz Fritz	Musketier	6	4-May-1916	Fricourt	
Müller, Paul	Unteroffizier	M.G.	8-May-1916	Fricourt	
Benedum, Karl	Schütze	4	10-May-1916	St. Quentin	
Fuchs, Constantin	Landsturmmann	12	13-May-1916	Fricourt	
Urbanik, Paul Hermann	Ersatz Reservist	12	14-May-1916	Fricourt	
Huck, August	Ersatz Reservist	2	15-May-1916	Fricourt	
Neidhart, Fritz	Unteroffizier	9	15-May-1916	Fricourt	
Berger, Hermann	Unteroffizier	9	15-May-1916	Fricourt	

RIR 111

NAME	RANK	CO.	DATE OF DEATH	LOCATION	NOTES
Neder, Ernst Willi	Musketier	9	15-May-1916	Fricourt	
Schneider, Andreas	Landsturmmann	M.G.	16-May-1916	Fricourt	
Knab, Christian	Kriegsfreiwilliger	4	18-May-1916	Fricourt	Died in 2nd Field Hospital, 52nd Infantry Division.
Haas, Augustin	Wehrmann	5	18-May-1916	Fricourt	
Häsele, Christian	Ersatz Reservist	3	23-May-1916	Fricourt	C.I.A., W.I.A., died 22-Jul-1916 in Dartford War Hospital
Sulzmann, Otoo	Gefreiter	4	23-May-1916	Fricourt	
Schmidt, Theodor	Unteroffizier	4	23-May-1916	Fricourt	
Wacker, Josef	Ersatz Reservist	12	24-May-1916	Fricourt	
Sütterlin, Hermann	Gefreiter	M.G.	25-May-1916	Flers	
Gries, Johann	Musketier	M.G.	25-May-1916	Fricourt	
Schmidt, Ernst	Schütze	8	26-May-1916	Dortmund	Died in Reserve Hospital 3, Brüderkrankenhaus, Dortmund
Haug, Josef	Wehrmann	10	26-May-1916	Fricourt	
Fritschi, Karl	Gefreiter	M.G.	30-May-1916	Fricourt	
Götzelmann, Wilhelm	Landsturmmann	9	31-May-1916	Fricourt	
Volk, Franz	Ersatz Reservist	6	3-Jun-1916	Fricourt	
Walter, Stefan	Ersatz Reservist	10	5-Jun-1916	Fricourt	
Scwarz, Paul	Landsturmmann	M.G.	5-Jun-1916	Fricourt	
Herget, Johann	Gefreiter	6	6-Jun-1916	Fricourt	
Lenz, Bernhard	Ersatz Reservist	5	9-Jun-1916	Fricourt	
Bühler, Johann	Landsturmmann	5	14-Jun-1916	Flers	
Stegmaier, Karl	Ersatz Reservist	10	14-Jun-1916	Fricourt	
Kupferschmidt, Johann Anton	Ersatz Reservist	6	16-Jun-1916	Fricourt	
Dold, Karl	Landsturmmann	5	17-Jun-1916	Fricourt	
Düsch, Edwin	Gefreiter	5	17-Jun-1916	Fricourt	
Ehescheid, Franz Karl Friedrich	Ersatz Reservist	4	19-Jun-1916	Fricourt	
Seger, Julius	Wehrmann	12	22-Jun-1916	Fricourt	
Waldkirch, Leopold	Landsturmmann	1	24-Jun-1916	Fricourt	
Binder, Mathias	Gefreiter	4	24-Jun-1916	Fricourt	
Gretzmeier, Josef	Musketier	4	24-Jun-1916	Fricourt	
Haaser, Albert	Landsturmmann	3	25-Jun-1916	Mametz	
Huber, Josef	Musketier	3	25-Jun-1916	Bapaume	
Kaiser I, Josef	Wehrmann	5	25-Jun-1916	Fricourt	
Halder, Joachim	Gefreiter	12	25-Jun-1916	Fricourt	
Hurst, Franz Xaver	Ersatz Reservist	M.G.	25-Jun-1916	Fricourt	
Hecker, Hans	Vizefeldwebel	4	26-Jun-1916	Fricourt	
Schink, Emil Arno	Landsturmmann	4	26-Jun-1916	Fricourt	
Schitterer, Franz	Landsturmmann	6	26-Jun-1916	Fricourt	
Gockenbach, August	Gefreiter	10	26-Jun-1916	Fricourt	

RIR 111

NAME	RANK	CO.	DATE OF DEATH	LOCATION	NOTES
Hochsticher, Wilhelm	Landsturmmann	11	26-Jun-1916	Fricourt	
Streit, Josef	Ersatz Reservist	12	26-Jun-1916	Fricourt	
Hebling, Peter	Ersatz Reservist	5	27-Jun-1916	Fricourt	
Kirchgässner, Josef	Gefreiter	7	27-Jun-1916	Fricourt	
Thoma, Fridolin	Landsturmmann	M.G.	27-Jun-1916	Fricourt	
Schroff, Gottfried	Reservist	3	28-Jun-1916	Flers	
Kaiser I, Josef	Landsturmmann	4	28-Jun-1916	Fricourt	
Basler, Stefan	Landsturmmann		28-Jun-1916	Fricourt	Killed when shell penetrated battalion dug-out
Jansen, Karl	Leutnant der Landwehr II	4	29-Jun-1916	Fricourt	
Kuhn, Xaver	Musketier	5	29-Jun-1916	Fricourt	
Böhler, Gebhard	Ersatz Reservist	7	29-Jun-1916	Fricourt	
Geiger, Adolf	Ersatz Reservist	10	29-Jun-1916	Mametz/Carnoy	
Wiest, Josef	Vizefeldwebel	4	30-Jun-1916	Bapaume	Died in 2nd Field Hospital, 52nd Infantry Division
Melcher, Franz	Musketier	8	30-Jun-1916	Fricourt	
Martin, Ernst	Unteroffizier	8	30-Jun-1916	Bapaume	Died in 2nd Field Hospital, 52nd Infantry Division
Martin, Ernst	Unteroffizier der Landwehr	12	30-Jun-1916	Fricourt	
Zaunsi, Fitmo	Musketier	12	30-Jun-16	Fricourt	

Mass grave, RIR 119, September 1914 (Author's collection)

Lone grave, RIR 119 (*Kriegstagbuch aus Schwaben*)

RIR 119

NAME	RANK	CO.	DATE OF DEATH	LOCATION	NOTES
Müller, Andreas	Gefreiter der Reserve	1	26-Sep-1914	Pozières	
Maier, Christian	Landwehrmann	5	26-Sep-1914	Beugny	
Münz, Matthäus	Landwehrmann	5	26-Sep-1914	Beugny	
Schmid, Alfons	Landwehrmann	5	26-Sep-1914	Beugny	
Schneider, Wilhelm	Gefreiter der Reserve	5	26-Sep-1914	Beugny	
Eckert, Hermann	Landwehrmann	6	26-Sep-1914	Beugny	
Frank, Christian	Landwehrmann	6	26-Sep-1914	Beugny	
Mutz, Wilhelm	Landwehrmann	6	26-Sep-1914	Beugny	
Schwenk, Christian	Landwehrmann	6	26-Sep-1914	Beugny	
Uhl, Isidor	Reservist	6	26-Sep-1914	Beugny	
Wielath, Josef	Landwehrmann	6	26-Sep-1914	Beugny	
Gross, Johannes	Landwehrmann	7	26-Sep-1914	Beugny	
Kunz, Joseph	Landwehrmann	7	26-Sep-1914	Beugny	
Wuhrer, Johann	Reservist	7	26-Sep-1914	Beugny	W.I.A., died 28-Sep-1914, Military hospital, 14 R.C., Cambrai.
Fackler, Friedrich	Landwehrmann	8	26-Sep-1914	Beugny	W.I.A., died 27-Sep-1914 in Military Hospital, Cambrai.
Holzwarth, Gotthilf	Landwehrmann	8	26-Sep-1914	Beugny	W.I.A., died 28-Sep-1914, Military Hospital Abteilung 1, Cambrai.

RIR 119

NAME	RANK	CO.	DATE OF DEATH	LOCATION	NOTES
Huber, Robert	Landwehrmann	8	26-Sep-1914	Beugny	W.I.A., died 16-Nov-1914, Reserve Hospital 1, Stuttgart
Keinath, Gottlieb	Gefreiter der Landwehr	8	26-Sep-1914	Beugny	
Willmann, Josef	Reservist	8	26-Sep-1914	Beugny	
Messerle, Gottlieb	Gefreiter der Reserve	1 M.G.	26-Sep-1914	Beugny	
Kohler, Friedrich	Reservist	2	27-Sep-1914	Pozières	W.I.A., died 30-Oct-1914, Reserve Field Hospital 1, Bapaume.
Reiniger, Gottlieb	Reservist	2	27-Sep-1914	Ovillers-La Boisselle	W.I.A., died 30-Sep-1914, Reserve Field Hospital 1, Bapaume.
Gräther, Heinrich	Landwehrmann	3	27-Sep-1914	Pozières	
Ernst, Hermann	Reservist	10	27-Sep-1914	Pozières	W.I.A., died 28-Sep-1914, Military Hospital, St. Quentin.
Bulmer, Friedrich	Vizefeldwebel der Reserve, Offiz. Asp.	12	27-Sep-1914	Morchies	
Ohngemach, Christian	Reservist	1	28-Sep-1914	Pozières	W.I.A., died 13-Oct1914, Reserve Hospital 1, Mariah. Aachen.
Fischer, Friedrich	Active Unterof-fizier	4	28-Sep-1914	Ovillers-La Boisselle	
Roth, Johann Georg	Landwehrmann	4	28-Sep-1914	Ovillers-La Boisselle	
Bitzer, Hermann	Reservist	6	28-Sep-1914	Ovillers-La Boisselle	
Mack, Wilhelm	Landwehrmann	6	28-Sep-1914	Ovillers-La Boisselle	
Bulling, Matthias	Landwehrmann	7	28-Sep-1914	Ovillers-La Boisselle	
Handmann, Gustav	Landwehrmann	7	28-Sep-1914	Ovillers-La Boisselle	
Kern, Otto	Landwehrmann	7	28-Sep-1914	Ovillers-La Boisselle	
Mey, Rudolf	Landwehrmann	7	28-Sep-1914	Ovillers-La Boisselle	
Alber II, Karl	Gefreiter	8	28-Sep-1914	Ovillers-La Boisselle	
Göhring, Jakob	Reservist	8	28-Sep-1914	Ovillers-La Boisselle	
Fuchs, Karl	Reservist	11	28-Sep-1914	Pozières	
Lauer, Gottlob	Reservist	11	28-Sep-1914	Pozières	
Neu, Reinhold	Reservist	11	28-Sep-1914	Pozières	W.I.A., died 30-Sep-1914, Reserve Field Hospital 1, Bapaume.
Rebmann, Ludwig	Landwehrmann	11	28-Sep-1914	Pozières	W.I.A., died 1-Oct-1914, Reserve Field Hospital 1, Bapaume.

RIR 119 NAME	RANK	CO.	DATE OF DEATH	LOCATION	NOTES
Wörner, Jakob	Reservist	11	28-Sep-1914	Pozières	
Bühler, Jakob	Landwehrmann	1	29-Sep-1914	Ovillers-La Boisselle	
Fischer, Walter	Leutnant der Reserve	1	29-Sep-1914	Ovillers-La Boisselle	W.I.A., died 30-Sep-1914, Reserve Field Hospital 1, Bapaume.
Kugler, Karl	Reservist	1	29-Sep-1914	Pozières	
Philippin, Wilhelm	Gefreiter der Reserve	1	29-Sep-1914	Ovillers-La Boisselle	
Weber, Karl	Landwehrmann	1	29-Sep-1914	Ovillers-La Boisselle	W.I.A., died 9-Oct-1914, Reserve Hospital Perleberg.
Bahnmüller, Gottlob	Reservist	2	29-Sep-1914	Ovillers-La Boisselle	
Bürkle, Martin	Reservist	2	29-Sep-1914	Ovillers-La Boisselle	
Calmbach, Christian	Reservist	2	29-Sep-1914	Ovillers-La Boisselle	
Finkbeiner, Gotthilf	Reservist	2	29-Sep-1914	Ovillers-La Boisselle	
Kirchherr, Karl	Reservist	2	29-Sep-1914	Ovillers-La Boisselle	W.I.A., died 1-Oct-1914, Reserve Field Hospital 1, Bapaume.
Lebherz, Karl	Unteroffizier der Reserve	2	29-Sep-1914	Ovillers-La Boisselle	
Marquart, Karl	Reservist	2	29-Sep-1914	Ovillers-La Boisselle	
Mössner, Ernst	Reservist	2	29-Sep-1914	Ovillers-La Boisselle	
Müller, Albert	Reservist	2	29-Sep-1914	Ovillers-La Boisselle	
Notter, Wilhelm	Reservist	2	29-Sep-1914	Ovillers-La Boisselle	
Reisser, Georg	Reservist	2	29-Sep-1914	Ovillers-La Boisselle	
Schnürle, Adam	Reservist	2	29-Sep-1914	Ovillers-La Boisselle	
Schnürle, Georg	Reservist	2	29-Sep-1914	Ovillers-La Boisselle	
Schrafft, Gustav	Reservist	2	29-Sep-1914	Ovillers-La Boisselle	
Stoll I, Friedrich	Reservist	2	29-Sep-1914	Ovillers-La Boisselle	
Möhrmann, Friedrich	Reservist	4	29-Sep-1914	Ovillers-La Boisselle	W.I.A., died 8-Oct-1914, Reserve Hospital Köln-Niehl.
Dold, Johannes	Landwehrmann	5	29-Sep-1914	Ovillers-La Boisselle	W.I.A., died 14-Oct-1914, Reserve Field Hospital 1, Bapaume.
Ehmann, Christian	Landwehrmann	5	29-Sep-1914	Ovillers-La Boisselle	

RIR 119

NAME	RANK	CO.	DATE OF DEATH	LOCATION	NOTES
Raible, Viktor	Landwehrmann	5	29-Sep-1914	Ovillers-La Boisselle	
Schmid, Fidel	Landwehrmann	5	29-Sep-1914	La Boisselle	W.I.A., died in hospital Fürst Karl, Sigmaringen.
Stapf, Georg	Landwehrmann	5	29-Sep-1914	Ovillers-La Boisselle	
Stocksisch, Ludwig	Landwehrmann	5	29-Sep-1914	Ovillers-La Boisselle	W.I.A., died 30-Sep-1914, Reserve Hospital 1, Bapaume.
Träger, Anton	Reservist	5	29-Sep-1914	La Boisselle	W.I.A., died 17-Oct-1914, Fortress Hospital Ulm.
Letsch, Hermann	Landwehrmann	7	29-Sep-1914	Ovillers-La Boisselle	W.I.A., died 29-Sep-1914, Main Dressing Station, 26th Reserve Division.
Wolf, Imanuel	Gefreiter der Landwehr	7	29-Sep-1914	Ovillers-La Boisselle	
Fetzer, Adolf	Reservist	10	29-Sep-1914	Ovillers/La Boisselle	
Kämmerle, August	Reservist	10	29-Sep-1914	Ovillers/La Boisselle	
Früh, Jakob	Landwehrmann	12	29-Sep-1914	Ovillers/La Boisselle	
Zeiler, Philipp	Landwehrmann	2	30-Sep-1914	Ovillers-La Boisselle	W.I.A., died 30-Sep-1914, Reserve Field Hospital 1, Bapaume.
Roos, Paul	Landwehrmann	7	30-Sep-1914	Ovillers-La Boisselle	W.I.A., died 30-Sep-1914 in Battle Headquarters dug-out.
Kübler, Johannes	Reservist	1 M.G.	30-Sep-1914	Ovillers/La Boisselle	
Wenzler, Hermann	Landwehrmann	6	1-Oct-1914	Ovillers-La Boisselle	W.I.A., died 1-Oct-1914, Reserve Field Hospital 1, Bapaume.
Müller, Eberhard	Gefreiter	3	2-Oct-1914	Ovillers-La Boisselle	
Eble, Karl	Landwehrmann	4	2-Oct-1914	Ovillers-La Boisselle	W.I.A., died 22-Oct-1914, Military Hospital Lüttich.
Schmälzle, Albert	Reservist	12	5-Oct-1914	St. Pierre-Divion	
Keppler II, Friedrich	Reservist	2	6-Oct-1914	Ovillers-La Boisselle	
Gauss, Gotthilf	Gefreiter der Reserve	3	20-Oct-1914	Ovillers-La Boisselle	
Kielwein, Karl	Reservist	3	20-Oct-1914	Ovillers-La Boisselle	
Ohngemach, Jakob	Reservist	3	20-Oct-1914	Ovillers-La Boisselle	
Selzer, Wilhelm	Active Unterof-fizier	3	20-Oct-1914	Ovillers-La Boisselle	
Stocker, Christian	Gefreiter	12	30-Oct-1914	Fricourt	W.I.A., died 30-Oct-1914, Field Hospital 2, Flers.
Taigel, Georg	Ersatz Reservist	12	30-Oct-1914	Fricourt	

RIR 119

NAME	RANK	CO.	DATE OF DEATH	LOCATION	NOTES
Walker, Adam	Landwehrmann	10	4-Nov-1914	Fricourt	
Weber, Hermann	Landwehrmann	10	4-Nov-1914	Fricourt	
Astfalk, Christian	Landwehrmann	12	21-Nov-1914	Ovillers/La Boisselle	W.I.A., died 26-Nov-1914, Reserve Field Hospital 1, Bapaume.
Walz, Adolf	Gefreiter der Reserve	12	21-Nov-1914	Miraumont	W.I.A., died 22-Nov-1914, Reserve Field Hospital 1, Bapaume.
Kirchherr, Gottlob	Reservist	4	24-Nov-1914	Ovillers-La Boisselle	Accidentally killed.
Keiper, Gustav	Leutnant	8	24-Nov-1914	Ovillers-La Boisselle	W.I.A., died 26-Nov-1914, Field Hospital 1, Bapaume.
Bezel, Karl	Leutnant der Reserve	5	25-Nov-1914	Ovillers-La Boisselle	W.I.A., died 17-Dec-1914, Reserve Field Hospital 1, Bapaume.
Steinhäuser, Georg	Landwehrmann	5	28-Nov-1914	Ovillers-La Boisselle	
Sturm, Georg	Kriegsfreiwilliger	2	4-Dec-1914	Ovillers-La Boisselle	
Danner, Friedrich	Unteroffizier der Reserve	7	8-Dec-1914	Ovillers-La Boisselle	
Burger, Jakob	Gefreiter der Landwehr	4	14-Dec-1914	Ovillers-La Boisselle	W.I.A., Military Hospital, Cambrai.
Hennefarth, Georg	Unteroffizier der Landwehr	4	14-Dec-1914	Ovillers-La Boisselle	
Kühn, Karl	Landwehrmann	4	14-Dec-1914	Ovillers-La Boisselle	W.I.A., died 14-Dec-1914, Field Hospital 1, Bapaume.
Linn, Karl	Vizefeldwebel, Offiz. Aspir.	7	16-Dec-1914	Ovillers-La Boisselle	
Bott I, Eugen	Reservist	2	17-Dec-1914	Ovillers-La Boisselle	
Klemm, Adolf	Vizefeldwebel, Offiz. Stellv.	2	17-Dec-1914	Ovillers-La Boisselle	
Weiss, Friedrich	Reservist	2	17-Dec-1914	Ovillers-La Boisselle	
Vogt, Paul	Kriegsfreiwilliger	4	17-Dec-1914	Ovillers-La Boisselle	
Mägerle, Bonifazius	Landwehrmann	5	17-Dec-1914	Ovillers-La Boisselle	
Bøcheler, Albert	Kriegsfreiwilliger	6	17-Dec-1914	Ovillers-La Boisselle	
Rode, Karl	Landwehrmann	6	17-Dec-1914	Ovillers-La Boisselle	
Günther, Alfred	Kriegsfreiwilliger	7	17-Dec-1914	Ovillers-La Boisselle	
Löffler, Viktor	Reservist	7	17-Dec-1914	Ovillers-La Boisselle	W.I.A., died 18-Dec-1914, Reserve Field Hospital 1, Bapaume.
Duffner, Josef	Reservist	8	17-Dec-1914	Ovillers-La Boisselle	

RIR 119

NAME	RANK	CO.	DATE OF DEATH	LOCATION	NOTES
Geiger, Alfred	Landwehrmann	8	17-Dec-1914	Ovillers-La Boisselle	
Jetter, Karl	Gefreiter der Reserve	8	17-Dec-1914	Ovillers-La Boisselle	
Pault, Josef ***	Reservist	8	17-Dec-1914	Ovillers-La Boisselle	
Drodofsky, Karl	Gefreiter	11	17-Dec-1914	Ovillers/La Boisselle	
Fetzer, Max	Kriegsfreiwilliger	11	17-Dec-1914	Ovillers/La Boisselle	
Mann, Gottlob	Landwehrmann	11	17-Dec-1914	Ovillers/La Boisselle	W.I.A., died 26-Dec-1914, Reserve Hospital, Krefeld.
Müller, Jakob	Sergeant	11	17-Dec-1914	Ovillers/La Boisselle	
Nauer, Franz	Gefreiter	11	17-Dec-1914	Ovillers/La Boisselle	
Baumann, Karl	Reservist	1 M.G.	17-Dec-1914	Ovillers/La Boisselle	
Geiger, Gustav	Gefreiter	1 M.G.	17-Dec-1914	Ovillers/La Boisselle	
Keller, Paul	Gefreiter der Landwehr	1 M.G.	17-Dec-1914	Ovillers/La Boisselle	
Klenk, Ludwig	Gefreiter der Landwehr	1 M.G.	17-Dec-1914	Ovillers/La Boisselle	
Schurer, Jakob	Reservist	1 M.G.	17-Dec-1914	Ovillers/La Boisselle	
Schütz, Eugen	Reservist	1 M.G.	17-Dec-1914	Ovillers/La Boisselle	
Zagst, Philipp	Landwehrmann	2	18-Dec-1914	Ovillers-La Boisselle	W.I.A., died 9-Jan-1915, Reserve Field Hospital 3, Vélu.
Eissler, Wilhelm	Landwehrmann	6	18-Dec-1914	Ovillers-La Boisselle	
Kleinhans, Adolf	Gefreiter der Reserve	6	18-Dec-1914	Ovillers-La Boisselle	
Mayer, Engelbert	Kriegsfreiwilliger	6	18-Dec-1914	Ovillers-La Boisselle	
Streib, Jakob	Landwehrmann	6	18-Dec-1914	Ovillers-La Boisselle	
Kopp, Friedrich	Landwehrmann	8	18-Dec-1914	Ovillers-La Boisselle	
Moosmann, Josef	Landwehrmann	8	18-Dec-1914	Ovillers-La Boisselle	
Baumann, Hermann	Reservist	11	20-Dec-1914	Beaumont	
Kraiss, Hermann	Leutnant der Reserve	11	20-Dec-1914	Beaumont	
Bäurle, Engelbert	Reservist	12	20-Dec-1914	Pozières	
Härdter, Karl	Gefreiter der Landwehr	6	21-Dec-1914	Ovillers-La Boisselle	W.I.A., died 22-Sdec-1914, Reserve Medical Company, Miraumont.

RIR 119 NAME	RANK	CO.	DATE OF DEATH	LOCATION	NOTES
Gamerdinger, Christian	Reservist	3	24-Dec-1914	Ovillers-La Boisselle	
Bentel, Friedrich	Kriegsfreiwilliger	12	24-Dec-1914	Irles	Accidentally killed.
Volz, Georg	Reservist	2	27-Dec-1914	Ovillers-La Boisselle	W.I.A., died 1-Jan-1915, Military Hospital 7, St. Quentin.
Wandel, Samuel	Reservist	1 M.G.	27-Dec-1914	Ovillers/La Boisselle	W.I.A., died 29-Dec-1914 in Military Hospital Palais de Justice, St. Quentin.
Stanger, Ernst	Gefreiter der Landwehr	3	29-Dec-1914	Ovillers-La Boisselle	W.I.A., died 29-Jan-1914, Field Hospital 1, Bapaume.
Digel, Gottlob	Ersatz Reservist	9	3-Jan-1915	La Boisselle	W.I.A., died 17-Jan-1915 in Military Hospital Palais de Justice, St. Quentin.
Gruner, Wilhelm	Gefreiter, Tambour	9	3-Jan-1915	La Boisselle	
Wolpert, Albert	Unteroofizier	9	3-Jan-1915	La Boisselle	
Gras, Gottlob	Landwehrmann	6	4-Jan-1915	Frankfurt	Died from an illness.
Keitel, Paul	Kriegsfreiwilliger	5	5-Jan-1915	Ovillers-La Boisselle	
Strobel, Martin	Gefreiter der Reserve	11	8-Jan-1915	Pozières	
Wohnsiedler, Richard	Kriegsfreiwilliger	11	8-Jan-1915	Pozières	
Linder, Friedrich	Reservist	2	9-Jan-1915	Ovillers-La Boisselle	
Wagner, Karl	Kriegsfreiwilliger	10	10-Jan-1915	La Boisselle	
Birkenmaier, Karl	Kriegsfreiwilliger	5	11-Jan-1915	Ovillers-La Boisselle	
Mayer, Gustav	Kriegsfreiwilliger	10	12-Jan-1915	La Boisselle	
Stoss, Friedrich	Landwehrmann	10	12-Jan-1915	La Boisselle	W.I.A., died 13-Jan-1915, Reserve Field Hospital 1, Bapaume.
Braun, Karl	Landwehrmann	11	12-Jan-1915	La Boisselle	W.I.A., died in Reserve Field Hospital 1, Bapaume
Pekari, Bernhard	Landwehrmann	10	14-Jan-1915	La Boisselle	
Häring, Karl	Kriegsfreiwilliger	12	14-Jan-1915	La Boisselle	
Maus, August	Feldwebel	1 M.G.	14-Jan-1915	Pozières	
Koch, Jakob	Landwehrmann	9	15-Jan-1915	La Boisselle	
Schmid, Wilhelm	Sergeant	10	16-Jan-1915	La Boisselle	
Haug, August	Reservist	10	17-Jan-1915	La Boisselle	
Leuze, Johannes	Unteroffizier der Reserve	10	17-Jan-1915	La Boisselle	M.I.A., declared dead.
Nill, Robert	Reservist	10	17-Jan-1915	La Boisselle	W.I.A., died 13-Feb-1915, Reserve Hospital 3, Frankfurt a.M.
Nisch, Johannes	Gefreiter der Landwehr	10	17-Jan-1915	La Boisselle	M.I.A., declared dead.
Nedele, Wilhelm	Landwehrmann	9	18-Jan-1915	La Boisselle	

RIR 119

NAME	RANK	CO.	DATE OF DEATH	LOCATION	NOTES
Wiedmann, Xaver	Landwehrmann	11	18-Jan-1915	La Boisselle	W.I.A., died 19-Jan-1915, Reserve Field Hospital 1, Bapaume.
Mayer, Karl	Landwehrmann	1 M.G.	18-Jan-1915	Ovillers/La Boisselle	
Rist, Christian	Unteroffizier der Reserve	9	20-Jan-1915	La Boisselle	
Maier, Robert	Musketier	1	24-Jan-1915	Stuttgart	
Müller, Pius	Landwehrmann	11	28-Jan-1915	La Boisselle	
Schwaiger, Gottlob	Reservist	4	7-Feb-1915	La Boisselle	
Gander, Friedrich	Landwehrmann	10	10-Feb-1915	La Boisselle	Killed on the road from Contalmaison to La Boisselle.
Bock, Johannes	Landwehrmann	2	23-Feb-1915	Beaumont	
Bauer, Alfred	Reservist	7	26-Feb-1915	Bapaume	Died of illness, Reserve Field Hospital 1, Bapaume.
Buchheim, Paul	Unteroffizier	7	10-Mar-1915	La Boisselle	
Hörter, Ernst	Reservist	1	11-Mar-1915	La Boisselle	W.I.A., died 12-Mar-1915, Reserve Field Hospital 1, Bapaume.
Dürr, Gottlieb	Landwehrmann	2	12-Mar-1915	La Boisselle	
Krauss, Jakob	Reservist	4	12-Mar-1915	La Boisselle	
Scholter, Erwin	Kriegsfreiwilliger	7	15-Mar-1915	La Boisselle	
Franz, Johannes	Musketier	1	17-Mar-1915	La Boisselle	
Kittel, Gottfried	Landwehrmann	4	20-Mar-1915	La Boisselle	
Keller, Paul	Reservist	8	20-Mar-1915	La Boisselle	
Rominger, Johannes	Landwehrmann	8	21-Mar-1915	La Boisselle	
Wetzel, Georg	Ersatz Reservist	4	22-Mar-1915	La Boisselle	
Stingel, Christian	Landwehrmann	6	22-Mar-1915	Beaumont	
Entenmann, Friedrich	Landwehrmann	4	23-Mar-1915	La Boisselle	W.I.A., died 29-Mar-1915, Reserve Field Hospital 1, Bapaume.
Fahrner, Johannes	Musketier	6	23-Mar-1915	La Boisselle	W.I.A., died 23-Mar-1915, Field Hospital 1, Bapaume.
Walter, Wilhelm	Kriegsfreiwilliger	11	26-Mar-1915	La Boisselle	W.I.A., died 31-Mar-1915, Reserve Field Hospital 1, Bapaume.
Hieber, Eugen	Landwehrmann	12	26-Mar-1915	La Boisselle	
Kalmbach, Georg	Reservist	12	26-Mar-1915	La Boisselle	
Schweizer, Adolf	Ersatz Reservist	12	26-Mar-1915	La Boisselle	
Weber, Anton	Musketier	4	27-Mar-1915	La Boisselle	
Frey, Hermann	Gefreiter der Landwehr	9	28-Mar-1915	La Boisselle	W.I.A., died 31-Mar-1915, Reserve Hospital 1, Bapaume.
Weber, Gottlob	Landwehrmann	9	31-Mar-1915	Ohmenhausen	Died from an illness.
Wurst, Otto	Kriegsfreiwilliger	7	4-Apr-1915	La Boisselle	
Mahler, Wilhelm	Reservist	4	2-May-1915	Thiepval	
Steimle, Albrecht	Ersatz Reservist	2	9-May-1915	Beaumont	

RIR 119

NAME	RANK	CO.	DATE OF DEATH	LOCATION	NOTES
Herre, Friedrich	Reservist	5	10-May-1915	Thiepval	W.I.A., died in the Palais de Justice, St. Quentin.
Leonhardt, Max	Kriegsfreiwilliger	10	12-May-1915	Beaumont	
Kozel, August	Landwehrmann	8	13-May-1915	La Boisselle	
Opferkuch, Eugen	Ersatz Reservist	2	14-May-1915	Beaumont	
Hartmann, Michael	Reservist	4	21-May-1915	Beaumont	
Kreutter, Felix	Landwehrmann	7	21-May-1915	Beaumont	W.I.A., died 23-May-1915, Military Hospital 7 A.C., St. Quentin.
Sattler, Johannes	Landwehrmann	1	24-May-1915	Beaumont	W.I.A., died 24-May-1915 in Battle Headquarters dug-out.
Langerer, Johann	Reservist	1	25-May-1915	Beaumont	W.I.A., died en route to Main Dressing Station, 26th Reserve Div.
Müller I, Otto	Gefreiter Kriegs-freiwilliger	2	25-May-1915	Beaumont	W.I.A., died 27-May-1915, Reserve Field Hospital 1, Bapaume.
Eisele, Gottlob	Kriegsfreiwilliger Schütze	1 M.G.	26-May-1915	Beaumont	
Müller, Wilhelm	Reserve Tambour	8	28-May-1915	Beaumont	
Wiedenmayer, August	Landwehrmann	3	31-May-1915	Beaumont	W.I.A., died 4-Jun-1915, Military Hospital, Palais de Justice, St. Quentin.
Bacher, Karl	Ersatz Reservist	2	2-Jun-1915	Beaumont	W.I.A., died 4-Jun-1915 at the Medical Company, Miraumont.
Klumpp, Christian	Reservist	1	7-Jun-1915	Beaumont	W.I.A., died en route to Main Dressing Station, 26th Reserve Div.
Bodenmüller, Adolf	Ersatz Reservist	2	7-Jun-1915	Beaumont	
Keppler, Karl	Unteroffizier der Reserve	2	7-Jun-1915	Beaumont	
Faul, Maximilian	Musketier	4	7-Jun-1915	Beaumont	
Löffler, Reinhold	Ersatz Reservist	4	7-Jun-1915	Beaumont	
Arnold, Karl	Gefreiter	7	7-Jun-1915	Beaumont	
Wagner, Georg	Reservist	7	7-Jun-1915	Beaumont	
Weigel, Ernst	Landwehrmann	8	7-Jun-1915	Beaumont	
Preisendanz, Gottlob	Landwehrmann	10	7-Jun-1915	Beaumont	
Schneiderhahn, Max	Musketier	11	7-Jun-1915	Beaumont	
Wenger, Wilhelm	Kriegsfreiwilliger	1 M.G.	7-Jun-1915	Beaumont	
Müller, Gotthilf	Grenadier	2	8-Jun-1915	Beaumont	
Seitz, Julius	Grenadier	2	8-Jun-1915	Beaumont	
Hank, Anton	Landwehrmann	1	9-Jun-1915	Beaumont	
Munding, Karl	Landwehrmann	1	9-Jun-1915	Beaumont	
Braun, Gottlob	Ersatz Reservist	8	9-Jun-1915	Beaumont	W.I.A., died -Jul-1915, Reserve Field Hospital 1, Bapaume.

RIR 119

NAME	RANK	CO.	DATE OF DEATH	LOCATION	NOTES
Bühler, Wilhelm	Reservist	1	10-Jun-1915	Beaumont	
Frey, Karl	Grenadier	1	10-Jun-1915	Beaumont	
Graf, Paul	Gefreiter	1	10-Jun-1915	Beaumont	W.I.A., died 10-Jun-1915 at Reserve Medical Company, Miraumont.
Schechinger, Friedrich	Reservist	1	10-Jun-1915	Beaumont	
Wagner, Paul	Kriegsfreiwilliger	1	10-Jun-1915	Beaumont	
Finkbeiner, Wilhelm	Reservist	4	10-Jun-1915	Beaumont	
Riedle, Hermann	Kriegsfreiwilliger	7	10-Jun-1915	Beaumont	
Weinläder, Jakob	Gefreiter der Reserve	1 M.G.	10-Jun-1915	Beaumont	
Herrmann, Karl	Landwehrmann	1	11-Jun-1915	Beaumont	
Riepp, Adolf	Kriegsfreiwilliger	1	11-Jun-1915	Beaumont	
Haap, Josef	Landwehrmann	9	11-Jun-1915	Beaumont	
Blaich, Gottlieb	Reservist	1	12-Jun-1915	Beaumont	
Braun, Jakob	Ersatz Reservist	1	12-Jun-1915	Beaumont	
Müller, Otto	Kriegsfreiwilliger	4	12-Jun-1915	Beaumont	
Schänzle, Max	Musketier	4	12-Jun-1915	Beaumont	
Graf, Hans	Kriegsfreiwilliger	2	13-Jun-1915	Beaumont	
Bub, Albert	Ersatz Reservist	4	13-Jun-1915	Beaumont	
Decker, Gustav	Landwehrmann	4	13-Jun-1915	Beaumont	
Graf, Ignaz	Reservist	4	13-Jun-1915	Beaumont	
Henssler, Rudolf	Active Haupt-mann	4	13-Jun-1915	Beaumont	W.I.A., died 13-Jun-1915, Main Dressing Station, Miraumont.
Weiss, Jakob	Unteroffizier der Reserve	4	13-Jun-1915	Beaumont	
Emanuel, Johann	Unteroffizier der Landwehr	4	15-Jun-1915	Beaumont	
Conzelmann, Konrad	Reservist	8	15-Jun-1915	Beaumont	
Haux, Alfred	Musketier	8	15-Jun-1915	Beaumont	
Maier, Wilhelm	Gefreiter der Landwehr	8	15-Jun-1915	Beaumont	
Moltenbrei, Wilhelm	Landwehrmann	2	16-Jun-1915	Beaumont	
Zepf, Johann	Landwehrmann	8	17-Jun-1915	Beaumont	
Maier, Wilhelm	Kriegsfreiwilliger	9	26-Jun-1915	Beaumont	
Keck, Friedrich	Reservist	3	3-Jul-1915	Beaumont	
Hofmann, Wilhelm	Reservist	1 M.G.	4-Jul-1915	Beaumont	
Roller, Friedrich	Sanitäts Gefreiter	2	8-Jul-1915	Beaumont	
Wagner, Julius	Landwehrmann	6	8-Jul-1915	St. Quentin	Died of illness, Lycée Henri Martin Military hospital.
Zimmermann, Andreas	Reservist	1 M.G.	11-Jul-1915	Beaumont	
Kübler, Eugen	Kriegsfreiwilliger	9	13-Jul-1915	Beaumont	
Schneider, Franz	Ldstpfl.	10	15-Jul-1915	Beaumont	

RIR 119

NAME	RANK	CO.	DATE OF DEATH	LOCATION	NOTES
Steudle, Karl	Leutnant der Landwehr	5	24-Jul-1915	Beaumont	W.I.A., died 28-Jul-1915, Reserve Field Hospital 1, Bapaume.
Birk, Karl	Gefreiter	9	30-Jul-1915	Beaumont	W.I.A., died 10-Aug-1915 in Military Hospital Orphelinat, St. Quentin.
Cleef, Johann	Reservist	1	3-Aug-1915	Beaumont	
Volle, Johannes	Landwehrmann	1	11-Aug-1915	Beaumont	W.I.A., died 17-Sep-1915, Reserve Hospital, Siegburg.
Herzog, Georg	Landsturmmann	1 Recruit	23-Aug-1915	Beaumont	W.I.A., died 24-Aug-1915, Main Dressing Station, Miraumont.
Eissler, Christian	Reservist	12	25-Aug-1915	Beaumont	
Maier, August	Kriegsfreiwilliger	5	27-Aug-1915	Beaumont	
Oesterle, Heinrich	Landwehrmann	11	27-Aug-1915	Beaumont	
Schäfer, Josef	Ldstpfl.	11	27-Aug-1915	Beaumont	
Hahn, Johannes	Reservist	2	1-Sep-1915	Beaumont	W.I.A., died 3-Oct-1915, Military Hospital 7 A.C., St. Quentin.
Rebstock, Eugen	Reservist	2	1-Sep-1915	Beaumont	W.I.A., died 1-Sep-1915 at the Medical Company, Miraumont.
Harr, Georg	Reservist	3	19-Sep-1915	Beaumont	
Staiger, Georg	Reservist	10	20-Sep-1915	Miraumont	
Weippert, Karl	Ersatz Reservist	10	20-Sep-1915	Miraumont	
Link, Wilhelm	Landwehrmann	4	21-Sep-1915	Beaumont	W.I.A., died in the evening of 21-Sep-1915, in Battle Headquarters dug-out.
Kleinfelder, Hermann	Landwehrmann	10	26-Sep-1915	Beaumont	
Benz, Robert	Unteroffizier	1	1-Oct-1915	Beaumont	W.I.A., died 13-Oct-1915, Reserve Field Hospital 1, Bapaume.
Weinmann, Friedrich	Gefreiter der Landwehr	9	3-Oct-1915	Beaumont	
Heckele, Johannes	Musketier	1	5-Oct-1915	Thiepval	
Gehring, Josef	Kriegsfreiwilliger	12	12-Oct-1915	Beaumont	
Müller, Gottlieb	Gefreiter, Kriegsfreiwilliger	12	12-Oct-1915	Beaumont	
Schmid, Gmund	Musketier	6	15-Oct-1915	Beaumont	
Wacker, Johann	Landwehrmann	1	17-Oct-1915	Westfalia	Died of illness, Reserve Hospital Bottrop.
Hähnle, Reinhold	Ersatz Reservist	9	22-Oct-1915	Beaumont	
Maisch, Christian	Gefreiter der Landwehr	10	3-Nov-1915	Baillescourt	
Möck, Johannes	Landwehrmann	11	8-Nov-1915	Miraumont	
Himmler, Georg	Ersatz Reservist	1 Recruit	10-Nov-1915	Vélu	Died from an illness, Field Hospital 2.

RIR 119

NAME	RANK	CO.	DATE OF DEATH	LOCATION	NOTES
Haller, Johannes	Ersatz Reservist	7	15-Nov-1915	Beaumont	W.I.A., died at the Reserve Medical Company 13, Miraumont.
Nagel, Wilhelm	Reservist	10	23-Nov-1915	Beaumont	W.I.A., died 24-Nov-1915, Reserve Field Hospital 1, Bapaume.
Denzinger, Otto	Landwehrmann	2	3-Dec-1915	Beaumont	W.I.A., died 4-Dec-1915, Reserve Field Hospital 1, Bapaume.
Maier, Richard	Kriegsfreiwilliger	9	3-Dec-1915	Beaumont	
Fritz, Wilhelm	Ersatz Reservist	12	3-Dec-1915	Beaumont	W.I.A., died 3-Dec-1915, Reserve Hospital 1, Bapaume.
Eberle, Melchior	Unteroffizier der Reserve	12	5-Dec-1915	near Beaumont	Accidentally killed.
Steinhardt, Josef	Musketier	3	7-Dec-1915	Beaumont	W.I.A., died 13-Dec-1915, Reserve Field Hospital 1, Bapaume.
Bihl, Franz	Reservist	7	12-Dec-1915	Beaumont	
Stier, Albert	Ersatz Reservist	7	12-Dec-1915	Beaumont	W.I.A., died 13-Dec-1915, Field Hospital 2, Bapaume.
Weiler, Christian	Ldstpfl.	7	12-Dec-1915	Beaumont	
Wörle, Karl	Landwehrmann	7	12-Dec-1915	Ovillers-La Boisselle	
Hartmayer, Gustav	Ersatz Reservist	9	16-Dec-1915	Beaumont	
Felder, Immanuel	Ldstpfl.	8	25-Dec-1915	Beaumont	
Ihle, Friedrich	Ersatz Reservist	10	29-Dec-1915	Beaumont	
Abelein, Karl	Ersatz Reservist	Recruit	31-Dec-1915	St. Pierre-Divion	
Webber, Jakob	Ersatz Reservist	Recruit	31-Dec-1915	St. Pierre-Divion	W.I.A., died 15-Jan-1916, Reserve Field Hospital 1, Bapaume.
Alb, Heinrich	Kriegsfreiwilliger	11	17-Jan-1916	Beaumont	
Alber, David	Infanterie Pionier	3	18-Jan-1916	Serre	W.I.A., died 22-Jan-1916, Reserve Field Hospital 1, Bapaume.
Stahl, Georg	Ersatz Reservist	1	24-Jan-1916	Beaumont	W.I.A., died 25-Jan-1916, Reserve Field Hospital 1, Bapaume.
Hutt, Ernst	Landwehrmann	10	29-Jan-1916	Beaumont	
Hoffmann, Richard	Ldstpfl.	8	30-Jan-1916	Beaumont	
Kotz, Josef	Musketier	2	2-Feb-1916	Beaumont	W.I.A., died 3-Feb-1916, Reserve Field Hospital 1, Bapaume.
Dirr, Matthias	Unteroffizier	12	14-Feb-1916	Beaumont	
Renz, Friedrich	Ldstpfl.	Recruit	15-Feb-1916	Beaumont	
Haizmann, Christian	Musketier	7	24-Feb-1916	Beaumont	Accidentally killed.
Schneider, Josef	Gefreiter der Landwehr	5	26-Feb-1916	Beaumont	

RIR 119

NAME	RANK	CO.	DATE OF DEATH	LOCATION	NOTES
Bitzer, Andreas	Gefreiter der Reserve	9	26-Feb-1916	Beaumont	W.I.A., died 28-Feb-1916, Reserve Field Hospital 1, Bapaume.
Pfund, Eugen	Vizefeldwebel, Offiz. Aspir.	8	11-Mar-1916	Beaumont	
Baumann, Georg	Ldstpfl.	8	15-Mar-1916	Beaumont	
Frölich, Ludwig	Reservist	1	22-Mar-1916	Beaumont	
Henninger, Gottlieb	Reservist	1	24-Mar-1916	Beaumont	
Heinzelmann, Matthias	Reservist	7	3-Apr-1916	Beaumont	W.I.A., died 3-Apr-1916, Reserve Field Hospital 1, Bapaume.
Bigiel, Maximilian	Musketier	5	6-Apr-1916	Beaumont	
Brucklacher, Otto	Unteroffizier	5	6-Apr-1916	Beaumont	
Stapf, Karl	Musketier	5	6-Apr-1916	Beaumont	
Böcker, Hermann	Vizefeldwebel der Landwehr	6	9-Apr-1916	Beaumont	
Jedele, Albert	Reservist	10	16-Apr-1916	Beaumont	
Mühlhöfer, Ferdinand	Sanitäts Unteroffizier	1 M.G.	17-Apr-1916	Bapaume	Died from an illness, Reserve Field Hospital 1.
Bühler, Jakob	Landwehrmann	5	24-Apr-1916	Miraumont	Accidentally killed.
Forell, Alois	Musketier	2	26-Apr-1916	Beaumont	
Spöhr, Friedrich	Reservist	3	29-Apr-1916	Beaumont	W.I.A., died 29-Apr-1916 at the Main Dressing Station, Reserve Medical Company, Miraumont.
Maier, Otto	Vizefeldwebel, Offiz. Aspir.	5	30-Apr-1916	Beaumont	
Jetter, Karl	Unteroffizier der Landwehr	Regt. Staff	30-Apr-1916	Klein Miraumont	W.I.A., died 30-Apr-1916, Main dressing station, 26th Reserve Division, Miraumont.
Mattes, Eugen	Reservist	9	5-May-1916	Beaumont	W.I.A., died 7-May-1916, Reserve Field Hospital 1, Bapaume.
Lebherz, August	Gefreiter der Reserve	6	7-May-1916	Beaumont	W.I.A., died 8-May-1916, Reserve Field Hospital 1, Bapaume.
Fichter, August	Gefreiter der Landwehr	5	19-May-1916	Beaumont	
Digeser, Fridolin	Reservist	7	28-May-1916	Beaumont	
Buz, Wilhelm	Vizefeldwebel, Offiz. Aspir.	4	29-May-1916	Beaumont	
Grosshans, Adam	Landsturmmann	1	30-May-1916	Beaumont	W.I.A., died 8-Jun-1916, Reserve Field Hospital 1, Bapaume.
Bommas, Oskar	Vizefeldwebel, Offiz. Aspir.	4	6-Jun-1916	Beaumont	
Müller, Albert	Landwehrmann	2	9-Jun-1916	Beaumont	
Reinwald, Heinrich	Kriegsfreiwilliger	7	11-Jun-1916	Beaumont	
Schüle, Ernst	Grenadier	9	11-Jun-1916	Beaumont	

RIR 119

NAME	RANK	CO.	DATE OF DEATH	LOCATION	NOTES
Röcker, Hermann	Kriegsfreiwilliger	10	11-Jun-1916	Beaumont	
Heckel, Karl	Unterozzizier, Offiz. Asp.	11	11-Jun-1916	Beaumont	
Weiss, Karl	Ldstpfl.	12	11-Jun-1916	Beaumont	W.I.A., died 23-Jun-1916, Military Hospital Palais de Justice, St. Quentin.
Hähnle, Lukas	Ldstpfl.	6	15-Jun-1916	Beaumont	
Dietrich, Wilhelm	Leutnant der Reserve	2	17-Jun-1916	Beaumont	W.I.A., died en route to Main Dressing Station, Miraumon
Berner, Gottlob	Musketier	5	19-Jun-1916	Beaucourt	
Kress, Georg	Landwehrmann	4	21-Jun-1916	Villers au Flos	Died as a result of illness, Reserve Hospital 55.
Alf, Anton	Musketier	7	23-Jun-1916	Beaumont	W.I.A., died 4-Jul-1916, Military hospital, Orphelinal, St. Quentin.
Engstler, Albert	Kriegsfreiwilliger	9	24-Jun-1916	Beaumont	W.I.A., died 16-Jul-1916 in Military Hospital, Le Cateau.
Hamman, Jakob	Ersatz Reservist	1	25-Jun-1916	Beaumont	W.I.A., died 27-Jun-1916, Reserve Field Hospital 1, Bapaume.
Gührer, Johann	Reservist	2	25-Jun-1916	Beaumont	
Sigle, Albert	Gefreiter Kriegs-freiwilliger	2	25-Jun-1916	Beaumont	W.I.A., died 28-Jun-1916, Württemberg Field Hospital 1, Bapaume.
Seemann, Karl	Vizefeldwebel, Offiz. Aspir.	6	25-Jun-1916	Beaumont	W.I.A., died 26-Jun-1916, Reserve Field Hospital 1, Bapaume.
Walker, Christian	Landwehrmann	10	25-Jun-1916	Beaumont	W.I.A., died 2-Aug-1916, Field Hospital 1, Oldenburg.
Hack, Georg	Ersatz Reservist	2	26-Jun-1916	Beaumont	W.I.A., died en route to Main Dressing Station.
Brumm, Georg	Ersatz Reservist	4	26-Jun-1916	Beaumont	
Gall, Karl	Reservist	4	26-Jun-1916	Beaumont	
Götsch, Gustav	Gefreiter	4	26-Jun-1916	Miraumont	
Aronsohn, Viktor	Ersatz Reservist	5	26-Jun-1916	Beaumont	W.I.A., died 27-Jun-1916 in Military Hospital, Caudry.
Benzing, Josef	Landwehrmann	5	26-Jun-1916	Beaucourt	
Golz, Paul	Kriegsfreiwilliger Vizef., Offiz. Aspir.	5	26-Jun-1916	Beaucourt	
Henke, David	Ldstpfl.	6	26-Jun-1916	Beaumont	W.I.A., died 21-Aug-1916, Reserve Hospital 1, Aachen.
Gehring, Bernhard	Unteroffizier der Landwehr	9	26-Jun-1916	Beaumont	
Grimm, Leonhard	Reservist	10	26-Jun-1916	Beaumont	W.I.A., died 7-Sep-1916, Reserve Hospital 7, Stuttgart
Beuter, Josef	Vizefeldwebel, Offiz. Aspir.	11	26-Jun-1916	Beaumont	W.I.A., died 12-Jul-1916, Reserve Hospital 3, Aachen.
Weiss, Johannes	Reservist	12	26-Jun-1916	Beaumont	

RIR 119

NAME	RANK	CO.	DATE OF DEATH	LOCATION	NOTES
Staiger, Wilhelm	Musketier	1 Recruit	26-Jun-1916	Beaumont-Pys	W.I.A., died 29-Jun-1916, Reserve Field Hospital 1, Bapaume.
Steckeler, Lorenz	Musketier	1 Recruit	26-Jun-1916	Beaumont-Pys	W.I.A., died 27-Jun-1916, Reserve Field Hospital 1, Bapaume.
Mäntele, Hermann	Musketier	1	27-Jun-1916	Beaumont	W.I.A., died 27-Jun-1916 in Battle Headquarters dug-out.
Glaser, Christian	Reservist	2	27-Jun-1916	Beaumont	
Fritz, Friedrich	Landwehrmann	5	27-Jun-1916	Beaucourt	K.I.A.
Häge, Adolf	Vizefeldwebel der Landwehr	11	27-Jun-1916	Beaumont	
Kemmler, Christian	Gefreiter der Landwehr	11	27-Jun-1916	Grandcourt	
Kussmaul, Johannes	Landwehrmann	1	28-Jun-1916	Beaumont	
Kromer, Emil	Kriegsfreiwilliger	9	28-Jun-1916	Beaumont	
Oesterle, Paul	Schütze	1 M.G.	28-Jun-1916	Beaumont	
Kottler, Robert	Schütze	2 M.G.	28-Jun-1916	Beaumont	
Weller, Georg	Schütze	2 M.G.	28-Jun-1916	Beaumont	W.I.A., died 6-Jul-1916, Military Hospital Palais de Justice, St. Quentin.
Sigler, Wilhelm	Musketier	2 Recruit	28-Jun-1916	Feste Alt Württemberg	W.I.A., died 30-Jun-1916, Reserve Field Hospital 1, Bapaume.
Sinn, Eugen	Ersatz Reservist	2 Recruit	28-Jun-1916	Feste Alt Württemberg	W.I.A., died 29-Jun-1916, Reserve Field Hospital 1, Bapaume.
Wenzler, Josef	Musketier	2 Recruit	28-Jun-1916	Beaumont	W.I.A., died 29-Jun-1916 in Battle Headquarters dug-out.
Haischer, Ignaz	Landwehrmann	1	29-Jun-1916	Beaumont	W.I.A., died en route to Main Dressing Station.
Seeger, Wilhelm	Ersatz Reservist	1	29-Jun-1916	Beaumont	W.I.A., died 30-Jun-1916, Reserve Field Hospital 1, Bapaume.
Möhler, Eduard	Unteroffizier, Offiz. Asp.	9	29-Jun-1916	Beaumont	W.I.A., died 1-Jul-1916, Reserve Field Hospital 1, Bapaume.
Baur, Friedrich	Feldwebel	11	29-Jun-1916	Beaumont	
Schneider, Gottlieb	Landwehrmann	1	30-Jun-1916	Beaumont	
Reicherter, Albert	Unteroffizier der Landwehr	2	30-Jun-1916	Beaumont	
Ruoff, Jakob	Musketier	2	30-Jun-1916	Beaumont	
Schedel, August	Musketier	2	30-Jun-1916	Beaumont	
Hettler, Wilhelm	Gefreiter	9	30-Jun-1916	Beaumont	W.I.A., died 1-Jul-1916, Main Dressing Station, 26th Reserve Division, Miraumont.
Wegmann, Jakob	Landwehrmann	12	30-Jun-1916	Beaucourt	K.I.A.

RIR 119

NAME	RANK	CO.	DATE OF DEATH	LOCATION	NOTES
Wetzel, Julius	Ldstpfl.	12	30-Jun-1916	Beaumont	

RIR 121

NAME	RANK	CO.	DATE OF DEATH	LOCATION	NOTES
Bullinger, Martin	Wehrmann	4	28-Sep-1914	Thiepval	W.I.A., died 5-Oct-1914, Reserve Field Hospital 1, Bapaume.
Wagner, Gottlob	Feldwebel	4	28-Sep-1914	Thiepval	
Beyl, Gottlob	Gefreiter	5	28-Sep-1914	Thiepval	
Heilmann, Ludwig	Wehrmann	8	28-Sep-1914	Thiepval	
Klimm, Josef	Gefreiter	8	28-Sep-1914	Authuille	
Schneider, Eberhard	Gefreiter	11	28-Sep-1914	Thiepval	
Walter, Hermann	Tambour Wehrmann	1	29-Sep-1914	Authuille	
Weippert, Friedrich	Wehrmann	1	29-Sep-1914	Authuille	
Ade, Karl	Reservist	2	29-Sep-1914	Authuille	M.I.A., declared dead.
Berner, Karl	Gefreiter	2	29-Sep-1914	Authuille	M.I.A., declared dead.
Bollinger, Gottlieb	Wehrmann	2	29-Sep-1914	Authuille	W.I.A., C.I.A., died 11-Oct-1914, Hospital 5, Amiens, French P.O.W. Camp.
Fischer, Adolf	Wehrmann	2	29-Sep-1914	Authuille	M.I.A., declared dead.
Gehring, Ferdinand	Wehrmann	2	29-Sep-1914	Authuille	M.I.A., declared dead.
Haag, Friedrich	Wehrmann	2	29-Sep-1914	Authuille	M.I.A., declared dead.
Henssler, Imanuel	Unteroffizier	2	29-Sep-1914	Authuille	M.I.A., declared dead.
Hering, Wilhelm	Wehrmann	2	29-Sep-1914	Authuille	W.I.A., died 3-Oct-1914, Hospital, Bapaume.
Hezel, August	Wehrmann	2	29-Sep-1914	Authuille	M.I.A., declared dead.
Hiller, Gottlob	Wehrmann	2	29-Sep-1914	Authuille	M.I.A., declared dead.
Hohenrein, Friedrich	Wehrmann	2	29-Sep-1914	Authuille	M.I.A., declared dead.
Jäger, Wilhelm	Wehrmann	2	29-Sep-1914	Authuille	M.I.A., declared dead.
Kleemann, David	Wehrmann	2	29-Sep-1914	Authuille	M.I.A., declared dead.
Kruck, Gottlieb	Gefreiter	2	29-Sep-1914	Authuille	M.I.A., declared dead.
Künzinger, Gotthilf	Wehrmann	2	29-Sep-1914	Authuille	W.I.A., died in hospital, date unknown.
Laier, Karl	Wehrmann	2	29-Sep-1914	Authuille	M.I.A., declared dead.
Läpple, Gustav	Wehrmann	2	29-Sep-1914	Authuille	
Lude, Johannes	Unteroffizier	2	29-Sep-1914	Authuille	W.I.A., died 26-Oct-1914, Reserve Field Hospital 1, Bapaume.
Raith, Karl	Wehrmann	2	29-Sep-1914	Authuille	M.I.A., declared dead.
Schatz, Gottlob	Wehrmann	2	29-Sep-1914	Authuille	M.I.A., declared dead.
Scholl, Johannes	Wehrmann	2	29-Sep-1914	Authuille	M.I.A., declared dead.
Schweizer, Gottlob	Wehrmann	2	29-Sep-1914	Authuille	M.I.A., declared dead.

RIR 121 NAME	RANK	CO.	DATE OF DEATH	LOCATION	NOTES
Stauch, Georg	Wehrmann	2	29-Sep-1914	Authuille	M.I.A., declared dead.
Stecher, Gottlob	Gefreiter	2	29-Sep-1914	Authuille	M.I.A., declared dead.
Wolf, Friedrich	Gefreiter	2	29-Sep-1914	Authuille	W.I.A., C.I.A., died 15-Oct-1914 in French P.O.W. Camp, Saint Brieue.
Wolpert, Johann	Wehrmann	2	29-Sep-1914	Authuille	M.I.A., declared dead.
Dempel, Albert	Wehrmann	4	29-Sep-1914	Thiepval	M.I.A., declared dead.
Kraft, Eberhard	Reservist	4	29-Sep-1914	Thiepval	
Laufter, Paul	Wehrmann	4	29-Sep-1914	Thiepval	
Wöhr, Hermann	Wehrmann	4	29-Sep-1914	Authuille	W.I.A., died 29-Sep-1914, Reserve Medical Company 14, Pozières.
Wörner, Gottlob	Unteroffizier	4	29-Sep-1914	Thiepval	M.I.A., declared dead.
Bächler, Christian	Wehrmann	5	29-Sep-1914	Thiepval	M.I.A., declared dead.
Englert, Friedrich	Wehrmann	5	29-Sep-1914	Thiepval	W.I.A., died 4-Oct-1914, Reserve Field Hospital 1, Bapaume.
Frommer, Georg	Wehrmann	5	29-Sep-1914	Thiepval	
Grün, Karl	Wehrmann	5	29-Sep-1914	Thiepval	M.I.A., declared dead.
Müller, Karl	Wehrmann	5	29-Sep-1914	Thiepval	M.I.A., declared dead.
Ott, Wilhelm	Hornist, Gefreiter	5	29-Sep-1914	Thiepval	W.I.A., M.I.A., died 8-Dec-1914 in French P.O.W. camp, Amiens.
Pierro, August	Wehrmann	5	29-Sep-1914	Thiepval	M.I.A., declared dead.
Rapp, Wilhelm	Wehrmann	5	29-Sep-1914	Thiepval	M.I.A., declared dead.
Schick, Gottlob	Wehrmann	5	29-Sep-1914	Thiepval	M.I.A., declared dead.
Altmann, Gottfried	Reservist	6	29-Sep-1914	Thiepval	M.I.A., declared dead.
Dobler, Karl	Wehrmann	6	29-Sep-1914	Thiepval	M.I.A., declared dead.
Gebert, Gottlieb	Wehrmann	6	29-Sep-1914	Thiepval	M.I.A., declared dead.
Hamann, Jakob	Wehrmann	6	29-Sep-1914	Thiepval	M.I.A., declared dead.
Heim, Otto	Gefreiter	6	29-Sep-1914	Thiepval	W.I.A., died 29-Sep-1914, main dressing station, Poziéres.
Hermann, Wilhelm	Reservist	6	29-Sep-1914	Thiepval	M.I.A., declared dead.
Hübsch, Johann	Wehrmann	6	29-Sep-1914	Thiepval	W.I.A., died 29-Sep-1914, dressing station, Thiepval.
Neutz, Gustav	Wehrmann	6	29-Sep-1914	Thiepval	W.I.A., M.I.A., died 7-Nov-1914, French P.O.W. camp, St. Briene.
Riexinger, Julius	Wehrmann	6	29-Sep-1914	Thiepval	W.I.A., M.I.A., died 31-Oct-1914, French P.O.W. camp, Bayonne.
Roth, August	Wehrmann	6	29-Sep-1914	Thiepval	
Ruckwied, Ludwig	Wehrmann	6	29-Sep-1914	Thiepval	
Schwarz, Gottlob	Wehrmann	6	29-Sep-1914	Thiepval	M.I.A., declared dead.
Sieber, Friedrich	Reservist	6	29-Sep-1914	Thiepval	W.I.A., died 30-Sep-1914, Reserve Field Hospital 1, Bapaume.

RIR 121 NAME	RANK	CO.	DATE OF DEATH	LOCATION	NOTES
Zeyer, Hermann	Wehrmann	6	29-Sep-1914	Thiepval	M.I.A., declared dead.
Brahner, Ernst	Reservist	8	29-Sep-1914	Thiepval	M.I.A., declared dead.
Sieber, Karl	Reservist	8	29-Sep-1914	Thiepval	
Wecker, Friedrich	Oberleutnant der Reserve	8	29-Sep-1914	Authuille	
Weimar, Friedrich	Reservist	8	29-Sep-1914	Thiepval	
Werner, Alfred	Unteroffizier	8	29-Sep-1914	Thiepval	
Fick, Georg	Hornist	9	29-Sep-1914	Ovillers	W.I.A., died 1-Oct-1914, Field Hospital 1, Bapaume.
Hinderer, Hermann	Reservist	9	29-Sep-1914	Thiepval	W.I.A., died 4-Oct-1914, in hospital, Ligny-Thilloy.
Merk, Wunibald	Musketier	9	29-Sep-1914	Thiepval	M.I.A., declared dead.
Müller, Friedrich	Reservist	9	29-Sep-1914	Thiepval	
Koppenhöfer, Jakob	Unteroffizier	11	29-Sep-1914	Thiepval	M.I.A., declared dead.
Lehmann, Christian	Wehrmann	11	29-Sep-1914	Thiepval	W.I.A., determined death occurred 5-Oct/6-Oct-1914 in Thiepval Wood.
Übelmesser, Georg	Wehrmann	11	29-Sep-1914	Thiepval	W.I.A., died 29-Sep-1914, Poziéres.
Lipp, Oskar	Oberleutnant/ Supply Officer	II Bn.	29-Sep-1914	Authuille	W.I.A., died 2-Oct-1914, Reserve Field Hospital 1, Bapaume.
Hoser, Friedrich	Wehrmann	1	30-Sep-1914	Authuille	W.I.A., died 19-Oct-1914, Reserve Hospital I, Ludwigsburg.
Weisshaar, Christian	Wehrmann	1	30-Sep-1914	Thiepval	
Felger, Karl	Wehrmann	4	30-Sep-1914	Authuille	M.I.A., declared dead.
Kübler, Karl	Wehrmann	4	30-Sep-1914	Authuille	M.I.A., declared dead.
Merkle, Alfons	Ersatz Reservist	4	30-Sep-1914	Authuille	
Mezger, Gottlob	Wehrmann	4	30-Sep-1914	Authuille	
Weiss, Johannes	Wehrmann	4	30-Sep-1914	Authuille	M.I.A., declared dead.
Auderer, Karl	Wehrmann	7	1-Oct-1914	Thiepval	M.I.A., declared dead.
Alt, Heinrich	Ersatz Reservist	8	1-Oct-1914	Thiepval	M.I.A., declared dead.
Gauer, Wilhelm	Reservist	8	1-Oct-1914	Thiepval	M.I.A., died 18-Oct-1918 inBritish P.O.W. camp.
Baumann, Karl	Wehrmann	8	2-Oct-1914	Thiepval	
Pfuhlmann, Johann	Wehrmann	2	5-Oct-1914	Thiepval	M.I.A., declared dead.
Haass, Wilhelm	Unteroffizier	5	5-Oct-1914	Thiepval	W.I.A., died 8-Oct-1914, Field Hospital 4, Miraumont.
Haberkern, Richard	Reservist	5	5-Oct-1914	Thiepval	
Hessel, Wilhelm	Wehrmann	5	5-Oct-1914	Thiepval	
Köbele, Traugott	Vizefeldwebel, Offiz. Asp.	5	5-Oct-1914	Thiepval	W.I.A., died 8-Oct-1914, Reserve Field Hospital 1, Bapaume.
Krauth, Alois	Reservist	5	5-Oct-1914	Thiepval	
Leiss, Wilhelm	Reservist	5	5-Oct-1914	Thiepval	
Mack, Friedrich	Reservist	5	5-Oct-1914	Thiepval	

RIR 121 NAME	RANK	CO.	DATE OF DEATH	LOCATION	NOTES
Rauth, Hermann	Unteroffizier	5	5-Oct-1914	Thiepval	
Röslen, Karl	Wehrmann	5	5-Oct-1914	Thiepval	
Schneider, August	Wehrmann	5	5-Oct-1914	Thiepval	
Spaich, Hermann	Wehrmann	5	5-Oct-1914	Thiepval	
Stein, Theodor	Wehrmann	5	5-Oct-1914	Thiepval	
Sautter, Friedrich	Hornist	7	5-Oct-1914	Thiepval	W.I.A., died 7-Oct-1914, Hospital 4, Miraumont.
Mayer, Karl	Vizefeldwebel, Offiz. Asp.	9	5-Oct-1914	Ovillers	W.I.A., died 7-Oct-1914, hospital, Miraumont.
Schlichenmayer, Gottlob	Wehrmann	9	5-Oct-1914	Ovillers	
Frey, Wilhelm	Wehrmann	10	5-Oct-1914	Thiepval	
Wahl, Christoph	Wehrmann	10	5-Oct-1914	Thiepval	W.I.A., died 14-Oct-1914, hospital, Bochum.
Baumann, Georg	Unteroffizier	11	5-Oct-1914	Thiepval	
Bräuninger, Karl	Reservist	11	5-Oct-1914	Thiepval	W.I.A., died 10-Oct-1914 in hospital, Miraumont.
Wieland, Wilhelm	Reservist	11	5-Oct-1914	Thiepval	
Kugler, Michael	Wehrmann	12	5-Oct-1914	Thiepval	
Möhle, Ernst	Reservist	12	5-Oct-1914	Thiepval	
Schmidt, Karl	Wehrmann	12	5-Oct-1914	Thiepval	
Wied, Friedrich	Reservist	12	5-Oct-1914	Thiepval	
Bürkle, Anton	Reservist	2	6-Oct-1914	Authuille	
Kirchner, Bernhard	Gefreiter	2	6-Oct-1914	Authuille	M.I.A., declared dead.
Maurer, Karl	Wehrmann	2	6-Oct-1914	Authuille	
Schert, Gottlob	Unteroffizier	2	6-Oct-1914	Authuille	
Weisser, Christian	Wehrmann	2	6-Oct-1914	Authuille	M.I.A., declared dead.
Häcker, Paul	Wehrmann	3	6-Oct-1914	Thiepval	
Kögel, Friedrich	Wehrmann	3	6-Oct-1914	Thiepval	
Mergenthaler, Reinhold	Wehrmann	3	6-Oct-1914	Thiepval	
Münzenmayer, Hermann	Vizefeldwebel	3	6-Oct-1914	Authuille	
Schnaitmann, Karl	Reservist	3	6-Oct-1914	Thiepval	
Weng, Friedrich	Reservist	3	6-Oct-1914	Thiepval	W.I.A., died 6-Oct-1914 en route to Reserve Medical Company.
Münzer, Franz	Reservist	6	6-Oct-1914	Thiepval	W.I.A., died 25-Oct-1914, Reserve Hospital, Aachen.
Mauk, Karl	Reservist	7	6-Oct-1914	Thiepval	
Fuchs, Gustav	Wehrmann	8	6-Oct-1914	Thiepval	
Küstner, Heinrich	Wehrmann	10	6-Oct-1914	Thiepval	
Frenz, Karl	Wehrmann	11	6-Oct-1914	Thiepval	
Giebler, Karl	Reservist	11	6-Oct-1914	Thiepval	
Glück, Hermann	vizefeldwebel	11	6-Oct-1914	Thiepval	
Vogel, Ernst	Reservist	11	6-Oct-1914	Thiepval	W.I.A., died 10-Oct-1914, Miraumont.

RIR 121 NAME	RANK	CO.	DATE OF DEATH	LOCATION	NOTES
Wahl, Wilhelm	Gefreiter	11	6-Oct-1914	Thiepval	
Schäfer, Friedrich	Gefreiter	12	6-Oct-1914	Thiepval	W.I.A., died 8-Oct-1914, Bapaume.
Kaiser, Gottlob	Reservist	M.G.	6-Oct-1914	Thiepval	W.I.A., died 24-Oct-1914, Bapaume.
Dagenbach, Wilhelm	Wehrmann	7	7-Oct-1914	Thiepval	
Künzel, Gustav	Reservist	7	7-Oct-1914	Thiepval	
Müller, Gottlieb	Wehrmann	7	7-Oct-1914	Thiepval	
Retz, Christian	Gefreiter	7	7-Oct-1914	Thiepval	
Schwarz, Friedrich	Wehrmann	7	7-Oct-1914	Thiepval	
Kern, Hermann	Wehrmann	8	7-Oct-1914	Thiepval	
Stahl, Karl	Reservist	8	7-Oct-1914	Thiepval	
Weiss, Wilhelm	Unteroffizier	10	7-Oct-1914	Thiepval	
Schilling, Hermann	Reservist	1	8-Oct-1914	Authuille	M.I.A., declared dead.
Knepper, Max	Gefreiter	11	10-Oct-1914	Thiepval	
Griesshaber, Ferdinand	Wehrmann	2	11-Oct-1914	Thiepval	
Linsenmaier, Wilhelm	Wehrmann	2	11-Oct-1914	Thiepval	K.I.A.
Plapp, Louis	Wehrmann	2	11-Oct-1914	Thiepval	Severely wounded, died 5-Jul-1915, Fortress Hospital Koblenz.
Knauss, Gustav	Wehrmann	4	11-Oct-1914	Bois Brule	???
Banhart, Otto	Reservist	2	12-Oct-1914	Authuille	M.I.A., declared dead.
Jud, Karl	Wehrmann	2	12-Oct-1914	Authuille	M.I.A., declared dead.
Vogt, Wilhelm	Reservist	2	12-Oct-1914	Authuille	Died en route to Lüttich.
Bäuerle, Paul	Gefreiter	M.G.	12-Oct-1914	Thiepval	
Roller, Karl	Reservist	1	13-Oct-1914	Thiepval	
Seemüller, Otto	Reservist	3	13-Oct-1914	Thiepval	
Seeüller, Otto	Reservist	3	13-Oct-1914	Thiepval	
Kern, Ludwig	Reservist	8	13-Oct-1914	Thiepval	W.I.A., died 16-Oct-1914, Military Hospital XI, Bapaume.
Heiss, Wilhelm	Reservist	9	13-Oct-1914	Thiepval	
Röhrle, Wilhelm	Wehrmann	12	13-Oct-1914	Thiepval	W.I.A., died 15-Oct-1914, Miraumont.
Bauer, Friedrich	Wehrmann	10	14-Oct-1914	Thiepval	
Dautel, August	Wehrmann	2	15-Oct-1914	Thiepval	
Hartmann, Gottlob	Wehrmann	2	15-Oct-1914	Authuille	
Krauss, Friedrich	Wehrmann	2	15-Oct-1914	Thiepval	
Meckes, Johannes	Wehrmann	2	15-Oct-1914	Thiepval	
Zeile, Karl	Wehrmann	2	15-Oct-1914	Thiepval	
Bürkle, Adolf	Gefreiter	2	16-Oct-1914	Thiepval	
Hild, Otto	Wehrmann	5	16-Oct-1914	Thiepval	
Weber, Karl	Reservist	12	16-Oct-1914	Thiepval	
Kaufmann, Karl	Gefreiter	M.G.	16-Oct-1914	Thiepval	

RIR 121 NAME	RANK	CO.	DATE OF DEATH	LOCATION	NOTES
Schlotterbeck, Robert	Wehrmann	2	17-Oct-1914	Beaumont	
Sommer, Hermann	Reservist	2	17-Oct-1914	Beaumont	
Zahner, Oskar	Wehrmann	2	17-Oct-1914	Beaumont	
Huber, August	Wehrmann	3	17-Oct-1914	Beaumont	
Klein, Karl	Wehrmann	7	17-Oct-1914	Thiepval	W.I.A., M.I.A., died 18-May-1915 in French hospital, Chartres.
Krapf, Karl	Unteroffizier	7	17-Oct-1914	Thiepval	M.I.A., declared dead.
Speth, Eugen	Wehrmann	10	17-Oct-1914	Thiepval	M.I.A., declared dead.
Truckses, Richard	Ersatz Reservist	10	17-Oct-1914	Thiepval	
Kuhn, Emil	Kriegsfreiwilliger	11	18-Oct-1914	Thiepval	
Schmidt, Philipp	Wehrmann	8	19-Oct-1914	Thiepval	
Ruckhaberle, Wilhelm	Wehrmann	3	20-Oct-1914	Beaumont	
Bauer, Ernst	Wehrmann	4	20-Oct-1914	Beaumont	W.I.A., died 29-Oct-1914 en route to hospital in Bapaume.
Fröschle, Paul	Wehrmann	4	20-Oct-1914	Beaumont	W.I.A., died 21-Oct-1914, Reserve Field Hospital 4.
Lederer, Karl	Reservist	4	20-Oct-1914	Beaumont	
Müller, Adolf	Reservist	4	20-Oct-1914	Beaumont	
Blankenhorn, Karl	Reservist	6	20-Oct-1914	Thiepval	
Bürkle, August	Wehrmann	6	20-Oct-1914	Bapaume	Sick, died 11-Nov-1914, Military Hospital.
Haag, Martin	Wehrmann	6	22-Oct-1914	Thiepval	W.I.A., died 23-Oct-1914, dressing station Thiepval.
Herrmann, Otto	Vizefeldwebel, Offiz. Asp.	12	22-Oct-1914	Thiepval	
Ragg, Wilhelm	Ersatz Reservist	1	23-Oct-1914	Beaucourt	
Bader, Emil	Reservist	5	23-Oct-1914	Thiepval	
Hanselmann, Albert	Wehrmann	10	23-Oct-1914	Thiepval	W.I.A., died 27-Oct-1914, hospital, Miraumont.
Hörrmann, Wilhelm	Gefreiter	11	23-Oct-1914	Thiepval	
Hehr, Karl	Wehrmann	7	25-Oct-1914	Thiepval	
Meissner, August	Wehrmann	10	25-Oct-1914	Thiepval	
Roth, Christian	Reservist	9	26-Oct-1914	Thiepval	
Clauss, August	Wehrmann	8	31-Oct-1914	Thiepval	W.I.A., died 1-Nov-1914, Reserve Hospital 4, Miraumont.
Klumpp, Theodor	Kriegsfreiwilliger	8	31-Oct-1914	Thiepval	
Wäller, Hermann	Wehrmann	1	6-Nov-1914	Thiepval	
Rössler, Georg	Reservist	11	6-Nov-1914	Thiepval	
Kaufmann, Ludwig	Gefreiter	2	7-Nov-1914	Authuille	
Baumann, Ernst	Reservist	10	9-Nov-1914	Thiepval	
Kögel, Wilhelm	Wehrmann	2	11-Nov-1914	Authuille	
Drechsel, Friedrich	Unteroffizier	10	13-Nov-1914	Frankfurt a.M.	Sick, died 19-Jan-1915, Reserve Hospital II.

RIR 121 NAME	RANK	CO.	DATE OF DEATH	LOCATION	NOTES
Hubele, Karl	Wehrmann		13-Nov-1914	St. Brieur	M.I.A., 29-Sep-1914 Authuille, died 11/13/1914 as P.O.W. in French hospital
Wurst, Wilhelm	Ersatz Reservist	9	14-Nov-1914	Thiepval	W.I.A., died 15-Nov-1914, wounded collecting point, Miraumont.
Bäuerle, Friedrich	Wehrmann	3	19-Nov-1914	Thiepval	
Beck, Gustav	Reservist	3	19-Nov-1914	Thiepval	
Wolf, Gottlob	Reservist	3	19-Nov-1914	Thiepval	
Burckhardt, Christian	Wehrmann	6	19-Nov-1914	Thiepval	W.I.A., died 20-Nov-1914, Field Hospital 1, Bapaume.
Fischer, Hermann	Kriegsfreiwilliger	11	25-Nov-1914	Courcelette	
Hirth, otto	Reservist	6	5-Dec-1914	Thiepval	W.I.A., died 5-Dec-1914 en route to dressing station Thiepval.
Mayer, Hermann	Leutnant der Reserve	6	5-Dec-1914	Thiepval	
Schweikle, Eugen	Leutnant der Reserve	6	5-Dec-1914	Thiepval	
Noller, Ernst	Reservist	9	8-Dec-1914	Thiepval	
Schmidt, Karl	Wehrmann	11	8-Dec-1914	Thiepval	W.I.A., died 9-Dec-1914, Miraumont.
Goldschmidt, Julius	Reservist	2 Ersatz	9-Dec-1914	Thiepval	Died in hospital as a result of wounds.
Kächele, Karl	Vizefeldwebel, Offiz. Asp.	5	11-Dec-1914	Thiepval	
Schramm, Karl	Wehrmann	5	11-Dec-1914	Thiepval	
Wöhrle, Hermann	Ersatz Reservist	10	11-Dec-1914	Thiepval	
Läpple, Wilhelm	Wehrmann	12	11-Dec-1914	Thiepval	W.I.A., died 12-Dec-1914, Miraumont.
Mütschele, Gotthold	Wehrmann	10	14-Dec-1914	Thiepval	
Ehmeneck, Ernst	Reservist	12	14-Dec-1914	Thiepval	
Eisele, Ernst	Ersatz Reservist	2	17-Dec-1914	Thiepval	
Faas, Eduard	Ersatz Reservist	2	17-Dec-1914	Thiepval	
Fischer, Otto	Ersatz Reservist	2	17-Dec-1914	Thiepval	
Zerrer, Wilhelm	Ersatz Reservist	2	17-Dec-1914	Thiepval	
Buck, Friedrich	Ersatz Reservist	5	17-Dec-1914	Thiepval	Injured by Very Light accident, died 17-Jan-1915, Reserve Field Hospital 1, Bapaume.
Hermann, Friedrich	Wehrmann	5	17-Dec-1914	Thiepval	
Kemmer, Karl	Kriegsfreiwilliger	5	17-Dec-1914	Thiepval	
Kühnle, Johann	Reservist	9	17-Dec-1914	Thiepval	
Kramer, Anton	Wehrmann	11	17-Dec-1914	Thiepval	
Röger, Leonhard	Wehrmann	11	17-Dec-1914	Thiepval	W.I.A., died 18-Dec-1914, Main Dressing Station, Miraumont.
Schmid, Georg	Reservist	11	17-Dec-1914	Thiepval	

RIR 121 NAME	RANK	CO.	DATE OF DEATH	LOCATION	NOTES
Bochert, Ernst	Ersatz Reservist	2 Ersatz	17-Dec-1914	Thiepval	
Lebzelter, Karl	Ersatz Reservist	2 Ersatz	17-Dec-1914	Thiepval	
Müller, Christian	Ersatz Reservist	2 Ersatz	17-Dec-1914	Thiepval	
Pfähler, Georg	Reservist	2 Ersatz	17-Dec-1914	Thiepval	
Röger, Rudolf	Gefreiter	2 Ersatz	17-Dec-1914	Thiepval	
Winkhardt, Josef	Wehrmann	6	20-Dec-1914	Thiepval	
Kölz, Gottlob	Ersatz Reservist	7	24-Dec-1914	Thiepval	W.I.A., died Reserve Field Hospital 2, Filers, date unknown.
Feinler, Lorenz	Wehrmann	4	25-Dec-1914	Thiepval	W.I.A., 27-Dec-1914, VII Army Corps Hospital, St. Quentin.
Frank, Christian	Wehrmann	9	25-Dec-1914	Thiepval	
Hirsch, Eugen	Wehrmann	1	29-Dec-1914	La Boisselle	
Klaiber, Georg	Reservist	10	31-Dec-1914	Thiepval	
Kircher, Karl	Reservist	10	6-Jan-1915	Thiepval	
Müller, Paul	Reservist	6	7-Jan-1915	Thiepval	W.I.A., died 8-Jan-1915, main dressing station, Miraumont.
Wamsler, Albert	Kriegsfreiwilliger	9	7-Jan-1915	Thiepval	
Nachbar, August	Reservist	5	8-Jan-1915	Thiepval	W.I.A., died 13-Jan-1915, Reserve Field Hospital 1, Bapaume.
Klenk, Christian	Gefreiter	9	8-Jan-1915	Thiepval	
Holzwarth, Gottlob	Wehrmann	10	8-Jan-1915	Thiepval	
Pommerer, Gottlieb	Reservist	10	8-Jan-1915	Thiepval	
Sauther, Wilhelm	Reservist	3	10-Jan-1915	Thiepval	W.I.A., died 14-Jan-1915, Reserve Field Hospital 1, Bapaume.
Bauer, Gottlieb	Wehrmann	4	10-Jan-1915	Thiepval	
Deiss, Karl	Ersatz Reservist	2 Ersatz	13-Jan-1915	Linz am Rhein	Died in Reserve Hospital as a result of wounds.
Wohlfarth, Wilhelm	Wehrmann	10	14-Jan-1915	Thiepval	W.I.A., died 15-Jan-1915, Bapaume.
Adis, Xaver	Unteroffizier	7	17-Jan-1915	Thiepval	
Kohler, Adolf	Reservist	M.G.	17-Jan-1915	Thiepval	
Ruth, Georg	Reservist	9	18-Jan-1915	Thiepval	
Huss, Johannes	Tambour	11	19-Jan-1915	Thiepval	W.I.A., died 28-Feb-1915, Military Hospital b, VII Army Corps.
Karle, Georg	Wehrmann	1	20-Jan-1915	Bapaume	Died of illness.
Laib, Gotthilf	Gefreiter	11	20-Jan-1915	Thiepval	
Fleiner, Wilhelm	Reservist	10	22-Jan-1915	Thiepval	
Widmann, Wilhelm	Reservist	9	23-Jan-1915	Thiepval	W.I.A., died 19-Feb-1915, Reserve Field Hospital 1, Bapaume.
Sinn, Friedrich	Reservist	12	26-Jan-1915	Thiepval	
Schopf, Wilhelm	Ersatz Reservist	1 Ersatz	26-Jan-1915	Thiepval	

RIR 121 NAME	RANK	CO.	DATE OF DEATH	LOCATION	NOTES
Harsch, Friedrich	Gefreiter	5	27-Jan-1915	Thiepval	W.I.A., 20-Jun-1915, Reserve Hospital III< Tübingen.
Schöneck, Christian	Reservist	3	29-Jan-1915	Thiepval	
Kämmle, Jakob	Wehrmann	5	30-Jan-1915	Thiepval	W.I.A., died 25-Feb-1915, Corps Hospital, Hotel Dieu, St. Quentin.
Bender, Friedrich	Reservist	12	30-Jan-1915	Thiepval	
Offenhäuser, Georg	Reservist	12	30-Jan-1915	Thiepval	
Schuhmacher, Andreas	Reservist	12	30-Jan-1915	Thiepval	
Schneller, Christian	Reservist	3	31-Jan-1915	Thiepval	
Ungerer, Friedrich	Gefreiter	9	31-Jan-1915	Thiepval	
Lust, Eugen	Leutnant der Reserve	4	2-Feb-1915	Thiepval	
Josenhans, Otto	Leutnant der Reserve	4	4-Feb-1915	Thiepval	W.I.A., died 24-Feb-1915, Field Hospital XIV Reserve Corps, Bapaume.
Hofmann, August	Wehrmann	5	6-Feb-1915	Thiepval	
Fröschle, Hermann	Reservist	2	16-Feb-1915	Mouquet Farm	
Spleiss, August	Musketier	Recruit	28-Feb-1915	St. Quentin	Died of illness in Military Hospital VII Army Corps.
Laidig, Georg	Reservist	12	4-Mar-1915	Neuss	Sick, died 13-Jun-1915 in Reserve Hospital I.
Neukamm, Anton	Musketier	7	14-Mar-1915	Thiepval	W.I.A., died 22-Mar-1915, Reserve Field Hospital 1, Bapaume.
Mayerdörfer, Josef	Musketier	7	15-Mar-1915	Thiepval	W.I.A., died 16-Mar-1915, Main Dressing Station, Miraumont.
Scheyerle, Georg	Musketier	3	27-Mar-1915	Thiepval	W.I.A., died 27-Mar-1915, in the position.
Kurz, Karl	Musketier	2	28-Mar-1915	Thiepval	W.I.A., died 8-Apr-1915, Reserve Field Hospital 1, Bapaume.
Alt, Wilhelm	Leutnant der Reserve	9	1-Apr-1915	Thiepval	
Häsel, Alfred	Reservist	1	7-Apr-1915	Thiepval	
Wolf, David	Wehrmann	3	7-Apr-1915	Thiepval	W.I.A., died 8-Apr-1915, Reserve Field Hospital 1, Bapaume.
Schneider, Josef	Musketier	3	11-Apr-1915	Thiepval	
Beker, Ludwig	Wehrmann	7	12-Apr-1915	Ovillers	W.I.A., died 12-Apr-1915, Sick Room II/R121, Ovillers-La Boisselle.
Eckstein, Karl	Musketier	4	14-Apr-1915	Thiepval	
Wieland, Gottlob	Reservist	10	22-Apr-1915	Thiepval	
Wagner, Richard	Kriegsfreiwilliger	10	28-Apr-1915	Beaucourt	

RIR 121 NAME	RANK	CO.	DATE OF DEATH	LOCATION	NOTES
Stegmaier, Karl	Kriegsfreiwilliger	10	12-May-1915	Thiepval	
Braun, Karl	Musketier	6	16-May-1915	Ovillers	
Ruff, Gustav	Gefreiter	6	16-May-1915	Ovillers	W.I.A., died 31-May-1915, Reserve Field Hospital 1, Bapaume.
Jäger, Wilhelm	Reservist	10	17-May-1915	Thiepval	W.I.A., died 17-May-1915, Mouquet Farm near Thiepval.
Käser, August	Kriegsfreiwilliger	2	31-May-1915	Thiepval	W.I.A., died 7-Jun-1915, Reserve Field Hospital 1, Bapaume.
Schickert, Karl	Reservist	12	5-Jun-1915	Thiepval	W.I.A., died 12-Jun-1915, Bapaume.
Röser, Robert	Wehrmann	8	8-Jun-1915	Beaumont	W.I.A., died 8-Jun-1915, Krk. S. St., Miraumont
Schmid, Christoph	Ersatz Reservist	8	8-Jun-1915	Beaucourt	
Neukamm, Johann	Musketier	8	9-Jun-1915	Beaumont	
Rummel, Stefan	Musketier	9	9-Jun-1915	Thiepval	
Barthelmeh, Karl	Musketier	6	10-Jun-1915	Beaumont	
Häfner, Gottlieb	Musketier	6	10-Jun-1915	Beaumont	
Völmle, Hugo	Kriegsfreiwilliger	7	10-Jun-1915	Serre	
Abele, Ernst	Wehrmann	8	10-Jun-1915	Beaumont	
Dambacher, Hermann	Ersatz Reservist	8	10-Jun-1915	Beaumont	
Herrlinger, Jakob	Reservist	8	10-Jun-1915	Beaumont	
Keicher, Josef	Ersatz Reservist	8	10-Jun-1915	Beaumont	M.I.A., declared dead.
Lees, Konrad	Musketier	8	10-Jun-1915	Beaumont	
Möhle, Hermann	Wehrmann	8	10-Jun-1915	Beaumont	
Rechkemmer, Ernst	Unteroffizier	8	10-Jun-1915	Beaumont	
Rössler, Georg	Wehrmann	8	10-Jun-1915	Beaumont	
Scharpf, Adolf	Musketier	8	10-Jun-1915	Beaumont	
Schillinger, Wilhelm	Wehrmann	8	10-Jun-1915	Beaumont	
Krämer, Friedrich	Wehrmann	5	11-Jun-1915	Beaumont	W.I.A., died 12-Jun-1915, Reserve Hospital 3, Vélu.
Nädele, Christian	Ersatz Reservist	5	11-Jun-1915	Beaumont	
Öttinger, Adolf	Unteroffizier	5	11-Jun-1915	Beaumont	W.I.A., died 12-Jun-1915, Reserve Field Hospital 1, Bapaume.
Lierheimer, Theodor	Reservist	7	11-Jun-1915	Serre	
Thielecke, Albert	Vizefeldwebel	7	11-Jun-1915	Serre	
Traunecker, Erwin	Kriegsfreiwilliger	8	11-Jun-1915	Grandcourt	
Abele, Johannes	Musketier	5	12-Jun-1915	Beaumont	W.I.A., died 12-Jun-1915, main dressing station, Miraumont.
Enderle, Sebastian	Musketier	5	12-Jun-1915	Beaumont	W.I.A., died 3-Jul-1915, Reserve Field Hospital 1, Bapaume.
Karlein, Alfons	Wehrmann	5	12-Jun-1915	Beaumont	

RIR 121 NAME	RANK	CO.	DATE OF DEATH	LOCATION	NOTES
Krieg, Emil	Wehrmann	5	12-Jun-1915	Beaumont	W.I.A., died 1-Jun-1915, Reserve Field Hospital 1, Bapaume.
Rick, Jakob	Wehrmann	7	12-Jun-1915	Serre	
Waldbauer, Christian	Wehrmann	7	12-Jun-1915	Serre	
Kuhnle, Eduard	Reservist	M.G.	12-Jun-1915	Serre	
Auracher, Friedrich	Ersatz Reservist	5	13-Jun-1915	Beaumont	
Bässler, Richard	?	5	13-Jun-1915	Beaumont	
Benz, Friedrich	Reservist	5	13-Jun-1915	Beaumont	
Blankenhorn, Valentin	Musketier	5	13-Jun-1915	Beaumont	
Brändle, Karl	Kriegsfreiwilliger	5	13-Jun-1915	Beaumont	W.I.A., died 13-Jun-1915, Beaumont.
Bruckgolz, Gustav	Reservist	5	13-Jun-1915	Beaumont	
Goss, Eduard	Gefreiter	5	13-Jun-1915	Beaumont	
Hornberger, Gustav	Hauptmann der Reserve	5	13-Jun-1915	Serre	
Kapfer, Alois	Unteroffizier	5	13-Jun-1915	Beaumont	
Kemmler, Ernst	Musketier	5	13-Jun-1915	Beaumont	
Mayer, Wilhelm	Unteroffizier	5	13-Jun-1915	Beaumont	
Präg, Karl	Musketier	5	13-Jun-1915	Beaumont	
Rudolph, Friedrich	Unteroffizier	5	13-Jun-1915	Beaumont	W.I.A., died 22-Jun-1915, Military Hospital VII Army Corps, St. Quentin.
Sick, Richard	Musketier	5	13-Jun-1915	Beaumont	
Spriegel, Johann	Reservist	5	13-Jun-1915	Beaumont	W.I.A., died 21-Jun-1915, Military Hospital VII Army Corps, St. Quentin.
Stuber, Friedrich	Unteroffizier	5	13-Jun-1915	Beaumont	W.I.A., died 13-Jun-1915, dressing station Beaumont.
Weber, Karl	Ersatz Reservist	5	13-Jun-1915	Beaumont	
Bauer, Karl	Wehrmann	7	13-Jun-1915	Serre	
Belstler, Albert	Musketier	7	13-Jun-1915	Serre	
Bidermann, Reinhold	Musketier	7	13-Jun-1915	Serre	
Braster, Eugen	Musketier	7	13-Jun-1915	Serre	
Buyer, Gottlob	Reservist	7	13-Jun-1915	Serre	
Dietz, Hermann	Musketier	7	13-Jun-1915	Serre	
Handschuh, Xaver	Ersatz Reservist	7	13-Jun-1915	Serre	W.I.A., M.I.A., died 2-Oct-1918 in French P.O.W. camp, Rennes.
Heinzinger, Johann	Musketier	7	13-Jun-1915	Serre	
Heiss, Karl	Reservist	7	13-Jun-1915	Serre	W.I.A., M.I.A., died 16-May-1917, in French P.O.W. camp, Le Chas D'or.
Hildenbrand, Alfons	Reservist	7	13-Jun-1915	Serre	

RIR 121 NAME	RANK	CO.	DATE OF DEATH	LOCATION	NOTES
Hirschmüller, Gottlieb	Gefreiter	7	13-Jun-1915	Serre	M.I.A., declared dead.
Hönes, Jakob	Wehrmann	7	13-Jun-1915	Serre	
Hösle, Karl	Ersatz Reservist	7	13-Jun-1915	Serre	
Jetter, Albert	Musketier	7	13-Jun-1915	Serre	M.I.A., declared dead.
Kaiser, Anselm	Reservist	7	13-Jun-1915	Serre	W.I.A., died 17-Jun-1915, Field Hospital 2, Bapaume.
Kirchner, Karl	Reservist	7	13-Jun-1915	Serre	
Köber, Karl	Musketier	7	13-Jun-1915	Serre	
Lutz, Friedrich	Ersatz Reservist	7	13-Jun-1915	Serre	M.I.A., declared dead.
Müller, August	Wehrmann	7	13-Jun-1915	Serre	M.I.A., declared dead.
Müller, Georg	Wehrmann	7	13-Jun-1915	Serre	W.I.A., died 15-Jun-1915, Field Hospital 1, Bapaume.
Müller, Wilhelm	Unteroffizier	7	13-Jun-1915	Serre	W.I.A., M.I.A., died inBritish P.O.W. camp.
Schäufele, Friedrich	Wehrmann	7	13-Jun-1915	Serre	
Schleh, Albert	Vizefeldwebel	7	13-Jun-1915	Serre	W.I.A., died 6-Jul-1915, Military Hospital VII, St. Quentin.
Seez, Ernst	Wehrmann	7	13-Jun-1915	Serre	
Semet, Albert	Gefreiter	7	13-Jun-1915	Serre	M.I.A., declared dead.
Sommer, Gottlob	Wehrmann	7	13-Jun-1915	Serre	
Stäudle, Wilhelm	Musketier	7	13-Jun-1915	Serre	
Vogelmann, Adolf	Musketier	7	13-Jun-1915	Serre	W.I.A., died 17-Jun-1915, Reserve Field Hospital 2, Bapaume.
Vollmer, Wilhelm	Reservist	7	13-Jun-1915	Serre	
Westen, Johannes	Musketier	7	13-Jun-1915	Serre	M.I.A., declared dead.
Wild, Karl	Musketier	7	13-Jun-1915	Serre	
Nagel, Guido	Hauptmann	II Bn.	13-Jun-1915	Serre	
Bonhorst, Ernst	Schütze	M.G.	13-Jun-1915	Serre	W.I.A., died 14-Jun-1915, Main Dressing Station, Miraumont.
Käss, Gottlieb	Wehrmann	M.G.	13-Jun-1915	Serre	
Löffler, Christian	Gefreiter	M.G.	13-Jun-1915	Serre	
Mühlhaupt, Friedrich	Reservist	M.G.	13-Jun-1915	Serre	M.I.A., died 16-Aug-1917 in French P.O.W. camp, Montfort.
Wolpert, Christian	Unteroffizier	M.G.	13-Jun-1915	Serre	
Breuninger, Heinrich	Musketier	9	14-Jun-1915	Thiepval	
Schwarz, Wilhelm	Wehrmann	6	16-Jun-1915	Ovillers	
Zimmermann, Gottlieb	Wehrmann	4	20-Jun-1915	Thiepval	
Holstein, Otto	Kriegsfreiwilliger, Gefreiter	2	21-Jun-1915	Thiepval	W.I.A., died 22-Jun-1915, Main Dressing Station, Miraumont.

RIR 121 NAME	RANK	CO.	DATE OF DEATH	LOCATION	NOTES
Leins, Wilhelm	Musketier	1	2-Jul-1915	Thiepval	W.I.A., died 30-Aug-1915, St. Quentin
Öckler, Wilhelm	Unteroffizier	9	6-Jul-1915	Thiepval	W.I.A., died 7-Jul-1915, hospital, Miraumont.
Wegmann, Christian	Wehrmann	6	8-Jul-1915	Gmünd	Sick, died 15-Jan-1916, Reserve Hospital 1.
Schiller, Friedrich	Reservist	1	9-Jul-1915	Thiepval	
Noller, Gottlob	Landsturmmann	6	13-Jul-1915	Thiepval	W.I.A., died 14-Jul-1915, Reserve Field Hospital 1, Bapaume.
Fröhlich, Friedrich	Ersatz Reservist	3	15-Jul-1915	Miraumont	
Bässler, Gottlob	Wehrmann	10	19-Jul-1915	Thiepval	W.I.A., died 19-Jul-1915, village sick room, Thiepval .
Heinrich, Gottlob	Wehrmann	10	19-Jul-1915	Thiepval	
Loos, Josef	Musketier	7	24-Jul-1915	Thiepval	
Glaser, Friedrich	Reservist	11	29-Jul-1915	Thiepval	
Zeltwanger, Gottlob	Reservist	11	29-Jul-1915	Thiepval	
Ungerer, Heinrich	Reservist	11	1-Aug-1915	Thiepval	W.I.A., died 2-Aug-1915, Miraumont.
Wied, Gottlieb	Ersatz Reservist	12	6-Aug-1915	Thiepval	W.I.A., died 7-Aug-1915, Miraumont.
Franz, Eugen	Kriegsfreiwilliger	1	9-Aug-1915	Thiepval	
Ludwig, Michael	Landsturm Recruit	5	19-Aug-1915	Gmünd	Died in Reserve Hospital 1.
Weeber, Otto	Gefreiter	6	22-Aug-1915	Thiepval	W.I.A., died 14-Jul-1916, Reserve hospital, Heilbronn.
Dettinger, Franz Josef	Musketier	2	26-Aug-1915	Thiepval	W.I.A., died 26-Aug-1915, in vicinity of Thiepval.
Alber, Werner	Unteroffizier, Kriegsfreiwilliger	4	26-Aug-1915	Authuille	
Maier, Gottlieb	Gefreiter	1	4-Sep-1915	Thiepval	
Falk, Karl	Schütze	M.G.	9-Sep-1915	Thiepval	W.I.A., died 9-Sep-1915, sick room, I/R121, Thiepval.
Weggenmann, Alois	Musketier	5	15-Sep-1915	Thiepval	
Atz, Paul	Ersatz Reservist	8	17-Sep-1915	Thiepval	W.I.A., died 20-Sep-1915, Main Dressing Station, Miraumont.
Niedermaier, Josef	Musketier	9	17-Sep-1915	Thiepval	
Fischer, Friedrich	Musketier	7	18-Sep-1915	Thiepval	W.I.A., died 18-Sep-1915, sick room, Thiepval.
Helmle, Alois	Musketier	7	18-Sep-1915	Thiepval	W.I.A., died 18-Sep-1915, sick room, Thiepval.
Siegle, Albert	Wehrmann	9	19-Sep-1915	Thiepval	
Jenner, Hermann	Musketier	2	21-Sep-1915	Thiepval	W.I.A., died 23-Sep-1915, Reserve Field Hospital 1, Bapaume.
Angerbauer, Jakob	Musketier	12	24-Sep-1915	Thiepval	
Wieland, Hermann	Musketier	5	25-Sep-1915	Thiepval	

RIR 121 NAME	RANK	CO.	DATE OF DEATH	LOCATION	NOTES
Horlacher, Friedrich	Musketier	9	25-Sep-1915	Thiepval	W.I.A., died 26-Sep-1915, main dressing station.
Sammet, Wilhelm	Kriegsfreiwilliger	5	26-Sep-1915	Thiepval	W.I.A., died 26-Sep-1915, dressing station Thiepval.
Strähle, Josef	Landsturmmann	9	26-Sep-1915	Thiepval	W.I.A., died 27-Sep-1915, hospital, Bapaume.
Räuchle, Gotthilf	Ersatz Reservist	5	29-Sep-1915	Thiepval	W.I.A., died 25-Oct-1915, Field Hospital 4, Achiet le Grande.
Meissner, Richard	Reservist	9	5-Oct-1915	Thiepval	W.I.A., died 21-Oct-1915, Military hospital VII Army Corps, St. Quentin.
Hoger, Anton	Musketier	5	6-Oct-1915	Mametz	
Schneider, Gottlieb	Reservist	3	7-Oct-1915	Thiepval	
Fröschle, Albert	Wehrmann	3	8-Oct-1915	Thiepval	
Schäfter, Hermann	Ersatz Reservist	5	9-Oct-1915	Mametz	
Kiemele, Matthäus	Ersatz Reservist	6	11-Oct-1915	Montauban	
Schüle, Wilhelm	Ersatz Reservist	7	12-Oct-1915	Montauban	W.I.A., died 13-Oct-1915, Field Hospital 1, Bapaume.
Müller, Karl	Ersatz Reservist	9	16-Oct-1915	Thiepval	
Wolf, Eugen	Unteroffizier	11	16-Oct-1915	Thiepval	
Hampele, Adolf	Musketier	6	18-Oct-1915	Montauban	
Scheffbuch, Johannes	Ersatz Reservist	10	23-Oct-1915	Thiepval	W.I.A., died 24-Oct-1915, Field Hospital 1, Miraumont.
Riekert, Christian	Landsturmmann	1	27-Oct-1915	Nagold	Sick 27-Oct-1915, died 6-Oct-1916, Reserve Hospital.
Fröscher, Wilhelm	Reservist	3	12-Nov-1915	Thiepval	W.I.A., died 13-Nov-1915, Reserve Hospital 1, Bapaume.
Sulzberger, Christian	Reservist	5	19-Nov-1915	Thiepval	
Dollmann, Karl	Musketier	5	22-Nov-1915	Thiepval	W.I.A., died 22-Nov-1915, dressing station, Thiepval.
Hess, Edwin	Musketier	2	26-Nov-1915	Thiepval	
Schuhmann, Josef	Hornist	10	26-Nov-1915	Thiepval	
Bader, Alois	Wehrmann	11	29-Nov-1915	Thiepval	Killed by accident.
Laauser, Ernst	Reservist	10	5-Dec-1915	Thiepval	
Scheerer, Karl	Unteroffizier	10	5-Dec-1915	Thiepval	
Weber, Karl	Wehrmann	10	7-Dec-1915	Thiepval	
Würtele, Karl	Ersatz Reservist	12	8-Dec-1915	Thiepval	W.I.A., died 9-Dec-1915, Miraumont.
Durner, Georg	Musketier	4	14-Dec-1915	Gmünd	Died of illness, Reserve Hospital I.
Ade, Johann	Unteroffizier	12	15-Dec-1915	Thiepval	
Riehle, Adolf	Wehrmann	2	19-Dec-1915	Gmünd	Died of illness, Reserve Hospital I.
Dölker, Gottlieb	Ersatz Reservist	12	23-Dec-1915	Thiepval	
Geiss, Anton	Gefreiter	12	23-Dec-1915	Thiepval	

RIR 121 NAME	RANK	CO.	DATE OF DEATH	LOCATION	NOTES
Lindner, Wilhelm	Musketier	12	23-Dec-1915	Thiepval	
Schmelzle, Georg	Gefreiter	1	24-Dec-1915	Thiepval	W.I.A., died 25-Dec-1915, Reserve Hospital 1, Bapaume.
Laier, Christian	Ersatz Reservist	4	24-Dec-1915	Thiepval	
Thaiss, Alfred	Wehrmann	4	24-Dec-1915	Thiepval	
Köhler, Friedrich	Wehrmann	10	24-Dec-1915	Thiepval	
Killinger, Karl	Unteroffizier	7	25-Dec-1915	Courcelette	W.I.A., died 26-Dec-1915, Field Hospital 1, Bapaume.
Vollert, Karl	Unteroffizier	12	27-Dec-1915	Thiepval	
Hofmann, Georg	Reservist	12	28-Dec-1915	Thiepval	
Dolderer, Hermann	Wehrmann	10	30-Dec-1915	Marbach	Sick, died 16-Apr-1916, in hospital.
Kleinknecht, Wilhelm	Reservist	9	3-Jan-1916	Thiepval	W.I.A., died 15-Jan-1916, Reserve Field Hospital 1, Bapaume.
Strecker, Karl	Reservist	12	13-Jan-1916	Thiepval	
Gäusbauer, Hermann	Wehrmann	6	14-Jan-1916	Thiepval	
Schöneck, Hermann	Reservist	8	19-Jan-1916	Thiepval	W.I.A., died 20-Jan-1916, Miraumont.
Walter, Augustin	Ersatz Reservist	10	22-Jan-1916	Gmünd	W.I.A., died 22-Jan-1916 from wounds suffered earlier.
Murr, Gustav	Kriegsfreiwilliger	12	24-Jan-1916	Thiepval	
Häfele, Heinrich	Musketier	6	30-Jan-1916	Beaucourt	
Guberau, Wilhelm	Gefreiter	4	2-Feb-1916	Courcelette	
Schneider, Franz	Kriegsfreiwilliger	11	3-Feb-1916	Thiepval	
Wagner, Valentin	Musketier	5	5-Feb-1916	Thiepval	W.I.A., died 6-Feb-1916, Main Dressing Station, Miraumont.
Burger, Gottlob	Kriegsfreiwilliger	11	9-Feb-1916	Thiepval	W.I.A., died 11-Feb-1916, Field Hospital 1, Bapaume.
Frand, Gustav	Ersatz Reservist	1	15-Feb-1916	Thiepval	
Haag, Gottfried	Gefreiter	10	20-Feb-1916	Thiepval	
Reber, Paul	Gefreiter	12	20-Feb-1916	Thiepval	
Tränkle, Karl	Wehrmann	3	26-Feb-1916	Thiepval	
Weihenmayer, Gotthilf	Gefreiter	4	29-Feb-1916	Thiepval	
Breuninger, Wilhelm	Wehrmann	9	2-Mar-1916	Thiepval	
Hohenberger, Karl	Sergeant	12	2-Mar-1916	Thiepval	
Grün, Emil	Reservist	4	13-Mar-1916	Thiepval	
Bässler, Karl	Wehrmann	2	14-Mar-1916	Thiepval	
Hirtreiter, Rupert	Musketier	10	20-Mar-1916	Thiepval	W.I.A., died 20-Mar-1916 in Thiepval.
Megerle, Christian	Reservist	10	3-Apr-1916	Osnabrück	Sick, died 23-Jan-1917 in hospital.

RIR 121 NAME	RANK	CO.	DATE OF DEATH	LOCATION	NOTES
Weiss, Josef	Musketier	4	12-Apr-1916	Gmünd	Died of illness, Reserve Hospital I.
Endriss, Hugo	Musketier	8	15-Apr-1916	Serre	M.I.A., reported killed by enemy.
Dierolf, Wilhelm	Musketier	9	17-Apr-1916	Serre	
Schreiber, Johannes	Gefreiter	9	17-Apr-1916	Serre	W.I.A., died 18-Apr-1916, Reserve Field Hospital 1, Bapaume.
Mannsperger, Wilhelm	Ersatz Reservist	6	21-Apr-1916	Serre	W.I.A., died 21-Apr-1916, dressing staion Serre.
Krimmer, Karl	Kriegsfreiwilliger	5	30-Apr-1916	Serre	
Stephan, Hermann	Wehrmann	10	5-May-1916	Beaumont	Heart attack
Diebold, Friedrich	Musketier	12	10-May-1916	Beaumont	
Fischer, Christian	Musketier	11	11-May-1916	Beaumont	W.I.A., died 12-May-1916, Field Hospital 1, Bapaume.
Oppenländer, Wilhelm	Reservist	6	20-May-1916	Serre	W.I.A., died 24-May-1916, Reserve Field Hospital 1, Bapaume.
Bockstatt, Karl	Landsturmmann	2	21-May-1916	Serre	
Marquardt, Erich	Vizefeldwebel, Offiz. Asp.	2	22-May-1916	Serre	W.I.A., died 23-May-1916, Main Dressing Station, Miraumont.
Wolfart, Otto	Musketier	2	22-May-1916	Serre	M.I.A. Later changed to K.I.A.
Wurster, Franz	Kriegsfreiwilliger	2	22-May-1916	Serre	M.I.A., Killed according to an English list.
Knecht, Johannes	Vizefeldwebel, Offiz. Asp.	2	23-May-1916	Serre	K.I.A.
Dietz, Erwin	Gefreiter	8	23-May-1916	Serre	M.I.A., 23-24-May-1916, declared dead.
Rommel, Emil	Vizefeldwebel, Offiz. Asp.	8	23-May-1916	Beaumont	Severely wounded. Died 29-Oct-1916, Reserve Hospital II, Ludwigsburg.
Weiss, Christian	Musketier	8	23-May-1916	Serre	M.I.A., 23-24-May-1916, declared dead.
Ebert, Johann	Reservist	1	26-May-1916	Serre	Died from wounds
Kuttruff, Wilhelm	Ersatz Reservist	1	26-May-1916	Serre	
Rieger, Johannes	Musketier	1	26-May-1916	Serre	
Allmendinger, Gottlieb	Wehrmann	2	27-May-1916	Serre	W.I.A., died 27-May-1916, Main Dressing Station, Miraumont
Schönherr, Josef	Musketier	2	27-May-1916	Serre	
Sommer, Heinrich	Leutnant der Landwehr	2	1-Jun-1916	Serre	
Mayer, Karl	Wehrmann	3	2-Jun-1916	Thiepval	
Öhler, Gotthilf	Gefreiter	7	3-Jun-1916	Beaumont	W.I.A., died 30-Jun-1916 in the position.

RIR 121 NAME	RANK	CO.	DATE OF DEATH	LOCATION	NOTES
Soulier, Wilhelm	Reservist	4	9-Jun-1916	Caudry	Died in Military Hospital Abteilung 2/IX of blood poisoning.
Michelfelder, Karl	Unteroffizier	3	10-Jun-1916	Serre	
Sigle, Friedrich	Ersatz Reservist	8	10-Jun-1916	Beaumont	W.I.A., died 10-Jun-1916, Field Hospital 1, Bapaume.
Maier, Christian	Wehrmann	4	16-Jun-1916	Serre	
Brukner, Gustav	Gefreiter	6	17-Jun-1916	Beaumont	W.I.A., died 17-Jun-1916, dressing station Beaumont.
Laissle, Ludwig	Landsturmmann	10	18-Jun-1916	Beaumont	
Müller, Alfons	Ersatz Reservist	12	18-Jun-1916	Beaumont	
Lemmermeier, Alois	Musketier	3	19-Jun-1916	Serre	
Gumpfer, Richard	Landsturmmann	4	21-Jun-1916	Serre	
Käs, Eugen	Leutnant der Landwehr	8	21-Jun-1916	Beaumont	W.I.A., died 21-Jun-1916, Dressing Station II/R121.
Frick, Hermann	Ersatz Reservist	6	24-Jun-1916	Serre	W.I.A., died 2-Jun-1917, Reserve Hospital IX, Stuttgart.
Geprägs, Gottfried	Musketier	6	24-Jun-1916	Beaumont	
Reinig, Karl	Gefreiter	3	25-Jun-1916	Serre	W.I.A., died 25-Jun-1916, Reserve Field Hospital 1, Bapaume.
Schippert, Wilhelm	Musketier	3	25-Jun-1916	Serre	Gassed, died 26-Jun-1916, Main Dressing Station, Miraumont.
Schradi, Wilhelm	Unteroffizier	10	25-Jun-1916	Beaumont	W.I.A., died 27-Jun-1916, hospital, Bapaume.
Miller, Georg	Musketier	12	25-Jun-1916	Beaumont	W.I.A., died 25-Jun-1916, Bapaume.
Schlör, Julius	Reservist	12	25-Jun-1916	Beaucourt	
Frhr. von Ziegesar, Hans	Hauptmann	I Bn.	25-Jun-1916	Serre	W.I.A., died 26-Jun-1916, Reserve Field Hospital 1, Bapaume.
Lachenmayer, Ferdinand	Reservist	M.G.	25-Jun-1916	Beaucourt	
Maisch, Karl	Wehrmann	4	26-Jun-1916	Miraumont	
Schaile, Karl	Wehrmann	10	26-Jun-1916	Beaumont	
Kohnle, Albert	Ersatz Reservist	12	26-Jun-1916	Beaumont	
Haug, Karl	Unteroffizier	1	27-Jun-1916	Serre	
Kost, Eugen	Reservist	3	27-Jun-1916	Serre	W.I.A., died 29-Jun-1916, Reserve Field Hospital 1, Bapaume.
Schlaich, Friedrich	Musketier	6	27-Jun-1916	Beaumont	
Bertsch, Karl	Musketier	7	27-Jun-1916	Beaumont	
Rupp, Johann	Musketier	7	27-Jun-1916	Beaumont	
Kögel, Jakob	Hornist	9	27-Jun-1916	Serre	W.I.A., died 28-Jun-1916, Reserve Field Hospital 1, Bapaume.

RIR 121 NAME	RANK	CO.	DATE OF DEATH	LOCATION	NOTES
Stetter, Hermann	Wehrmann	1	28-Jun-1916	Serre	
Klein, Wilhelm	Kriegsfreiwilliger	2	28-Jun-1916	Serre	
Hirner, Alois	Musketier	5	28-Jun-1916	Beaumont	
Reich, Friedrich	Wehrmann	5	28-Jun-1916	Beaumont	
Clauss, Ernst	Musketier	6	28-Jun-1916	Beaumont	
Schilpp, Friedrich	Wehrmann	6	28-Jun-1916	Beaumont	
Hägele, Johann	Ersatz Reservist	7	28-Jun-1916	Beaumont	W.I.A., died 1-Jul-1916, Reserve Field Hospital 2, Vélu.
Daub, Eugen	Ersatz Reservist	M.G.	28-Jun-1916	Beaumont	
Krapf, Karl	Musketier	3	29-Jun-1916	Serre	
Gann, Gottlob	Wehrmann	9	29-Jun-1916	Serre	W.I.A., died 3-Jul-1916, Military Hospital 1, X Army Corps.
Müller, Viktor	Recruit	M.G.	29-Jun-1916	Beaumont	
Kanzler, Georg	Musketier	5	30-Jun-1916	Beaumont	
Merz, Konrad	Ersatz Reservist	5	30-Jun-1916	Beaumont	
Sauter, Rafael	Ersatz Reservist	5	30-Jun-1916	Beaumont	
Schurr, Johannes	Landsturmmann	5	30-Jun-1916	Beaumont	
Blind, Karl	Reservist	8	30-Jun-1916	Beaumont	

IR 180 NAME	RANK	CO.	DATE OF DEATH	LOCATION	NOTES
Digel, Adolf	Reservist	4	27-Sep-1914	Bihucourt	K.I.A., shot in head
Häusler, Wilhelm	Landsturmmann	4	27-Sep-1914	Bihucourt	K.I.A., shot in head
Singer, Lorenz	Musketier	1	29-Sep-1914	Thiepval	Severely wounded right leg, died 4-Dec-1914 at Ver. Hospital Marien Hospital, Münster
Weber, Wilhelm	Reservist	1	29-Sep-1914	Thiepval	Severely wounded in stomach, died
Sauter, Klaus	Leutnant	2	29-Sep-1914	Thiepval	Severely wounded in stomach, died 2-Oct-1914, Field Hospital 1, Bapaume
Bödding, Bernhard	Kriegsfreiwilliger	3	29-Sep-1914	Authuille	Severely wounded in back, died 18-Oct-1914, Auxiliary Hospital Burgsteinfurt
Bofinger, Gustav	Ersatz Reservist	3	29-Sep-1914	Authuille	M.I.A., declared dead.
Bölzle, Heinrich	Reservist	3	29-Sep-1914	Authuille	Severely wounded in leg, died 27-Nov-1914 Reserve Hospital III, Aachen, Luisen Hospital
Fritz, Albrecht	Reservist	3	29-Sep-1914	Thiepval	
Froriep, Max	Kriegsfreiwilliger	3	29-Sep-1914	Authuille	M.I.A., declared dead.
Fuchs, Gustav	Musketier	3	29-Sep-1914	Authuille	M.I.A., declared dead. (Severely wounded in leg)

IR 180

NAME	RANK	CO.	DATE OF DEATH	LOCATION	NOTES
Gnamm, Hans	Fahnenjunker/ Unteroffizier	3	29-Sep-1914	Authuille	M.I.A., declared dead.
Guhl, Friedrich	Reservist	3	29-Sep-1914	Authuille	M.I.A., declared dead.
Haug, Johannes	Reservist	3	29-Sep-1914	Authuille	Severely wounded both legs, died 21-Oct-1914 Württemberg Reserve Field Hospital 1, Bapaume
Jahn, Hermann	Musketier	3	29-Sep-1914	Authuille	M.I.A., declared dead.
Kaltenmark, Paul	Reservist	3	29-Sep-1914	Authuille	
Mack, Theodor	Gefreiter	3	29-Sep-1914	Authuille	M.I.A., declared dead. (Slightly wounded right leg)
Merz, Eugen	Musketier	3	29-Sep-1914	Authuille	Severely wounded right leg, died 30-Sep-1914, Field Hospital I, Bapaume
Neuscheler, Christian	Reservist	3	29-Sep-1914	Authuille	M.I.A., declared dead.
Reusch, Georg	Ersatz Reservist	3	29-Sep-1914	Authuille	M.I.A., declared dead.
Thaler, Joseph	Reservist	3	29-Sep-1914	Authuille	M.I.A., declared dead.
Tröscher, Wilhelm	Tambour	3	29-Sep-1914	Authuille	
Wanderer, Traugott	Kriegsfreiwilliger	3	29-Sep-1914	Authuille	M.I.A., declared dead.
Wittel, Aloisius	Reservist	3	29-Sep-1914	Authuille	M.I.A., declared dead. (Slightly wounded)
Zwanger, Karl	Musketier	3	29-Sep-1914	Authuille	M.I.A., declared dead.
Boley, Heinrich	Gefreiter der Landwehr	4	29-Sep-1914	Pozières	M.I.A., declared dead.
Duttlinger, Fritz	Unteroffizier	4	29-Sep-1914	Pozières	K.I.A., shot in head
Finkbeiner, Georg	Wehrmann	4	29-Sep-1914	Pozières	M.I.A., declared dead. (Slightly wounded)
Karrer, Gottlieb	Reservist	4	29-Sep-1914	Pozières	
Knecht, Anton	Musketier	4	29-Sep-1914	Pozières	M.I.A., declared dead.
Kost, Paul	Unteroffizier	4	29-Sep-1914	Pozières	M.I.A., declared dead.
Kuhn, Albert	Wehrmann	4	29-Sep-1914	Pozières	M.I.A., declared dead.
Lang, Ludwig	Gefreiter der Reserve	4	29-Sep-1914	Pozières	M.I.A., declared dead.
Lemmerz, Richard	Unteroffizier	4	29-Sep-1914	Pozières	K.I.A., shot in head
Reichle, Johannes	Vizefeldwebel	4	29-Sep-1914	Pozières	K.I.A., shot in head
Schöllkopf, Christian	Musketier	4	29-Sep-1914	Pozières	M.I.A., declared dead. (Slightly wounded right leg)
Trück, Christian	Wehrmann	4	29-Sep-1914	Pozières	M.I.A., declared dead.
Uber, Gerhard	Gefreiter der Reserve	4	29-Sep-1914	Pozières	W.I.A., C.I.A., died of wounds 4-Oct-1914 in French P.O.W. Camp. Senlis, Somme
Wagner, Maximilian	Unteroffizier	4	29-Sep-1914	Pozières	M.I.A., declared dead.
Welsch, Friedrich	Reservist	4	29-Sep-1914	Pozières	M.I.A., declared dead.
Frisch, Hermann	Unteroffizier	5	29-Sep-1914	Thiepval	
Kicherer, Wilhelm	Musketier	5	29-Sep-1914	Thiepval	

IR 180

NAME	RANK	CO.	DATE OF DEATH	LOCATION	NOTES
Mahle, Karl	Gefreiter der Reserve	5	29-Sep-1914	Thiepval	
Schaal, Karl	Reservist	5	29-Sep-1914	Thiepval	
Traub, Hermann	Reservist	5	29-Sep-1914	Thiepval	
Geck, Otto	Gefreiter der Reserve	6	29-Sep-1914	Thiepval	
Krebser, Paul	Vizefeldwebel der Reserve	6	29-Sep-1914	Thiepval	Severely wounded in head, died 8-Oct-1914, Württemberg Reserve Field Hospital 3, Ligny-Thilloy
Rieder, Julius	Kriegsfreiwilliger	6	29-Sep-1914	Thiepval	Severely wounded right arm, left leg, died 10-Oct-1914, Military Hospital 4, Augusta Hospital Köln
Schüle, Christian	Reservist	6	29-Sep-1914	Thiepval	
Stegmaier, Johannes	Gefreiter der Reserve	6	29-Sep-1914	Thiepval	K.I.A., shot in head
Traub, Gottfried	Reservist	6	29-Sep-1914	Thiepval	K.I.A., shot in head
Volkland, Emil	Musketier	6	29-Sep-1914	Thiepval	
Britsch, Friedrich	Kriegsfreiwilliger	8	29-Sep-1914	Thiepval	W.I.A., C.I.A., died 25-Nov-1914 in P.O.W. Camp Hop. Tarbes
Holder, Adam	Musketier	8	29-Sep-1914	Thiepval	W.I.A., C.I.A., died 8-Oct-1914 in French P.O.W. Camp Caserne Guebriant St. Brieux
Holzschub, Viktor	Kriegsfreiwilliger	8	29-Sep-1914	Thiepval	M.I.A., declared dead
Koch, Otto	Reservist	8	29-Sep-1914	Thiepval	W.I.A., died 15-Oct-1914, Reserve Hospital Julius-Spital, Würzburg
Kochendörfer, Martin	Gefreiter	8	29-Sep-1914	Thiepval	M.I.A., declared dead. (Wounded)
Lamotke, Otto	Unteroffizier der Reserve	8	29-Sep-1914	Thiepval	M.I.A., declared dead. (Wounded)
Metzger, Julius	Reservist	8	29-Sep-1914	Thiepval	M.I.A., declared dead.
Schmid, Martin	Unteroffizier der Landwehr	8	29-Sep-1914	Thiepval	
Auwärter, Ernst	Reservist	9	29-Sep-1914	Thiepval	
Bässler, Karl	Reservist	9	29-Sep-1914	Thiepval	
Beck, Friedrich	Musketier	9	29-Sep-1914	Thiepval	
Benzenhöfer, Ernst	Reservist	9	29-Sep-1914	Thiepval	Severely wounded right leg and right arm, died 29-Sep-1914 in Württemberg Reserve Field Hospital 1, Bapaume
Bulling, Bernhard	Musketier	9	29-Sep-1914	Thiepval	Severely wounded right leg, left arm. Died from wounds
Eisele, Johannes	Krankenträger	9	29-Sep-1914	Thiepval	
Fetscher, August	Musketier	9	29-Sep-1914	Thiepval	

IR 180

NAME	RANK	CO.	DATE OF DEATH	LOCATION	NOTES
Frank, Friedrich	Musketier	9	29-Sep-1914	Thiepval	Severely wounded left leg and head, died 31-Oct-1914, Reserve Hospital II, Aachen
Heinzmann, Johannes	Landsturmmann	9	29-Sep-1914	Thiepval	K.I.A. Shot in chest
Hohlbauch, Otto	Musketier	9	29-Sep-1914	Thiepval	
Joos, Jakob	Reservist	9	29-Sep-1914	Thiepval	Severely wounded in chest, died 14-Oct-1914, Reserve Hospital II, Aachen
Kaiser, Joseph	Medical Gefreiter	9	29-Sep-1914	Thiepval	K.I.A., shot in head
Kottler, Philipp	Musketier	9	29-Sep-1914	Thiepval	Severely wounded in head, died 29-Sep-1914, before hospital treatment
Pfitzenmaier, Albert	Musketier	9	29-Sep-1914	Thiepval	Slightly wounded left leg, died 30-Oct-1914, Reserve Hospital II, Aachen
Riffel, Karl	Musketier	9	29-Sep-1914	Thiepval	K.I.A., shot in back
Ruoff, Friedrich	Musketier	9	29-Sep-1914	Thiepval	
Schäffler, Ernst	Reservist	9	29-Sep-1914	Thiepval	Died from wounds
Schmid, Xaver	Reservist	9	29-Sep-1914	Thiepval	Severely wounded, head, died 22-Oct-1914, Reserve Hospital St. Vonzenz, Köln-Nippes
Staudt, Gottlieb	Reservist	9	29-Sep-1914	Thiepval	Severely wounded right leg, died 8-Oct-1914, Reserve Hospital 5, Jünglingsheim, Aachen
Stippler, Friedrich	Reservist	9	29-Sep-1914	Thiepval	Severely wounded right leg, died 5-Oct-1915, Military Hospital, Mons
Lang, Artur	Musketier	10	29-Sep-1914	Thiepval	
Sanwald, August	Reservist	10	29-Sep-1914	Thiepval	K.I.A., shot in head
Strohmaier, Wilhelm	Musketier	11	29-Sep-1914	Thiepval	
Aufschlag, Ernst	Reservist	12	29-Sep-1914	Thiepval	K.I.A., shot in head
Votteler, Wilhelm	Musketier	12	29-Sep-1914	Thiepval	K.I.A., shot in chest
von Haldenwang, Hermann	Oberstleutnant	Regt. Staff	29-Sep-1914	Thiepval	W.I.A., died 29-Sep-1914 in Württemberg Reserve Field Hospital 1, Bapaume. (K.I.A.)
List, Karl	Wehrmann	1	30-Sep-1914	Pozières	K.I.A., shot in head
Dannecker, Georg	Musketier	2	30-Sep-1914	Authuille	
Roeker, Daniel	Musketier	3	30-Sep-1914	Thiepval	W.I.A., died 1-Oct-1914, Main Dressing Station
Baumann, Josef	Reservist	5	30-Sep-1914	Thiepval	
Closs, Rudolf	Musketier	5	30-Sep-1914	Thiepval	Severely wounded. Died from wounds
Dannenmann, Karl	Kriegsfreiwilliger	5	30-Sep-1914	Thiepval	Severely wounded. Died from wounds
Frech, Alois	Hornist	5	30-Sep-1914	Thiepval	

IR 180

NAME	RANK	CO.	DATE OF DEATH	LOCATION	NOTES
Götze, Gustav	Musketier	5	30-Sep-1914	Thiepval	
Grupp, Bernhard	Reservist	5	30-Sep-1914	Thiepval	Severely wounded, died 1-Oct-1914, Württemberg Field Hospital, Bapaume
Hopphan, Friedrich	Ersatz Reservist	5	30-Sep-1914	Thiepval	
Kottmann, Augustin	Reservist	5	30-Sep-1914	Thiepval	Severely wounded, died 1-Oct-1914, Reserve Medical Company 26, Le Sars
Rommel, Robert	Musketier	5	30-Sep-1914	Thiepval	Severely wounded, died 2-Oct-1914, Württemberg Field Hospital 3, Ligny-Tilloy
Schlotterbeck, Christian	Musketier	5	30-Sep-1914	Thiepval	Severely wounded, died 5-Oct-1914, Württemberg Reserve Field Hospital 3, Ligny-Tilloy
Sontheim, Ludwig	Musketier	5	30-Sep-1914	Thiepval	
Weber, Karl	Gefreiter der Reserve	5	30-Sep-1914	Thiepval	
Albrecht, Andreas	Musketier	6	30-Sep-1914	Thiepval	
Angele, Heinrich	Reservist	6	30-Sep-1914	Thiepval	Severely wounded, right leg, died 2-Oct-1914, Württemberg Field Hospital 3, Ligny-Tilloy
Bauer, Gottlob	Musketier	6	30-Sep-1914	Thiepval	
Baur, Elias	Reservist	6	30-Sep-1914	Thiepval	
Bosch, Gustav	Reservist	6	30-Sep-1914	Thiepval	
Braun, Friedrich	Unteroffizier der Reserve	6	30-Sep-1914	Thiepval	
Erhard, Anton	Reservist	6	30-Sep-1914	Thiepval	
Göggelmann, Christian	Musketier	6	30-Sep-1914	Thiepval	
Klein, Gottlieb	Musketier	6	30-Sep-1914	Thiepval	
Remmlinger, Franz	Reservist	6	30-Sep-1914	Thiepval	
Sauer, Friedrich	Reservist	6	30-Sep-1914	Thiepval	
Schäfer, Hermann	Reservist	6	30-Sep-1914	Thiepval	
Schempp, Christian	Reservist	6	30-Sep-1914	Thiepval	
Schneckenburger, Wilhelm	Reservist	6	30-Sep-1914	Thiepval	
Wokenmann, Alfred	Vizefeldwebel	6	30-Sep-1914	Thiepval	
Bertiller, Gustav	Wehrmann	7	30-Sep-1914	Thiepval	
Birkelmann, Georg	Musketier	7	30-Sep-1914	Thiepval	
Blatt, Eugen	Musketier	7	30-Sep-1914	Thiepval	Severely wounded, right arm and back, died 24-Oct-1914, Military Hospital, Mons
Eitelhuber, Ludwig	Reservist	7	30-Sep-1914	Thiepval	Severely wounded, head and hip, died 11-Mar-1915, Aachen
Knoblich, Karl	Unteroffizier	7	30-Sep-1914	Thiepval	K.I.A.

IR 180

NAME	RANK	CO.	DATE OF DEATH	LOCATION	NOTES
Speidel, Markus	Wehrmann	7	30-Sep-1914	Thiepval	Severely wounded left leg, died 8-Oct-1914, Reserve Hospital Aachen
Spörner, Karl	Gefreiter der Reserve	7	30-Sep-1914	Thiepval	Severely wounded, head and left leg, died 16-Oct-1914, Reserve Hospital II, Aachen
Trinkle, Albert	Reservist	7	30-Sep-1914	Thiepval	Severely wounded, left leg and hip, died 30-Sep-1914 during transport to the dressing station in Le Sars
Dennochweiler, Alfons	Gefreiter	8	30-Sep-1914	Thiepval	
Hiemer, Alfred	Kriegsfreiwilliger	8	30-Sep-1914	Thiepval	
Göhring, Hermann	Musketier	10	30-Sep-1914	Thiepval	W.I.A., died 1-Feb-1915, Military Hospital 4, Augusta Hospital, Koblenz
Haug, Georg	Reservist	10	30-Sep-1914	Thiepval	
Koppenhöfer, Georg	Tambour	10	30-Sep-1914	Thiepval	
Nübel, Wilhelm	Musketier	10	30-Sep-1914	Thiepval	
Schwab, Ernst	Reservist	10	30-Sep-1914	Thiepval	
Steinle, Wilhelm	Musketier	10	30-Sep-1914	Thiepval	
Diebold, Oskar	Reservist	12	30-Sep-1914	Thiepval	
Knödler, Florian	Reservist	12	30-Sep-1914	Thiepval	Died from wounds
Möck, Karl	Gefreiter der Reserve	12	30-Sep-1914	Thiepval	
Beisser, Johann	Musketier	5	1-Oct-1914	Thiepval	
Egner, Otto	Reservist	5	1-Oct-1914	Thiepval	
Häderle, Gustav	Kriegsfreiwilliger	5	1-Oct-1914	Thiepval	
Epple, Wilhelm	Musketier	6	1-Oct-1914	Thiepval	
Kugler, Gotthilf	Reservist	6	1-Oct-1914	Thiepval	
Schmid, Friedrich	Reservist	6	1-Oct-1914	Thiepval	
Seifried, Wilhelm	Musketier	6	1-Oct-1914	Thiepval	W.I.A., died 12-Oct-1914, Military Hospital 3, Brussels
Scheubing, Hermann	Musketier	7	1-Oct-1914	Thiepval	
Birk, Christian	Musketier	8	1-Oct-1914	Thiepval	
Eifrig, Kurt	Musketier	8	1-Oct-1914	Thiepval	
Pietzcker, Franz	Leutnant der Reserve	8	1-Oct-1914	Thiepval	
Enz, Wilhelm	Musketier	9	1-Oct-1914	Thiepval	
Oesterle, Friedrich	Ersatz Reservist	9	1-Oct-1914	Thiepval	
Haiber, Emil	Reservist	6	2-Oct-1914	Thiepval	
Maier, Friedrich	Unteroffizier der Reserve	6	2-Oct-1914	Thiepval	
Richter, Hugo	Reservist	6	2-Oct-1914	Thiepval	
Anderer, Josef	Musketier	12	2-Oct-1914	Thiepval	W.I.A., died 4-Oct-1914, Reserve Field Hospital III, Ligny-Tilloy

IR 180

NAME	RANK	CO.	DATE OF DEATH	LOCATION	NOTES
Kromer, Hermann	Ersatz Reservist	12	2-Oct-1914	Thiepval	M.I.A., declared dead.
Nubing, August	Reservist	12	2-Oct-1914	Thiepval	
Walter, Christian	Musketier	12	2-Oct-1914	Thiepval	
Kehret, Friedrich	Unteroffizier	1 MG Co.	2-Oct-1914	Thiepval	
Kingeter, Eugen	Schütze	1 MG Co.	2-Oct-1914	Thiepval	
Weber, Albert	Schütze	1 MG Co.	2-Oct-1914	Thiepval	
Mangold, Georg	Musketier	10	3-Oct-1914	Thiepval	W.I.A., died 3-Oct-1914 during transport to the rear
Daferner, Wilhelm	Musketier	12	3-Oct-1914	Thiepval	
Rall, August	Musketier	12	3-Oct-1914	Thiepval	
Storz, Heinrich	Vizefeldwebel der Reserve	12	3-Oct-1914	Thiepval	
Neher, Heinrich	Musketier	2	4-Oct-1914	Pozières	W.I.A., died 11-Oct-1914, Field Hospital 1, Bapaume
Storz, Karl	Reservist	2	4-Oct-1914	Pozières	W.I.A., died 5-Oct-1914, Württemberg Field Hospital 1, Bapaume
Glein, Karl	Kriegsfreiwilliger	12	4-Oct-1914	Thiepval	M.I.A., declared dead.
Hägele, Johannes	Musketier	12	4-Oct-1914	Thiepval	W.I.A., died 4-Oct-1914 during transport to dressing station
Kuttler, Ulrich	Wehrmann	4	5-Oct-1914	Pozières	W.I.A., died 7-Oct-1914, Reserve Field Hospital IV, Miraumont
Wiech, Anton	Reservist	4	5-Oct-1914	Thiepval	
Bohm, Josef	Vizefeldwebel	6	5-Oct-1914	Thiepval	
Lutz, Heinrich	Musketier	6	5-Oct-1914	Thiepval	W.I.A., died 7-Oct-1914, Württemberg Reserve Field Hospital 3, Ligny-Thilloy
Stiefel, Jakob	Musketier	10	5-Oct-1914	Thiepval	
Mauz, Karl	Musketier	12	5-Oct-1914	Thiepval	
Steinorth, Karl	Unteroffizier der Reserve	1	6-Oct-1914	Pozières/Thiepval	K.I.A. either 5 Oct or 6-Oct-1914, shot in head
Allmendinger, Edmund	Unteroffizier	5	6-Oct-1914	Thiepval	W.I.A., died 12-Oct-1914, Military Hospital 4, Cöln zu Brüssel
König, Hugo	Musketier	9	6-Oct-1914	Paris	W.I.A., C.I.A., died in French P.O.W. Camp, L'Hopital Militaire du Walde de Garce, Paris
Haller, Wilhelm	Landsturmmann	10	6-Oct-1914	Thiepval	
Kirn, Johannes	Kriegsfreiwilliger	10	6-Oct-1914	Thiepval	
Steinhilber, Ernst	Kriegsfreiwilliger	12	6-Oct-1914	Thiepval	W.I.A., died 21-Oct-1914, Military Hospital, Cambrai
Blessing, Franz-Xaver	Reservist	10	7-Oct-1914	Thiepval	
Müller, Alfred	Musketier	11	7-Oct-1914	Thiepval	
Schneider, Friedrich	Musketier	11	7-Oct-1914	Thiepval	

IR 180

NAME	RANK	CO.	DATE OF DEATH	LOCATION	NOTES
Schneider, Gottlob	Reservist	11	7-Oct-1914	Thiepval	M.I.A., declared dead.
Abele, Franz	Gefreiter der Reserve	12	8-Oct-1914	Thiepval	
Herzer, Anton	Musketier	12	8-Oct-1914	Thiepval	W.I.A., died 10-Oct-1914, Reserve Field Hospital 3, Miraumont
Leinmüller, Josef	Reservist	10	9-Oct-1914	Thiepval	
Wössner, Adolf	Reservist	10	9-Oct-1914	Thiepval	W.I.A., died 6-Nov-1914, Reserve Hospital Sick House, Reutlingen
Grau, Hermann	Reservist	10	10-Oct-1914	Thiepval	
Dreber, Albert	Musketier	10	11-Oct-1914	Thiepval	
Sauter, Joseph	Wehrmann	10	11-Oct-1914	Thiepval	
Ballreich, Friedrich	Leutnant	11	12-Oct-1914	Thiepval	
Weiss, Max	Musketier	1	14-Oct-1914	Thiepval	
Getto, Oskar	Gefreiter der Reserve	7	15-Oct-1914	Thiepval	W.I.A., died 18-Oct-1914, Reserve Field Hospital 1, Miraumont
Ammann, Karl	Musketier	11	15-Oct-1914	Thiepval	Died from wounds, 14-Oct/15-Oct-1914
Maile, Johannes	Musketier	12	15-Oct-1914	Thiepval	Died from wounds
Frank, Hermann	Gefreiter der Reserve	12	16-Oct-1914	Thiepval	W.I.A., 16-Oct-1914, Reserve Hospital 4, Miraumont
Krauss, Gottlob	Gefreiter der Reserve	2	18-Oct-1914	Thiepval	
Stahl, Richard	Kriegsfreiwilliger	2	18-Oct-1914	Thiepval	
Ortlieb, Ernst	Musketier	6	19-Oct-1914	Thiepval	W.I.A., died 20-Sep-1914, Dressing Station Miraumont
Steeb, Alfons	Unteroffizier	6	19-Oct-1914	Thiepval	W.I.A., died 22-Oct-1914, Field Hospital 4, Miraumont
Ballweg, Karl	Kriegsfreiwilliger	10	20-Oct-1914	Thiepval	M.I.A., declared dead.
Holzinger, Theodor	Kriegsfreiwilliger	10	20-Oct-1914	Thiepval	M.I.A., declared dead.
Kürner, Gotthilf	Kriegsfreiwilliger	10	20-Oct-1914	Thiepval	M.I.A., declared dead.
Wenzel, Hermann	Kriegsfreiwilliger	5	21-Oct-1914	Thiepval	W.I.A., died 24-Oct-1914, Field Hospital4, Miraumont
Richter, Mortiz	Kriegsfreiwilliger	2	22-Oct-1914	Thiepval	W.I.A., died 23-Oct-1914, Field Hospital 4, Miraumont
Kern, Karl	Kriegsfreiwilliger	10	22-Oct-1914	Thiepval	W.I.A., died 22-Oct-1914, Grandcourt
Geist, Adolf	Reservist	6	25-Oct-1914	Thiepval	
Rieth, Friedrich	Reservist	5	26-Oct-1914	Thiepval	
Schweizer, Theodor	Kriegsfreiwilliger	10	26-Oct-1914	Thiepval	
Klein, Georg	Reservist	6	27-Oct-1914	Thiepval	W.I.A., died 30-Oct-1914, Württemberg Reserve Field Hospital, Miraumont
Flogaus, Christian	Oberleutnant der Reserve	4	28-Oct-1914	Mouquet Farm	

IR 180

NAME	RANK	CO.	DATE OF DEATH	LOCATION	NOTES
Krause, Artur	Major	I Bn. Staff	28-Oct-1914	Mouquet Farm	Died 24-Apr-1915 with III/RIR247 as a result of his wound
Kurz, Albert	Musketier	1	31-Oct-1914	Courcelette	W.I.A., died 31-Oct-1914 in Reserve Hospital 4, Miraumont
Schnizer, Friedrich	Kriegsfreiwilliger	7	1-Nov-1914	Thiepval	
Schnizer, Otto	Kriegsfreiwilliger	7	1-Nov-1914	Thiepval	
Röder, Hermann	Musketier	5	2-Nov-1914	Thiepval	W.I.A., 12-Nov-1914, Military Hospital, Mons
Frech, Eugen	Musketier	11	4-Nov-1914	Thiepval	
Munk, Otto	Musketier	1 MG Co.	4-Nov-1914	Thiepval	
Dietz, Karl	Reservist	5	6-Nov-1914	Thiepval	W.I.A., died 7-Nov-1914, Reserve Hospital 4, Miraumont
Keller, Max	Kriegsfreiwilliger	5	9-Nov-1914	Thiepval	W.I.A., died 9-Nov-1914, Württemberg Reserve Field Hospital 4, Miraumont.
Mosthaf, Karl	Unteroffizier	1 MG Co.	10-Nov-1914	Thiepval	Died from illness
Sigel, Karl	Vizefeldwebel/Off. Replacement	1 MG Co.	10-Nov-1914	Thiepval	Died from illness
Riester, Anton	Gefreiter Krankenträger	5	11-Nov-1914	Thiepval	W.I.A., died 12-Nov-1914, Military Hospital, Bapaume
Trosse, Paul	Reservist	5	11-Nov-1914	Thiepval	
Maher, Matthias	Reservist	5	14-Nov-1914	Thiepval	
Wacker, Thomas	Kriegsfreiwilliger	9	14-Nov-1914	Thiepval	W.I.A., died 19-Nov-1914, Field Hospital 1, Bapaume
Gogel, Albert	Gefreiter der Reserve	8	16-Nov-1914	Thiepval	
Maier, Johann	Reservist	6	22-Nov-1914	Thiepval	W.I.A., died 22-Nov-1914, Main Dressing Station Württemberg Reserve Medical Company Miraumont
Strotbeck, Albert	Musketier	8	24-Nov-1914	Thiepval	
Schmidt, Karl	Gefreiter der Reserve	6	25-Nov-1914	Thiepval	
Rädle, Hermann	Kriegsfreiwilliger	5	27-Nov-1914	Thiepval	W.I.A., died 14-Dec-1914, Field Hospital 1, Bapaume
Gölz, Karl	Reservist	8	30-Nov-1914	Thiepval	
Harr, Erich	Fahnenjunker	8	30-Nov-1914	Thiepval	
Hirsch, Milton	Reservist	8	30-Nov-1914	Thiepval	
Legat, Ferdinand	Kriegsfreiwilliger	8	30-Nov-1914	Thiepval	
Heinel, Friedrich	Landsturmmann	3	4-Dec-1914	Tübingen	Died from illness, Reserve Hospital 1, Tübingen
Hähnle, Eugen	Reservist	10	8-Dec-1914	Thiepval	W.I.A., died 16-Dec-1914, Württemberg Field Hospital 1, Bapaume
Kirch, Hermann	Kriegsfreiwilliger	6	9-Dec-1914	Thiepval	

IR 180

NAME	RANK	CO.	DATE OF DEATH	LOCATION	NOTES
Fischer, Rudolf	Reservist	6	10-Dec-1914	Thiepval	
Maier, Albert	Reservist	2	17-Dec-1914	Authuille	
Mändle, August	Musketier	2	17-Dec-1914	Authuille	
Rieth, Paul	Unteroffizier	2	17-Dec-1914	Authuille	
Schurr, Julius	Ersatz Reservist	5	17-Dec-1914	Thiepval	
Bulling, Matthäus	Reservist	5	19-Dec-1914	Thiepval	Died from wounds
Bopp, Josef	Reservist	8	19-Dec-1914	Thiepval	
Lieb, Wilhelm	Vizefeldwebel	5	20-Dec-1914	Thiepval	
Bürle, August	Reservist	8	24-Dec-1914	Thiepval	
Leuze, Wilhelm	Gefreiter	7	26-Dec-1914	Thiepval	
Alf, Wilhelm	Musketier	11	27-Dec-1914	Thiepval	W.I.A., died 7-Jan-1915, Württemberg Reserve Field Hospital 1, Bapaume
Zeller, Friedrich	Kriegsfreiwilliger	10	3-Jan-1915	Thiepval	
Schmierer, Johannes	Ersatz Reservist	12	3-Jan-1915	St. Pierre-Divion	W.I.A., died 5-Feb-1915, Reserve Field Hospital 1, Bapaume
Sattler, Matthäus	Reservist	2	5-Jan-1915	Thiepval	
Langenbucher, Michael	Reservist	9	11-Jan-1915	Thiepval	W.I.A., died 12-Jan-1915, Württemberg Reserve Field Hospital, Bapaume
Stöcker, Hermann	Musketier	10	11-Jan-1915	Thiepval	W.I.A., died 27-Jan-1915, Military Hospital 7, St. Quentin
Kraut, Max	Leutnant der Reserve	11	11-Jan-1915	Serre	W.I.A., died 7-Nov-1915, Württemberg Reserve Field Hospital 1, Bapaume
Haag, Friedrich	Musketier	12	11-Jan-1915	Thiepval	
Eisler, Martin	Musketier	5	12-Jan-1915	Thiepval	W.I.A., died 23-Feb-1915, Württemberg Field Hospital 1, Bapaume
Schradin, Heinrich	Kriegsfreiwilliger	5	12-Jan-1915	Thiepval	
Käfel, Hermann	Reservist	4	14-Jan-1915	Courcelette	
Junginger, Leonhard	Musketier	11	14-Jan-1915	Thiepval	
Stalter, Josef	Unteroffizier	8	15-Jan-1915	Serre	Died from wounds
Gauss, Anton	Unteroffizier	12	21-Jan-1915	Thiepval	W.I.A., died 28-Jan-1915, Württemberg Reserve Field Hospital 1, Bapaume
Hieber, Eugen	Kriegsfreiwilliger	8	25-Jan-1915	Thiepval	
Keck, Wilhelm	Musketier	12	25-Jan-1915	Thiepval	W.I.A., died 5-Feb-1915, Auxiliary Hospital Schlüchtern-Kassel
Schwarz, Hermann	Gefreiter	1MGCo.	29-Jan-1915	Thiepval	Died from wounds
Ruoff, Ludwig	Musketier	11	31-Jan-1915	Thiepval	
Greiner, Karl	Musketier	2	5-Feb-1915	Thiepval	W.I.A., died 5-Feb-1915, barracks, Thiepval
Mayer, August	Reservist	7	9-Feb-1915	St. Pierre-Divion	W.I.A., died 14-Feb-1915, Bapaume

IR 180

NAME	RANK	CO.	DATE OF DEATH	LOCATION	NOTES
Hutt, Ferdinand	Reservist	11	9-Feb-1915	Thiepval	W.I.A., died 2-Apr-1915, Württemberg Reserve Field Hospital 1, Bapaume
Müller, Ernst	Musketier	Ersatz Bn	14-Feb-1915	Tübingen	Died from illness, Reserve Hospital 1, Tübingen
Alle, Wilhelm	Ersatz Reservist	5	16-Feb-1915	Thiepval	
Baumann, Ernst	Landsturmmann	Ersatz Bn	17-Feb-1915	Herthausen-Hechingen	Died from illness
Kunkel, Jakob	Kriegsfreiwilliger	10	18-Feb-1915	Thiepval	Died from wounds
Riehle, Jakob	Kriegsfreiwilliger	10	18-Feb-1915	Thiepval	W.I.A., died 19-Feb-1915, Reserve Hospital, Miraumont
Bührle, Rudolf	Reservist	11	18-Feb-1915	Thiepval	W.I.A., died 21-Feb-1915, Field Hospital 1, Bapaume
Abele, Albert	Kriegsfreiwilliger	10	19-Feb-1915	Thiepval	
Falter, Gottlob	Musketier	9	21-Feb-1915	Thiepval	
Retter, Karl	Musketier	9	21-Feb-1915	Thiepval	
Schloz, Otto	Kriegsfreiwilliger	11	21-Feb-1915	Thiepval	
Koch, Ernst	Reservist	11	22-Feb-1915	Thiepval	
Weber, Johannes	Reservist	8	23-Feb-1915	Thiepval	Died from wounds
Lutz, Heinrich	Unteroffizier der Reserve	5	25-Feb-1915	Thiepval	
Seyboldt, Julius	Unteroffizier der Reserve	1	13-Mar-1915	Thiepval	W.I.A., died 15-Mar-1915 at Field Hospital 1, Bapaume
Marstaller, Johannes	Reservist	12	15-Mar-1915	St. Pierre-Divion	
Lemke, Ernst	Kriegsfreiwilliger	11	20-Mar-1915	Thiepval	
Faisst, Karl	Kriegsfreiwilliger	12	22-Mar-1915	St. Pierre-Divion	
Beiswenger, Josef	Ersatz Reservist	10	23-Mar-1915	Thiepval	
Schloz, Gustav	Musketier	5	24-Mar-1915	Thiepval	W.I.A., died 24-Mar-1915, Main Dressing Station
Riehm, Friedrich	Kriegsfreiwilliger	8	30-Mar-1915	Thiepval	
Klooster, Kornelius	Landsturmmann	Ersatz Bn	31-Mar-1915	Tübingen	Died from illness, Reserve Hospital 3, Tübingen
Tebben, Heinrich	Landsturmmann	Ersatz Bn	1-Apr-1915	Tübingen	Died from illness, Reserve Hospital 3, Tübingen
Gerdes, Martin	Landsturmmann	Ersatz Bn	2-Apr-1915	Tübingen	Died from illness, Reserve Hospital 2, Tübingen
Lude, Gottlieb	Musketier	1	4-Apr-1915	Thiepval	
Lutz, Wilhelm	Reservist	4	6-Apr-1915	Thiepval	Died from wounds
Steck, Gottlieb	Unteroffizier	8	6-Apr-1915	Thiepval	
Hartenstein, Otto	Kriegsfreiwilliger	1	11-Apr-1915	Thiepval	
Nerz, Jakob	Reservist	1	11-Apr-1915	Thiepval	
Schäfer, Oskar	Reservist	1	11-Apr-1915	Thiepval	
Arnold, Hermann	Kriegsfreiwilliger	2	11-Apr-1915	Thiepval	W.I.A., died.
Fritz, Gottlob	Kriegsfreiwilliger	2	11-Apr-1915	Thiepval	W.I.A., died 23-Apr-1915, Württemberg Field Hospital, Bapaume
Sailer, Gottlieb	Musketier	2	11-Apr-1915	Thiepval	

IR 180

NAME	RANK	CO.	DATE OF DEATH	LOCATION	NOTES
Klein, Fritz	Gefreiter	7	11-Apr-1915	Thiepval	
Schuster, Josef	Kriegsfreiwilliger	7	11-Apr-1915	Thiepval	
Weit, Otto	Kriegsfreiwilliger	10	11-Apr-1915	St. Pierre-Divion	
Bittlingmaier, Wilhelm	Reservist	11	11-Apr-1915	St. Pierre-Divion	K.I.A. either 10-Apr or 11-Apr-1915
Dammenmiller, Anton	Reservist	11	11-Apr-1915	St. Pierre-Divion	
Drechsel, Karl	Musketier	11	11-Apr-1915	St. Pierre-Divion	M.I.A., declared dead.
Jaissle, Hugo	Musketier	11	11-Apr-1915	St. Pierre-Divion	
Müller II, Valentin	Musketier	11	11-Apr-1915	St. Pierre-Divion	
Müller, Josef	Musketier	11	11-Apr-1915	St. Pierre-Divion	W.I.A., died 11-Apr-1915, Württemberg Reserve Field Hospital 1, Bapaume
Schrack, Ernst	Leutnant der Reserve	11	11-Apr-1915	St. Pierre-Divion	M.I.A., declared dead.
Schwarzwälder, Gustav	Wehrmann	11	11-Apr-1915	St. Pierre-Divion	
Sessler, Wilhelm	Vizefeldwebel	11	11-Apr-1915	St. Pierre-Divion	
Heim, Christian	Unteroffizier	12	11-Apr-1915	Thiepval	
Rath, Johann	Landsturmmann	Ersatz Bn	11-Apr-1915	Tübingen	Died from illness, Reserve Hospital 1, Tübingen
Schäfer, Johannes	Wehrmann	4	12-Apr-1915	Thiepval	
Schallenmüller, Heinrich	Reservist	8	12-Apr-1915	Thiepval	W.I.A., died 13-Apr-1915, Thiepval
Fink, Friedrich	Gefreiter der Reserve	1	14-Apr-1915	Thiepval	
Bächle, Karl	Musketier	2	14-Apr-1915	Thiepval	
Fink, Gotthilf	Reservist	2	14-Apr-1915	Thiepval	
Gaffner, Adam	Musketier	2	14-Apr-1915	Thiepval	
Hartnagel, Jakob	?	2	14-Apr-1915	Thiepval	W.I.A., died 15-Apr-1915, Dressing Station
Schenk, johannes	kriegsfreiwilliger Gefreiter	6	14-Apr-1915	Thiepval	W.I.A., died 26-Apr-1915, Field Hospital 1, Bapaume
Mozer, Otto	Kriegsfreiwilliger	4	15-Apr-1915	Thiepval	W.I.A., died 16-Apr-1915, Main Dressing Station, Miraumont
Schreiner, Eugen	Reservist	2	16-Apr-1915	Bapaume-Le Sars road	Died from an accident
Holder, Johannes	Musketier	12	20-Apr-1915	Thiepval	
Gutekunst, Johann	Musketier	3	26-Apr-1915	St. Quentin	Died of illness, Military Hospital St. Quentin, Lycée Henri Martin
Preuninger, Hermann	Musketier	2	3-May-1915	Thiepval	M.I.A., declared dead.
Allgaier, Ludwig	Reservist	12	4-May-1915	Thiepval	W.I.A., died 12-May-1915, Württemberg Reserve Field Hospital 1, Bapaume
Delle, Georg	Landsturmmann	12	5-May-1915	Thiepval	

IR 180

NAME	RANK	CO.	DATE OF DEATH	LOCATION	NOTES
Kern, Lorenz	Unteroffizier der Reserve	1	8-May-1915	Köln am Rhine	Died of illness in Fortress Hospital 11 School in Dau, Köln am Rhine
Sulz, Georg	Reservist	8	9-May-1915	Thiepval	W.I.A., died 5-Jun-1915, Military Hospital, Palais de Justice, St. Quentin
Grau, Karl	Reservist	11	15-May-1915	Thiepval	
Sayer, Christian	Kriegsfreiwilliger	6	20-May-1915	Thiepval	
Maier, August	Gefreiter	12	22-May-1915	Thiepval	W.I.A., died 26-May-1915, Württemberg Reserve Field Hospital 1, Beaumetz
Maier, Friedrich	Musketier	11	26-May-1915	Thiepval	
Kienzle, Theodor	Musketier	4	4-Jun-1915	St. Pierre-Divion	W.I.A., died 5-Jun-1915, Main Dressing Station, Miraumont
Baisch, Otto	Reservist	6	4-Jun-1915	Thiepval	
Keller, Friedrich	Unteroffizier der Reserve	6	4-Jun-1915	Thiepval	
Wieland, Max	Gefreiter	6	4-Jun-1915	Thiepval	M.I.A., declared dead.
Blumenstock, Friedrich	Vizefeldwebel	7	4-Jun-1915	Thiepval	W.I.A., died 6-Jul-1915, Mainz
Hieber, Bernhard	Gefreiter der Reserve	7	4-Jun-1915	Thiepval	
Steinhilber, Jakob	Musketier	2	7-Jun-1915	St. Pierre-Divion	W.I.A., died 16-Jun-1915, Bapaume
Sautter, Wilhelm	Reservist	1	8-Jun-1915	Grandcourt/ Thiepval	W.I.A., died 9-Jun-1915 in Bapaume
Chrissler, Eugen	Musketier	9	8-Jun-1915	Hébuterne	
Huttenlocher, Wilhelm	Musketier	9	8-Jun-1915	Hébuterne	
Kicherer, Jakob	Musketier	9	8-Jun-1915	Hébuterne	
Kirn, Richard	Leutnant der Landwehr	9	8-Jun-1915	Hébuterne	
Klink, Gustav	Kriegsfreiwilliger	9	8-Jun-1915	Hébuterne	
Spissmann, Gustav	Musketier	9	8-Jun-1915	Hébuterne	
Staib, Friedrich	Reservist	9	8-Jun-1915	Hébuterne	
Weymüller, Karl	Musketier	9	8-Jun-1915	Hébuterne	
Wirtensohn, Josef	Kriegsfreiwilliger	9	8-Jun-1915	Hébuterne	
App, Vincenz	Kriegsfreiwilliger	10	8-Jun-1915	Hébuterne	W.I.A., died 16-Jun-1915, Field Hospital 1, Favreuil
Arsan, Egbert	Leutnant der Reserve	10	8-Jun-1915	Hébuterne	
Bäuerle, Erwin	Musketier	10	8-Jun-1915	Hébuterne	
Beilbarz, Ambros	Landsturmmann	10	8-Jun-1915	Hébuterne	
Biberger, Andreas	Musketier	10	8-Jun-1915	Hébuterne	
Bihr, Eugen	Kriegsfreiwilliger	10	8-Jun-1915	Hébuterne	
Dörr, Eugen	Musketier	10	8-Jun-1915	Hébuterne	
Gittinger, Franz	Musketier	10	8-Jun-1915	Hébuterne	

IR 180

NAME	RANK	CO.	DATE OF DEATH	LOCATION	NOTES
Heintzeler, Gerhard	Kriegsfreiwilliger	10	8-Jun-1915	Hébuterne	
Hugger, Hermann	Unteroffizier	10	8-Jun-1915	Hébuterne	
Keller, Wilhelm	Ersatz Reservist	10	8-Jun-1915	Hébuterne	M.I.A., declared dead.
Kopp, Eugen	Vizefeldwebel	10	8-Jun-1915	Hébuterne	
Lauterwasser, Paul	Gefreiter	10	8-Jun-1915	Hébuterne	
Lötterle, Robert	Musketier	10	8-Jun-1915	Hébuterne	
Maier, Georg	Musketier	10	8-Jun-1915	Hébuterne	M.I.A., declared dead.
Märkle, Georg	Wehrmann	10	8-Jun-1915	Hébuterne	
Möricke, Paul	Leutnant der Reserve	10	8-Jun-1915	Hébuterne	
Raich, August	Musketier	10	8-Jun-1915	Hébuterne	
Rempfer, Jakob	Ersatz Reservist	10	8-Jun-1915	Hébuterne	
Rothenbacher, Josef	Musketier	10	8-Jun-1915	Hébuterne	
Ruoss, Georg	Musketier	10	8-Jun-1915	Hébuterne	
Schmid, Karl	Ersatz Reservist	10	8-Jun-1915	Hébuterne	
Schöll, Hermann	Musketier	10	8-Jun-1915	Hébuterne	M.I.A., declared dead.
Sommer, Karl	Musketier	10	8-Jun-1915	Hébuterne	
Spohn, Theodor	Kriegsfreiwilliger	10	8-Jun-1915	Hébuterne	
Strähle, Robert	Ersatz Reservist	10	8-Jun-1915	Hébuterne	
Vögtle-Matta, Johannes	Ersatz Reservist	10	8-Jun-1915	Hébuterne	
Widmann, Wilhelm	Musketier	10	8-Jun-1915	Hébuterne	W.I.A., died 12-Jun-1915, Field Hospital 4, Achiet-le Grand
Wolfensberger, Karl	Kriegsfreiwilliger	10	8-Jun-1915	Hébuterne	
Wurster, Ernst	Wehrmann	10	8-Jun-1915	Hébuterne	M.I.A., declared dead.
Ziegele, Wilhelm	Ersatz Reservist	10	8-Jun-1915	Hébuterne	W.I.A., died 22-Aug-1915, Field Hospital 3, Bapaume
Benzinger, Karl	Unteroffizier der Reserve	11	8-Jun-1915	Hébuterne	
Hees, Wilhelm	Ersatz Reservist	11	8-Jun-1915	Hébuterne	
Kielwein, Friedrich	Leutnant der Reserve	11	8-Jun-1915	Hébuterne	
Mühlhäuser, Hermann	Musketier	11	8-Jun-1915	Hébuterne	
Pfrommer, Friedrich	Musketier	11	8-Jun-1915	Hébuterne	M.I.A., declared dead.
Reiff, Karl	Musketier	7	9-Jun-1915	Thiepval	
Messer, Wilhelm	Reservist	9	9-Jun-1915	Hébuterne	
Bauer, Alfons	Musketier	1	10-Jun-1915	Beaumont-Hamel	
Bauer, Christian	Reservist	1	10-Jun-1915	Beaumont-Hamel	M.I.A., declared dead.
Bertsch, Eberhardt	Musketier	1	10-Jun-1915	Beaumont-Hamel	
Buck, Karl	Landsturmmann	1	10-Jun-1915	Beaumont-Hamel	M.I.A., declared dead.
Dinkelacker, Max	Musketier	1	10-Jun-1915	Beaumont-Hamel	
Drechsler, Eugen	Unteroffizier	1	10-Jun-1915	Beaumont-Hamel	
Eisinger, Karl	Musketier	1	10-Jun-1915	Beaumont-Hamel	

IR 180

NAME	RANK	CO.	DATE OF DEATH	LOCATION	NOTES
Frick, Jakob	Wehrmann	1	10-Jun-1915	Beaumont-Hamel	
Grauer, Friedrich	Kriegsfreiwilliger	1	10-Jun-1915	Beaumont-Hamel	
Grauer, Jakob	Musketier	1	10-Jun-1915	Beaumont-Hamel	
Hepperle, Gottlob	Ersatz Reservist	1	10-Jun-1915	Beaumont-Hamel	M.I.A., declared dead.
Hipp, Gottlieb	Tambour	1	10-Jun-1915	Beaumont-Hamel	
Höschle, Franz	Reservist	1	10-Jun-1915	Beaumont-Hamel	
Kurfess, Josef	Musketier	1	10-Jun-1915	Beaumont-Hamel	
Lang, Ernst	Musketier	1	10-Jun-1915	Beaumont-Hamel	
Leibssle, Karl	Unteroffizier der Reserve	1	10-Jun-1915	Beaumont-Hamel	
Lutz, Eugen	Unteroffizier der Reserve	1	10-Jun-1915	Beaumont-Hamel	
Lutz, Friedrich	Reservist	1	10-Jun-1915	Beaumont-Hamel	
Mäder, Matthäus	Wehrmann	1	10-Jun-1915	Beaumont-Hamel	W.I.A., died 13-Jun-1915 in Military Hospital 7th Army Corps, St. Quentin, Palais de Justice
Mozer, Karl	Reservist	1	10-Jun-1915	Beaumont-Hamel	M.I.A., declared dead.
Raible II, Karl	Wehrmann	1	10-Jun-1915	Beaumont-Hamel	
Reichardt, August	Musketier	1	10-Jun-1915	Beaumont-Hamel	M.I.A., declared dead.
Reichle, Gottlieb	Unteroffizier der Reserve	1	10-Jun-1915	Beaumont-Hamel	M.I.A., declared dead.
Schaal, Gottfried	Musketier	1	10-Jun-1915	Beaumont-Hamel	
Schnitzer, Gottlob	Unteroffizier der Reserve	1	10-Jun-1915	Beaumont-Hamel	
Schuch, Karl	Reservist	1	10-Jun-1915	Beaumont-Hamel	
Seemann, Gottlieb	Musketier	1	10-Jun-1915	Beaumont-Hamel	
Steinmetz, Adolf	Musketier	1	10-Jun-1915	Beaumont-Hamel	
Straub, Josef	Reservist	1	10-Jun-1915	Beaumont-Hamel	
Votteler, Gottlob	Reservist	1	10-Jun-1915	Beaumont-Hamel	
Walker, Adam	Reservist	1	10-Jun-1915	Beaumont-Hamel	M.I.A., declared dead.
Weisser, Stefan	Musketier	1	10-Jun-1915	Beaumont-Hamel	W.I.A., C.I.A., died 17-Mar-1916 in Reserve Hospital 1, Stuttgart as exchanged Prisoner of War
Wild, Jakob	Musketier	1	10-Jun-1915	Beaumont-Hamel	M.I.A., declared dead.
Wurster I, Wilhelm	Musketier	1	10-Jun-1915	Beaumont-Hamel	
Frank, Friedrich	Ersatz Reservist	11	10-Jun-1915	Hébuterne	
Nuoffer, Martin	Reservist	11	10-Jun-1915	Hébuterne	
Bitzer, Eugen	Musketier	1	12-Jun-1915	Beaumont-Hamel	
Maute, Wilhelm	Musketier	5	12-Jun-1915	Beaumont-Hamel	
Feifel, Josef	Gefreiter der Reserve	10	12-Jun-1915	Hébuterne	Died from wounds
Gross, Friedrich	Musketier	10	12-Jun-1915	Hébuterne	W.I.A., died 13-Jun-1915, Field Hospital 2, Bapaume
Holzwarth, Gottlieb	Musketier	10	12-Jun-1915	Hébuterne	W.I.A., died 12-Jun-1915 during transport to the hospital

IR 180

NAME	RANK	CO.	DATE OF DEATH	LOCATION	NOTES
Seibold, Rudolf	Musketier	10	12-Jun-1915	Hébuterne	
Stickel, Theodor	Musketier	10	12-Jun-1915	Hébuterne	W.I.A., died 13-Jun-1915, Field Hospital 2, Bapaume
Wiedmann, Ernst	Kriegsfreiwilliger	10	12-Jun-1915	Hébuterne	W.I.A., died 12-Jun-1915 during transport to the hospital
Schlichter, Anton	Gefreiter	12	12-Jun-1915	Thiepval	
Jehle, Georg	Vizefeldwebel	Ersatz Bn	12-Jun-1915	Tübingen	Died from illness
Bühner, Karl	Gefreiter der Reserve	9	13-Jun-1915	Hébuterne	
Frasch, Georg	Musketier	9	14-Jun-1915	Hébuterne	W.I.A., died 6/15/1915, Field Hospital 4, Achiet le Petit
Buck, Hermann	Schütze	1 MG Co.	16-Jun-1915	Beaumont-Hamel	W.I.A., died 7/6/1915, Württemberg Field Hospita1, Bapaume
Kraus, Hermann	Kriegsfreiwilliger	8	17-Jun-1915	La Louviere Farm	W.I.A., died 6/18/1915, Field Hospital 4, Achiet le Grand
Maass, Johann	Musketier	7	19-Jun-1915	Thiepval	W.I.A., died 6/19/1915, Dressing Station, Miraumont
Finkbeiner, Matthäus	Wehrmann	1	20-Jun-1915	Beaumont-Hamel	Captured 6/10/1915, died 6/20/1915 in French P.O.W. camp
Münst, Franz	Hauptmann	11	20-Jun-1915	Hébuterne	W.I.A., died 7/5/1915, Field Hospital 4, Achiet-le Grand
Hild, Eugen	Gefreiter der Reserve	11	22-Jun-1915	Hébuterne	
Falch, Hans	Ersatz Reservist	5	24-Jun-1915	Thiepval	
Hetzer, Karl	Wehrmann	10	2-Jul-1915	Miraumont	W.I.A., died 7/2/1915, Reserve Field Hospital, Bapaume
Wüst, Georg	Landsturmmann	Ersatz Bn	5-Jul-1915	Tübingen	Died from illness
Epple, Friedrich	Unteroffizier	4	11-Jul-1915	Thiepval	
Kielwein, Georg	Unteroffizier	4	11-Jul-1915	Thiepval	
Klauser, Hermann	Gefreiter	4	11-Jul-1915	Thiepval	
Kloz, Adolf	Feldwebel	4	11-Jul-1915	Thiepval	W.I.A., died 11-Jul-1915, Dressing Station, Miraumont
Wörz, Jakob	Musketier	12	17-Jul-1915	Serre	
Deiss, Alfred	Leutnant der Landwehr	7	21-Jul-1915	Serre	W.I.A., died 2-Aug-1915, Field Hospital 1, Bapaume
Kimmerle, Gotthilf	Reservist	7	21-Jul-1915	Serre	
Merz, Kaspar	Reservist	7	21-Jul-1915	Serre	
Rapp, Otto	Musketier	7	21-Jul-1915	Serre	W.I.A., died 27-Jul-1915, Field Hospital 1, Bapaume
Wist, Wilhelm	Musketier	10	23-Jul-1915	Serre	
Büttner, Otto	Kriegsfreiwilliger	8	25-Jul-1915	Serre	W.I.A., died 26-Jul-1915, Dressing Station, Miraumont
Schlayer, Otto	Musketier	5	2-Aug-1915	Serre	

IR 180

NAME	RANK	CO.	DATE OF DEATH	LOCATION	NOTES
Klein, Hermann	Ersatz Reservist	11	3-Aug-1915	Serre	
Klemmer, Xaver	Reservist	10	5-Aug-1915	Serre	
Class, Wilhelm	Musketier	1	14-Aug-1915	Serre	
Nagel, Heinrich	Reservist	11	20-Aug-1915	Serre	W.I.A., died 25-Aug-1915, Württemberg Reserve Field Hospital 1, Bapaume
Seibel, Emanuel	Landsturmmann	1	21-Aug-1915	Serre	
Holzapfel, Georg	Musketier	Ersatz Bn	21-Aug-1915	Tübingen	Died from illness, Reserve Hospital 3, Tübingen
Heilig, Friedrich	Gefreiter	10	22-Aug-1915	Ludwigsburg	Died as a result of illness, Reserve Hospital I, Ludwigsburg
Käftle, Karl	Landsturm Recruit	Ersatz Bn	27-Aug-1915	Reutlingen	Died from an accident
Wernz, Eugen	Musketier	5	29-Aug-1915	Serre	W.I.A., died 2-Oct-1915, Reserve Field Hospital1, Bapaume
Aufschlag, Friedrich	Reservist	12	31-Aug-1915	Miraumont	Died from an accident
Häussler, Gotthilf	Unteroffizier	11	1-Sep-1915	Serre	W.I.A., died 2-Sep-1915, Reserve Medical Company 26, Miraumont
Schmälzle, Friedrich	Musketier	7	4-Sep-1915	Serre	W.I.A., died 4-Sep-1915, Reserve Field Hospital 1, Bapaume
Eiffler, Ludwig	Landsturmmann	10	4-Sep-1915	Serre	W.I.A., died 6-Oct-1917, Reserve Hospital I, Tübingen
Weiblen, Christian	Musketier	6	8-Sep-1915	Serre	W.I.A., died 9-Sep-1915, Miraumont
Allgaier, Albert	Kriegsfreiwilliger	10	9-Sep-1915	Serre	
Bäder, Karl	Gefreiter	7	10-Sep-1915	Serre	W.I.A., died 11-Sep-1915, Dressing Station Reserve Medical Company 26, Miraumont
Eberspächer, Karl	Musketier	8	10-Sep-1915	Serre	W.I.A., died during transport to the dressing station
Steinberger, Ludwig	Ersatz Reservist	10	10-Sep-1915	Serre	
Schmollinger, Kurt	Kriegsfreiwilliger	8	11-Sep-1915	Serre	Died from wounds
Steudle, Friedrich	Gefreiter	10	13-Sep-1915	Serre	
Reuchlen, Georg	Kriegsfreiwilliger	7	15-Sep-1915	Serre	W.I.A., died 16-Sep-1915, Main Dressing Station, Miraumont
Leopold, Anton	Musketier	6	18-Sep-1915	Serre	
Schaupp, Wilhelm	Kriegsfreiwilliger	5	20-Sep-1915	Serre	
Hirschburger, Georg	Reservist	6	22-Sep-1915	Serre	W.I.A., died 22-Sep-1915, Dressing Station II Battalion, Serre
Mettmann, Karl	Leutnant der Reserve	12	22-Sep-1915	Serre	
Dussler, Johannes	Kriegsfreiwilliger	10	26-Sep-1915	Serre	

IR 180

NAME	RANK	CO.	DATE OF DEATH	LOCATION	NOTES
Link, Karl	Musketier	6	3-Oct-1915	Serre	W.I.A., died 4-Oct-1915, Reserve Field Hospital 1, Bapaume
Meth, Herbert	Gefreiter	6	3-Oct-1915	Serre	
Sailer, Felix	Kriegsfreiwilliger	6	3-Oct-1915	Serre	
Blank, Josef	Leutnant	5	8-Oct-1915	Serre	
Stängle, Gustav	Musketier	5	8-Oct-1915	Serre	
Buchele, Christian	Reservist	10	17-Oct-1915	Serre	
Müller, Bernhard	Reservist	10	17-Oct-1915	Serre	
Hermann, Alfons	Vizefeldwebel der Reserve	5	21-Oct-1915	Serre	
Bihr, Josef	Kriegsfreiwilliger	8	4-Nov-1915	Serre	W.I.A., died 11-Apr-1916, Reserve Medical Company 26, Miraumont
Hoss, Karl	Landsturmmann	6	5-Nov-1915	Serre	Died from wounds
Krohmer, Paul	Musketier	12	14-Nov-1915	Thiepval	W.I.A., 15-Nov-1915, Main Dressing Station Rserve Medical Company 26, Miraumont
Baumann, Viktor	Musketier	6	22-Nov-1915	Serre	
Rempfer, Johannes	Unteroffizier der Reserve	1	2-Dec-1915	Serre	
Buck, Robert	Musketier	1	7-Dec-1915	Serre	
Erb, Josef	Ersatz Reservist	6	7-Dec-1915	Serre	W.I.A., died 12-Jan-1916, Württemberg Reserve Field Hospital 1, Bapaume
Zimmerer, Hermann	Musketier	6	7-Dec-1915	Serre	
Fischer, Rudolf	Landsturmmann	10	7-Dec-1915	Serre	
Sing, Johannes	Ersatz Reservist	10	8-Dec-1915	Serre	
Nussbaum, Erwin	Musketier	Ersatz Bn	12-Dec-1915	Tübingen	Died from illness, Reserve Hospital 1, Tübingen
Koch, Wilhelm	Kriegsfreiwilliger	4	14-Dec-1915	Serre	
Thudium, Wilhelm	Musketier	3	15-Dec-1915	Serre	W.I.A., died 15-Dec-1915 during transprt to Bapaume
Klotz, Friedrich	Kriegsfreiwilliger	2	18-Dec-1915	Serre	
Gern, Karl	Kriegsfreiwilliger	4	18-Dec-1915	Serre	
Dölker, Martin	Vizefeldwebel	9	18-Dec-1915	Serre	
Eisele, Gustav	Ersatz Reservist	1	19-Dec-1915	Serre	W.I.A., died 20-Dec-1915 Main Dressing Station Miraumont
Fausel, Theodor	Musketier	2	22-Dec-1915	Serre	W.I.A., died 28-Dec-1915, Württemberg Reserve Field Hospital 1, Bapaume
Schneck, Karl	Ersatz Reservist	5	24-Dec-1915	Serre	Died from wounds
Nonnenmacher, Gottlob	Landsturmmann	3	26-Dec-1915	Tübingen	Died from illness, Reserve Hospital 1, Tübingen
Queissner, Eberhardt	Musketier	10	28-Dec-1915	Serre	W.I.A., died 2-Jan-1916, Reserve Medical Company 26, Miraumont

IR 180

NAME	RANK	CO.	DATE OF DEATH	LOCATION	NOTES
Ruoff, Josef	Gefreiter	1 MG Co.	30-Dec-1915	Serre	W.I.A., died 9-Jan-1916, Württemberg Reserve Field Hospital I, Bapaume
Berthele, Karl	Ersatz Reservist	7	2-Jan-1916	Bapaume	Died from illness, Württemberg Field Hospital 1, Bapaume
Müller, Wilhelm	Landsturmmann	3	6-Jan-1916	Serre	
Speier, Gottlob	Landsturmmann	Ersatz Bn	8-Jan-1916	Tübingen	Died from an accident
Treiber, Wilhelm	Unteroffizier	2	14-Jan-1916	Serre	
Muff, Johannes	Landsturmmann	8	14-Jan-1916	Serre	W.I.A., died 21-Jan-1916, Württemberg Reserve Field Hospital 1, Bapaume
Bausinger, Ernst	Gefreiter	8	15-Jan-1916	Serre	
Seybold, August	Ersatz Reservist	8	15-Jan-1916	Serre	M.I.A., declared dead.
Schneider, Jakob	Reservist	3	22-Jan-1916	Serre	
Vogt, Eugen	Gefreiter	3	22-Jan-1916	Serre	
Strohmann, Theodor	Landsturmmann	Ersatz Bn	23-Jan-1916	Tübingen	Died from illness, Reserve Hospital 1, Tübingen
Bundschub, Josef	Musketier	3	30-Jan-1916	Serre	
Rehkugler, Eugen	Gefreiter	3	30-Jan-1916	Serre	W.I.A., died 27Feb-1916, Military Hospital, St. Quentin
Frommer, Emil	Landsturmmann	Ersatz Bn	31-Jan-1916	Tübingen	Died from illness, Reserve Hospital 2, Tübingen
Fuchs, Hermann	Musketier	1	3-Feb-1916	Serre	
Franke, Alfred	Kriegsfreiwilliger	8	19-Feb-1916	Serre	
Schwertfeger, Fritz	Vizefeldwebel	8	19-Feb-1916	Serre	M.I.A., declared dead.
Unrath, Johannes	Unteroffizier	9	19-Feb-1916	Serre	W.I.A., died 20-Feb-1916, Württemberg Reserve Field Hospital 1, Bapaume
Ulmer, Josef	Musketier	Ersatz Bn	25-Feb-1916	Tübingen	Died from illness, Reserve Hospital 2, Tübingen
Kurz, Gotthilf	Unteroffizier	Ersatz Bn	27-Feb-1916	Tübingen	Died from illness, Reserve Hospital 3, Tübingen
Sigel, Friedrich	Musketier	12	18-Mar-1916	Serre	
Seyfried, Emil	Ldstpfl.	Ersatz Bn	18-Mar-1916	Tübingen	Died from illness, Reserve Hospital 2, Tübingen
Staiger, Karl	Musketier	11	21-Mar-1916	Serre	W.I.A., died 22-Mar-1916, Württemberg Reserve Field Hospital 1, Bapaume
Schnizler, Karl	Musketier	2	1-Apr-1916	Serre	
Huttelmaier, August	Reservist	6	20-Apr-1916	Serre	W.I.A., died 24-Apr-1916, Dressing Station, Serre
Sontheimer, Ludwig	Leutnant der Reserve	2	25-Apr-1916	Irles	Accidentally killed
Müller, Albert	Gefreiter	11	25-Apr-1916	Serre	
Flaig, Johann	Gefreiter	11	26-Apr-1916	Serre	
Wiech, Josef	Kriegsfreiwilliger	12	26-Apr-1916	Serre	

IR 180

NAME	RANK	CO.	DATE OF DEATH	LOCATION	NOTES
Holz,	Unteroffizier	6	8-May-1916	Miraumont	W.I.A., died 8-May-1916, Dressing Station, Miraumont
Staiger, Christian	Feldwebel-Leutnant	Ersatz Bn	11-May-1916	Stuttgart	Died of illness, Auxiliary Hospital, Karl Olga Sick House, Stuttgart
Ehscheid, Ferdinand	Landsturmmann	11	14-May-1916	Serre	
Schumacher, Christoph	Ersatz Reservist	11	14-May-1916	Serre	
Arnold, Josef	Schütze	1MGCo.	15-May-1916	Serre	
Preuss, Anton	Landsturmmann	2	18-May-1916	Serre	
Butterstein, Hermann	Schütze	1MGCo.	7-Jun-1916	Ovillers	W.I.A., died 7-Jun-1916 at Dressing Station
Gaibler, Albert	Schütze	1MGCo.	7-Jun-1916	Ovillers	W.I.A., died 8-Jun-1916, in hospital, Reserve Medical Company 14, Flers
Reiff, Christian	Reservist	9	10-Jun-1916	Ovillers	
Schwarzkopf, Alfons	Ersatz Reservist	10	11-Jun-1916	Ovillers	
Gmelin, Gotthard	Vizefeldwebel	8	16-Jun-1916	Ovillers	
Kuch, Georg	Musketier	8	16-Jun-1916	Ovillers	W.I.A., died shortly after being wounded on the same day
Mack, Hermann	Kriegsfreiwilliger	9	21-Jun-1916	Ovillers	
Döttinger, Gotthilf	Musketier	3	22-Jun-1916	Ovillers	
Späth, Josef	Schütze	2MGCo.	23-Jun-1916	Ovillers	
Hiller, Johannes	Musketier	6	24-Jun-1916	Ovillers	W.I.A., died 7-Jul-1916, Auxiliary Hospital Catholic Sick House Rheinberg
Hering, Karl	Musketier	3	25-Jun-1916	Ovillers	
Liebling, Eugen	Musketier	3	25-Jun-1916	Ovillers	
Müller, Hermann	Wehrmann	3	25-Jun-1916	Ovillers	W.I.A., died 6-Jul-1916, Reserve Hospital I, Aachen
Kächele, Emil	Musketier	6	25-Jun-1916	Ovillers	
Biehler, Wilhelm	Krankenträger	7	25-Jun-1916	Ovillers	
Walz, Eugen	Musketier	12	25-Jun-1916	Ovillers	
Theis, Philipp	Landsturm Recruit	2	26-Jun-1916	Ovillers	
Rupp, Christian	Gefreiter	4	26-Jun-1916	Ovillers	
Linder, Georg	Musketier	8	26-Jun-1916	Ovillers	W.I.A., died 27-Jun-1916, Reserve Medical Company 26, Miraumont
Nadler, Anton	Kriegsfreiwilliger	8	26-Jun-1916	Ovillers	Died from wounds
Baier, Andreas	Unteroffizier	9	26-Jun-1916	Ovillers	
Barner, Ernst	Musketier	9	26-Jun-1916	Ovillers	
Gaab, Erwin	Ersatz Reservist	9	26-Jun-1916	Ovillers	
Möhrmann, Karl	Musketier	10	26-Jun-1916	Ovillers	

IR 180 NAME	RANK	CO.	DATE OF DEATH	LOCATION	NOTES
Grünewald, Otto	Unteroffizier	11	26-Jun-1916	Ovillers	W.I.A., died 28-Jun-1916, Württemberg Reserve Field Hospital 1, Bapaume
Ricker, Max	Leutnant der Reserve	11	26-Jun-1916	Ovillers	
Seibold, Karl	Musketier	11	26-Jun-1916	Ovillers	
Keinath, Johannes	Schütze	1 MG Co.	26-Jun-1916	Ovillers	
Hübner, Josef	Landsturmmann	1	27-Jun-1916	Ovillers	
Keinath, Martin	Wehrmann	3	27-Jun-1916	Ovillers	
Link, Christian	Landsturmmann	7	27-Jun-1916	Ovillers	W.I.A., died 29-Jun-1916, Württemberg Reserve Field Hospital 1, Bapaume
Benseler, Ernst	Reservist	9	27-Jun-1916	Ovillers	
Hörmann,	Vizefeldwebel	9	27-Jun-1916	Ovillers	
Krieg, Christian	Musketier	9	27-Jun-1916	Ovillers	
Remppis, Hans	Vizefeldwebel	9	27-Jun-1916	Ovillers	
Säufferer, Otto	Unteroffizier	9	27-Jun-1916	Ovillers	
Siegel, Walter	Vizefeldwebel	9	27-Jun-1916	Ovillers	
Stöckle, Hermann	Leutnant der Reserve	9	27-Jun-1916	Ovillers	
Finkbeiner, Albert	Musketier	10	27-Jun-1916	Ovillers	
Meschenmoser, Franz	Musketier	10	27-Jun-1916	Ovillers	
Schenk, Karl	Ersatz Reservist	10	27-Jun-1916	Ovillers	
Strauss, Ernst	Ersatz Reservist	10	27-Jun-1916	Ovillers	
Waldmann, Heinrich	Landsturmmann	11	27-Jun-1916	Ovillers	
Kuppler, Johann	Reservist	2	28-Jun-1916	Ovillers	
Lutz, Wilhelm	Musketier	2	28-Jun-1916	Ovillers	
Rüdiger, Friedrich	Gefreiter	2	28-Jun-1916	Ovillers	W.I.A., died from wounds
Steinhilber, Richard	Gefreiter	5	28-Jun-1916	Ovillers	W.I.A., died 8-Jul-1916, State Hospital Cöln-Deutz.
Stähle, Sebastian	Musketier	10	28-Jun-1916	Ovillers	
Glaser, Gottlob	Musketier	11	28-Jun-1916	Ovillers	
Kastenholz, Anton	Landsturmmann	11	28-Jun-1916	Ovillers	
Rappold, Wilhelm	Kriegsfreiwilliger	11	28-Jun-1916	Ovillers	W.I.A., died 29-Jun-1916, Dressing Station, Miraumont
Rupp, Johannes	Reservist	11	28-Jun-1916	Ovillers	
Steller, Ernst	Landsturmmann	11	28-Jun-1916	Ovillers	
Spitz, Wilhelm	Musketier	2	29-Jun-1916	Ovillers	W.I.A., died from wounds
Bauer, Gustav	Musketier	2	30-Jun-1916	Ovillers	
Hasler, August	Landsturm Recruit	2	30-Jun-1916	Ovillers	
Drohmann, Albert	Unteroffizier	11	30-Jun-1916	Ovillers	

Monument to the fallen from RFAR 26 and RIR 99. Dedicated 7 December 1914. Designed by III/R99 Adjutant G. Müller. Constructed by *Wehrmann* Otto Ritter, 12/R99 and *Wehrmann* Karl Schäfer, 9/R99. (Author's collection)

Grave of *Hauptmann* Braumüller, RIR 99. (Author's collection)

RFAR 26

NAME	RANK	CO.	DATE OF DEATH	LOCATION	NOTES
Bernhard, Georg	Fahrer	6	29-Sep-14	Pys	
Riesser, Franz	Kanonier	6	29-Sep-14	Pys	W.I.A., died 3-Oct-1914 in Reserve Field Hospital 3, Ligny-Thilloy.
Efinger, Franz	Kanonier	8	29-Sep-14	Pys	W.I.A., died 30-Sept-1914 in Reserve Field Hospital 1, Bapaume.
Müller I, Wilhelm	Kanonier	9	29-Sep-14	Pys	W.I.A., died 11-Oct-1914 in auxiliary hospital Leverkufen (Rheinland).
Erz, Johannes	Gefreiter	1	30-Sep-14	Pys	
Lamparter, Michael	Gefreiter	L.M.C. II	1-Oct-14	Ligny-Thilloy	
Schmid VI, David	Kanonier	L.M.C. II	1-Oct-14	Ligny-Thilloy	
Hander, Alfred	Unteroffizier	4	3-Oct-14	Thiepval	W.I.A., died 5-Oct-1914 in Reserve Field Hospital 3, Miraumont.
Hauser, Friedrich	Kanonier	Staff I	6-Oct-14	Grandcourt	Injured in accident, died 25-Oct-1914 in Military Hospital, 21st Army Corps, Bapaume.
Veigel, August	Kanonier	1	7-Oct-14	Pozières	
Hirner, Julius	Fahrer	3	7-Oct-14	Grandcourt	
Schmäh, Anton	Unteroffizier	4	7-Oct-14	Grandcourt	W.I.A., died 11-Oct-1914 in Reserve Field Hospital 4, Miraumont.
Wurst, Georg	Kanonier	8	7-Oct-14	Pozières	
Weerth, Hans	Vizewachtmeister	1	15-Oct-14	Beaumont	
Beck, Friedrich	Kanonier	4	18-Oct-14	Thiepval	W.I.A., died 29-Nov-1914 in Reserve Hospital, Crefeld.
Brischar, Friedrich	Gefreiter	2	19-Oct-14	Beaucourt	
Geldin, Johannes	Kanonier	2	19-Oct-14	Beaucourt	
Wetzel, Johannes	Kanonier	2	19-Oct-14	Beaucourt	
Wiedmann, Sigmund	Kanonier	2	19-Oct-14	Beaucourt	
Schock, Ludwig	Fahrer	L.M.C. III	23-Oct-14	Beaucourt	
Zehender, Georg	Fahrer	3	26-Oct-14	Beaumont	W.I.A., died 26-Nov-1914 in Reserve Hospital 1, Aachen.
Mann, Christian	Kanonier	1	29-Oct-14	Beaucourt	M.I.A.
Merz, Friedrich	Fahrer	3	2-Nov-14	Beaucourt	
Schädler, Georg	Gefreiter	5	14-Nov-14	Grandcourt	
Köder, Albert	Fahrer	2	19-Nov-14	Beaucourt	W.I.A., died 21-Feb-1915 in Reserve Field Hospital 4, Miraumont.
Held, Andreas	Fahrer	6	3-Dec-14	Thiepval	W.I.A., died 4-Dec-1914 in Reserve Field Hospital 3, Miraumont.
Härle, Theodor	Gefreiter	3	8-Dec-14	Beaucourt	
Knaupp, Albert	Kanonier	9	6-Jan-15	Pozières	

RFAR 26

NAME	RANK	CO.	DATE OF DEATH	LOCATION	NOTES
Auchenberg, Josef	Kanonier	1	11-Jan-15	Beaumont	W.I.A., died en route to the wounded collecting station, Miraumont.
Messner, Georg	Fahrer	3	15-Jan-15	Beaucourt	
Hausser, Max	Leutnant der Res.	9	18-Jan-15	La Boisselle	Ordered to the Staff of RIR 120.
Mensch, Franz	Kanonier	6	22-Jan-15	Thiepval	
Zondler, Paul	Unteroffizier	8	24-Jan-15	Pozières	W.I.A., died 29-Jan-1915 in Field Hospital 1, Bapaume.
Härlin, Walter	Kriegsfreiwilliger, Gefreiter	6	7-Feb-15	Thiepval	
Balbach, Johann	Gefreiter	LM.C.II	7-Feb-15	Grandcourt	
Neumeyer, Erich	Kriegsfreiwilliger, Fahrer	LM.C.II	7-Feb-15	Grandcourt	
Epp, Mathias	Kanonier	6	16-Feb-15	Thiepval	
Mauz, Gottlieb	Kanonier	6	16-Feb-15	Thiepval	W.I.A., died en route to Reserve Field Hospital 4, Miraumont.
Konzelmann, Karl	Kanonier	8	10-Mar-15	Pozières	
Deubel, Franz	Kanonier	9	16-Mar-15	Grandcourt	
Müller, Christian	Fahrer	7	4-Apr-15	Oberhausen	Died as a result of sickness, in Reserve Hospital, Oberhausen (Rheinland).
Mauser, Friedrich	Kanonier	1	10-May-15	Beaucourt	
Lay, Wilhelm	Kanonier	LM.C.I	13-May-15	Béaulencourt	Accidentally killed.
Wolf II, Jakob	Kanonier	9	5-Jun-15	Beaucourt	
Floruss, Wilhelm	Kanonier	9	7-Jun-15	Miraumont	
Autenrieth, Ernst	Vizewachtmeister	Staff I	9-Jun-15	Beaucourt	
Catoir, Richard	Gefreiter	1	10-Jun-15	Beaucourt	
Hund, Konrad	Kanonier	1	10-Jun-15	Beaucourt	
Egeler, Martin	Kanonier	2	12-Jun-15	Beaucourt	
Merkle, Hugo	Gefreiter	8	15-Jun-15	Courcelette	Accidentally killed.
Hohl, Georg	Landwehrmann	5	20-Jul-15	Grandcourt	W.I.A., died in Field Hospital 1, Bapaume.
Hörer, Hermann	Kanonier	LM.C.I	13-Aug-15	Beaucourt	
Sengel, David	Fahrer	6	15-Jan-16	Grandcourt	Accidentally killed.
Burkhardt, Friedrich	Vizewachtmeister	8	12-Feb-16	Grevillers Wood	Accidentally killed.
Jetter, Johannes	Kanonier	1	12-May-16	Beaucourt	
Bardanischeck, Karl	Fahrer	LM.C.I	12-May-16	Beaucourt	
Pfrommer, Hermann	Fahrer	LM.C.I	12-May-16	Beaucourt	W.I.A., died 21-May-1916 in Field Hospital 1, Bapaume.
Mugele, Paul	Kanonier	6	6-Jun-16	St. Pierre-Divion	
Dörr, Friedrich	Unteroffizier	Staff I	14-Jun-16	Miraumont	Died in Reserve Medical Compay 26 of sickness.

RFAR 26					
NAME	RANK	CO.	DATE OF DEATH	LOCATION	NOTES
Welte, Eugen	Leutnant der Res.	3	25-Jun-16	Grevillers	Commanding a Balloon Detachment, shot down. Died en route to Field Hospital 1, Bapaume.
Auchter, Thomas	Kriegsfreiwilliger, Vizewachtmeister	6	25-Jun-16	Grevillers	Killed as a result of injuries suffered in a burning observation balloon.
Brodbeck, Otto	Unteroffizier	5	26-Jun-16	Grandcourt	
Clauss, Immanuel	Gefreiter	5	26-Jun-16	Grandcourt	Buried, died 29-Apr-1918 in hospital in Esslingen.
Decker, Heinrich	Kanonier	5	26-Jun-16	Grandcourt	
Geiger, Gottlieb	Fahrer	LMC.I	27-Jun-16	Beaucourt	
Hink, David	Gefreiter	LMC.II	27-Jun-16	Courcelette	
Bergmann, Christian	Fahrer	5	28-Jun-16	Courcelette	
Reichle, Xaver	Gefreiter	LMC.I	28-Jun-16	Miraumont	
Hofsäss, Karl	Kanonier	6	30-Jun-16	Courcelette	

Bibliography

Unpublished sources
Feldpost Letters (1915), *Telegrafist* Alois Eisele, XIV Reserve Corps *Fernsprech Abteilung.*
Feldpost Letters (1915-1916), *Kriegsfreiwilliger* Karl Losch, 3rd Company, RIR 119.
Feldpost Letters (1914-1915), *Unteroffizier der Reserve* Fritz Rohr, 2nd Company, RIR 111.
Feldpost Letters (1915-1916), *Gefreiter der Reserve* Rudolf Siegele, 4th Battery, RFAR 29.
Feldpost Letters (1914-1915), *Wehrmann* Xavier Straub, 9th Company, RIR 111.

Diary of Hans Ludwig, 6th Coy, RIR 120.
Diary of Ernest Shephard, 1st Dorset Regiment

Hauptstaatsarchiv Stuttgart, Kriegsstammrolle 7/RIR 121 HstAS M 478-13

Public Records office – Kew:
PRO W0157/171
PRO WO95/2389
PRO W095/1482
General Staff (Intelligence), General Headquarters, *Summary of recent information regarding the German army and its methods*, Ia/24495, January 1917
The Principles in Trench Warfare as laid down in the XIV Reserve Corps, Ia/13590, 19th May 1916. Document SS 490

Newspapers
The Londonderry Sentinel
Peterborough Advertiser
The People's Journal
The New York Times

Printed sources (books and articles)
Anon, *Deutsche Verlustlisten*, (1914-1916), Berlin, 1914-1916
Anon, *Die 26. Reserve Division 1914-1918,* Stuttgart, 1920
Anon, *Kriegstagbuch aus Schwaben*, Stuttgart, 1914-1919
Atkinson, C.T., *The History of the South Wales Borderers 1914-1918,* London, 1931
Bachelin, Major Eduard, *Das Reserve-Infanterie-Regiment Nr. 111 im Weltkrieg 1914 bis 1918,* Karlsruhe, 1938
Baumgartner, Richard (Ed.), 'An der Somme, An interview with Soldat Emil Geobelbecker', *Der Angriff, A Journal of World War I History,* 1979, No. 3
Baumgartner, Richard (Ed.), 'The Somme 1 July 1916', *Der Angriff, A Journal of World War 1 History*, 1981, No. 13
Bayerisches Kriegsarchiv, *Die Bayern im Grossen Krieg 1914-1918,* München, 1923

Bezzel, Oberst a.D. Dr. Oskar, *Das Königlich Bayerische Reserve-Infanterie-Regiment Nr. 6*, München, 1938

Brown, Malcolm, *The Imperial War Museum Book of the Somme*, London, 1996

Delmensingen, General der Artillerie Konrad Kraft von & Feeser, Generalmajor a.D. Friedrichfranz, *Das Bayernbuch vom Weltkriege 1914-1918*, Stuttgart, 1930

Douie, Charles, *The Weary Road*, London, 1929

Edmonds, Brigadier-General Sir James E., *History of the Great War. Military Operations France and Belgium 1916. Sir Douglas Haig's Command to the 1st July: Battle of the Somme*, London, 1932

Ehrler, Hans Heinrich, *Ehrenbuch der Gefallenen Stuttgarts 1914-1918*, Stuttgart, 1925

Fabeck, Hans von, *Im Orkan der Sommeschlacht. Ein Abschnitt aus der Kriegsgeschichte des Reserve-Infanterie-Regiment Nr. 99*, Berlin, 1930

Falls, Cyril, *History of the Ulster Division*, Belfast, 1991 reprint

Feldmann, Heinrich, *Unsere Taten und Fahrten. Das Grossherzoglich Mecklenburgische Reserve-Jäger-Bataillon Nr. 14 im Weltkrieg 1914-1918*, Oldenburg, 1929

Freydorf, Rudolf von, *Das 1. Badische Leib-Grenadier-Regiment Nr. 109 im Weltkrieg 1914-1918*, Karlsruhe i.B., 1927

Fiedel, Paul, *Geschichte des Infanterie Regiments von Winterfeldt (2, Oberschlesisches) Nr. 23, Das Regiment im Weltkriege*, Berlin, 1929

Forstner, Major a.D. Kurt Freiherr von, *Das Königlich-Preussische Reserve-Infanterie-Regiment Nr. 15*, Oldenburg, 1929

Fraser, Alastair, 'Finding Jakob', *Battlefields Annual Review*, Singapore, 2005

Frick, Leutnant der Landwehr Albert, *Erlebnisse in den Ersten Tagen der Somme-Schlacht (24 Juni bis 7 Juli 1916)*, 1916

Frisch, Georg, *Das Reserve-Infanterie-Regiment Nr. 109 im Weltkrieg 1914 bis 1918*, Karlsruhe, 1931

Fromm, Oberst a.D, *Das Württembergische Reserve-Infanterie-Regiment Nr. 120 im Weltkrieg 1914-1918*, Stuttgart, 1920

Gallion, Lt d. R. Dr. Wilhelm, *Das Reserve-Infanterie-Regiment Nr. 40 im Weltkrieg*, Mannheim, 1936

General Staff, *Handbook of the German Army in War, January 1917*, Wakefield, 1973

Gerster, Matthäus, *Das Württembergische Reserve-Infanterie-Regiment Nr. 119 im Weltkrieg 1914-1918*, Stuttgart, 1920

Gerster, Matthäus, *Die Schwaben an der Ancre*, Heilbronn a.N., 1918

Gerster, Matthäus, *Treffen der 26.R.D. am 5 Juli 1936*, Stuttgart, 1936

[Greiner & Vulpius], *Reserve-Infanterie-Regiment Nr. 110 im Weltkrieg 1914-1918*, Karlsruhe, 1934

Hedin, Sven, *With the German Armies in the West*, Plymouth, 1915

Holtz, Hauptmann Freiherr Georg vom, *Das Württembergische Reserve-Infanterie-Regiment Nr. 121 im Weltkrieg 1914-1918*, Stuttgart, 1921

Horsfall, Jack & Cave, Nigel, *Serre, Somme*, London, 1996

Ihlenfeld, Oberst a.D. v. & Engle, Major a.D., *Das 9. Badische Infanterie-Regiment Nr. 170 im Weltkrieg*, Oldenburg, 1926

Jäger, Herbert, *German Artillery of World War One*, Marlborough, 2001

Jecklin, Königlich Preussischer Major a.D. Wilhelm von, *Das Reserve-Jäger-Bataillon Nr. 8 im Weltkrieg 1914-1918*, Erfurt, 1930

Kaiser, Generalmajor a.D. Franz, *Das Königlich Preussen Infanterie-Regiment Nr. 63 (4. Oberschlesisches)*, Berlin, 1940

Kameradschaftsbund, *Ehrentafel Res. Inf. Regt. 119*

Klaus, Major a.D. Justizrat Max, *Das Württembergisches Reserve-Feldartillerie-Regiment Nr. 26 im Weltkrieg 1914-1918*, Stuttgart, 1929

Klett, Fritz, *Das Württembergische Reserve-Dragoner-Regiment im Weltkrieg 1914-1918*, Stuttgart, 1935

Knies, Oberstleutnant L., *Das Württembergishe Pionier Bataillon Nr. 13 im Weltkrieg 1914-1918*, Stuttgart, 1937

Kölbig, Kurt Siegfried, Kuhn, Hans-Karl, *Gedanken an der Westfront 1914-1917. Das Tagesbuch des Leutnants der Reserve Karl August Zwiffelhoffer*, 2003

Korfes, Hauptmann a.D. Dr. Otto, *Das 3.Magdeburgische Infanterie-Regiment Nr. 66 im Weltkriege*, Berlin, 1930

Korps Buchhandlung, *Der Schützengraben, Feldzeitung des XIV Reservekorps (1915-1917)*, Bapaume, 1915-1917

Korpsverlagsbuchhandlung, *An der Somme*, Bapaume, 1917

Korpsverlagsbuchhandlung, *Zwischen Arras und Péronne*, Bapaume, 1916

Kümmel, Leutnant d.Res. a.D. Studienrat Dr. Phil., *Reserve-Infanterie-Regiment Nr. 91 im Weltkriege 1914-1918*, Oldenburg, 1926

Lais, Otto, *Die Schlacht an der Somme*, Karlsruhe, 1940

Lehmann, Generalleutnant a.D. August, *Das K.B. Pionier-Regiment*, München, 1927

Lutz, Hauptmann Ernst Freiherr von, *Das Königlich bayerische 16.Infanterie-Regiment im Kriege 1914-1918*, Passau, 1920

Macdonald, Lyn, *Somme*, London, 1983

Marx, Julius, *Kriegs Tagebuch eines Juden*, Frankfurt am Main, 1964

Metzger, Karl, *Vom Weltkrieg 1914/18. Selbsterlebnisse eines Frontsoldaten*, Grossachsenheimer Zeitung, 1935

Middlebrook, Martin, *First Day on the Somme*, New York, 1972

Moos, Leutnant d. R. a.D. Ernst, *Das Württembergische Res.-Feld-Artillerie Regiment Nr. 27 im Weltkrieg 1916-1918*, Stuttgart, 1925

Moser, Generalleutnant Otto von, *Die Württemberger im Weltkriege*, Stuttgart, 1938

Mücke, Kgl. Preuss. Rittmeister a.D. Kurt von, *Das Grossherzoglich Badische Infanterie-Regiment Nr. 185*, Oldenburg, 1922

Müller, Major d.R. Paul, Fabeck, Oberst a.D. Hans von & Riesel, Oberstleutnant a.D. Richard, *Geschichte des Reserve-Infanterie-Regiment Nr. 99*, Zeulenroda, 1936

Müller-Loebnitz, Oberstleutnant Wilhelm, *Die Badener im Weltkrieg*, Karlsruhe, 1935.

Neubronn, Leutnant Dr. Carl & Pfeffer, Leutnant d. R. Dr. Georg, *Geschichte des Infanterie-Regiments 186*, Oldenburg, 1926

Offiziersverein des I.R. 180, *Totenbuch des 10.Württembergischen Infanterie-Regiment Nr. 180. Namentliches Verzeichnis der im Weltkrieg 1914-1918 gefallenen Offiziere, Unteroffiziere und Mannschaften*, Stuttgart, 1936

Orr, Philip, *The Road to the Somme, Men of the Ulster Division tell their story*, Belfast, 1992

Reichskriegsministerium, *Der Weltkrieg 1914 bis 1918. Die Militärischen Operationen zu Lande, Zehnter Band*, Berlin, 1936

Reymann, Oberleutnant a.D. H., *3.Oberschlesische Infanterie-Regiment Nr. 62 im Kriege 1914-1918*, Zeulenroda, 1930

Robertshaw, Andy, 'Hell in the Heidenkopf', *Battlefields Annual Review,* Singapore, 2005

Shephard, Ernest, *A Sergeant-Major's War. From Hill 60 to the Somme,* Trowbridge, 1988

Silbereisen, Leutnant der Reserve, Ehrler, Landsturmmann Hans Heinrich, Eisenmann, Landsturmmann Alexander & Schulze-Etzel, Gefreiten Theodor, *Schwäbische Kunde aus den grossen Krieg,* Stuttgart, 1918

Soden, General der Infanterie a.D. Freiherr von, *Die 26.(Württembergische) Reserve-Division im Weltkrieg 1914-1918,* Stuttgart, 1939

Stedman, Michael, *Salford Pals,* London, 1993

Stein, General von, *A War Minister and his work,* London, n.d.

Stosch, Oberstleutnant a.D. Albrecht von, *Somme-Nord I.Teil: Die Brennpunkte der Schlacht im Juli 1916,* Oldenburg, 1927

Swinson, Arthur, 'Race to the Sea', *History of the First World War,* 1969, Vol. 1, No. 11

Taylor, James W., *The 1st Royal Irish Rifles in the Great War,* Dublin, 2002

Turner, William, *Accrington Pals,* London, 1992

Vischer, Oberstleutnant Alfred, *Das 10. Württembergische Infanterie-Regiment Nr. 180 in der Somme-Schlacht 1916,* Stuttgart, 1917

Vischer, Oberstleutnant Alfred, *Das 10. Württembergische Infanterie-Regiment Nr. 180 im Weltkrieg 1914-1918,* Stuttgart, 1921

Volksbund Deutsche Kriegsgräberfürsorge e.V., *Deutsche Kriegsgräber, Am Rande der Strasse, Frankreich, Belgien, Luxemburg und Niederlande,* Kassel, n.d.

Wissmann, Oberst von, *Das Reserve-Infanterie-Regiment Nr. 55 im Weltkrieg,* Berlin, n.d.

Wohlenberg, Oberleutnant d.R. a.D. Rektor Alfred, *Das Reserve-Infanterie-Regiment Nr. 77 im Weltkriege 1914-18,* Hildesheim, 1931

Wurmb, Herbert Ritter von, *Das K. B. Reserve-Infanterie-Regiment Nr. 8,* München, 1929

Related titles published by Helion & Company

Imperial German Army 1914-18:
Organisation, Structure, Orders of Battle
Herrmann Cron & Duncan Rogers
416pp Paperback
ISBN 978-1-874622-29-1

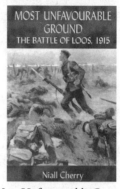

Most Unfavourable Ground.
The Battle of Loos 1915
Niall Cherry
384 pages Hardback
ISBN 978-1-906033-21-7

A selection of forthcoming titles:

Landrecies to Cambrai. Case Studies of German Offensive and
Defensive Operations on the Western Front 1914-17
Duncan Rogers (ed.)   ISBN 978-1-906033-76-7

Sniping in France 1914-18. With Notes on the Scientific
Training of Scouts, Observers and Snipers
Major H. Hesketh-Prichard DSO MC   ISBN 978-190603349-1

The Road to Königgratz. Helmuth von Moltke and the Austro-Prussian War 1866
Quintin Barry   ISBN 978-1-906033-37-8

The Silent General. Horne of the First Army. A Biography of
Haig's trusted Great War Comrade-in-Arms
Don Farr   ISBN 978-190603347-7

The Science of War. A Collection of Essays and Lectures 1892–
1903 by the late Colonel G. F. R. Henderson, C.B.
Capt Neill Malcolm, D.S.O. (ed.)   ISBN 978-1-906033-60-6

HELION & COMPANY
26 Willow Road, Solihull, West Midlands B91 1UE, England
Telephone 0121 705 3393   Fax 0121 711 4075
Website: http://www.helion.co.uk